Ethics and Professionalism for Healthcare Managers

HAP/AUPHA Editorial Board for Undergraduate Studies

Monica L. Rasmus, DrPH, Chairman
Texas Southern University

Ana A. Abad-Jorge, EdD
University of Virginia

Bryan K. Breland, DrPH, JD
University of Alabama at Birmingham

Tina DiFranco
University of Baltimore

Lennox Graham, DM
Howard University

Holly Hampe, DSc
Robert Morris University

Lori Peterson, PhD
Northeastern State University

Jessica L. Ryan, PhD
University of West Florida

Dale L. Sanders, DO, DHA
Alma College

Mark Sciegaj, PhD
Pennsylvania State University

Geoffrey Silvera
Auburn University

James H. Tiessen, PhD
Ryerson University

Ethics and Professionalism for Healthcare Managers

SECOND EDITION

Leigh W. Cellucci | Tony Cellucci | Tracy J. Farnsworth

AUPHA

Health Administration Press, Chicago, Illinois
Association of University Programs in Health Administration, Washington, DC

Your board, staff, or clients may also benefit from this book's insight. For information on quantity discounts, contact the Health Administration Press Marketing Manager at (312) 424-9450.

This publication is intended to provide accurate and authoritative information in regard to the subject matter covered. It is sold, or otherwise provided, with the understanding that the publisher is not engaged in rendering professional services. If professional advice or other expert assistance is required, the services of a competent professional should be sought.

The statements and opinions contained in this book are strictly those of the authors and do not represent the official positions of the American College of Healthcare Executives or the Foundation of the American College of Healthcare Executives.

Copyright © 2022 by the Foundation of the American College of Healthcare Executives. Printed in the United States of America. All rights reserved. This book or parts thereof may not be reproduced in any form without written permission of the publisher.

26 25 24 23 22   5 4 3 2 1

Library of Congress Cataloging-in-Publication Data

Names: Cellucci, Leigh W., author. | Cellucci, Anthony J., author. | Farnsworth, Tracy J., author. | Forrestal, Elizabeth. Ethics and professionalism for healthcare managers. | Association of University Programs in Health Administration, issuing body.
Title: Ethics and professionalism for healthcare managers / Leigh W. Cellucci, Tony Cellucci, Tracy J. Farnsworth.
Other titles: Gateway to healthcare management.
Description: Second edition. | Chicago, Illinois : Health Administration Press ; Washington, DC : Association of University Programs in Health Administration, [2022] | Series: Gateway to healthcare management | Preceded by Ethics and professionalism for healthcare managers / Elizabeth J. Forrestal, Leigh W. Cellucci. 2016. | Includes bibliographical references and index. | Summary: "This book prepares readers to recognize and respond to the ethical dilemmas they will encounter on a regular basis during their career in healthcare management. Through cases, exercises, and self-quizzes, readers can apply the theories and tools presented in the text to actual situations they may find themselves facing"— Provided by publisher.
Identifiers: LCCN 2021053183 (print) | LCCN 2021053184 (ebook) | ISBN 9781640553125 (paperback ; alk. paper) | ISBN 9781640553095 (epub)
Subjects: MESH: Health Services Administration—ethics | Delivery of Health Care—ethics | Professional Role | Ethics, Clinical | United States
Classification: LCC R724 (print) | LCC R724 (ebook) | NLM W 84 AA1 | DDC 174.2—dc23/eng/20211209
LC record available at https://lccn.loc.gov/2021053183
LC ebook record available at https://lccn.loc.gov/2021053184

The paper used in this publication meets the minimum requirements of American National Standard for Information Sciences—Permanence of Paper for Printed Library Materials, ANSI Z39.48-1984. ∞™

Acquisitions editor: Jennette McClain; Manuscript editor: Deborah Ring; Project manager: Andrew Baumann; Cover designer: James Slate; Layout: Integra

Found an error or a typo? We want to know! Please e-mail it to hapbooks@ache.org, mentioning the book's title and putting "Book Error" in the subject line.

For photocopying and copyright information, please contact Copyright Clearance Center at www.copyright.com or at (978) 750-8400.

Health Administration Press
A division of the Foundation of the
  American College of Healthcare Executives
300 S. Riverside Plaza, Suite 1900
Chicago, IL 60606-6698
(312) 424-2800

Association of University Programs
  in Health Administration
1730 M Street, NW
Suite 407
Washington, DC 20036
(202) 763-7283

"The family is our refuge and our springboard; nourished on it we can advance to new horizons. In every conceivable manner, the family is link to our past, bridge to our future."
—*Alex Haley*

*To our families, who have shown faith in us and our work
and have done so with love and a lot of humor.*
—*L. W. C., T. C., and T. J. F.*

BRIEF CONTENTS

Foreword xvii
Preface xxi
Acknowledgments xxv

PART I Ethics and the Profession of Healthcare Management

Chapter 1 Healthcare Management as a Profession 9
Chapter 2 Basic Concepts of Ethics 26
Chapter 3 Professionalism 45
Chapter 4 Stewardship 63
Chapter 5 Professional Codes of Ethics and Ethical Principles 84

PART II Ethical Decision-Making in the Healthcare Environment

Chapter 6 Ethical Framework 109
Chapter 7 Ethical Decision-Making Process 127
Chapter 8 Research in Healthcare Organizations 147
Chapter 9 Clinical Interactions 170

PART III Ethical Applications in the Healthcare Environment

Chapter 10 Human Resources 209
Chapter 11 Strategic Planning 229
Chapter 12 Operations Management 251

Chapter 13	Health Informatics	274
Chapter 14	Health Policy, Health Disparities, and Ethics	301
Chapter 15	Healthcare Management Consulting	333
Chapter 16	Building Your Future as a Healthcare Manager	349

Glossary 377

Index 389

About the Authors 415

DETAILED CONTENTS

Foreword xvii
Preface xxi
Acknowledgments xxv

PART I   Ethics and the Profession of Healthcare Management

        Case Study: Should Hospital Emergency Departments Be Used as
           Revenue Streams Despite Needs to Curb Overutilization? 2

Chapter 1   Healthcare Management as a Profession 9

        Important Terms 9
        Learning Objectives 9
        What Is a Profession? 10
        Characteristics 11
        Values 14
        Stages of Professionalization 16
        Mini-Case Study: Coding Error in Orthopedics 22
        Points to Remember 22
        Challenge Yourself 23
        For Your Consideration 23
        References 24

Chapter 2   Basic Concepts of Ethics 26

        Important Terms 26
        Learning Objectives 26
        Why Study Ethics? 27

	Ethical Branches	27
	Ethical Theories	32
	Behaving Ethically	36
	Mini-Case Study	37
	Points to Remember	38
	Challenge Yourself	39
	For Your Consideration	40
	References	40
Chapter 3	Professionalism	45
	Important Terms	45
	Learning Objectives	45
	What Is Professionalism?	49
	Effective and Moral Leadership	54
	Corporate Social Responsibility Engagement	55
	The Healthcare Manager's Role in CSR	56
	Mini-Case Study: Settlement in HCA Fraud Probe	58
	Points to Remember	58
	Challenge Yourself	59
	For Your Consideration	59
	Check These Out	60
	References	60
Chapter 4	Stewardship	63
	Important Terms	63
	Learning Objectives	63
	The Role of Stewardship in Healthcare Managers' Duties	64
	Fiduciary Duty	68
	Environmental Sustainability as a Moral Imperative	70
	Responsibility of Organizational Stewards to Stakeholders	72
	Mini-Case Study: Medical Malpractice and the Healthcare Facility's Responsibility	75
	Points to Remember	76
	Challenge Yourself	77
	For Your Consideration	77
	Check These Out	78
	References	78
Chapter 5	Professional Codes of Ethics and Ethical Principles	84
	Important Terms	84
	Learning Objectives	84

ACHE's Code of Ethics 85
MGMA's Code of Ethics 90
ACHCA's Code of Ethics 90
Internalized Codes Lead to Professional Norms 91
Application of Codes of Ethics 93
Mini-Case Study: The Dining Rooms at the Legacy 93
Points to Remember 95
Challenge Yourself 95
For Your Consideration 96
Check These Out 98
References 98

PART II Ethical Decision-Making in the Healthcare Environment

Case Study: How Should Complex Communication Responsibilities
   Be Distributed in Surgical Education Settings? 102

Chapter 6 Ethical Framework 109

Important Terms 109
Learning Objectives...109
Ethical Conflicts..111
The Four-Quadrant Model 112
Unawareness of Ethical Implications 118
Mini-Case Study: Vaping Becomes a Health Epidemic Among
   Youth 120
Points to Remember 121
Challenge Yourself 122
For Your Consideration 123
References 124

Chapter 7 Ethical Decision-Making Process...127

Important Terms 127
Learning Objectives...127
When Medical Futility and Ethical Principles Collide 128
Steps in the Ethical Decision-Making Process.....................132
Related Resources and Use of Ethics Consultation..............135
Recognizing Nonrational Elements in Ethical Deliberations.................135
Common Errors in Decision-Making and Strategies to
   Avoid Them 137
Recognizing and Managing Moral Distress..........................138
Mini-Case Study: Obligations to Staff 141

Points to Remember 142
Challenge Yourself 142
For Your Consideration 143
References 144

Chapter 8 Research in Healthcare Organizations 147
Important Terms 147
Learning Objectives..147
Unethical Human Experimentations in US Healthcare....................149
Major Documents Detailing Ethical Research Standards in
  Healthcare...150
Institutional Review Board 153
Federal Agencies Responsible for the Oversight of Research in
  Healthcare...154
Future Ethical Challenges...158
Mini-Case Study: Groupthink and the Tuskegee Study.................159
Points to Remember 163
Challenge Yourself 163
For Your Consideration 164
Check These Out..166
References 166

Chapter 9 Clinical Interactions 170
Important Terms 170
Learning Objectives..170
Principles in Clinical Ethics..172
Access to Healthcare Services and Distributive Justice 180
Telemedicine and Telehealth..181
End-of-Life Decisions..184
Institutional Ethics Committee and Ethics Support....................186
Preventing Medical Errors 187
Mini-Case Study: Surgical Errors Persist...................................189
Points to Remember 190
Challenge Yourself 191
For Your Consideration 192
References 192

PART III Ethical Applications in the Healthcare Environment

Case Study: Should a Good Risk Manager Worry About Cost and
  Price Transparency in Health Care? 200

| **Chapter 10** | Human Resources | 209 |

    Important Terms 209
    Learning Objectives..209
    Ethical Principles in HR..211
    HR and Confidentiality...214
    HR and Honesty 217
    The Role of HR Managers in Ethical Human Resources....................217
    Mini-Case Study: Serving as a Patient Advocate 220
    Points to Remember...222
    Challenge Yourself 222
    For Your Consideration 223
    Check These Out..224
    References 224

Chapter 11   Strategic Planning 229

    Important Terms 229
    Learning Objectives..229
    What Is Strategic Planning?..233
    CVS's Strategy..234
    Vidant Health's Strategy 236
    Lessons from the US Military's Humanitarian Efforts.......................238
    Mini-Case Study: Cooperative Strategy for 21st Century
        Seapower..241
    Points to Remember..243
    Challenge Yourself...243
    For Your Consideration 244
    Check These Out..245
    References 245

Chapter 12   Operations Management 251

    Important Terms 251
    Learning Objectives..251
    What Is Operations Management? 254
    Applying Ethical Principles to the Case from the Field 255
    Connecting the CFR Definition to Operational Actions 257
    Healthcare Managers' Role in Ethical Operations Management........264
    Mini-Case Study: Change for the Better..266
    Points to Remember..267
    Challenge Yourself...268
    For Your Consideration 268

	Check These Out	269
	References	270
Chapter 13	Health Informatics	274
	Important Terms	274
	Learning Objectives	274
	Health Informatics	275
	What Is an Electronic Health Record?	277
	Growth and Current Status of EHR Utilization	279
	Ethical Conflicts in Health Informatics	282
	Mini-Case Study: Ethical Principles of Physician Rating Websites	291
	Points to Remember	292
	Challenge Yourself	292
	For Your Consideration	293
	Check These Out	295
	References	295
Chapter 14	Health Policy, Health Disparities, and Ethics	301
	Important Terms	301
	Learning Objectives	301
	Pandemic and All-Hazards Preparedness Acts of 2006, 2013, and 2019	304
	Social Marketing	307
	Public Health Initiatives	310
	Health Disparities	313
	Mini-Case Study: The Structural Roots of Racism and Discrimination in Lactation Care	321
	Points to Remember	323
	Challenge Yourself	323
	For Your Consideration	323
	Check These Out	324
	References	325
Chapter 15	Healthcare Management Consulting	333
	Important Terms	333
	Learning Objectives	333
	What Is Healthcare Consulting?	334
	Ideal Characteristics of Healthcare Management Consultants	336
	Mini-Case Study: Consultants Settle, Pay $3.13 million	341

	Points to Remember	342
	Challenge Yourself	343
	For Your Consideration	344
	Check These Out	346
	References	346
Chapter 16	Building Your Future as a Healthcare Manager	349
	Important Terms	349
	Learning Objectives	349
	Professional Development	354
	Emotional Intelligence	355
	Personal Mission Statement	359
	Earning Trust by Walking the Talk	361
	Mini-Case Study: Problems at the VA Healthcare System (2013–21)	361
	Points to Remember	363
	Challenge Yourself	364
	For Your Consideration	364
	References	365
	Appendix: Carson Dye's Emotional Intelligence Valuation Form	368

Glossary 377
Index 389
About the Authors 415

FOREWORD

THE BIG PICTURE

As healthcare undergoes tremendous change amid the reverberations brought on by COVID-19 and its delta and omicron variants, the movement toward value-based care, and the push to provide virtual care, healthcare providers and those in academia who teach and train future healthcare providers and administrators face tremendous ethical challenges. COVID-19 is a worldwide phenomenon that has garnered the attention of governments, pharmaceutical companies, regulators, insurance companies, distributors, providers, and the general public. It has brought global health, public health, and healthcare management into the spotlight.

Beginning in 1945, as World War II concluded and troops returned home from Europe and the Pacific, healthcare was transformed from a public good into a commodity, access to which was based on the ability to pay for services. The economic interests of providers outweighed patients' ability to receive comprehensive and compassionate services. The American College of Healthcare Executives first published its Code of Ethics to govern individual behavior in 1941 and has updated it periodically over the years. The latest iteration of the Code of Ethics states that individual behavior should maintain or enhance the overall quality of life, dignity, and well-being of those needing healthcare services and help create an equitable, accessible, effective, and efficient healthcare executive (ACHE 2017).

Healthcare has evolved since the Hill-Burton Act of 1946, which supported hospital construction to accommodate soldiers returning from World War II. Major legislative disruptors in healthcare since that time have included the Prospective Payment System of 1983, the Health Insurance Portability and Accountability Act of 1996, the Health Information Technology for Economic and Clinical Health Act of 2009, and the Affordable Care Act of 2010. These laws created bureaucratic bloat, rules, regulations, and management procedures that accelerated the growth of health care management. Healthcare cost increases followed as a result of more people requiring healthcare services, an aging population, changes in disease prevalence and incidence, increasing use of healthcare services, and increases in the price and intensity of services (Dieleman et al. 2017).

US healthcare spending grew 4.6 percent in 2019, reaching $3.8 trillion or $11,582 per person (CMS 2020). This amounted to 17 percent of US gross domestic product (Commonwealth Fund 2021). Healthcare created 346,000 new jobs in 2018, up from 284,000 jobs in 2017; this number includes 219,000 jobs in ambulatory services and 107,000 hospital jobs. In response to economic growth in healthcare, universities expanded their academic programs devoted to training professionals for careers in healthcare. Healthcare occupations are expected to grow more than 20 percent from 2016 to 2026 (BLS 2021). Support occupations (23 percent) and healthcare practitioners and technical occupations (15 percent) are projected to be among the fastest-growing careers during this period. As the economic interests of providers become more urgent, we must focus on the ethics of management and the structure of healthcare to ensure that the needs of the community are served.

THE WORKFORCE

The number of physicians in the United States grew 150 percent between 1975 and 2010, roughly in keeping with population growth, while the number of healthcare administrators increased 3,200 percent during the same period (Cantlupe 2021).

Preparing students for success includes readying them for the job market (Burning Glass Technologies 2017). In the United States, 637 programs offer undergraduate and graduate degrees in health management, up 43 percent since 2014. In total, 22,347 degrees were conferred, up 29.4 percent since 2014 (Burning Glass Technologies 2017). The growth in healthcare as a result of legislation, facilities expansion, and increasing numbers of professionals providing care and managing resources requires a renewed focus on ethics and professionalism.

ETHICS AND PROFESSIONALISM IN THE CLASSROOM

What does this mean for ethics and professionalism, and what is the difference between ethics and professionalism? Academic programs, through their accreditation processes, focus on competencies to determine whether students have benefited from their educational experience. Several competency models are currently in use. The most important consideration for academic programs is identifying student's skills gaps and closing them. These gaps primarily pertain to financial skills, project management, team leadership, communication skills, information technology, and process management (Howard, Howard, and Scott 2017).

Ethics are guidelines that state the do's and don'ts in a specific context. Professionalism refers to specific traits that are expected of a professional. Ethics are stated, whereas professionalism is cultivated by individuals. Student competencies for professionalism and ethics include accountability, integrity, achievement orientation, ethical decision-making, lifelong learning, and self-confidence (Slomka et al. 2008).

Ethics and Professionalism for Healthcare Managers is a timely reminder of what healthcare leaders do. This book provides a theoretical and conceptional framework for ethics and defines key terminology. Most importantly, this text presents Cases from the Field that are relevant to healthcare. The case studies are followed by questions that require the reader to think more deeply about decision-making. Each chapter concludes with superb references for additional research. This book makes a major contribution to the field of healthcare administration by elevating ethics and reaffirming its relevance to daily healthcare decision-making. The book will have a profound impact on faculty and students because it reinforces the philosophy that patients, along with the efficiency and effectiveness in the healthcare system, need to be at the center of all we do.

Diane M. Howard, PhD, FACHE
Chicago, IL

References

American College of Healthcare Executives (ACHE). 2017. "Code of Ethics." Amended November 13. www.ache.org/-/media/ache/ethics/code_of_ethics_web.pdf.

Burning Glass Technologies. 2017. *Labor Insight Version 5.5*. Accessed November 10, 2021. https://www.burning-glass.com/labor-insight-version-5-5/.

Cantlupe, J. 2017. "Expert Forum: The Rise (and Rise) of the Healthcare Administrator." Athena Insight. Published November 7. www.athenahealth.com/knowledge-hub/practice-management/expert-forum-rise-and-rise-healthcare-administrator.

Centers for Medicare and Medicaid Services (CMS). 2020. Accessed December 7, 2021. www.CMS.gov.

Commonwealth Fund. 2020. "Health Care System Profiles: United States." Accessed November 30, 2021. www.commonwealthfund.org/international-health-policy-center/countries/united-states.

Dieleman, J., E. Squires, M. Campbell, et. al. 2017. "Factors Associated with Increases in U.S. Health Care Spending, 1996–2013." *JAMA* 318 (17): 1668–78.

Howard, D., J. Howard, and L. Scott. 2017. "From the Classroom to the Workforce: Empowering Students to Find Their Career Passion." *Journal of Health Administration Education* 34 (3): 395–405.

Slomka, J., B. Quill, M. DesVignes-Kendrick, and L. E. Lloyd. 2008. "Professionalism and Ethics in the Public Health Curriculum." *Public Health Reports* 123 (Suppl. 2): 27–35.

US Bureau of Labor Statistics (BLS). 2021. *Occupational Outlook Handbook*. Retrieved December 7. www.bls.gov/ooh/.

PREFACE

One of the compelling benefits of authoring a book for Health Administration Press (HAP) is having a home base at the HAP exhibition table at all Association of University Programs in Health Administration (AUPHA) meetings. This important connection enables professors who adopted the first edition to give valuable feedback about the text, including suggestions for improvement. We have enjoyed meeting our colleagues; many of their comments inspired and informed this second edition, which we hope brings the best of teaching into the health services management classroom, for both students and professors. For the past two annual meetings, we have not been able to meet this way because of COVID-19 and the imperative to shift from a face-to-face conference to a virtual one. We first met to plan this new edition during the 2019 AUPHA annual meetings in New Orleans. Little did we know that the COVID-19 pandemic would end our traditional ways of collaborating, but it spurred us to find new ways to work productively. With virtual meetings and interviews, telephone calls, and emails, we were able to develop the structure and content for this edition.

We knew we wanted to retain the richness and detail that had been well received in the first edition and include substantial and comprehensive updates where appropriate. Also, we wanted to provide information centered on health policy, health disparities, and ethics. Legislation and politics influence healthcare delivery with respect to the costs incurred, the quality of care provided, and patient access to care. In this text, we focus on why this matters ethically for healthcare managers so you can perform your responsibilities with the knowledge, skills, ability, and conduct expected. Moreover, we have emphasized the importance of interprofessional collaboration for successful management. Further, we wanted to keep the same balance of theory and application to help you make the cognitive leap from passive reading to active understanding.

To this end, we present three parts—(1) Ethics and the Profession of Healthcare, (2) Ethical Decision-Making in the Healthcare Environment, and (3) Ethical Applications in the Healthcare Environment—to ensure that you are prepared for ethical and professional management. We have added three case studies, previously published in the American Medical Association's *AMA Journal of Ethics*, to introduce each part. In addition, we have revised and added chapters to address moral distress, moral stance, and situational context; included revisions to the Common Rule and the definition of what is classified as a "human subject"; and focused on health policy, health disparities, structural racism, and social determinants of health to provide current, relevant information that we believe will improve your performance in the health services management field.

We know you will be more effective if you are prepared for ethical dilemmas and understand that you have a significant role in addressing and resolving them. We begin this second edition with the case study examining whether hospital emergency departments should be used as revenue streams despite needs to curb overutilization. Informal feedback suggests that this case has resulted in engaged and lively class discussion (in face-to-face and virtual classes) about patient needs and hospital fiduciary responsibilities. Also, it sets the stage for instructors to illustrate the importance of ethics and professionalism for healthcare managers who work with clinicians and staff to provide better healthcare. Chapters 1–5 lay the foundation by elaborating the concepts of ethics and professionalism, discussing the importance of interprofessional collaboration between clinicians and administrators, detailing stewardship, and interviewing an administrator who reflects on what professionalism means in her daily life and work.

Then, we turn our attention to the importance of ethical decision-making with a case study that asks how complex communication responsibilities should be distributed in surgical education. This case focuses on the reality that although many hospital and healthcare administrators are not professionally trained clinicians, your understanding of clinical issues and the complex decision-making and communications challenges that your clinical colleagues face is crucial. In Chapters 6–9, we discuss law and ethics and present a model illustrating the relationship between the two. We explain the ethical decision-making process and present an ethical decision-making model, incorporating the positions of the American College of Healthcare Executives and the National Center for Ethics in Health Care. We examine healthcare research, including discussion of landmark cases that prompted the development of research oversight and the policies and procedures that have been put in place to ensure ethical research conduct. Moreover, we include a chapter on clinical ethics, including the use of telehealth, so that you are familiar with the ethical issues faced by licensed providers.

In the third and last section of the text, we focus on ethical applications in the healthcare environment, beginning with an AMA case that asks whether a good risk manager should worry about cost and price transparency in healthcare. This case is about issues associated with price practices through the ethical lenses of justice and autonomy. In chapters 10–16, we consider human resources, including social media and social media guidelines in healthcare, health informatics, and ethical conflicts in the use of health information, the ethics of consulting, and the strategic planning process and implementation to address community needs. The COVID-19 pandemic highlighted the need for ethical and professional managers to respond effectively in difficult times, exemplified in the ways in which they addressed supply chain disruptions and how they monitored and adjusted hospital visitation policies for the safety of employees, patients, and their families. The final chapter is about your future, highlighting important points made throughout the text and discussing concepts such as emotional intelligence and professional accountability.

Each chapter in this text offers the following:

- **Important Terms** that identify the major topics discussed and terminology.

- **Learning Objectives** that summarize what readers will be able to do after reading and studying the chapter content.

- Case studies that translate theories into real-life scenarios. Each chapter begins with a **Case from the Field** to set the stage for the concepts to be discussed and ends with a **Mini-Case Study** highlighting a topic covered in the chapter. Each Mini-Case Study includes discussion questions that will help readers make decisions regarding actions that should be taken or assess the actions that were taken.

- **Definitions** of important terms on the page.

- **Challenge Yourself** questions that serve as a framework for student reflection on the material.

- Class-tested **For Your Consideration** exercises intended to spur class discussion or provide team-based assignments.

- A list of online resources mentioned in the chapter, called **Check These Out**.

- **Points to Remember** that summarize the main concepts presented in the chapter.

- **References** that include both classic and current publications.

Writing this second edition has been a collaborative, team effort that we found to be a rewarding experience. We hope this work adds value to your educational and career experiences.

Leigh W. Cellucci
East Carolina University
Greenville, North Carolina

Tony Cellucci
East Carolina University
Greenville, North Carolina

Tracy J. Farnsworth
Idaho College of
   Osteopathic Medicine
Meridian, Idaho

> ## INSTRUCTOR RESOURCES
>
> This book's instructor resources include PowerPoint slides and an instructor guide containing answers to the book's mini-case study questions, self-quizzes, exercises, lists of additional reading materials, and links to related websites.
>
> For the most up-to-date information about this book and its instructor resources, go to ache.org/HAP and browse for the book's order number: 2449I.
>
> This book's instructor resources are available to instructors who adopt this book for use in their course. For access information, please email hapbooks@ache.org.

ACKNOWLEDGMENTS

We thank all our faculty colleagues and friends who let us discuss with them the healthcare ethics and professionalism issues, challenges, and opportunities that we encountered as we researched the Cases from the Field and Mini-Case Studies presented in the chapters. We wrote this text during a pandemic, and we appreciated the contact and conversation—virtually via Teams and Zoom—to discuss and exchange ideas.

We also thank Tami Marie Santeramo, the interlibrary loan coordinator at the Laupus Health Sciences Library at East Carolina University. Her unwavering enthusiasm for our work and her help securing materials for us are appreciated. Special appreciation also goes to Danielle Braley-Winkle, who, as the administrative assistant in East Carolina University's Psychological Assessment and Specialty Services Clinic, kept the clinic going strong using telehealth during a pandemic. Dr. Bob Orlikoff, dean of the College of Allied Health Sciences at East Carolina University, deserves special mention for his continued support and selfless leadership.

We thank those who took time from their busy careers to speak with us about their work. In particular, we thank Caroline Doherty, chief development and programs officer at Roanoke Chowan Community Health Center, for her willingness to provide, review, and approve the interview material we used in chapter 3. We acknowledge Dr. Lisa Campbell at East Carolina University for her teaching and expertise on health disparities and particularly for sharing information about the National CLAS Standards. We also thank the alumnae of East Carolina University and Idaho State University—Mindy Stosich-Benedetti, Jen Harris, Shalina Patel, Chelsea Richards, Meghan Scherer, and Kendra Worth—who are working in specialty clinics, Federally Qualified Health Centers, hospitals and health systems, and an insurance brokerage firm. Even though they are working in different healthcare environments, they voiced similar thoughts about the importance of ethics and professionalism. Each interview included examples that illustrated overarching themes of the need for lifelong learning, working collaboratively in teams, being prepared to lead when needed, and treating others with respect, kindness, and compassion, all while being mindful that they are professionals in a field driven by service. This service they expressed gave them a deeper sense of purpose. The authors of this text hope that this book will help provide students and entry-level to mid-level managers with the foundations and tools they need to achieve this deeper sense of purpose, too.

We also thank Erik Schiller, editorial assistant for the *AMA Journal of Ethics*, for his assistance in helping us reproduce and properly present the case studies that introduced each part in this text.

Finally, we acknowledge the professionals at Health Administration Press. Jennette E. McClain served as our acquisitions editor, and her steadfast support is greatly appreciated. She was a champion of our work on this second edition, and we value her calm leadership. Deborah Ring served as our copyeditor, and we appreciate her expert attention to detail and careful reading of our drafts. She has a special talent of making track changes fun, and we appreciated that. Joe Misulonas, marketing specialist, deserves a special thanks as he quickly supplied us with electronic access to ACHE texts as needed. We also thank Drew Baumann, editorial production manager, who led the entire production process from editing through final typeset files, and Nancy Vitucci, marketing manager for the American College of Healthcare Executives, who led the marketing efforts.

On a personal note, Leigh W. Cellucci thanks Elizabeth J. Forrestal, Professor Emerita, for her friendship and mentorship. Dr. Forrestal served as the lead author of the first edition of this book, and we hope we have honored her vision regarding our discipline as one of service for the betterment of others. Her legacy continues. Also, Leigh thanks her two dear friends, Susan M. Lackey and Donna B. Owns, who exemplify ethics and professionalism in their everyday lives—thank you for continuing to inspire me.

PART I
ETHICS AND THE PROFESSION OF HEALTHCARE MANAGEMENT

This book addresses many of the issues and challenges related to ethics and professionalism that healthcare managers commonly face. The material covered in part I includes foundational information about the profession of healthcare management and what it means to be a professional; the evolution and importance of medical and managerial codes of ethics—and what it means to be an ethical leader; and the fiduciary role of a healthcare manager as wise and trusted steward—taking into account the varied and oftentimes conflicting needs, rights, and interests of myriad organizational stakeholders.

The following case and commentary are about balancing patient needs and hospital fiduciary responsibilities. Consider the following questions as you read:

1. Briefly describe one or more reasons why hospital leaders should not view the emergency department (ED) as a primary revenue stream for their organization.

2. What are the obligations of hospital leaders and emergency department personnel when their hospital chooses to receive Medicare funding?

3. Describe the "middle ground" position that hospital and medical leaders often take to reconcile the apparent conflict between business and patient or community needs.

4. Briefly describe other solutions that General Hospital's leaders might pursue to reconcile or justify the conflict of operating an ED-based revenue center.

5. What are some of the recent innovations in the US healthcare system that could help hospital and medical leaders reconcile the apparent conflict(s) between actions that advance the financial "margin" versus the "mission" of their organization?

Case Study: Should Hospital Emergency Departments Be Used as Revenue Streams Despite Needs to Curb Overutilization?

Abstract

This case asks how a hospital should balance patients' health needs with its financial bottom line regarding emergency department utilization. Should hospitals engage in proactive population health initiatives if they result in decreased revenue from their emergency departments? Which values should guide their thinking about this question? Drawing upon emerging legal and moral consensus about hospitals' obligations to their surrounding communities, this commentary argues that treating emergency departments purely as revenue streams violates both legal and moral standards.

Case

General Hospital, located in a downtown urban center, serves a wide variety of patients from its immediate neighborhood and surrounding suburbs and counties. A significant percentage of the patient population is drawn from General's adjacent blocks, where the community has high rates of poverty and crime and many residents tend to have poor health status. Traditionally, General's programs offer charity care to local, underserved patients.

Dr. Z, a health professional and senior executive, meets quarterly with each department to discuss successes, challenges, and plans moving forward. One particular area of concern has been emergency department overutilization. During this meeting, Dr. X, director of emergency medicine, and Dr. Y, a third-year emergency medicine resident, propose a plan to address overutilization. Dr. Y presents data on asthma-related emergency department visits, which illustrates that most patients with asthma-related complaints have lower-than-average household incomes and come from demographically similar neighborhoods within 3 miles of General's campus.

Drs. X and Y propose a plan to send physicians and community health workers to patients' homes to try to help reduce asthma triggers; this plan would likely improve health outcomes over the long term but would be costly to implement.

Dr. Z reiterates General's commitment to treating any patient who presents to the emergency room (ER), regardless of ability to pay. Dr. Z expresses concern that shifting charity efforts from emergency service provision to community outreach could compromise an important current revenue stream for General, as the hospital collected millions in revenue for asthma-related emergencies over the past 2 years. The physicians wonder what they should do to balance their competing obligations—to address emergency department overutilization and build community programs that improve health outcomes.

COMMENTARY

How should hospitals improve community health without compromising the quality of emergency care or their bottom line? Ultimately, we argue, treating emergency departments as a major revenue source violates legal standards and core values. However, hospitals are obligated to try to reduce ER utilization not by erecting barriers but by improving communities so that local residents rely less on emergency care to meet their acute health care needs in the first place.

Hospitals' Legal Obligations to Communities

We assume that General Hospital is, like most US hospitals, a nonprofit hospital that receives funding from Medicare. As such, it is bound by 3 major legal obligations. First, the Emergency Medical Treatment and Labor Act (EMTALA) requires that emergency departments accept walk-in patients regardless of ability to pay and provides them (at a minimum) with direct medical services to a point of stabilization.[1] Second, Section 501(r)(3) of the Internal Revenue Code requires that nonprofit hospitals provide "community benefit" under the Affordable Care Act (ACA), with the aim of improving the health of their communities.[2] Accordingly, they must undertake community health needs assessments every 3 years and develop an accompanying implementation strategy to address those needs.[3] Third, a requirement found in Section 501(r) of the Internal Revenue Code has long mandated that nonprofits provide charity care to patients who need it, particularly by ensuring that patients who qualify for assistance get it.[4]

The ACA expanded these requirements, ensuring that hospitals make public their financial assistance policy and provide services either for free or at a reduced rate to patients who qualify.[5] Hospitals also must make an effort to determine patient eligibility for financial assistance and, if patients meet these criteria, forego extensive collection practices.[6]

General Hospital's nonprofit status potentially tells us a great deal about how this dilemma should be resolved. While we do not know any details about General Hospital's financial status, we can assume that the institution receives a variety of tax benefits as a nonprofit. These benefits include not only the direct benefits of not having to pay numerous federal and state income taxes but also indirect benefits, such as being exempt from taxation on donations and opportunities to invest in tax-free bonds.[7] Although we do not know the scope or depth of General Hospital's community benefit work, we can assume that, as required by law, the hospital has a financial assistance program in place and provides charity care as a primary source of its community benefit activities.[8] Like all nonprofit hospitals,

General has an ethical obligation to its ER patients to provide them the best possible care, whether in the acute setting or through community-building initiatives that reduce the need for emergency care.

General Hospital's Deliberation About Values

In her aim to provide the best possible care to the surrounding community, Dr. Y, an ER resident (hereafter "the resident"), represents ideals for which physicians should strive. A widely cited 1964 interpretation of the Hippocratic Oath, a foundation of medical ethics, makes a critical distinction between prevention and treatment: "I will apply, for the benefit of the sick, all measures [that] are required. . . . I will prevent disease whenever I can, for prevention is preferable to cure."[9] The Hippocratic Oath is taken by just about every medical professional at some point in his or her training, and it delivers an ethical blueprint for medical practice. Nevertheless, health care systems have responsibilities that transcend ethical patient care, including administrative and financial responsibilities. Given the multifaceted nature of hospitals as both businesses and sites for medical care, how should these institutions weigh their various responsibilities?

Enter Dr. Z, the hospital administrator (hereafter "the administrator"). The case characterizes the administrator as concerned about both patients and the hospital's financial viability. Looking more closely, the administrator casts the hospital as a business in which asthma-related emergencies are viewed in one light as an "important current revenue stream." "Charity care," however, only serves to hurt hospital margins. Asthma control, in this context, becomes a commodity. Framing the administrator's outlook in this way is not to say that she lacks regard for the health of patients; she very well may, or at least may have convinced herself that she does. But how can the administrator promote health in the organization if she does not meet the bottom line? The administrator's main concern appears to be that shifting General Hospital's charity care program from emergency service provision to community outreach would compromise an important revenue stream. General would not only sacrifice current monies generated from patients with asthma in the emergency room but also lose all potential revenue from now-healthier community members who would no longer visit the ER at the same rate.

Dr. X, the emergency medicine director (hereafter "the director"), attempts to provide a solution to this conflict. The director, as a physician, aims for the same ideals of health as the resident by virtue of the core professional ethics principles he has vowed to uphold. As the emergency medicine point of contact for the administrator, however, he is also tasked with making sure these ideals fit within a successful business model. More succinctly, the director represents the middle ground between the goals of improving health outcomes and maintaining financial viability within the hospital. This middle ground reflects a more general tension within the US health care system today, as financial realities constrain health care decision making and subsequent health outcomes. And this middle ground too often becomes necessary to navigate for physicians such as the director, who are stuck between administrators' concerns about the bottom line and their own commitment to the health of their patients.

Ultimately, the above conflict requires that a choice be made that weighs moral responsibilities to ensure optimal health outcomes and protect the financial viability of the institution. Clearly both must be addressed in this scenario; however, the moral path aligns significantly better with the core values of health care professionals and the interests of patients alike. Thus, it becomes necessary to examine the current health care system and to explore meaningful changes that would both protect patient care and population health while promoting a successful business model for health care institutions.

Exploring Solutions to General Hospital's Dilemma
While EMTALA is a long-established federal law, true community outreach requires more of hospitals. Just as medicine itself is increasingly shifting to models of active (e.g., preventive) engagement, community-building activities can be considered "active" while charity care is mostly "reactive." Charity care is, at the end of the day, aimed not at improving health conditions in communities but rather at swallowing the bill for care—either entirely or by delivering it at a reduced rate. Yet, as enforcement and oversight of charity care is weak, it is likely that General Hospital will face no consequences if it meets even bare minimum standards. Only a handful of hospitals have lost their nonprofit status under community benefit laws.[10]

This reality raises the question of whether new incentives are needed to push hospitals toward a more active approach to community health. Innovative models used by hospitals across the country demonstrate many ways that General could improve the quality of life for the surrounding community. One way would be implementing public health programs, such as the one presented by the resident. By shifting to preventive medicine, General Hospital would spend more time educating the community and providing tools to promote wellness. The hope is that such a shift would result in patients coming to the ER only when they truly need emergent care while the hospital would still benefit both morally and financially by keeping its patients.

One consideration with regard to ER use and reimbursement is that, while Medicaid and the Medicaid expansion have greatly reduced uncompensated care provided by US hospitals,[11] the only truly profitable patients are those who have private insurance. And, even here, a sobering fact underpins this profitability: regardless of their payer (Medicare, Medicaid, private insurance), patients not experiencing a true emergency—meaning that their care could have been managed in an outpatient setting—are rarely profitable.[12] By implementing preventive measures, General Hospital would shift nonemergent care to its more appropriate outpatient setting while allowing emergency department resources to be utilized more as they were intended.

Another possible solution is to zoom out on the presented case and look at how this situation might be different within value-based payment structures that are currently being tested in the US health care system. Coverage is undoubtedly one of the core issues that helps to drive General Hospital's conflict, as those who depend on Medicaid or self-pay account for 48% of non-urgent emergency room visits.[13] Universal health care proposals such as Medicare for All have gained significant traction among lawmakers, health care practitioners, and the public at large,[14] and such proposals would ensure that coverage is not a prohibitive factor in meeting basic health needs. In the near future, however, the move away from fee-for-service payment models toward systems that pay for value and demonstrated outcomes will force hospitals such as General to think more comprehensively about the relationship between patient care and financial considerations. Avoidable emergency department visits, in particular, jeopardize hospital profitability. Indeed, if these trends toward value-based payment continue, hospitals will no longer be paid for services provided that do not have enduring positive effects on patients—including through prevention.

Yet another option is increasing the focus on preventative social services in hospitals and having that focus reflected in compensation, a possibility discussed by Stuart Butler and Carmen Diaz of the Brookings Institution with regard to hospitals and schools as community "hubs."[15] Shifting health care further into a central role in the community could feasibly shift perception of disease from an emergent issue needing a quick fix to a preventable entity. Developing hospital-based programs to promote access to affordable, healthy food and safe housing provides an opportunity to strengthen moral commitments to local communities and develop new revenue streams for hospitals.

Conclusion

This case raises a number of difficult questions for hospitals operating in a fast-changing health care environment. The different perspectives that comprise the case's ethical core—those of Drs X, Y, and Z—represent ideal types and possibly even stereotypes of positions that certainly do exist within US hospitals. At the same time, we assume that all clinicians, be they emergency room physicians or hospital leadership, care (albeit to potentially different degrees) about health outcomes, patient needs, and ethics. Yet, this case makes clear that ethics may not always be enough to force different actors, driven by divergent roles and interests, to provide patient-centered care. Rather, legal structures such as those put in place by EMTALA, nonprofit tax code, and the Affordable Care Act serve as a guardrail for ethical lapse. Indeed, in an age of mergers, consolidation, and system competition, when patient-centricity risks being reduced to a buzzword or branding campaign, the case of General Hospital illustrates the need for strong legal requirements, backed up by enforcement, to ensure that medical professionals put their obligations to patients first.

In recent years, innovations have arisen both in the way health care is delivered and in methods of payment. It is therefore important, as well, to consider the fast-changing nature of medicine itself in assessing this case. Promising models such as accountable care organizations, medical homes, and payment reforms emphasizing value over volume—especially those receiving strong financial and logistic support from the Centers for Medicare and Medicaid Services—are likely to both force and incentivize hospitals to take more responsibility for the well-being of the populations surrounding their campuses.

References

1. Zibulewsky J. The Emergency Medical Treatment and Active Labor Act (EMTALA): what it is and what it means for physicians. *Proc (Bayl Univ Med Cent)*. 2001;14(4):339–346.
2. Internal Revenue Service. Community health needs assessment for charitable hospital organizations—section 501(r)(3). https://www.irs.gov/charities-non-profits/community-health-needs-assessment-for-charitable-hospital-organizations-section-501r3. Accessed December 22, 2018.
3. Internal Revenue Service. Requirements for 501(c)(3) hospitals under the Affordable Care Act. https://www.irs.gov/charities-non-profits/charitable-organizations/new-requirements-for-501c3-hospitals-under-the-affordable-care-act. Updated July 2, 2018. Accessed August 22, 2018.
4. Internal Revenue Service. Charitable hospitals—general requirements for tax-exemption under section 501(c)(3). https://www.irs.gov/charities-non-profits/charitable-hospitals-general-requirements-for-tax-exemption-under-section-501c3. Accessed December 22, 2018.
5. Internal Revenue Service. Financial assistance policy and emergency medical care policy—section 501(r)(4). https://www.irs.gov/charities-non-profits/financial-assistance-policy-and-emergency-medical-care-policy-section-501r4. Accessed December 22, 2018.
6. Internal Revenue Service. Billing and collections—section 501(r)(6). https://www.irs.gov/charities-non-profits/billing-and-collections-section-501r6. Accessed December 22, 2018.
7. Rosenbaum S, Kindig DA, Bao J, Byrnes MK, O'Laughlin C. The value of the nonprofit hospital tax exemption was $24.6 billion in 2011. *Health Aff (Millwood)*. 2015;34(7):1225–1233.
8. Young GJ, Flaherty S, Zepeda ED, Singh SR, Cramer GR. Community benefit spending by tax-exempt hospitals changed little after ACA. *Health Aff (Millwood)*. 2018;37(1):121–124.
9. Lasagna L. Modern physician's oath. Quoted by: Hospice Patients Alliance. http://www.hospicepatients.org/modern-physicians-oath-louis-lasagna.html. Accessed August 22, 2018.
10. LaPointe J. In IRS first, non-profit hospital loses status under ACA rules. *RevCycleIntelligence*. August 24, 2017. https://revcycleintelligence.com/news/in-irs-first-non-profit-hospital-loses-status-under-aca-rules. Accessed November 20, 2018.
11. Schubel J, Broaddus M. Uncompensated care costs fell in nearly every state as ACA's major coverage provisions took effect. Center on Budget and Policy Priorities. https://www.cbpp.org/research/health/uncompensated-care-costs-fell-in-nearly-every-state-as-acas-major-coverage. Published May 23, 2018. Accessed January 2, 2019.
12. Wilson M, Cutler D. Emergency department profits are likely to continue as the Affordable Care Act expands coverage. *Health Aff (Millwood)*. 2014;33(5):792–799.

13. Honigman LS, Wiler JL, Rooks S, Ginde AA. National study of non-urgent emergency department visits and associated resource utilization. *West J Emerg Med*. 2013;14(6):609–616.
14. Kirzinger A, Wu B, Brodie M. Kaiser Health tracking poll—March 2018: views on prescription drug pricing and Medicare-for-all proposals. Henry J. Kaiser Family Foundation. https://www.kff.org/health-costs/poll-finding/kaiser-health-tracking-poll-march-2018-prescription-drug-pricing-medicare-for-all-proposals/. Published March 23, 2018. Accessed November 20, 2018.
15. Butler S, Diaz C. Hospitals and schools as hubs for building healthy communities. Brookings Institution. https://www.brookings.edu/wp-content/uploads/2016/12/hospitalsandschoolsashubs_butler_diaz_120516.pdf. Published November 2016. Accessed August 28, 2018.

Source: Myers, A., A. Cain, B. Franz, and D. Skinner. 2019. "Should Hospital Emergency Departments Be Used as Revenue Streams Despite Needs to Curb Overutilization?" *AMA Journal of Ethics* 21 (3): E207–14. Reprinted with permission.

CHAPTER 1
HEALTHCARE MANAGEMENT AS A PROFESSION

At the end of the day, we all should have the same goal, and that is to make a difference in patients' lives.

— Christine M. Candio, 2019 ACHE Gold Medal Award recipient

IMPORTANT TERMS

- Altruism
- Code of ethics
- Competencies
- Profession
- Professional norms
- Referent
- Self-regulation
- Systematic knowledge
- Values

LEARNING OBJECTIVES

Studying this chapter will help you to

➤ explain the concept of a profession,

➤ identify characteristics of professions and professionals,

➤ appreciate the values of professionals, and

➤ understand the process of professionalization and the stages of healthcare management's evolution as a profession.

> **profession**
> A body of knowledge shared by a group of individuals with specialized education and training and common values.

The purpose of this chapter is to guide you—a future healthcare manager—in developing a sense of healthcare management as a **profession** and healthcare managers as professionals. In this chapter, we explore the meaning of a profession in general and in the healthcare field particularly. We also discuss the characteristics, values (such as altruism), and stages of professionalization in healthcare administration. (Professionalism is discussed fully in chapter 3.)

WHAT IS A PROFESSION?

In everyday language, when we ask people what their "profession" is, we are actually asking about their job. Sociologists such as Talcott Parsons (1954), however, are more specific in their use of the word, defining a profession by its core set of components. One such definition includes the following core components (in italics) (Australian Council of Professions 2003):

> A profession is a *disciplined* group of individuals who adhere to *high ethical standards* and uphold themselves to, and are accepted by, the public as possessing *special knowledge and skills* in a widely recognized, organized *body of learning* derived from *education and training at a high level*, and who are prepared to exercise this knowledge and these skills in the *interest of others*.

Professionalism is related to this definition. According to the Healthcare Leadership Alliance, a consortium of healthcare professional associations, professionalism is "the ability to align personal and organizational conduct with ethical and professional standards that include a responsibility to the patient and the community, a service orientation, and a commitment to lifelong learning and improvement" (Garman et al. 2006, 219).

These definitions support our belief that ethics and professionalism are necessarily intertwined. One enhances or strengthens the other. Achieving the high-level education, training, and public service expected of a professional is equally important to your career. As you move through this book, you will repeatedly encounter the core components of a profession, so keep them in mind:

- Disciplined
- High ethical standards
- Special knowledge and skills
- Body of learning
- Education and training at a high level
- Interest of others

> **CASE FROM THE FIELD**
> **Exemplary Leadership**
>
> In 2019, Christine M. Candio was one of two recipients of the Gold Medal Award, the highest honor of the American College of Healthcare Executives (ACHE). The Gold Medal Award recognizes executives who exemplify the highest qualities of leadership to improve healthcare services and the health of their communities. Candio first worked as a medical-surgical nurse and then rose through the ranks as a healthcare manager and leader to become the president and CEO of St. Luke's Health Corporation in suburban St. Louis, Missouri.
>
> In this position, Candio manages an independent network of 32 entities, including acute care facilities, a skilled nursing facility, a rehabilitation hospital, outpatient care facilities, and group medical practices covering the full continuum of care. She credits the success of her organization to her people—all 5,000 team members. In an interview with Eric W. Ford, editor of the *Journal of Healthcare Management*, she stated, "They make the difference. Every single day, I see people here who care deeply about doing the right thing and who want to make a difference" (Ford 2019, 202). Candio also highlighted the importance of transparency and inclusiveness: "The leadership lesson I have learned in addressing shared concerns is that you must bring people to the table." She went on: "You also have to be a very good listener. There is great value in that. As a leader, I keep an ear to the ground as well as an eye to the future" (Ford 2019, 203–4).

CHARACTERISTICS

Experts often describe professions and professionals in terms of their characteristics. Two characteristics common to professions and professionals are *possessing systematic knowledge* and *adhering to professional norms* (Larson 1977).

POSSESSING SYSTEMATIC KNOWLEDGE

Systematic knowledge is the hallmark of a profession. In our list of the core components of a profession, it is represented as *special knowledge and skills* and *body of learning*. Professionals use their systematic knowledge to solve problems and make decisions. For example, healthcare managers use their knowledge of healthcare operations and their computer skills to manage medical supply inventories.

Both the general public and individuals in a field recognize that systematic knowledge belongs exclusively to a specific profession. This knowledge—published in textbooks, journals, manuals, and other authoritative sources—defines the profession's scope of activities and

systematic knowledge
Facts, tools, and theories of a field organized into a unique body of knowledge.

responsibilities. According to the Association of University Programs in Health Administration (2017), undergraduate students in healthcare management should have systematic knowledge in the following content areas:

- US healthcare system
- Population or community health
- Cultural competence and diversity
- Organizational development and organizational behavior theory
- Management of healthcare organizations
- Operations assessment and improvement
- Management of human resources and health professionals
- Information systems management and assessment
- Healthcare law
- Governance
- Health policy
- Leadership
- Statistical analysis and application to decision-making
- Healthcare economics
- Post-acute care
- Healthcare marketing
- Financial analysis and management
- Ethics in business and clinical decision-making
- Strategy formulation and implementation
- Quality assessment for patient care improvement

Several of these content areas may be covered in a single course, or a content area may be integrated into multiple courses to provide the necessary fundamental knowledge. These broad topics are then further broken down into specific units known as **competencies**.

Competency-based education has become the norm in professional education. Professional competencies involve the demonstration of specialized knowledge, skills, and abilities. For example, competency in communication might be shown by preparing a formal business proposal. An example of a management competency is applying inventory

competencies
The knowledge and skills needed to be considered proficient in a profession.

management measurements and techniques. Competencies can be assessed through many methods, including a minimum grade of B in specified courses, qualifying exams, required papers or portfolio work samples, preceptor ratings, and alumni surveys. Accreditation entities require education programs to define and assess the specific competencies they teach as part of their formal program review (Cellucci, Molinari, and Young 2018).

Education and training at a high level are the best methods for acquiring systematic knowledge and competencies. For example, healthcare management students pursue an extensive and defined course of study at a college or university. Systematic knowledge acquired through experience only, such as on-the-job training or an apprenticeship, is not itself a sufficient substitute for formal education and training. Competencies are systematically acquired through participation in an organized formal academic program, although this often includes supervised experiences by way of internships. Later work and career experience can certainly reinforce and bolster academic learning. In fact, over time, the results of experience—after they are verified and then published by researchers—may become part of the systematic knowledge for future professionals. The key point, however, is that professionals attain systematic knowledge after a long and intense period of formal academic study.

Adhering to Professional Norms

Professionals follow the standards of behavior or **professional norms** of their chosen profession. Exhibit 1.1 provides examples of these norms. High behavioral standards are taught, modeled, and instilled during a student's education and training in the field, interactions with established professionals, and internships (if applicable). William Sullivan (2015) persuasively argues that professional work includes social responsibilities that involve fiduciary and ethical duties. Often, professional norms are implied or understood, rather than openly

professional norms
Internalized standards of conduct to which professionals automatically and unconsciously conform.

Commitment to each of the following norms is critical for healthcare professionals:

- Public service through education and promotion of the health and well-being of patients (including clients and residents) and society in general
- Integrity and respect for others
- Honesty with patients, peers, subordinates, associated organizations, and oversight entities
- Fairness in the distribution of resources among patients, employees, departments, organizations, and community members or the public
- Loyalty through stewardship, fiduciary responsibility, and avoidance of conflicts of interest
- Mentoring and training the next generation of professionals
- Self-regulation, which protects the public from harm
- Lifelong learning to elevate skills, knowledge, and awareness

Exhibit 1.1
Examples of Professional Norms

stated. Because compliance with these norms is assumed, professional norms are a form of control, dictating the behavior of every member of a profession.

VALUES

value
A basic and fundamental belief of the members of a profession.

Professional **values** represent the basic and fundamental beliefs of the profession's members. In this sense, values define a profession and guide its members. As professionals make work-related decisions and take actions, they uphold and apply these values daily.

As a profession develops, its members form a disciplined group known as a professional association, organization, or society. Members of an association share a bond with, or feel a sense of connectedness to, their fellow members. This bond is the result of (1) having similar educational and work experiences and (2) being held to the same norms and values.

referent
An entity, such as a professional association, to which its members look for guidance.

Associations influence the actions and attitudes of their members by serving as **referents** for their members; that is, members look or refer to them for guidance on a variety of matters. Formally, associations may administer disciplinary actions—such as censure or revocation of credentials—to members who violate standards and ethical codes. Informally, members may ostracize other members who breach the rules or disobey norms.

In short, as a referent, the association essentially sets the values of its membership. The membership, in turn, preserves and perpetuates these values by applying them and expecting others to live by them. In healthcare management, professional values include public service, respect for others and fairness, self-regulation, a sense of calling and meaningful work, and autonomy.

PUBLIC SERVICE

altruism
Sacrificing oneself for the public good.

One value that healthcare professionals share is public service. To uphold this value, professionals need to be altruistic or willing to sacrifice personal needs or gains for the good of others. **Altruism** is the quality that makes professionals think and act in the interest of serving the community. Without it, healthcare could become a profession of people pursuing their own interests or selfish goals, instead of a public service that everyone can rely on.

RESPECT FOR OTHERS AND FAIRNESS

In a diverse society, a critical professional value is respect for others and a sense of fairness in the delivery and management of healthcare. Society increasingly expects professionals to avoid prejudice and other forms of injustice in their work. More and more, healthcare is perceived as a basic human right. While acknowledging the complexity of health disparities, health professions are increasingly asked to rectify disparities in healthcare delivery and outcomes. These topics are addressed more fully in chapter 14.

An example of a leader who exemplifies these values is A. Hugh Greene, the president and CEO of Baptist Health in Jacksonville, Florida, and a fellow of ACHE, the premier credential in the healthcare management profession. In 2013, Greene was honored with *Modern Healthcare*'s 2013 Community Leadership Award for his work over 20 years to provide access to healthcare to the homeless and uninsured populations in his area. The president of the Florida Hospital Association explained that Greene "advocates for the greater goal and pitches in even when it isn't going to benefit him directly" (Landen 2013, 19).

Of note, the ACHE Code of Ethics regards public service as a responsibility "to community and society." Consequently, it advises healthcare executives to (1) "identify and meet the healthcare needs of the community" and, importantly, (2) "support access to healthcare services for all people" (ACHE 2017). By using their systematic knowledge of the healthcare system (including managerial skills and tools), healthcare professionals can do a lot to serve their patients and communities, as well as to improve healthcare delivery and promote health for the good of society overall.

Self-Regulation

Self-regulation is another value in healthcare management. It is a privilege that society grants to members of a profession to govern themselves. This includes determining educational standards, establishing qualifications for practice, and disciplining members (White 2014). For example, state statutes establish boards of nursing home administrators to administer training programs, set qualifications, develop and administer tests, issue licenses, investigate complaints of noncompliance with state statutes, and build enforcement programs for disciplinary actions for nursing home administrators. In exchange for the privilege of self-regulation, the public expects members of a profession to

- be competent and practice within their scope or domain,
- behave ethically and adhere to a code of ethics, and
- serve the greater good.

self-regulation
The ability to govern or monitor oneself.

In healthcare, the primary purpose of self-regulation is to improve society's health. To this end, professional associations have policies, standards, and rules intended to support and promote achievement of high-quality care.

A Calling and Meaningful Work

Many professionals consider their work a *calling*, something they are born to do and thus want to pursue at all costs. For example, in describing his public service, Greene said, "I see it [public service] as fundamental to who we are" (Landen 2013, 19). This is also exemplified by the quotation opening this chapter by Christie Candio: "At the end of the day, we all should have the same goal, and that is to make a difference in patients' lives" (Ford 2019, 203).

Answering this professional calling and doing meaningful work are values, and they are highly valued in any profession. Professionals believe that their work is a large part of their being. As such, they are devoted to helping their profession flourish.

Autonomy

Professionals value their *autonomy*—the ability to independently (1) organize their own work, (2) make decisions that affect them, and (3) take actions. The basis of this autonomy is the professional's systematic knowledge, values and standards, and commitment to public service (Irvine 1997).

The extent of a professional's autonomy depends on the work setting. For example, in private healthcare management consulting firms, decisions made by professionals are subject only to their own review and their professional association's review. On the other hand, in hospitals, large healthcare organizations, and government agencies, professionals' work is subject to complex external legislative and administrative rules and to routine supervision.

Stages of Professionalization

Through the process of professionalization, occupations evolve into professions (Hall 1968; Wilensky 1964). Professionalization is generalized into stages, based on the evolution of the early professions of law, medicine, and the ministry. Not all professions follow the exact same sequence of evolution, and not all professions fully demonstrate all the stages.

The evolution of the healthcare management profession and a brief description of each evolutionary stage are discussed in this section.

DID YOU KNOW?
Professional Autonomy Versus Patient Autonomy

Professional autonomy and patient autonomy differ. The former is a professional's "authority and freedom to regulate themselves and act within their spheres of competence" (Wilensky 1964, 146). Professionals believe that they are "free to exercise" their decision-making and only other peer professionals are "competent to question" their decisions (Hall 1968, 93).

Patient autonomy, on the other hand, is about self-determination, or the right to make decisions regarding one's own healthcare. To exercise autonomy, patients (and their families) should be fully informed of their options, and healthcare providers (professionals) should respect their rights. Patient autonomy is discussed fully in chapter 9.

STAGE 1: FULL-TIME OCCUPATION

The process of professionalization begins when an occupation becomes a full-time job. For example, hospital administration started as a profession in the early 1900s, when the concept of the modern hospital emerged. At that time, hospitals, seeking to dispel their image as disease-ridden poorhouses, began to adopt the latest medical technology to emphasize that they were modern, scientific institutions (Arndt and Bigelow 2007). Full-time hospital administrators, then known as *superintendents*, were needed to manage the acquisition of and payment for the technology.

Once full-time, professionals devote time, money, and attention to their profession—unlike amateurs and temporary practitioners, who are generally excluded from the status of professional.

STAGE 2: FORMAL TRAINING

The second stage of professionalization is formal training. Professions establish formal education and training programs in colleges and universities as a prerequisite for full-time practice. In the past, professionals in a field received their training on-site or on the job (as an apprentice, for example) or were hired from related or other disciplines. For example, in the early 1900s, hospital administrators were initially managers in manufacturing companies, and they applied general business practices from that industry to hospital operations (Arndt and Bigelow 2007).

In the 1930s, the first master's degree program in hospital administration (now referred to as "health administration," "healthcare management," or "healthcare system administration") was established at the University of Chicago (Davis 1984). Other professions followed a pattern similar to that followed by the healthcare management profession. Today, possessing a college degree, at a minimum, is often associated with (and often a requirement for) being a professional.

STAGE 3: PROFESSIONAL ASSOCIATION

Graduates of formal training programs and veteran practitioners and leaders formed the first professional associations, ushering in the third evolutionary stage. Exhibit 1.2 presents some examples of professional associations in the healthcare management field; the list presented here is not at all exhaustive.

Professional associations serve as a platform for gaining recognition for the profession and its practitioners. Associations define their areas of expertise and educational domain, standards for competent practice, and appropriate behaviors for members. Qualification for membership includes the individual's work functions and responsibilities as well as academic and professional credentials. Exhibit 1.3 lists some of these credentials.

EXHIBIT 1.2
Selected Professional Associations in Healthcare Management

American Academy of Medical Administrators
American College of Health Care Administrators
American College of Healthcare Executives
American Hospital Association
Association of University Programs in Health Administration
Healthcare Financial Management Association
Medical Group Management Association
Professional Association of Healthcare Office Management

The primary purpose of associations is twofold: to advance the profession and to advocate for their members. As a public service and on behalf of their members, associations issue press releases or statements about current events in their area of expertise. They respond privately or publicly to proposals that affect their membership. For example, in June 2019, the Healthcare Financial Management Association sent a letter to the Centers for Medicare & Medicaid Services regarding proposed rule changes for hospital Inpatient Prospective Payment Systems in fiscal year 2020 (HFMA 2019). Additionally, associations offer

EXHIBIT 1.3
Selected Academic and Professional Credentials

Academic Credentials
Master of Business Administration (MBA)
Master of Health Administration (MHA)
Master of Health Services Administration (MHSA)
Master of Public Administration (MPA)
Master of Public Health (MPH)
Master of Science (MS)

Professional Credentials
Certified Administrator in Physician Practice Management (CAPPM)
Certified Assisted Living Administrator (CALA)
Certified Healthcare Financial Professional (CHFP)
Certified Medical Manager (CMM)
Certified Medical Practice Executive (CMPE)
Certified Nursing Home Administrator (CNHA)
Certified Professional in Healthcare Risk Management (CPHRM)
Credentialed by the American Academy of Medical Administrators (CAAMA)
Fellow of the American College of Healthcare Executives (FACHE)
Fellow in the American College of Medical Practice Executives (FACMPE)
Fellow of the Healthcare Financial Management Association (FHFMA)

their members access to job postings; opportunities for networking; continuing education programs; publications and other resources; and discounted rates on products and services, such as books, guides, and advertising. Through myriad activities, associations increase the visibility of their profession and membership as well as give them a clear, united voice.

STAGE 4: SELF-REGULATION

The fourth stage of professionalization is self-regulation, the privilege of a profession to govern itself. To do this, professions control entry into the field and monitor the quality of practice by developing and enforcing standards for

- educational and training programs,
- academic and professional certification or credentials, and
- the licensure process.

First, educational and training standards include a curriculum defined by an accreditation or certification body in the field. To be accredited or certified, educational and training programs must provide evidence that they teach the curriculum. In the 1900s, associations served as accreditation or certification bodies; however, in the twenty-first century, accountability shifted to stand-alone entities that are associated with but independent of associations. In healthcare administration, graduate programs are accredited by the Commission on Accreditation of Healthcare Management Education, and undergraduate programs are certified by the Association of University Programs in Health Administration.

Second, associations control the eligibility requirements to earn individual certification or credentials, which represents excellence in practice and service. One type of certification is based on *academic credentials*, such as the MHA. Another type of certification is based on *professional credentials*, such as FACHE; see exhibit 1.3 for a list of some of the credentials in healthcare management. Both academic and professional achievements and experiences are part of the eligibility criteria, and so is passing a rigorous test. In healthcare administration, a certification test includes items on operations, management and leadership, finance, statutes and regulations, facility design and maintenance, quality and risk management, strategic planning, and human relations. Professionals are expected to maintain their certification by participating in continuing education.

Third, through licensure, professions have the legal right to exclude nonqualified individuals. State legislatures pass statutes that (1) define the profession and its scope of practice and then (2) delegate the authority to enforce rules to the profession's regulatory body (such as a board of examiners), which then issues licenses. In healthcare management, professionals who need a license to practice include nursing home administrators, assisted living administrators, and risk managers.

To apply for a state license, qualified candidates must provide several documents, including (but not limited to) the following:

- Official transcripts of academic degrees from accredited institutions
- Other educational records, such as courses or training completed
- References, at least one of which from an employer
- National examination score of at least 75 percent (passing)

Licenses are issued for a specified period, so the documents for a renewal application must show the specified time span. Renewal often requires documentation of continuing education.

The regulatory body (or state) maintains a registry of licensed individuals and sanctions those who are incompetent or violate codes of ethics. These sanctions vary, depending on the severity of the violation, but may involve the following:

- Official letter of reprimand or censure with public notification
- Restriction in the scope of practice, such as requiring a preceptor present during practice or banning an individual from performing certain procedures
- Suspension of the license to practice for a period or until a stipulation has been met, such as completion of a remedial course
- Permanent revocation of license

Stage 5: Code of Ethics

code of ethics
Standards of behavior and conduct for members of a profession.

The final stage of professionalization is the development and enforcement of a **code of ethics**. The primary purpose of the code of ethics is to hold members of a profession to high ethical standards.

While all health providers (e.g., physicians, nurses, psychologists) have an ethical code, these codes vary somewhat by discipline. However, they share the same underlying values or ethical principles, emphasizing

- beneficence (doing good) and avoiding harm (nonmaleficence),
- honesty and integrity,
- justice,
- fidelity, and
- sanctity (respect for all individuals' dignity and life).

> **DID YOU KNOW?**
> **Claims**
>
> A claim is a request for payment that itemizes services, dates, and costs. *Healthcare providers* (such as hospitals, physicians, and other practitioners) submit claims to *payers* (such as Medicare, Medicaid, healthcare insurance plans, and workers' compensation programs). Patients may also submit claims for benefits based on the terms of their health insurance policy.

Students-in-training must integrate these professional values into their own moral code and ethical decision-making process. Associations, which develop and disseminate their own codes, expect members to uphold the standards in their professional dealings and relationships—with patients and their families, employees, colleagues, superiors, and the community. Codes also serve as the basis of disciplinary actions taken against members who violate accepted behaviors and practice. Examples of codes of ethics for healthcare managers are the Code of Ethics of the American College of Healthcare Executives (ACHE 2017) and the Code of Ethics and Disciplinary Procedures of the Medical Group Management Association (MGMA 2015).

Chapter 5 discusses codes of ethics in the healthcare management profession in more detail.

> **DID YOU KNOW?**
> **Coding**
>
> Healthcare providers use codes when they submit claims to payers. Payers use these codes—rather than any clinical narrative statements—to determine payment to providers. Coding is the process of transforming clinical narrative statements for diagnoses and procedures into numerical or alphanumerical representations. Two commonly used sets of codes are the International Classification of Diseases (ICD) and the Current Procedural Terminology (CPT). For example, orthopedic surgeons use ICD codes to represent their patients' diagnoses (such as knee pain) and CPT codes to represent the services they rendered to patients (such as evaluation and management of knee pain). Several codes exist for evaluation and management, representing different settings (office or emergency department), levels of difficulty (returning patient or consult), and levels of complexity (problem focused or comprehensive). To submit an accurate claim, and therefore receive correct payment, providers should make sure that the code recorded matches the service rendered.

Mini-Case Study: Coding Error in Orthopedics

For six months now, you have been an assistant administrator in a large orthopedic group practice. You feel fortunate because your capstone experience as a student in a healthcare management program took place in a similar physician practice.

Currently, you are reviewing reimbursements received from Blue Cross. Several large federal agencies are based in your city, so many Blue Cross payments are for patients enrolled in the Federal Employee Health Benefits Program. You are confused by a discrepancy that you found while matching patient medical records with corresponding claims and reimbursements. The claims for office visits for returning patients were submitted using a higher code of consultation.

From your capstone experience, you learned that office visits for returning patients generally are *not* coded as consultations. It appears, then, that this practice is upcoding services to fraudulently inflate its reimbursements. You bring your concerns to your boss, the practice's CEO, who says, "Our coders are certified. Plus, our orthopedic surgeons are the best in the area. They only treat the most complex cases, which are equal to consultations. Don't worry about it." The CEO then reassigns you to updating the practice's strategic plan and tells you to drop the reimbursement review.

After thought and preparation, you set up an appointment to meet with the practice's medical director.

Mini-Case Study Questions

1. What documents would you bring to your meeting with the medical director?
2. What professional standards has the CEO violated?
3. Is it likely that the CEO is licensed?
4. Which credentials—academic and professional—could the CEO hold?
5. Would you immediately report the CEO to an association's professional standards committee (or a similar entity that investigates violations of professional standards)?
6. What laws have been broken? Who should be held responsible?
7. Should you find another job?

Points to Remember

- A profession is a body of knowledge shared by a group of individuals with specialized education and training and common values.

- Two common characteristics of professionals are possessing systematic knowledge and adhering to professional norms.

- Values important to professionals include public service, respect for others and fairness, self-regulation, a sense of calling and meaningful work, and autonomy.
- Professions evolve through a multistage professionalization process. Although the stages generally are similar, they may vary slightly from one profession to another.
- The development and enforcement of a profession's code of ethics is one important stage. The code of ethics not only sets the ethical standards for professional conduct but also serves as the basis of disciplinary actions taken against those who violate accepted behaviors and practice.

Challenge Yourself

1. Based on what you've read in this chapter, are "professional athletes" professionals? Why or why not?
2. Ask the program director whether your program has developed a set of competencies expected of all graduates and review these documents. How are these competencies assessed? If necessary, how would failure to obtain a particular competency at the expected level be remediated?
3. As a healthcare management trainee, do you find any of the professional or ethical values discussed in this chapter surprising or different from your experience? How can you incorporate the healthcare management profession's norms and values into your daily thoughts, beliefs, and actions?
4. Find and categorize examples of behaviors or actions, excluding examples given in this book, for *each* of the values of healthcare administrators. The behaviors and actions may come from your personal experiences, work experiences, recent events, or historical events.
5. What professionals are licensed in your state? Do you think all healthcare administrators should be licensed, not just those who work in certain settings? What are the advantages and disadvantages of licensure?

For Your Consideration

1.1 What similarities and differences can you find between the codes of ethics of ACHE and MGMA?
1.2 The ACHE Code of Ethics, section I, states that healthcare executives shall "comply with all laws and regulations pertaining to healthcare management in the jurisdictions in which the healthcare executive is located or conducts professional activities." In your other courses, have you learned about laws or regulations to which this responsibility might be referring? Why would the code make compliance with laws and regulations a responsibility?

References

American College of Healthcare Executives (ACHE). 2017. "Code of Ethics." Amended November 13. www.ache.org/-/media/ache/ethics/code_of_ethics_web.pdf.

Arndt, M., and B. Bigelow. 2007. "Hospital Administration in the Early 1900s: Visions for the Future and the Reality of Daily Practice." *Journal of Healthcare Management* 52 (1): 34–47.

Association of University Programs in Health Administration. 2017. "Criteria for AUPHA Undergraduate Program Certification." Revised June. https://higherlogicdownload.s3.amazonaws.com/AUPHA/5c0a0c07-a7f7-413e-ad73-9b7133ca4c38/UploadedImages/Certification/Guidelines_for_Undergraduate_Certification_rev_2017.pdf.

Australian Council of Professions. 2003. "What Is a Profession?" Accessed January 6, 2021. www.professions.org.au/what-is-a-professional/.

Cellucci, L. W., C. Molinari, and J. Young. 2018. "Competency-Based Education in Undergraduate Programs Certified by the Association of University Programs in Health Administration." *Journal of Health Administration Education* 35 (2): 175–85.

Davis, M. M. 1984. "Development of the First Graduate Program in Hospital Administration." *Journal of Health Administration Education* 2 (2): 121–34.

Ford, E. 2019. "Interview: Christine M. Candio, FACHE, President and CEO, St Luke's Health Corporation." *Journal of Healthcare Management* 64 (4): 201–4.

Garman, A. N., R. Evans, M. K. Krause, and J. Anfossi. 2006. "Professionalism." *Journal of Healthcare Management* 51 (4): 219–22.

Hall, R. H. 1968. "Professionalization and Bureaucratization." *American Sociological Review* 33 (1): 92–104.

Healthcare Financial Management Association (HFMA). 2019. "HFMA Comments on FY2020 IPPS Proposed Rule." Published July 2. www.hfma.org/industry-initiatives/regulatory-and-accounting-resources/comment-letters/hfma-comments-fy2020-ipps-proposed-rule.html.

Irvine, D. 1997. "The Performance of Doctors. I: Professionalism and Self Regulation in a Changing World." *British Medical Journal* 314 (7093): 1540–42.

Landen, R. 2013. "Offering Service, Leadership When It's Needed Most." *Modern Healthcare* 43 (46): 18–19.

Larson, M. S. 1977. *The Rise of Professionalism: A Sociological Analysis.* Berkeley, CA: University of California Press.

Medical Group Management Association (MGMA). 2015. "MGMA-ACMPE Code of Ethics." Published September 29. www.mgma.com/MGMA/media/files/about/Code-of-Ethics-Approved.pdf.

Parsons, T. 1954. "The Professions and Social Structure." In *Essays in Sociological Theory*, revised ed., edited by T. Parsons, 34–49. Glencoe, IL: Free Press.

Sullivan, W. M. 2015. "Professional Responsibility: Its Nature and New Demands." In *Professional Responsibility*, vol. 4, *Advances in Medical Education*, edited by D. Mitchell and R. K. Ream, 59–74. Cham, Switzerland: Springer.

White, W. D. 2014. "Professional Self-Regulation in Medicine." *AMA Journal of Ethics* 16 (4): 275–78.

Wilensky, H. L. 1964. "The Professionalization of Everyone?" *American Journal of Sociology* 70 (2): 137–58.

CHAPTER 2
BASIC CONCEPTS OF ETHICS

Moral courage isn't an esoteric branch of philosophy; it's a practical necessity for modern life.
—Rushworth M. Kidder, journalist and ethicist

Important Terms

- Casuistry
- Categorical imperative
- Ethical branch
- Ethics
- Moral agent
- Moral courage
- Moral disengagement
- Principle
- Principlism
- Stakeholder theory
- Utility

Learning Objectives

Studying this chapter will help you to

➤ explain the concept of ethics,

➤ enhance your awareness of the ethical perspectives of healthcare professionals,

➤ become familiar with ethical theories and traditions,

➤ learn about the factors that influence ethical behavior,

➤ understand the need for moral courage in living ethically, and

➤ examine your own values and ethics.

Chapter 2: Basic Concepts of Ethics

This chapter introduces you to the different branches of **ethics** and its theories. In studying ethics, you examine how you relate to others and to the world in terms of the general nature of morals, specific choices you (or others) make, conflicts you (or others) may face, and processes you use in making moral judgments.

> *ethics*
> A system of beliefs and behaviors that people value and use to guide their conduct; the study of the moral life.

Why Study Ethics?

The study of ethics in philosophy dates to humanity's earliest times. Beginning in the fifth century BCE, the Greeks pondered the meaning of life and the rightness or wrongness of actions.

You may have taken an ethics course in college, examining the principles and theories that historically have been used to determine whether actions are ethical and then applying them to such controversial subjects as capital punishment, the use of stem cells in medicine, or animal rights. Moreover, as we saw in chapter 1, ethical obligations are an expected part of business and professional life.

In today's healthcare world, the study of ethics is alive and well, helping healthcare providers, administrators, researchers, and policymakers grapple with questions and challenges. One such question involves the increasing use of technology in healthcare. Because technology advances so quickly, ethical issues and laws always lag behind technological developments (Wadhwa 2014). Many technologies that are emerging today will likely affect healthcare delivery in the future, including artificial intelligence and robotics, sophisticated medical devices and sensors, 3D printing of tissues, health information systems using cloud computing, CRISPR and genetic engineering, and life enhancement and extension technologies (Ellis 2019; Sadiku, Akhare, and Musa 2019). The use of these technologies and devices raises ethical issues for both healthcare providers and regulators (Harbut 2019; Walker 2017), including their possible misuse as well as privacy and security concerns.

Although the use of technology may improve care and even survival for patients, and it may improve overall quality and efficiency in healthcare, the expense also results in unequal access, creating thorny questions for healthcare policy. When medical technologies are expensive and budgets are tight, for example, should the healthcare system invest its limited dollars in (1) ever more sophisticated and costly technologies that help a select few, or (2) less costly preventive medicine and health promotion that have the potential to help many? Examining the ethical components of the many decisions and choices encountered in healthcare enables healthcare managers to develop a more comprehensive response or approach.

Ethical Branches

An **ethical branch** is a major category of ethics composed of clusters and families of theories that share characteristics or functions. The four common branches are descriptive ethics, normative ethics, moral psychology, and applied ethics.

> *ethical branch*
> A major category of ethics composed of clusters and families of theories that share characteristics or functions.

> **CASE FROM THE FIELD**
> Acting on Behalf of the Federal Government and Saving Healthcare Resources
>
> Amanda Cashi was a district sales manager for a medical device manufacturer. The manufacturer—then called Fox Hollow Technologies, Inc., and now known as ev3—made and sold the SilverHawk peripheral plaque excision system. The SilverHawk was a small cutting device that removed atherosclerotic plaque from blood vessels.
>
> Cashi, as a whistleblower acting on behalf of the federal government, filed a lawsuit alleging that the manufacturer had violated the federal False Claims Act. According to the US Department of Justice (DOJ), the manufacturer had caused 12 hospitals in nine states to admit patients to the hospital for procedures involving its SilverHawk device, even though many of those patients should have been treated in an outpatient setting at significantly less cost. As a result of this scheme, the hospitals received higher Medicare payments, and the manufacturer received higher sales.
>
> In February 2015, the DOJ announced that the manufacturer would pay $1.25 million to resolve allegations that it had caused hospitals to submit false claims to Medicare. Commenting on the settlement, the acting assistant attorney of the DOJ's Civil Division said, "Charging the government for higher-cost inpatient services that patients do not need wastes the country's precious health care resources." Cashi, under the False Claims Act's whistleblower provisions, received $250,000 as her portion of the government's settlement (DOJ 2015).

Descriptive Ethics

Descriptive ethics—also called *comparative ethics* or *empirical ethics*—describes how people actually behave in the face of ethical problems and choices. It does not prescribe what people ought to do or proscribe (forbid) what they ought *not* do. Descriptive ethics can be applied at the level of the individual or the society, providing valuable insights into how people reason, how corporations conduct business, and how societies function.

This ethical branch arose because people and cultures have different values. When social scientists—such as anthropologists, sociologists, and organizational theorists—write about descriptive ethics, they usually discuss different societies' definitions of moral behavior and norms (internalized societal expectations). For example, organizational theorists may explain what people do and what they believe in a particular corporate culture of deceit and trickery (in this case, the corporation is a mini-society). No value judgments are made in these writings.

In descriptive ethics, behavior is not judged, because universal truths and ethical **principles** do not exist. As a consequence, some people negatively label descriptive ethics *relativism*, which means that judgments of moral values, truth, and goodness vary by the individual's or society's historical, religious, or cultural perspective.

principle
A general prescriptive judgment.

NORMATIVE ETHICS

Normative ethics—also called *prescriptive ethics*—stipulates what people should do or should not do in the face of ethical problems and choices. Its name is derived from norms, and as such, it prohibits courses of action or behaviors that violate societal standards.

To help people determine the proper actions and behaviors, normative ethicists precisely define terms such as *right, wrong, good, obligation,* and *duty.* In this ethical branch, universal truths, such as good and right, do exist. Ethical theories that make normative claims are described later.

MORAL PSYCHOLOGY

Moral psychology examines how people develop moral reasoning through intellectual development. Similar to physical and mental growth, moral reasoning begins during childhood and continues to mature throughout adulthood.

Psychologist Lawrence Kohlberg (1981) theorized that moral reasoning develops across levels and stages (from childhood, through adolescence, and into adulthood). He hypothesized three levels of moral thinking—preconventional, conventional, and postconventional morality—using moral dilemmas to study the reasons that individuals give for their moral choices. Kohlberg's most famous moral dilemma asked whether a man should steal an expensive drug to save his wife from a serious disease. Individuals in earlier stages of moral reasoning cited concrete consequences of their decision (e.g., I would get arrested), or the need to follow conventional rules (e.g., it is always wrong to steal), while those at the highest level emphasized abstract principles of justice (e.g., preserving human life is a more important value than money, or it is wrong to deprive others who also need the drug). For Kohlberg, it was not the decision but the rationale that determined one's stage of moral reasoning.

However, Kohlberg's work was later criticized for its gender bias, because his study sample was largely composed of males from Western cultures. Carol Gilligan (1982) proposed that Kohlberg's theory conflated morality with an understanding of rules and justice while overlooking other ethical concerns such as compassion and care. As a result, moral psychology today includes not only the principles of justice but also of harmony, responsibility, and caring.

APPLIED ETHICS

Applied ethics—also called *practical ethics* or *professional ethics*—is the use of general ethical theories, moral reasoning, and professional codes of ethics and conduct to make decisions and solve problems. Practical, real-world moral concerns in professions, technology, public policy, and other areas are the focus of applied ethics. In healthcare organizations, the types of applied ethics include bioethics, business ethics, organizational ethics, and profession-specific ethics, such as nursing ethics and occupational therapy ethics. Healthcare managers use applied ethics when they do the following:

- Ensure access to health services by garnering adequate resources and determining effective means to recruit professional and administrative staff
- Allocate resources fairly and with beneficence across their units
- Ensure that policies, procedures, and operations are universally fair and serve employees, patients, and other stakeholders from all socioeconomic strata
- Resolve issues that could be conflicts of interest
- Serve as wise stewards of limited resources by decreasing fraud, waste, and abuse
- Protect patients and employees by fostering efforts to increase quality and safety and to eliminate bullying and sexual harassment

Bioethics

Bioethics is a type of normative applied ethics that deals with moral conflicts stemming from or related to the practice of biological, health, and life sciences; it includes areas of medicine, law, agriculture, ecology, biotechnology, research, sociology, and behavioral studies. Two common approaches to bioethics are **principlism** and **casuistry**.

In principlism, bioethicists base their judgment or resolution of cases on the four ethical principles: respect for autonomy (self-determination), nonmaleficence (do no harm), beneficence (do good), and justice (fairness) (Beauchamp and Childress 2013). Such middle-level principles are an alternative to complex theories as a basis and common morality for making applied moral decisions.

In casuistry, on the other hand, bioethicists work on a case-by-case basis, exploring each case's facts, complexity, relevant laws, and unusual circumstances before making a decision. According to this approach, moral understanding rests on the concrete understanding of particular cases, which give rise to rules or principles (Cudney 2014). Each of these two approaches separately generates a unified and coherent set of moral judgments or rules that can be used as resources for future cases.

Business Ethics

Business ethics—also called *managerial ethics* or *corporate ethics*—is a type of descriptive or normative applied ethics that managers and leaders use to make operational decisions and resolve behavioral problems or conflicts. Healthcare managers use business ethics when they

---

principlism
An ethical decision-making approach that uses the four ethical principles—respect for autonomy (self-determination), nonmaleficence (do no harm), beneficence (do good), and justice (fairness)—as a standard for judgment or resolution.

casuistry
An ethical decision-making approach that relies on a case's facts, complexity, relevant laws, and unusual circumstances to determine a judgment.

consciously verify that cost reports to Medicare are accurate or when they gauge patients' access to health services in establishing hours of operation.

Stakeholder theory extends business ethics to address the rights and interests of people who interact with the business and are affected by its decisions (Freeman, Wicks, and Parmar 2004). These people—such as employees, customers, suppliers, and members of the surrounding community—have a stake in the business's success. The successful manager effectively maintains the support of all stakeholders by fairly balancing their interests with maximizing profits. Patricia Werhane, the founder of the *Journal of Business Ethics*, is perhaps best known for applying this perspective to healthcare (Dmytriyev and Wicks 2018; Werhane 2000).

stakeholder theory
A theory that extends business ethics to address the rights and interests of people who interact with the business and are affected by its decisions.

Organizational Ethics

Organizational ethics is a type of applied ethics that holds an organization accountable for the values and moral positions it articulates and applies. Specifically, it is an "organization's efforts to *define* its own core values and mission, *identify* areas in which important values come into conflict, *seek* the best possible resolution of these conflicts, and *manage* its own performance to ensure that it acts in accord with espoused values" (Pearson, Sabin, and Emanuel 2003, 32). As managed care expanded, organizational ethics took shape, with the Office of Inspector General releasing a model compliance plan and The Joint Commission issuing accreditation standards related to organizational ethics.

The collective moral choices of organizational members—including the board and administrators; physicians, nurses, and other clinicians; and professional, technical, and support staff—should be congruent with the organization's core values and aimed at achieving its mission and goals. Organizational ethics overlaps with business ethics; the focus is quality improvement and aligning decision-making with the values of the organization. Collective moral choices thus enable the accomplishment of organizational goals (Lahey et al. 2020).

Profession-Specific Ethics

The academic preparation of all professions includes the study of ethics. Typically, this study covers ethical theories and principles, allocation of scarce resources, responsible use of advanced technologies, and appropriate relationships with clients and subordinates. Each profession pays particular attention to ethical issues that arise within their work and to advancing and applying its ethical code. As a result, profession-specific ethics emerged, such as bioinformatics ethics, clinical ethics, computer ethics, health informatics ethics, nursing ethics, psychology ethics, physical therapy ethics, and so on. Ethical codes specific to healthcare professions include both general aspirational principles and values and specific codes of conduct (e.g., maintaining confidentiality of medical information, avoiding harmful dual relationships).

ETHICAL THEORIES

Ethical theories are derived from philosophical traditions and provide insight into ethical questions. Healthcare managers can use them as guides to action. This section explains the ethical theories known as deontology, utilitarianism, virtue ethics, John Rawls's principles of justice, and the ethics of care.

DEONTOLOGY

Deontology—also known as *formalism* or *ethics of duty*—is a normative ethical theory that determines the rightness or wrongness of an act by its conformity to a universal moral rule or duty. The word comes from the Greek, combining *deon* (obligation or duty) and *logos* (science). Simply, deontology is about doing the right things for the right reasons (Robertson, Morris, and Walter 2007).

This approach to ethics is most associated with the philosopher Immanuel Kant (1785). According to Kant, we all have an ethical duty to ourselves and to others—which he calls a **categorical imperative**—that obliges us to follow maxims or rules of conduct. Two important maxims are as follows:

categorical imperative
An unconditional, absolute (without exceptions or qualifiers) moral requirement.

1. An act should be capable of becoming a universal law applicable to everyone across space and time.

2. Rational beings are never solely a means to an end; they are ends in and of themselves. Personal value is not relative; no person has more value or less value than anybody else.

Contemporary deontologists are called *neo-Kantians*. Their influences on today's ethics include the recognition of individual rights, the emphasis on people's intrinsic value, and the doctrine that an act's rightness or wrongness lies in the act itself and not in the consequences the act produces (i.e., an act is right because it is inherently honest, irrespective of the outcome). This tradition gave rise to the concept of ethical duties and is prominent in professional ethics education.

Utilitarianism

In contrast, other theories are termed *consequential* because the moral rightness or wrongness of an act is determined by its end result or consequence. When consequentialists weigh an issue, they consider (1) the person's goal in committing the act, (2) the act's long-term effects on others or society, and (3) the potential costs and benefits of the act.

Utilitarianism, associated with the philosophers Jeremy Bentham and John Stuart Mill, is one such theory. Bentham (1789, I.3) defined utility as "that property in any object, whereby it tends to produce benefit, advantage, pleasure, good, or happiness . . . or . . . to prevent the happening of mischief, pain, evil, or unhappiness to the party whose interest is considered." Bentham and Mill argued that an action's rightness is determined by its **utility** or capacity to maximize happiness (or pleasure) and minimize pain. Mill related having a conscience to a felt obligation to promote the general happiness, even of strangers, and saw such morality as the most basic way to achieve personal happiness and noble character.

> *utility*
> The worth or value of an object to someone; in utilitarianism utility was proposed as a measure of goodness in promoting happiness.

Utilitarianism applies to both individuals and governments. Many government policies, including healthcare policies, are based on utilitarianism. In utilitarian-based policies, the net effects of competing proposals' capacities to maximize advantages and minimize disadvantages are calculated. (This calculation is called *hedonic calculus*; *hedonic* is Greek for "pleasure.") The proposal that produces the most pleasure and the least pain is selected.

For example, two types of economic evaluations follow this process. The first is cost–utility analysis, which measures outcomes in utilities. In healthcare, this analysis identifies the treatment, among several proposed treatments, that gives patients the most years of quality life. The second is cost–benefit analysis, which puts a dollar amount on life outcomes.

Virtue Ethics

Virtue ethics is a normative ethical theory that determines rightness by the quality of a person's character rather than the nature of a person's act or its consequences. In virtue ethics, people are viewed as **moral agents**. A virtue is seen as a disposition or trait of character to behave in a certain way. Virtue ethics can be traced back to Aristotle, who proposed four cardinal virtues: prudence (practical wisdom), fairness (justice), courage, and temperance (self-control). Aristotle (350 BCE) wrote of these virtues as habits, explaining that originally the virtuous traits were innate to our nature; however, we perfected them by habitually using them.

> *moral agent*
> A person who can rationally evaluate right and wrong; who has the power to take voluntary action; who has moral obligations, duties, and responsibilities to act; whose action can be evaluated; and who is accountable for his or her actions.

In a classic paper, Patti Gardiner (2003) explains how virtue ethics might enhance moral sensitivity and actions in the practice of medicine, providing several examples of its application to moral dilemmas (e.g., a patient's refusal of a blood transfusion). She argues that a virtue ethics approach better considers the relationship and emotional factors that are part of being human. Whereas deontology focuses on what ethical duties apply, virtue ethics asks, who should I be?

The concept of virtuous traits that can be perfected by constant practice is important to remember. In healthcare administration, for example, as managers perform their duties, they can strengthen their virtuous character traits by consistently being honest, compassionate, inclusive, respectful, and so on. Additionally, virtue ethics can serve as a guide to professional development and organizational enhancement (Dawson 2018; McCammon and Brody 2012). For example, healthcare managers who want to improve their ability to communicate in an inclusive and respectful manner could focus their continuing education on communicating effectively with culturally diverse communities.

JOHN RAWLS'S PRINCIPLES OF JUSTICE

John Rawls's principles of justice theory is derived from the social contract framework and posits that people agree to organize themselves on the basis of justice and the benefits of mutual cooperation. This agreement has enabled the formation of governments, societies, communities, and other social organizations. Although it was developed within a political framework, the principles of justice theory has relevance for healthcare managers because it focuses on the concept of justice as fairness.

Rawls (1985), a twentieth-century political philosopher, is the father of this theory. He proposed principles that serve as guidelines to social organizations:

- *Liberty principle.* "Each person has an equal right to a fully adequate scheme of equal basic rights and liberties, which scheme is compatible with a similar scheme for all" (Rawls 1985, 227). This principle means that all citizens have the equal right to exercise free speech, vote, hold public office, and take part in other rights and liberties under the law. This principle is more important than the next principle.

- *Equal opportunity principle and the difference principle.* "Social and economic inequalities are to satisfy two conditions: first, they must be attached to offices and positions open to all under conditions of fair equality of opportunity; and second, they must be to the greatest benefit of the least advantaged members of society" (Rawls 1985, 227). This principle means that inequalities in society may exist. Some people may have higher incomes or more power (such as healthcare executives) than other people (such as clerks and receptionists). However, these inequalities may exist *only* if everyone has an equal opportunity to obtain those positions and statuses, and if the least advantaged groups in society receive the greatest benefit from the inequality (such as the improvement of the health outcomes in the poorest neighborhoods).

Rawls's theory emphasizes that, *ideally*, people should be guided solely by justice and the benefits of mutual cooperation when determining society's structures, such as the distribution of rights and resources. However, in *reality*, people are often influenced and prejudiced by their own particular and morally irrelevant circumstances, such as age, gender, race, religion, physical and intellectual abilities, and economic and social status.

Healthcare managers should be aware that their own circumstances may affect their decisions. As ethical managers, they should minimize their biases and maximize justice when developing or weighing solutions or options to ethics-related problems. For example, healthcare managers should ensure that policies and procedures are fair for all patients, regardless of whether those policies and procedures will apply to them or their family sometime in the future.

ETHICS OF CARE

Ethics of care—also known as *care ethics, ethic of caring, ethics of caring,* or *caring ethic*—is a cluster of normative ethical theories focused on relationships, interconnectedness, and harmony. This approach is sometimes identified with Gilligan and feminist approaches to ethics. It emphasizes caring itself as a basis for a moral action (Steyl 2020).

Care ethicists pay attention to the specific or unique details of interpersonal situations. They view ethical conflicts holistically, recognizing that ethical choices are heavily influenced by the conflict's contextual factors, such as family relationships and economic status. They value the experiences of the decision maker and others involved in a situation because these experiences provide real, practical, firsthand knowledge (Benner et al. 2008; Hardin 2018).

The key concerns of care ethicists are as follows:

- Use and misuse of power in relationships
- Lack of empowerment and feelings of powerlessness
- Poor treatment of vulnerable populations as a reflection of society's overall ethical behavior

For example, care ethics is troubled by *brain drain*, the exodus of talented, highly educated, and skilled professionals from their own (typically poor and developing) countries to pursue high-paying jobs and other opportunities in other (typically rich and developed) countries (Raghuram 2009). Note that the relevance of ethics of care has expanded beyond personal relationships and into the realms of politics, government, social policy, and international relations (Held 2006; Kim 2021).

Healthcare managers may apply ethics of care principles when dealing with a patient who has complex, chronic disease. Suppose, for example, that an elderly female patient with Alzheimer's disease is determined to stay in her home no matter what. Her family is concerned that she is no longer able to care for herself and seeks support from her medical providers to place her in a nursing home. Under the ethics of care, the ultimate decision—which is tailored to the patient's particular circumstances—is made in cooperation with the patient, family members, physicians, nurses, and members of the healthcare team, who share information and work together in assuming responsibility. Focusing on interrelatedness, the ethics of care aligns with healthcare's current emphasis on integration and coordination.

In summary, there are many ethical theories and frameworks that provide useful perspectives for healthcare management. While arguably none is fully adequate or without criticism, each theory illuminates important aspects for moral deliberations. Consequences do matter, but sometimes principles are more important. Being moral is about character. While all these theories reject relativism, virtue ethics and care ethics allow for more consideration of relationships and community context.

BEHAVING ETHICALLY

Ethical theories necessarily focus on moral reasoning. Behavior is more complex and affected by personality and situational factors. Behaving ethically requires character, moral awareness and sensitivity, and a commitment to implement moral values. Every day, some individuals ignore misconduct or act unethically themselves when given opportunities to do so. Social psychologists have studied the conditions under which people behave dishonestly (Gino, Ayal, and Ariely 2009; Gino and Bazerman 2009; Gino et al. 2011). For example, cheating among college students increases when they see a peer cheating. Our emotional state, such as being stressed or exhausted, reduces self-control. Dishonesty and even minor infractions reduce trust in one another and can lead to more serious ethical violations (Welsh et al. 2015).

By studying the conditions that affect unethical behavior, these psychologists are able to suggest ways that organizations and society can encourage moral behavior, such as making actions more visible and reminding individuals of ethical standards. For example, a simple sign stating "be kind to one another" reduced illegal parking in accessible spaces. Also, increasing personal engagement and commitment (e.g., signing a statement that you are reporting expenses accurately) promoted more ethical behavior (Ayal et al. 2015).

As evidenced by widely publicized corporate scandals, organizations may be even more vulnerable to ethical violations than individuals. In this context, the organizational climate may encourage **moral disengagement**, allowing individual decision makers to justify unethical conduct (Welsh et al. 2015).

moral disengagement
The process of convincing the self that ethical standards do not apply to oneself in a particular context.

The theory of moral engagement (Bandura 1999) is concerned with how individuals rationalize unethical or unjust actions that depart from usual ethical principles to avoid self-condemnation. This involves processes such as reconstructing immoral conduct, diffusing responsibility, dehumanizing the victim, and misrepresenting injurious consequences. Particularly relevant to organizational ethical issues is diffusion of responsibility. Managers may say that they were merely following the dictates of a board or organizational leader and cannot be held responsible. Moreover, when an executive group decides a policy, no single person feels responsible for any negative consequences. Clear and communicated ethical norms can help prevent inappropriate, deceitful, or illegal practices and emphasize the organization's commitment to ethical principles. Moreover, managers and leaders should always model ethical behavior by conducting themselves in an ethical manner.

Although some researchers have investigated dark personality traits (e.g., Machiavellianism, narcissism) in unethical conduct (Somma et al. 2020), most health professionals likely wish to behave ethically. Their violations may reflect a lapse of judgment or sensitivity to a situation that has ethical implications. Consider the case of a hospital administrator who lost his job because he accepted a surgeon's invitation to make an incision on a patient. It is likely that he quickly regretted this action, after considering how it affected the hospital's reputation and how he was clearly outside his competence (Gooch 2020).

Moreover, behaving ethically is sometimes presented as being virtuous and feeling good. Behaving ethically more often involves a choice between unattractive alternatives. For example, Bill is an effective healthcare administrator in a medical center who is respected and liked by the physician staff, many of whom have become his friends. Dr. Smith, who Bill has known for years, is aging and has begun to experience cognitive difficulties, which he doesn't acknowledge and some of his colleagues dismiss. As these cognitive difficulties are apparent to him, Bill must decide whether he should put his friend on administrative leave, even though this would end their friendship and perhaps negatively affect his relations with the medical staff. Such situations demand that healthcare managers not only engage in a process of ethical reasoning but also exhibit **moral courage**.

In his highly recommended book of that name, Rushworth Kidder (2006, 72) defines moral courage as "the quality of mind and spirit that enables one to face up to ethical challenges firmly and confidently, without flinching or retreating." He describes how moral courage involves drawing on moral values, understanding the risks, and enduring the hardships that may flow from ethical action. The latter draws on trust in past experiences, character, personal intuition, and faith.

moral courage
The ability to stand up for what is ethically right with confidence and commitment.

Mini-Case Study

Individuals are said to need moral courage when they are faced with challenging policies or practices in their work organization that they believe are wrong (i.e., whistleblowing). Often, such cases involve fraud. For example, Comprehensive Pain Specialists (CPS), a national company of pain clinics (a laboratory and 60 clinics across six states), was accused of fraudulently billing Medicare for expensive and unnecessary urine tests. A news report (McLaren 2019) explained that it is standard procedure in pain clinics to initially assess new patients with a drug test to ensure that they are not already taking opioids; most clinics screen for opiates only at that initial visit. However, CPS's policy was to opt for expensive qualitative tests for every patient at every visit. According to court documents, "This testing was commonly referred to as 'liquid gold'—leaving no doubt that profit was Defendants' primary objective in performing urine drug testing."

CPS providers mostly ignored or overlooked these test results in making patient decisions. Multiple employees then brought lawsuits against CPS stating that the company had retaliated against them for questioning company policies. Dr. Suzanne Alt was one such whistleblower, reporting that CPS had inflated bills for unnecessary tests. When she asked a supervisor why CPS never used cheaper drug tests, she was advised to "test the CPS way." A month later, she was fired. Another employee who worked as an insurance specialist for CPS alleged that she had been made to repeatedly forge a founding physician's signature. Upon investigation, the US Department of Justice joined the suit against CPS, alleging that it had defrauded the government out of more than $25 million by submitting "thousands of false claims to federal and state-funded health care programs" (McLaren 2019).

In a review of the research literature on whistleblowing in healthcare, John Blenkinsopp and colleagues (2019, 738) distinguished between studies focusing on clinical matters and those focusing on financial wrongdoing, which dominates the general literature on whistleblowing. They defined whistleblowing as "raising concerns about unsafe, unethical or poor quality care to persons able to effect action." The authors reviewed 55 such studies conducted internationally (9.5 percent in the United States), most of which involved nurses highlighting their role as patient advocates. In addition, most of the studies focused on individuals and their decisions to report, although other influences were highlighted in their review. Education and professional socialization by strong mentors was found to be important. Also, those in management roles were more likely to report with organizational culture perhaps the strongest influence. The climate of an organization was viewed as influencing and being affected by having clear whistleblowing policies and the organization's response to reported concerns. Individuals who report wrongdoing are likely to experience emotional distress and negative consequences, including peer rejection, so external whistleblowing is generally considered a last resort.

Of relevance to healthcare managers is the importance of moral leadership and the challenging perception that complaints often are not dealt with appropriately. There is a need for healthcare managers to develop policies and practices, including staff training that emphasizes putting patient care first. In focusing on organizational responses, whistleblowing might be reframed for healthcare managers not as a threat, but as providing valuable information that can help organizations improve services (Blenkinsopp et al. 2019).

MINI-CASE STUDY QUESTIONS

1. If you were a new employee in a healthcare setting and had concerns about a financial or clinical practice in the organization, what steps would you consider taking to address your concern? What are some resources that you might use?
2. Have you ever experienced any situation (e.g., cheating on an exam, alcohol or other drug misuse, misrepresentation) that you believed negatively affected the behavior of individuals or eroded ethics? What did you do? Can you think of interventions that might encourage appropriate behavior and higher ethical standards?
3. How can you avoid the erosion of your own ethics?
4. How can you prevent the erosion of others' ethics?

POINTS TO REMEMBER

➤ Ethics is a system of beliefs and behaviors that people value and use to control their conduct.

➤ The four branches of ethics are descriptive ethics, normative ethics, moral psychology, and applied ethics.

➤ Healthcare managers use applied ethics, which includes bioethics, business ethics, organizational ethics, and profession-specific ethics.

- Ethical theories in philosophy includes deontology, utilitarianism, virtue ethics, John Rawls's principles of justice, and the ethics of care.
- Behaving ethically involves more than moral reasoning, as many situational variables affect our behavior. Unfortunately, others and social context may influence good people to sometimes behave badly.
- Responding to and implementing ethical decisions in challenging situations requires moral courage.

Challenge Yourself

1. Have you ever used a system to decide the rightness or wrongness of your own actions? Someone else's actions? How did you make your determination? Were any of the ethical branches or theories similar to your way of thinking?
2. Research an emerging technology that interests you, along with its uses in healthcare. Briefly describe the advantages and possible risks of this technology.
3. Can you identify situations in which bioethics and organizational ethics overlap? How might the beliefs of clinicians (professionals providing hands-on care) differ from the beliefs of healthcare managers?
4. You and a group of five friends purchased tickets for a play at your local community theater. Your plan is to meet at your home at 6:00 p.m., go to a nice restaurant for dinner, and then proceed to the theater. The plan is to be at the theater by 7:45 p.m. for the 8:00 p.m. play. Timing is essential. One of your friends is known to be consistently and significantly late, and you and the others know that she will not show up on time. So, secretly, the four of you have decided to tell her that the meeting time is at 5:30 p.m., giving her enough time to be tardy without messing up the schedule. How would utilitarianists and deontologists judge your act?
5. Now, imagine that you are a manager in a large, multifacility physician practice. You are formulating your unit's budget request, and you have asked the unit supervisors to turn in their reports by May 1 to ensure that the request is reviewed, revised, and aggregated into the organizational budget by June 15. One of the supervisors always submits his work late. His reports are three to five days late. You have decided to tell him that his report is due April 20. Consider your decision from the points of view of utilitarianists and deontologists.
6. In the United States, most health insurance is linked to employment. Using Rawls's principles of justice theory, make an argument for unlinking health insurance from employment.
7. How would you evaluate whistleblowing and laws that protect whistleblowers? What is society's interest in whistleblowing? What do you see as the advantages or disadvantages of whistleblowing?

For Your Consideration

2.1 According to ethicist William Nelson (2005), healthcare managers and leaders should use the approach of procedural justice when making decisions. Procedural justice is similar to stakeholder theory in that it "takes into account the rights, values, and interests of the broad range of individuals and groups who are affected by" an ethical conflict and "will be harmed by or will benefit from the decision" (Nelson 2005, 10). In applying procedural justice to ethical conflicts, one challenge is how to prioritize the competing values. Werhane (2000) suggests that for healthcare organizations, the appropriate prioritization should be (1) patients or the population served, (2) clinicians and staff, and (3) the organization, including its financial stability.

Review the example of the elderly patient with Alzheimer's disease in the "Ethics of Care" section and then consider the following:
   a. Prioritize the interests of the affected individuals and groups according to Nelson's definition of procedural justice.
   b. What happens to the interests of family members, neighbors, friends, and lay volunteers (such as Meals on Wheels staff)?
   c. Do the presence or absence of public transportation and community services and the elderly patient's personal social support system (such as religious organizations) matter in procedural justice?
   d. What would justify the decision *not* to prioritize the elderly patient's (or population's) interests first?

2.2 You have returned from vacation to find that your office has been moved.
   a. Under what conditions would a consequentialist conclude that the person or people who moved your office acted morally?
   b. Consider the actions of the person or people who moved your office using principlism. Do you have enough information to resolve your ethical concerns?
   c. What additional information would help you reach a decision about the morality of this situation?
   d. As a moral agent, how should you respond to this situation?

References

Aristotle. 350 BCE. "Book II, Section 4." In *Nicomachean Ethics*. Internet Classics Archive. Accessed August 30, 2021. http://classics.mit.edu/Aristotle/nicomachaen.2.ii.html.

Ayal, S., F. Gino, R. Barkan, and D. Ariely. 2015. "Three Principles to REVISE People's Unethical Behavior." *Perspectives on Psychological Science* 10 (6): 738–41.

Bandura, A. 1999. "Moral Disengagement in the Preparation of Inhumanities." *Personality and Social Psychology Review* 3: 193–209.

Beauchamp, T. L., and J. F. Childress. 2013. *Principles of Biomedical Ethics*, 7th ed. New York: Oxford University Press.

Benner, P., M. Sutphen, V. Leonard-Kahn, and L. Day. 2008. "Formation and Everyday Ethical Comportment." *American Journal of Critical Care* 17 (5): 473–76.

Bentham, J. 1789. *An Introduction to the Principles of Morals and Legislation*. Library of Economics and Liberty. Accessed January 13, 2021. www.econlib.org/library/YPDBooks/Jevons/jvnPE.html?chapter_num=7#book-reader.

Blenkinsopp, J., N. Snowden, R. Mannion, M. Powell, H. Davies, R. Millar, and J. McHale. 2019. "Whistleblowing over Patient Safety and Care Quality: A Review of the Literature." *Journal of Health Organization and Management* 33 (6): 737–56.

Cudney, P. 2014. "What Really Separates Casuistry from Principlism in Biomedical Ethics." *Theoretical Medicine and Bioethics* 35 (3): 205–29.

Dawson, D. 2018. "Organisational Virtue, Moral Attentiveness, and the Perceived Role of Ethics and Social Responsibility in Business: The Case of UK HR Practitioners." *Journal of Business Ethics* 148 (4): 765–81.

Dmytriyev, S., and A. C. Wicks. 2018. "Building Bridges: Patricia Werhane, Business Ethics and Health Care." In *The Moral Imagination of Patricia Werhane: A Festschrift*, edited by R. Freeman, S. Dmytriyev, and A. Wicks, 143–63. Champaign, IL: Springer.

Ellis, M. 2019. "Top 10 Medical Technologies of 2019." Proclinical. Published February 27. www.proclinical.com/blogs/2019-2/top-10-new-medical-technologies-of-2019.

Freeman, R. E., A. C. Wicks, and B. Parmar. 2004. "Stakeholder Theory and the Corporate Objective Revisited." *Organization Science* 15 (3): 364–69.

Gardiner, P. 2003. "A Virtue Ethics Approach to Moral Dilemmas in Medicine." *Journal of Medical Ethics* 29 (5): 297–302.

Gilligan, C. 1982. *In a Different Voice: Psychological Theory and Women's Development*. Cambridge, MA: Harvard University Press.

Gino, F., S. Ayal, and D. Ariely. 2009. "Contagion and Differentiation in Unethical Behavior: The Effect of One Bad Apple on the Barrel." *Psychological Science* 20 (3): 393–98.

Gino, F., and M. H. Bazerman. 2009. "When Misconduct Goes Unnoticed: The Acceptability of Gradual Erosion in Others' Unethical Behavior." *Journal of Experimental Social Psychology* 45 (4): 708–19.

Gino, F., M. E. Schweitzer, N. L. Mead, and D. Ariely. 2011. "Unable to Resist Temptation: How Self-Control Depletion Promotes Unethical Behavior." *Organizational Behavior and Human Decision Processes* 115 (2): 191–203.

Gooch, K. 2020. "Former Tennessee Hospital CEO Says He Was Asked to Resign After Participating in Surgery." *Becker's Hospital Review*. Published August 25. www.beckershospitalreview.com/hospital-management-administration/former-tennessee-hospital-ceo-says-he-was-asked-to-resign-after-participating-in-surgery.html.

Harbut, R. F. 2019. "AMA Code of Medical Ethics' Opinions Related to Ethics of Life-Sustaining Technologies." *AMA Journal of Ethics* 21 (5): E416–20.

Hardin, J. 2018. "Everyday Ethical Comportment: An Evolutionary Concept Analysis." *Journal of Nursing Education* 57 (8): 460–68.

Held, V. 2006. *The Ethics of Care: Personal, Political, and Global.* New York: Oxford University Press.

Kant, I. 1785. *Fundamental Principles of the Metaphysic of Morals*, translated by T. K. Abbott. London: Longmans, Green & Co.

Kidder, R. M. 2006. *Moral Courage.* New York: HarperCollins.

Kim, H.-K. 2021. "Care Ethics as a Challenge to the Structural Oppression Surrounding Care." *Ethics and Social Welfare* 15 (2): 151–66.

Kohlberg, L. 1981. *The Philosophy of Moral Development.* San Francisco: Harper & Row.

Lahey, T., E. G. DeRenzo, J. Crites, J. Fanning, B. J. Huberman, and J. P. Slosar. 2020. "Building an Organizational Ethics Program on a Clinical Ethics Foundation." *Journal of Clinical Ethics* 31 (3): 259–67.

McCammon, D., and H. Brody. 2012. "How Virtue Ethics Informs Medical Professionalism." *HEC Forum* 24 (4): 257–72.

McLaren, M. L. 2019. "Government Joins Seven Whistleblowers in $50 Million Lawsuit Against Sen. Steve Dickerson and CPS Pain Clinics over Fraudulent Urine Test Billings." *Whistleblower News Review*. Published August 20. www.whistleblowergov.org/healthcare-and-pharma.php?article=government-joins-7-whistleblowers-in-50m-lawsuit-against-senator-and-clinics_154.

Nelson, W. A. 2005. "An Organizational Ethics Decision-Making Process." *Healthcare Executive* 20 (4): 8–14.

Pearson, S. D., J. E. Sabin, and E. J. Emanuel. 2003. *No Margin, No Mission: Health-Care Organizations and the Quest for Ethical Excellence*. New York: Oxford University Press.

Raghuram, P. 2009. "Caring About 'Brain Drain' Migration in a Postcolonial World." *Geoforum* 40 (1): 25–33.

Rawls, J. 1985. "Justice as Fairness: Political Not Metaphysical." *Philosophy and Public Affairs* 14 (3): 223–51.

Robertson, M., K. Morris, and G. Walter. 2007. "Overview of Psychiatric Ethics V: Utilitarianism and the Ethics of Duty." *Australasian Psychiatry* 15 (5): 402–10.

Sadiku, M., Y. P. Akhare, and S. M. Musa. 2019. "Emerging Technologies in Healthcare: A Tutorial." *International Journal of Advances in Scientific Research and Engineering* 5 (7): 199–204.

Somma, A., S. Borroni, M. Sellbom, K. E Markon, R. F Krueger, and A. Fossati. 2020. "Assessing Dark Triad Dimensions from the Perspective of Moral Disengagement and DSM-5 Alternative Model of Personality Disorder Traits." *Personality Disorders* 11 (2): 100–107.

Steyl, S. 2020. "A Care Ethical Theory of Right Action." *Philosophical Quarterly* 71 (3): 502–23.

US Department of Justice (DOJ). 2015. "Minnesota-Based ev3 to Pay United States $1.25 Million to Settle False Claims Act Allegations." Published February 5. www.justice.gov/opa/pr/minnesota-based-ev3-pay-united-states-125-million-settle-false-claims-act-allegations.

Wadhwa, V. 2014. "Laws and Ethics Can't Keep Pace with Technology." *MIT Technology Review*. Published April 15. www.technologyreview.com/2014/04/15/172377/laws-and-ethics-cant-keep-pace-with-technology/.

Walker, M. J. 2017. "Ethics and Advanced Medical Devices: Do We Need a New Approach?" *Health Voices* 21. Published November. https://healthvoices.org.au/issues/november-2017/ethics-advanced-medical-devices-need-new-approach/.

Welsh, D. T., L. D. Ordóñez, D. G. Snyder, and M. S. Christian. 2015. "The Slippery Slope: How Small Ethical Transgressions Pave the Way for Larger Future Transgressions." *Journal of Applied Psychology* 100 (1): 114–27.

Werhane, P. H. 2000. "Business Ethics, Stakeholder Theory, and the Ethics of Healthcare Organizations." *Cambridge Quarterly of Healthcare Ethics* 9 (2): 169–81.

CHAPTER 3
PROFESSIONALISM

Never let your sense of morals prevent you from doing what is right.
—Isaac Asimov, science writer

Important Terms

- Charisma
- Corporate social responsibility
- Evidence-based management
- Health Insurance Portability and Accountability Act of 1996 (HIPAA)
- Integrity
- Internship preceptor
- Interprofessionalism
- Moral leadership
- Professionalism
- Professional role

Learning Objectives

Studying this chapter will help you to

➤ explain the concept of professionalism,

➤ explain the concept of interprofessionalism,

➤ describe the importance of healthcare managers' participation as equal members of the interprofessional team,

➤ discuss healthcare managers as ethical leaders, and

➤ evaluate the role of healthcare managers in corporate social responsibility.

Healthcare managers—whether they work in a hospital, physician practice, community clinic, long-term care facility, or government health agency—are expected to have mastered several competencies. One of those competencies is the focus of this chapter: professionalism.

> **CASE FROM THE FIELD**
> **Becoming Professionals**
>
> College senior Rob Marley enters the student lounge of his university's Department of Health Services Management for the first fall semester meeting of the Future Healthcare Managers (FHM) student organization. At the end of the last semester, he was elected to serve as FHM's president. In that role, he is now responsible for planning and holding events where health services management majors can network with each other and with local health administration leaders. Rob also wants to lead two service projects during the school year—(1) a fundraiser for the local HIV/AIDS service organization and (2) a volunteering opportunity for FHM in a community hospital's annual Teddy Bear Clinic, designed to help children become more comfortable and at ease in a hospital setting. He knows that FHM's events will help him and his fellow students become more professional and will prepare them to work in healthcare leadership roles.
>
> Rob's immediate career plans are to complete an undergraduate degree in health services management and then earn a master's degree in health informatics and information management. Afterward, he wants to work in a hospital setting and use his computer and technical skills to manage and coordinate healthcare data. Ultimately, he wants to be a chief information officer (CIO) of a large (more than 300 beds) acute care hospital. He learned of the CIO position when he attended a tour (arranged by FHM) of a university medical center's information systems department. The CIO spoke to the visiting group, and right then, Rob knew he wanted to follow the CIO's career path.
>
> Meanwhile, college senior Maria Diaz arrives at a healthcare clinic for the first day of her internship, a partial requirement for her bachelor's degree in health administration. In this position, she is assisting with the clinic's public outreach efforts. Specifically, she will be creating and designing a clinic brochure for an upcoming diabetes prevention program and contributing to grant writing for the clinic's five service delivery locations.
>
> Maria applied to intern for the clinic because it delivers primary care regardless of patients' ability to pay. Working in the healthcare field really matters to her, and being an intern for an organization like the clinic is one way she can start to help families in a situation similar to what she had experienced. During the COVID-19 pandemic, her mom was laid off, and the family lost their health insurance coverage. This, in turn, caused a financial hardship for the family because Maria's dad had diabetes and was insulin dependent. A healthcare clinic similar to the one where she is interning helped them. Her professional goal is to be a manager and eventually a leader for the clinic or one just like it.
>
> *(continued)*

> **CASE FROM THE FIELD**
> **Becoming Professionals** (continued)
>
> Rob and Maria are examples of students of the healthcare management profession who are advancing their understanding of the field's professionals, their roles and responsibilities, and the required technical and interpersonal skills—hands-on. While Rob and Maria plan to pursue their career goals in different healthcare settings, both are developing skills that will help them become professionals.
>
> Rob sits down at the conference table and greets the members of the FHM, while Maria shakes hands with her internship supervisor, the clinic's outreach director. Both students are beaming with nervous energy, excited that today they are a student leader and an intern, respectively, but tomorrow a CIO and an administrator.

One of the lessons learned by students of health administration is that healthcare is always changing, and these changes place new demands on healthcare managers. Currently, the demands focus on lowering costs but improving health outcomes for patients. To this end, healthcare managers are constantly looking for ways to provide the safest environment possible that leads to high quality of care and brings about measurably better outcomes without adding significant costs to the already stretched organizational budget. Healthcare managers can determine what works best through a practice known as **evidence-based management**, whereby the approaches that consistently yield desirable results (according to research findings) are examined, tailored to fit a specific need, and strategically applied. According to Mary Stefl (2008, 360), this "shift to evidence-based management has led to numerous efforts to define the competencies most appropriate for healthcare." Stefl served as a consultant to the task force of the Healthcare Leadership Alliance (HLA) charged with determining such competencies, which have become integral in healthcare management education.

evidence-based management
A practice whereby the approaches that consistently yield desirable results are examined, tailored to fit a specific need, and strategically applied.

> **DID YOU KNOW?**
> Healthcare Leadership Alliance
>
> The Healthcare Leadership Alliance is composed of six professional associations in healthcare. This brief list highlights each organization's features.
> 1. American College of Healthcare Executives (www.ache.org)
>   • Professional society for healthcare executives
>   • More than 48,000 members
>
> *(continued)*

> **DID YOU KNOW?**
> **Healthcare Leadership Alliance** *(continued)*

- Offers student-associate level of membership to students enrolled in an undergraduate or a graduate health administration program of a regionally accredited university

2. American Organization of Nurse Executives (www.aone.org)
   - Professional society for nurse executives
   - Subsidiary of the American Hospital Association
   - Focuses on shaping healthcare through nursing leadership
   - Offers student memberships to full-time, pre-licensure nursing students

3. Healthcare Financial Management Association (www.hfma.org)
   - Professional society for healthcare financial management executives
   - Serves as a resource on healthcare financial issues, information, and education
   - Offers student memberships at reduced fee to full-time college students interested in healthcare finance and not currently employed in the profession

4. Healthcare Information and Management Systems Society (www.himss.org)
   - Professional society for healthcare information technology professionals
   - More than 80,000 members
   - Focuses on how information technology can help improve healthcare
   - Offers student membership to full-time students who attend an accredited college or university and who are interested in health information and management

5. Medical Group Management Association (www.mgma.com)
   - Professional society for administrators in medical group practices
   - More than 55,000 members
   - Offers student memberships to full-time students

6. American College of Medical Practice Executives (www.mgma.com)
   - Merged with MGMA in 2011
   - Prior to the merger, served as the educational resource and provider organization for MGMA

Members of these professional associations have much in common. First and most, they all work in the healthcare field. Second, they share similar expertise (management) and language (terms used in healthcare delivery generally and in healthcare administration specifically). Third, they are educated in college and university programs, many of which have undergone accreditation or certification reviews to ensure that their programs offer students the opportunity to achieve a level of performance that is consistent with industry expectations. The members of the associations that make up with HLA include alumni of some of the certified or accredited programs as well as professors who are educating future healthcare executives.

The HLA task force identified five competency domains for the healthcare management profession (Stefl 2008). Since the publication of the HLA task force's five competency domains, they have become commonly used in program assessment, and they are now the standard for programs certified by the Association of University Programs in Health Administration (Cellucci, Molinari, and Young 2018). The five domains are as follows:

1. Communication and relationship management
2. Professionalism
3. Leadership
4. Knowledge of the healthcare system
5. Business skills and knowledge

We discuss two of these areas in this chapter: professionalism and leadership.

What Is Professionalism?

In its simplest form, **professionalism** can be defined as the knowledge, skills, abilities, and conduct expected of practitioners of a profession. The HLA task force offers a more elaborate definition: "the ability to align personal and organizational conduct with ethical and professional standards that include a responsibility to the patient and the community, a service orientation, and a commitment to lifelong learning and improvement" (Garman et al. 2006, 219). Both of these definitions imply a foreknowledge, a prerequisite ability, or know-how—and that is true. For a student of a profession to become a professional, the student should first learn the basics (through formal education and training) and accumulate firsthand experience in and exposure to the field (through internships, on-the-job training, site visits, and other means).

professionalism
The knowledge, skills, abilities, and conduct expected of practitioners of a profession.

Exhibit 3.1 details how professionalism develops at each career level (entry, middle, and senior); recent college graduates without experience typically fall into the entry-level category. This list includes competency areas, such as the following:

- *Understanding professional roles and norms.* **Professional role** refers to the assigned and expected functions, responsibilities, and working relationships of a person in a professional position. A professional norm, as defined in chapter 1, is an internalized standard of conduct to which professionals automatically and unconsciously conform. For example, if you are in a healthcare manager role (regardless of career level), a norm is to remain up to date on current management practices by attending continuing education events, such as seminars or workshops and annual association meetings. For more examples of professional norms, see exhibit 1.1 in chapter 1.

professional role
The assigned and expected functions, responsibilities, and working relationships of a person in a professional position.

EXHIBIT 3.1
Professionalism and Its Development at Different Career Levels

	Entry level	Middle level	Senior level
Definition	First position out of graduate school up to first level of leadership	"Manager of managers" roles up to service-line level	From vice president up
Competency areas			
Understanding of professional roles and norms	Joining relevant professional associations; attending events; getting involved in committees	Maintaining professional activities; seeking out opportunities to observe and model senior-level norms	Modeling professionalism within one's organization; encouraging professionalism in others
Working with others	Developing skills in giving and receiving feedback; strategically developing work relationships across the organization	Cultivating working relationships across the organization; developing relationships with others in similar positions at other organizations; actively seeking and providing feedback	Cultivating a feedback-rich environment; helping direct reports align career goals with organizational objectives; encouraging others to pursue professional development
Self-management	Developing balance between roles within and outside of work; actively planning and managing one's career	Maintaining an effective work–life integration; continuing to monitor and manage time and stress; planning for career and postcareer life	Ensuring that roles within and outside work blend effectively; actively planning postcareer transition; preparing successors
Contribution	Directly contributing one's time and resources to help others; seeking others to help develop one's expertise	Contributing expertise and resources, both within and outside the organization through activities such as mentoring, writing/presenting, and advocacy	Modeling and promoting the importance of contributing; developing a climate that facilitates others' contributions

Source: Adapted with permission from Garman et al. (2006), 221.

- *Working with others.* This entails giving and accepting both positive and negative feedback as well as developing and maintaining working relationships with people in similar or different roles. For example, you will need to work effectively with other healthcare administrators and clinicians as a member of the team. This working well together—as a member of the team dedicated to patient care—illustrates the value of interprofessionalism, a concept elaborated later in this chapter.

- *Self-management.* This is associated with time management, maintaining high ethical standards, and career planning (especially if you are in entry- and middle-level positions).

- *Contributing or giving back.* This involves providing free or volunteer service to the community, the profession, and the people you work with, as well as those who have served you.

Achieving competency in these four areas is a step toward professionalism. Importantly, doing so will familiarize you with a multitude of concepts, including ethical standards, career evolution, continuing professional education, and serving others. The ethical standards you learn at this stage of your career (such as the profession's codes of ethics, the organization's values, and the culture's practices or norms) will not only guide your decision-making and behavior but also prompt you to examine your own long-held moral views and convictions. You may fully determine whether your personal values and mission fit with the values and mission of the organization and the profession you want to join or have joined. To assess your mastery of these competencies, you can use the *Healthcare Executive Competencies Assessment Tool* developed by the American College of Healthcare Executives (ACHE 2021).

Simply put, ethics is the cornerstone of professionalism. You will be working in a field in which the decisions you make will affect the health and well-being of others. Ethical standards will guide you in making the best possible choices.

INTERPROFESSIONALISM

Interprofessionalism is defined by the Institute of Medicine (2003, 54) as an interdisciplinary team "composed of members from different professions and occupations with varied and specialized knowledge, skills, and methods." As part of an interdisciplinary team, healthcare administrators and clinicians (e.g., physicians, nurses, physical therapists, speech pathologists, occupational therapists, and other health professionals) help determine and implement policies and actions to ensure better patient care. Key to success is each person understanding their distinct and critical role on a team, which is part of mastering the professional competency of working well with others. Thus, a necessary step is to communicate the value that each team member offers to achieve role clarity (Bittner 2018).

interprofessionalism
Healthcare professionals from different disciplines working together collaboratively for better patient care.

The case that introduced part I of this text asked how a hospital should balance patients' health needs with its financial bottom line in the utilization of the emergency department. Should hospitals engage in proactive population health initiatives if they result in decreased revenue from their emergency departments? What values should guide their thinking about this question? Grounded in an emerging legal and moral consensus on hospitals' obligations to their surrounding communities, the commentary on this case study proposes that treating emergency departments purely as revenue streams violates both legal and moral standards.

This case highlights a situation in which interprofessional collaboration could help General Hospital's physicians and executives affirm what it means to be a professional and an ethical leader as they deliberate their responsibilities and obligations and guide their best course of action. Their decisions will influence their entire career as professionals who are charged with bringing about better patient care and provide service to their community.

The benefits of interprofessional collaboration are illustrated by the increase in telehealthcare delivery during the COVID-19 pandemic. Patient needs continued even though the pandemic made face-to-face patient encounters difficult and potentially unsafe for both providers and patients (the virus is transmitted mainly from person to person within close contact through respiratory droplets). Telehealth emerged as a partial solution that would allow providers and patients to meet virtually. The term *telehealth* refers to "any health care services delivered at a distance" (Mahoney 2020, 439). Healthcare providers turned to this modality, when appropriate, to offer virtual patient care.

Interprofessional teams maintained quality care delivered by telehealth and, in the process, discovered benefits for both patients and healthcare professionals. According to the US Department of Health and Human Services (2021), the benefits of telehealth delivery include limiting exposure to COVID-19, reducing transit time for both patients and providers, and expanding patient access to providers who are located elsewhere. Telehealth interprofessional teams are composed of administrative and clinical team members to ensure quality care. For example, University of Virginia healthcare teams working with cystic fibrosis patients found that telehealth enabled them to develop an interprofessional virtual clinic to provide continued coordinated care throughout the pandemic (Compton et al. 2020). Health information managers provided data management and ensured the availability of health information technology needed for telehealth delivery, and healthcare managers coordinated activities to ensure compliance with the **Health Insurance Portability and Accountability Act (HIPAA)** of 1996 and to maintain appropriate staffing for administrative actions (scheduling patient appointments, billing) and clinical encounters (occupational therapists, physical therapists, nurses).

Clinicians followed a clinic flow sheet, so that virtual meetings allowed the patient to enter a HIPAA-compliant virtual room, and then clinicians could enter one at a time, notifying the next provider to enter when it was their time to meet with the patient. Moreover, the team met following each appointment to review the process, work together, and offer ideas for quality improvement. As a result, patient care continued during the pandemic, and the telehealth interprofessional team delivery was recognized as both "feasible and sustainable" (Compton et al. 2020, 983).

Health Insurance Portability and Accountability Act of 1996 (HIPAA)
A federal law that set the standards for protecting the privacy of patients' health information.

Internship Professionalism

Undergraduate students' journey to professionalism may be evidenced by their activities, conduct, and performance during their internship experience (which is at least 120 hours in a healthcare setting) and program portfolio (which consists of written materials that represent the internship experience) (Casciani 2012). An **internship preceptor** serves as an intern's practitioner supervisor. In this role, the preceptor is responsible for guiding the intern's work and performance, encouraging the intern to behave professionally (such as working well with others and following the code of ethics), and assessing the intern's level of professionalism.

Preceptors' responses to specific student behaviors allow for them and the program director to evaluate progress toward mastery of specific competencies. Exhibit 3.2 lists criteria for the assessment of the competency domain of professionalism in undergraduate interns.

internship preceptor
An intern's practitioner supervisor.

EXHIBIT 3.2
Evaluating the Professionalism of Undergraduate Interns

Professionalism	Competency	Measurement
Ability to align personal conduct with ethical and professional standards that include a service orientation and a commitment to lifelong learning	Be attentive, proactive, and ready to learn	Preceptor evaluation
	Meet commitments and complete tasks according to assigned requirements	Preceptor evaluation
	Treat others with respect; show sensitivity to their views, values, and customs	Preceptor evaluation
	Demonstrate ethical behavior consistent with professional code of ethics	Preceptor evaluation
	Prepare for lifelong learning and career planning	Program portfolio
	Assume responsibility for one's own career management and goal setting	Program portfolio
	Demonstrate effective resume and interviewing skills	Program portfolio

Source: Reprinted with permission from Casciani (2012). All rights reserved.

As you experience your internship, keep in mind that that your preceptor will be asked to evaluate your performance. One note of caution is in order here, however: Do not expect to master all competencies during your entry-level years. Throughout your course of study, you will be learning to think like an administrator, applying principles to healthcare situations. These courses will prepare you for the internship experience (Wilson 2016). Nonetheless, mastery does not come about quickly; it is achieved throughout a career.

Effective and Moral Leadership

The HLA task force defined leadership as "the ability to inspire individual and organizational excellence, to create and attain a shared vision, and to successfully manage change to attain the organization's strategic ends and successful performance" (Stefl 2008, 364). This definition can be broken down into three leadership competencies (Garman, Butler, and Brinkmeyer 2006, 362):

1. Establishing a compelling vision and developing energizing goals
2. Enhancing organizational climate by building trust, facilitating individual motivation, encouraging teamwork, and supporting and valuing diversity
3. Developing leaders by supporting and mentoring high-potential talent as well as planning for leadership succession

With the help of their professors and cooperation from their peers, students can begin developing these competencies during their undergraduate years.

Volunteering to fill a leadership role and engaging followers are good ways to practice the first competency. For example, Rob—the newly elected student leader of FHM (see the Case from the Field earlier in this chapter)—plans to coordinate two events that will not only serve his community and introduce his group to different aspects of the healthcare profession but also create energy and excitement among FHM members.

The second competency may be developed through team classwork and assignments. Team members can assess one another on leadership criteria such as team management, individual motivation, and inspiring team members (Casciani 2012; Chhabria et al. 2019).

The third competency depends on one's position in a healthcare organization. It is seen at the middle and senior career levels—not entry level—and it signals that leadership evolves and involves different activities and focus over time. As a student, you may enter a mentoring relationship and build on what you learn from the experience to benefit you and someone else later in your career.

Being an effective leader is evidenced by what the professional actually does—that is, their actions, behaviors, and performance, and not just their words, intentions, or plans. In his classic 1988 article "Leadership: More Doing than Dash," Peter F. Drucker—known as the father of business management—wrote that leadership is *not* about **charisma** or a set of personality traits. Rather, it is about **integrity**, responsibility, and adherence to goals and standards.

Integrity is a characteristic that is also associated with **moral leadership**. Robert Coles (2000, xiv)—professor emeritus at Harvard University, Pulitzer Prize winner, and recipient of the Presidential Medal of Freedom—defined moral leaders in his book as those who exhibit "courage and idealism, and a capacity for effectiveness, an ability to get things done." As an example, Coles profiled people—both famous and not famous, official and unofficial leaders—who were involved in the 1960s civil rights movement in the United States. One of those moral leaders was Albert Jones, a parent who volunteered to drive the bus that transported the first African American children to a newly integrated school in Boston. When asked why he had acted as he did, Jones answered, "[S]o I could look at myself in the mirror and not want to run away in shame: that's the explanation, for sure" (Coles 2000, 211).

Moral leadership requires professional leaders to understand that it does matter that they like what they see in the mirror. It requires leaders to do, not just think of, what is right. For example, Maria (see the Case from the Field in this chapter) plans to work in an organization whose value is to provide healthcare to people who need it, regardless of their ability to pay. While such organizations must earn enough income to keep their doors open, they prioritize people before profit.

The characteristics associated with leadership are as pertinent today as they were when the HLA identified them in 2006. Healthcare managers' moral leadership is key to establishing and maintaining an ethical culture at the workplace. So is their work as members of interprofessional teams with their clinical and administrative colleagues to identify and address any barriers to an ethical workplace. ACHE (2020) encourages such actions and reaffirms its position by stating that they are a "professional obligation."

charisma
The special personal appeal that disarms and draws in other people.

integrity
A person's honest, virtuous, and thus trustworthy quality.

moral leadership
Leadership characterized by courage to do the right or ethical thing no matter what.

Corporate Social Responsibility Engagement

Corporations—such as hospitals, pharmaceutical companies, and healthcare clinics—play a significant role in creating social value in their community. For example, some local health centers hold fairs to educate the public about a disease and to provide disease screenings. Other healthcare organizations offer charity care to those who cannot afford services, and still others provide tuition reimbursement or free continuing education to their staff. Sustainability is also important to creating social value, as some organizations ensure that new buildings constructed for their healthcare facilities use solar energy and that water use is efficient (Haddiya, Janfi, and Guedira 2020). These efforts are known as **corporate social responsibility (CSR)**, or simply *community benefit*. CSR can be defined as the "context-specific organizational actions and policies that take into account stakeholders' expectations and the triple bottom line of economic, social, and environmental performance" (Aguinis

corporate social responsibility (CSR)
A concept that refers to companies' commitment to working ethically, mindful of the social, economic, and environmental concerns of their stakeholders and the communities in which they work.

and Glavas 2012, 933). Simply put, healthcare organizations have an ethical obligation to act in a socially responsible way and to create a positive impact for their patients and community.

CSR applies not just to the strategic decisions made by hospital leaders, but also to the decisions you make and the actions you will take as a professional. "The socially responsible healthcare organization has to help every health professional to work well and with strong ethical roots" (Russo 2016, 325). Ethics matter.

The Healthcare Manager's Role in CSR

A review of the literature on CSR noted some predictors of CSR engagement, including management commitment, alignment of personal values and corporate mission, and a real concern for community issues (Aguinis and Glavas 2012). These predictors depend on a number of factors, such as the level of staff support for CSR engagement and whether staff members share the values and morals underlying the organization's mission, vision, and CSR endeavors. For example, if healthcare managers personally believe in giving back to the community, then they will more likely to champion and promote the organization's initiatives to be a good corporate citizen—locally, nationally, and internationally.

In addition, healthcare managers are compelled by the healthcare profession to get involved in enriching their community. In chapter 1, we discussed ACHE's Code of Ethics. Section V of that code directly refers to healthcare executives' responsibilities (ACHE 2017):

The healthcare executive shall:
A. Work to identify and meet the healthcare needs of the community;
B. Work to identify and seek opportunities to foster health promotion in the community;
C. Work to support access to healthcare services for all people;
D. Encourage and participate in public dialogue on healthcare policy issues, and advocate solutions that will improve health status and promote quality healthcare;
E. Apply short- and long-term assessments to management decisions affecting both community and society; and
F. Provide prospective patients and others with adequate and accurate information, enabling them to make enlightened decisions regarding services.

The role of healthcare managers in CSR initiatives is threefold:

1. Identify goals that meet the healthcare needs of the community and that fit with the organization's mission

2. Motivate stakeholders to get involved in initiatives
3. Plan and implement actions to ensure the initiatives are successful

As an illustration of this role, consider the work of Caroline Doherty, chief development and programs officer at Roanoke Chowan Community Health Center (RCCHC). RCCHC is a federally funded community health center that serves five rural counties in eastern North Carolina and treats patients regardless of their ability to pay. The mission of RCCHC (www.rcchc.org) is

> to provide patient centered, high quality, compassionate health care, responsive to the diverse needs of the people we serve.

In 2019, 80 percent of RCCHC's patients were living below 200 percent of the federal poverty level, and its payer mix included 8 percent who did not have health insurance, 44 percent covered by Medicare, 31 percent with private or third-party insurance, and 17 percent covered by Medicaid (Doherty 2021; RCCHC 2019). In that same year, the facility served almost 17,000 patients with more than 51,000 patient visits (RCCHC 2019).

At RCCHC, diabetes is a health condition that warrants serious attention. About 5,000 of its 17,000 patients are diabetic, and another 5,000 are considered prediabetic. Knowing that helping patients make changes to adopt healthier lifestyle behaviors can reduce their chances of becoming diabetic (Cardel et al. 2020), Doherty secured grant funding to train RCCHC staff to serve as facilitators for the Centers for Disease Control and Prevention's Diabetes Prevention Program, a yearlong experience in which patients meet regularly to motivate one another and learn how to adopt healthier lifestyles (Ely et al. 2017). The program allows RCCHC to provide quality services and supports its mission to be responsive to the diverse needs of the people they serve.

As mentioned earlier, the manager's role in CSR is threefold. Doherty and her team illustrate these responsibilities at RCCHC by (1) identifying important actions needed, (2) involving stakeholders, and (3) securing funding and implementing a plan to help those with diabetes manage the disease well and to help prediabetic patients reduce their chances of becoming diabetic. Doherty (2021) noted that she could not do this work without being passionate about the purpose:

> I have committed my life to community health; my first job was in 1988 when I worked at the Office of Rural Health in Raleigh, North Carolina, and I continue to do this work today because we are all called upon to be each other's keepers, looking out for each other's health and well-being, especially when there are obstacles. I believe that access to basic healthcare that keeps you healthy is a right—a fundamental human right.

Mini-Case Study: Settlement in HCA Fraud Probe

Rita Cabell, a third-year student in an undergraduate health administration program, is taking a Legal Issues and Ethics course. Her professor has asked the class to research HCA (or Columbia/HCA), the largest for-profit owner and operator of healthcare facilities in the United States.

Rita's research brings up a seemingly endless list of criminal and civil charges against the company in the late 1990s through early 2000s. In 2000, HCA was ordered to pay more than $840 million as restitution for fraudulent actions to which the company admitted guilt (DOJ 2000). Moreover, the company paid to resolve its outpatient laboratory billing to Medicare, Medicaid, and TRICARE for tests that were either unnecessary or had not been ordered by a physician. Fines addressed the practice of marketing HCA facilities as community education and then billing Medicare to pay for those services.

All told, HCA committed ten kinds of fraud, including overcharging, unlawful Medicare billing, paying kickbacks to physicians, reporting of false data, and making illegal deals. The fraudulent activities were systemic, pervading every HCA site—from home health agencies to hospitals to outpatient laboratories. In 2003, HCA was ordered to pay an additional $631 million (DOJ 2003), bringing the total fines and penalties to about $1.7 billion.

Rita recalls an earlier lecture about ACHE's Code of Ethics; she decides to visit the website to give her some perspective on all the information she has gathered and to prepare herself for the in-class discussion.

Mini-Case Study Questions

1. If you were an HCA executive, what would have been your ethical obligation to prevent or report the fraudulent activities? What does ACHE's Code of Ethics say about this?
2. Are you concerned by HCA's actions leading up to its guilty plea and multimillion-dollar settlements? Why or why not?

Points to Remember

➤ Professionalism can be defined as the knowledge, skills, ability, and conduct expected of practitioners of a profession.

➤ Professional role refers to the assigned and expected functions, responsibilities, and working relationships of a person in a professional position.

➤ Corporate social responsibility is the "context-specific organizational actions and policies that take into account stakeholders' expectations and the triple bottom line of economic, social, and environmental performance" (Aguinis and Glavas 2012, 933).

➤ The role of healthcare managers in CSR initiatives is threefold: (1) identify goals that meet the healthcare needs of the community and that fit with the organization's mission, (2) motivate stakeholders to get involved in initiatives, and (3) plan and implement actions to ensure the initiatives are successful.

CHALLENGE YOURSELF

1. Consider the chapter-opening quote by Isaac Asimov: "Never let your sense of morals prevent you from doing what is right." What do you think it means? Give an example that is true for you as you prepare to become a healthcare manager.
2. As a student in a healthcare management program, what factors do you consider important in choosing an internship? Why are those factors important to you?
3. Identify CSR activities conducted by a local health center, hospital, or clinic. Read the organization's mission statement on its website. How do these CSR activities relate to its mission?

FOR YOUR CONSIDERATION

3.1 ACHE offers an ethics self-assessment that may help you identify your ethical strengths and weaknesses. The results of this self-assessment should not be shared with others or in class. Take ACHE's Ethics Self-Assessment. Afterward, reflect on the strengths and weaknesses that you identified. What strengths do you want to build on, and what weaknesses do you want to improve?

3.2 In 2015, professional football player Jason Pierre-Paul of the New York Giants was involved in a fireworks accident that resulted in the amputation of his right index finger at Jackson Memorial Hospital in Miami, Florida (Chang 2016). An ESPN reporter posted a photo of Pierre-Paul's medical records, which showed that his finger had been amputated. According to HIPAA, patients have the right to confidentiality. HIPAA requires providers to protect patients against "reasonably anticipated" disclosures of personal information.

An investigation conducted by the US Department of Health and Human Services' Office of Civil Rights (OCR) uncovered that two hospital employees had inappropriately accessed Pierre-Paul's medical records. Moreover, the investigation determined that an employee had been selling personal health information and had accessed more than 24,000 patient records without a job-related purpose. The OCR imposed a $2.15 million penalty on Jackson Memorial (HHS 2019).

Imagine that you are an intern at this hospital, assigned to help the hospital administrator who is investigating the confidentiality breaches. The administrator has asked you to propose a guideline or procedure that could help prevent future breaches in patient confidentiality. According to ACHE's Code of Ethics, what are the healthcare executive's responsibilities in the event of such a breach? What ideas will you propose for the guideline? How are your ideas supported by ACHE's Health Information Confidentiality policy statement?

Check These Out

Want more information about the organizations and concepts discussed in this chapter? Check these websites out.

- ACHE Code of Ethics: www.ache.org/ABT_ACHE/code.cfm
- ACHE Ethics Self-Assessment: www.ache.org/newclub/career/ethself.cfm
- ACHE Healthcare Executive 2020 Competencies Assessment Tool: www.ache.org/-/media/ache/career-resource-center/competencies_booklet.pdf
- ACHE Health Information Confidentiality policy statement: www.ache.org/about-ache/our-story/our-commitments/ethics/ache-code-of-ethics/health-information-confidentiality
- Roanoke Chowan Community Health Center: www.rcchc.org

References

Aguinis, H., and A. Glavas. 2012. "What We Know and Don't Know About Corporate Social Responsibility: A Review and Research Agenda." *Journal of Management* 38 (4): 932–68.

American College of Healthcare Executives (ACHE). 2021. "ACHE Healthcare Executive 2021 Competencies Assessment Tool." Accessed January 18, 2021. www.ache.org/-/media/ache/career-resource-center/cat_2021.pdf.

———. 2020. "Creating an Ethical Culture Within the Healthcare Organization." Published November. www.ache.org/about-ache/our-story/our-commitments/ethics/ache-code-of-ethics/creating-an-ethical-culture-within-the-healthcare-organization.

———. 2017. "Code of Ethics." Amended November 13. www.ache.org/-/media/ache/ethics/code_of_ethics_web.pdf.

Bittner, C. 2018. "The Importance of Role Clarity for Development of Interprofessional Teams." *Journal of Continuing Education in Nursing* 49 (8): 345–47.

Cardel, M., K. Ross, M. Butryn, W. Donahoo, A. Eastman, J. Dillard, A. Grummon, P. Hopkins, L. Whigham, and D. Janicke. 2020. "Acceptance-Based Therapy: The Potential to Augment Behavioral Interventions in the Treatment of Type 2 Diabetes." *Nutrition & Diabetes* 10: Article 3.

Casciani, S. 2012. "The Development of a Set of Program Competencies for an Undergraduate Healthcare Administration Program." *Journal of Health Administration Education* 29 (2): 163–72.

Cellucci, L. W., C. Molinari, and J. Young. 2018. "Competency-Based Education in Undergraduate Programs Certified by the Association of University Programs in Health Administration." *Journal of Health Administration Education* 35 (2): 175–85.

Chang, D. 2016. "Fired After NFL Player's Medical Chart Leaked to ESPN, Worker Sues." *Miami Herald*. Published July 11. www.miamiherald.com/news/health-care/article88913872.html.

Chhabria, K., E. Black, C. Giordano, and A. Blue. 2019. "Measuring Health Professions Students' Teamwork Behavior Using Peer Assessment: Validation of an Online Tool." *Journal of Interprofessional Education & Practice* 16: 100271.

Coles, R. 2000. *Lives of Moral Leadership: Men and Women Who Made a Difference.* New York: Random House.

Compton, M., M. Soper, B. Reilly, L. Gettle, R. List, M. Bailey, H. Bruschwein, L. Somerville, and D. Albon. 2020. "A Feasibility Study of Urgent Implementation of Cystic Fibrosis Multidisciplinary Telemedicine Clinic in the Face of COVID-19 Pandemic: Single-Center Experience." *Telemedicine and e-Health* 26 (8): 978–85.

Doherty, C. 2021. Interview with L. Cellucci, January 23.

Drucker, P. 1988. "Leadership: More Doing Than Dash." *Wall Street Journal*, January 6.

Ely, E., S. Gruss, E. Luman, E. Gregg, M. Ali, K. Nhim, D. Rolka, and A. Albright. 2017. "A National Effort to Prevent Type 2 Diabetes: Participant-Level Evaluation of CDC's National Diabetes Prevention Program." *Diabetes Care* 40 (1): 1331–41.

Garman, A. N., P. Butler, and L. Brinkmeyer. 2006. "Leadership." *Journal of Healthcare Management* 51 (6): 360–64.

Garman, A. N., R. Evans, M. Krause, and J. Anfossi. 2006. "Professionalism." *Journal of Healthcare Management* 51 (4): 219–22.

Haddiya, I., T. Janfi, and M. Guedira. 2020. "Application of the Concepts of Social Responsibility, Sustainability, and Ethics to Healthcare Organizations." *Risk Management and Healthcare Policy* 13: 1029–33.

Institute of Medicine. 2003. *Health Professions Education: A Bridge to Quality*. Washington, DC: National Academies Press.

Mahoney, M. 2020. "Telemedicine, and Related Technologic Platforms: Current Practice and Response to COVID-19 Pandemic." *Journal of Wound, Ostomy, and Continence Nursing* 47 (5): 439–44.

Roanoke Chowan Community Health Center (RCCHC). 2019. *Annual Report: 2019*. Accessed January 24, 2021. www.rcchc.org/news/203-roanoke-chowan-community-health-center-s-2019-annual-report.html.

Russo, F. 2016. "What Is the CSR's Focus in Healthcare?" *Journal of Business Ethics* 134 (2): 323–34.

Stefl, M. 2008. "Common Competencies for All Healthcare Managers: The Healthcare Leadership Alliance Model." *Journal of Healthcare Management* 53 (6): 360–73.

US Department of Health and Human Services (HHS). 2021. "What Is Telehealth?" Updated May 19. https://telehealth.hhs.gov/patients/understanding-telehealth/.

———. 2019. "OCR Imposes a $2.15 Million Civil Monday Penalty Against Jackson Health System for HIPAA Violations." Published October 23. www.hhs.gov/hipaa/for-professionals/compliance-enforcement/agreements/jackson/index.html.

US Department of Justice (DOJ). 2003. "Largest Health Care Fraud Case in U.S. History Settled." Published June 26. www.justice.gov/archive/opa/pr/2003/June/03_civ_386.htm.

———. 2000. "HCA–The Health Care Company & Subsidiaries to Pay $840 Million in Criminal Fines and Civil Damages and Penalties." Published December 14. www.justice.gov/opa/pr/2000/December/696civcrm.htm.

Wilson, A. 2016. "Think Like an Administrator: An Instructional Design and Delivery Template for Healthcare Administration." *Journal of Health Administration Education* 33 (1): 179–90.

CHAPTER 4
STEWARDSHIP

Morality is the basis of things and truth is the substance of all morality.
—Mahatma Gandhi, India's independence leader

IMPORTANT TERMS

- Climate-smart healthcare
- Duty of care
- Fiduciary duty
- The Joint Commission
- LEED-certified
- Stakeholder
- Stewardship
- Third-party payer

LEARNING OBJECTIVES

Studying this chapter will help you to

➤ define stewardship and its role in healthcare managers' duties,

➤ explain the fiduciary duty of healthcare managers,

➤ explain environmental sustainability as a moral imperative, and

➤ discuss the responsibility of organizational stewards to stakeholders.

stewardship
Acts that enhance the sense of the healthcare organization's commitment to the community and increase public trust in the healthcare organization.

stakeholder
A person or group that has a stake in the organization and is affected by the organization's actions and decisions.

third-party payer
An entity that pays or reimburses a healthcare provider for the services rendered to a patient.

Stewardship, according to the World Health Organization, is "the careful and responsible management of the well-being of the population" (Travis et al. 2002, 1). To elaborate, Gerard Magill and Lawrence Prybil (2020, 18) offer this definition:

> Stewardship requires us first to treasure the trust we have received from the community as the necessary context for pursuing a prudent use of limited resources. Stewardship invites us to recall who we are via our organization mission as the context that will inspire us to meet in an ethical manner the needs of financing, delivery, and care in the field today.

As stewards, healthcare managers take into account the needs, rights, and interests of the organization's **stakeholders**. In hospitals, community health clinics, and physician practices, for example, stakeholders include patients, healthcare providers, administrators and other leaders, other employees, the public or community, and **third-party payers** (such as an insurance company, Medicare, or Medicaid). In for-profit organizations, stakeholders include stockholders, who are interested in the organization's financial viability and general welfare.

By always putting the stakeholders *first*, healthcare managers earn and maintain the stakeholders' trust. This notion of integrity—a quality that enables trust—relates to our discussion in chapter 3 of integrity as a necessary prerequisite for effective leadership. Integrity is an indicator of healthcare managers' stewardship; managers "model the way" and encourage others to behave accordingly (Kouzes and Posner 2007). Your engagement in modeling the way to keep stakeholders first is not solely dependent on you alone. In chapter 3, we introduced the concept of *interprofessionalism*, which refers to clinical and administrative professionals working collaboratively as part of a team to improve health outcomes. The key to successful interprofessional collaboration is for team members to model the way as well (Grady and Hinings 2019; Orchard, Rykhoff, and Sinclair 2020).

Consider the following case from the field, in which we describe the experience of Virginia Mason Medical Center (VMMC)—the first medical center to change its practice from encouraging employees to receive the flu vaccination to implementing a mandatory flu vaccination program. The decision was made as a team, with direction and support from the senior leader of the medical center. The team members modeled the way to bring about better health outcomes for the center's stakeholders.

The Role of Stewardship in Healthcare Managers' Duties

Healthcare managers have a broad set of duties covering administrative, operational, clinical, financial, staffing, community benefit, and other areas. Stewardship is the responsibility of healthcare managers throughout their professional careers. Healthcare managers understand that organizational resources "including financial resources and real property, are held in

> **CASE FROM THE FIELD**
> Stewards of the Community's Health
>
> Influenza (the flu) is a contagious viral respiratory infection. It is transmitted when an infected person coughs or sneezes, producing droplets that another person inhales or touches on a surface. People who are infected with the flu report symptoms such as fever, cough, sore throat, body aches, headache, fatigue, or runny or stuffy nose. Although most people recover from the flu without lasting effects, the World Health Organization (2021) estimates that severe complications from the illness result in about 290,000 to 650,000 deaths annually worldwide. According to the Centers for Disease Control and Prevention (CDC 2021a), the combination of the flu and pneumonia in 2019 ranked ninth in the top ten leading causes of death in the United States. In 2020–21, people responded to the COVID-19 pandemic by implementing precautionary measures such as wearing masks, staying home, reducing travel, and practicing physical distancing. Moreover, more people received the flu vaccine during this time (CDC 2021b). These precautionary measures likely reduced the number of flu and pneumonia deaths.
>
> Both the WHO and the CDC recommend annual vaccinations against the flu (CDC 2019), but the WHO calls on healthcare workers specifically to get vaccinated yearly. Healthcare associations—including the American Hospital Association, American Medical Directors Association, American Nurses Association, American Public Health Association, Association for Professionals in Infection Control and Epidemiology, American Academy of Family Physicians, American Academy of Pediatrics, American College of Physicians, and Veterans Health Administration—have all issued strong support for mandatory vaccination of healthcare workers.
>
> Virginia Mason Medical Center in Seattle, Washington, was the first health center to mandate the flu vaccine for all employees. The center's leadership team first introduced a campaign for voluntary vaccinations but met with little success. The experience illustrates that the commitment to the goal of providing better care for patients outranked individual choice, a decision that was not taken lightly. This is VMMC's story.
>
> VMMC is a tertiary care organization with 336 beds, outpatient care, regional clinics, a research center, and residency programs (Rakita et al. 2010, 882). In 1998, VMMC's leadership implemented a voluntary influenza vaccination program to provide free flu shots to all its employees. Six years later, however, VMMC's numbers showed that only about 55 percent of the 5,000 or so employees had taken advantage of the offer (Rakita et al. 2010).
>
> In 2004, during a rapid process improvement workshop attended by internal stakeholders—including physicians, nurses, frontline staff, and administrators—the proposal was made to make flu vaccinations mandatory throughout VMMC. This decision illustrated the organization's commitment "to put the patient first—in reality, not just rhetorically" (*Virginia Mason Blog* 2012). With leadership support, especially from the CEO, the mandatory policy was implemented in 2005.
>
> *(continued)*

> **CASE FROM THE FIELD**
> Stewards of the Community's Health *(continued)*
>
> An interdisciplinary team, including a senior vice president and the deputy chief of medicine, was formed to lead the program in its first year (Rakita et al. 2010). To educate employees about the program and encourage their compliance with it, the team launched a website, brought in grand-round speakers, offered one-on-one meetings with interested staff members, and held fun events, such as a vaccination party. Exceptions for health or religious reasons were allowed; in 2006, exempted employees or those who refused vaccinations were required to wear surgical masks while at work during the flu season. By 2010, VMMC was reporting a vaccination rate of 98.9 percent, although seven employees had quit because of the policy and two had been fired for noncompliance.
>
> Since VMMC's pioneering decision in 2005, many healthcare organizations have developed and implemented their own mandatory flu vaccination programs for workers. These organizations are spread across all 50 states, with more than 1,100 listed on the Influenza Vaccination Mandates Honor Roll by the Immunization Action Coalition (Immunize.org 2021). Examination of both voluntary and mandatory efforts in the United States and abroad revealed that mandatory policies plus education and promotion campaigns yielded higher vaccination compliance with mandatory policies having the highest impact on employee behavior (Schumacher et al. 2020).

trust by the organization for the good of others" (Wallenhorst 2014, 51). Let's consider how stewardship is reflected in the duties of healthcare managers by using the framework of VMMC's efforts (see Case from the Field).

IDENTIFY AND PRIORITIZE STAKEHOLDERS

Healthcare managers identify the people they serve or those affected by their decisions—both inside and outside the organization—and then prioritize the stakeholders in order of need. At VMMC, the targets of the mandatory flu vaccination program were the healthcare workers (including doctors, nurses, assistants, and administrators). However, the patients were the first priority because their already compromised health could worsen as a result of contracting the illness from their caregivers.

Patients especially vulnerable are those under age two, those over age 65, and those for whom the flu would likely bring about complications, such as pregnant women and immunosuppressed individuals. In fact, a policy statement issued by the American Academy of Pediatrics (2015, 809) to support mandatory vaccination of all healthcare personnel noted that doing so is "ethical, just, and necessary." The statement referenced two published cases of providers infecting patients with the flu. The first involved 19 infants in a neonatal intensive care unit, resulting in the death of one baby; the second was an outbreak in a bone marrow transplant unit, causing the death of two patients (American Academy of Pediatrics 2015, 812).

Although the workers were a second priority, they were no less important in VMMC's case. At first, the organization gave employees a chance to exercise their right of autonomy (to decide for themselves whether to receive the flu shot). The voluntary program became mandatory only after many years of minimal employee participation—and even at that point, those who opted out for religious and other personal reasons were given choices out of respect.

Identifying stakeholders (and then prioritizing them) is a duty of stewardship. Managers honor people's autonomy but, at the same time, weigh the consequences of that decision for the people they serve.

Support and Sustain the Organizational Mission

Stewardship calls on managers to reflect on their work to understand how it helps or hampers the organization's mission. This is exactly what happened at VMMC. When internal stakeholders recommended that flu vaccinations be mandatory for all employees, they were following the organization's stated mission:

> Our mission is to improve the health and well-being of the patients we serve—Healing illness is our first priority and is what gives our people the energy for our vision. We are also committed to providing a broad range of services that improve one's sense of well-being and which prevent illness.

The mandatory policy helped prevent patients from being exposed to the flu virus—at least by the hospital workers. This policy exhibits that VMMC, given its mission, is putting patients first.

Maintain Organizational Integrity Through Reciprocity

A trust-based relationship between the organization and the community it serves offers reciprocal benefits. While acts of stewardship build and maintain stakeholder trust in the healthcare organization, they also encourage commitment to personal and organizational integrity within the healthcare organization (Magill and Prybil 2020, 18). By making vaccination mandatory for all its workers, VMMC sent a message that it is a safe provider and cares about the well-being of those who work and seek services there. In turn, this message spread and was endorsed not only by the community but also by other healthcare organizations, which then adopted the same stance as VMMC.

FIDUCIARY DUTY

fiduciary duty
The duty of an individual or a group to act in the best interest of another individual or group.

Fiduciary duty requires professionals to "act in good faith with the care an ordinarily prudent person would exercise under similar circumstances" (Office of Inspector General 2003). When healthcare managers act as stewards or for the good of others, they are exercising their fiduciary duty. The three responsibilities of fiduciary duty are duty of care, duty of loyalty, and duty of obedience.

Consider, for example, the fiduciary duty of a customer service representative for an insurance company. (Graduates of health administration programs may work in the insurance industry, sometimes beginning their career as customer service representatives.) These representatives typically work in high-volume call centers, responding to inquiries regarding healthcare coverage, enrollment, billing, claims adjustments, and coordination of care. Specifically, they answer questions such as "Is hospital stay covered under my plan?" and "Is my doctor inside or outside of my network?" Typically, fees are lower for the patient if the provider is inside, rather than outside, of the insurance network. Knowing this, representatives have a fiduciary duty to exercise **duty of care** by accurately and completely responding to customers or their representatives as a reasonable person would. If customers find this response to be honest, then they will begin to trust the insurance company and the representative. A breach of fiduciary duty—and broken trust—occurs when a representative lies, misinforms, or misleads the customer.

duty of care
A responsibility under fiduciary duty that requires an individual or a group to act with the care and prudence any reasonable entity would do.

Consider as another example the fiduciary duty of a member of a board of directors. The board acts to "create and maintain a foundation for relationships among the stakeholders that identifies and implements their healthcare goals as effectively as possible" (Griffith and White 2019, 100). Those who accept the responsibility of serving on the board are expected to act on behalf of the organization to ensure they effectively meet stakeholders' needs. Typically, board members hold jobs outside the organization and serve on the board for a limited period (such as one year or three years). During their service, they are expected to exercise their *duty of loyalty* and *duty of obedience*. The duty of loyalty prohibits board members from gaining advantages (such as money, favors, and other benefits) at the organization's expense. The duty of obedience requires adherence to the organization's mission. Thus—in addition to fulfilling the usual board member responsibilities of attending and being prepared for board meetings, disclosing any conflicts of interest, and keeping confidential the board's activities and discussions—board members must maintain their focus on the organizational mission (Curran 2016; Sundean et al. 2019).

The case of *Manhattan Eye, Ear & Throat Hosp. v. Spitzer* (N.Y. Sup. Ct., 186 Misc.2d 126, 715 N.Y.S.2d 575 [1999]) illustrates the duty of obedience. The nonprofit Manhattan Eye, Ear and Throat Hospital (MEETH) in New York City was founded in 1869 with the following mission:

> To establish, provide, conduct, operate and maintain a hospital in the City, County and State of New York for the general treatment of persons suffering from acute short-term

illnesses; performing general plastic surgery; treating persons suffering from diseases of the eye, ear, nose or throat; and maintaining a school for post graduate instruction in the treatment of such illnesses, performing such surgery, and the treatment of such diseases, and conducting associated and basic research.

MEETH's board of directors placed "monetize the assets" as the top priority over shoring up and continuing the organization's healthcare mission. The board, facing budgetary problems, voted to sell MEETH's medical complex to two entities—a hospital with a plan to open a breast cancer facility and a real estate developer with a plan to build an apartment building. The sale would have shuttered facilities that provided eye, ear, nose, and throat services—as defined in MEETH's mission—to the community. The board did not pursue or entertain other offers that would have preserved MEETH's original mission. Eliot Spitzer, New York State's attorney general at the time, did not approve the sale, saying, "It is my duty to ensure the fair value of MEETH and that any such transaction promotes its not-for-profit health purposes" (New York State Office of the Attorney General 1999).

The New York State Court agreed with Spitzer and pointed out that MEETH's board members should have attended to their fiduciary duty to preserve MEETH's mission. The sale was denied, which gave other interested healthcare organizations, which promised to remain true to MEETH's mission, the chance to compete to purchase the medical complex. Today, MEETH is affiliated with Lenox Hill Hospital and continues to operate according to MEETH's original mission. As this case illustrates, the duty of obedience is a serious and complicated expectation.

The **Joint Commission** addresses the importance of fiduciary duty as well. The Joint Commission issues white papers to guide accredited healthcare organizations and programs through the standards it expects them to meet or exceed. One of these white papers explains what fiduciary means in the healthcare context (Joint Commission 2009, 3):

> That one acts to the best of one's ability in the interest of another, not in self-interest. The "other" can trust the fiduciary . . . And that ethical obligation has been taken on by those who choose to work in healthcare—not just those trained as clinicians, the doctors and nurses, but also the managers, executives, and trustees.

Joint Commission
An independent, not-for-profit organization that provides accreditation or certification to healthcare organizations and programs in the United States.

Moreover, The Joint Commission's Code of Conduct (2020, 16) underscores the importance of their fiduciary duty by asserting that their "employees and board members owe a duty of undivided and unqualified loyalty to the organization." The expectations of health professionals in organizations that The Joint Commission reviews are the same as those for their own employees, contractors, and board members.

Healthcare managers in entry-, middle-, and senior-level positions are bound by their duty of care, duty of loyalty, and duty of obedience to their patients and employees. Moreover, they are responsible to the communities in which they live and work. To further illustrate the concept of fiduciary duty and violation of this duty, we consider the case of *Kenseth v. Dean Health Plan, Inc.*

KENSETH V. DEAN HEALTH PLAN, INC.

In 1987, Deborah Kenseth underwent vertical gastric banding, a surgical weight-loss procedure designed to control the amount of food that passes into the stomach. By 2005, Kenseth was experiencing acid reflux and other complications from the procedure and was advised by her physician to have corrective surgery.

As directed by the information printed on her health insurance card, Kenseth phoned Dean Health Plan, her insurance company. She explained to Dean's customer service representative the type of surgery to be performed and the date of the operation. When the representative asked the nature of the procedure, Kenseth said it was to address her acid reflux, but she did not elaborate that the problem was related to the gastric banding she had had in 1987 (*Kenseth v. Dean Health Plan, Inc.*, 610 F.3d. 452 [7th Cir., June 28, 2010]).

The representative put Kenseth on hold and then later returned to inform her that the insurance coverage had been verified and a $300 copayment was expected. After the surgery, however, Dean denied the claim, citing that its policy excluded coverage for surgical treatment of morbid obesity and for any services related to a noncovered benefit. Kenseth was billed $77,974. After internal appeals with Dean failed, Kenseth sued in court over breach of fiduciary duty. The case made its way to the US Court of Appeals for the Seventh Circuit, which in 2013 ruled that Dean had indeed violated its fiduciary duty to Kenseth. Simply put, "an insurer has an affirmative obligation to provide accurate and complete information when a beneficiary inquires about her insurance coverage" (*Kenseth v. Dean Health Plan, Inc.*, No. 11-1560 [7th Cir., June 13, 2013]).

This case underscores the valuable concept of duty of care. Dean, through its representatives, violated Kenseth's trust by not providing complete and accurate information as reasonable entities involved in the same situation would. This is a basic responsibility of fiduciary duty that professionals even in an entry-level position are expected to know.

ENVIRONMENTAL SUSTAINABILITY AS A MORAL IMPERATIVE

An organization's corporate social responsibility (CSR) activities are a reflection of its stewardship. (See chapter 3 for more discussion of CSR.) Both CSR and stewardship take into consideration the effects that the organization's policies have on stakeholders, which, in the process, garner goodwill and trust. A policy becomes a moral imperative if it is something that should happen because it is the right thing to do. Environmental sustainability policy, like mandatory flu vaccination policy, has become a moral imperative for many healthcare organizations.

Using tools and techniques that result in less waste, creating local solutions for residents' needs, and consuming fewer resources all help create environmental sustainability in the healthcare workplace. Examples include a new physician practice building an energy-efficient clinic, a long-term care facility creating a vegetable garden in its courtyard that provides fresh vegetables for consumption by residents, and a hospital reducing paper use by adopting electronic health records. Such efforts create an eco-friendlier and greener environment that helps improve "operational efficiencies, driven by strong pressure to reduce costs while maintaining high quality service" (Zhu, Johnson, and Sarkis 2018, 25). This is the reason environmental sustainability is a moral imperative. It is the right thing to do for many reasons.

Take the focus on **climate-smart healthcare**, for example. The World Bank (2017) proposes that climate-smart healthcare is a method to address climate change and provide quality healthcare through low-carbon and resilience strategies. Low-carbon healthcare includes actions such as waste reduction in hospitals and clinics and building and remodeling facilities to be more energy efficient (World Bank 2017, 13). Climate-smart healthcare is a relatively recent strategy to address healthcare's contributions and climate change, but the concept is already being adopted throughout the healthcare industry. For example, in 2010, Austin-Travis County Emergency Management Service adapted ambulances to be more environmentally friendly by adding solar panels to improve battery use during patient transfer (Careless 2011). By 2017, it had added green-powered electrical systems in more than 40 ambulances so that the vehicles need not remain idling outside emergency departments. This shift to green-powered electrical systems helped reduce fuel costs and greenhouse gas emissions. Moreover, employees and patients in emergency departments were not confronted with the loud noise of idling engines (Benavides 2017).

climate-smart healthcare
The implementation of resilient healthcare strategies for the more efficient use of materials and wise waste management to produce a healthier environment.

Kaiser Permanente—the largest integrated managed care organization, which operates hospitals and medical groups in eight states and the District of Columbia and serves more than 12 million members—defines environmental stewardship as an obligation to minimize environmental impact. It self-identifies as a steward, as endorsed in its environmental stewardship statement (Kaiser Permanente 2021):

> At Kaiser Permanente, we believe it is our obligation as a health care provider to minimize our environmental impact. We embed efforts to be environmentally responsible throughout our organization—in how we power our facilities, purchase food and medical supplies and equipment, manage waste, and invest in our communities. We also prioritize partnerships with others to develop policies and systems that strengthen community health and protect our environment.

Kathy Gerwig, environmental stewardship officer for Kaiser Permanente, leads the organization's strategic initiatives for sustainability issues, including overseeing the reduction of energy emissions and toxic chemical use, as well as increasing water conservation and providing more fresh local foods to employees and patients in their facilities.

Practice Greenhealth, an organization that honors healthcare institutions for their sustainability efforts, has recognized Kaiser Permanente with several environmental excellence awards (Kaiser Permanente 2017; Practice Greenhealth 2020).

For example, Kaiser Permanente has been **LEED-certified** (Leadership in Energy and Environmental Design) for designing, constructing, operating, and maintaining its building according to environmental standards. LEED was created by the US Green Building Council (2014), an organization of professionals that endorses green living and the construction of "a sustainable built environment for all within the next generation." In 2019, San Diego Medical Center achieved LEED, earning the double LEED Platinum rating for environmentally friendly practices that are part of everyday life, such as the use of recycled materials, local building materials to reduce transport costs, and air filters (Kaiser Permanente 2019).

Kaiser Permanente's commitment to environmental sustainability is not just a part of its values, but also a moral imperative.

> **LEED-certified**
> Certification provided when a building is designed, constructed, operated, and maintained according to set environmental standards.

RESPONSIBILITY OF ORGANIZATIONAL STEWARDS TO STAKEHOLDERS

The term *stakeholder* derives from a theory that asserts "there is always a context to business theory, and that context is moral in nature" (Freeman 1994, 412). This moral context refers to the responsibility that stewards of the organization—board members, leaders, or managers—have to those who have a *stake* (an interest) in the organization. Here are two scenarios that show how stewards can fulfill this responsibility in an ethical manner.

DOWNSIZING THE WORKFORCE

The board of directors of a for-profit hospital is considering downsizing personnel to reduce costs and increase profits. According to stakeholder theory, board members should first study the impact or outcome of such an action on its stakeholders. Specifically, they should address questions such as the following:

- How would it affect the *patient* quality of care, appointment scheduling, and waiting times for services?
- How would it affect the *physicians'* schedules?
- How would it affect the livelihood, career, and morale of *employees* whose positions are slated to be terminated?
- How would it affect the hospital's ability to serve or provide access to the *community*?

On top of these, the potential effects on the organization's bottom line should be considered.

With regard to the personnel who may lose their livelihoods, board members should "take account of the fact that those people will be affected in significant ways and perhaps there is more [of a] duty to afford some dignity and respect to workers who may be laid off" (Gibson 2000, 248).

Taking stakeholders' interests into account, however, can reveal competing or conflicting stakeholder interests (Mainardes, Alves, and Raposo 2011). For instance, consider the practice of disclosing medical errors.

DISCLOSING MEDICAL ERRORS

The Joint Commission first required accredited healthcare organizations to develop a process for disclosing unanticipated outcomes of care in 2001 (Singh et al. 2012). Since that time, healthcare managers ensure that they train providers in this disclosure and assess the process to ensure compliance. This task may be allocated to risk managers—administrators charged with ensuring the delivery of "safe and trusted health care" (ASHRM 2021). To this end, risk managers may be involved in training providers to communicate effectively with patients and their families to mitigate the risk of misunderstanding. Misunderstanding often encourages litigation, which, in turn, damages the reputation of providers and the hospital.

The following stakeholders are involved in the disclosure of medical errors:

1. *Providers*. Some of the reasons providers may resist disclosure include the following (Amori 2013; ASHRM 2006, 2017):
   - Concern that they may cause more upset to the patient and family members
   - Concern they may receive retribution from colleagues and the hospital
   - Belief that the disclosure is not necessary
   - Belief that the same negative outcome would have resulted regardless of the process
   - Concern that an apology is an admission of guilt
   - Concern that disclosure increases lawsuit risk

2. *Patients*. Reasons for disclosure are based on the assumption that patients have the right to know and to have access to their personal health information. Patients (and their families) depend on their providers' medical expertise and assume that these providers will act on their benefit, will not cause them harm, and will be honest with them regarding their health, treatments, and other issues.

3. *Public*. The community trusts that the healthcare organization or facility in the area credentials or employs providers who are qualified and will act ethically, which includes disclosing errors and other adverse events. Violation of that trust is detrimental to the relationship between the organization and its public.

4. *Board of directors.* As the representing authority of the healthcare organization, the board is responsible for actions that affect patient safety. Their actions or inactions may reflect poorly on the hospital and its providers—or, worse, the organization could be liable for medical errors made as a result.

The American Society for Healthcare Risk Management (ASHRM) published *Risk Management Pearls on Disclosure of Adverse Events*, a guideline for healthcare professionals charged with policy disclosure. The recommendations—which underscore the responsibility of providers, leadership, and administrators—focus on presenting the facts about the events, the outcome, the patient plan of care, and the plan to ensure the event does not happen again. Moreover, it recommends an apology be made when appropriate (Amori 2013; ASHRM 2006, 2017).

The literature that examines litigation and disclosure rulings indicates that having **transparency** does not necessarily decrease the number of lawsuits, but it does influence the amount of damages awarded to plaintiffs. The Veterans Health Administration (VHA) follows the **Lexington Model** for disclosure (Eaves-Leanos and Dunn 2012). In 1987, a patient died at the Lexington Veterans Affairs Medical Center because of an error. The center made a decision to communicate openly and honestly with the patient's family about the error and the cause of the patient's death. The Lexington Model was adopted as a risk management program to provide transparency to patients. The program includes (Eaves-Leanos and Dunn 2012, 164)

transparency
A policy of sharing information and communicating directly, honestly, and in a timely manner.

Lexington Model
A risk management program for disclosing errors that was instituted at Lexington Veterans Affairs Medical Center following a patient's death.

◆ a face-to-face meeting with the patient and family,

◆ an apology from those who committed the error,

◆ a monetary compensation, and

◆ an action plan detailing how the organization will minimize the risk that the error will reoccur.

Since the implementation of the Lexington Model, lawsuits continue to be filed, but the litigation awards have been lower. The Lexington facility is in the top 25 percent of claims among VHA medical centers, but its litigation costs are in the bottom 25 percent (Eaves-Leanos and Dunn 2012).

Similarly, the University of Michigan implemented a medical disclosure process in 2001 with full transparency that included offers of compensation. Reviewing records from 1995 through 2007, Allen Kachalia and colleagues (2010, 214) found that the "disclosure-with-offer approach to medical errors did not increase legal claim and costs." An examination of malpractice claims among US physicians found that payouts had declined. Adam Schaffer and colleagues (2017, 714) speculate that "disclosure, apology, and offer" may have positively influenced this reduction. Also, after four Massachusetts hospitals implemented communication, apology, and resolution programs for medical errors, Kachalia and colleagues (2018, 1842) found that these programs helped reduce the need for litigation and allowed institutions to "work with patients to reach a speedy resolution." These examples show that an effective disclosure program is stewardship in action.

Mini-Case Study: Medical Malpractice and the Healthcare Facility's Responsibility

In 1965, the Illinois Supreme Court ruled that Charleston Community Memorial Hospital was liable for negligent actions taken by the providers who practiced in the hospital (*Darling v. Charleston Community Memorial Hospital*, 33 Ill.2d 326, 211, N.E.2d 253, 14 A.L.R.3d 860 [Ill. September 29, 1965]). Before this decision, hospitals argued that because the organization itself did not practice medicine, it was not responsible for medical errors committed by its clinical staff—even though it provided credentials that allowed clinicians to practice medicine in their facilities.

In 1960, a university student named Dorrence Darling II broke his right leg while playing football at Eastern Illinois University. He was taken to Charleston Community Memorial Hospital (a facility accredited by The Joint Commission), where Dr. Alexander casted his leg and, along with staff nurses, provided subsequent treatment and care. The next day, Darling complained of severe pain, and the toes visible outside the cast turned dark and became swollen. After a two-week stay at Charleston Community Memorial Hospital, he was transferred to Barnes Hospital in St. Louis, Missouri; there, Dr. Reynolds, the head of orthopedic surgery, took charge of his care. He found a "considerable amount of dead tissue" as a result of the lack of blood circulation to the improperly casted leg. After several surgical attempts to save the leg, Dr. Reynolds had to amputate Darling's leg below the knee (Wiet 2005).

Because Darling was a minor, his father (acting on his behalf) sued Dr. Alexander and Charleston Community Memorial Hospital for negligence. (Dr. Alexander reached a separate settlement with the family.) The suit against the hospital contended that it should not have allowed Dr. Alexander to perform the orthopedic procedure in the hospital, that the medical and nursing staff did not perform appropriate follow-up care, and that a consulting physician was not brought in when complications arose (Marren, Feazell, and Paddock 2003, 197). Further, the suit argued that the hospital was responsible for the work of the medical staff who practiced in its facilities, as well as for the quality of care provided to Darling.

The hospital responded that it was not liable (Marren, Feazell, and Paddock 2003, 197):

> [O]nly an individual properly educated and licensed, and not a corporation, may practice medicine. Accordingly, a hospital is powerless under the law to forbid or command any act by a physician or surgeon in the practice of his profession. A hospital is not an insurer of the patient's recovery, but only owes the patient the duty to exercise such reasonable care as his known condition requires and that degree of care, skill and diligence used by hospitals generally in the community.

Charleston Community Memorial Hospital's defense relied on the historical assumption that hospitals are similar to hotels in that they are merely places in which independent practitioners perform their craft. The *Darling* ruling asserted, however, that hospitals do have a responsibility for the care of their patients and held Charleston Community Memorial Hospital directly liable (Wiet 2005, 400). The hospital, in turn, appealed the decision to the US Supreme Court, but its appeal was denied.

The case was labeled the "Big Bang" event for hospitals. It caused hospitals to ensure that their providers were adequately trained; that their boards of directors played a more active role in overseeing policy on patient care quality; and that administrative positions, such as risk managers, were added to create and oversee a variety of quality and safety programs and tasks, such as event and incident management and regulatory and accreditation compliance. This case and the subsequent hospital actions helped define healthcare organizations' fiduciary duty to their patients and their communities.

Mini-Case Study Questions

1. Identify the stakeholders in *Darling v. Charleston Community Memorial Hospital*.
2. Identify a hospital-based program designed to improve the quality of care. One example is Yale New Haven Hospital's (2019) Hand Hygiene Campaign, which provides a hands-on approach to promoting proper hand hygiene habits to help prevent infection. You may choose to search the databases at your university library to find a quality and safety program at a hospital of your choice, or you may contact the risk manager at your local hospital. Summarize the program and explain why and how it illustrates stewardship.

Points to Remember

- In healthcare delivery, stewardship of healthcare managers means acting in the best interests of patients, providers and staff, and the community, which helps build and maintain a trust relationship.
- Healthcare managers fulfill fiduciary duty responsibilities by acting in good faith with the care that an ordinarily prudent person would exercise under similar circumstances.
- The three responsibilities of fiduciary duty are duty of care, duty of loyalty, and duty of obedience.
- Environmental sustainability is a moral imperative because it is the right thing to do for a variety of reasons.
- The moral context of stakeholder theory refers to the responsibility that stewards—board members, leaders, or managers—have to those who have a *stake* (an interest) in the organization.

Challenge Yourself

1. Consider the chapter-opening quote by Mahatma Gandhi: "Morality is the basis of things and truth is the substance of all morality." Think of how this might be true for you as you prepare to become a healthcare manager.
2. When Virginia Mason Medical Center implemented its mandatory influenza vaccination policy, the interests of different stakeholders conflicted. Explain this conflict between the healthcare workers who did not want a flu shot and the patients and broader community who needed protection from the virus.
3. Based on what you learned in this chapter, explain how the disclosure of unintended outcomes illustrates fiduciary duty. Why is disclosing an unintended outcome representative of the commitment to duty of care, duty of loyalty, and duty of obedience?
4. Since The Joint Commission mandated that healthcare organizations disclose medical errors, healthcare risk managers have worked to implement communication, apology, and resolution programs. Research indicates that such programs have a positive effect on litigation and costs to the healthcare organization. Why do you think such programs have this effect?

For Your Consideration

4.1 Idaho has proclaimed one day in May as "Idaho Gives" day. During this 24-hour period, people donate money to a designated nonprofit organization (Bryce 2014). In 2013, the state received $600,000 in donations for the first annual "Idaho Gives" day. In 2014, Idaho Gives generated $778,000 (Berry 2014; Dunlap 2014). By 2019, donations had increased to more than $1.8 million, distributed to about 600 nonprofits (KPVI 2019). The Pocatello Free Clinic (www.pocatellofreeclinic.com) was one of the nonprofit healthcare organizations that received designated funds in 2014, collecting more than $3,825. Along with other fundraisers dedicated to the free clinic, and an increase in the number of nonprofits listed, the clinic received $2,840, which is less than what it had received five years earlier.

The Pocatello Free Clinic provides medical and dental care at no cost. It also partners with the local university's healthcare internship programs for the students.

Assume that you are doing your undergraduate health services management internship at the Pocatello Free Clinic. You agree to honor the fiduciary duty of this position. One of your projects is to help lead a public relations effort to educate the public about the clinic, its need for donations, and the upcoming Idaho Gives day. Write a one-page report that explains how this project does or does not exemplify your fiduciary duty (duty of care, duty of loyalty, and duty of obedience). (Hint: To determine your answer, ask yourself, would the project fit the clinic's mission? Would it help clinicians provide better patient care? Would it be in the best interest of the organization?)

4.2 To ensure that future healthcare managers can continue to meet the sustainability demands in decades to come, an idea has been proposed to integrate green assignments or projects into the established health administration program curriculum (Olden and Friedman 2010). The revisions may be simple, such as calculating the return on investment (ROI) of a green product or service (for a finance class), or a little more involved, such as planning and implementing a green project (for a leadership class) (Olden and Friedman 2010, 130–31). In the finance class, students may be taught to calculate the ROI of new fixtures that reduce or eliminate water waste. In the leadership class, students may roll out a green change among their classmates such as biking or carpooling to class instead of driving alone. Other possibilities include assessing a case study of a real-life systemwide green project. These small revisions in curriculum will encourage students to at least think about sustainability in the healthcare workplace and their daily life.

Propose an environmental or green assignment or project that could be integrated into your health administration class or curriculum.

Check These Out

Want more information about the organizations and concepts discussed in the chapter? Check these websites out.

- American Academy of Family Physicians: www.aafp.org
- American Academy of Pediatrics: www.aap.org
- American College of Physicians: www.acponline.org
- American Hospital Association: www.aha.org
- American Public Health Association: www.apha.org
- American Society for Healthcare Risk Management: www.ashrm.org
- Association for Professionals in Infection Control and Epidemiology: www.apic.org
- Centers for Disease Control and Prevention: www.cdc.gov
- Immunization Action Coalition: www.immunize.org
- Joint Commission: www.jointcommission.org
- US Green Building Council: www.usgbc.org
- World Health Organization: www.who.int

References

American Academy of Pediatrics. 2015. "Policy Statement—Recommendation for Mandatory Influenza Immunization of All Health Care Personnel." *Pediatrics* 136 (4): 809–18.

American Society for Healthcare Risk Management (ASHRM). 2021. "Health Care Risk Management Professional Overview." Accessed March 7, 2021. www.ashrm.org/about/hrm_overview.

———. 2017. "Communication and Resolution Programs: Where Are We Now?" Published June 28. https://forum.ashrm.org/2017/06/28/communication-and-resolution-programs-where-are-we-now/.

———. 2006. *Risk Management Pearls on Disclosure of Adverse Events*. Chicago: ASHRM.

Amori, G. 2013. "Disclosure of Unanticipated Events in 2013." American Society for Healthcare Risk Management. Accessed May 28, 2021. www.ashrm.org/sites/default/files/ashrm/Disclosure-of-Unanticipated-Events-in-2013_Prologue.pdf.

Benavides, M. O. 2017. "Austin-Travis County EMS Leads the Way with Sustainable, Cost-Efficient Ambulance Innovations." *Journal of Emergency Medical Services*. Published October 4. www.jems.com/operations/austin-travis-county-ems-leads-the-way-with-sustainable-cost-efficient-ambulance-innovations/.

Berry, H. 2014. "'Idaho Gives' Raises Nearly $780K, Sets Date for 2015." *Boise Weekly*. Published May 2. www.boiseweekly.com/CityDesk/archives/2014/05/02/idaho-gives-raises-nearly-780k-sets-date-for-2015.

Bryce, D. 2014. "Idaho Gives Registers Another Monetary Success." *Idaho State Journal*. Published May 2. www.idahostatejournal.com/members/idaho-gives-registers-another-monetary-success/article_77bda76a-d1c0-11e3-91fb-0019bb2963f4.html.

Careless, J. 2011. "Austin's Ambulances Go Green." *EMSWorld*. Published March. www.emsworld.com/article/10318930/austins-ambulances-go-green.

Centers for Disease Control and Prevention (CDC). 2021a. "Leading Causes of Death." Updated April 9. www.cdc.gov/nchs/fastats/deaths.htm.

———. 2021b. "2020–21 Flu Season Summary FAQ." Updated July 22. www.cdc.gov/flu/season/faq-flu-season-2020-2021.htm#anchor_1627000307956.

———. 2019. "Key Facts About Influenza (Flu) & Flu Vaccine." Updated September 13. www.cdc.gov/flu/keyfacts.htm.

Curran, C. 2016. *Nurse on Board: Planning Your Path to the Boardroom*. Indianapolis, IN: Sigma Theta Tau International.

Dunlap, T. 2014. "Idaho Gives Raises More Than $700,000." MagicValley.com. Published May 6. https://magicvalley.com/news/local/idaho-gives-raises-more-than-700-000/article_d08965e8-d4cf-11e3-a840-0019bb2963f4.html.

Eaves-Leanos, A., and E. Dunn. 2012. "Open Disclosure of Adverse Events: Transparency and Safety in Health Care." *Surgical Clinics of North America* 92 (1): 163–77.

Freeman, E. 1994. "The Politics of Stakeholder Theory: Some Future Directions." *Business Ethics Quarterly* 4 (4): 409–21.

Gibson, K. 2000. "The Moral Basis of Stakeholder Theory." *Journal of Business Ethics* 26 (3): 245–57.

Grady, C., and C. Hinings. 2019. "Turning the Titanic: Physicians as Both Leaders and Managers in Healthcare Reform." *Leadership in Health Services* 32 (3): 338–47.

Griffith, J., and K. White. 2019. *The Well-Managed Healthcare Organization*, 9th ed. Chicago: Health Administration Press.

Immunize.org. 2021. "Influenza Vaccination Honor Roll." Accessed February 21. www.immunize.org/honor-roll/influenza-mandates/.

Joint Commission. 2020. *Code of Conduct*. Accessed July 26, 2021. www.jointcommission.org/-/media/tjc/documents/about-us/code-of-conduct-manual-121520-final.pdf.

———. 2009. "Leadership in Healthcare Organizations: A Guide to Joint Commission Leadership Standards." Accessed July 26, 2021. www.jointcommission.org/assets/1/18/WP_Leadership_Standards.pdf.

Kachalia, A., S. Kaufman, R. Boothman, S. Anderson, K. Welch, S. Saint, and M. Rogers. 2010. "Liability Claims and Costs Before and After Implementation of a Medical Error Disclosure Program." *Annals of Internal Medicine* 153 (4): 213–21.

Kachalia, A., K. Sands, M. Van Niel, S. Dodson, S. Roche, V. Novack, M. Yitshak-Sade, P. Folcarelli, E. Benjamin, A. Woodward, and M. Mello. 2018. "Effects of a Communication-and-Resolution Program on Hospitals' Malpractice Claims and Costs." *Health Affairs* 37 (11): 1836–44.

Kaiser Permanente. 2021. "Environmental Stewardship." Accessed August 30. https://about.kaiserpermanente.org/community-health/improving-community-conditions/environmental-stewardship.

———. 2019. "World's First Double LEED Certified Hospital." Published October. https://about.kaiserpermanente.org/our-story/our-history/a-history-of-leading-the-way.

———. 2017. "Kaiser Permanente Honored with 17 Environmental Excellence Awards." Published May 2. https://about.kaiserpermanente.org/our-story/news/accolades-and-awards/kaiser-permanente-honored-17-environmental-excellence-awards.

Kouzes, J., and B. Posner. 2007. *The Leadership Challenge*, 4th ed. San Francisco: Jossey-Bass.

KPVI. 2019. "Idaho Gives 2019 Surpasses $1.7 Million Fundraising Goal." Published May 2. www.ktvb.com/article/news/local/idaho-gives-2019-surpasses-17-million-fundraising-goal/277-40fab658-646b-49d5-9967-6b6934fde6db.

Magill, G., and L. Prybil. 2020. *Governance Ethics in Healthcare Organizations*. New York: Routledge.

Mainardes, E., H. Alves, and M. Raposo. 2011. "Stakeholder Theory: Issues to Resolve." *Management Decision* 49 (2): 226–52.

Marren, J., G. Feazell, and N. Paddock. 2003. "The Hospital Board at Risk and the Need to Restructure the Relationship with the Medical Staff: Bylaws, Peer Review and Related Solutions." *Annals of Health Law* 12 (2): 179–234.

New York State Office of the Attorney General. 1999. "Spitzer Opposes Sale of MEETH." Published September 30. www.ag.ny.gov/press-release/spitzer-opposes-sale-meeth.

Office of Inspector General, US Department of Health and Human Services. 2003. *Corporate Responsibility and Corporate Compliance: A Resource for Health Care Boards of Directors*. Accessed March 6, 2021. http://oig.hhs.gov/fraud/docs/complianceguidance/040203corpresprsceguide.pdf.

Olden, P., and L. Friedman. 2010. "Preparing Today's Students to Lead Tomorrow's Green Healthcare Organizations." *Journal of Health Administration Education* 27 (2): 127–34.

Orchard, C., M. Rykhoff, and E. Sinclair. 2020. "Interprofessional Collaborative Leadership in Health Care Teams: From Theorising to Measurement." In *Sustainability and Interprofessional Collaboration*, edited by C. Orchard, M. Rykhoff, and E. Sinclair, 291–322. Cham, Switzerland: Palgrave Macmillan.

Practice Greenhealth. 2020. "Circles of Excellence Award Honorees." Accessed March 6, 2021. https://practicegreenhealth.org/sites/default/files/2020-05/2020%20Awards%20List%20for%20website.pdf.

Rakita, R., B. Hagar, P. Crome, and J. Lammert. 2010. "Mandatory Influenza Vaccination of Healthcare Workers: A 5-Year Study." *Infection Control and Hospital Epidemiology* 31 (9): 881–88.

Schaffer, A., A. Jena, S. Seabury, H. Singh, V. Chalasani, and A. Kachalia. 2017. "Rates and Characteristics of Paid Malpractice Claims Among U.S. Physicians by Specialty, 1992–2014." *JAMA Internal Medicine* 177 (5): 710–18.

Schumacher, S., J. Salmanton-Garcia, O. Cornely, and S. Mellinghoff. 2020. "Increasing Influenza Vaccination Coverage in Healthcare Workers: A Review on Campaign Strategies and Their Effect." *Infection* 49 (3): 387–99.

Singh, V., C. Cunningham, M. Panda, D. Hetzler, and D. Stanley. 2012. "Disclosure and Documentation of Reported Unanticipated Medical Events or Outcomes: Need for Healthcare Provider Education." *Journal of Healthcare Risk Management* 32 (1): 14–22.

Sundean, L., K. White, L. Thompson, and L. Prybil. 2019. "Governance Education for Nurses: Preparing Nurses for the Future." *Journal of Professional Nursing* 35 (5): 346–52.

Travis, P., D. Egger, P. Davies, and A. Mechbal. 2002. "Towards Better Stewardship: Concepts and Critical Issues." World Health Organization. Accessed July 26, 2021. www.who.int/healthinfo/paper48.pdf.

US Green Building Council. 2014. "About." Accessed April 27. www.usgbc.org/about.

Virginia Mason Blog. 2012. "Mandatory Flu Shots: A Defining Moment." Published September 12. https://vmcares.wordpress.com/2012/09/12/mandatory-flu-shots/

Wallenhorst, J. 2014. "Ethics and Governance." In *Managerial Ethics in Healthcare: A New Perspective*, edited by G. Filerman, A. Mills, and P. Schyve, 51–77. Chicago: Health Administration Press.

Wiet, M. 2005. "Darling v. Charleston Community Memorial Hospital and Its Legacy." *Annals of Health Law* 14 (2): 399–408.

World Bank. 2017. "Climate-Smart Healthcare: Low-Carbon and Resilience Strategies for the Health Sector." Accessed March 6, 2021. http://documents1.worldbank.org/curated/en/322251495434571418/pdf/113572-WP-PUBLIC-FINAL-WBG-Climate-smart-Healthcare-002.pdf.

World Health Organization (WHO). 2021. "Influenza (Seasonal)." Accessed February 19. www.who.int/en/news-room/fact-sheets/detail/influenza-(seasonal).

Yale New Haven Hospital. 2019. "Hospital to Take Hands-On Approach to Hand Hygiene." Published May 2. www.ynhh.org/publications/bulletin/050219/hospital-to-take-hands-on-approach-to-hand-hygiene.

Zhu, Q., S. Johnson, and J. Sarkis. 2018. "Lean Six Sigma and Environmental Sustainability: A Hospital Perspective." *Supply Chain Forum: An International Journal* 19 (1): 25–41.

CHAPTER 5

PROFESSIONAL CODES OF ETHICS AND ETHICAL PRINCIPLES

Right is right, and wrong is wrong, and a body ain't got no business doing wrong when he ain't ignorant and knows better.

—Mark Twain, *The Adventures of Huckleberry Finn*

Important Terms

- American College of Health Care Administrators (ACHCA)
- American College of Healthcare Executives (ACHE)
- Medical Group Management Association (MGMA)
- National Alliance on Mental Illness (NAMI)

Learning Objectives

Studying this chapter will help you to

➤ understand the codes of ethics of healthcare management professional associations,

➤ explain the relationship between codes of ethics and professional norms, and

➤ describe how codes of ethics can be applied by healthcare managers at all career levels.

Chapter 5: Professional Codes of Ethics and Ethical Principles

This chapter presents the codes of ethics of three professional associations for healthcare managers: the **American College of Healthcare Executives (ACHE)**, the **Medical Group Management Association (MGMA)**, and the **American College of Health Care Administrators (ACHCA)**.

The MGMA Code of Ethics (2015) notes the expectation that administrators act in matters and behaviors consistent with MGMA's mission to "empower practices, providers, and patients to create meaningful change in healthcare" (MGMA 2021). To that end, the code focuses on members' professional conduct to promote better performance of medical practice leaders and their organizations "by connecting members, building partnerships, setting the standards for certification, advocating for physician practice and providing innovative solutions" (MGMA 2015).

The codes of ethics for ACHE (2017) and ACHCA (2014) emphasize the ethical treatment of patients or residents, loyalty to the profession, and conduct becoming of a professional (such as honesty, integrity, and respect). Moreover, they note that professionals have an additional duty to the public. ACHCA (2016) calls on its members to "participate with others in the community to plan for and provide a full range of health care services." ACHE (2017) promotes six responsibilities that healthcare executives have to their community and to society at large:

A. Work to identify and meet the healthcare needs of the community;
B. Work to identify and seek opportunities to foster health promotion in the community;
C. Work to support access to healthcare services for all people;
D. Encourage and participate in public dialogue on healthcare policy issues, and advocate solutions that will improve health status and promote quality healthcare;
E. Apply short- and long-term assessments to management decisions affecting both community and society; and
F. Provide prospective patients and others with adequate and accurate information, enabling them to make enlightened decisions regarding services.

As discussed in chapter 1, the codes spell out behaviors that members learn, follow, and conform to. Healthcare professionals internalize the codes, which then become professional norms. The crisis at Mountain State Hospital (see the following Case from the Field) illustrates the importance of codes of ethics in guiding an administrator's duty or responsibility to stakeholders.

ACHE's Code of Ethics

ACHE is the professional association for those in the healthcare management profession. Its membership of about 48,000 comes from all career levels and from all settings, including

---

American College of Healthcare Executives (ACHE)
The professional association for those in the healthcare management profession.

Medical Group Management Association (MGMA)
The professional association for medical practice administrators.

American College of Health Care Administrators (ACHCA)
The professional association for administrators of long-term care facilities.

> **CASE FROM THE FIELD**
> Crises Reveal Our Character

Bob Allred, the administrator at Mountain State Hospital, reflected on a crisis that occurred at the hospital some years ago. Although he admitted that he might have handled some of the conversations with stakeholders differently, he stood by his final decision.

A US District Court judge had ordered Mountain State Hospital to admit Harold Bentley, an accused murderer who had been found not competent to stand trial (Farnsworth and Cellucci 2011). Bentley allegedly had murdered his boss because he thought the boss was the devil and was out to kill him. While awaiting the state's decision regarding his competency to stand trial, he languished in the state prison for four years in a 4- by 8-foot cell, 23 hours a day. Thus, he could do no physical harm to anyone else, but he had not been receiving appropriate mental healthcare. He received limited psychotropic medications but had few mental health evaluations and little treatment (Farnsworth and Cellucci 2011).

The **National Alliance on Mental Illness (NAMI)** has challenged the appropriateness of treating people with mental illness—such as Bentley—in correctional settings. NAMI (2016, 71) articulated its policy position as follows:

> *NAMI believes that persons who have committed offenses due to states of mind or behavior caused by a serious mental illness do not belong in penal or correctional institutions. Such persons require treatment, not punishment. A prison or jail is never an optimal therapeutic setting.*

State statutes require the US Department of Health and Human Services (HHS) to evaluate and treat chronically and severely mentally ill patients who are not being treated by private providers. State hospitals and clinics serve as this safety net. Moreover, state law mandates that dangerous and violent mentally ill patients be treated in locked-down and secure facilities (Farnsworth and Cellucci 2011). However, at the time of the incident, the only locked-down and secure facilities in the state where Mountain State Hospital is located were the state prisons, where mental healthcare was not provided. The hospital that could provide the needed care (medications and medical attention) for the violent mentally ill was not equipped as a secure environment in which the patients could not hurt themselves or others. As a result, dangerous mentally ill patients were denied access to healthcare.

Most states had addressed the issue of providing a locked-down and secure mental health facility, but Mountain State Hospital's state had not. The state was not rich, it was predominantly rural and thus had limited funds, and it had conservative policies on welfare and state-paid care for the mentally ill. Further, the state did not operate or contract with other states to provide a secure forensic mental hospital.

Mountain State Hospital was a state facility with Joint Commission accreditation. It had 120 beds for patients with severe mental and emotional disorders. These patients were determined

(continued)

National Alliance on Mental Illness (NAMI)
A national mental health organization dedicated to building better lives for Americans affected by mental illness.

> **CASE FROM THE FIELD**
> *Crises Reveal Our Character (continued)*
>
> to be a threat to themselves or others, but the authorities (mental health professionals and local judges) deemed them sufficiently safe for the mental hospital because they did not have a history of violent behavior. Seven psychiatrists, four clinical psychologists, and 20 master's-prepared mental health clinicians—along with nurses, social workers, and support personnel—staffed the hospital at the time. Staff members were regularly trained about safety and the potential risks they may encounter as they cared for mentally disturbed patients. At times, employees and patients did get injured on the job, but the injuries had not been life-threatening.
>
> Allred was an experienced administrator, having served as vice president, chief operating officer, and chief executive officer of both freestanding community hospitals and multihospital systems. Moreover, he had master's degrees in health administration and business administration. Before taking the administrator position at Mountain State Hospital, he worked for a hospital that had undergone a merger, which eliminated his position. While at Mountain State Hospital, he received an offer to serve as CEO of a hospital in a different state, but he turned it down because his family had already settled in the community. His children liked their schools, and he and his wife enjoyed their church and community involvement and had many friends. Personnel at the facility were pleased that a person with his experience had accepted the leadership role—that is, until the Bentley case arose.
>
> Some of the medical staff members confronted Allred and opposed Bentley's admission. Two psychiatrists threated to resign if Allred did not ignore the judge's ruling. Their plea was emotional, stating that their purpose was to treat mentally ill patients and that they had the legal right to accept or reject patients if they could not provide care in a safe environment. Admitting Bentley, they argued, would violate the safe environment factor. One employee even exclaimed, "We should care for our patients—the nonviolent mentally ill; the violent should not be allowed in the facility. I can't keep my vulnerable patients safe with dangerous and violent patients around!" (Farnsworth and Cellucci 2011, 37). Other staff members—clinical psychologists, nurses, and social workers—supported Bentley's admittance because they saw his mental healthcare need. They said, as the experts in mental healthcare, "We are or should be the obvious providers of that care" (Farnsworth and Cellucci 2011, 37).
>
> As the person in charge of Mountain State Hospital and reporting to HHS (because the hospital is a state facility), Allred was the one to decide whether to obey the judge's order to admit Bentley. While Allred responded to the staff members' concerns and focused on understanding their competing points of view, he also had to decide whether to honor the judge's order. Bentley's crime, imprisonment, mental competency, and court-ordered stay at Mountain State Hospital received frequent media attention that further stimulated stakeholder opinions and expectations.
>
> *(continued)*

> **CASE FROM THE FIELD**
> Crises Reveal Our Character *(continued)*
>
> ### THE STAKEHOLDERS
>
> *The state* received an F grade from NAMI because of its inadequate or lack of mental health per capita spending, infrastructure, information access, and service availability.
>
> *The public*, responding to local television and newspaper coverage of the events, was critical. Opinions fell into two categories: (1) The state's job was to protect its citizens, and (2) the state should protect the patients in the hospital and the employees who served them.
>
> *The district court judge* focused on the need to provide healthcare to all. Bentley's mental condition had to be evaluated, treated, and stabilized. These needs could not be met in prison but in Mountain State Hospital.
>
> *Hospital staff members* held differing positions based on their priorities. Some were concerned about patient and staff safety. Others were focused on the patient's need and their responsibility as professionals to provide care regardless of the situation.
>
> *HHS leaders* were interested in following the law and managing public perception at the same time.
>
> *Bentley* was a citizen in the state who needed mental healthcare.
>
> ### THE DECISION
>
> After listening to hospital staff and HHS leaders, Allred followed the judge's order and admitted Bentley. Four psychiatrists resigned as a result. He communicated with the medical community and found visiting psychiatrists who practiced in the region and offered part-time, temporary assistance until full-time replacements were hired. In addition, he employed a physician assistant and a clinical nurse practitioner trained in mental health. He assigned one-on-one staffing for Bentley, and he increased security in the facility by adding locks on doors.
>
> At the time of this writing, Bentley is receiving mental healthcare and appropriate medications at Mountain State Hospital. No incident of harm to providers or other patients involving Bentley has occurred.

hospitals, healthcare systems, long-term care facilities, physician practices, and consultancies. Eighty chapters are active that allow members to network, receive more training or continuing education, and advance their careers. ACHE's activities, programs, reports, and publications are planned with its vision, mission, and values in mind (see exhibit 5.1).

The ACHE Code of Ethics is divided into seven parts: a preamble followed by six points that address specific responsibilities. The preamble asserts that members' responsibilities

> **EXHIBIT 5.1**
> ACHE Vision, Mission, and Values

- **Vision:** To be the preeminent professional society for leaders dedicated to advancing health
- **Mission:** To advance our members and healthcare leadership excellence
- **Values:** Integrity, lifelong learning, leadership, diversity and inclusion

Source: ACHE (2021).

extend to everyone they encounter—including patients, colleagues, and employees of the organization, the community served and the public at large, and the profession itself. In addition, members are expected to be positive role models for others as "decisions and actions will reflect personal integrity and ethical leadership that others will seek to emulate." Most important, the preamble puts forward that the patient comes first (ACHE 2017):

> The fundamental objectives of the healthcare management profession are to maintain or enhance the overall quality of life, dignity and well-being of every individual needing healthcare service and to create a more equitable, accessible, effective and efficient healthcare system.

The six points cover members' distinct responsibilities to the profession (part I), to patients or others served (part II), to the organization (part III), to employees (part IV), and to the community and society (part V), as well as their duty to report infractions of the code (part VI).

ETHICAL PRINCIPLES

The preamble and six parts of the ACHE Code of Ethics are based on the following ethical principles, which members are expected to adopt and then apply to their daily lives—professional and otherwise:

- *Honesty* in both personal and professional interactions and activities
- *Integrity* in character, decision-making, and actions
- *Respect* for self and others, including customs, beliefs, and practices
- *Justice* in thought and action, such as treating employees and patients fairly, allocating resources equitably, and supporting healthcare access for all people
- *Loyalty* to the profession and the organization in which one works; this includes promptly reporting, addressing, and preventing potential threats and negative events
- *Beneficence* toward others and mindfulness that every decision has consequences for people

- *Autonomy* in decision-making, such as to protect the rights and interests of patients and other stakeholders
- *Honor* in serving as a moral advocate

Let's apply this code to Allred's experience at Mountain State Hospital. As a member of ACHE, he knew well ACHE's Code of Ethics and the ethical principles behind it. His behavior and decisions during the crisis reflect those ethical principles. He showed honesty, integrity, respect, and beneficence when addressing the conflicting demands and perspectives of the many stakeholders. He was loyal, just, autonomous, and honorable when making the final decision to admit Bentley. The fact that several psychiatrists in the region voluntarily stepped in to cover for the psychiatrists who quit after Bentley was admitted is a testament to Allred's ethical foundation and the respect he had earned in the profession and the community. In Allred's words, "I have found in my work in healthcare that situations present themselves that are complex. Bentley's case was an example of such situations that end up on an administrator's desk. Part of my job is to navigate and negotiate solutions with reference to my ethical code, which was certainly influenced by my profession. It was the right thing to do to admit Bentley."

MGMA's Code of Ethics

MGMA is a professional society for medical practice administrators with a membership of more than 55,000. This association has 50 state affiliates, which allow local members to network, take advantage of training and continuing education courses, and advance their careers. The mission of MGMA (2021) is to "elevate the performance of medical practice leaders and their organizations by connecting members, building partnerships, setting the standards for certification, advocating for physician practice and providing innovative solutions."

The Code of Ethics of MGMA endorses appropriate professional behaviors for all its members to act professionally and in keeping with the association's mission, goals, and objectives. Moreover, it cautions members from misusing the information received from the association, a statement similar to the loyalty ethical principle in ACHE's Code of Ethics.

ACHCA's Code of Ethics

ACHCA is the association for administrators of long-term care facilities. With nearly 2,000 members, the association has six regional directors across the country and chapters in 22 states (ACHCA 2020). Like ACHE and MGMA, ACHCA offers networking opportunities, resources, and seminars and other educational events. Its vision, mission, and values are

> **EXHIBIT 5.2**
> ACHCA Vision, Mission, and Values

- **Vision:** To be the premier organization providing professional leadership and professional development opportunities for post-acute and aging services health care leaders.
- **Mission:** The American College of Health Care Administrators (ACHCA) is the catalyst for excellence in post-acute and aging services leadership.
- **Values:**
  - Identifies post-acute and aging services leaders
  - Recognizes post-acute and aging services leaders
  - Supports post-acute and aging services leaders
  - Advocates for the role of post-acute and aging services leaders
  - Promotes professional excellence among post-acute and aging services leaders

Source: ACHCA (2020).

shown in exhibit 5.2. Activities, programs, reports, and publications from the association are planned with its vision, mission, and values in mind.

Divided into five parts, ACHCA's Code of Ethics contains a preamble and four expectations of members. The preamble asserts that long-term care administrators must live by the "highest standards of integrity and ethical principles." The four expectations are as follows (ACHCA 2014):

1. Expectation I: Hold paramount the welfare of persons for whom care is provided. (This expectation echoes the respect, justice, and beneficence ethical principles.)

2. Expectation II: Maintain high standards of professional competence and personal conduct.

3. Expectation III: Maintain a professional posture that places paramount the interests of the facility and its residents.

4. Expectation IV: Honor responsibilities to the public, profession, and relationships with colleagues and members of related professions.

These expectations are founded on the same ethical principles as honesty, integrity, loyalty, and honor (described in ACHE's Code of Ethics).

INTERNALIZED CODES LEAD TO PROFESSIONAL NORMS

As defined in chapter 1, professional norms are internalized standards to which professionals automatically and unconsciously conform. These norms influence behavior in any situation, especially during times of conflict. Exhibit 1.1 in chapter 1 lists examples of professional norms. Consider a few of these examples as they pertain to Allred's experience.

- *Public service through education and promotion of the health and well-being of patients (including clients and residents) and society in general.* Bentley had a violent history, but he was still a patient who was mentally ill and needed treatment. Plus, Mountain State Hospital was the only option in a state that offered limited resources for mentally ill offenders. By following the court order to admit him, Allred was promoting the health and well-being of a patient in dire need and (perhaps indirectly) educating the public about the need for more mental health services. His decision to add locks on doors in the facility and to assign one-on-one care for Bentley showed his concern for the safety of other patients, the employees, and society in general. In Allred's words, "I knew we could receive and treat him and keep others safe. I knew because I knew my staff members . . . were well-trained. Working together, we strategically plan[ned] and then provide[d] a place and treatment for Bentley."

- *Fairness in the distribution of resources among patients, employees, departments, organizations, and community members or the public.* Giving Bentley one-on-one staffing, adding locks throughout the facility, and hiring replacements for professionals who left after his admission cost money. Indeed, Mountain State Hospital put more resources into him than into other patients. However, Bentley's case was unusual and necessitated extreme measures. In the end, the extra lengths Allred took to receive Bentley ensured that the environment was as safe as possible for the rest of the patient population and the staff members. In Allred's words, "The fact is some patients command more resources than others because of the nature of what they need. We are committed to treating patients as individuals, regardless of their ability to pay. By that standard, it was a fair distribution based on need."

- *Lifelong learning, which elevates skills, knowledge, and awareness.* Reflecting on this crisis allowed Allred to identify what was done well and what could have been done better. The experience itself reaffirms or challenges personal and professional ethical values. More important, it strengthens character, and a strong character indicates that the professional has internalized the codes of ethics and applies them as norms without thinking about them. In Allred's words, "In times of crisis we don't really have an opportunity to develop character. Instead, a crisis presents an opportunity to reveal character. And so, if you haven't taken time in the front end to learn about values and ethics and views on important issues, you are likely to be weak when you are needed to be strong. Clarity and strength are needed. Take time now to get familiar with codes, reflect upon them. When the hour of truth arrives, you will be able to take a stand."

Application of Codes of Ethics

Codes of ethics can be applied over the course of your career in healthcare management. As a student or an early careerist, you have already been exposed to these codes through your college coursework, internship, or entry-level position. As your career advances—from entry to middle to senior levels—you will encounter plenty of opportunities to apply the code's ethical principles to specific work situations. This is why learning or internalizing these codes is so important.

Consider, for example, Margaret, a recent graduate of a master of health administration program. She first learned of the codes in an undergraduate healthcare class and had a chance to apply them during her internship at a local nursing home. Now that she works at the nursing home full-time, she has become reliant on that knowledge, especially ACHCA's Code of Ethics. Her responsibilities include meeting potential residents and their family members, giving them a tour of the facility, and educating them about costs and daily routines and activities.

One of these potential clients asked her about the facility's policy on visiting animals—specifically, her beloved dog, which was now in the care of her nephew. Margaret disclosed that the facility had a no-pets visitor policy, but she offered the potential client an alternative: Check out Therapy Dogs International (TDI), an organization that assesses dogs for the purpose of becoming therapy dogs. If her dog passed TDI's evaluation test, then the dog could visit as a therapy dog, although the client would have to share the visit with other residents. (See www.tdi-dog.org for more information.)

This response is a direct application of what Margaret learned from codes of ethics. She was honest, informative, respectful of and sensitive to the potential client's need, and professional (by knowing the facility's rules and the options available in the community). Her actions exhibited not only Expectation I and Expectation III of ACHCA's Code—(1) "hold paramount the welfare of persons for whom care is provided" and (2) "maintain a professional posture that places paramount the interests of the facility and its residents"—but also the ethical principles espoused by ACHE's Code of Ethics.

At middle and senior levels, professionals both practice and teach the codes. At this point, the codes have become internalized and manifest themselves as professional norms.

Mini-Case Study: The Dining Rooms at The Legacy

The Legacy was a 132-bed skilled nursing facility providing around-the-clock care to residents. Owned and operated by the Williams family, The Legacy opened its doors in 1994 with the mission of delivering high-quality care to older adults while treating them and their families with dignity and respect. The Williamses trained all personnel and volunteers at the facility and insisted that they all learn and live by the mission. Family members of the residents were welcome at The Legacy and visited often.

One of the residents at The Legacy was Mrs. Hightower. She had an incurable brain disorder, which had deteriorated the brain cells that controlled her body movements. When her family brought her to The Legacy two years ago, she could no longer walk or hold items that had weight, such as a book. The disorder had progressed to the point that swallowing had become a problem for her. She could choke on or inhale food or drink (possibly leading to pneumonia), so she had to be carefully monitored. To this end, she received speech therapy that helped her practice swallowing techniques and one-on-one nursing care to meet her nutrition needs. Her advance healthcare directive (living will) indicated that she chose not to receive a feeding tube.

Mrs. Hightower's daughter Amy served as her mother's healthcare power of attorney, and she visited her each morning before work. Amy's children were also frequent visitors. In fact, the elementary school–aged granddaughter once sought (and received) permission from Mrs. Williams to bring her ballet classmates and teachers to perform for all the residents. Amy consulted with The Legacy's care planning team about her mother's care. For example, when swallowing first became difficult for Mrs. Hightower, Amy asked the team if she could bring a straw to help her mother sip the coffee she brought every morning. This was currently working, but all knew that it was only a matter of time before Mrs. Hightower would no longer be able to swallow, even with a straw.

When Mrs. Williams was informed about Mrs. Hightower's condition, she had to make some decisions. First, she discussed the situation with the care planning team. Second, she determined that Mrs. Hightower would have to be transferred from the Magnolia dining room to the Azalea dining room. Third, she scheduled a meeting with Amy to inform her of the change and to involve her in preparing her mother for the dining room transition. Mrs. Williams wanted to treat this as gently as possible, because this was yet another experience that Mrs. Hightower would lose.

At The Legacy, eating dinner in the Magnolia room was a highlight of the day for many residents. It certainly had been Mrs. Hightower's favorite activity. Residents loved it because, as one resident said, it was "the way we all used to enjoy our dinner, with our friends and family as we shared a meal." But the Magnolia was reserved for residents who did not need constant assistance with eating. Given Mrs. Hightower's difficulty with swallowing, she would not function well in the independent setting of Magnolia. The Azalea dining room, which was just as nice as the Magnolia, was more suited to her needs. There, a staff member would be by her side while she ate to attend to her specific needs; she would not be alone.

At the meeting with Mrs. Williams and the care planning team, Amy learned that Mrs. Hightower's favorite certified nursing assistant had volunteered to sit with her throughout the first few meals until she became used to the Azalea. Moreover, the nutritionist planned on serving Mrs. Hightower's favorite dishes for her first few dinners. Mrs. Williams also promised to visit Mrs. Hightower at the end of the day to show support and check on her. After the meeting, Mrs. Williams and Amy talked with Mrs. Hightower about the change in dining rooms and the plans to help her through it. While Mrs. Hightower was sad about the news and found it difficult to speak (another complication from her brain disorder), she expressed that she knew the change was coming and thanked Mrs. Williams for coming to her in person.

Amy's comment about the whole situation was nothing but complimentary: "We all knew it was only a matter of time because there is no cure. This disorder only progresses. I and the rest of my family are grateful to the Williamses and The Legacy staff because they always treated my mother with kindness, respect, and caring. This event was more than about where my mother ate dinner, and they understood that."

Mini-Case Study Questions

1. Explain how Mrs. Williams followed The Legacy's mission when she engaged Amy, the care planning team, and Mrs. Hightower in the process of transferring Mrs. Hightower from the Magnolia to the Azalea dining room.
2. Discuss at least two ethical principles that relate to this case. Consider, for example, how autonomy and respect may have influenced the actions taken.
3. Do you think Mrs. Williams followed the ACHCA code? Explain why or why not.

Points to Remember

- Professional associations in healthcare, such as ACHE, MGMA, and ACHCA, issue their own codes of ethics.
- Codes of ethics spell out standards of behavior that the professionals learn, follow, and internalize. Once internalized, the codes become professional norms.
- Codes of ethics can be applied throughout a healthcare manager's career and influence behavior.

Challenge Yourself

1. Consider the chapter-opening quote by Mark Twain: "Right is right, and wrong is wrong, and a body ain't got no business doing wrong when he ain't ignorant and knows better." Think of how this might be true for you as you prepare to become a healthcare manager.
2. The court order mandating that Mountain State Hospital admit Harold Bentley brought the interests of the hospital's stakeholders into conflict. Explain the conflict between the psychiatrists who did not want Bentley admitted and the judge's and HHS's support for his admittance.
3. Based on what you learned in this chapter, give an example of a code you have internalized to become a professional norm.

For Your Consideration

5.1 The Mini-Case Study in this chapter, "The Dining Rooms at the Legacy," noted that Mrs. Hightower was losing her ability to swallow and that she had an advance healthcare directive (living will) indicating she did not wish to receive a feeding tube. Review and understand the Mayo Clinic's information about living wills, advance directives, power of attorney, and physician orders for life-sustaining treatment at www.mayoclinic.org/healthy-lifestyle/consumer-health/in-depth/living-wills/art-20046303. Note that states have different laws pertaining to living wills; so, there is no universal template that will serve you if and when you decide to finalize a living will.

For this exercise, download the Advance Care Planning Expanded Toolkit from Vidant Health (2019). The document outlines five steps for developing a living will. The first step asks you to think about what is important to you. Complete this step alone or with someone you trust (e.g., a classmate, friend, family member, or religious leader):

STEP 1—Think About

Think about the questions in the rest of this section and write down your thoughts. This can help you sort out your feelings about what matters most to you.

Quality of Life
- What gives your life value, meaning, and purpose?
- What does "quality of life" mean to you?
- What would you miss most if you couldn't walk, talk, eat, or think normally?
- What would you be willing to give up or tolerate to keep what matters most to you?
- Is quality of life more important to you than how long you live?
- Or do you want to live as long as possible, no matter what?

Healthcare Experiences
- Think about good or bad health experiences you know about. How have those experiences influenced your choices for future healthcare?
- Has anyone close to you died? Do you think their death was a "good" death or "bad" death? Why?
- Do you have any medical problems or conditions? Do you expect them to get worse?
- Will your medical problems change your quality of life? If so, how?
- Are you having medical treatments for your problem/condition?
- Are you thinking about having any new medical treatment(s)?
- Will this affect your quality of life? If so, how?

Chapter 5: Professional Codes of Ethics and Ethical Principles

End-of-Life Care
- Think about medical treatments near the end of your life. Are there circumstances when you would want CPR, mechanical ventilation, artificial nutrition, or artificial hydration?
- Are there treatments you know you would want?
- Are there treatments you know you would NOT want?
- Can you imagine a time you would you want to stop having treatments just to keep you alive longer and only use comfort measures to keep you as comfortable as possible in the time you have left?
- Where would you prefer to spend your last few months, weeks, or days? In your home? Nursing Home? Hospital?

Someone to Speak for You
- Who would you want to speak for you about healthcare decisions if you could not communicate for yourself? Would they be able to make decisions based on what you want?
- Have you told this person what you would want? Have you told anyone?
- How much do you want your family or other loved ones to be involved in your healthcare?

Final Wishes
- What do you want to do or say before you die?
- Do you want your organs donated after you die? Have you discussed this with your family or loved ones?
- Would you prefer to be buried or cremated? Do you have instructions about what should happen to your body after you die?

    Upon completing this step, summarize what you learned about what matters to you. What surprised you as you identified what matters? What role did the ethical principle of autonomy play when you considered your answers? How does this exercise influence you as a future healthcare manager who will be acting on behalf of your institution's policies regarding end of life?

5.2 Allred said the following in reflecting on the Mountain State Hospital events: "In times of crisis we don't really have an opportunity to develop character. Instead, a crisis presents an opportunity to reveal character. And so, if you haven't taken time in the front end to learn about values and ethics and views on important issues, you are likely to be weak when you are needed to be strong. Clarity and strength are needed. Take time now to get familiar with codes, reflect upon them. When the hour of truth arrives, you will be able to take a stand."

With this advice, develop your own personal mission statement. This exercise will help prepare you one day "to take a stand." Peruse the internet for helpful guidelines on creating a mission statement; you can also visit these free resources:
- Cabral, C. 2020. "Personal Mission Statements (7 Habits)." Published April 5. www.shortform.com/blog/personal-mission-statement-7-habits/.
- Forbes Coaches Council. 2017. "13 Ways You Can Craft a Strong Personal Mission Statement." Published November 7. www.forbes.com/sites/forbescoachescouncil/2017/11/07/13-ways-you-can-craft-a-strong-personal-mission-statement/?sh=25c55cb22dee.
- Forsey, C. 2019. "Here's How to Write an Impressive Personal Mission Statement." Published January 3. https://blog.hubspot.com/marketing/personal-mission-statement.

Check These Out

Want more information about the organizations and concepts discussed in the chapter? Check these websites out.

- American College of Health Care Administrators: www.achca.org
- American College of Health Care Administrators Code of Ethics: https://achca.memberclicks.net/assets/code%20of%20ethics_achca%20non-member_140430.pdf
- American College of Healthcare Executives: www.ache.org
- American College of Healthcare Executives Code of Ethics: www.ache.org/-/media/ache/ethics/code_of_ethics_web.pdf
- Medical Group Management Association: www.mgma.com
- Medical Group Management Association Code of Ethics: www.mgma.com/MGMA/media/files/about/Code-of-Ethics-Approved.pdf
- National Alliance on Mental Illness: www.nami.org
- Therapy Dogs International: www.tdi-dog.org

References

American College of Health Care Administrators (ACHCA). 2020. *2019–2020 Annual Report*. Accessed March 13, 2021. https://achca.memberclicks.net/assets/site/FY2019-2020%20ACHCA%20Annual%20Report%20document%20Final.pdf.

———. 2016. "Strategic Goals 2016 and Beyond." Published September. https://achca.memberclicks.net/assets/docs/Conferences/achca%20strategic%20goals%20and%20plan.pdf.

———. 2014. "Code of Ethics." Accessed March 13, 2021. https://achca.memberclicks.net/assets/docs/code%20of%20ethics_achca%20non-member_140430.pdf.

American College of Healthcare Executives (ACHE). 2021. "About ACHE." Accessed August 31. www.ache.org/about-ache.

———. 2017. "Code of Ethics." Amended November 13. www.ache.org/-/media/ache/ethics/code_of_ethics_web.pdf.

Farnsworth, T., and L. W. Cellucci. 2011. "The Decision to Admit or Not to Admit." *Journal of Critical Incidents* 4: 34–37.

Medical Group Management Association (MGMA). 2021. "About MGMA." Accessed March 12. www.mgma.com/about/organization.

———. 2015. "Code of Ethics." Published September 29. www.mgma.com/MGMA/media/files/about/Code-of-Ethics-Approved.pdf.

National Alliance on Mental Illness (NAMI). 2016. *Public Policy Platform of the National Alliance on Mental Illness*, 12th ed. Published December. www.nami.org/getattachment/Learn-More/Mental-Health-Public-Policy/Public-Policy-Platform-December-2016-(1).pdf.

Vidant Health. 2019. "Advance Care Planning Toolkit." Revised December. www.vidanthealth.com/wp-content/uploads/2020/11/Advance-Care-Planning-Toolkit-1-7-20-Web.pdf.

PART II
ETHICAL DECISION-MAKING IN THE HEALTHCARE ENVIRONMENT

The material covered in part II includes a deeper look into ethical decision-making processes; common ethical issues and interactions in the clinical setting, including challenging exchanges between and among medical professionals, patients, and their families; and the important role and contribution of the human resources manager in establishing and ensuring organizational ethics.

This case and commentary focus on the reality that although many hospital and healthcare administrators are not professionally trained clinicians, they must understand clinical issues and the complex decision-making and communications challenges that their clinical colleagues face. Consider the following questions as you read:

- Poor communication can lead to ethical dilemmas and poor ethical decision-making. The reasons for poor communication in end-of-life care are multifactorial. What are some of the factors in poor communications presented in this case?

- What are some of the core competencies needed for leading difficult conversations in the clinical/patient care environment?

- Complex, highly emotional conversations are often fraught with communication challenges. These conversations often involve concerns beyond the medical issues being discussed. What are some of these considerations?

Case Study: How Should Complex Communication Responsibilities Be Distributed in Surgical Education Settings?

Abstract

Part of any trauma surgeon's job is communicating effectively in difficult, often time-limited, situations. The ability to effectively discuss topics like goals of care in these settings has a direct effect on patient care. Many factors contribute to the complexity of these conversations, including patient, physician, surrogate, and system-specific factors. In responding to the case of Mr. D and Dr. J, we attempt to outline and analyze some of the moral challenges and ethical questions that this professional responsibility poses to trauma surgeons and trainees.

Case

Mr. D is a 19-year-old man severely injured after his motorcycle collided with oncoming traffic. He was not helmeted—either because his helmet came off or because he was not wearing one—at the time of the collision. He was unresponsive and intubated at the scene. Initial trauma workup reveals a Glasgow Coma Scale score of 3T, indicative of severe traumatic brain injury, although he received no medications from emergency medical service professionals in the field or while being transported to the emergency department. After being initially stabilized in the trauma bay, Mr. D was transferred to the surgical intensive care unit (SICU). A head computerized tomography (CT) scan obtained just prior to transfer reveals significant intracranial trauma including multiple foci of intracranial hemorrhage, mild midline shift (movement of the brain or part of the brain past its center line), and a moderate-sized subdural hematoma. Aside from his severe intracranial injuries, Mr. D has no major intrathoracic or intra-abdominal injuries. He continues to be unresponsive to noxious stimulation but has pupillary constriction, and he is breathing spontaneously on the ventilator, indicating exceedingly poor brain function but not brain death.

Dr. J is the second-year resident physician in the SICU who performed Mr. D's initial neurosurgical examination and is taking care of him. Dr. J has spoken with Dr. S, the chief neurosurgical resident, about Mr. D's poor prognosis. Based on Dr. S's assessment, Mr. D suffered devastating intracranial injuries and has little hope for meaningful recovery. Dr. J and Dr. S discuss Mr. D's case and consider whether a decompressive craniectomy (a partial skull removal that would allow expansion of a swelling brain) would help him. After further deliberation, however, they agree that it would probably not. No surgery is planned, and Dr. S plans to talk to the attending physician about Mr. D in the morning.

At 2 a.m., Mr. D's mother, father, siblings, and extended family arrive. His bedside nurse asks Dr. J to provide Mr. D's family with an update and escorts Mr. D's family to the conference room. Dr. J has never led a discussion with a patient's family about the goals of care, and she hesitantly agrees to meet with Mr. D's family. Dr. J clarifies that it is likely that Mr. D's injuries will result in brain death. "Brain death?" Mr. D's mother asks as she begins to weep. "What's that?" Dr. J ponders how to explain brain death to the grieving mother. Then Mr. D's father, who introduces himself as a family practice physician, asks Dr. J if there is anything the team can do to save his son. He has heard about decompressive craniectomy helping "brain-injured" patients and asks whether this procedure can be done. Dr. J states that she and Dr. S considered it and agree that this procedure would not benefit Mr. D. Mr. D's father then asks, "And your attending physician agrees?" Dr. J wonders how to respond.

COMMENTARY

The case of Mr. D and Dr. J highlights some relevant issues in ethical communication and surgical education. Communication is a professional duty of all physicians. McCullough notes that sound, trustworthy information is a patient right.[1] Dr. J has never led a family discussion about goals of care and is understandably hesitant. However, she is correct in proceeding with the family update despite never having done it before. Alternatively, she could call her attending physician (who presumably is not in the hospital) to come in and have the goals-of-care discussion with Mr. D's family. This would have left Mr. D's family sitting at the hospital, maybe even at their son's bedside, without any update or information for an extended period of time. Given the nature of the patient's injuries, progression to brain death prior to the arrival of the attending physician is also possible. In this case, it is important to have the goals-of-care discussion as soon as possible. Dr. J's inexperience, combined with her respect for surrogate autonomy, presents a dilemma for Dr. J and the potential for missteps in communication.

Factors in Poor Communication

Communication, in and of itself, is not really an ethical issue. When effective, it can be a vehicle that facilitates good ethical decision making. Unfortunately, the opposite is true as well. Poor communication can lead to ethical dilemmas and poor ethical decision making. The reasons for poor communication in end-of-life care are multifactorial.[2,3] Patient, physician, surrogate, and system-specific factors are all contributors to the complexity of the communication.

Patient Factors

A few patient-specific factors are relevant, and chief among these factors is the sudden, severe nature of a patient's injuries. Such injuries result in loss of patient decision-making capacity, a major factor in the complexity of communication. The patient's pre-injury state of health, the patient's value system, and what the patient would consider an acceptable quality of life are also significant contributors. In this case, none of these contributing patient factors is known, although it can be assumed that Mr. D was most likely healthy since he was 19 years old and riding a motorcycle. Previously healthy patients who suffer catastrophic injuries that will significantly alter their quality of life will likely have perspectives on quality of life that are very different from those of chronically ill patients who sustain similar injuries. Each of these cases presents different communication challenges.

Physician Factors

There are numerous physician-specific factors that affect communication in these kinds of situations, and this case highlights two of them: relevant experience in discussing end-of-life issues and the ability to impart pertinent information. Dr. J lacks clinical experience but also experience in holding difficult conversations. It is important for her to provide clear medical information about the total injury burden and prognosis. Dr. J recognizes the need for input from a more experienced surgeon such as Dr. S, the neurosurgery chief resident. The information exchanged between Dr. J and Dr. S was useful because it included information that any meaningful discussion about goals of care requires, including specifics of the injury and current condition, the patient's prognosis, and treatment options.[3] The end result of this conversation between these two residents is that surgery is not an option for this patient. Unfortunately, this same conversation does not take place with the neurosurgery attending physician in order to verify that this is the best course of action for this patient.

This failure to close the loop presents both moral and medicolegal issues that are related more to the medical training paradigm than to communication or end-of-life care. Suffice it to say that a decision as consequential as the decision to operate (or not operate) ideally should be vetted by an attending surgeon. In situations in which the decision to operate is closely linked to decisions regarding end-of-life care, it becomes absolutely essential to have the attending surgeon confirm the plan. In this case, Dr. J should confirm the plan with the attending surgeon by phone rather than deferring the conversation until the surgeon arrives in the morning.

Surrogate Factors

Surrogate decision-maker factors are also some of the most challenging ones in difficult conversations. Surrogates are often unprepared to be thrust into the role of decision maker. They may have little or no knowledge of the patient's desires regarding advance directives. This is especially true of younger patients and trauma patients like Mr. D. Emotions are a tremendously important factor to consider in these conversations. They affect surrogates' ability to think and process information as well as their ability to make decisions. Surrogate cognitive ability and familiarity with the medical environment can be important factors to consider as well. In this particular case, the experience of Mr. D's father as a family physician is an important detail for Dr. J to consider.

The mature practitioner who leads these discussions recognizes that these factors can be helpful or harmful in these conversations. Using some medical terminology in conversation can give the false impression of medical literacy that can easily be misinterpreted by treating physicians. Therefore, communication expertise involves developing skills to confirm that information is understood correctly while simultaneously facilitating a natural and open flow to the conversation. As a physician inexperienced in leading difficult conversations, Dr. J should focus on the immediate issue, which is the goals-of-care conversation. She should proceed using language that is clear and easy for all members of the family to understand.

System Factors

There is a pair of system-specific barriers to effective communication that are present in this scenario: time constraints and inexperience of the on-call team. When Mr. D's family arrives, it is appropriate to provide them with an update on their son's condition even though it is the middle of the night. Ideally, the attending physicians for the SICU and the neurosurgery team would lead this conversation. But, in this case, waiting until morning would likely worsen the fears and anxieties of Mr. D's family and would delay communicating critical information that is already available. Unfortunately, it is one of the realities of trauma and surgical critical care that resident-led family meetings are both unavoidable and essential. This fact points to the need for intentional education for surgical trainees in this key area. Junior residents themselves acknowledge much more anxiety than senior residents when faced with having difficult conversations with patients or families.[4] This anxiety is often related to uncertainty about the patient's diagnosis or prognosis.[5]

Communication Education for Trainees

The need for formalized and intentional education of trainees in this particular area has been recognized across medical specialties.[4-11] To date, no large-scale studies on communication skills training for difficult conversations have been performed, but smaller studies show promising results.[5, 9-11] Simulation and case-based discussion modules have both been described in the literature.[5, 6, 9-11] A well-rounded training model in this area likely requires a multifaceted approach with a tiered progression of responsibility. Didactic lectures, simulations, and case-based discussions should provide a good foundation.

On clinical services, though, a tiered progression of trainee responsibility seems most logical. Initially, this would likely begin with observation of attending surgeons and senior residents adept at this type of communication. Then partial participation, likely starting conversations with less severely ill patients, can occur under direct supervision. Ideally, this training would progress to more involvement of the trainee as competency is demonstrated, culminating with the trainee leading a discussion about severely ill patients with family or surrogates, again under adequate attending supervision. This tiered progression of responsibility would equip the resident physician to independently lead difficult conversations before being thrust into a difficult situation, as in this case, because of the attending physician's absence.

A key component of this approach is defining the core communication competencies for leading difficult conversations. At present, there is no widely accepted standard. A number of authors have attempted to define these competencies in a series of small trials and in recommendations based on expert consensus.[2, 3, 6, 11]

Table 1 shows a list of suggested core competencies adapted from these publications. Demonstrating competency in conducting difficult conversations requires skill in both verbal and nonverbal communication. Specific components integral to verbal communication include clear transmission of information, appropriate empathic acknowledgment, and providing the opportunity to ask questions. Nonverbal skills are also essential to reflect the importance of the conversation, to demonstrate reflexive listening, and to provide appropriate emotional support.

TABLE 1
Core Competencies for Leading Difficult Conversations

Nonverbal skills
Chooses an appropriate location for meeting
Sits down with family
Makes good eye contact
Uses good posture and body language
Demonstrates care and concern through tone of voice and pace of conversation
Allows some silence for family to absorb information
Uses reflexive listening skills

Verbal skills
Leads introductions of all parties present (clinicians and family)
Gives news in direct, succinct manner
Explains information clearly, using appropriate language (avoids jargon)
Is respectful of patient
Offers emotional support
Asks open-ended questions
Acknowledges emotions of family and patient
Attempts to elicit treatment goals and expectations
States prognosis clearly
Discusses treatment options
Restates and summarizes as needed
Invites questions

Addressing Futility

This particular scenario suggests the patient's father's concern about futility; the case states that he asks "if there is anything the team can do to save [my] son." Concern about futility seems to underlie the residents' decision to forego surgical intervention. There are generally considered to be two types of futility, quantitative and qualitative,[12] and the distinction between these types of futility is germane to the moral dilemma faced by Dr. J.

Quantitative futility refers to the inability of an intervention to achieve the intended physiological outcome. In this scenario, the decompressive craniectomy is intended to decrease intracranial hypertension, which is possible, so would not be futile in a quantitative sense.[13] Qualitative futility, on the other hand, is the term applied to an intervention that results in an outcome that is below a standard that the patient would consider acceptable.[14]

Discussions about qualitative futility are often more complex and more individualized as they center on things like benefit to the patient and quality of life. In this case, the family wants to know if anything can be done "to save" their son. This question is much more difficult question to answer because it's unclear what exactly Mr. D's father means by "save." Is saving merely maintaining pulse? Does it mean restoring Mr. D to his pre-injury functional status? Perhaps it is somewhere in between. In this scenario, Dr. J tells Mr. D's family that decompressive craniectomy "would not benefit Mr. D."

Without having a conversation with the family about what would be an acceptable outcome, it would be difficult for Dr. J to know whether the procedure would in fact benefit the patient. To address the family's question of what can be done to save Mr. D, it would have been more appropriate for Dr. J to discuss the available treatment options and expected outcomes of each. This approach could have provided information that could have allowed the family and Dr. J to determine whether any of the available treatments could result in outcomes that the patient would consider acceptable.

Conclusion

Leading complex, highly emotional conversations involving brain death and severe traumatic brain injury is fraught with communication challenges. These conversations often involve issues beyond the medical issues being discussed. Ethical considerations such as quantitative futility, qualitative futility, respect for patient or surrogate autonomy, and surrogate decision making are all prominently featured in end-of-life conversations. Inadequate communication can make these ethical considerations problematic. Patient, physician, surrogate, and system-specific factors all can potentially contribute to inadequate communication.

The urgency of trauma situations often thrusts trainees into a lead role before they are entirely ready to lead. At present, most trainees, both surgical and medical, are not given adequate formal training in leading difficult discussions about end-of-life care.[4,5,7,8,10] As a result, they are justifiably anxious about engaging in these conversations. These considerations underscore the importance of a multifaceted educational approach to communication that begins early in training and emphasizes tiered responsibility.

References

1. McCullough LB, Jones JW, Brody BA. *Surgical Ethics*. New York, NY: Oxford University Press; 1998.
2. Cooper Z, Courtwright A, Karlage A, Gawande A, Block S. Pitfalls in communication that lead to nonbeneficial emergency surgery in elderly patients with serious illness: description of the problem and elements of a solution. *Ann Surg*. 2014;260(6):949–957.
3. Cooper Z, Koritsanszky LA, Cauley CE, et al. Recommendations for best communication practices to facilitate goal-concordant care for seriously ill older patients with emergency surgical conditions. *Ann Surg*. 2016;263(1):1–6.
4. Centofanti J, Swinton M, Dionne J, et al. Resident reflections on end-of-life education: a mixed-methods study of the 3 Wishes Project. *BMJ Open*. 2016;6(3):e010626.
5. Curtis JR, Back AL, Ford DW, et al. Effect of communication skills training for residents and nurse practitioners on quality of communication with patients with serious illness: a randomized trial. *JAMA*. 2013;310(21):2271–2281.
6. Falcone JL, Claxton RN, Marshall GT. Communication skills training in surgical residency: a needs assessment and metacognition analysis of a difficult conversation objective structured clinical examination. *J Surg Educ*. 2014;71(3):309–315.
7. Kawaguchi S, Mirza R, Nissim R, Ridley J. Internal medicine residents' beliefs, attitudes, and experiences relating to palliative care: a qualitative study. *Am J Hosp Palliat Care*. 2017;34(4):366–372.
8. Rhodes RL, Tindall K, Xuan L, Paulk ME, Halm EA. Communication about advance directives and end-of-life care options among internal medicine residents. *Am J Hosp Palliat Care*. 2015;32(3):262–268.
9. Trickey AW, Newcomb AB, Porrey M, et al. Two-year experience implementing a curriculum to improve residents' patient-centered communication skills. *J Surg Educ*. 2017;74(6):e124–e132.
10. Raoof M, O'Neill L, Neumayer L, Fain M, Krouse R. Prospective evaluation of surgical palliative care immersion training for general surgery residents. *Am J Surg*. 2017;214(2):378–383.
11. Haglund MM, Rudd M, Nagler A, Prose NS. Difficult conversations: a national course for neurosurgery residents in physician-patient communication. *J Surg Educ*. 2015;72(3):394–401.
12. Jecker NS, Pearlman RA. Medical futility. Who decides? *Arch Intern Med*. 1992;152(6):1140–1144.
13. Hutchinson PJ, Kolias AG, Timofeev IS, et al; RESCUEicp Trial Collaborators. Trial of decompressive craniectomy for traumatic intracranial hypertension. *N Engl J Med*. 2016;375(12):1119–1130.
14. Solomon MJ, Brasel KJ. End-of-life issues: how to respect patients' wishes and prevent futility. In: Ferreres AR, Angelos P, Singer EA, eds. *Ethical Issues in Surgical Care*. Chicago, IL: American College of Surgeons; 2017:191–193.

Source: Dennis, B. M., and A. B. Peetz. 2018. "How Should Complex Communication Responsibilities Be Distributed in Surgical Education Settings?" *AMA Journal of Ethics* 20 (5): 431–38. Reprinted with permission.

CHAPTER 6
ETHICAL FRAMEWORK

Ethics is knowing the difference between what you have a right to do and what is right to do.
—Potter Stewart, former US Supreme Court justice

Important Terms

- Beneficent
- Certificate of need (CON)
- Civil disobedience
- Claim
- Defense mechanism
- Ethical conflict
- False Claims Act
- Federally Qualified Health Center
- Fee schedule
- Law
- Law fallacy
- Moral blindness
- Qui tam
- Rationalization
- Whistleblower

Learning Objectives

Studying this chapter will help you to

➤ appreciate the relationship between ethics and law,

➤ categorize the relationship between ethics and law using the four-quadrant model, and

➤ understand the implications of ethical unawareness.

law
A rule enacted by a legislative body, such as the US Congress or a state legislature; regulation is a rule established by an executive agency to carry out a law.

Ethics requires critical thinking. As a starting point, healthcare managers determine the relationship between ethics and **law** in the conflict they face. This chapter uses a four-quadrant model to explain the relationship between ethics and law. Applying the four-quadrant model helps healthcare managers sort through this relationship as well as categorize the ethical conflicts they face.

CASE FROM THE FIELD
Man of the Year, 1930

Mahatma Gandhi was an ethical leader who broke the law and became *Time* magazine's "Man of the Year" in 1930. Born in 1869 in western India, he was given the name Mohandas Karamchand Gandhi. He became known as Mahatma—or "Great Soul"—in the early twentieth century as he worked for the rights of Indian people in India (Severance 1997).

When Gandhi was born, India was a colony of the British Empire. As his family was poor and his mother had been widowed, Gandhi decided that if he became a lawyer, he could attain an administrative post to support his mother. Therefore, in 1888, at the age of 18, he left India, defying his caste leader, to study law in London (Hay 1989). There, he became a member of activist intellectual societies such as the Theosophical Society. Henry David Thoreau's essay on civil disobedience would greatly influence Gandhi's future political thinking (Hendrick 1956). He passed the bar examinations in 1890 and returned to India in 1891.

Gandhi worked for India's independence from Great Britain. His actions were grounded in *satyagraha*, a concept referring to nonviolent political action. The word itself has no equivalent in English, but it implies a convergence of truth, noninjury, and self-suffering (Hettne 1976).

In 1930, Gandhi mobilized the Indian people to show their support for the independence cause by walking in the Salt March (or Dandi March) (Suchitra 1995; Weber 2002). The Salt March focused attention on the injustice of the British salt tax. India has salt deposits, but the British monopolized salt manufacturing and retailing (Varshney 2003). The British salt laws not only levied a heavy tax on salt but also made illegal the manufacturing, purchase, sale, and even possession of salt (Suchitra 1995). Essential to health, salt had a universal impact on all segments of Indian society.

The Salt March drew the world's attention and empathy. Over 25 days—between March 12 and April 6—Gandhi and his 78 followers marched 240 miles from the city of Ahmedabad near the northwest coast of India to the seaside town of Dandi farther down the coast (Habib 1997; Suchitra 1995; Weber 2002). Stopping along the way to speak to villagers, he reached approximately 500,000 people (Suchitra 1995). At Dandi, he extracted salt, which was a violation of the law (Habib 1997).

Other salt marches were undertaken throughout the country; people made contraband salt. To demonstrate their support, 227 village headmen resigned as a means of noncooperation

(continued)

Chapter 6: Ethical Framework   **111**

CASE FROM THE FIELD
Man of the Year, 1930 (continued)

(Habib 1997). The nationalist movement of civil disobedience resulted in the arrest and imprisonment of Gandhi and 90,000 supporters (Suchitra 1995). While full independence did not come for India until 1947, his campaign of civil disobedience has been credited as the greatest nonviolent battle in history (Weber 2002). In 1931, Gandhi appeared on the cover of *Time* magazine as its Man of the Year for 1930 (*Time* 1931).

Civil disobedience is illegal, but Gandhi's behavior is considered by many to be ethical.

DID YOU KNOW?
Salt Hunger

The human body needs salt (sodium) to function properly. Salt is essential to maintaining blood pressure and to the functioning of muscles and nerves. Without salt, the human body develops salt depletion or hyponatremia (low blood sodium). Hyponatremia may result in muscle weakness, vomiting, and possible convulsions and coma (Buffington and Abreo 2016). Today, however, we are more focused on the negative effects of excessive salt, such as hypertension.

Ethical Conflicts

Healthcare managers face many difficult situations that may pose **ethical conflicts** for them. The following are some examples of possible ethical conflicts:

- Taking the right action, such as giving a negative performance appraisal, is necessary, but doing so is difficult or uncomfortable for the people involved and their relationship.

- Expanding services at a small, rural hospital to include obstetrics would be good for the community's families, but the costs of obstetric services would make the hospital unprofitable, which is a violation of fiduciary duty (see chapter 4 for more discussion of this duty).

- Choosing between two equally negative alternatives is stressful but may be inevitable.

ethical conflict
Any problem or situation that has an ethical component; a situation in which ethical principles seem to collide.

Sometimes, the ethical conflict is resolved by a relevant mandate, such as a law, policy, or rule. Often, however, healthcare managers must deal with ethical conflicts that are *not* covered by some edict—for instance, when they feel pressured to do something that they are uncomfortable with, that they know to be wrong, or that requires them to bend the rules (Dean, Beggs, and Keane 2010). Thus, laws, policies, and rules can only cover *some* of the ethical conflicts that managers face. For other conflicts, managers may find that relying on laws or other mandates to provide the answer is not a viable option.

THE FOUR-QUADRANT MODEL

Ethics and law are distinct but related. The four-quadrant model (see exhibit 6.1) graphically depicts these relationships. This model provides a conceptual framework to classify corporate decision-making (Henderson 1982). It was meant to prepare business executives for public scrutiny of their company's internal decisions.

The model shows that ethics and law, although related, do not have a one-to-one relationship. For example, an act that is ethical is not necessarily legal. Conversely, an act that is unethical is not necessarily illegal. Instead, the relationship is categorized into four quadrants:

- Quadrant I: Ethical and Legal
- Quadrant II: Ethical and Illegal
- Quadrant III: Unethical and Legal
- Quadrant IV: Unethical and Illegal

Of the four quadrants, only two are straightforward—Quadrants I and IV. The other two quadrants—Quadrants II and III—require more thought, work, and disentanglement

EXHIBIT 6.1
Four-Quadrant Model of Ethics and Law

Quadrant I Ethical and Legal	**Quadrant II** Ethical and Illegal
Quadrant III Unethical and Legal	**Quadrant IV** Unethical and Illegal

Source: Henderson (1982, 42). Used and adapted with permission.

than the straightforward quadrants. We examine each of the four quadrants from the viewpoint of healthcare managers.

QUADRANT I: ETHICAL AND LEGAL

Healthcare managers are ethical and legal when they perform their routine duties honestly and justly. The following examples represent ethical and legal acts from each function of management:

- *Planning.* Healthcare managers act with beneficence and follow the law when they provide information to support a healthcare organization's planning activities, such as applying for a **certificate of need (CON)**. In many states, healthcare organizations must obtain CON approval before they can plan certain new services or construct new buildings.

- *Organizing.* Healthcare managers act both ethically and legally when they schedule clinicians to provide services within their scope of practice or licensure. For example, in skilled nursing facilities, clinical managers schedule occupational and physical therapists to provide specific therapies to residents.

- *Leading and directing.* Healthcare managers consciously exercise ethics when they put aside personal biases (justice) and act for the good of the unit (beneficence) during the hiring process. They follow the law when they do not question job applicants about their religion, national origin, marital status or pregnancy plans, or other personal details.

- *Controlling.* During routine quality audits, healthcare managers may discover errors in practice management software or other systems. For example, during software upgrade and testing, a duplicate of charges was created. The practice's manager discovered that these duplicate charges were submitted to Medicare along with the "real" charges, creating duplicate **claims**. The duplicate claims were paid by the Medicare administrative contractor, resulting in overpayment to the physician practice. The healthcare manager acted ethically (honestly) and within the law (complying with Medicare regulations) when he contacted the contractor to report the overpayment and arrange repayment.

Acting ethically and legally may seem easy but doing what is right and legally permissible can be difficult. For example, as discussed in chapter 2, **whistleblowers** who accurately report corporate misdeeds to the authorities are acting ethically and legally. Often, however, whistleblowers become the target of organizational disapproval and criticism, which could make whistleblowers feel as if they have done something wrong. Fortunately, federal law

certificate of need (CON)
Required written approval issued by a state agency for proposed new services, buildings, and other plans.

claim
An itemized request that a provider (organization or individual practitioner) submits to a payer (health insurance plan, Medicare, or another payer) for reimbursement of services rendered.

whistleblower
An individual who exposes and reports corporate wrongdoing.

and many state laws protect whistleblowers. Despite having the high ethical ground and legal protections, whistleblowers know that facing the censure of colleagues takes courage.

Quadrant II: Ethical and Illegal

In the United States, ethical but illegal behavior can be described as **civil disobedience**. The following are three examples of individuals and groups who refused to follow the law but arguably did the right thing nonetheless:

civil disobedience
The concept of resisting a law for the sake of standing up for what is morally right.

1. For six years, Henry David Thoreau (1849) refused to pay taxes because he disagreed with the US government's actions regarding slavery and the Mexican-American War. He spent one night in jail for this offense.

2. In 1961, the Freedom Riders—a group of civil rights activists—rode interstate buses in the South to test the states' compliance with the desegregation ruling of the US Supreme Court. These southern states still upheld segregation for their transit facilities (Ling 2007), so the Freedom Riders were breaking local statutes while supporting the greater cause of justice.

3. Healthcare professionals and activists protested the decision of North Carolina's legislature to forgo Medicaid expansion under the Affordable Care Act. In 2013, many of these protesters were arrested and subsequently charged with disorderly conduct, trespassing, and violating building rules. In the protesters' view, civil disobedience was necessary to protest the loss of benefits (such as preventive care) for poor patients (Morgan 2015; van der Horst 2014).

Quadrant III: Unethical and Legal

People can be dishonest, unprincipled, untrustworthy, unfair, and uncaring without breaking the law. Actions that are unethical and legal often represent circumstances in which the legal system and social customs have failed to keep pace with change or new knowledge. Often, areas that outpace legal and social processes are scientific research, technology, and environmental issues. For example, scientists *could* clone sheep before members of society decided whether they *should* clone living beings.

Before 2007, a hospital could be reimbursed for preventable conditions that patients acquired in the hospital (even if the hospital or provider caused the condition because of an error or an unsanitary practice). No law or regulation existed that prohibited payment for these charges or claims. Therefore, if a hospitalized patient contracted an infection from a dirty urinary catheter, for example, the hospital could receive Medicare payment not only for the care related to the patient's actual condition but also for the services related to the infection.

Evidence-based medicine, however, has advanced our knowledge of quality in medical care. As a result, the Deficit Reduction Act of 2005 (which became effective in 2007) eliminated Medicare payments for preventable hospital-acquired medical conditions. However, a loophole existed: The hospital could still receive Medicaid payments. The Patient Protection and Affordable Care Act of 2010 eliminated this loophole. Effective July 1, 2011, Medicaid no longer reimburses for healthcare-acquired conditions and other provider-preventable conditions (HHS 2011). Simply put, although receiving payment for preventable conditions or medical errors committed by the provider was unethical, such claims were not illegal until 2005 and 2010, respectively.

Another example is government regulation related to "surprise billing"—that is, when patients receive an unexpected bill for services from a hospital, provider, or medical transport service that is outside their insurance plan's provider network (Steinbrook 2019). Often in emergency or other circumstances, the use of out-of-network services is necessary, yet without insurance covering a major portion of the cost, the patient may receive bills that would be considered astronomical—for example, $7,000 for emergency jaw surgery performed by an out-of-network physician or $20,000 for an out-of-network emergency department visit—that they must pay out of pocket. These bills reveal the high medical prices that hospitals and providers list as their charges compared with the discounted charges negotiated by insurance networks. The federal No Surprises Act, passed in 2021, instituted patient protections from liability beyond what they might pay for in-network care, increased transparency in medical billing, and provided for arbitration of billing disputes (Hoadley, Keith, and Lucia 2020). This example illustrates the need for government regulation to prevent what was widely seen as abusive billing practices.

Quadrant III is difficult because the healthcare sector is dynamic, constantly inundated with new laws, advances in technologies, and new interpretations of existing regulations. Technology and biomedical knowledge, in particular, are advancing faster than laws and regulations can be written and passed. Consider a recent publication on the ethical and legal implications of the use of artificial intelligence in breast cancer care (i.e., the development of machine learning to read mammographic images and developing treatment algorithms for care) (Carter et al. 2020). Artificial intelligence offers great potential to improve patients' quality of care and life outcomes, yet this developing technology raises ethical concerns about patient choice, privacy, clinician responsibility, automation bias, and use in nontransferable settings with worse outcomes. Addressing these challenges will require discussion about how to implement such technologies and a proactive role by developers, providers, regulators, and professional groups with public input. Research ethics is discussed more fully in chapter 8.

To be on the safe side and avoid this quadrant, healthcare managers should consider not only what is legal but also the ethical implications of healthcare practices and policies. They should align their actions with those proposed in the Code of Ethics of the American College of Healthcare Executives and consciously check their decision-making for potential ethical conflicts.

Quadrant IV: Unethical and Illegal

Healthcare managers fall into this quadrant when they deliberately commit acts that are criminal, morally corrupt, and socially unacceptable. Examples include preparing inflated **fee schedules**, submitting fraudulent reports, and issuing inflated patient or client bills. For these actions, managers and their organizations could face legal liability under the **False Claims Act**.

Here are some examples of how healthcare managers may act unethically and illegally as they perform the functions of management:

- *Planning.* By law, 51 percent of the governing board of a **Federally Qualified Health Center** must be composed of members who are active consumers of the health center's services. The director of one health center is aware that several members of the board want to expand substance abuse services to homeless women of childbearing age and their children. The director is opposed to this idea. To prevent the discussion of this topic during an upcoming strategic planning session with the board, the director appoints to the board several former citizens of the community, each of whom she knows is vehemently against providing support to homeless people. Thus, her action does not promote beneficence, and it is illegal.

- *Organizing.* Arranging the physical layout of a facility is a component of organizing. The manager of a patient accounts department of a rehabilitation facility reorganized the department's layout so that its main aisles are narrower—only 32 inches rather than the required 36 inches. As a result, clients in wheelchairs cannot access several public areas or offices in the department. This outcome is the manager's intention, because she believes that some of her staff members were spending too much time straightening out the bills for clients in wheelchairs. By limiting access to public areas, the manager is acting unethically and violating the Americans with Disabilities Act of 1990.

- *Leading and directing.* Established acts guarantee civil rights, nondiscrimination, and equal pay for equal work for all employees in all industries in the United States. Noncompliance with these federal equal employment opportunity laws is both unethical and illegal for hiring organizations and their managers or leaders.

- *Controlling.* In 2014, as result of a "takedown" by the Medicare Fraud Strike Force teams in six cities, 90 people—including doctors, nurses, healthcare company owners, healthcare executives, and other personnel—were charged with Medicare fraud. Their alleged crimes included fraudulently billing for medically unneeded, phony, or fake services totaling about $260 million, violating the antikickback statute and money laundering laws (HHS 2014).

---

fee schedule
A list of medical services and procedures and their costs developed by healthcare providers for billing and claims purposes.

False Claims Act
A federal law passed in 1863 that prohibits businesses, groups, and individuals from defrauding the US government; healthcare organizations are subject to this law because Medicare and Medicaid are government programs involving claims and payments.

Federally Qualified Health Center
A clinic that receives government funds for providing affordable, good-quality, comprehensive healthcare services to an underserved community.

> **DID YOU KNOW?**
> False Claims Act
>
> The False Claims Act (FCA) is a federal law (Title 13 of the US Code) that prohibits businesses, groups, and individuals from defrauding the US government. In 1863, Congress passed the FCA in response to contractors who sold the Union Army shoddy provisions during the Civil War. Making or receiving improper payments to or from the government is included in this law (although tax fraud is separate). Healthcare organizations are subject to the FCA because Medicare and Medicaid are government programs involving claims and payments.
>
> Under the FCA, private citizens may sue on behalf of the government. This type of suit, derived from English law, is known as a **qui tam** (short for the Latin phrase *qui tam pro domino rege quam pro se ipso in hac parte sequitur*, meaning "who pursues this action on the king's behalf as well as his own"). Private citizens, known as *relators*, receive 15 percent to 30 percent of the recovered settlement if the defendants are found guilty of fraud. A 1986 amendment (Public Law 99-562) strengthened the FCA. The FCA imposes triple damages and civil fines of $5,000 to $10,000 per false claim. Subsequent amendments in 2009 (under the Fraud Enforcement and Recovery Act) and 2010 (under the Patient Protection and Affordable Care Act) expanded the scope of the FCA.
>
> The FCA's scope is broad. Conspiring to commit a violation is unlawful, even if the conspiracy is unsuccessful. Of particular relevance to healthcare managers is the provision that makes retaining overpayments—even those accidentally received—a violation of the law. Providers who receive Medicare or Medicaid overpayments must return the money to the government within 60 days of discovering the error or when the next government report is due. Moreover, many states have their own FCA.
>
> In 2014, Duke University Health System Inc. agreed to repay $1 million for falsely billing federal and state health insurance programs. This repayment was a settlement of an FCA suit filed by a medical biller in 2012 and joined by the federal and state governments in 2014 (Murawski 2014a, 2014b). In the suit, the plaintiffs (the biller and the governments) alleged that Duke had (1) billed separately (instead of together) for services that were required to be bundled and, in the process, added an unjustifiable code and (2) falsely billed for the presence of physician assistants at coronary artery bypass surgeries when residents were also present, a prohibited practice (DOJ 2014). The biller had raised concerns about the billing practices to her supervisor, who responded, "There's a right way, a wrong way, and the Duke way," rather than take action to correct the erroneous billing practices (Murawski 2014a). However, Duke admitted no wrongdoing in the settlement, instead blaming an undetected software problem.
>
> Duke was ordered to repay an additional $626,000 for overbilling. These bills were inflated by the billing department for inpatient hospital discharges that were transfers, coded for the costliest medical conditions and drugs, and failed to credit rebates from medical device manufacturers. The US Department of Health and Human Services found the overbilling during an audit (Murawski 2014b). Representatives of Duke University Health System stated that the system was improving its compliance with federal billing requirements.

qui tam
A legal action, under the False Claims Act, filed by an individual (e.g., a whistleblower) on behalf of the government.

Overall, healthcare managers act ethically when they are good stewards of their organizations' resources. Stewardship (see chapter 4) enables more people to access and receive quality healthcare services (beneficence and utility) because there is less inefficiency and waste. For example,

- as *human resources stewards*, healthcare managers treat their subordinates, peers, and superiors honestly. They practice open and fair employee recruitment, and they conduct just performance evaluations.
- as *financial stewards*, healthcare managers establish accurate fee schedules, submit truthful government reports, and prepare correct patient or client bills.
- as *community stewards*, healthcare managers promote good health in their community and the responsible use of the country's healthcare dollars.

Unawareness of Ethical Implications

Every day presents opportunities for people to do what is right *or* what is wrong. Unawareness of the ethical implications of actions can lead to **moral blindness** or the **law fallacy**. We discuss both concepts in this section.

Moral Blindness

People with moral blindness do not "see" or realize that an action has underlying ethical implications. This blindness may stem from self-centeredness, disregard for others, or general incomprehension of ethics. Many people might say they understand ethics on a theoretical level, but they may not apply ethics at the practical level.

Two common reactive effects of moral blindness are **defense mechanisms** and **rationalization**. Both minimize the consequences of moral blindness. For healthcare managers, the most important consequence is acting in a manner that is inconsistent with the profession's ethical standards.

Defense Mechanisms

People use defense mechanisms when they have committed an act that they know is wrong on some level, so they let their unconscious mind take over to avoid the anxiety or guilt from the act. These thoughts or feelings may be too difficult to handle, while forgetting or avoiding the ethical implications is easier; this may be why people frequently rely on defense mechanisms. Those who put up a defense mechanism may say, "I didn't know it was wrong" or "I just did what I was told to do."

---

moral blindness
Insensitivity to or ignorance of the ethical implications of one's actions.

law fallacy
Invocation of the law when faced with an ethical conflict.

defense mechanism
A mental and emotional strategy to avoid feelings of anxiety or guilt over a wrongdoing.

rationalization
Justification or plausible excuse for inappropriate actions or decisions.

Healthcare managers can counter the tendency to use defense mechanisms by focusing on the accuracy of the information they obtain, receive, and share and on their responsibility to face the consequences if the information is incorrect. Accuracy and responsibility may have fewer emotionally charged connotations than honesty and justice. In addition, healthcare managers can help their subordinates avoid the use of defense mechanisms by supporting those who admit to errors and take responsibility for them.

Rationalization

Rationalization is justification for unacceptable or undesirable actions or decisions. Such reasoning is often filled with excuses rather than actual explanations of motives or intentions. In healthcare management, rationalization does not advance the goal of the organization to improve health. Candid assessment and factual depiction of motives and intentions can lessen rationalization.

Law Fallacy

The law fallacy is the invocation of the law when faced with an ethical conflict. It can occur in two ways: (1) when taking the easy or undemanding way out of a difficult situation (e.g., "We didn't treat the visitor who collapsed in our parking lot because our rule is . . .") and (2) when there are misconceptions about the relationship between ethics and law (e.g., "Our policy is based on the law, so our policy is ethical").

Healthcare managers are particularly prone to seek the first way when they are stressed or if they are inexperienced in dealing with complicated ethical conflicts. Following a law or rule is much easier than thinking through the context and implications of a situation. On the surface, defaulting to a law or rule may appear to be the simplest response. However, healthcare administration is a complex field, so straightforward or simple solutions may exacerbate the ethical conflict in the long term. For example, not treating the visitor who collapsed in the parking lot because of a rule could ultimately damage the relationship between the administration and stakeholders (such as clinicians and the community). The stakeholders may believe that the healthcare organization's duty is to do good, particularly by caring for the sick and injured. The second way relates to what we discussed earlier in this chapter—that ethics and law are related but are not equivalent. Some ethically unaware healthcare managers may mistakenly believe that ethical principles are articulated in or established by legal standards. Ethics, though, is the moral choice to do the right thing. It represents the ideal of how people ought to behave. Laws, on the other hand, are *minimum* standards. They define the misbehavior that deserves punishment. Healthcare management must be aware of this fundamental difference.

The legalistic approach to ethics assumes that anything not prohibited by law is then, by definition, ethical. This approach is embodied in the misleading and incomplete statement, "If it's legal, it's ethical." Nothing could be further from the truth.

Mini-Case Study: Vaping Becomes a Health Epidemic Among Youth

Luca, a 14-year old student, was attending a Friday night football game when several friends introduced him to vaping. E-cigarette devices first appeared around 2007, originally proposed as a method of delivering nicotine without smoking cigarettes, ostensibly as an aid to quitting. Within ten years, "Juuling" had become a craze among youth. The company Juul successfully marketed its innovative e-cigarette product, including flavors such as mint and bubblegum through aggressive advertising targeting young people.

E-cigarettes are often styled after pens. The battery-powered devices ignite and burn a flavored liquid contained in a cartridge; vaping is the act of inhaling the vaporized liquid aerosol. While the dangers of smoking were well known at the time, we knew little about this product and its safety. What could go wrong? You might ask Luca—he had a seizure as a teenager, attributed to the high quantity of nicotine he was consuming. Vaping nicotine equates to smoking about 20 conventional cigarettes (Newman 2019; Williams 2019).

As the popularity of e-cigarettes grew, "mysterious" medical issues, and particularly respiratory illnesses associated with vaping (e.g., "popcorn lung"), began appearing across the United States. Physicians and the Centers for Disease Control and Prevention (CDC) increasingly raised alarms. By November 2018, more than 2,000 known cases of lung disease and 39 deaths had been linked to vaping.

Initially, e-cigarette advertising to youth was permitted, even though advertising of conventional tobacco products was prohibited, and the products were unregulated. In 2010, the US Food and Drug Administration (FDA) attempted to reclassify e-cigarettes as pharmaceuticals, as their stated purpose was smoking cessation, but the industry balked and filed suit in federal court to block the agency from doing so. Instead, companies such as Juul sought to have e-cigarettes regulated as a tobacco product (Newman 2019; Williams 2019). In 2016, the FDA announced its intention to do just that.

Meanwhile, an epidemic was already underway. According to the Monitoring the Future Survey, which tracks changes in attitudes and use of drugs among youth, by 2019, more than one-quarter of high school seniors had tried vaping, and 12 percent were vaping almost daily, compared with less than 5 percent of adults (McPhillips 2019). In 2020, the CDC reported that 3.6 million middle and high school students had used vaping products in the previous 30 days.

It is not clear why e-cigarettes were considered safer than cigarettes. The aerosol contains numerous organic compounds, heavy metals, and flavoring chemicals such as diacetyl (known to cause serous lung disease). Moreover, e-cigarettes can give off formaldehyde (Jensen et al. 2015). We now can quantify the diacetyl risk by measuring diacetyl exposure (Stephens 2021). Most teenagers who began vaping had never smoked cigarettes, but now many are addicted to nicotine. The tobacco industry maintains that was never its purpose, but others studying the companies' marketing strategies are skeptical why they might market bubble gum flavors to adults. Moreover, the FDA granted an application period for manufacturers to apply for clearance to market e-cigarettes as having a therapeutic cessation purpose; none has ever been approved.

As the crisis continued, communities and several states (e.g., New York, Michigan, Washington) began to restrict sales, and eventually the FDA made selling e-cigarettes to youth under 18 years of age illegal under its authority granted under the federal Family Smoking Prevention and Tobacco Control Act. In June 2021, Juul agreed to pay the state of North Carolina $40 million to settle a lawsuit over the marketing of e-cigarettes to teenagers; several other suits were pending. The FDA must now rule whether and how any e-cigarettes will be allowed to be marketed to adults (Lindblom 2021).

The vaping epidemic story involves an emerging health crisis, the need for government regulation of an industry that sprung up quickly, and a continuing need for public health education. Some public education efforts have been initiated (CDC 2020), such as the "Real Cost" campaign for tobacco prevention, which disseminates materials about e-cigarettes in schools. In addition, the website Safer ≠ Safe offers resources for quitting e-cigarettes (www.thetruth.com/article/safer-safe). There is also guidance for communities to create protective prevention policies (see Public Health Law Center 2020).

Mini-Case Study Questions

1. What ethical principles are illustrated in this Mini-Case Study? In what quadrant (see exhibit 6.1) would you put Juul's actions? Were its actions legal? Ethical? Do you think this has changed over time?
2. Do you think teenagers like Luca have an expectation that advertised products are safe? Do the tobacco companies marketing e-cigarettes have an ethical duty to protect the public? Do they have a duty to comply with applicable laws?
3. Is targeting a consumer segment though marketing strategies ethical? Legal? Does the age or other demographics of the consumer segment affect your opinion?
4. What are the ethical obligations of federal agencies such as the FDA? What are their legal duties?
5. What roles might a healthcare organization and manager play in addressing a health crisis like the one involved in vaping?

Points to Remember

- Ethics is the differentiation between right and wrong, irrespective of law.
- Laws define misconduct warranting punishment.
- Ethics and law are related but are not identical.
- The relationship between ethics and law can be categorized into four quadrants: ethical and legal, ethical and illegal, unethical and legal, and unethical and illegal.
- Healthcare managers face ethical and legal conflicts while performing their daily managerial and supervisory duties.

➤ Unawareness of the ethical implications of actions can lead to moral blindness or the law fallacy.

➤ Defaulting to legality represents a misunderstanding of ethics and law.

Challenge Yourself

1. Find and categorize examples of behaviors or actions, excluding examples from this textbook, for each of the four quadrants (see exhibit 6.1).
   a. The behaviors and actions may come from the following:
      - Personal experiences
      - Work experiences
      - Recent events
      - Historical events
   b. For each behavior or action, identify the ethical principle(s) and the relevant law or laws.
   c. Based on what you learned in this chapter, do you see the examples that you found and categorized in question 1 differently than you did before?
   d. As a healthcare manager, how could you use what you learned about the quadrants?
   e. For which quadrant(s) did you have the most trouble finding examples?

2. Although most people would agree that fraud is a problem that should be addressed under the False Claims Act, David Hyman (2001) proposes that attempts at legislative and enforcement using this framework are poorly designed for our current healthcare system, which involves managed care agreements and service delivery arrangements to serve program ends. Yet providers are liable for actions that are not abusive or intentionally fraudulent. Moreover, Hyman suggests that our understanding of fraud does not take into account the attitudes and social norms of stakeholders such as providers, insurers, program administrators, and public consumers.

   Hyman argues that there are, in fact, a number of rationales for committing fraud, such as the following: (1) insurance companies have deep pockets, and thus they can pay for care that providers deem necessary; (2) providing the right care is more important than cost considerations; and (3) corrective action, not criminal action, is the right moral choice to respond, since the action was made on behalf of providing care, or it was unintentional. In other words, doing the right thing overrides fraud, ethically speaking.

   Examine the perspectives of these stakeholder groups (providers, insurers, program administrators, and public consumers) on what constitutes unethical referral and billing practices and assess the following cases of Medicaid fraud:
   - A personal care worker charged Medicaid for services provided in a particular state when the patient was not present in that state when the services were said to have been provided.

- A personal care worker unintentionally submitted false timesheets when she made an error in data entry times and dates that resulted in false billings to Medicaid.
- An administrative assistant billed Medicaid under her boss's (a physician) billing identification number, even though she is responsible for all charges billed under that number.
- Physicians received payments from a dialysis clinic in exchange for patient referrals; the physicians received shares in the dialysis center for less than fair-market value.

FOR YOUR CONSIDERATION

6.1 For each of the following scenarios, determine which quadrant the action belongs in, and why:

   a. You are late to an important meeting at the community health center's corporate office. The route from your facility to the corporate office is congested and busy and has a speed limit of 45 miles per hour. Today, unfortunately, traffic is heavier than usual on this route because of road construction. To avoid the delay, you cut through a residential neighborhood on a side street. Although the posted speed limit there is 25 miles per hour, you drive through at 45 miles per hour because you are late.

   b. Nine months ago, after a computer system upgrade, you noticed that the new software had been miscalculating and underreporting the amount of money collected under drug rebates. While the discrepancy is extremely small, it affects the report that you submit to the state for your organization's uncompensated care (services for which no payment was received). You are concerned about the accuracy of the report. As soon as you noticed the discrepancy, you reported it, along with its origin and potential consequences, to your superior. Your superior said that she would check with the "IT people." She did not say that she would get back to you with an update, but you assumed she would tell you when the problem was fixed. A week ago, you found out that the miscalculation is still occurring. When you completed your report, you added an asterisk next to the uncompensated care amount to indicate that it is incorrect.

   c. You are the administrator of a free clinic, and many of its patients are poor. A disposable diaper vendor approaches you about its community outreach program, which provides newborns with free diapers for two months. To participate, your clinic has to give the vendor two patient lists on an ongoing basis—(1) mothers who have had their first postnatal visit and (2) babies who have had their first newborn visit. The vendor will cross-reference the lists so that families are not contacted twice. To help your clinic's poorest patients, you authorize the clinic staff to list only patients with Medicaid coverage.

   d. You are purchasing a laptop for your administrative associate. Two laptops—TopProcess and BestElectronic—meet your administrative associate's processing needs, and their costs and features are equal. However, TopProcess comes with a free cell phone, and you need a new cell phone. You decide to buy the TopProcess laptop and keep the cell phone for yourself.

6.2 Quadrant II involves civil disobedience under the law and might seem warranted only retrospectively, as in the historical examples of the civil rights movement and the North Carolina protest. In your view, under what conditions should we take seriously the argument that disobeying a law is the higher moral choice?

REFERENCES

Buffington, M. A., and K. Abreo. 2016. "Hyponatremia: A Review." *Journal of Intensive Care Medicine* 31 (4): 223–36.

Carter, S. M., W. Rogers, K. T. Win, H. Frazer, B. Richards, and N. Houssami. 2020. "The Ethical, Legal and Social Implications of Using Artificial Intelligence Systems in Breast Cancer Care." *Breast* 49: 25–32.

Centers for Disease Control and Prevention (CDC). 2020. "Quick Facts on the Risks of E-cigarettes for Kids, Teens, and Young Adults: What Is in E-cigarette Aerosol?" Reviewed December 16. www.cdc.gov/tobacco/basic_information/e-cigarettes/Quick-Facts-on-the-Risks-of-E-cigarettes-for-Kids-Teens-and-Young-Adults.html#e-cigarette-aerosol.

Dean, K. L., J. M. Beggs, and T. P. Keane. 2010. "Mid-Level Managers, Organizational Context, and (Un)ethical Encounters." *Journal of Business Ethics* 97 (1): 51–69.

Habib, I. 1997. "Civil Disobedience 1930–31." *Social Scientist* 25 (9): 43–66.

Hay, S. 1989. "The Making of a Late-Victorian Hindu: M. K. Gandhi in London, 1888–1981." *Victorian Studies* 33 (1): 74–98.

Henderson, V. E. 1982. "The Ethical Side of Enterprise." *Sloan Management Review* 23 (3): 37–47.

Hendrick, G. 1956. "The Influence of Thoreau's 'Civil Disobedience' on Gandhi's Satyagraha." *New England Quarterly* 29 (4): 467–71.

Hettne, B. 1976. "The Utility of Gandhian Tradition." *Journal of Peace Research* 13 (3): 227–45.

Hoadley, J., K. Keith, and K. Lucia. 2020. "Unpacking the No Surprises Act: An Opportunity to Protect Millions." *Health Affairs Blog*. Published December 18. www.healthaffairs.org/do/10.1377/hblog20201217.247010/full/.

Hyman, D. A. 2001. "Health Care Fraud and Abuse: Market Change, Social Norms, and the Trust 'Reposed in the Workmen.'" *Journal of Legal Studies* 30 (Suppl. 2): 531–67.

Jensen, R. P., W. Luo, J. F. Pankow, R. M. Strongin, and D. H. Peyton. 2015. "Hidden Formaldehyde in E-Cigarette Aerosols." *New England Journal of Medicine* 372 (4): 392–93.

Lindblom, E. N. 2021. "All Eyes on the FDA: The Upcoming Regulation of Juul E-Cigarettes." *Medpage Today*. Published August 6. www.medpagetoday.com/opinion/second-opinions/93938.

Ling, P. J. 2007. "Tracing the Movement's Path." *Reviews in American History* 35 (2): 289–96.

McPhillips, D. 2019. "Vaping in America, by the Numbers." *US News & World Report*. Published September 30. www.usnews.com/news/healthiest-communities/articles/2019-09-30/vaping-in-america-by-the-numbers.

Morgan, P. 2015. "Handcuffs." *Journal of the American Academy of Physician Assistants* 28 (5): 12–13.

Murawski, J. 2014a. "Duke to Pay $1M for False Billing." *News & Observer* (Raleigh, NC), March 22.

———. 2014b. "Duke to Repay Medicare $626K." *News & Observer* (Raleigh, NC), May 3.

Newman, K. 2019. "Vaping and E-Cigarettes: The New Public Health Problem." *US News & World Report*. Published Sept 30. www.usnews.com/news/healthiest-communities/articles/2019-09-30/vaping-and-e-cigarettes-a-new-public-health-problem.

Public Health Law Center. 2020. "States and Tribes Stepping In to Protect Communities from the Dangers of E-Cigarettes: Actions and Options." Published February 25 www.publichealthlawcenter.org/resources/states-and-tribes-stepping-protect-communities-dangers-e-cigarettes-actions-and-options.

Severance, J. B. 1997. *Gandhi: Great Soul*. New York: Clarion.

Steinbrook, R. 2019. "Ending Surprise Medical Bills." *JAMA Internal Medicine* 179 (11): 1465–66.

Stephens, S. 2021. "E-cigarette Flavoring Risks: ECU Researcher Studies Risks of Lung Injury from E-cigarette Flavoring Compound." East Carolina University. Published February 17. https://news.ecu.edu/2021/02/17/e-cigarette-flavoring-risks/.

Suchitra. 1995. "What Moves Masses: Dandi March as Communication Strategy." *Economic and Political Weekly* 30 (14): 743–46.

Thoreau, H. D. 1849. "Resistance to Civil Government: A Lecture Delivered in 1847." In *Aesthetic Papers*, edited by E. P. Peabody, 189–211. New York: G. P. Putman. www.archive.org/details/aestheticpapers00peabrich.

Time. 1931. "'Saint Gandhi': Man of the Year 1930." Published January 5. http://content.time.com/time/magazine/article/0,9171,930215,00.html.

US Department of Health and Human Services (HHS). 2014. "Medicare Strike Force Charges 90 Individuals for Approximately $260 Million in False Billing." Published May 13. www.hhs.gov/about/news/2014/05/13/medicare-fraud-strike-force-charges-90-individuals-for-approximately-260-million-in-false-billing.html.

———. 2011. "Medicaid Program; Payment Adjustment for Provider-Preventable Conditions Including Health Care-Acquired Conditions; Final Rule." *Federal Register* 76 (108): 32816–38.

US Department of Justice (DOJ). 2014. "Duke University Health System, Inc. Agrees to Pay $1 Million for Alleged False Claims Submitted to Federal Health Care Programs." Published March 21. www.justice.gov/usao/nce/press/2014/2014-mar-21.html.

US Food and Drug Administration (FDA). 2020. "FDA Finalizes Enforcement Policy on Unauthorized Flavored Cartridge-Based E-cigarettes That Appeal to Children, Including Fruit and Mint." Published January 2. www.fda.gov/news-events/press-announcements/fda-finalizes-enforcement-policy-unauthorized-flavored-cartridge-based-e-cigarettes-appeal-children.

van der Horst, C. 2014. "Civil Disobedience and Physicians—Protesting the Blockade of Medicaid." *New England Journal of Medicine* 371 (21): 1958–60.

Varshney, A. 2003. "Nationalism, Ethnic Conflict, and Rationality." *Perspectives on Politics* 1 (1): 85–99.

Weber, T. 2002. "Gandhian Nonviolence and the Salt March." *Social Alternatives* 21 (2): 46–51.

Williams, J. P. 2019. "Vaping: From 'Safer Than Cigarettes' to Public Health Crisis." *US News & World Report*. Published September 30. www.usnews.com/news/healthiest-communities/articles/2019-09-30/vaping-from-safer-than-cigarettes-to-public-health-crisis.

CHAPTER 7
ETHICAL DECISION-MAKING PROCESS

Ethical ambiguities are an inevitable part of healthcare, but the ability to have a systematic approach to review and address them is key.
—Deborah J. Bowen, FACHE, CAE, president and CEO, American College of Healthcare Executives

Important Terms

- Advance healthcare directive
- Direct report
- Ethical decision-making process
- Medical futility
- Moral distress
- Moral injury
- Precautionary principle
- Situational context
- Surrogate

Learning Objectives

Studying this chapter will help you to

➤ recognize ethical conflicts in the problems that healthcare managers face,

➤ analyze and resolve problems using an ethical decision-making process,

➤ recognize the role of ethical principles and philosophies in decision-making,

➤ become proficient in ethical decision-making and implementing decisions, and

➤ respond to situations involving moral distress in healthcare settings.

ethical decision-making process
The rational, step-by-step process of weighing facts, emotional and situational concerns, and ethical principles.

Understanding and using an **ethical decision-making process** promotes better decisions. Following a rational, step-by-step process, ethical decision makers explicitly and consciously weigh facts, recognize their emotions and situational concerns, and consider ethical principles. This chapter draws from the ethical decision-making process of healthcare ethicist William A. Nelson (2005, 2015). Nelson's process—part of the Ethics Toolkit of the American College of Healthcare Executives (ACHE)—was originally developed from an organizational point of view. In his 2015 revision, however, Nelson stresses the importance of a uniform process that can address both clinical and administrative issues. Decision-making models invoke intentional systematic reflection that enhances rational analysis of the issues involved and result in an ethically justifiable decision. Critiques of such models (e.g., Rogerson et al. 2011) highlight the role of nonrational and intuitive factors in ethical judgments. After reviewing the ACHE model, we will discuss such factors and additional considerations in ethical decision-making, concluding this chapter with a discussion of moral distress.

medical futility
The professional opinion that continuing medical treatment is no longer a viable option for a patient.

When Medical Futility and Ethical Principles Collide

As a result of advances in technology and medical care, members of the healthcare community and society sometimes face the issue of **medical futility**. Medical futility refers to situations in which treatment is no longer considered to have value. More specifically, Lawrence Schneiderman (2011, 125) defines medical futility as "the unacceptable likelihood of achieving an effect that the *patient* has the capacity to appreciate as a *benefit*." According to Schneiderman, both the patient and the benefit are central to the healing process and the goals of medicine, including the alleviation of suffering. Moreover, medical futility has both quantitative (i.e., the likelihood that further treatment will be of value) and qualitative (i.e., the painfulness of procedures and quality of life) elements.

surrogate
An individual appointed to make healthcare decisions for a person if that person becomes incapacitated or can no longer make decisions; also known as an *agent*, *proxy*, or *representative*.

Ethical principles collide, though, when healthcare professionals believe that treatment is futile and should be discontinued, while patients (clients or residents) and their **surrogates** (parents, agents, or proxies) believe that treatment that maintains life should be continued. The use of an **advance healthcare directive**—a document that outlines a patient's preferences for treatments, life-sustaining technology, and other medical care—generally reduces the likelihood of an ethical conflict arising when patients are facing the end of life.

advance healthcare directive
A legal document that specifies a person's preferences for treatments, life-sustaining technology, and other medical care; written before and used after the person becomes incapacitated or can no longer make decisions.

Ethical conflicts involving clinical care, such as medical futility, require practical management and leadership engagement as well as the medical knowledge of clinicians. In situations of medical futility, the ethical principles of autonomy (or self-determination), beneficence, and fidelity (or loyalty) collide. This situation can be especially difficult with seriously ill children. Healthcare managers and clinicians may use the ethical decision-making

> **? DID YOU KNOW?**
>
> In cases involving disputes over the medical treatment of seriously ill children, the courts sometimes have even been called upon to resolve ongoing conflicts between hospitals and parents (Glover-Thomas 2020). Consider the case of Alfie Evans, who was born in May 2016 in Great Britain and entered the hospital that December when he started experiencing seizures. Alfie was diagnosed with a rare degenerative neurological condition that left him in a semivegetative state, dependent on artificial ventilation. His medical providers believed that catastrophic degradation of brain tissue had occurred and that he had no hope of improvement. They felt that further treatment, including prolonging the child's breathing on a ventilator, was not only futile but inhumane.
>
> However, Alfie's parents were not convinced that their son was unresponsive to them and wanted to transfer him to a hospital in another country that might keep him alive for longer. The hospital sought a declaration from a British court, which ruled that continued ventilator support was not in Alfie's best interest. The parents' appeal drew considerable media attention to the conflict between their desire to keep Alfie alive artificially and the hospital's view that prolonging his life would cause more distress.
>
> Nicola Glover-Thomas (2020) reviews several such cases from the perspective of the legal standard of "best interests" and the factors that affect judicial interpretation. In a Texas case involving an infant named Tinslee Lewis, who had a rare heart defect and lung disease, parental wishes to sustain life support were upheld despite a medical consensus regarding her care (Flanders 2021). Clearly, such cases involve heartbreaking and difficult situations for all involved, bringing the concept of medical futility into focus.
>
> A healthcare manager faced with this type of situation would consider broadening the decision-making process to include a hospital ethics committee and avenues of dispute resolution. Sergeant (2021) suggests such a process approach and the use of the **precautionary principle** to privilege patient decision-making in medical futility cases, thus shifting the burden of proof as a safeguard against actions causing premature death.

precautionary principle
A decision-making rule developed in environmental law stating that in cases of serious or irreversible threats to the health of humans or ecosystems, acknowledged scientific uncertainty should not be used as a reason to postpone preventive measures (i.e., err on the side of prevention).

process to sort through and weigh the ethical principles and options to resolve this conflict. They also try to avoid ethical conflicts, as evidenced in the following cases.

- *Autonomy.* Members of the healthcare community respect the right of patients and their surrogates to make informed decisions—either consenting to or refusing treatment. In the United States, this right is protected under the Patient Self-Determination Act of 1990.

♦ *Beneficence.* Healthcare providers are morally bound to provide healthcare services that benefit (or are good for) patients and, at the same time, to do no harm. Medical futility cases are not focused solely on *not* providing an intervention; they also should consider the standard for palliative care as well as the patient's comfort and quality of life.

♦ *Fidelity.* Healthcare providers have a duty to follow their codes of ethics and to deliver appropriate healthcare services as defined by their professional practice guidelines. In this way, they can keep their promises and be faithful to their duties.

In the cases described here, the patients' right to self-determination for their children collided with the healthcare providers' right to practice within their professions' standards of care. Decisions involving medical futility require careful thought on a case-by-case basis.

In both life-or-death decisions and routine business decisions, the ethical decision-making process is a resource. This process is illustrated in exhibit 7.1 and elaborated in the next section. This process provides a way for decision makers to obtain stakeholders' opinions and gather all the facts and perspectives; to identify, consider, and weigh the ethical principles involved in the decision; to thoroughly develop and analyze multiple options; to assess each option's moral consequences and implications; and to arrive at a decision and course of action. This process requires knowledge, skill, and practice. It is not a spreadsheet that computes and spits out an answer for you. After all, quick fixes cannot resolve complex human ethical conflicts.

A prerequisite to engaging in the process of ethical decision-making is having moral awareness and a commitment to adopting a moral stance. The failure to recognize when a situation involves an ethical conflict is a critical leadership oversight. An ethical conflict is likely present when any of the following are present: (1) employees use terms such as *right, wrong, ought,* or *should*; (2) the rights of individuals are involved, such as the right to

> **DID YOU KNOW?**
> What Is an Ethical Conflict?
>
> "An ethical conflict occurs when an uncertainty, a question or a controversy arises regarding competing ethical principles, personal values, or organizational and professional ethical standards of practice" (Nelson 2015, 46). It is a dilemma because competing principles are at play, and often it involves a choice between two undesirable alternatives.

> **EXHIBIT 7.1**
> Ethical Decision-Making Process Framework
>
> 1. Understand the background and circumstance leading to an ethical conflict
>   Gather all the facts
>   Understand the context and social meaning of the problem
>   Identify all the affected stakeholders and their perspectives and values
>   Revise initial appraisal
>
> 2. Identify the specific ethical question needing clarification
>   Articulate the ethical conflict in terms of competing values or principles
>
> 3. Consider the related ethical principles and organizational values
>   Acknowledge relevant principles and organizational values
>   Identify the ethical drivers—the principles at the core of the problem
>
> 4. Determine the options for action
>   Consider all potential options
>   Review their justification in terms or ethical principles and theories
>   Identify probable consequences for stakeholders
>
> 5. Choose or recommend from among the response options
>   Prioritize options based on the identified core principles and values
>   Consider the selected action in terms of organization's mission and values
>   Share decision and justification with involved parties
>   Review action plan and implement intentionally
>
> 6. Review the outcome and anticipate reoccurrence of the conflict
>   Define evaluation criteria and obtain feedback adjusting as needed
>   Consider what might be learned going forward
>
> *Source:* Information from ACHE (2018); Nelson (2005, 2015).

privacy; (3) duties are involved, such as the duty to avoid conflicts of interest; and (4) the decision's outcome may harm an individual or a group.

Even seemingly routine managerial decisions commonly involve ethical principles such as fairness, honesty, and loyalty. For example, keeping the contents of an employee's performance evaluation private (inaccessible even to other managers) is a routine ethical decision. Contrast that behavior with the decision of a healthcare manager who gossips and thus reveals the confidential contents of an employee's performance review. Revealing confidential contents is a violation of trust and a breach of the ethical principle of fidelity. The employee would no longer trust the manager, nor would the manager's other direct reports who learned of this violation of trust. However, not all leadership actions or decisions involving ethical principles are ethical conflicts—the latter involves conflict between such principles.

Adopting a moral stance involves taking responsibility for building and fostering an environment that supports ethical decision-making. As president and CEO of ACHE, Deborah J. Bowen, FACHE, CAE (2019) proposed that as the healthcare industry faces change, executives are steadied by having a code of ethics as a moral compass. Moreover, they are responsible for creating an ethics-focused culture in their organization. Talking about ethics helps build and foster that supportive environment. Therefore, while the emphasis is on acting ethically, healthcare managers also talk ethics by explaining the ethical principles involved in their decisions. For example, healthcare managers communicate a moral point of view when they explain to their staff and others how to uphold the spirit of a policy rather than just meeting the letter of a procedure.

Before considering a problem or situation, ascertain boundaries and ownership of the situation, problem, or question. Given that healthcare organizations are systems, will you as the healthcare manager be able to make the decision alone? The decision maker should have the authority and responsibility to implement the decision. (For our purposes in this chapter, we appoint you—as a future healthcare manager—as the decision maker. It is important that you are aware, though, that you will not always be the decision maker.)

STEPS IN THE ETHICAL DECISION-MAKING PROCESS

Following explicit steps in the decision-making process will ensure that sufficient attention is brought to situations involving possible ethical conflict and that the decision made is ethically justifiable.

STEP 1: UNDERSTAND THE BACKGROUND AND CIRCUMSTANCE LEADING TO THE ETHICAL CONFLICT

Gather the facts by interviewing the people involved; consulting with experts and superiors; observing the situation; obtaining and inspecting relevant policies, procedures, laws, and regulations; and conducting pertinent investigations. For a clinical case, it is important to know the medical issues involved, including the diagnosis, prognosis, treatment options, and goals of care, in addition to the patient's values and preferences. If the patient lacks capacity, determine the appropriate decision maker. Is there disagreement as to the facts or their interpretation? Achieving consensus on the facts helps reduce conflict. What is the context (timing, setting, culture, and social meaning) of the problem?

Identify all affected stakeholders and their perspectives and values. All the stakeholders may not be obvious. Consider who will be directly affected by the decision, who might be indirectly affected, and who might suffer collateral damage. Obvious internal stakeholders are patients, their families, and the professionals involved in delivering care. Less obvious internal stakeholders are board members, administrators, staff members in related departments, and technical personnel. External stakeholders may include former patients and employees; populations similar to the patient, such as other patients with the same religious beliefs or disease; oversight, regulatory, and accrediting agencies; politicians, advocacy groups, and the general public; vendors, business associates, and professional associations; and friends of the organization. All the stakeholders' perspectives and values should be defined (if possible) and the primary stakeholder identified.

As a decision maker, you begin with an initial appraisal of the situation. However, as you gather and synthesize facts into information, you may revise this initial appraisal. Take your time and be thorough; your search should be vigilant.

STEP 2: IDENTIFY THE SPECIFIC ETHICAL QUESTION NEEDING CLARIFICATION

Articulate the ethical conflict in terms of competing values or principles. For example, the decision to close a medical facility in a rural community that is losing money might involve a conflict between addressing community healthcare needs and the organization's obligation to function as a fiscally responsible medical center. Stakeholders should reach a consensus about the underlying issues that are at stake. (For examples of this scenario, see the closure of Pungo Hospital in chapter 11 and the discussion of emergency department closures in chapter 14.)

STEP 3: CONSIDER THE RELATED ETHICAL PRINCIPLES AND ORGANIZATIONAL VALUES

The next step is closely related and involves acknowledging the ethical principles and organizational values related to the specific ethical conflict. As described in earlier chapters, central ethical principles are honesty, integrity, respect for self and others, justice (fairness), loyalty (fidelity or good faith), beneficence, autonomy, honor, nonmaleficence (not doing bad), and utility. Are there particular organizational values, policies, or, in some cases, legal perspectives that are relevant? Identify the ethical drivers—the principles at the core of the problem. Note that drivers are different from principles, which may be tangential to the problem or situation.

STEP 4: DETERMINE THE OPTIONS FOR ACTION

The decision makers should recognize and list all options for responding to the ethical question presented by the situation, including their ethical justifications. Ethical theories and perspectives (see chapter 5 for a discussion of the ethical principles of the

American College of Health Care Administrators and ACHE) may be useful in formulating options and the rationale for each option. When identifying options, healthcare managers should identify the probable consequences of each option for each stakeholder. Long-term and short-term consequences should be considered. What are the arguments for and against each alternative? Perhaps several options can be combined. This type of ethical analysis prevents decision makers from choosing the first action that is suggested. Novice healthcare managers should be aware that doing nothing is always an option in the decision-making process.

STEP 5: CHOOSE OR RECOMMEND FROM AMONG THE RESPONSE OPTIONS

Following the ethical analysis, choose a recommended response. This involves prioritizing the principles and values identified earlier for this situation. Assessing the likely consequences of each option (i.e., benefits and costs) is another aspect of this choice. The selected option should be not only practical but also based on clinical and organizational ethical principles and in keeping with the organization's mission and values. The goal is to arrive at an ethical outcome that minimizes harm—although at times, this may limit other values. Once selected for implementation, the recommended option and the ethical justification for this course of action are shared with all involved parties. Discussion might also focus on how best to implement the decision. Finally, the decision is implemented. Gathering facts, analyzing, and reflecting are much easier than acting. It takes energy and motivation to act. More important, it often takes moral character—courage, integrity, and self-sacrifice—to act (Kidder 2006).

STEP 6: REVIEW THE OUTCOME AND ANTICIPATE REOCCURRENCE OF THE CONFLICT

The process of ethical decision-making should always include feedback. Define the criteria for evaluating both the consistency of the implementation of the action plan and the outcome of the decision. The outcome of the selected decision can be assessed formally or informally, although this is an important step. Ethical decision makers are willing to adjust to new data and feedback. If the problem remains unsolved, they repeat the ethical decision-making process, modify their course of action, and implement the modification.

Moreover, ethical healthcare managers learn from this decision-making process. Nelson (2015) posits that the process should not end with the resolution of the specific conflict but anticipation of what can be learned from the experience of the conflict. Healthcare managers may explore how the conflict arose and how future reoccurrences of such conflicts might be prevented. Perhaps the chosen decision will shape responses to other dilemmas, and documenting the process of resolution will build an organizational resource.

RELATED RESOURCES AND USE OF ETHICS CONSULTATION

In addition to the ACHE Code of Ethics, Bowen (2019) highlights additional resources in the ACHE toolkit for healthcare managers, including guidance on establishing an executive-driven ethical culture, an ethics self-assessment, and ethical policy statements. Ethical policy statements apply the ethical code to address specific ethical issues facing healthcare organizations, such as patient confidentiality, end-of-life concerns, and workplace violence. Being familiar with current best practice guidelines is part of professionalism and lifelong learning (see chapter 3).

Another aspect of ethical decision-making is the use of ethics consultation. This may be a beneficial step at each stage of the ethical decision-making process. Ethics consultation might involve the formal use of an organization's ethics committee or individual consultation with a valued colleague or mentor. Consultation may be considered a final check of our decision-making process and recognition of our limitations and potential for bias. Documenting such consultation in difficult situations is evidence of professional deliberation and ethical conduct. The National Center for Ethics in Health Care (2015) provides an overview of formal ethics consultation.

RECOGNIZING NONRATIONAL ELEMENTS IN ETHICAL DELIBERATIONS

Although ethical decision-making models are useful in that they allow us to pause and reflect on ethical principles in difficult situations, they are necessarily limited in that they rest on the assumption that such decisions are based only on rational conscious thought.

A large body of literature indicates that actual decision-making is more complex. We are all affected by personal and interpersonal influences, and automatic nonrational processes are at play in our intuitive response to such situations (Cristofaro et al. 2021; Rogerson et al. 2011). It can be said that the way people grasp moral truth is akin to intuitive perception, which is followed by reasoning to justify decisions.

Two types of information processing may interact when people make ethical decisions. Either type can be prominent in determining behavior, as shown by psychologists Daniel Kahneman and Amos Tversky in their classic work (Kahneman 2003; Tversky and Kahneman 1981). Our emotions or affective responses particularly influence our judgments, and thus they can influence our response to a patient or employee more than objective considerations. Loyalty to a friend may be more salient than justice in a situation, or it may cause us to be complacent or fail to act when confronted with an ethical dilemma. Because our affective responses are powerful, the framing of choices can lead to different decisions. For example, physicians respond differently to a 10 percent mortality rate compared with a 90 percent survival rate.

Kahneman and Tversky describe the heuristics, or mental shortcuts, that people use in decision-making; these heuristics are generally helpful in understanding the world, but they can also lead to bias or error in decision-making. An example is the representativeness heuristic, in which people use a prototypical example to estimate the likelihood of an event, while ignoring important statistical information such as the base rate or overall probability. We might also seek out information selectively to confirm our existing beliefs. Moreover, people exhibit a blind spot in that they are better able to recognize such biases in others than themselves. These nonrational and automatic processes have implications for understanding and improving ethical decision-making.

In reviewing descriptive models of ethical decision-making, Mark Schwartz (2016) described both rationally based and more affective-intuitive perspectives. He proposed an integrated ethical decision-making model for understanding all the factors that influence such decisions in organizational settings. Both individual and situational factors contribute to decisions and behavior. Individual factors are assumed under the general construct of the individual's moral capacity, which includes character disposition, stage of moral development, moral identity, and integrity. Demographics, personality facets, religious background, and ethical experience and training all influence a person's moral capacity. Situational factors also influence our decisions and actions. Here, aspects of the issue, its complexity, and its importance are relevant, as is the organizational environment infrastructure. Organizations with a strong ethical culture and climate are assumed to promote ethical sensitivity and the importance of behaving in a way that is considered ethical within the organization. A more personal aspect of the situation is the person's ethical vulnerability because of their own life circumstances. In this way, ethical behavior is the result of an interaction between the person and the situational context in which an ethical issue arises. Both individual factors and the **situational context** moderate the ethical decision-making-process, which includes recognizing emotions, intuition, ethical reasoning, and rationalization—all leading to an evaluative judgment and an intention to act.

Students come to the healthcare field with their own personal backgrounds and moral perspectives. Ethics education should address the influence of emotion and nonrational elements affecting our judgments, as well as reflective analysis. Developing as a healthcare administrator requires integrating our personal history and moral identity with the profession's ethics code and decision-making process to develop an integrated professional identity (Rogerson et al. 2011).

Even for those with strong moral character, decisions can remain ideas because they first have to overcome opposition, resist distractions, and develop tactics and strategies for implementation (Johnson 2021). Moreover, we all can find plausible reasons for *not* acting. For that reason, recognizing the human tendency to rationalize or harmonize beliefs is an important consideration. Unfortunately, humans use defense mechanisms and rationalization very adeptly (see chapter 6). Being aware of errors in decision-making is one aspect of decision-making competence. Developing decision-making competence and skills provides healthcare managers the confidence that they need to carry through their decisions.

---

situational context

The circumstances of a decision, such as aspects of the issue, organizational structure, ethical climate, leadership's expectations, and peers' influence, as well as the person's personal situation.

COMMON ERRORS IN DECISION-MAKING AND STRATEGIES TO AVOID THEM

Common errors can occur during decision-making. Even when they follow the steps of the ethical decision-making process presented in this chapter, healthcare managers can still get caught in *decision traps* (another name for these common errors). Strategies to avoid these traps are discussed in this section.

Two common decision traps are moral blindness and the law fallacy (discussed in chapter 6). Morally blind healthcare managers are insensitive to or ignorant of the ethical implications of actions—their own, other people's, and their healthcare organization's. Healthcare managers may also operate using a law fallacy mindset, in which they erroneously assume that anything not prohibited by law is ethical. These two traps often come into play when healthcare managers must adopt a moral stance and decrease their moral awareness.

Other traps relate to cognitive heuristics, such as anchoring, confirming evidence, estimating and forecasting, framing, status quo, and sunk cost (Hammond, Keeney, and Raiffa 1998; Korhonen and Wallenius 2020). Exhibit 7.2 provides brief descriptions of these decision traps, which can have negative effects at several steps in the ethical decision-making process, such as gathering the facts, conducting an ethical analysis, and selecting a response option.

EXHIBIT 7.2 Descriptions of Major Decision Traps

Decision trap	Description
Anchoring	Making an initial estimate and, after receiving additional evidence, adjusting the estimate (as the adjustments are typically insufficient and biased toward the initial estimate)
Confirming evidence	Seeking and excessively weighting evidence that supports an existing hunch or idea, and avoiding and minimizing contradictory evidence
Estimating and forecasting	Biasing decisions because of overcautiousness and exaggeration of extreme events when assessing probabilities
Framing	Biasing decisions toward the original formulation of a problem or situation because the decision maker's norms, habits, and personal characteristics determine one set of choices
Status quo	Biasing decisions by making choices that continue to preserve the status quo
Sunk cost	Biasing current decisions to justify past decisions that may now be invalid (sunk cost is a resource, such as time and money, that can no longer be recouped)

Sources: Referenced in Bostrom and Ord (2006); Hammond, Keeney, and Raiffa (1998); Kahneman (2003); and Korhonen and Wallenius (2020).

Healthcare managers can use three general strategies for avoiding decision traps:

1. *Be alert*. Being aware that decision traps exist makes avoiding them easier. Moreover, as decision makers progress through the decision-making steps outlined here, they should be alert to the traps that threaten the quality of decisions reached at a particular step. For example, a healthcare manager who immediately obtains data confirming a hunch may stop gathering data too soon, falling into the "confirming evidence" trap. The contradictory data that go undetected could have been important and could have reversed the decision.

2. *Be knowledgeable*. Knowledge includes defining what the traps are, how they can negatively affect decisions, and which steps are susceptible to errors. Healthcare managers should seek input from superiors, peers, and direct reports about potential biases in formulating and analyzing a problem and implementing the plan of action. Fresh eyes could identify a trap to which the decision maker is blind.

3. *Stop to think*. Too often, healthcare managers believe they need to decide immediately—on the spot. Without taking time to think first, they may rush to judgment and make a decision that could later prove flawed. Systematically reflecting and using the steps in the ethical decision-making process takes time. Those who have courage—especially the courage to say, "I need to research this problem, but I'll get back to you"—are better equipped to avoid decision traps. Courageous healthcare managers are consciously putting their integrity into action. They are acting on their moral point of view.

Recognizing and Managing Moral Distress

Ann Hamric, Elizabeth Epstein, and Kenneth White (2014) were among the first researchers to discuss the relevance of **moral distress** to healthcare and healthcare managers. This concept was introduced by Andrew Jameton (1984) in the context of nursing to describe the distress that nurses experience when they encounter constraints in providing care. As seen in this chapter, both healthcare providers and administrators face ongoing ethical issues in their work that demand a response. Moral distress occurs when individuals feel powerless to carry out what they believe to be the ethically appropriate action; it can be viewed as a struggle to uphold ethics and professional standards in the healthcare environment (Mooney 2021). Moral distress is increasingly seen as an important topic in medicine (Dean, Talbot, and Caplan 2020; Perni 2017).

In their discussion of moral distress and healthcare organizations, Hamric, Epstein, and White (2014) describe the evolution of the concept of moral distress and its relevance to healthcare managers. Originally, moral distress was believed to occur because a person's

moral distress
Psychological distress that occurs when individuals perceive a moral obligation and feel constrained from acting ethically; consequently, they may experience symptoms and a compromised sense of agency.

actions are limited by institutional factors; today, however, the causes of moral distress are seen as arising from multiple factors within the individual, the clinical situation, the organization, and the external environment. Importantly, it may affect healthcare managers directly in their decision-making capacity or indirectly in their role of promoting a positive ethical climate in the organization.

Moral distress may manifest at multiple levels, such as a healthcare practitioner providing patient care in a particular situation, the functioning of a medical team or unit, or the structure of the organization. In end-of-life situations, nurses who feel that a patient is being provided inadequate pain relief or futile treatment may experience a range of emotions, such as frustration, anger, and guilt, and they may develop physical symptoms of stress, particularly if they feel powerless to express their perspective. Hamric, Epstein, and White (2014) note that the discussion of individual cases often reveals other issues that contribute to moral distress—such as communication issues within a unit, inadequate policies covering the situation, or perhaps a hierarchical hospital structure that prevents staff from feeling heard. In framing moral distress, it is important to recognize both individual concerns (e.g., important values, perceived constraints, personal integrity) and the broader structural factors in which moral distress arises (Pauly, Varcoe, and Storch 2012).

The failure to address the factors that contribute to moral distress may result in increasing levels of distress and lingering bad feelings among providers, known as *moral residue* (Hamric, Epstein, and White 2014). **Moral injury** occurs when the cumulative negative effects of moral distress become long-lasting (e.g., physical and emotional exhaustion) and interfere with professional functioning, causing individuals to question the morality of the system and their ability to work within it. In this way, ongoing moral distress can lead to negative consequences such as diminished morale, lost productivity, poor job satisfaction, burnout, and employee turnover (Lamiani, Borghi, and Argentero 2017).

moral injury
The end state of an egregious violation or repeated moral distresses that interfere with the ability to provide care in keeping with moral beliefs and expectations, leading to a state of burnout.

Scholars have developed and modified specialized measures of moral distress within healthcare (Epstein et al. 2019; Giannetta et al. 2020); the research findings from these studies add to our understanding of the construct. A comprehensive review identified a variety of strategies and instruments for studying moral distress in different settings, within professional groups, and across countries. For example, a single visual analogue scale ranging from 0 (absence of distress) to 10 (worst moral distress) has been used to measure moral distress in nurses over time. Most studies use a version of the moral distress scale that has been adapted for different groups.

The Measure of Moral Distress for Healthcare Professionals (MMD-HP) was designed to capture key components of the construct, such as unethicality, external pressure, feeling complicit in the situation, distress associated with the violation of professional standards, and perceived lack of voice (Epstein et al. 2019). Respondents indicate the frequency and distress level associated with 27 items targeting three perceived sources or causes of moral distress: patient situation, unit or team functioning, and system level. This revised scale specifically included more items at the system level based on responses from earlier studies.

In a study that included 706 individuals in healthcare professions (e.g., nurses, physicians, and other providers, including some pharmacists), this measure demonstrated good overall reliability or internal consistency (alpha = .93). The investigators reported a four-factor structure reflecting the perceived sources of distress: (1) systems level (e.g., being required to care for more patients than staff can handle safely; excessive documentation interfering with care); (2) patient clinical concerns (e.g., family is aggressive in the treatment of a dying patient); (3) factors pertaining to the team unit, such as personal vulnerability to one's moral code (e.g., working within a unit that does not respect or treat vulnerable or stigmatized patients well); and (4) breakdown in team functioning (e.g., poor continuity of care, communication).

As hypothesized, this measure demonstrated evidence of construct validity. Epstein and colleagues (2019) found that nurses scored higher than physicians in moral distress, although they did not differ from other professionals. Moral distress was also higher among those working in intensive care settings. In addition, there was a significant negative association (–.55) between moral distress scores and a measure of perceived hospital ethical climate. Significantly, moral scores were also higher for participants (20 percent of this sample) who indicated that they were considering leaving their position.

It is apparent that healthcare professionals perceive moral distress as impacting patient care, although more research is needed in this area. Turnover is costly to organizations in terms of the time and cost of hiring and onboarding new staff. For administrators, this research literature underscores the importance of understanding the moral distress experienced in healthcare organizations and considering appropriate responses.

Multiple strategies at different levels are needed to manage and prevent moral distress. One strategy for addressing moral distress in critical care situations is the *debriefing*, in which a trained facilitator allows those directly affected to process their feelings and help each other cope. Shilpa Shashidhara and Shaylona Kirk (2020) offer a framework for conducting a debriefing that includes the preparation and assessment needed and a stepwise approach to the conduct of the meeting, including reflection and emotional experiences, sharing coping strategies, and identifying takeaways for the future. Most efforts are directed at strengthening providers' coping skills and resilience.

Focus group research conducted with middle- and late-career healthcare providers working in intensive care (Helmers, Palmer, and Greenberg 2020) identified three strategies for addressing moral distress: (1) active personal coping (e.g., gathering more facts, confronting distress situation head-on, and self-care efforts), (2) reflection strategies (e.g., perspective taking, compartmentalization, hopes for the future), and (3) use of resources (e.g., ethics debriefs, consultation with bioethics experts, and use of mentors). Healthcare leaders typically have directed intervention efforts at enhancing the healthcare environment by implementing ethics and moral distress education programs and providing needed resources. Attempts to improve team and system functioning should involve interdisciplinary collaboration, as multiple perspectives are needed to improve future care at this level. More research is needed on the effectiveness of these strategies and on the role of structural inequalities (Pauly, Varcoe, and Storch 2012).

Finally, healthcare managers and leaders can also experience moral distress, although this has been studied much less systematically. Hamric, Epstein, and White (2014) observed that this topic is more often discussed in the management literature. Craig Mitton and colleagues (2011), the first researchers to examine moral distress among nonclinical managers, identified several sources of moral distress among healthcare managers: having to communicate decisions that they did not agree with, causing them to feel dishonest or untruthful; and having to implement an organizational decision that might be for the good of the whole organization, but whose consequences fall disproportionately on one staff group or community; having to make choices that they perceive as violating their obligations to others given the constraints imposed by patient care and allocation of limited resources. Although some mid-level managers expressed that higher levels of management may not experience moral distress to the same degree because they are more removed from the patient care experience, senior leaders refuted this idea, citing their concern for how the functioning of the healthcare system affects the patient experience.

Yvonne Denier and colleagues (2019) describe the difference between being concerned about ethical decision-making from a business perspective (e.g., clinical and financial data, legal issues, etc.) and values-based leadership in healthcare. The latter requires managers to integrate ethical values into their daily lived experience on the job. Leaders committed to values-based leadership describe it in terms of metaphors—for example, tending a garden, learning a language, trekking with an ethical compass, and giving people wings. Such leaders do all this from a community-model perspective because it "is about care and not about cookies" (Denier, Dhaene, and Gastmans 2019, 14).

Mini-Case Study: Obligations to Staff

Moral distress can arise when managers perceive a conflict between their perceived obligations to their staff and the organizational decisions that they are directed to carry out. Mitton and colleagues (2011, 113) provide a poignant example in which a nurse manager discussed how night shifts in her facility were often short-staffed. The manager stated that if she were in the evening nurse's place, she would feel that it was not safe to only leave two registered nurses to cope. The manager brought her concerns to upper-level management but did not receive a successful response, causing her to experience considerable angst. To resolve these feelings, the manager often chose to join the night staff on the floor, even if this meant working an additional full shift on top of her own day's work.

Mini-Case Study Questions

1. How is this case an example of *moral* distress, rather than the stress of the manager's ongoing responsibilities?
2. What are some reasons for understaffing?

3. As a healthcare manager, how would you define the core problem in this case, and what are some potential solutions? In your view, has this nurse manager solved her conflict? What else might she have done? What options would a nonclinical manager consider?

Points to Remember

- Many decisions and routine actions by healthcare managers can have significant ethical implications, which often go unrecognized.
- Ethical decision-making is a reflective process that promotes ethical outcomes.
- Ethical decision-making is a process that can be learned. Developing awareness of affective and potential biases is important in developing this competency.
- Ethical decision makers explicitly consider the right thing to do, the impact of their decisions on others, and the consequences of their decisions.
- Healthcare managers can avoid common errors in decision-making, known as decision traps, by being alert to their existence, being knowledgeable about them, and stopping to think.
- Recognizing and managing moral distress is important for healthcare managers and their organizations.

Challenge Yourself

1. The difficult medical cases discussed at the beginning of this chapter might suggest the concept of medical futility is of recent origin. However, some experts believe that Hippocrates himself addressed this issue (Jones 1923, 193):

    First I will define what I conceive medicine to be. In general terms, it is to do away with the sufferings of the sick, to lessen the violence of their diseases, and to refuse to treat those who are overmastered by their diseases, realizing that in such cases medicine is powerless.

    Ask yourself: Does placing medical futility within the historical tradition of modern medicine change the underlying ethical problem? Do healthcare managers and other administrators have a role in decisions involving medical futility and the care of patients? Do participants other than patients (or surrogates) have autonomy?

    Many third-party payers, such as Medicare, require treatments to be medically necessary to qualify for coverage and reimbursement. What is the relationship between medical futility, medical necessity, and rationing? Earlier, we discussed the collision of autonomy, beneficence, and fidelity. What other ethical principles do you believe are involved in medical futility?

2. The chapter proposed that the routine decision to maintain the confidentiality of an employee's performance evaluation contains an ethical element. Name several other routine managerial decisions or problems that you believe contain ethical elements. For each decision or problem, identify the associated ethical principle(s). Name one managerial problem that contains an ethical conflict, and then identify the ethical principles involved.
3. Review the steps of the ethical decision-making process. Thinking as a healthcare manager, which step do you think is the most difficult? Why? Which step do you think determines the quality of your decision? Why?
4. Explain how one of the ethical theories (see chapter 2)—deontology, consequentialism, Rawls's principle of justice, or the ethics of care—aligns with your values. Explain how that theory affects and guides your ethical analyses.

For Your Consideration

7.1 In the 1991 movie *What About Bob?* Bill Murray plays Bob Wiley, a kindhearted and witty New Yorker with many phobias. Richard Dreyfuss plays Bob's successful and arrogant psychiatrist, Dr. Leo Marvin. When Dr. Marvin leaves for his month-long vacation at his summer home in New Hampshire, Bob follows him and ingratiates himself into Dr. Marvin's family. Dr. Marvin becomes increasingly annoyed with Bob's dependency and comes to view him as a stalker. Dr. Marvin's own mental health deteriorates to the point that he begins plotting Bob's death through what he calls "death therapy."

In business, the question "What do we do about Bob?" has become a code. "Bob" refers to a particularly opinionated set of customers, a market segment with a certain profile, or a problematic employee or coworker. The business needs to consider Bob's views, skills, informal leadership, political clout, or some other aspect.

You are Pat, a department head in a tertiary care center. Bob, a unit supervisor, is one of your **direct reports**. He graduated from college about seven years ago with a bachelor's degree in health services management and joined your department two years ago as a unit supervisor. Before that, he worked as an assistant manager at a midsized medical group practice.

direct report
An employee who works under and is managed by an immediate superior or boss.

Bob is eager and articulate, and he has a strong work ethic. He is always the first person to arrive at the office and the first to respond enthusiastically to proposals in leadership meetings. Claiming you as his mentor in his first year of employment, he asks for your ideas or comments on every step of every project or task that you assign him. Often, he submits extremely rough outlines or a set of bullets, not finished reports. This makes you feel as if you are doing his work for him. As a result, in his last performance review, you rated him as "needs improvement" on initiative. You explained that he needs to use his education and work experience to justify his assumptions and decisions and complete assignments on his own.

Jane, another one of your direct reports, informs you that since Bob's performance review, he has been asking her and other coworkers for their ideas and comments on his outlines and bullets. Jane quotes him: "Can I run this past you for feedback so we're all on the same page before sending it up to Pat?"

What are you going to do about Bob?

   a. Use the ethical decision-making process to address this problem. What is the most critical step in the process? Justify your selection.
   b. Describe the ethical implications of doing nothing.
   c. What is the potential impact on the process of labeling someone a "Bob"?

7.2 Read the article by Denier, Dhaene, and Gastmans (2019) on values-based leadership and discuss the appropriateness of the metaphors they use to describe the behavior and functioning of successful healthcare managers. Which of these metaphors do you see as the most critical or embodying aspects that you wish to cultivate in yourself as a manager?

References

American College of Healthcare Executives (ACHE). 2018. "Ethics Toolkit." Accessed March 19, 2021. www.ache.org/about-ache/our-story/our-commitments/ethics/ache-code-of-ethics/creating-an-ethical-culture-within-the-healthcare-organization/ethics-toolkit.

Bostrom, N., and T. Ord. 2006. "The Reversal Test: Eliminating Status Quo Bias in Applied Ethics." *Ethics* 116 (4): 656–79.

Bowen, D. J. 2019. "Transformational Times Steadied by Code of Ethics." *Healthcare Executive*, March/April, 8–9.

Cristofaro, M., M. J. Sousa, J. Sanchéz-Garcia, and A. Larsson. 2021. "Contextualized Behavior for Improving Managerial and Entrepreneurial Decision-Making." *Administrative Sciences* 11 (1): 14.

Dean, W., S. G. Talbot, and A. Caplan. 2020. "Clarifying the Language of Clinician Distress." *Journal of the American Medical Association* 323 (10): 923–24.

Denier, Y., L. Dhaene, and C. Gastmans. 2019. "'You Can Give Them Wings to Fly': A Qualitative Study on Values-Based Leadership in Health Care." *BMC Medical Ethics* 20: Article 35.

Epstein, E. G., P. B. Whitehead, C. Prompahakul, L. R. Thacker, and A. B. Hamric. 2019. "Enhancing Understanding of Moral Distress: The Measure of Moral Distress for Health Care Professionals." *AJOB Empirical Bioethics* 10 (2): 113–24.

Flanders, N. 2021. "U.S. Supreme Court Declines Hospital's Appeal to Remove Tinslee Lewis from Life Support." Live Action News. Published January 13. www.liveaction.org/news/supreme-court-declines-appeal-tinslee-lewis-life/.

Giannetta, N., G. Villa, F. Pennestrì, R. Sala, R. Mordacci, and D. F. Manara. 2020. "Instruments to Assess Moral Distress Among Healthcare Workers: A Systematic Review of Measurement Properties." *International Journal of Nursing Studies* 111: 103767.

Glover-Thomas, N. 2020. "Getting the Balance Right: Medical Futility, Scientific Advancement, and the Role of Law." *Medical Law Review* 28 (3): 573–94.

Hammond, J. S., R. L. Keeney, and H. Raiffa. 1998. "The Hidden Traps in Decision Making." *Harvard Business Review* 76 (5): 47–58.

Hamric, A. B., E. G. Epstein, and K. R. White. 2014. "Moral Distress and the Healthcare Organization." In *Managerial Ethics in Healthcare: A New Perspective*, edited by G. Filerman, A. Mills, and P. Schyve, 137–57. Chicago: Health Administration Press.

Helmers, A., K. D. Palmer, and R. A Greenberg. 2020. "Moral Distress: Developing Strategies from Experience." *Nursing Ethics* 27 (4): 1147–56.

Jameton, A. 1984. *Nursing Practice: The Ethical Issues*. Englewood Cliffs, NJ: Prentice-Hall.

Johnson, C. E. 2021. *Meeting the Ethical Challenges of Leadership: Casting Light or Shadow*, 7th ed. Thousand Oaks, CA: Sage.

Jones, W. H. S. (trans.). 1923. *Hippocrates, Vol. II*, 190–217. London: William Heinemann Ltd.

Kahneman, D. 2003. "A Perspective on Judgment and Choice: Mapping Bounded Rationality." *American Psychologist* 58 (9): 697–720.

Kidder, R. M. 2006. *Moral Courage*. New York: HarperCollins.

Korhonen P. J., and J. Wallenius. 2020. *Making Better Decisions*. Cham, Switzerland: Springer.

Lamiani, G., L. Borghi, and P. Argentero. 2017. "When Healthcare Professionals Cannot Do the Right Thing: A Systematic Review of Moral Distress and Its Correlates." *Journal of Health Psychology* 22 (1): 51–67.

Mitton, C., S. Peacock, J. Storch, N. Smith, and E. Cornelissen. 2011. "Moral Distress Among Health System Managers: Exploratory Research in Two British Columbia Health Authorities." *Health Care Analysis* 19 (2): 107–21.

Mooney, J. 2021. "Moral Distress: The Struggle to Uphold Ethics in Healthcare." *Behavioral Health Partners Blog*. Published January. www.urmc.rochester.edu/behavioral-health-partners/bhp-blog/january-2021/moral-distress-the-struggle-to-uphold-ethics-in-he.aspx.

National Center for Ethics in Health Care. 2015. *Ethics Consultation: Responding to Ethics Questions in Health Care*, 2nd ed. Accessed September 8, 2021. www.ethics.va.gov/docs/integratedethics/ec_primer_2nd_ed.pdf.

Nelson, W. A. 2015. "A Six-Step Process Should Guide Ethical Decision-Making in Healthcare." *Healthcare Executive* 30 (4): 46–48.

———. 2005. "An Organizational Ethics Decision-Making Process." *Healthcare Executive* 20 (4): 8–14.

Pauly, B. M., C. Varcoe, and J. Storch. 2012. "Framing the Issues: Moral Distress in Healthcare." *HEC Forum* 24 (1): 1–11.

Perni, S. 2017. "Moral Distress: A Call to Action." *AMA Journal of Ethics* 19 (6): 533–36.

Rogerson, M. D., M. C. Gottlieb, M. M. Handelsman, S. Knapp, and J. Younggren. 2011. "Nonrational Processes in Ethical Decision Making." *American Psychologist* 66 (7): 614–23.

Schneiderman, L. J. 2011. "Defining Medical Futility and Improving Medical Care." *Bioethical Inquiry* 8 (2): 123–31.

Schwartz, M. S. 2016. "Ethical Decision-Making: An Integrated Approach." *Journal of Business Ethics* 139 (4): 755–76.

Sergeant, C. S. 2021. "Playing God: Faulty Decision-Making in Medical Futility Disputes." *Mitchell Hamline Law Review*. Published February 12. https://open.mitchellhamline.edu/mhlr/vol47/iss1/12.

Shashidhara, S., and S. Kirk. 2020. "Moral Distress: A Framework for Offering Relief Through Debrief." *Journal of Clinical Ethics* 31 (4): 364–71.

Tversky, A., and D. Kahneman. 1981. "The Framing of Decisions and the Psychology of Choice." *Science* 211 (4481): 453–58.

CHAPTER 8
RESEARCH IN HEALTHCARE ORGANIZATIONS

The Commission finds that many of the actions of the researchers were morally wrong and the individual researchers and institutional officials were morally blameworthy.
—Presidential Commission for the Study of Bioethical Issues

IMPORTANT TERMS

- *Belmont Report*
- Civil monetary penalties
- Common Rule
- Federal-wide assurance of compliance (FWA)
- Groupthink
- Institutional review board (IRB)
- Nuremburg Code
- Office for Civil Rights (OCR)
- Office for Human Research Protection (OHRP)
- Office of Research Integrity (ORI)
- Privacy Rule
- Study protocols
- Tuskegee Study

LEARNING OBJECTIVES

Studying this chapter will help you to

➤ be familiar with frequently cited cases of breaches of ethics in US biomedical research,

➤ summarize key documents underpinning current ethical perspectives and regulations,

➤ outline the responsibilities of institutional review boards, and

➤ explain the roles of federal agencies responsible for the oversight of research conducted in healthcare organizations.

This chapter introduces ethical concerns related to research conducted in healthcare organizations. Research occurs in academic health centers, community hospitals, physician offices, community health centers, and other healthcare organizations. The goal of this chapter is to familiarize you with the vocabulary, important concepts, and topics of biomedical research ethics. As the chapter-opening quotation makes clear, institutional officials—such as healthcare managers—are just as morally responsible for the ethical conduct of research studies being done in their institutions as the researchers doing the studies.

> **LANDMARK CASES FROM THE FIELD**
> Unethical US Public Health Service Studies
>
> Hippocrates (400 BCE) wrote that the "physician must . . . have two special objects in view with regard to disease, namely, to do good or to do no harm."
>
> In two notorious studies, members of the US Public Health Service (PHS) violated Hippocrates's call to do good and to do no harm: the Tuskegee Study of Untreated Syphilis in the Negro Male (commonly known as the **Tuskegee Study**) and the Sexually Transmitted Disease Inoculation Study (conducted in Guatemala).
>
> From 1932 through 1972, the Tuskegee Study was conducted in rural Macon County, Alabama, to obtain information on the course of untreated syphilis in African American men. During this 40-year period, PHS researchers did not tell the African American men who participated or the community the true purpose of the study. Instead, the men were told that the PHS was studying "bad blood." Of the 600 total participants, 399 had syphilis, but the researchers did not inform them of their disease. Moreover, after the discovery in 1947 that penicillin was the definitive treatment for syphilis, the researchers blocked treatment for the men. As a result, the men infected their wives, who passed the disease to their unborn children, who then were born with congenital syphilis (Jones 1981). (Read more about the PHS and the Tuskegee Study in the Mini-Case Study later in this chapter.)
>
> In another study, PHS researchers, working with four Guatemalan government agencies, conducted a study in Guatemala from 1946 through 1948 to determine penicillin's effectiveness as a preventive treatment after exposure to a sexually transmitted disease (STD) (Reverby 2011). The researchers deliberately exposed a total of 1,308 people—including prisoners, psychiatric patients in an asylum, soldiers, and prostitutes—to syphilis, gonorrhea, and chancroid. Most of the participants were in their twenties. About half of them received some form of treatment, and 83 died. In addition, through 1953, to improve the diagnosis of STDs, the researchers drew blood and cerebrospinal fluid from 5,128 subjects, including soldiers, prisoners, psychiatric patients, children, leprosy patients, and US Air Force personnel at a base in Guatemala. According to the Presidential Commission for the Study of Bioethical Issues (2011, v), the "Guatemala experiments involved gross violations of ethics as judged against both the standards of today and the researchers' own understanding of applicable contemporaneous practices."

Tuskegee Study
A 40-year syphilis study on 600 African American men in Macon County, Alabama, that misinformed its subjects and prevented treatment for the syphilitic men in the group.

Unethical Human Experimentations in US Healthcare

The primary purpose of human experimentation is to acquire new scientific knowledge rather than to provide therapy. During the past 100 years, biomedical researchers in the United States have conducted experiments on vulnerable populations, such as prisoners, children and minors, intellectually disabled people, terminally ill or comatose patients, and economically or educationally disadvantaged people. Researchers have also conducted experiments on military service members and civilians (Advisory Committee on Human Radiation Experiments 1995; US House of Representatives 1986). This section introduces you to four frequently cited cases of ethical breaches in biomedical research in the United States.

1. *Willowbrook Hepatitis Studies.* Conducted from 1956 to about 1976, these studies not only deliberately infected children who had severe intellectual disabilities and were institutionalized at the Willowbrook State School in New York, but also deceived their parents to give consent. In the 1950s, Willowbrook had about 6,000 residents, 77 percent of whom were severely or profoundly intellectually disabled. Hepatitis was widespread there. Researchers exposed newly admitted children to the hepatitis virus to learn more about the natural course of the disease and its prevention. The consent obtained from the children's parents was deceptive because it was worded as though the children were receiving a vaccine against the virus rather than being infected with the virus (Rothman 1982).

2. *Jewish Chronic Disease Hospital Study.* In 1963, researchers injected 22 weak and chronically ill patients at the Jewish Chronic Disease Hospital with live cancer cells (Katz 1992). The purpose of the study was to investigate the ability of chronically ill patients to reject foreign cells. Because of their mental conditions, some of the patients were incapable of understanding the experiment, and none of the patients were informed that they were subjects in an experiment. Instead, they were told that the injections were "skin tests." The Board of Regents of the University of the State of New York (the state medical licensing board) gave the study's two lead physician-researchers only one year of probation each, with the condition that both conducted themselves "in a manner befitting his professional status" (Katz, Capron, and Glass 1972, 62).

3. *Fernald School Study.* In the late 1940s through the early 1950s, 32 intellectually disabled children at the residential Fernald School in Massachusetts were fed oatmeal with milk containing radioisotopes (Buchanan 1996; Mann 1994). The purpose of the study was to determine the effect of oat cereals on the absorption of calcium in milk (Mann 1994). Researchers, with the

collusion of the school's administrator, tricked parents into giving consent for their children's "participation" by describing the activity as a "science club" (Buchanan 1996). Additionally, 17 other children at the school were fed radioactive iron so that the researchers could learn about iron absorption in the body (Mann 1994).

4. *Wrentham State School Study.* In 1961, researchers from Harvard Medical School, Massachusetts General Hospital, and Boston University School of Medicine went to the residential Wrentham State School in Massachusetts to study the effectiveness of a proposed method to block the absorption of radioactive iodine—a type of material that would be released in a nuclear explosion (Advisory Committee on Human Radiation Experiments 1995). To that end, the researchers gave radioactive iodine to 70 intellectually disabled children living in the school.

In these four human experiments, the researchers and administrators involved, in pursuit of their own agenda, were willing to

- take advantage of vulnerable populations,
- deceive patients and their families,
- violate human rights and patients' rights,
- ignore the necessity of obtaining patients' informed consent,
- conduct experiments of no therapeutic value to patients, and
- perform experiments in which the risks outweighed any potential benefits for patients.

Major Documents Detailing Ethical Research Standards in Healthcare

Protections for human research subjects have evolved over time. The origins of informed consent for research participants can be traced to the Nuremberg Trials of 1945–46, which documented the horrendous treatment of individuals in Nazi concentration camps during World War II under the guise of medical research. Exhibit 8.1 summarizes key international and federal documents that provide protections for research participants.

In the United States, the Tuskegee Study is arguably the most notorious violation of ethics in human experimentation. Congressional and public outrage about that study resulted in the passage of the National Research Act of 1974, which, in turn, created the

EXHIBIT 8.1
Key Documents Establishing Protections for Human Research Subjects

Document	Description
Nuremberg Code (1947)	Set of ten statements requiring that human participation in research be voluntary and informed
	The code was a result of the Nuremberg Military Tribunals Doctors' Trial, in which Nazi doctors were tried for performing torturous medical experiments on civilian prisoners—specifically, those in concentration camps—during World War II.
Declaration of Helsinki (1964)	International ethics guide for physicians conducting research using human subjects
	Outside the United States, the Declaration of Helsinki is the mostly widely adopted set of ethical guidelines for biomedical research (WMA 2013).
Policy and Procedure Order 129, US Surgeon General (1966)	Directive regulating clinical research funded by the US Public Health Service
	This document requires that an institutional standing committee review researchers' proposals to ensure the (1) protection of the rights and welfare of human subjects, (2) appropriateness of the methods used to secure informed consent, and (3) determination of the risks and potential medical benefits of the investigation.
National Research Act (Public Law 93-348, 1974) and Subsequent Regulations	Legislation providing a framework for the protection of human subjects of biomedical and behavioral research
	This act was implemented in several US Department of Health and Human Services (HHS) regulations, which are based on the *Belmont Report* of 1979 and have been expanded over the years. In 1991, most other federal departments and agencies joined the HHS in adopting a uniform set of rules for the protection of human subjects.
Belmont Report (1979)	Report of the National Commission for the Protection of Human Subjects of Biomedical and Behavioral Research
	This report (1) identified the basic ethical principles that should underlie biomedical and behavioral research on human subjects and (2) developed guidelines to ensure that research is conducted in accordance with those principles; the report is formally known as *Ethical Principles and Guidelines for the Protection of Human Subjects of Research*.

National Commission for the Protection of Human Subjects of Biomedical and Behavioral Research (1979). This commission was charged with the following responsibilities:

- Identify the basic ethical principles that should underlie biomedical and behavioral research on human subjects
- Develop guidelines to ensure that research is conducted in accordance with those principles

Belmont Report
A report that provides the ethical foundation for biomedical and behavioral research in the United States; published in 1979 as *Ethical Principles and Guidelines for the Protection of Human Subjects of Research*.

Subsequent Commissions for the Study of Bioethics have been formed by presidents or the US Congress for the continued analysis of ethical considerations underlying the nation's activities in science, medicine, and technology.

Fulfilling its charge in 1979, the commission published *Ethical Principles and Guidelines for the Protection of Human Subjects of Research*, which is more commonly known as the **Belmont Report**, named for the Belmont Conference Center where the commission met to draft it. In the *Belmont Report*, protections for human research subjects are based on three key ethical principles: respect for persons, beneficence, and justice (see exhibit 8.2).

EXHIBIT 8.2
Three Ethical Principles of the *Belmont Report*

Principle	Descriptions	Application	Requirements
Respect for persons	• Individuals should be treated as autonomous agents • Persons with diminished autonomy are entitled to protection	Informed consent	• Subjects, to the degree they are capable, must be given the opportunity to choose what shall or shall not happen to them • Process contains three elements: information, comprehension, and voluntariness
Beneficence	• Do no harm • Maximize possible benefits and minimize possible harms	Assessment of risks and benefits	Nature and scope of risks and benefits are carefully and systematically assessed
Justice	Fair distribution of the risks and benefits of research	Selection of subjects	Procedures and outcomes in the selection of research subjects must be fair

Source: Adapted from the National Commission for the Protection of Human Subjects of Biomedical and Behavioral Research (1979).

Subsequently, the US Department of Health, Education, and Welfare (now known as the Department of Health and Human Services, or HHS) adopted the *Belmont Report* as a statement of its policy. In the late 1970s and early 1980s, the content of the *Belmont Report* was incorporated into federal regulations governing research using human subjects. Researchers in the HHS or funded by the HHS who conduct biomedical or behavioral research are required to (1) get voluntary informed consent from all human subjects in the research study, and (2) obtain an approval from an institutional review board, a committee whose members read **study protocols** to decide whether the study meets ethical standards.

These regulations were first published in the *Code of Federal Regulations*, Title 45, Part 46 (45 CFR 46). The HHS continues to revise and expand the protections for human subjects. Generally, the expansions and revisions have added protections for specific vulnerable populations who are perceived to be at greater risk of coercion in research, such as children, prisoners, those suffering from emotional difficulties or cognitive impairment, and individuals who are economically disadvantaged.

Researchers and managers of healthcare organizations now have a uniform set of rules for the protection of human subjects called the Federal Policy for the Protection of Human Subjects, informally known as the **Common Rule**. The Common Rule outlines the basic provisions for institutional review boards, informed consent, and the **federal-wide assurance of compliance (FWA)**.

Almost all federal agencies have adopted the Common Rule. The latest revision to the rule was fully implemented in 2019. The revised rule strengthens protections for people who volunteer to participate in research while ensuring that the oversight system does not add inappropriate administrative burdens, particularly to low-risk research. It also allows more flexibility in keeping with today's dynamic research environment. The rule now expects consent forms to include a concise explanation—at the beginning of the document—of the key information that would be most important to individuals contemplating participation in a particular study, including the purpose of the research, the risks and benefits, and appropriate alternative treatments that might be beneficial to the prospective subject (OHRP 2017).

Several federal departments and agencies outside the HHS have additional regulations in place for research involving special populations or for human experimentation in general.

Institutional Review Board

To comply with the Common Rule, organizations that have researchers who conduct human experimentation have in place an **institutional review board (IRB)**, sometimes called a *human subjects committee*. As an administrative body, the IRB exists to protect the rights and welfare of human subjects recruited to participate in research activities associated with institutions. You should familiarize yourself with the policies and procedures that govern research at your university.

---

study protocols
A preestablished set of procedures for ethical research.

Common Rule
Uniform set of regulations on the ethical conduct of research involving human subjects established by the federal agencies that fund such research; formally, the *Federal Policy for the Protection of Human Subjects*.

federal-wide assurance of compliance (FWA)
A written, binding, formal commitment by an institution to comply with applicable regulations on research using human subjects.

institutional review board (IRB)
An administrative body established to protect the rights and welfare of human subjects recruited to participate in research activities.

The composition of an IRB is described in the *Code of Federal Regulations*. The IRB must have at least five diverse members; of these five, at least one member must have a scientific background, one member must have a nonscientific background, and one member must be unaffiliated with the institution conducting the research. Most IRBs have 10 to 14 members, including experts in vulnerable subjects and in a variety of research designs and methods. In addition, an IRB may use consultants with special expertise in research or the area of proposed experiments. IRB meetings are scheduled according to the needs of the institution, and minutes are kept. Most studies undergo full review, although some that pose minimal risk (e.g., a survey of needs or satisfaction with a service) and do not involve vulnerable populations may undergo expedited review. Studies involving patients, and therefore protected health information, may undergo two reviews to ensure compliance with the research obligations under the Health Insurance Portability and Accountability Act (HIPAA) of 1996 as well as the broader IRB protections for research participants.

The Common Rule requires that research be (1) reviewed and approved by an IRB and (2) subject to continuing review by the IRB. The IRB has the authority to suspend or terminate any approved research that is not being conducted in accordance with its requirements. Per the federal-wide assurance of compliance, institutions are responsible for protecting the rights and welfare of human subjects of research conducted at or sponsored by the institution, *regardless of whether the research is subject to federal regulation.*

FEDERAL AGENCIES RESPONSIBLE FOR THE OVERSIGHT OF RESEARCH IN HEALTHCARE

Healthcare managers need to be aware of the federal agencies that govern the research in their organization. These agencies may contact the organization to request information or issue notices. Agencies that commonly interact with healthcare organizations include the Office for Human Research Protections, the Office of Research Integrity, and the Office for Civil Rights.

OFFICE FOR HUMAN RESEARCH PROTECTIONS

The **Office for Human Research Protections (OHRP)** is the agency within the HHS that is charged with protecting the rights, welfare, and well-being of subjects involved in research conducted or supported by the HHS. The OHRP fulfills this responsibility through three strategies:

1. *Influence the design of human subject protection at regulated institutions through the FWA.* In the FWA document, institutions promise to comply with applicable regulations on research using human subjects and stipulate the procedures for achieving compliance.

Office for Human Research Protections (OHRP)
The agency within the US Department of Health and Human Services that protects the rights, welfare, and well-being of subjects involved in research conducted or supported by the HHS.

2. *Conduct compliance (not-for-cause) audits and complaint (for-cause) investigations.* Compliance audits are general surveillance site visits during which the OHRP evaluates the institution's overall compliance. Complaint investigations deal with specific complaints received by the OHRP regarding investigators' misconduct or reports of a serious incident, such as the death of a healthy subject.

3. *Provide educational programs and materials on ethics and produce guidelines and interpretations of specific regulatory provisions.*

Healthcare managers should be aware of the OHRP's enforcement powers. These powers include requiring corrective actions, freezing expenditures of federal research grant funds, and barring individuals or entire institutions from receiving federal research funds.

OFFICE OF RESEARCH INTEGRITY

The **Office of Research Integrity (ORI)** is the agency within the HHS that oversees and directs activities for research integrity in the PHS (except the regulatory activities of the Food and Drug Administration). The ORI's mission is to prevent research misconduct and promote research integrity principally through oversight, education, and review of institutional findings and recommendations. In the 1980s, several occurrences of research misconduct—such as falsifying studies, fabricating data and results, and plagiarism—were reported, including these two well-known cases:

Office of Research Integrity (ORI)
The agency within the US Department of Health and Human Services that oversees and directs activities for research integrity in the US Public Health Service.

1. *Darsee affair.* John Darsee fabricated research data during his undergraduate years at the University of Notre Dame; his medical residency at Emory University; and his cardiology fellowship at Brigham and Women's Hospital, a teaching affiliate of Harvard University. These faked data were central to many of the papers he published in reputable scientific publications. Upon investigation based on the suspicions of associates, his entire fraudulent career unraveled, and journal editors published retractions reflecting on the limitations of peer review and how science might be better protected (Relman 1983).

2. *Stephen E. Breuning case.* Breuning faked his research and results, which influenced the development of drug therapy for developmentally delayed children displaying self-injurious behavior. The investigative team from the National Institute of Mental Health found that none of the studies on psychopharmacologic treatment reported in Breuning's published articles and federal grant applications had actually been conducted. This case was one of the first criminal convictions prosecuted in federal court for scientific fraud, and it continues to be analyzed (Garfield and Welljams-Dorof 1990; Sottile 2018).

As a result of the public outcry over these and other cases of misconduct, Congress passed the Health Research Extension Act of 1985. Federal grant applicants or awardee institutions must establish an administrative process to review reports of scientific fraud and to report any investigation of alleged scientific fraud.

Research misconduct violates the ethical principles of fidelity and responsibility as well as integrity. Factors that may contribute to research fraud include personal character, institutional pressures to publish, a desire to gain prestige in the field, academic traditions and the assumption of honesty, and limited oversight. Commentators have particularly highlighted the need for supervision and institutional integrity, the role and ethical responsibilities of coauthors, and ways to strengthen the review process (Garfield and Welljams-Dorof 1990; Relman 1983; Sottile 2018).

OFFICE FOR CIVIL RIGHTS

The **Privacy Rule** under HIPAA works with the Common Rule. That is, HIPAA requires researchers to obtain a signed authorization before using or disclosing protected health information for research. The **Office for Civil Rights (OCR)** is the agency within the HHS that protects people's basic rights and investigates allegations of violations of the HIPAA Privacy Rule.

If the OCR finds evidence that supports the complaint, it requires the offending organization to voluntarily comply or take corrective action. If the organization does not take satisfactory action to resolve the matter, the OCR may impose fines, known as **civil monetary penalties**. If the complaint could be a violation of the criminal provision of HIPAA, the OCR may refer the complaint to the US Department of Justice for investigation. Additionally, the OCR conducts compliance reviews and provides education and outreach to foster compliance with the requirements of the Privacy Rule.

It is educational to review the OHRP's Compliance and Reporting website (www.hhs.gov/ohrp/compliance-and-reporting/determination-letters/index.html). For example, in 2019, a complaint alleged that a major medical institution had failed in its efforts to protect patient confidentiality. Specifically, participants in a research study who were living with HIV were recruited by email to assess their interest in a new study. However, the recruitment email visibly contained the email addresses of 145 individuals, some of whom were recognized by the complainant. Findings suggested that while the medical institution was apparently reviewing this incident, it failed in its duty to immediately report it. In response, the medical institution suspended email recruitment and required the investigators to write an apology letter to those whose confidentiality had been inadvertently breached. The website also includes an example of a determination letter sent to a major cancer research center for a not-for-cause evaluation or audit of its informed consent processes and other procedures to protect research participants.

Privacy Rule
A regulation under the Health Insurance Portability and Accountability Act of 1996 that protects the privacy, use, and disclosure of people's own medical records and other health information.

Office for Civil Rights (OCR)
An office within the US Department of Health and Human Services that protects people's basic rights and investigates complaints of violations of the Privacy Rule of the Health Insurance Portability and Accountability Act of 1996.

civil monetary penalties
Fines imposed by federal agencies for violating laws or regulations.

Similarly, a review of the ORI's Research Misconduct Summaries involving specific investigators and projects will dispel the erroneous notion that IRBs, laws, and regulations have eliminated individual ethical misconduct or abuses in biomedical research.

Scientific misconduct has the potential for great harm, not only to the research community but also to the public's trust in science and healthcare. A cogent example is the long-lasting impact of a paper published by a Dr. Wakefield in the medical journal *The Lancet*. Wakefield reported on a possible link between autism and childhood vaccination for diseases such as rubella and mumps. Other investigators reported no such relationship, and this paper was eventually retracted under allegations of fraud. Nevertheless, based on this proposed link and parental concern, childhood vaccination rates decreased, and distrust of vaccines persists (Godlee, Smith, and Marcovitch 2011).

Although criminalization of the most severe forms of misconduct, such as fabrication and falsification of data, has been proposed, this measure, by itself, is not seen as a complete solution to ensuring the integrity of research findings (Bülow and Helgesson 2019; Dal-Re et al. 2020).

Erik Boetto and colleagues (2020) discuss the difficulties of ensuring the integrity of research submitted during the COVID-19 pandemic amid the pressing need to share discoveries and the overwhelming number of submissions to healthcare journals. They call for strengthening journal policies on data sharing and potential use of new computer technologies in data collection that allow for ongoing review.

> **? DID YOU KNOW?**
> **The Legacy of Henrietta Lacks**
>
> Henrietta Lacks (1920–51) was a young Black mother living in Virginia who developed cervical cancer. In 1951, she sought treatment at Johns Hopkins University Hospital for pain and bleeding and was diagnosed with late-stage cervical cancer. At that time, the hospital treated African American patients, but on segregated wards (full integration of inpatient care did not occur until 1973).
>
> Although Lacks died, some of her cancer cells retrieved during a biopsy were sent to the research lab of Dr. George Otto Gey, who was studying cancer. He discovered that, unlike many of the other samples he was sent, these cells were able to be replicated every 24 hours. They became known as the HeLa cell line, and he shared the cloned cells freely with medical researchers around the world. The immortalized cell line has contributed for many years to medical research on many diseases such as polio, leukemia, and HIV.
>
> Consistent with medical research at that time, however, there was no informed consent for tissue samples, and Lacks's family only learned about their mother's contribution decades
>
> *(continued)*

> ** DID YOU KNOW?**
> **The Legacy of Henrietta Lacks** *(continued)*
>
> later. For many, this failure was part of a culture of historical exploitation, and the case spurred discussion of the bioethical issues involved.
>
> Lacks's life story was told in the 2010 book *The Immortal Life of Henrietta Lacks* by Rebecca Skloot. In 2013, an agreement was reached with her family, Johns Hopkins, and the National Institutes of Health (NIH) that now requires scientists to receive permission from a committee to use Lacks's genetic blueprint or HeLa cells in NIH-funded research. Further, Johns Hopkins and the family announced in 2018 that a new research building on the university's East Baltimore campus would be named in her honor (Johns Hopkins Medicine 2021).
>
> In the revised Common Rule, the definition of "human subject" has been modified to now include identifiable biospecimens. Identifiable biospecimens and identifiable private data are now treated in the same way.

FUTURE ETHICAL CHALLENGES

Many of the early examples in this chapter involving research ethics were historical cases. These cases have led to a better understanding of ethical principles in research and subsequent regulations to protect the health of research participants while enhancing medical care. The *Belmont Report* highlighted this balance of risks and benefits—not just to future patients or society, but the participants themselves.

Ethical issues in research are and will continue to be relevant to healthcare in the future. Current and future ethical issues are discussed as part of the Varsity Medical Ethics Debates, which have been conducted since 2008 between students at Oxford and Cambridge Universities. The debates focus on controversial topics in healthcare involving ethics and policy, such as whether genetic information should be patented and whether cognitive enhancement drugs should be available by prescription.

The latest published debate concerned the increased use of constant health monitoring devices. These include devices for self-diagnosis, such as small electrocardiogram recorders to diagnose atrial fibrillation, continuous glucose monitoring devices for diabetic patients, MHealth apps, and telemonitoring devices (Gilmartin et al. 2018). Chapter 6 discussed the use of artificial intelligence (AI) technology to provide breast cancer care. Looking to the future, AI is likely to revolutionize many aspects of our lives, including healthcare delivery. These technologies offer the potential to increase patient autonomy, simplify disease management, and improve connections between patients and providers. But achieving the benefits of associated research on medical technologies will require developers, providers, regulators, and healthcare managers to work together to fully consider the biomedical research risks related to respect for patients, beneficence, and justice.

Mini-Case Study: Groupthink and the Tuskegee Study

Why did the researchers involved in the Tuskegee Study continue their experiment long after the discovery of penicillin as a treatment for syphilis and after the development of the **Nuremberg Code**? Experts suggest that **groupthink** is the answer (Braithwaite, Griffin, and De La Rosa 2011).

    Groupthink exists in cohesive groups—groups with an "esprit de corps." Irving Janis (1971, 43), the research psychologist who developed the theory and coined the term, defined groupthink as the "mode of thinking that persons engage in when concurrence-seeking becomes so dominant in a cohesive ingroup that it tends to override realistic appraisals of alternative courses of action." Three types of groupthink exist:

- Type I: Overestimation of the group's power and morality
- Type II: Closed-mindedness
- Type III: Pressure of uniformity

    To understand how groupthink played a role in the decisions of the PHS researchers involved in the Tuskegee Study, consider the following background information about the PHS and its researchers.

> **Nuremberg Code**
> A set of ten statements requiring that human participation in research must be voluntary and informed.
>
> **groupthink**
> A manner of thinking in which every member of the group supports the dominant perspective and thus fails to consider alternative or contradictory ideas.

The US Public Health Service in Historical Context

The PHS dates back to 1798, when it was called the Marine Hospital Service and provided hospital care for sick merchant seamen (Reverby 2009). In 1912, it became officially known as the Public Health Service and was charged by the federal government with overseeing all its health activities.

    The PHS was built on a military model; it had a commissioned corps of medical officers led by a surgeon general. The commissioned officers were considered the medical elite, as passing the PHS exams to become an officer was more difficult than passing state medical board exams (Reverby 2009). Once commissioned, officers were moved from station to station and taught by experienced senior medical officers. This model engendered esprit de corps, loyalty to the PHS, and a cohesive network of officers who had the special relationship of being friends, teachers, and students.

    As part of their medical research, PHS researchers conducted auto-experimentation—that is, they exposed themselves to diseases and thus made themselves the subjects of their research. Walter Reed and his three colleagues—Jesse Lazear, James Carroll, and Aristides

Agramonte—conducted auto-experimentation on yellow fever from 1900 through 1901. In August 1900, at Columbia Barracks, a US military base near Havana, Cuba, Carroll and Lazear allowed mosquitoes to bite them. Both men developed yellow fever, and Lazear's case turned fatal on September 25, 1900. This tradition of self-sacrifice imbued the PHS medical researchers with a sense of martyrdom in the name of science (Reverby 2009).

The Tuskegee Study

In 1918, under congressional mandate, the PHS created a special unit to combat venereal diseases, called the Division of Venereal Diseases (or VD Division). PHS officers of the VD Division saw themselves as elite crusaders and called themselves "syphilis men" (Jones 2008).

In the late 1920s, researchers from the VD Division conducted studies to determine the prevalence of syphilis among African Americans in the rural South and to investigate the possibilities of mass treatment (Brandt 1978). These studies were funded by the Julius Rosenwald Fund. After the Wall Street crash of 1929, however, the Rosenwald Fund could no longer finance the studies. To "salvage" what the researchers had found during their initial studies, the chief of the VD Division, Dr. Taliaferro Clark, proposed an experiment using living people (Thomas and Quinn 1991). That was the root of the Tuskegee Study, which began in 1932 and over the years enrolled 600 African American men—399 of whom had untreated syphilis and 201 of whom did not have the disease.

High-ranking PHS medical officers and researchers were involved in the Tuskegee Study. Dr. Clark was not only the chief of the VD Division but also the assistant surgeon general at the time. Other officers involved during the first ten years of the Tuskegee Study were Dr. Hugh Cumming, the surgeon general when the study commenced, and Dr. Raymond A. Vonderlehr, the assistant surgeon general who succeeded Dr. Clark. All three officers were graduates of the medical school at the University of Virginia (Lombardo and Dorr 2006). In 1933, when Dr. Clark retired, Dr. Vonderlehr became chief of the VD Division. He was especially committed to continuing the experiment because of his scientific interest in the cardiovascular complications of syphilis. Over the next 40 years, the PHS's policy of promoting from within resulted in VD Division chiefs who had worked on the Tuskegee Study early in their careers (Jones 2008). Beginning in 1936, the researchers published their findings in scholarly medical journals, such as the *Journal of the American Medical Association* and *Public Health Reports*. By the end of the Tuskegee Study in 1972, the researchers had published more than a dozen research articles about the men in the study and the toll of their disease (Reverby 2009).

Initially, the study was meant to be short term, lasting six months to eight months. However, after Dr. Vondelehr became chief of the VD Division, the Tuskegee Study was modified to become a "death as end-point study" (Brandt 1978). The researchers did not tell the 399 men who had syphilis that they had the disease. Instead, the men were led to believe that they were receiving special treatment for their "bad blood" (Katz 1992). This "treatment," however, was not the conventional treatment for syphilis but rather consisted only of vitamins and aspirin (Reverby 2001).

Efforts to retain the men as experiment subjects and to prevent the treatment of their syphilis were extraordinary (Thomas and Quinn 1991). For example, the PHS researchers tracked the men to other public health departments, intervened with local physicians, and blocked them from being drafted into military service during World War II (drafted soldiers were routinely treated) (Katz 1992; Reverby 2001). In 1951, when penicillin became the standard medical intervention for syphilis, the researchers continued to deny treatment, insisting that the study was all the more urgent because it afforded a unique opportunity that would not come again (Jones 1981). As a result, the Tuskegee Study became the "longest nontherapeutic experiment on human beings in medical history" (Jones 1981, 91).

For the first 24 years of the study, no one in the PHS ordered or performed a periodic reassessment of the study's scientific value or ethics. However, in 1956, its first external criticism was made. Dr. Count Gibson heard Dr. Sidney Olansky of the PHS speak about the Tuskegee Study. After reading published articles on the study, Dr. Gibson wrote Dr. Olansky to question its ethics. However, Dr. Gibson was convinced by colleagues that questioning the PHS was inadvisable if he wanted a successful career (Reverby 2009). In 1957, in the 25th year of the study, the PHS held a meeting at which the decision was made to continue the study and to give the subjects fake treatments of iron tonics and aspirin, "special certificates of participation" signed by the surgeon general, and $1.00 for every year of "service."

In the late 1950s and the 1960s, discussions of ethics in medical research began in earnest. In the mid-1960s, the PHS and the Tuskegee Study came under the oversight of the Communicable Disease Center (now the Centers for Disease Control and Prevention [CDC]). In 1965, PHS researchers decided that the study still served a purpose and rationalized the "racial aspects of the experiment" (Brandt 1978, 26; Reverby 2009). In 1966, the surgeon general issued Policy and Procedure Order 129 (see exhibit 8.1), which required institutions receiving PHS research grants to put mechanisms in place to protect human subjects. Technically, the order did not apply to the PHS's own research studies; ethically, however, PHS researchers should have complied in the true spirit of the order. Unfortunately, they remained morally blind.

THE WHISTLEBLOWER

Fortunately, Peter Buxton was not blind to the immorality of the Tuskegee Study. Buxton was a PHS psychiatric social worker who investigated cases of venereal disease in San Francisco (Jones 2008). Upon learning about the study in 1966, he conducted his own investigation, wrote multiple letters, and met with PHS officials to express his concerns (Jones 2008). He made parallels between the study and the Nazi's experiments at concentration camps (Reverby 2009). As a result of his complaints, in 1969, the CDC convened a blue-ribbon panel to consider whether the Tuskegee Study should be continued. Only one panel member—who was unfamiliar with the study—insisted that the study be terminated and that the men receive treatment for their condition (Lederer 2005). That panel member was outvoted. In 1967, Buxton resigned from the PHS to attend law school.

In 1972, Buxton, after finishing law school, decided to pursue the termination of the Tuskegee Study. He showed copies of the published research articles and his correspondence with PHS officials to Edith Lederer, an Associated Press reporter (Jones 2008). Lederer forwarded the materials to her superiors at the Associated Press, who gave the story to Jean Heller, another of its reporters. Heller conducted telephone interviews with CDC officials who confirmed the study's existence (Jones 2008). The CDC officials stated that the PHS physicians were rendering medical services to the survivors and continuing to investigate syphilis's effects on the men (Heller 1972). On July 25, 1972, Heller broke the story, titled "Syphilis Victims in U.S. Study Went Untreated for 40 Years," in the *Washington Star*, and it was reprinted by the *New York Times* the following day. A public outcry ensued. In August 1972, the CDC convened the Tuskegee Syphilis Study Ad Hoc Advisory Panel. On the panel's recommendation, HHS Assistant Secretary of Health Dr. Merlin K. DuVal terminated the Tuskegee Study on November 16, 1972 (DuVal 1972).

MINI-CASE STUDY QUESTIONS

1. Which types of groupthink do you believe the PHS researchers and CDC officials showed? Support your choices with evidence from the Mini-Case Study.
2. How do the historical and cultural background of the PHS, its researchers, and the CDC relate to the groupthink types you chose?
3. Janis (1982) explains that groupthink leads to poor decision-making as a result of seven defects:

    a. Incomplete survey of alternatives
    b. Incomplete survey of objectives
    c. Failure to examine the risks of the preferred choice
    d. Failure to reappraise initially rejected alternatives
    e. Poor information search
    f. Selective bias in processing information at hand
    g. Failure to work out contingency plans

    Which defects of decision-making do you see in the decisions of the PHS researchers and the CDC?
4. To avoid poor decision-making as a result of groupthink, how can you, as a healthcare manager, use the ethical decision-making process framework and steps described in chapter 7 (see exhibit 7.1)?
5. What forces other than groupthink could explain the PHS researchers' decisions?

Points to Remember

➤ US biomedical researchers have conducted experiments on vulnerable human beings, such as prisoners, children and minors, intellectually disabled people, terminally ill or comatose patients, and economically or educationally disadvantaged people.

➤ Commonly cited examples of notorious US human experiments are the Tuskegee Study, the Sexually Transmitted Disease Inoculation Study, the Willowbrook Hepatitis Studies, the Jewish Chronic Disease Hospital Study, the Fernald School Study, and the Wrentham State School Study.

➤ Key documents that underpin ethical perspectives and current regulations in the United States are the National Research Act, the *Belmont Report*, and the Common Rule.

➤ An institutional review board is an administrative body established to protect the rights and welfare of human research subjects recruited to participate in research activities associated with healthcare organizations and other institutions.

➤ Several past cases of research misconduct—such as falsifying studies, fabricating data and results, and plagiarism—resulted in federal regulation over research integrity, but such examples of misconduct continue today.

➤ The Health Insurance Portability and Accountability Act of 1996 requires that researchers obtain a signed authorization before using or disclosing protected health information for research.

➤ Federal agencies enforcing the rules and regulations protecting the rights and welfare of research subjects and research integrity include the Office for Human Research Protections, the Office of Research Integrity, and the Office for Civil Rights, all under the US Department of Health and Human Services.

➤ The prevention of scientific misconduct and ways to ensure the integrity of findings and public trust in the science behind healthcare remain important topics.

Challenge Yourself

1. The term "research subjects" has been replaced with "research participants." What do you see as the significance of this change in language? Is the term "subjects" dehumanizing?
2. You are the associate vice president for operations at a large academic health center. One of your subordinates, the director of facilities and capital planning, who recently earned a master of health administration degree, has expressed interest in serving on the health center's IRB. What response will you give this subordinate?

3. List three experiments discussed in the chapter that violated all three ethical principles on which, per the *Belmont Report*, responsible research must be founded. Explain how these experiments violated the three principles.
4. You receive a letter from the OHRP. The letter states that its team will be visiting your site on a compliance audit. What are your thoughts?
5. You are a healthcare manager. You have heard through the grapevine that a few of your organization's researchers on a project involving patients are "exploiting" what they believe to be a loophole in the Common Rule. Should you be concerned?
6. Most universities require ethical training for students involved in research. One such study course is provided by the Collaborative Institutional Training Initiative (CITI). Learn whether your institution provides access to CITI or a similar training course and complete the research ethics course provided.

For Your Consideration

8.1 People use a variety of heuristics (rules of thumb) as quick checks on the ethics and ethical implications of their behavior or intended actions. These ethics heuristics include the following:

- *Golden rule.* Do unto others as you would have them do unto you. Put yourself in other people's shoes.
- *Media attention.* Can your reasoning, justification, and actions withstand public scrutiny? Would your parents, teachers, religious leaders, and friends be proud or ashamed to read about you and your actions on the front page of your local newspaper? What if the local television news team arrived with its reporter and camera operator to interview you, your staff, and your superiors? What if your actions went viral on the internet or social media?
- *Role model.* Would you be comfortable for a young person who looks up to you as a role model to see and understand your actions? Are you setting the example of practicing what you preach? Do you want that young person to emulate your behavior?
- *Worst-case scenario.* What is the worst possible outcome of this action? Can you, and are you willing, to live with this bad outcome? Would you be proud of yourself and be willing to share the outcome with your college classmates?

Reliance on heuristics can undermine decision-making and problem-solving. Therefore, while heuristics can function as quick checks, they should not be used as a substitute for systematic and methodical ethical decision-making.

    a. Prioritize the heuristics. Which rule of thumb makes the most sense for you? Why?
    b. Describe a time that you used a heuristic. How did that work for you?

c. As a healthcare manager, what could possibly go wrong if you always followed the golden rule?
d. Can you think of some potential negative effects of using heuristics?

8.2 From 1845 to 1849, Dr. J. Marion Sims experimented on several African American slaves to develop a surgical treatment for vesicovaginal fistula, a common debilitating condition of the era (Sims 1852, 1884). Three of these subjects were Anarcha, Betsey, and Lucy. Their suffering led to the discovery of a successful treatment for the condition.

Vesicovaginal fistula is an abnormal tract or hole that develops between the bladder and the vagina following an obstructed childbirth. The abnormal tract allows urine to continuously flow into the vagina. Sometimes the tract extends to the rectum (rectovaginal fistula), causing a constant dribble of fecal matter and the release of gas. The condition is miserable for women as it produces a stench, skin ulceration, and infection.

For discovering the successful treatment for vesicovaginal fistula and other innovative inventions, Dr. Sims became known as the father of gynecology. While searching for treatment, he designed medical instruments, including the speculum, and discovered a position for gynecological examination and surgery (Sartin 2004). Initially reluctant to treat gynecological problems, he planned to send Lucy back to her owner, who had sent her to him for treatment of her condition (which turned out to be vesicovaginal fistula). But that very day, while figuring out a way to manipulate a white patient's inverted uterus, he discovered a position that would enable him to perform gynecological examinations. He then knew how to examine Lucy.

From that point on, Dr. Sims "ransacked the county" for cases of vesicovaginal fistula (Sims 1884, 236). He first found Anarcha and Betsey and then other women slaves. He obtained their owners' permission to keep them for surgical experiments. Anarcha, Betsey, Lucy, and the other women were kept in what he termed a "little hospital," which actually was an "old hut" at the back of his property (Moir 1940, 778; Sims 1884, 230).

The surgeries were performed without anesthesia, as the use of ether was still relatively unknown and controversial (Wall 2006). Anarcha, who had both a vesicovaginal fistula and a rectovaginal fistula, underwent 30 surgeries to repair the holes. Betsey, Lucy, and the other women also underwent up to 30 surgeries each. About 40 surgeries failed because of infections and wound breakdown. He persevered because he believed he "was on the eve of one of the greatest discoveries of the day" and could improve the operation with each attempt (Sims 1884, 235, 237).

In 1853, Dr. Sims moved to New York City and became a teacher and leading surgeon on the medical staff of Women's Hospital, a charity hospital. There, throughout the 1850s and 1860s, he performed surgeries on poor female Irish immigrants (Sartin 2004).

a. Under what circumstances is it appropriate to use people as a means to an end, such as a medical discovery that alleviates pain and suffering for humanity?

b. Were Anarcha, Betsey, Lucy, and the other women able to give voluntary consent?
c. What ethical principles related to conducting research are involved in this case?
d. Do you perceive other ethical issues in this case?

CHECK THESE OUT

Want more information about the organizations and concepts discussed in the chapter? Check these websites out.

- *Belmont Report*: www.hhs.gov/ohrp/regulations-and-policy/belmont-report/index.html
- *Code of Federal Regulations*: www.ecfr.gov
- HIPAA Privacy Rule: www.hhs.gov/ocr/privacy/hipaa/administrative/privacyrule/
- Nuremberg Code: https://history.nih.gov/display/history/Nuremberg+Code
- Office for Civil Rights (OCR): www.hhs.gov/ocr/office/
- Office for Human Research Protections (OHRP): www.hhs.gov/ohrp/
  - Compliance Oversight: www.hhs.gov/ohrp/compliance/
- Office of Research Integrity (ORI): https://ori.hhs.gov/
- ORI Misconduct Case Summaries: https://ori.hhs.gov/case_summary
- Presidential Commission for the Study of Bioethical Issues: https://bioethicsarchive.georgetown.edu/pcsbi/history.html

REFERENCES

Advisory Committee on Human Radiation Experiments. 1995. *Final Report: White House Advisory Committee on Human Radiation Experiments*. Accessed September 8, 2021. http://archive.org/details/advisorycommitte00unit.

Boetto, E., D. Golinelli, G. Carullo, and M. P. Fantini. 2020. "Frauds in Scientific Research and How to Possibly Overcome Them." *Journal of Medical Ethics*. Published October 6. https://doi.org/10.1136/medethics-2020-106639.

Braithwaite, R., J. Griffin, and M. De La Rosa. 2011. "The Southern Male Placebo Study: The Good, the Bad, and the Ugly." In *The Search for the Legacy of the USPHS Syphilis Study at Tuskegee*, edited by R. V. Katz and R. C. Warren, 59–68. Lanham, MD: Rowman & Littlefield.

Brandt, A. M. 1978. "Racism and Research: The Case of the Tuskegee Syphilis Study." *Hastings Center Report* 8 (6): 21–29.

Buchanan, A. 1996. "Judging the Past: The Case of the Human Radiation Experiments." *Hastings Center Report* 26 (3): 25–30.

Bülow, W., and G. Helgesson. 2019. "Criminalization of Scientific Misconduct." *Medicine, Health Care, and Philosophy* 22 (2): 245–52.

Dal-Re, R., L. Bouter, P. Cuijpers, C. Gluud, and S. Holm. 2020. "Should Research Misconduct be Criminalized?" *Research Ethics* 16 (1–2): 1–12.

DuVal, M. K. 1972. "Memorandum Terminating the Tuskegee Syphilis Study, 11/16/1972." Accessed August 5, 2021. http://research.archives.gov/description/650716.

Garfield, E., and A. Welljams-Dorof. 1990. "The Impact of Fraudulent Research on the Scientific Literature: The Stephen E. Breuning Case." *Journal of the American Medical Association* 263 (10): 1424–26.

Gilmartin, C., E. H. Arbe-Barnes, M. Diamond, S. Fretwell, E. McGivern, M. Vlazaki, and L. Zhu. 2018. "Varsity Medical Ethics Debate 2018: Constant Health Monitoring—the Advance of Technology into Healthcare." *Philosophy, Ethics, and Humanities in Medicine* 13: Article 12.

Godlee, F., J. Smith, and H. Marcovitch. 2011. "Wakefield's Article Linking MMR Vaccine and Autism Was Fraudulent." *British Medical Journal* 342: c7452.

Heller, J. 1972. "Syphilis Victims in U.S. Study Went Untreated for 40 Years." *New York Times*, July 26.

Hippocrates. 400 BCE. "Book I. Section II. Second Constitution." In *Of the Epidemics*, translated by F. Adams. Internet Classics Archive. Accessed August 5, 2021. http://classics.mit.edu//Hippocrates/epidemics.html.

Janis, I. L. 1982. *Groupthink: Psychological Studies of Policy Decisions and Fiascoes*, 2nd ed. Boston: Houghton Mifflin.

———. 1971. "Groupthink." *Psychology Today Magazine* 5 (6): 43–44, 74–76.

Johns Hopkins Medicine. 2021. "The Legacy of Henrietta Lacks." Accessed April 3. www.hopkinsmedicine.org/henriettalacks/index.html.

Jones, J. H. 2008. "The Tuskegee Syphilis Experiment." In *The Oxford Textbook of Clinical Research Ethics*, edited by E. J. Emanuel, C. Grady, R. A. Crouch, R. K. Lie, F. G. Miller, and D. Wendler, 86–96. New York: Oxford University Press.

———. 1981. *Bad Blood: The Tuskegee Syphilis Experiment*. New York: Free Press.

Katz, J. 1992. "Abuse of Human Beings for the Sake of Science." In *When Medicine Went Mad: Bioethics and the Holocaust*, edited by A. L. Caplan, 233–70. Totowa, NJ: Humana Press.

Katz, J., A. M. Capron, and E. S. Glass. 1972. *Experimentation with Human Beings: The Authority of the Investigator, Subject, Professions, and State in the Human Experimentation Process*. New York: Russell Sage Foundation.

Lederer, S. E. 2005. "Experimentation on Human Beings." *OAH Magazine of History* 19 (5): 20–22.

Lombardo, P. A., and G. M. Dorr. 2006. "Eugenics, Medical Education, and the Public Health Service: Another Perspective on the Tuskegee Syphilis Experiment." *Bulletin of the History of Medicine* 80 (2): 291–316.

Mann, C. C. 1994. "Radiation: Balancing the Record." *Science* 263 (5146): 470–73.

Moir, C. 1940. "J. Marion Sims and the Vesico-Vaginal Fistula: Then and Now." *British Medical Journal* 2 (4170): 773–78.

National Commission for the Protection of Human Subjects of Biomedical and Behavioral Research. 1979. *The Belmont Report: Ethical Principles and Guidelines for the Protection of Human Subjects of Research*. Accessed August 5, 2021. www.hhs.gov/ohrp/regulations-and-policy/belmont-report/index.html.

Office for Human Research Protections (OHRP). 2017. "Revised Common Rule." Accessed March 28, 2021. www.hhs.gov/ohrp/regulations-and-policy/regulations/finalized-revisions-common-rule/index.html.

Presidential Commission for the Study of Bioethical Issues. 2011. *"Ethically Impossible" STD Research in Guatemala from 1946 to 1948*. Accessed August 5, 2021. https://bioethicsarchive.georgetown.edu/pcsbi/sites/default/files/Ethically%20Impossible%20(with%20linked%20historical%20documents)%202.7.13.pdf.

Relman, A. S. 1983. "Lessons from the Darsee Affair." *New England Journal of Medicine* 308 (23): 1415–17.

Reverby, S. 2011. "'Normal Exposure' and Inoculation Syphilis: A PHS 'Tuskegee' Doctor in Guatemala, 1946–1948." *Journal of Policy History* 23 (1): 6–28.

———. 2009. *Examining the Tuskegee Study: The Infamous Syphilis Study and Its Legacy*. Chapel Hill, NC: University of North Carolina Press.

———. 2001. "More Than Fact and Fiction: Cultural Memory and the Tuskegee Syphilis Study." *Hastings Center Report* 31 (5): 22–28.

Rothman, D. J. 1982. "Were Tuskegee and Willowbrook 'Studies in Nature'?" *Hastings Center Report* 12 (2): 5–7.

Sartin, J. S. 2004. "J. Marion Sims, the Father of Gynecology: Hero or Villain?" *Southern Medical Journal* 97 (5): 500–505.

Skloot, R. 2010. *The Immortal Life of Henrietta Lacks*. New York: Broadway Paperbacks.

Sims, J. M. 1884. *The Story of My Life*. New York: D. Appleton and Company.

———. 1852. "On the Treatment of Vesico-Vaginal Fistula." *American Journal of the Medical Sciences* 23 (45): 59–82.

Sottile, D. 2018. "The Ethical Dilemma of Blowing the Whistle: Research Misconduct and Its Reporters." *Hilltop Review* 10 (2): 50–55.

Thomas, S. B., and S. C. Quinn. 1991. "Public Health Then and Now: The Tuskegee Syphilis Study, 1932 to 1972: Implications for HIV Education and AIDS Risk Education Programs in the Black Community." *American Journal of Public Health* 81 (11): 1498–505.

US House of Representatives, Committee on Energy and Commerce, Subcommittee on Energy Conservation and Power. 1986. *American Nuclear Guinea Pigs: Three Decades of Radiation Experiments on U.S. Citizens*. Accessed August 5, 2021. www.osti.gov/opennet/servlets/purl/16007522-IV9agR/16007522.pdf.

Wall, L. L. 2006. "The Medical Ethics of Dr. J. Marion Sims: A Fresh Look at the Historical Record." *Journal of Medical Ethics* 32 (6): 346–50.

World Medical Association (WMA). 2013. "World Medical Association Declaration of Helsinki: Ethical Principles for Medical Research Involving Human Subjects." Accessed August 5, 2021. www.wma.net/policies-post/wma-declaration-of-helsinki-ethical-principles-for-medical-research-involving-human-subjects/.

CHAPTER 9
CLINICAL INTERACTIONS

Ethics is an inherent and inseparable part of clinical medicine as the physician has an ethical obligation (i) to benefit the patient, (ii) to avoid or minimize harm, and to (iii) respect the values and preferences of the patient.
—Basil Varkey, physician and professor emeritus, Medical College of Wisconsin

Important Terms

- Accountability for reasonableness (A4R)
- Best interests standard
- Boundary crossing
- Boundary violation
- Case consultation
- Clinical ethics
- Clinicians
- Cultural humility
- Distributive justice
- Informed consent
- Institutional ethics committee (IEC)
- Mandated reporter
- Persistent vegetative state (PVS)
- Root-cause analysis
- Substituted judgment standard
- Tarasoff duty

Learning Objectives

Studying this chapter will help you to

➤ become familiar with clinical ethics,

➤ summarize the common concerns in clinical ethics,

- describe the history of telehealth and related ethical and legal issues,
- articulate the purposes of an institutional ethics committee and ethics support, and
- understand and discuss the problem of medical errors in healthcare.

This chapter introduces ethical concerns related to the hands-on provision of healthcare and services. Professionals who directly deliver such care and services are generally called **clinicians** (from *clinical*, meaning at the bedside). Clinicians include physicians, nurses, physician assistants, advanced practice nurses, physical therapists, clinical psychologists, social workers or counselors, and other clinical practitioners. This chapter will familiarize you with the common issues in **clinical ethics**. As you read this chapter, reflect on the case presented at the beginning of part II, "How Should Complex Communication Responsibilities Be Distributed in Surgical Education Settings?" The case illustrates some of the difficult ethical questions faced by residents in a medical center when communicating about end-of-life decisions. While some healthcare managers may be clinicians as well, all should be familiar with the ethical issues faced by licensed providers. In this chapter, we examine these ethical issues and illustrate them using some well-known legal cases. In addition, we present an overview of institutional ethics committees and ethical support programs in healthcare organizations.

Clinical ethics and professional codes emphasize the same ethical traditions and principles discussed in previous chapters. These include autonomy, beneficence and nonmaleficence, respect for self and others, honesty and integrity, justice, fidelity, and sanctity of life.

clinician
A professional—such as a physician, nurse, physician assistant, advanced practice nurse, physical therapist, counselor, clinical psychologist, or other clinical practitioner—who provides hands-on healthcare and services.

clinical ethics
A subset of bioethics in which the moral issues arise from the delivery of healthcare and services or from general clinical practice.

> **CASE FROM THE FIELD**
> One Lone Voice
>
> Dr. Frances Oldham Kelsey was a medical reviewer for the US Food and Drug Administration (FDA). In 1960, her very first assignment was to review a drug company's application to market thalidomide in the United States. (Thalidomide was already widely used in Europe to treat nausea in pregnancy.) Dr. Kelsey found the data submitted by the pharmaceutical company to be insufficient, so she requested better data. In response, the company pressured her and her supervisors at the FDA for approval by calling, sending letters, and visiting them "at least weekly over the next two years" (Kuehn 2010). But she held firm, refusing to approve thalidomide in the United States until more tests were conducted that proved its safety.
>
> During that time, reports began to emerge of thousands of infants being born (in other parts of the world) with no limbs or severely deformed limbs, a condition called *phocomelia*.
>
> *(continued)*

> **CASE FROM THE FIELD**
> One Lone Voice *(continued)*
>
> The mothers of these children had taken thalidomide during pregnancy (Kim and Scialli 2011). Subsequently, in late 1961, thalidomide was banned in most countries.
>
> Dr. Kelsey's insistence on putting the drug's approval on hold prevented this tragedy from happening in the United States. In 1962, her action was recognized, and she received the President's Award for Distinguished Federal Civilian Service, the highest honor given to a civilian in the United States.

Principles in Clinical Ethics

Several important considerations arise in discussing ethical issues in clinical care; although they may present in different ways across professions and settings, they are critical for all engaged in clinical care. You might remember the central principles of clinical ethics as the five Cs: competence, consent, confidentiality, crossing boundaries, and culture.

Competence

One might argue that competence is the first ethical directive, as providing less than competent care is unethical. Health professions, including healthcare management, have moved toward specifying the competencies (learned through professional training programs) that are necessary for licensure and practice. In chapter 2, we encountered an unthinking healthcare manager who participated in a surgical operation and lost his job for doing so. However, even among licensed professionals, there is an ethical obligation to know the limits of one's training and preparation.

Physicians, nurses, psychologists, and other healthcare professionals are not necessarily prepared to work with all clinical conditions or populations (e.g., pediatric or geriatric medicine), but limit their activities to areas in which they have received training and supervision. In situations in which they may have limited experience but are still the best provider (e.g., in a rural area), they may seek additional training and consultation in providing care. For example, psychologists trained as mental health professionals may not be prepared to work on an integrative primary care team without further training in health psychology, as the role and function of a psychologist in that setting are very different from a traditional mental health agency. Moreover, most clinicians are mandated by their professional boards to complete continuing education training throughout their career to maintain competence.

In addition to intellectual competence involving attaining the relevant knowledge and skills needed, competence also involves emotional competence. The latter refers to the capacity to manage affective reactions and personal problems that could interfere with providing care. Clinicians who are struggling with their own mental health issues, such as depression, substance use, or other forms of personal distress, must take the necessary actions to avoid practicing while impaired. These actions might include personal treatment, consultation, or even stepping away from practice temporarily. Thus, all clinicians have an ethical obligation to maintain self-care.

INFORMED CONSENT

All clinicians and members of the healthcare community respect the right of their patients (or clients and residents) and their healthcare surrogates (or agents) to make informed decisions that either consent to or refuse treatment.

Informed consent is an established patient right that is ensured by ethical standards, healthcare organizations' policies, accreditation standards, and federal and state laws. The ethical basis of informed consent is autonomy—the right of self-determination. Also known as "respect for persons," the concept of autonomy was fully developed in the *Belmont Report*, discussed in chapter 8 (National Commission for the Protection of Human Subjects of Biomedical and Behavioral Research 1979). Healthcare organizations' policies typically mirror patient bills of rights, such as the American Hospital Association's (2021) Patient Care Partnership and the education efforts on patient rights of accrediting bodies such as The Joint Commission (2019).

The legal framework for informed consent was established by a series of pivotal court decisions beginning in the early twentieth century (see exhibit 9.1). These decisions advanced the concept of consent, from requiring consent to touch to obtaining patient consent after the full disclosure of risks and benefits of a treatment or nontreatment.

Informed consent guarantees *competent adults* the right to make autonomous decisions about their health and medical treatment. Informed consent, for the most part, is founded on this competent adult model. Obtaining consent becomes complicated when patients are incompetent or incapacitated, or they are minors. Other difficult situations include patients' unreasonable requests for treatments or services, the use of physical or chemical restraints, and abandonment.

informed consent
A patient's written agreement to receive care, services, diagnostic or therapeutic procedures, and other medical interventions with full knowledge of the risks and benefits.

- ◆ *Incompetent or incapacitated patients.* Conflicts arise when an individual's capacity to decide is uncertain. *Competence* is a legal determination of the degree of mental soundness necessary for a person to make a decision about a specific issue or to carry out a specific act. *Capacity*, on the other hand, is an individual's ability to make an informed decision (Barstow, Shahan, and Roberts 2018). This can be determined by any licensed physician, although

EXHIBIT 9.1
Pivotal Court Decisions Related to Informed Consent

Decision	Year	Key point
Mohr v. Williams	1905	Physicians must obtain permission to violate the bodily integrity of patients.
Pratt v. Davis	1906	Implied consent is limited to emergencies and cases in which patients know the consequences and defer to physicians' professional judgment.
Rolater v. Strain	1913	Patients can set conditions on consent, and physicians cannot exceed the parameters of the agreement.
Schloendorff v. Society of New York Hospital	1914	Competent adults have the right to determine what happens to their bodies; physicians who operate without consent commit an assault and are liable for damages.
Salgo v. Leland Stanford Jr. University Board of Trustees	1957	First legal use of the term *informed consent*; full disclosure should be consistent with physician discretion.
Gray v. Grunnagle	1966	Lack of disclosure of risk resulted in a decision of battery.
Berkey v. Anderson	1969	Lack of disclosure of risk is fraud and deceit.
Canterbury v. Spence	1972	Information disclosed should be what a reasonable patient in a similar situation would require to make an informed decision.
Cobbs v. Grant	1972	The physician has a duty to disclose to the patient all significant perils of a procedure, such as death, bodily harm, and problems of recuperation.
Wilkinson v. Vesey	1972	Decisions to proceed with therapy are *not* solely medical determinations and must reference the patient's values.
Truman v. Thomas	1980	Duty to disclose the risks of no treatment goes beyond battery because there is no touching.

Sources: Data from Faden and Beauchamp (1986); Green and MacKenzie (2007).

physicians may seek a psychiatric or neuropsychological evaluation in making their determination. For these patients, healthcare surrogates or agents, the courts, or others make decisions based on what they believe to be the patient's preferences or in the patient's best interests.

◆ *Minors.* Parents and guardians are responsible for giving informed consent for their underage (minor) children. One complication involving minors is that the definition of the age of majority varies by state, from 18 to 21. Other complications are exceptions to parental consent, such as emancipation and minors' reproductive rights. Emancipated minors are children who are legally independent from their parents. Children who financially support themselves and live on their own are often considered emancipated. In some states, marriage and military service lead to emancipation. Regarding reproductive rights, nonemancipated minors can give legal consent (without their parents or guardians) to receive birth control, get tested for sexually transmitted diseases, obtain prenatal care, and obtain other reproductive services (except for abortion, which requires parental notification, consent, or both in most states). The right of minors to seek treatment varies by state; for example, in some states, teenagers (age 16 and above) may provide consent to receive substance abuse treatment services, although many providers would also try to persuade them to involve their parents. Clinicians working with minors at the behest of parents will also try to obtain the child's assent to treatment in addition to parental consent.

Institutional ethics committees (discussed later in the chapter), the state, and the courts may become involved when the parents' decision places a child's health, well-being, or life in jeopardy. While the state and the courts recognize parents' right of custody and seek to maintain family autonomy, they also protect children's best interests.

◆ *Other difficult issues.* Clinicians have no duty to concede to patients' unreasonable requests for medical services that are known to be ineffective. For example, if a patient requests antibiotics when she has no infection, her doctor is under no obligation to prescribe the antibiotics. Less clear, however, are instances in which the patient or his family members request services because they believe the services are beneficial to or maintain the life of the patient, but the team of clinicians deems them futile (see chapter 7 for the discussion of medical futility).

Physical and chemical restraints may be used when patients become agitated or delirious or endanger themselves or others. For example, if an agitated patient is pulling out her IV (intravenous) line and puts herself in harm's way, then the clinicians on duty can use physical restraints (such as vests, straps, belts, and limb ties) or chemical restraints (such as sedatives) to control the behavior.

Abandonment is the "unilateral withdrawal by a physician from a patient's care without first formally transferring that care to another qualified physician who is acceptable to the patient" (Pellegrino 1995, 377). In other words, clinicians cannot abandon—or "fire"—patients, even if they become uncooperative. If a patient refuses treatment or is otherwise unwilling to listen to a clinician, the clinician would ethically provide treatment alternatives and referral supporting the patient during the transition.

Informed consent—whether it is obtained from a competent adult, a parent or guardian (for a minor), a surrogate or agent (for an incapacitated person), or an emancipated minor—operates under the ethical principles of autonomy, beneficence, nonmaleficence, honesty, and justice.

Confidentiality

Another central ethical principle for all clinicians is respect for patient confidentiality, which is written into all professional ethics codes and usually state law. It is considered unethical for a healthcare provider to reveal a person's status as a patient and certainly any private health information. In addition to failing to meet an ethical obligation, such disclosures violate regulations under the Health Insurance Portability and Accountability Act (HIPAA) of 1996 and may result in legal actions.

Healthcare agencies are in violation of patient confidentiality when an employee leaks the status or clinical information of a celebrity patient. There have been numerous health record scandals (and HIPAA violations) involving celebrities who have had their medical records leaked to the public. For example, the University of California, Los Angeles, Health System agreed to pay $865,500 as part of a settlement with federal regulators after two celebrity patients alleged that hospital employees had broken the law and reviewed their medical records without authorization (Lewis 2011). As we have seen, patient information must not be shared with others who are not involved in their care, with the exception of the minimal information allowed to those involved in processing required insurance or billing information. Other disclosures require a signed authorization or release from the patient to share their clinical records.

Some limits to confidentiality have been recognized (e.g., when a person is considered an imminent danger to self or others); these exceptions generally are covered in the organization's informed consent policy. For example, clinicians may break confidentiality to protect a patient from death by suicide if there is no alternative to lower that risk. In some states, clinicians may also have a duty to warn potential or intended victims—if they are identifiable and in imminent danger—of a risk that is foreseeable and serious. This duty to warn is known as the **Tarasoff duty**, so called for the 1974 California court ruling that first articulated this responsibility. In healthcare, the duty to warn applies to counselors, psychologists, and psychiatrists, whose clients may make statements threatening other people. State laws vary in recognizing this duty and how this duty is best balanced with confidentiality. In some states, the duty to protect may be best fulfilled by hospitalizing or otherwise protecting the patient and others.

In addition, physicians and other clinicians who receive the results of diagnostic tests (such as a patient's HIV-positive status) may be **mandated reporters**, bound by a duty to report the findings to the area health department, which may engage in contact tracing and testing to prevent disease (Elger, Michaud, and Mangin 2010).

In the duty to warn, the ethical principles of beneficence and fidelity are in conflict. However, the duty to warn or protect may override patient confidentiality. Moreover, HIPAA recognizes that disclosing a patient's health information to law enforcement, family members, and other people may be necessary to protect the patient and others from serious and imminent harm.

Tarasoff duty
The duty to warn a potential or intended victim about an imminent danger or threat recognized in many jurisdictions.

mandated reporter
An individual who holds a professional position (e.g., healthcare provider, counselor, teacher) and is required by state law to report specified information to an appropriate agency (e.g., child abuse to social services).

> **DID YOU KNOW?**
> *Tarasoff v. Regents of the University of California*
>
> In August 1969, during an outpatient therapy session, Prosenjit Poddar, a student of the University of California, Berkeley, specifically told his psychologist at the university's hospital that he was going to kill Tatiana Tarasoff, another student, when she returned from a summer in Brazil. The psychologist diagnosed Poddar with paranoid schizophrenia and alerted campus police of his threat. Notably, however, the psychologist did not warn Tarasoff or her family. Campus police took Poddar into custody but released him after he promised to stay away from Tarasoff. The director of the hospital's psychiatry department declined to place Poddar in a 72-hour hold in the hospital. On October 27, 1969, when Tarasoff returned from Brazil, Poddar murdered her.
>
> Tarasoff's parents brought a wrongful death suit against the Regents of the University of California, the campus police, and the hospital's psychotherapists. In December 1974, the California Supreme Court ruled that all of these parties were immune from suit. However, the ruling specified that a psychologist has the duty to warn a potential victim. In 1985, the California legislature codified the Tarasoff rule in state law, stating that psychotherapists have a duty to protect or warn a third party if they believe a patient poses a serious risk of inflicting bodily injury to an identifiable person. This decision sparked a national conversation, and as a result, healthcare professionals today have the affirmative duty to warn and take action to protect potential targets of danger.

Relatedly, providing appropriate and accurate documentation of clinical services is a clinical, ethical, and legal responsibility for clinicians. Increasingly, clinical notes are written and maintained in electronic health records (discussed in chapter 13). The sharing of electronic health records among multiple professionals poses challenging questions in terms of confidentiality and what information is appropriate to share. For example, it may be appropriate for a psychologist to share that a patient undergoing surgery has a history of trauma without elaborating on the details of that trauma (Ashton and Sullivan 2018). Patients should be aware of what information will be shared with other professionals, and in all cases, notes should be brief, relevant, and respectfully written with the patient's interest and voice (empowerment) in mind.

Crossing/Not Crossing Boundaries

Clinicians take on a special professional role in providing healthcare in which it is understood that the purpose of the relationship is to aid the patient and improve their well-being. The term *boundaries* refers to the rules that guide the professional relationship and set it apart from other types of relationships. Ethical issues can arise when a provider interacts with patients in additional or multiple roles, crossing patient–clinician boundaries. For example, it is universally understood that providers should not date or become intimately involved with their patients; in fact, this is considered a crime in many states (LaMance 2018).

Other types of relationships can create conflicts of interest for healthcare providers and negatively affect clinical decisions or care. For example, if a provider has a secondary business relationship with a patient and the business venture is unsuccessful, this could negatively affect the patient–provider relationship and the patient's care. In addition, consider the situation of a physician who regularly works with geriatric patients as part of a hospital service. She decides to invest in a new private MRI center and begins to send her patients there. Although the referrals may be appropriate, it certainly has the appearance of a conflict of interest, because she has a financial interest at stake. There is even a danger that the physician could be accused of making some referrals that are unnecessary. Although this situation may be perhaps ambiguous, clinicians should never receive money directly from making referrals—referred to as *kickbacks*. Any payments received should be for providing clinical services and not for the referrals themselves.

Other dual or multiple roles (e.g., family friend, accepting invitations or gifts) fall into a gray area, particularly in smaller communities. Not every **boundary crossing** is a **boundary violation** or unethical. The Ethics Code for Nurses states that when acting within one's role as a professional, nurses recognize and maintain boundaries that establish appropriate limits on relationships (Washington State Nurses Service Organization 2016).

The ethics codes for the health professions vary somewhat in how they address the issue of multiple roles. The ethical guidelines of the American Medical Association allow physicians considerable autonomy but state that the responsibility to patient care should

---

boundary crossing
A deviation from an established professional role or boundary that may or may not be for a therapeutic purpose (e.g., provider self-disclosure, checking in on a former patient).

boundary violation
A boundary crossing that creates a reasonable risk of exploitation or harming the patient's care.

be paramount. In their ethics code, psychologists are advised to refrain from entering any relationship if it could reasonably be expected to impair their objectivity or effectiveness or risk harm to the patient. Randall Reitz and colleagues (2013) address navigating multiple roles in the special case of healthcare organizations involved in teaching or healthcare education, where clinicians may have complex relationships with learners whom they also supervise. For example, clinical supervisors should not prescribe medications to their students or serve as therapists, although they may provide support and referrals to those who need assistance. This model, which encourages greater role awareness and decision-making to ensure an appropriate level of engagement in roles other than the primary role (in this case, clinical faculty), is valuable for all clinicians to consider.

Cultural Competence

The final C for cultural competence refers to the obligation of clinicians to develop the knowledge and skills necessary to serve patients who are different from themselves. Although this duty is a part of overall professional competence, it is highlighted in training programs as a reminder that the United States is a diverse society and the ethical principle of justice requires clinicians to provide competent healthcare to all. Members of ethnic groups (e.g., Black or African Americans, Hispanic or Latino persons, Asian Americans, Muslims) bring their own specific cultural histories, cultural understandings of illness, and attitudes toward medical care. In chapter 8, we saw how the history of racism in the conduct of medical research, as in the Tuskegee Study, has affected attitudes toward hospitals and physicians among some Black or African Americans. Healthcare providers must understand the cultural factors affecting each patient and be able to engage in effective communication to establish a trusting relationship. They must be sensitive to language needs (including the appropriate use of medical interpreters), health literacy, and the role of the patient's family in care.

In addition to learning about the culture and community of patients, clinicians should adopt an attitude of **cultural humility** to be respectful of all patients' cultural identities and open to the opportunities to explore multicultural issues that affect them. Cultural humility is considered a necessary professional competence for healthcare administrators if they are to work effectively in today's healthcare environment. Curriculum content and experiential learning about diversity in training programs promotes awareness of personal blind spots and allows for more effective communication (Russell, Augustin, and Jones 2017).

The idea of culture encompasses many considerations beyond race and ethnicity. For example, clinicians serving patients in the armed forces need to understand military culture, and clinicians must also acquire professional competence in working with individuals with disabilities. Healthcare managers should be familiar with their organization's compliance with the federal Americans with Disabilities Act and any language or other special services offered. For example, is the organization's website accessible to those with visual impairments?

cultural humility
Taking a humble and respectful interpersonal stance toward individuals from other cultures that involves challenging one's own cultural biases and approaching learning about other cultures as a lifelong process.

Access to care is an important issue because it is a major contributor to societal healthcare inequities (discussed further in chapter 14).

Access to Healthcare Services and Distributive Justice

Individuals and groups may encounter limited access to healthcare and services primarily based on their ability to pay and insurance status in the United States. The ethical principles that pertain to access to care are beneficence, nonmaleficence, and justice.

Under the principles of beneficence and nonmaleficence, clinicians have an ethical duty to act in ways that promote good and minimize harm to their patients. However, ethical conflicts can arise in promoting beneficence. For example, a physician recommends that his 90-year-old male patient with multiple chronic diseases could benefit from a scarce, expensive, direct-acting antiviral drug for hepatitis C. On the other hand, also invoking beneficence, another physician counters that societal interests would be better served if that same drug were given instead to a young patient with hepatitis C, who may live longer than the elderly patient and thus could benefit more from the drug. From a clinical point of view, we must ask, for whom does beneficence prevail—the elderly patient or the young patient? From a societal point of view, the question is, should scarce healthcare resources be consumed by a few patients or distributed across entire populations?

Justice is a widely shared moral value in the United States (Gillon 2020; Menzel 2012). However, people differ in their views on how justice should be achieved. For example, during a pandemic, should vaccines be distributed on a first-come, first-served basis or based on individuals' risk of developing a severe illness? **Distributive justice** is one way to address this question. In this context, distributive justice refers to the unequal allocation of scarce resources according to morally relevant factors (McKneally et al. 1997, 163). More formally, the theory of distributive justice refers to the fair, equitable, and appropriate distribution of healthcare resources determined by justified norms (Varkey 2021, 20). According to this theory, the distribution of healthcare resources may be based on need, effort, contribution, merit, or free-market exchange.

Balancing these principles to arrive at a workable plan is difficult. To fairly prioritize these many considerations, leaders can apply the **accountability for reasonableness (A4R)** theory. A4R theory uses due process to set priorities in healthcare. Its key elements are (1) transparency and explicitness, (2) relevant rationales, (3) appeals procedures, and (4) decision-making that is legally or voluntarily regulated (Daniels 2000; Daniels and Sabin 2008). Physician Basil Varkey (2021) provides an illustrative example of distributive justice in which a city hospital must decide how to allocate an available ventilator between two patients so as to maximize benefits, such as life expectancy, likelihood of survival, and benefit to others. Varkey suggests that such decisions are best made by a select committee that excludes those directly caring for the patients involved.

---

distributive justice
The unequal allocation of scarce resources according to morally relevant factors.

accountability for reasonableness (A4R)
A theory that uses due process to set priorities in healthcare decision-making.

TELEMEDICINE AND TELEHEALTH

Although the terms *telemedicine* and *telehealth* are often used interchangeably, they should be distinguished from one another. The term *telemedicine* was originally used to denote the provision of medical services across distance using telecommunications technology. It first appeared in the literature in the 1970s, and its usage increased in the 1990s. *Telehealth* is an umbrella term that comprises a broader scope of health-related functions, such as education, case management, and administrative tasks. The term *e-health* includes these functions as well as computing applications (Fatehi and Wootton 2012).

It is important to put telemedicine in historical context. It was originally developed to extend access to healthcare services to places that were difficult to serve, such as rural areas and developing countries. It was different in many ways from telehealth today in that it relied on a medical center using older technologies to communicate consultations to on-site providers. For example, Ronald Weinstein and colleagues (2008) describe the development of the Arizona Telemedicine Program, which was centered at the state's medical school and served a variety of independent health organizations across the state. In this early study, the authors discuss the adoption of telehealth policies by the legislature, components of the telemedicine program, and lessons learned in developing, planning, and ongoing assessment of telemedicine services. Through this program, specialty consultations were provided to patients in correctional facilities and to Native Americans living on remote reservations. Importantly, these authors also highlight the need for provider training and having a champion. Many healthcare managers, including the authors of this book, saw organizations invest in telehealth technology, only to see it stored in a corner and not effectively used.

The growth of telehealth services has involved expanding applications and increasing interest in the way such services might reduce healthcare costs (Dorsey and Topol 2016; Kvedar, Coye, and Everett 2014). Joseph Kvedar, Molly Joel Coye, and Wendy Everett (2014), for example, give examples of telehealth applications, such as access to specialty physicians who can read radiologic images and provide consultations, telemonitoring for patients with congestive heart failure, medication adherence programs, and home health programs for veterans. Many of these telehealth projects resulted in positive patient satisfaction and cost savings through the reduction of hospital admissions and stays. There is now evidence that telehealth can positively affect patient outcomes in a variety of disease states relative to control (no telehealth) conditions (DelliFraine and Dansky 2008). For example, telehealth services for the elderly in skilled nursing facilities have been shown to reduce inappropriate use of medication (Badichek 2021).

Clearly, however, some aspects of health delivery, such as physical examinations, are not amenable to telehealth. Further research is needed to determine where and when telehealth services can improve care. Telehealth is no longer provided exclusively within hospitals (where there are large systems and technical support personnel) but increasingly is delivered by telehealth applications directly to the patient's home through a computer or mobile device. A particular area of growth is the use of telehealth to provide psychotherapy remotely (Luxton, Nelson, and Maheu 2016).

Despite the increasing adoption of telemedicine and telehealth, these services have several important limitations (Dorsey and Topol 2016; Nelson 2017), such as legal and regulatory issues involved in providing medical or health services across state jurisdictions, and issues with insurance coverage and reimbursement. In addition, the *digital divide*—the reality that many rural communities and patients of lower socioeconomic status do not have access to telecommunications technology—presents a barrier to the adoption and use of these services.

A number of ethical issues are involved in providing telehealth services (Ananfack Nguefack et al. 2020; Chaet et al. 2017). These include provider competence, providing the best patient care for the person, informed consent, protecting privacy and confidentiality, and promoting justice and equal access.

- *Competence.* Providers must be proficient in the basic use of the technology and able to use it comfortably with patients. Healthcare organizations must provide the necessary training and technical support to ensure that practice standards are met. Standards and guidelines in telemedicine and telehealth have been developed (Krupinski and Bernard 2014), along with interprofessional competencies for telebehavioral health (Maheu et al. 2018).

- *Providing the best patient care for the person.* Patients should be assessed to determine whether they are best served by in-person or telehealth care and which telehealth services best suit them. Often, this requires conducting an in-person assessment of the patient's needs and home environment and considering whether telehealth services can be used in conjunction with or as a supplement to scheduled visits. Some have questioned inappropriateness of a physician informing a patient of an incurable diagnosis using remote technology (Ananfack Nguefack et al. 2020). Providers must also plan to how they can handle any emergency needs that emerge during the practice of telehealth.

- *Informed consent.* As we have seen, providing fully informed consent is an ethical obligation for all care; in the context of telehealth, this includes addressing how telehealth will be employed in patient care, the necessary skills and equipment, and the risks to patient privacy and how they will be mitigated (e.g., encryption).

- *Protecting privacy and confidentiality.* In addition to sharing organizational privacy policies, providers must adhere to guidelines specific to the setting (e.g., providing telehealth in a clinic versus the provider's home), ensure that everyone involved in telehealth is aware of the confidentiality rules, and make certain that confidential information is safeguarded.

◆ *Promoting justice and equal access.* Although telehealth care can improve access to care, healthcare organizations and providers should also advocate for equal access to telehealth services to ensure that certain populations (e.g., the elderly, low-income patients) are not excluded from the benefits of participation in such programs. For example, computers or tablets could be loaned to patients, or providers could provide services by phone in addition to videoconferencing.

Consider what these guidelines might look like for a psychologist providing psychotherapy via telehealth to an adult patient with depression who lives in a remote area. First, the provider might meet with the patient in person to assess the patient's needs and diagnosis, including the risk of suicide. If appropriate, the provider would allow the patient to choose either in-person or telehealth sessions (after discussing the pros and cons of each option); offer a separate telehealth informed consent policy as a supplement to the clinic's regular informed consent policy, specifying the risks and rules of telehealth (e.g., sessions must be conducted at home in a private location); and then conduct an environmental scan of the patient's home and computer setup to ensure that it is appropriate for telehealth. The provider would also need to obtain permission and a release of information for an emergency contact person if they would be unable to reach the patient or have concerns about their welfare.

During the telehealth sessions, the provider would confirm the patient's location and might specify a "safe word" to be used if the patient was no longer in a private location (e.g., someone else walked into the room). The provider would also need to develop a plan (e.g., phone contact) in case the technology failed. This example shows that there is more to telehealth practice than just getting online. Adequate safeguards must be in place for a provider to use telehealth in an ethical manner.

The COVID-19 pandemic accelerated the adoption of telehealth services. Within weeks, many behavioral health providers were forced to go online to continue care. A national survey of more than 2,600 licensed psychologists indicated a 12-fold increase in clinical work using telepsychology, from about 7 percent before to 85 percent during the pandemic; the extent of telehealth use varied by geography, patient population served, and degree of organizational support provided (Pierce et al. 2021). These psychologists projected that they would perform approximately 35 percent of their work virtually after the pandemic. In 2020, telehealth services accounted for 23.6 percent of ambulatory encounters by working-age adults with health insurance. Behavioral health encounters using telehealth outpaced medical contacts, 46 percent to 22 percent (Weiner et al. 2021). In response, the Centers for Medicare & Medicaid Services broadened the range of telehealth services eligible for reimbursement under Medicare; advocates will likely want this greater access to continue after the pandemic.

Telehealth care was not uniformly embraced by everyone, however. For example, the CEO of a Federally Qualified Health Center reported that many of their patients preferred traditional in-person visits with medical providers, and some providers even volunteered to take on more shifts to avoid practicing via telehealth. Although the center had telehealth capabilities, many of its patients did not speak English or had poor Wi-Fi or privacy and therefore preferred to meet in person with their interdisciplinary team. From a high of 35 percent of total visits to this facility, telehealth visits fell over time to 15 percent, leading healthcare administrators to believe that telehealth would not replace traditional healthcare in their setting (Siwicki 2021).

Despite such conflicting experiences, it is likely that most healthcare organizations will provide some telehealth or e-health services in the future. Even before the pandemic, a number of trends pointed to the growth of telehealth services, including the development of innovative technologies, healthcare workforce shortages (especially in rural areas), reorganization of healthcare delivery systems and financial aspects of medical care, and growing consumerism in healthcare (Tuckson, Edmunds, and Hodgkins 2017). Overseeing this growth and the appropriate use of telehealth will be a vital part of healthcare management for the foreseeable future.

END-OF-LIFE DECISIONS

At the end of life, patients and clinicians face many ethical issues, such as the right to live, the right to die, and the quality of life. Our current medical technology has extended life far beyond an age that was only imagined in the past. As a result, decisions made at the end of life often involve the maintenance or withdrawal of life-prolonging equipment and treatments. Conflicts may arise between the patients (and family members) who desire a natural death and clinicians who feel compelled to continue administering advanced therapies. Considerations of the patients' current and future quality of life are often key components of these decisions. These decisions must be made across the span of life, from newborns to the "oldest-olds" (those aged 85 years and older).

This section focuses on the ethical conflicts that occur during the care of patients with severe brain injuries. Discussions about care and treatment at the end of life involve the ethical principles of autonomy, beneficence, nonmaleficence, and sanctity.

Profound injuries to the brain come in many different types and manifest in different ways. The causes of brain injuries include trauma, stroke, brain tumor, drug or alcohol intoxication, anoxia (lack of oxygen), poisoning, and underlying disease (such as diabetes or infections). Fine (2005) emphasizes that unconscious people cannot suffer. This consideration is important to decisions about maintaining or withdrawing medical treatments.

Patients lose their autonomy when they are unconscious or in a **persistent vegetative state (PVS)** because they are unaware of themselves and their surroundings. For autonomy to be relevant, the patient must have awareness. An advance healthcare directive—a legal

---

persistent vegetative state (PVS)
A clinical condition in which the patient is completely unaware of the environment or surroundings and is incapable of cognitive thinking or activity.

document that specifies a person's preferences for treatments, life-sustaining technology, and other medical care—is one way that patients can retain their autonomy, even when they are in a PVS. Without an advance healthcare directive, treatment decisions are made for the patients first under the **substituted judgment standard** or, later (if necessary), under the **best interests standard**.

Using substituted judgment, a surrogate—usually a family member—makes healthcare decisions on behalf of the patient and according to the patient's previously expressed preferences, values, and beliefs. This standard strives to preserve the patient's autonomy by honoring the patient's own wishes. If the patient's preferences are ambiguous or unknown, the surrogate bases decisions on what is in the best interests of the patient. The best interests standard relies on the information available. More recently, it has been proposed that such end-of-life decisions should be guided by the principle of reducing harm or pain (Bellieni 2020).

Those who oppose the withdrawal of life support cite the ethical principle of sanctity. That is, life or existence has an intrinsic value, and as such, it is worth preserving—regardless of what the body can or cannot do. Both proponents and opponents of withdrawal of life support ground their arguments in the ethical principles of beneficence and nonmaleficence. Proponents state that releasing someone from intractable pain and suffering is the ultimate beneficence. Opponents believe that terminating someone's life is the ultimate maleficence. Proponents use quality of life as a justification to withhold or forgo life-sustaining interventions (Maglio and Garcia 2020; Nantais and Kuczewski 2004). However, opponents resent the implication that severe illness or PVS serves to "disqualify." Judgments about quality of life are complex, subjective, and dependent on the culture and values (Hosaka 2017) of patients, their families, clinicians, and other involved persons.

substituted judgment standard
A standard whereby a patient's surrogate makes healthcare decisions based on the patient's previously expressed preferences or known values and beliefs.

best interests standard
A standard whereby the patient's surrogate (or a court) makes healthcare decisions based on the best interests of the patient.

> **DID YOU KNOW?**
> Right-to-Die Cases: Quinlan, Schiavo, and Cruzan
>
> Karen Quinlan and Terri Schiavo were each in a persistent vegetative state (PVS) following serious brain injuries. PVS is a clinical condition in which the patient is completely unaware of the environment or surroundings and incapable of cognitive thinking or activity. It is accompanied by sleep–wake cycles and spontaneous movements.
>
> Quinlan's case lasted from the mid-1970s through the mid-1980s. After realizing that her condition would not improve, her parents asked physicians to disconnect her respirator and thus end her life. Her physicians, however, refused, believing that they had a duty to protect her life and that termination of life support was the equivalent of murder. Her parents then
>
> *(continued)*

> **DID YOU KNOW?**
> Right-to-Die Cases: Quinlan, Schiavo, and Cruzan (continued)
>
> filed a petition to remove the respirator, but the court denied it. After an appeal, the New Jersey Supreme Court ruled in the parents' favor. Quinlan lived in a PVS for another ten years, sustained only by artificial nutrition and hydration (ANH). She died of pneumonia in 1985.
>
> Schiavo's case lasted from the late 1990s through the mid-2000s. She had been in a PVS for eight years before her husband petitioned the courts to stop ANH. Her parents opposed the petition. The disagreement led to many court challenges and appeals and involved state and national politicians such as the Florida governor, members of the US Congress, and even President George W. Bush. After seven years of court proceedings, ANH was finally withdrawn, and Schiavo died in 2005.
>
> In 1983, Nancy Cruzan was involved in an automobile crash that left her in a PVS. Much like the Quinlan and Schiavo cases, Cruzan's case generated much controversy and many court actions involving her parents, the state of Missouri, and right-to-life proponents. As Quinlan's parents did, Cruzan's parents petitioned the court to authorize her disconnection from her feeding tubes and thus allow her to die with dignity. Eventually, the US Supreme Court ruled that Cruzan had a right to die; it was the high court's first-ever ruling on a right-to-die case. Cruzan died in 1990, nearly eight years after her accident. Her case spurred much interest in advance healthcare directives. The Patient Self-Determination Act of 1990 requires healthcare providers to inform patients of their right to refuse treatment and have an advance directive in place.

INSTITUTIONAL ETHICS COMMITTEE AND ETHICS SUPPORT

An **institutional ethics committee (IEC)** is a permanent organizational committee that provides advice and support on clinical ethics issues. IECs differ from institutional review boards (IRBs) in that IECs focus on patient care, whereas IRBs focus on human research subjects and are governed by federal regulations (see chapter 8 for more information on IRBs). These bodies developed in the 1980s, and according to one survey more than 90 percent of US hospitals had ethics committees by 2001 (Hajibabaee et al. 2016). They are likely ubiquitous today.

IECs have three main goals or purposes (Hajibabaee et al. 2016; Mercurio 2011):

1. Conduct case analysis and **case consultations** in which the IEC reviews an ethical conflict and then advises the parties involved, including clinicians, administrators, other organizational members, and patients and family members

2. Educate organizational members and patients about ethics, ethical problems, and ethical decision-making

institutional ethics committee (IEC)
A permanent organizational committee that provides advice and support on clinical ethics issues.

case consultation
The institutional ethics committee process of hearing and reviewing an ethical conflict and then advising all the parties involved on the next most appropriate steps to take.

3. Assist in the development and revision of organizational policies and guidelines to facilitate ethical service provision

Based on an extensive review of the literature worldwide, Hajibabaee et al. (2016) elaborate on the functions and challenges of ethics committees in carrying out these goals.

Ethical conflicts under the purview of IECs typically pertain to informed consent, access to and use of healthcare and services, and decisions made at the beginning and end of life. Historically, ethics committees have played a critical role in advocating for the current shared decision-making model in difficult ethical situations, such as the care of critically ill infants in the neonatal intensive care unit (Sullivan and Cummings 2020). IECs are in place in hospitals, nursing facilities, managed care organizations, home health agencies, rehabilitation facilities, hospices, residential centers, and primary care clinics.

IECs are advisory bodies, not decision-making bodies. As such, their advice is merely a recommendation, not an order. However, their recommendations are influential and carry weight because IECs are regarded as "moral authorities" and conduct careful deliberations (Mercurio 2011, 2).

Today, ethics committees are one component of the ethics support provided to healthcare personnel, including clinical ethics consultation, moral case deliberations, and ethics rounds or ethics discussion and reflection groups (Rasoal et al. 2017). They may perform consultations, or consultations may be conducted by designated others who have broad competencies in ethical theory, health law, and the clinical context, as well as interpersonal process skills to facilitate communication. Consultations may be triggered by specific situations, but they also may be more general in focus—for example, to provide education to personnel on how to deal with moral distress (see chapter 7).

The moral case deliberation process involves a facilitator working with healthcare professionals (for an hour or an entire day) to engage in mutual reflection on difficult ethical situations in their practice. The facilitator conducts a theory-based conversation, such as Socratic dialogue or dilemmas to promote awareness but does not provide recommended actions. Ethics rounds or discussion and reflection groups are more ongoing, with the purpose of stimulating reflection and promoting mutual understanding among professional groups. Such groups may also provide emotional support to healthcare personnel and have been found to improve job satisfaction and increase understanding among interprofessional groups (Rasoal et al. 2017). Such groups take a more "bottom-up" perspective that complements formal ethical committee policies and decisions.

PREVENTING MEDICAL ERRORS

In late 1999, the Institute of Medicine (IOM) published a groundbreaking report titled *To Err Is Human: Building a Safer Health System*. It estimated that "at least 44,000 people, and perhaps as many as 98,000 people, die annually from medical errors" (IOM 2000). In fact, according to the report, more people died from preventable medical errors in hospitals than from motor vehicle accidents and breast cancer combined. Moreover, the total cost of preventable adverse events (including lost income, production, disability, and healthcare costs) was found to be substantial—between $17 and $19 billion—with healthcare costs accounting for approximately half of that amount.

In medicine, an *adverse event* is an injury caused by something other than the underlying medical condition of the patient. Adverse events are most frequently attributable to errors that are considered preventable. Medical errors include medication-related errors, diagnostic errors, treatment errors (e.g., wrong-site surgery or surgical injuries), inadequate monitoring, hospital-acquired or treatment-related infections, equipment failure, and communication or system failures.

In response to the report, the following actions were taken:

- The Joint Commission issued a cluster of standards in support of patient safety, which became effective in 2001. One standard specifically requires that all unanticipated outcomes of care be disclosed to patients (see the section on "Disclosing Medical Errors" in chapter 4).

- Congress enacted the Patient Safety and Quality Improvement Act of 2005, which became fully effective in 2009. The goal of the act is to improve patient safety by encouraging voluntary and confidential reporting of medical errors and other adverse events. Healthcare providers report data about adverse events to patient safety organizations, which, in turn, collect, aggregate, and analyze the data. The act provides federal legal privilege and confidentiality protections for conducting patient safety activities.

- The Joint Commission issued revised National Patient Safety Goals, which became effective in 2016 (Mascioli and Carrico 2016). Again, their intent is to reduce risks to the patient by implementing safety procedures in high-risk areas. These procedures include managing proper use of clinical alarms on equipment, ensuring the accuracy of patient identification, communicating effectively (e.g., critical test results), increasing safety regarding medication use (e.g., labeling, reconciliation of differences), and adopting universal protocols to prevent so-called sentinel events (i.e., unexpected occurrences involving death or serious physical or psychological injury).

There is no single solution for increasing patient safety across the healthcare field, although progress has been made in some areas (Bates and Singh 2018). For example, effective interventions have been developed to reduce hospital infections as well as medication errors. Surgical checklists are now used in the operating room to reduce surgical injuries. Hospitals also use standardized communications when patients are passed between providers at shift changes to ensure continuity of care. However, practices and progress remain inconsistent, such that the level of preventable harm remains high.

Risk management requires analytical work, such as conducing a **root-cause analysis** of sentinel events (McGowan, Wojahn, and Nicolini 2021). This type of analysis generally is undertaken by a diverse interprofessional team within days of an adverse or sentinel event requiring investigation; this team interviews everyone involved and develops a corrective action plan. The plan is based on the team's understanding of the factors that led to the event and includes specific corrective actions, responsibilities for implementation with timelines, and strategies for evaluating the effectiveness of the proposed changes. Daniel Neuspiel and Andrew Schuman (2018) provide a flowchart example of a root-cause analysis of medication errors in a pediatric practice.

Medical errors remain a problem in healthcare delivery. Nevertheless, providers are now being taught to disclose adverse events and medical errors (Borz-Baba, Johnson, and Gopal 2020), and some hospitals have introduced communication and resolution programs to proactively address instances of substandard care when they occur (Mayor 2017). For healthcare managers, addressing medical errors involves establishing a culture of safety (rather than assigning blame) though leadership and policies, such that the healthcare organization becomes a learning system focused on identifying needed quality improvements (McGowan, Wojahn, and Nicolini 2021; Rodziewicz, Houseman, and Hipskind 2018).

root-cause analysis A comprehensive systems-based investigation of the factor(s) that caused an adverse event; the analysis not only addresses the event under investigation but also results in action plans to prevent future events.

MINI-CASE STUDY: SURGICAL ERRORS PERSIST

In a paper on ethics in clinical practice, Basil Varkey (2021) describes the case of a 45-year-old woman presenting with fever, abdominal pain, and tenderness. She had undergone surgery to remove her gallbladder (a cholecystectomy) three weeks earlier. Upon further examination, the physicians determined that a sponge had been left inside the patient's abdomen during surgery. The sponge was removed, and the patient was successfully treated with antibiotics.

Similarly, Adriana Koek (2020) describes a male patient in his late 80s who presented with a mass on his right hip. A CT scan revealed "radiopaque surgical material"—a sponge—surrounding a soft tissue mass. Many years earlier, the patient had undergone a surgical fusion of vertebrae. Again, a sponge was left inside the patient. Although considerable progress has been made in preventing this type of error, the problem of retained surgical sponges persists. Most often, the surgical error is caught early—in fact, the second case was noteworthy for the patient's presentation decades after his original surgery.

MINI-CASE STUDY QUESTIONS

1. Why do healthcare organizations have an ethical obligation to provide a safe environment?

2. How do ethical principles support The Joint Commission's standard requiring that all unanticipated outcomes of care be disclosed to patients?
3. Another concern is the cooperation clause in policies for malpractice and professional liability insurance. An admission of error (fault) could void a physician's coverage for related claims. How do such policies affect the disclosure of unanticipated outcomes?
4. What ethical obligations do healthcare managers have to contribute to the safety of their organization's environment?
5. Which standards of professional codes of ethics relate to establishing and maintaining patient safety?

Points to Remember

- The moral issues involved in clinical ethics result from the delivery of healthcare and services and general clinical practice.
- The major ethical principles in clinical practice include autonomy, beneficence and nonmaleficence, respect for self and others, honesty and integrity, justice, fidelity, and sanctity of life.
- Clinical ethical issues commonly revolve around issues of (1) competence, (2) informed consent, (3) confidentiality, (4) crossing boundaries, and (5) cultural competence.
- Competence involves maintaining knowledge and skills relevant to the standards of practice, as well as the clinician's own emotional health.
- Informed consent supports a patient's right to accept or refuse healthcare or services. It is based on the adult competent model, although special issues arise related to minors and incapacitated patients.
- Confidentiality relates to fidelity and the recognized privacy granted to personal health information, although there are limits to confidentiality.
- Providers have a specific professional role with respect to their patients and reflect carefully on boundary crossings that might cause harm or negatively affect the patient's care.
- Developing cultural competence in providing care to all patients within a diverse society is an ethical issue.
- Access to healthcare raises the ethical issues of beneficence and distributive justice.
- As the use of telemedicine and telehealth increases, healthcare organizations must pay special attention to ethical concerns related to competence, best care, informed consent, privacy, and access.

- Ethical conflicts at the end of life often are related to the right to live, the right to die, and the quality of life and involve the ethical principles of autonomy, beneficence, nonmaleficence, and sanctity of life.
- An institutional ethics committee is a permanent organizational committee that provides advice and support on clinical ethics issues.
- The extent and costs of medical errors continue to concern healthcare organizations, providing the impetus to improve patient safety.

Challenge Yourself

1. You are asked to attend a meeting of your organization's healthcare ethics committee at which an ethical conflict that the organization is facing will be discussed. How will you prepare yourself for the meeting?
2. Healthcare ethicist William A. Nelson (2006) describes the following three situations involving ethical decisions. Which of these decisions involve ethical conflicts? Pretend that you are a patient safety officer.
   a. You need to choose among several software packages to track events involving patient safety. The decision is difficult to make, and you might need the assistance of a consultant to determine which software package has the best technical features and complies with organizational rules for return on investment, user-friendliness, and compatibility with existing computer systems.
   b. You have decided to purchase an excellent software package. Unfortunately, it exceeds the budget approved by the finance department. You split the order for the software package among three purchase orders, thereby concealing its true cost and staying within your purchasing authority amount and below finance's "radar."
   c. To facilitate your evaluation of a vendor's software package, the vendor offers to take you to a site in Florida where the software has been installed. The vendor will pay for your flight as well as your midweek, two-day stay at a hotel. You are tempted to take the offer because you are curious to see how the software works in real life. Besides, you rationalize, it has been a brutal winter, and you could use a short vacation.
3. Consider conducting some additional research on telehealth. For example, can you find an example of telehealth applications available in your community or state? What precautions are in place to ensure that telehealth services are provided ethically? Does your state allow providers living in other states to provide you with telehealth services?
   Here are some websites that may provide you with general information:
   https://intermountainhealthcare.org/health-information/telehealth
   https://telehealth.org/
   https://www.hhs.gov/hipaa/for-professionals/faq/telehealth/index.html

4. Clinicians' ethical obligations typically focus on promoting the best interests of their individual patients. Healthcare managers' obligations, however, often focus on the best interests of the patient population served by the organization. How might these different perspectives affect discussions of ethical conflicts?

For Your Consideration

9.1 For a moment, imagine that you are a patient seeking confidential help from a therapist for a personal problem. What would you want the provider to share with you as part of the informed consent process? Is informed consent something that is only relevant to the beginning of treatment, or might it evolve? Explain your answer.

9.2 Your healthcare organization has decided to develop a telehealth service program for diabetic patients in a rural area of the state with the explicit goal of helping them manage their disease more effectively. You will be the healthcare manager overseeing this program and are attending an interprofessional meeting describing the project. What questions might you have about the program and fulfilling the ethical and legal obligations associated with telehealth?

References

American Hospital Association. 2021. *The Patient Care Partnership: Understanding Expectations, Rights and Responsibilities*. Accessed April 23. www.aha.org/other-resources/patient-care-partnership.

Ananfack Nguefack, E. G., A. A. Essomba, G. N. Nkeng, S. P. Medoua Bella, N. V. Njedock Sontsa, and A. R. Nana. 2020. "Ethics in Telemedicine and Telehealth: A Literature Review." *International Research Journal of Advanced Engineering and Science* 5 (4): 67–70.

Ashton, K., and A. Sullivan. 2018. "Ethics and Confidentiality for Psychologists in Academic Health Centers." *Journal of Clinical Psychology in Medical Settings* 25 (3): 240–49.

Badichek, J. 2021. "Prescribe More Telehealth for the Elderly." Medpage Today. Published April 12. www.medpagetoday.com/practicemanagement/telehealth/92049.

Barstow, C., B. Shahan, and M. Roberts. 2018. "Evaluating Medical Decision-Making Capacity in Practice." *American Family Physician* 98 (1): 40–46.

Bates, D. W., and H. Singh 2018. "Two Decades Since *To Err Is Human*: An Assessment of Progress and Emerging Priorities in Patient Safety." *Health Affairs* 37 (11): 1736–43.

Bellieni, C. V. 2020. "The Pain Principle: An Ethical Approach to End-of-Life Decisions." *Ethics & Medicine: An International Journal of Bioethics* 36 (1): 41–49.

Borz-Baba, C., M. Johnson, and V. Gopal. 2020. "Designing a Curriculum for the Disclosure of Medical Errors: A Requirement for a Positive Patient Safety Culture." *Cureus* 12 (2): e6931.

Chaet, D., R. Clearfield, J. E. Sabin, and K. Skimming. 2017. "Ethical Practice in Telehealth and Telemedicine." *Journal of General Internal Medicine* 32 (10): 1136–40.

Daniels, N. 2000. "Accountability for Reasonableness: Establishing a Fair Process for Priority Setting Is Easier Than Agreeing on Principles." *British Medical Journal* 321 (7272): 1300–1301.

Daniels, N., and J. E. Sabin. 2008. "Accountability for Reasonableness: An Update." *British Medical Journal* 337: a1850.

Dellifraine, J. L., and K. H. Dansky. 2008. "Home-Based Telehealth: A Review and Meta-analysis." *Journal of Telemedicine and Telecare* 14 (2): 62–66.

Dorsey, E. R., and E. J. Topol. 2016. "State of Telehealth." *New England Journal of Medicine* 375 (2): 154–61.

Elger, B., K. Michaud, and P. Mangin. 2010. "When Information Can Save Lives: The Duty to Warn Relatives About Sudden Cardiac Death and Environmental Risks." *Hastings Center Report* 40 (3): 39–45.

Faden, R. R., and T. L. Beauchamp. 1986. *A History and Theory of Informed Consent*. New York: Oxford University Press.

Fatehi, F., and R. Wootton. 2012. "Telemedicine, Telehealth or e-Health? A Bibliometric Analysis of the Trends in the Use of These Terms." *Journal of Telemedicine and Telecare* 18 (8): 460–64.

Fine, R. L. 2005. "From Quinlan to Schiavo: Medical, Ethical, and Legal Issues in Severe Brain Injury." *Baylor University Medical Center Proceedings* 18 (4): 303–10.

Gillon, R. 2020. "Raising the Profile of Fairness and Justice in Medical Practice and Policy." *Journal of Medical Ethics* 46 (12): 789–90.

Green, D. S. T., and C. R. MacKenzie. 2007. "Nuances of Informed Consent: The Paradigm of Regional Anesthesia." *HSS Journal: The Musculoskeletal Journal of Hospital for Special Surgery* 3 (1): 115–18.

Hajibabaee, F., S. Joolaee, M. A. Cheraghi, P. Salari, and P. Rodney. 2016. "Hospital/Clinical Ethics Committees' Notion: An Overview." *Journal of Medical Ethics and History of Medicine* 9 (17): 1–9.

Hosaka, K. R. J. 2017. "The Politics of Palliative Care in Resource Limited Settings." *Journal for Undergraduate Ethnography* 7 (1): 47–67.

Institute of Medicine (IOM). 2000. *To Err Is Human: Building a Safer Health System*. Washington, DC: National Academies Press.

Joint Commission. 2019. "The Joint Commission Launches Educational Campaign on Patient Rights." Published November 14. www.jointcommission.org/resources/news-and-multimedia/news/2019/11/the-joint-commission-launches-educational-campaign-on-patient-rights/.

Kim, J. K., and A. R. Scialli. 2011. "Thalidomide: The Tragedy of Birth Defects and the Effective Treatment of Disease." *Toxicological Sciences* 122 (1): 1–6.

Koek, A. Y. 2020. "Retained Surgical Sponge Presenting Four Decades Later as a Rapidly Growing Soft Tissue Mass." *Case Reports in Surgery*. Published January 20. https://doi.org/10.1155/2020/1230173.

Krupinski, E. A., and J. Bernard. 2014. "Standards and Guidelines in Telemedicine and Telehealth." *Healthcare* 2 (1): 74–93.

Kuehn, B. M. 2010. "Frances Kelsey Honored for FDA Legacy: Award Notes Her Work on Thalidomide, Clinical Trials." *Journal of the American Medical Association* 304 (19): 2109–10, 2112.

Kvedar, J., M. J. Coye, and W. Everett. 2014. "Connected Health: A Review of Technologies and Strategies to Improve Patient Care with Telemedicine and Telehealth." *Health Affairs* 33 (2): 194–99.

LaMance, K. 2018. "Is It Malpractice for a Doctor or Therapist to Engage in a Sexual Relationship with a Patient?" LegalMatch. Updated April 16. www.legalmatch.com/law-library/article/sexual-relationships-with-patients.html.

Lewis, N. 2011. "UCLA Health System Pays $865,000 over Privacy Charges." Dark Reading. Published August 7. www.darkreading.com/risk/ucla-health-system-pays-865-000-over-privacy-charges.

Luxton, D. D., E. L. Nelson, and M. M. Maheu. 2016. *A Practitioner's Guide to Telemental Health: How to Conduct Legal, Ethical, and Evidence-Based Telepractice*. Washington, DC: American Psychological Association.

Maglio, M., and V. García. 2020. "Thinking 'Quality of Life': From Measures to Categorizations of the Human Beings." In *From Measuring Rods to DNA Sequencing: Assessing the Human*, edited by I. Voléry and M.-P. Julien, 97–121. Singapore: Palgrave Macmillan.

Maheu, M. M., K. P. Drude, K. M. Hertlein, and D. M. Hilty. 2018. "A Framework of Interprofessional Telebehavioral Health Competencies: Implementation and Challenges Moving Forward." *Academic Psychiatry* 42 (6): 825–33.

Mascioli, S., and C. B. Carrico. 2016. "Spotlight on the 2016 National Patient Safety Goals for Hospitals." *Nursing Critical Care* 11 (6): 19–22.

Mayor, S. 2017. "Explaining and Apologizing to Patients After Errors Does Not Increase Lawsuits, Finds Study." *British Medical Journal* 359: j4536.

McGowan, J., A. Wojahn, and J. R. Nicolini. 2021. "Risk Management Event Evaluation and Responsibilities." Updated February 16. www.ncbi.nlm.nih.gov/books/NBK559326/.

McKneally, M. F., B. M. Dickens, E. M. Meslin, and P. A. Singer. 1997. "Bioethics for Clinicians, 13: Resource Allocation." *Canadian Medical Association Journal* 157 (2): 163–67.

Menzel, P. T. 2012. "Justice and Fairness: A Critical Element in U.S. Health System Reform." *Journal of Law, Medicine & Ethics* 40 (3): 582–97.

Mercurio, M. R. 2011. "The Role of a Pediatric Ethics Committee in the Newborn Intensive Care Unit." *Journal of Perinatology* 31 (1): 1–9.

Nantais, D., and M. Kuczewski. 2004. "Quality of Life: The Contested Rhetoric of Resource Allocation and End-of-Life Decision Making." *Journal of Medicine and Philosophy* 29 (6): 651–64.

National Commission for the Protection of Human Subjects of Biomedical and Behavioral Research. 1979. *The Belmont Report: Ethical Principles and Guidelines for the Protection of Human Subjects of Research*. Accessed August 5, 2021. www.hhs.gov/ohrp/regulations-and-policy/belmont-report/index.html.

Nelson, R. 2017. "Telemedicine and Telehealth: The Potential to Improve Rural Access to Care." *American Journal of Nursing* 117 (6): 17–18.

Nelson, W. A. 2006. "Defining Ethics." *Healthcare Executive* 21 (4): 38–39.

Neuspiel, D. R., and A. J. Schuman. 2018. "Prevent Medical Errors in Your Practice." *Contemporary Pediatrics* 35 (7): 31–34.

Pellegrino, E. D. 1995. "Nonabandonment: An Old Obligation Revisited." *Annals of Internal Medicine* 122 (5): 377–78.

Pierce, B. S., P. B. Perrin, C. M. Tyler, G. B. McKee, and J. D. Watson. 2021. "The COVID-19 Telepsychology Revolution: A National Study of Pandemic-Based Changes in U.S. Mental Health Care Delivery." *American Psychologist* 76 (1): 14–25.

Rasoal, D., K. Skovdahl, M. Gifford, and A. Kihlgren. 2017. "Clinical Ethics Support for Healthcare Personnel: An Integrative Literature Review." *HEC Forum: An Interdisciplinary Journal on Hospitals' Ethical and Legal Issues* 29 (4): 313–46.

Reitz, R., P. D. Simmons, C. Runyan, C., Hodgson, J., S. Carter-Henry. 2013. "Multiple Role Relationships in Healthcare Education." *Families, Systems, & Health* 31 (1): 96–107.

Rodziewicz, T. L., B. Houseman, and J. E. Hipskind. 2018. "Medical Error Prevention." Published May 16. https://europepmc.org/article/nbk/nbk499956.

Russell, C. T. S., F. Augustin, and P. Jones. 2017. "Perspectives on the Importance of Integrating Diversity into the Healthcare Administration Curriculum: The Role of Cultural Humility." *Journal of Health Administration Education* 34 (3): 371–93.

Siwicki, B. 2021. "Telemedicine Didn't Work Well for This Provider—Here's Why." *Healthcare IT News*. Published April 7. www.healthcareitnews.com/news/telemedicine-didnt-work-well-provider-heres-why.

Sullivan, A., and C. Cummings. 2020. "Historical Perspectives: Shared Decision Making in the NICU." *NeoReviews* 21 (4): e217–25.

Tuckson, R. V., M. Edmunds, and M. L. Hodgkins. 2017. "Telehealth." *New England Journal of Medicine* 377 (16): 1585–92.

Varkey, B. 2021. "Principles of Clinical Ethics and Their Application to Practice." *Medical Principles and Practice* 30 (1): 17–28.

Washington State Nurses Service Organization. 2016. "Don't Cross the Line: Respecting Professional Boundaries." Published February 24. www.wsna.org/news/2016/dont-cross-the-line-respecting-professional-boundaries.

Weiner, J. P., S. Bandeian, E. Hatef, D. Lans, A. Liu, and K. W. Lemke. 2021. "In-Person and Telehealth Ambulatory Contacts and Costs in a Large US Insured Cohort Before and During the COVID-19 Pandemic." *JAMA Network Open* 4 (3): e212618.

Weinstein, R. S., A. M. Lopez, E. A. Krupinski, S. J. Beinar, M. Holcomb, R. A. McNeely, R. Latifi, and G. Barker. 2008. "Integrating Telemedicine and Telehealth: Putting It All Together." In *Current Principles and Practices of Telemedicine and e-Health*, edited by R. Latifi, 23–38. Amsterdam: IOS Press.

PART III
ETHICAL APPLICATIONS IN THE HEALTHCARE ENVIRONMENT

The material covered in part III includes an overview of ethical applications in the healthcare environment related to strategic planning, financial and operations management, health informatics, risk management, and external relations.

This case and commentary focus on issues associated with a price transparency policy that calls for more transparency in charges. It examines price practices through the ethical lenses of justice and autonomy. Consider the following questions as you read:

1. Historically, what has been the role of healthcare risk managers in addressing ethics and social justice issues?

2. What are some of the complexities and potential unintended consequences of a national policy to promote price transparency?

3. Explain why you agree with or oppose the first commenter's view that cost transparency is a matter of personal liberty.

4. What are some reasons for the seemingly inexplicable price variations that often occur across the healthcare industry?

5. How does transparency become a tool for the healthcare manager to advocate for patient autonomy and choice? Give examples from other professions.

6. How would you summarize a hospital risk manager's duties and responsibilities to patients and to the organization? How would a wise risk manager reconcile the real or perceived conflicts of interest between the two?

Case Study: Should a Good Risk Manager Worry About Cost and Price Transparency in Health Care?

Abstract

This case highlights the evolving and expanding role(s) of hospital risk managers over the last 30 years. Once largely focused on hospital liability risk management, risk managers today have a broader set of enterprise risk management responsibilities. The following commentary about a surprise billing case considers roles of risk managers in promoting cost and price transparency—a matter that in recent years has received extensive national attention.

Case

JJ and KJ co-parent EJ, their 16-year-old, who is recovering from being hospitalized for 8 days following a surgery. In the explanation of benefits they received from their insurer, a fraction of what the hospital charged was covered by the insurer, leaving JJ and KJ with a bill of about $190,000 for their child's inpatient care. Shocked and dismayed, JJ and KJ called the insurer to complain. Investigation ensued and revealed substantial variation in what different organizations charge for comparable surgical care. Results of the investigation were published by a national print media company. One organization offered the procedure with an inpatient stay of 8 days and estimated that the cost to the patient's family would be about $85,000. Another organization offered the procedure with 3 inpatient days for a total of about $35,000 with an estimated cost to the patient's family of about $25,000.

Members of the public began to ask, "Why is there such variation in what this procedure costs?" Recent responses to public concern about a lack of transparency in health care pricing and what's been called "no surprise billing" have prompted The White House to direct the US Department of Health and Human Services to develop rules requiring hospitals to publish prices "that reflect what people actually pay for services."[1]

A risk manager, GG, at the hospital where EJ had surgery is relieved that the organization seems to have weathered negative public attention generated by EJ's case. GG has been wondering, however, how other organizations offer the procedure at lower costs: Are they saving the money by cutting quality and thus increasing patients' risks of postsurgical complications that would probably be identified in an inpatient care setting? What should patients be told about this risk? GG notes that EJ's hospital and the 2 organizations that offered the same surgery at lower cost performed approximately the same number of procedures and suspects that pricing differences cannot be explained only in terms of volume or economies of scale.

GG also wonders, Why is our organization's length of stay (LOS) so much longer than some others'? If we can reduce LOS, we should, because each day in hospital increases a patient's risk of contracting a nosocomial infection. I wonder what our patients are told about this.

Aside from these questions facing the hospital, GG has broader concerns, too: If organizations respond to public and government demand for pricing transparency, health care networks might respond by consolidating prices. This move would result in less cost variation across a market and less competition and could raise overall costs of care. For example, GG recently read that the president and chief executive officer of America's Health Insurance Plans warned that price transparency rules requiring "publicly disclosing competitively negotiated, proprietary rates will reduce competition and push prices higher—not lower—for consumers, patients, and taxpayers."[2]

GG notes that markets tend to initially react negatively to concerns about increased prices: When stocks of major hospital operators and insurers fall, shareholder value falls, reducing organizational access to capital or increasing the cost of capital. As a result, strategic planning for broadening market share or making capital improvements necessary to remain competitive could be placed on hold. So, GG considers the scope of her responsibility to the organization's shareholders, too.

GG wonders what to do over the short and long terms.

COMMENTARY 1 BY JOSH CHARLES HYATT, DHSc, MHL, MBE(c)

Cost transparency in health care allows individual patients to exercise choice by deciding what is in their best physical and financial interests. According to the US Census Bureau, in 2018 there were 27.5 million uninsured in the United States; Blacks (9.7%) and Hispanics (17.8%) are uninsured at a higher rate than non-Hispanic Whites (5.4%).[3] Additionally, the number of underinsured people (whose out-of-pocket medical expenses are 5% to 10% of their annual income or who have deductibles that are more than 5% of their annual income[4]) grew to 44 million in 2018.[4] These inequities are at the heart of social justice, inhibiting fairness and placing an undue burden on the most vulnerable (who have the highest risk of harm and least ability to afford it). Hospital risk managers (hereafter, risk managers) have a stake in preserving justice—viz, fairness and equity as they concern patient rights, consent, satisfaction, and harm reduction.

As a profession, health care risk management has not been at the vanguard of social justice issues. Hospital executives, leadership teams, and ethics committee representatives generally discuss and develop policy related to ethical and values-based concerns without the input of risk managers who are responsible to manage the aftermath when those decisions result in liability exposure. The scope of risk management has traditionally encompassed daily firefighting (i.e., triaging and investigating events, managing sentinel events, engaging in institutional and clinician consultation) rather than ethically normative concerns (i.e., what we ought to do). Similar to bioethics, risk management was born of necessity. Risk management questions and concerns are rarely straightforward clinical, regulatory, or legal issues; rather, these inquiries, though not the traditional questions faced by an ethics committee, are multifaceted in nature, with values at their core and informed by ethical principles.

Justice advocacy expands the risk manager's role from managing loss, ensuring compliance, and overseeing billable services to augmenting risk mitigation (by taking steps to reduce the impact of liability) and addressing risk concerns from a morally courageous position (doing the right thing). The risk manager has a unique perspective on managing loss while being in a position to address broader elements of justice by reflecting on whose interests are predominant (patient, institution, profession, or society) and acting in a manner that seeks to balance the best interests of stakeholders. Reflecting both a moral and operational risk management imperative, this essay explores the issue of cost transparency as it relates to justice in health care.

Cost Transparency as a Moral Imperative

John Rawls suggests that a just society is a fair society, wherein all persons are equal, all have access to needed resources, and the least advantaged benefit.[5] All health care professionals, including risk managers, embracing their obligation to work toward health care equality—currently a mere aspiration—is axiomatic to promoting a society in which fairness prevails.[6] Ideally, access to needed services should be guaranteed and health care policies that emphasize equitable systems that benefit the vulnerable should be ubiquitous.[7] Unfortunately, these conditions for distributive justice are not met in US health care. A record 25% of Americans reported in 2019 that they or a family member put off treatment for a serious medical condition in the past year because of cost, and, within this group, the income gap between top and bottom earners was 23%.[8] One important step for the health care system to take is to cultivate transparency so that people are aware of the costs of care up front and can triage their options and plan their diagnostic testing and care with this information in mind, in consultation with their health care physician.

On November 15, 2019, the US Department of Health and Human Services, the US Department of Labor, and the US Department of the Treasury published the Transparency in Coverage Rule, which calls for health care price information to be accessible to the public to permit "easy comparison-shopping."[9] As of the writing of this essay, the rule has just completed the public comment phase. The principle argument against price transparency is that publishing fee schedules would affect hospitals' ability to negotiate lower contract rates with payers, resulting in a "floor" for prices that hospitals would be willing to accept.[10] This argument appears to disregard the justice concerns of patient access and individual affordability.

As a result of this lack of transparency, the most vulnerable in our society are the most likely victims of predatory pricing via *price fixing*, a financial agreement between 2 parties (in this case, the payers and the institutions negotiating rates), and price discrimination, selling a product at different prices to different groups based on willingness to pay.[11] Price fixing and price discrimination primarily affect those who are uninsured or underinsured, are designed to exclude lower-priced managed care companies and Medicaid (the lifeline for vulnerable populations) from provider networks, and limit competition (driving up costs and limiting access to care). Ultimately, these agreements are socially unjust because they pose barriers to access and disenfranchise vulnerable populations.

Personal Liberty and Cost Transparency

Why is cost transparency a matter of personal liberty? Making autonomous, noncoerced, and informed health care decisions is the cornerstone of medical ethics and fundamental to health care policy and health law. Nevertheless, cost transparency and the impacts of care costs on the individual are not given adequate attention during informed consent deliberations and are more rarely discussed by risk managers as a tool for risk mitigation. People cannot thrive if they avoid seeking health care due to cost and a lack of control in the planning of their care. Health care policies at all levels (government, insurance company, and health care organization) should regard individuals, in Kant's terms,[12] as "an end" in themselves by ensuring cost transparency, thereby promoting patients' autonomy and collaboration with their clinicians.[13]

One area of health care in which price disclosure is commonplace, highly efficient, and upholds the individual's moral agency is dentistry. Dentists are often heavily constrained by insurance policies with varying levels of reimbursement and significant out-of-pocket expenses for the patient. Knowing that patients will have high expenses, dentists often provide patients with a summary of recommended procedures, triaged as to importance, and priced out for the patient's review.

Operational (Normative) Concerns

Billing. Surprise billing and billing for services that the patient believes are substandard generally lead to grievances, which are often the risk manager's first indications that a larger problem may exist (e.g., quality of care concerns, patient injury, or interpersonal issues with the clinician or other staff). Risk managers walk a fine line between maintaining the institution's financial best interest and managing the patient's response to being blindsided by a surprise bill. Surprise billing has significant negative impacts on patient satisfaction (including by reducing patients' trust in the physician and institution); increases the risk of litigation and frivolous suits; consumes the time of the risk manager and staff; and increases conflict between clinicians, institutions, and patients. Effective transparency mitigates these concerns and time wasters.

Litigation risks. Patients who are harmed by or who are generally dissatisfied with care may not consider filing a lawsuit until they receive a bill for services they believe are substandard. This event might trigger distrust and rage in some people, leading to the first call to an attorney. Upstream actions, such as price transparency and discussing costs during informed consent deliberations, can avert litigation costs and the anxiety associated with them.

Safety risks. Patients with bills in collections for service they perceive as poor or for amounts they consider unreasonable can increase the risk of workplace harassment and violence. Workplace violence consists of both physical violence or threats and harassing or stalking behaviors. High concentrations of poverty and areas in which diminished economic opportunities exist are leading social and economic risk factors for type 2 (client-on-worker) workplace violence, per the Centers for Disease Control and Prevention classification.[14] Workplace violence has become a national epidemic and a significant cause of employment and vocational dissatisfaction.[15] For physicians and staff, violent behaviors consume time and energy, are morally distressing, and are potentially dangerous. Establishing clear billing expectations and having risk mitigation plans for when something unexpected occurs during treatment can decrease the risks of both litigation and workplace violence.

Limitations on Cost Transparency

I propose 2 specific reasons why risk managers may not see cost transparency as a social justice issue warranting their engagement. The first concerns the institutional burdens that it creates, and the second concerns the circumstances in which it is not feasible to get price consent prior to treatment.

Institutional burdens. Although transparency with patients regarding costs would preserve patients' autonomy and reduce their stress, it does present another unfunded burden with operational constrictions. Performing this function would involve either using clinical team members (i.e., physicians, nurses, or other medical professionals), which would not be a good use of their time, or having nonclinical staff well trained in insurance complement the informed consent discussion provided by the physician, which, in adding a new administrative layer, would increase an already bloated system. However, cost transparency could potentially reduce administrative costs related to billing grievances, potential litigation, and safety risks.

Emergency services and competency. There will be times when transparency is not realistic or safe. The Emergency Medical Treatment and Labor Act (EMTALA) requires medical screening and emergent stabilization without consideration of ability to pay in emergency room settings,[16] and there is a perceived ethical duty to rescue when a person's life is imminently threatened.[17] However, the duty to treat does not alleviate the duty to be fair in pricing and explain existing costs when it is reasonable to do so.

Conclusion

It is incumbent upon the health care system to take the morally defensible position of ensuring fairness and equity for all stakeholders. Risk managers should advocate for transparency in pricing not only because ethics is an aspect of risk managers' daily work but also because transparency promotes personal liberty and fairness in society. Transparency is a means for the risk manager to advocate for patient autonomy and choice, encourage beneficent treatment and shared decision making, avoid harm from crippling debt and unnecessary treatment or service, and promote the general welfare. It also serves the secondary interests of improved patient satisfaction, increased patient trust in the institution and physician, improved patient relationships with clinicians, and reduced conflicts resulting from surprise billing.

COMMENTARY 2 BY STEPHEN L. NEWMAN, MD

This case is familiar to clinicians, health care executives, payers, and many patients and their parents. The "balance after" is the amount a financially responsible party (EJ's family, in this case) owes after their insurance company pays its negotiated rate. For an 8-day, in-network hospitalization surgery, EJ's family owed $190,000; some individuals have been known to receive a $117,000 bill for surgical services provided at their local hospital, due to the assistant surgeon being out of network.[18] This article explains why pricing variations occur and considers hospital risk managers' responsibilities to serve both patients and organizations.

Chargemaster Manipulation

Variations in hospital inpatient and outpatient pricing schedules are the result of chargemaster manipulations that have occurred since Medicare adopted, in 1983, the Diagnosis Related Groups (DRGs) system for bundling payments for diagnosis-specific services.[19] A chargemaster is a hospital-specific database of billable services and supplies used to itemize procedure-specific charges that are aggregated in bills sent to patients and insurers, although the amounts actually paid by patients and insurers are less. In response to increasing government regulation of payments through Medicare and Medicaid, hospitals inflate chargemaster prices to optimize reimbursement from these government programs. Such manipulations are also used in the commercial insurance sector, as insurers tend to adopt regulatory and payment practices first used in government payment systems. For example, a hospital that performs many orthopedic procedures but few cardiac procedures would disproportionately raise prices on orthopedic care items. Conversely, a hospital that performs many cardiac procedures but few orthopedic procedures would disproportionately raise prices on cardiac care items. Chargemaster manipulation explains why there is so much variation—and seemingly unexplained and ridiculously large variation—in prices of hospital inpatient and outpatient services among organizations that can be located in the same region.

Risk Managers' Responsibilities

Unsurprisingly, some hospital business practices are designed to optimize revenue, so let's turn now to hospital risk managers' duties in cases of surprise billing. A risk manager has a duty to serve his or her organization (shareholders, in this case), clinicians, external parties (for example, attorneys, payers, and regulators), and patients and their loved ones; the services a risk manager provides to each of these stakeholders might be different.

Responsibilities to patients. The American Society for Health Care Risk Management (ASHRM) lists several duties a hospital risk manager has to patients and families[20] that apply to the above case. First, a "health care risk manager has a responsibility to practice the profession with honesty, fairness, integrity, respect and good faith" and, second, "to help promote the overall quality of life, dignity, safety, and wellbeing of every individual needing healthcare services."[20] ASHRM also states that it is a risk manager's duty to "Communicate honestly and factually with patients and their families, as well as colleagues and others."[20]

Of course, hospital risk managers do not typically interact with each patient in a hospital. However, in cases like this one, interaction is certainly appropriate and advisable, since a "balance after" bill of $190,000 would very likely be an unpleasant surprise that could lead to litigation.[21] Specifically, in this case, a risk manager, along with a patient financial services staff member, could have an adjunctive role in discussing surprise billing with EJ's parents; this role would include offering financial education and support and acting as a liaison to help EJ's parents interpret technical financial language.

Responsibility to an organization. A hospital's direct and indirect costs for delivering health care services performed by clinicians is confidential, but what a hospital charges payers and other financial guarantors is public. This distinction is important in the discussion of risk managers' roles and responsibilities, since risk managers are uniquely positioned to help organizations mitigate litigation risk that can be generated by surprise billing. Specifically, risk managers can advocate for up-front hospital inpatient and outpatient pricing transparency, such that financially responsible parties are informed about their copayment or coinsurance obligations before a hospital admission or before a health care service is rendered rather than after discharge, as occurred in EJ's case.

Distinguishing Financial Risk from Health Risk

The family's out-of-pocket financial responsibility is distinct from what a hospital charges, which is public information, and some have argued that, to motivate transparency, the coverage rates hospitals negotiate with insurers should also be public. Others have suggested that pricing transparency should be part of informed consent processes. Although risks and benefits are intended to be communicated during informed consent, financial risks differ importantly from health risks. Health risks should be conveyed and clarified by a clinician, and financial risk should be conveyed and clarified by a financial counselor, perhaps with a risk manager. If up-front disclosure of financial burden to patients and their families were adopted by an organization, a good risk manager could try to serve all constituents without compromising the protection of any constituent.

References

1. The White House. President Donald J. Trump is putting patients first by making healthcare more transparent. https://www.whitehouse.gov/briefings-statements/president-donald-j-trump-putting-american-patients-first-making-healthcare-transparent/. Published June 24, 2019. Accessed April 15, 2020.
2. Rosenberg J. Trump issues executive order intended to require disclosure of negotiated rates between insurers, hospitals. *AJMC Newsroom*. June 24, 2019. https://www.ajmc.com/newsroom/trump-issues-executive-order-intended-to-require-disclosure-of-negotiated-rates-between-insurers-hospitals. Accessed September 7, 2020.
3. Berchick ER, Barnett JC, Upton RD; US Census Bureau. Health Insurance Coverage in the United States: 2018. https://www.census.gov/content/dam/Census/library/publications/2019/demo/p60-267.pdf. Current Population Reports P60-267(RV). Published 2019. Accessed March 11, 2020.
4. Collins SR, Bhupal HK, Doty MM. Issue brief: health insurance coverage eight years after the ACA. Commonwealth Fund. https://www.commonwealthfund.org/publications/issue-briefs/2019/feb/health-insurance-coverage-eight-years-after-aca. Published February 7, 2019. Accessed March 11, 2020.
5. Sandel MJ. *Justice: What's the Right Thing to Do?* New York, NY: Farrar Straus & Giroux; 2009:chap9.
6. Beauchamp T, Childress J. *Principles of Biomedical Ethics*. 7th ed. New York, NY: Oxford University Press; 2009.
7. Farmer P, Campos NG. Rethinking medical ethics: a view from below. *Dev World Bioeth*. 2004;4(1):17–41.
8. Saad L. More Americans delaying medical treatment due to cost. Gallup. https://news.gallup.com/poll/269138/americans-delaying-medical-treatment-due-cost.aspx. Published December 9, 2019. Accessed May 7, 2020.
9. Centers for Medicare and Medicaid Services. Transparency in Coverage proposed rule (CMS-9915–P). https://www.cms.gov/newsroom/fact-sheets/transparency-coverage-proposed-rule-cms-9915-p. Published November 15, 2019. Accessed March 11, 2020.
10. Porter S. Trump issues executive order on healthcare price transparency. Health Leaders. https://www.healthleadersmedia.com/finance/trump-issues-executive-order-healthcare-price-transparency. Published June 24, 2019. Accessed March 11, 2020.

11. Guo V. Ethics and pricing: 5 must know pricing ethics issues and how to avoid them. *Price Intelligently Blog*. June 6, 2019. https://www.priceintelligently.com/blog/bid/164830/5-must-know-pricing-strategy-ethics-issues. Updated May 5, 2020. Accessed May 7, 2020.
12. Kant I. *Critique of Practical Reason*. Gregor M, trans-ed. Cambridge, UK: Cambridge University Press; 1997.
13. Schmidt H, Gostin LO, Emanuel EJ. Public health, universal health coverage, and Sustainable Development Goals: can they coexist? *Lancet*. 2015;386(9996):928–930.
14. National Institute for Occupational Safety and Health, Centers for Disease Control and Prevention. Social and economic risk factors. https://wwwn.cdc.gov/WPVHC/Nurses/Course/Slide/Unit3_10. Reviewed February 7, 2020. Accessed April 14, 2020.
15. Arnetz JE, Arnetz BB. Violence towards health care staff and possible effects on the quality of patient care. *Soc Sci Med*. 2001;52(3):417–427.
16. Examination and Treatment for Emergency Medical Conditions and Women in Labor, 42 USC §1395dd (1986).
17. McKie J, Richardson J. The rule of rescue. *Soc Sci Med*. 2003;56(12):2407–2419.
18. Rosenthal E. After surgery, surprise $117,000 medical bill from doctor he didn't know. *New York Times*. September 20, 2014. https://www.nytimes.com/2014/09/21/us/drive-by-doctoring-surprise-medical-bills.html#:~:text=Till%20It%20Hurts-,After%20Surgery%2C%20Surprise%20%24117%2C000%20Medical%20Bill%20From%20Doctor%20He%20Didn,know%20was%20on%20his%20case. Accessed July 29, 2020.
19. Cortes DA, Landman N, Smolders RK. Making bundled payments work: leveraging the CMS DRG experience. *NEJM Catalyst*. May 10, 2018. http://blog.iagsaude.com.br/wp-content/uploads/2018/05/Making-bundled-payments-work_CMS-DRG-exeprience_NEJM-maio-2018-2.pdf. Accessed September 7, 2020.
20. American Society for Health Care Risk Management. Healthcare Risk Management Code of Professional Responsibility. https://www.ashrm.org/sites/default/files/ashrm/Code_of_Conduct_2013.pdf. Published 2013. Accessed July 29, 2020.
21. Appleby J. Taking surprise medical bills to court. *Kaiser Health News*. December 19, 2018. https://khn.org/news/taking-surprise-medical-bills-to-court/. Accessed July 29, 2020.

Source: Hyatt, J., and S. Newman. 2020. "Should a Good Risk Manager Worry About Cost and Price Transparency in Health Care?" *AMA Journal of Ethics* 22 (11): E924–32. Reprinted with permission.

CHAPTER 10
HUMAN RESOURCES

I have no right, by anything I do or say, to demean a human being in his own eyes. What matters is not what I think of him; it is what he thinks of himself. To undermine a man's self-respect is a sin.

—Antoine de Saint-Exupery, aviator and author

Important Terms

- Autonomy
- Beneficence
- Credentialing
- Informational justice
- Justice
- Nonmaleficence
- Physician health program (PHP)
- Physician impairment
- Privileging
- Procedural justice

Learning Objectives

Studying this chapter will help you to

➤ explain the ethical principles of justice, beneficence, nonmaleficence, and autonomy in human resources (HR),

➤ discuss the promise of confidentiality and honesty, and

➤ describe the role of HR managers in ethical HR activities.

Regardless of the size and type of the healthcare facility—a small physician practice or a large regional medical center, for example—the human resources (HR) function exists. Although HR personnel do not directly provide patient care, they are very important to healthcare organizations. They not only tend to the HR needs of the people who make up the organization—clinicians, administrators, and support and maintenance staff—but also help establish and maintain the environment in which healthcare and services are provided. As a support function, HR helps managers with recruitment, selection, retention, performance review, retirement, and termination. Additionally, HR personnel verify the qualifications and credentials of job applicants, and HR managers are involved in the physician credentialing process (discussed later in this chapter). These tasks ensure that the organization has the capability to serve its patients and community. This chapter addresses the ethical issues in HR activities encountered by managers who perform HR tasks (for simplicity, we refer to them in this chapter as HR managers, although we note that not all facilities—such as physician practices—have designated HR managers).

As you read the following Case from the Field, consider what recommendations you might make to a nursing home manager confronted with a similar situation. In addition, consider what administrative actions might be introduced to ensure that such an event is not repeated—for example, discussion of the Nursing Home Reform Act of 1987 in employee orientation, explanation of nursing home management response if an employee engages in such behavior, or development and implementation of social media guidelines. The Nursing Home Reform Act was enacted to ensure that nursing home residents receive care that promotes quality of life. In December 2020, H.R. 9021 was introduced to Congress for consideration. The Nursing Home Reform Modernization Act of 2020 was designed to improve quality and transparency for nursing home residents and families.

CASE FROM THE FIELD
Social Media and the CNA Abusers

In December 2018, two certified nursing assistants (CNAs) at the Abington of Glenview Nursing Home in Illinois posted a snap on Snapchat showing their treatment of a 91-year-old woman resident. In the video, one of the CNAs was waving a hospital gown at the resident while the other CNA recorded it. The caption read, "Margaret hates gowns," accompanied by two laughing emojis (De Mar 2019). The resident's daughter reported that her mother had dementia and "a deep fear of being made to wear a hospital gown" (Meadows 2019). She felt the CNAs had "deliberately taunted and bullied my mom . . . And they're not even supposed to have phones when they're on duty" (Kukulka 2019). Moreover, the staff at the nursing home was aware of the resident's fear (Meadows 2019).

(continued)

> **CASE FROM THE FIELD**
> Social Media and the CNA Abusers *(continued)*
>
> The nursing home subsequently fired the two CNAs, and the Illinois Department of Public Health cited the nursing home for "failure to implement its own abuse prevention policy" (Krakow 2019). The CNA who recorded the event pleaded guilty to one count of attempted unauthorized recording and was sentenced to one year of supervision and 50 hours of community service (Meadows 2019). The CNA who waved the hospital gown was sentenced to 18 months of court supervision and 100 hours of community service. He pleaded guilty to disorderly conduct, stating that he had "knowingly and intentionally alarmed and disturbed" her (Meadows 2019).
>
> The resident's family sued the nursing home, claiming that it had failed to protect their mother from abuse and violated the Health Insurance Portability and Accountability Act (HIPAA) of 1996, which requires healthcare providers to protect the privacy of their patients' health information, including details shared electronically.

Nursing home residents have the right to privacy, and providers must ensure their confidentiality and protect against "reasonably anticipated" disclosures of personal information. HIPAA rules apply to the nursing home as it serves as a healthcare provider and conducts business electronically (i.e., billing). To ensure that such an incident never happens again, a nursing home manager could be assigned to develop a training session for all personnel on the appropriate use of social media and the consequences of posting about residents and their protected health information. Moreover, if a formal social media policy has not been implemented, one should be created (see exhibit 10.1 for an example). The manager should make himself or herself available to anyone who has questions about the social media policy. While personnel typically know not to discuss residents and their conditions in public areas, they may not apply the same rule when posting on social media platforms such as Snapchat, TikTok, Twitter, Instagram, and Meta.

Ethical Principles in HR

Ethical principles, introduced in chapter 1 and elaborated and illustrated in every chapter since, play an important part in healthcare. The same is true of HR activities. Take our Case from the Field as an example. You were asked to consider what administrative actions might be introduced to ensure that such an event is not repeated. The manager helps create and sustain a safe and compliant working environment for all personnel by developing and

> **EXHIBIT 10.1**
> Sample Social Media Guidelines for a Nursing Home
>
> - *Maintain confidentiality.* Do no harm by *not* posting confidential information about the nursing home, its employees, physicians, residents, and their families, visitors, and associates of the organization. Use good ethical judgment. As a general rule, do not post content that is not readily available to the public.
> - *Be accurate.* Double- or triple-check the facts or content of your post. If you make an error, correct it as quickly as possible.
> - *Be transparent and honest.* Do not misrepresent yourself as speaking on behalf of the nursing home. Write in the first person or include a disclaimer that you are voicing your opinions, not those of the organization.
> - *Maintain privacy.* Separate your personal from your professional social media activities.
> - *Contact the marketing department with questions.* If you are unsure about a post, ask the social media experts in the marketing department before you publish. They are here to help.
> - *Beware of the consequences.* Failure to follow these guidelines may result in disciplinary actions—including reprimand, termination, or revocation of clinical privileges.

implementing policies, procedures, and training. Your efforts would be guided by the ethical principles of justice, beneficence, nonmaleficence, and autonomy, which we review in this section as they apply to the case considered here.

Justice

Justice is the ethical principle of administering deserved rewards or penalties that are aligned with legal and moral standards. When HR managers operate with justice, they handle all issues fairly. **Procedural justice**, on the other hand, refers to fair procedures that ensure fair or equitable outcomes (Rawls 1971). Take cutting a birthday cake as an example. If you are cutting the cake, the assumption is that you will take the last piece, because you first distribute the slices to others. Because you are serving yourself last, you will make sure that you cut the cake as evenly as possible (fair process) so that your slice is the same size as others (fair outcome) (Rawls 1971, 84). (In the For Your Consideration section in chapter 2, you were asked to look at procedural justice from ethicist William Nelson's [2005] perspective.)

Tom Beauchamp and James Childress (2019) explain that justice rests on the notions of fairness and equality. In the nursing home case, the resident's right to care and privacy outweighed the behavior and posting by the staff members. Nonetheless, the CNAs were treated throughout the process as fairly as possible. They were charged, they admitted their actions, and their employment was subsequently terminated for cause. The same cannot be said for the resident, however. Her daughter relocated her to another facility, disrupting

---

justice
The ethical principle of administering deserved rewards or penalties that are aligned with legal and moral standards.

procedural justice
Fair procedures that ensure fair or equitable outcomes.

her routine but providing a safer environment. In this case, procedural justice was achieved for the employees, but not for the resident.

What information and how much information should be communicated matters as well. Everyone does not need to know everything about every situation. That is, managers should exercise **informational justice**, which refers to how much pertinent information is given to explain and justify decisions and the development of subsequent protocols (Greenberg and Colquitt 2005; Kurian 2018). For example, an HR manager may share with other employees that the CNAs' Snapchat post identified *a* resident, but the manager should not share the exact details so as not to bring harm to the resident again.

informational justice
The decision to give or share only pertinent information.

BENEFICENCE

Beneficence refers to actions that help or benefit others. It is based on the Hippocratic Oath, which states that physicians are to apply measures required to benefit the sick. An HR manager's adherence to beneficence would be exemplified by creating and implementing a social media training session to ensure that all staff are aware of the nursing home's social media policy and that such an incident does not happen again.

beneficence
The ethical principle of acting to help or benefit others.

NONMALEFICENCE

Nonmaleficence refers to actions one should not commit. It is different from doing good (beneficence); rather, it is about *refraining* from taking action that could do harm. In the Case from the Field, both CNAs violated the principle of nonmaleficence. They did not stop themselves from engaging in the incident or posting the video about a resident whom they were supposed to protect from harm.

nonmaleficence
The ethical principle of refraining from actions that could harm others.

AUTONOMY

Autonomy refers to people's ability to make decisions for themselves, being mindful of the importance of respect, truth, and confidentiality. As Beauchamp and Childress (2019, 105) explain, the moral rules that apply to autonomy expect us to do the following:

autonomy
The ethical principle of making decisions independently or for oneself.

- ◆ Tell the truth
- ◆ Respect the privacy of others
- ◆ Protect confidential information
- ◆ Obtain consent for interventions with patients
- ◆ When asked, help others make important decisions

Even though the resident's individual autonomy was limited because of her dementia and need for care, the CNAs provided poor care and little, if any, respect for her autonomy—precisely because their actions were potentially harmful and conducted without her knowledge or consent. They violated the resident's right to care and privacy. An important note is that their autonomous choices potentially harmed someone else. Hence, you should consider what limits are to be placed regarding your autonomous decisions. In the case of the CNAs, they acted with autonomy that caused harm, and their employment was terminated because of it. Simply put, act autonomously if the moral rules apply; otherwise, consider a decision prior to acting.

HR and Confidentiality

Patients may speak or share sensitive information with their healthcare providers in confidence. This type of confidentiality should apply to employee–employer relations (where the employer is represented by administrators and supervisors) as well. That is, there must be a mutual understanding that employee information is sensitive and should remain confidential. Moreover, this understanding should extend to physicians; although they often are not employees, they have practicing privileges. According to the 2018 Physician Practice Benchmark Survey conducted by the American Medical Association (AMA), about 46 percent of physicians in the United States owned their own practices, 47 percent were employees, and the remaining 7 percent of practicing physicians were independent contractors (Kane 2019).

Of these physicians, about 8 percent were directly employed or contracted by hospitals, while another 27 percent worked in practices that were partly or wholly owned by a hospital (Kane 2019). Physicians may work in private offices or clinics, but they need to be credentialed and have practice privileges in area hospitals to perform certain procedures that require a hospital setting.

HR managers (and anyone else with HR responsibilities) have the responsibility to maintain the confidentiality of personnel and physicians who work in the organization.

Personnel

The practice of keeping confidential the private information of prospective, current, and past employees is essential, both ethically and legally. During the application and selection processes, for instance, job candidates may submit personal information such as college transcripts; private telephone numbers and addresses; and workforce data such as race, ethnicity, and gender. Additionally, the search committee may have notes from the reference-checking process and interviews. Everyone who has access to a candidate's information should be cognizant of their responsibility not to diminish a prospective employee's autonomy; they accomplish this by ensuring that all information is kept confidential.

The Society for Human Resource Management (SHRM) is the largest international professional association of HR managers. SHRM offers sample policies for HR professionals to consult as they develop or update policies or procedures for their workplace. For example, its employee records confidentiality policy notes that all "pre-employment inquiry information" must be kept confidential (SHRM 2021). Moreover, throughout the hiring process, the transparency, fairness, and confidentiality of all persons involved in the process is paramount (Goldstein et al. 2017). After the hiring process, employees (including managers) have a responsibility to exercise discretion. For example, managers should curb negative gossiping because the behavior is associated with negative consequences in the workplace (Tian et al. 2019; Wilkie 2014). Negative gossiping violates confidentiality, and the sender may be communicating untrue information, thereby discounting the credibility of the gossip as well as the gossiper (Lee and Barnes 2021). The "dangers of gossip" include potential violations of trust (Wilkie 2014). The role of the HR manager is to ensure that employees understand the importance of maintaining confidentiality because it is the ethical thing to do.

Physicians

To illustrate the importance of maintaining confidentiality, we present the issue of **physician impairment**, in which confidentiality is critical. (Note that all types of healthcare and medical professionals, not just physicians, suffer from impairment. For our purposes, we focus this section on physician impairment.)

In 1973, the AMA addressed the issue of physician impairment in a paper titled "The Sick Physician" (Council on Mental Health 1973). Physician impairment is a physician's inability to provide safe, competent care to patients because of physical or mental illness and substance abuse, "including alcoholism or drug dependence" (Council on Mental Health 1973, 684). In 2021, about 10 to 15 percent of all doctors were abusing alcohol in the United States, about the same as or slightly higher than the general public (Murray 2021). However, the prescription drug abuse is five times higher among physicians compared with nonphysicians (McLellan et al. 2008; Mines et al. 2013). Perhaps one reason for this greater rate of abuse is that physicians have easier access to prescription drugs than those who do not have prescribing authority. The effect of physician impairment on the workplace is significant because physicians are in charge of people's health. The problem goes beyond impaired doctors showing up late for patient appointments and seeing fewer patients per day; it places patients' lives in danger. Thus, physician impairment is not just a personal but a public safety issue.

In 2001, The Joint Commission began to require hospitals to establish a confidential, nondisciplinary system to identify and assist impaired physicians (Krall, Niazi, and Miller 2012). In 2011, the Federation of State Medical Boards (FSMB) updated its policy on physician impairment, noting that confidentiality is a key incentive to "refer physicians into a PHP [**physician health program**] early rather than wait for frank impairment and

physician impairment
A physician's inability to provide safe, competent care to patients because of physical or mental illness or substance abuse or dependence.

physician health program (PHP)
A state-based program that helps impaired physicians get treatment and rehabilitation so that they can return to practice.

referral to the board for discipline" (FSMB 2011, 6). In 2019, FSMB expanded this policy to provide guidance to state boards regarding recommendations on "emerging issues" such as physician opioid use disorder (FSMB 2019, 1, 9–10). A PHP oversees an impaired physician's treatment, rehabilitation, and follow-up care.

The American College of Physicians issued a position paper on physician impairment and rehabilitation. It also emphasizes the importance of confidentiality. The paper states that impaired physicians have a duty to seek help, and other physicians have a responsibility to assist and report colleagues who appear to be impaired, starting with a "sensitive but forthright discussion" (Candilis, Kim, and Sulmasy 2019, 871).

Physicians have an ethical duty to seek help regarding their impairment because they are violating all of the ethical principles of justice, beneficence, nonmaleficence, and autonomy. They should not practice medicine while under the influence of drugs or alcohol, and they are duty-bound to report impaired colleagues (AMA 2021). Medical directors, administrators, and other colleagues may identify a physician and refer impaired physicians to a PHP, or a physician may voluntarily seek assistance. For example, the North Carolina Physicians Health Program (NCPHP) receives referrals from treatment centers as well as colleagues and spouses of impaired physicians (Pendergast and Scarborough 2009). The North Carolina Medical Board took the position that physicians have a "professional obligation to act." In 2017, the NCPHP assisted 225 physicians out of more than 15,000 physicians practicing in the state, and over 90 percent reported that the NCPHP program had helped them (Ellis 2018). HR professionals also may be involved in identification, referral, and follow-up by assisting or guiding medical directors or other relevant personnel throughout the process.

According to the FSMB (2019, 8), referrals to a PHP may follow one of two tracks:

- The voluntary track that includes participants who enter the PHP without the board's mandate. These physicians should be afforded anonymity from the board as long as they do not pose a risk of harm to the public. Cases that pose a danger of harm to the public should be reported to the board with laws or regulations in place that allow that reporting.
- The mandated track includes physicians that are required by the board to participate in a PHP. As such, their identities are known to the board.

Whichever track is assigned to the impaired physician, the *promise of confidentiality* must be fulfilled by everyone involved—as long as the physician is not deemed dangerous or a threat to anyone's health and well-being. In North Carolina, for example, confidentiality is maintained, and the identities of impaired physicians are unknown to the North Carolina Medical Board. To maintain this confidentiality status, impaired physicians who may be unsafe to practice (i.e., patient care could be negatively affected) must sign a binding agreement that they will not practice while under assessment and treatment (Huff 2011).

Moreover, the AMA (2021) extends confidentiality to physicians who report a suspected impaired physician.

A healthcare manager or HR manager should be aware of the signs of physician impairment. The indicators include too many missed patient appointments; an excessive number of prescription orders; gradual or drastic change in behavior that causes conflict with patients, employees, and others; and reports of decreased patient charting (Baldisseri 2007; Bright and Krahn 2010; Fitzgerald 2021; Mines et al. 2013). In such situations, the manager works with the medical director to investigate the suspicion, identify the type of impairment, approach the physician, refer the physician to a PHP, and support the physician and medical director (or other personnel) through treatment and recovery.

HR AND HONESTY

Ethical HR requires the *promise of honesty*. Just as clinicians are bound by their professions' ethical codes to share medical information to enable patients to exercise their autonomy (and to see that clinicians have their best interests at heart), managers should abide by their own ethical code, which emphasizes honesty. According to the Code of Ethics of the American College of Healthcare Executives (ACHE 2017), healthcare executives must be "[t]ruthful in all forms of professional and organizational communication, and avoid disseminating information that is false, misleading or deceptive."

In HR, truthful communication comes in the form of clear, straightforward, and regularly updated employee policies; timely, organization-wide explanations of changes to processes and policies; sharing of data and information to help people do their jobs well; use of all appropriate media (including employee newsletters, bulletin boards, flyers, emails, intranet, social media, and staff meetings) to ensure that HR information and announcements reach as many stakeholders as possible; and a transparent, open-door system that encourages employees and other internal stakeholders to be honest in return (such as when asking difficult questions, reporting errors, admitting mistakes, and airing grievances). As discussed in other chapters, honesty is a first step toward building trust—not only between managers and their direct reports, but also among leadership, employees, physicians, patients, and other stakeholders in between.

THE ROLE OF HR MANAGERS IN ETHICAL HUMAN RESOURCES

Physician credentialing and employment termination are two activities that HR managers are involved in but do not control. To be of assistance in these efforts, HR managers should ensure that the processes and policies followed by those in charge of credentialing and termination are both legal and ethical.

Physician Credentialing

Credentialing of physicians is usually conducted by HR managers in consultation with physicians. It is a peer-review process; thus, although managers gather and verify the necessary documentation, they are not involved in **privileging**—the approval of practice privileges based on verified credentials and other factors. Instead, privileging is determined by the medical staff. If all credentials are in order, the chief of the medical staff recommends to the board of directors that the physician be given privileges to perform designated procedures in the facility. If the board of directors agrees, the physician receives privileges.

Hospitals, health systems, and other types of healthcare providers have an ethical—and often a legal—duty to conduct a proper and careful credentialing process. In the 1965 case *Darling v. Charleston Memorial Hospital*, the Illinois Supreme Court found that Charleston Memorial was negligent in credentialing a doctor who set a patient's broken leg incorrectly and in doing so cut the blood circulation to the leg, leading to its amputation (Wiet 2005). Moreover, the nurses failed to see or report early signs of the problem or to serve as advocates for the patient. *Darling v. Charleston Memorial Hospital* is a landmark case that set a precedent for healthcare providers found legally liable for the incompetence of their credentialed clinicians (see the Mini-Case Study in chapter 4).

The legal responsibility for physician credentialing varies by state. For example, in Illinois, hospitals have legal responsibility, but that is not so in Utah. The Utah Code (§ 78B-3-425) does not allow medical malpractice lawsuits based on negligent credentialing (Utah State Legislature 2011; Utah Code 2011). In the absence of legal guidance or requirement, healthcare managers should rely on their ethics—specifically, the principles of beneficence and nonmaleficence—when doing their part in the credentialing process. Unlike Utah, other states allow for negligent credentialing claims; thus, hospitals and health systems must take seriously their legal duty to properly credential their clinicians. Adhering to the beneficence and nonmaleficence principles, some healthcare facilities even employ personnel designated to oversee physician recruitment and credentialing.

Employment Termination

HR managers usually do not decide who gets fired, but they assist the department manager or supervisor or advise them on what to do if termination is imminent or necessary. Every healthcare delivery organization has a different termination policy; for some, the policy is zero tolerance for violating rules, which is what happened when three clinical support staffers were fired by University Medical Center in Tucson, Arizona.

In 2011, US Representative Gabrielle Giffords was holding a "Congress on Your Corner" event in a grocery store parking lot in Tucson when a gunman opened fire at the crowd, wounding Giffords and 12 others and killing six people (Gassen and Williams 2013). Most of the injured were taken to University Medical Center. News of the shooting

---

credentialing
The process of collecting, evaluating, and verifying the education and training, license, work history, references, and criminal background of physicians who apply for practice privileges.

privileging
The approval of a physician's privileges to perform designated procedures in a facility.

flooded television, radio, newspapers, and websites for many weeks. Public services and vigils were held for the dead and the injured. The public's support for and interest in the victims were enormous.

Despite the constant coverage of the events after the shooting, updates about Giffords, and interviews with witnesses and families of the deceased, University Medical Center kept quiet about the conditions of the injured survivors in its care, precisely because such information is private. Adhering to HIPAA rules, University Medical Center allowed only select personnel to access these patients' charts or health records (HHS 2021). These authorized users included the clinicians who provided direct care and services to the patients, billing personnel, and other stakeholders who had a need-to-know, work-related reason. (See chapter 13 for more discussion of health records privacy and security.)

Three clinical support staff members who had nothing to do with the treatment of the injured patients looked at the private files, breaking HIPAA rules and hospital policy. The employees were immediately terminated. A hospital spokesperson explained that their firing was the result of "inappropriately accessing confidential medical records" (CNN 2011). University Medical Center has a zero-tolerance policy on any violations of patient privacy (Hensley 2011). HR has a role in communicating such a policy to all stakeholders of the organization, and all employees must be informed of the consequences (including termination) of violating the policy. When honestly and widely communicated, such a policy may serve as a deterrent or at least may come as no surprise when enforced.

An ethical termination process includes the four ethical principles discussed earlier. Let us examine each in the context of the events at University Medical Center.

- *Justice*. HR administered a penalty (termination) that was aligned with legal and hospital standards (HIPAA rules and hospital policy). The employees were aware of the zero-tolerance policy and the consequences of violating the patient privacy rule. The termination was the direct outcome of the employees' action.

- *Beneficence*. In an effort to help staff, HR communicated to all employees the zero-tolerance policy regarding inappropriately accessing private patient information. HR also conveyed the importance of upholding HIPAA standards.

- *Nonmaleficence*. HR never had a public discussion about who the employees were and why they accessed the information as doing so could do harm. Rather, it focused on what happened, when it happened, and what consequences resulted. The harm was already done, so there was no need to add more.

- *Autonomy*. To show respect for the autonomy of the employees involved, HR kept their identity confidential. Additionally, way before the events happened, HR gave all employees honest talk about the zero-tolerance policy that would help them make informed, independent decisions.

The University Medical Center case occurred in 2011. You might surmise that by now, healthcare workers would refrain from inappropriately accessing confidential medical records. However, even though the employees lost their jobs, the act of snooping, sharing, or selling patient records remains an issue that warrants attention. For example, in 2016 at Jackson Health System in Miami, Florida, two employees accessed a patient's electronic medical record. The patient happened to be a professional football player, and photos of his amputated finger were subsequently published by an ESPN reporter (HHS 2019). At the same facility in 2017, an employee was arrested for identity theft after it was discovered that she had been selling patients' personal health information for six years to others who used the information to file false tax returns in the patients' names (Sweeney 2017). In May 2020, 13 employees at Hennepin Healthcare in Minneapolis, Minnesota, were fired after they inappropriately accessed the medical records of a man who had died after an officer handcuffed him and pressed his knee into the back of the man's neck (Mannix 2020). Your responsibility as a healthcare manager to exhibit ethical behavior remains when you are interacting with employees, even when you are terminating their employment for cause.

Mini-Case Study: Serving as a Patient Advocate

A key ethic in the nursing profession is serving as an advocate for patients. At times, nurses may stand up for patients when their actions challenge authority. Provision 3 of the American Nurses Association's Code of Ethics focuses on patients' rights to privacy, confidentiality, and safety (Lachman 2009). The code directs nurses to report actions that may harm patients. That directive is clear, and it is taken seriously by professional nurses. HR support for nurses when they are advocating for their patients is important because the nurses are fulfilling their ethical duty.

Consider the following case, compiled from newspaper and blog accounts (see Elbein 2011; Lowes 2010; Sack 2010), of an incident that happened in Winkler County, Texas. As you read this summary, consider the role and ethical obligations of those involved to their patients and employees. What should hospital leaders have done for the nurses as they served as patient advocates?

Two nurses had worked at the same Winkler County hospital for more than 20 years. One of the nurses was in charge of quality assessment, and her responsibility included auditing hospital records to ensure that quality of care was maintained. The other nurse was the compliance officer, responsible for ensuring that hospital physicians and pharmacists were following state regulations. In 2007, the hospital hired a new administrator to serve as executive director and head manager; later, the compliance officer described him as "not a listener," saying, "He didn't want us looking at anything or making comments about anything" (Elbein 2011). In 2008, the hospital hired a new physician, who became friends with this administrator and the town's sheriff.

As the compliance officer, the nurse reviewed the charts (medical records) of patients, including those under the new physician's care. She found the new physician's treatments to be highly unsafe and discovered evidence of a conflict of interest. Specifically, he was giving patients samples of elixirs that were not approved by the US Food and Drug Administration (FDA). These elixirs consisted of fruit juice and dietary supplements, and they were sold only by the physician and through his website. Moreover, she found that the physician had prescribed thyroid medicine to patients who did not have thyroid issues, failed to appropriately treat a diabetic patient who should have been referred to another hospital for skin grafting, and performed surgeries at the hospital even though surgeries were not allowed at the hospital.

When the compliance officer expressed her concerns to the new administrator, his response was minimal. He instructed her to write a waiver for patients to sign; the waiver released the hospital from liability resulting from the elixirs. Additionally, he told her to write a letter to the physician to inform him about hospital policies (such as physicians were prohibited from prescribing medications that had not been approved by the FDA and from performing surgeries on site). The administrator refused to take further actions.

Next, the compliance officer, the quality assurance nurse, and a nurse who worked with the physician reported their concerns to the hospital's board of directors. One board member interrupted them and shut down their attempt to inform. Frustrated, the nurse who worked with the physician quit her job, but the compliance officer and quality assurance nurse continued to voice their concerns—to no avail. In fact, the administrator issued an order that no one employed in the hospital may report any doctors without his permission; the board passed this order as policy. In 2009, both nurses anonymously wrote a letter to the Texas Medical Board detailing the physician's unsafe clinical practices.

After the physician (who already had a restricted license) was informed that he was under review by the state board, the sheriff launched an investigation and obtained a warrant to search the nurses' computers. A copy of the complaint letter was found on the computer used by the quality assurance nurse. Both nurses were fired, arrested, and then indicted for misuse of official information, which carried a $10,000 fine and possible imprisonment of up to ten years. The Texas Nurses Association established a legal defense fund for the nurses, and other state nurse associations, as well as the national nurse association, contributed financial support. Letters and emails of support poured in for both nurses before and during the trial.

The outcomes of the case were as follows:

- The charges against the quality assurance nurse were dropped before trial.
- The compliance officer was found not guilty after a jury deliberation that lasted less than one hour.
- The two nurses sued the hospital, county, sheriff, and prosecutor in civil court and received damages of $750,000.
- The administrator resigned from the hospital, was charged with and pleaded guilty to a misdemeanor of abuse in an official capacity, and turned over evidence against the sheriff.

- The sheriff was found guilty of retaliation, misuse of official information, and two counts of official oppression and was subsequently removed from office, sentenced to four years of probation and 100 days in jail, and fined $6,000.
- The physician pleaded guilty to two felony charges of retaliation and misuse of official information, surrendered his medical license, was sentenced to 60 days in jail and five years of probation, and was fined $5,000.

MINI-CASE STUDY QUESTIONS

1. Review the events that occurred during this two-year conflict. What unethical HR practices took place?
2. If you worked in HR at the hospital, what were your ethical obligations to prevent these unethical practices? Consider, for example, the ethical standards of justice, beneficence, nonmaleficence, and autonomy and the responsibility to patients, employees, and physicians with practicing privileges.
3. Are you concerned by the administrator's actions (or lack of) that led up to one nurse leaving and two nurses getting fired? Why or why not?

POINTS TO REMEMBER

➤ Managers engaged in HR activities play a significant role in ensuring that employees, patients, and physicians with practicing privileges are treated ethically and treat others ethically.

➤ The ethical principles of justice, beneficence, nonmaleficence, and autonomy guide HR professionals as they support the efforts of the organization and its people.

➤ Justice is administering deserved rewards or penalties that are aligned with legal and moral standards.

➤ Beneficence is acting to help or benefit others.

➤ Nonmaleficence is refraining from actions that could harm others.

➤ Autonomy is making decisions independently or for oneself.

➤ Fulfilling the promise of confidentiality and the promise of honesty is both a legal and an ethical responsibility.

CHALLENGE YOURSELF

1. Consider the chapter-opening quote by Antoine de Saint-Exupery. Think of an example that might be true for you as you prepare to become a healthcare manager.

2. Review the Case from the Field. What important points should be included in an HR manager's new employee training session at the nursing home? Offer an example to illustrate.
3. The Society for Human Resource Management notes that the confidentiality of employee information is essential. Consider a physician recruiter's role in hiring a new physician. Why is confidentiality an important concept in this situation?

For Your Consideration

10.1 Imagine that you are the HR manager as you watch this video, posted on YouTube by emergency nurse Lillian Udell: www.youtube.com/watch?v=61VNJAJshwU. Udell works at Lincoln Hospital in the South Bronx, New York. She interviewed other healthcare workers on April 21, 2020, at the height of the COVID-19 pandemic. During the interview, a nurse educator is named and identified as a patient who died of the virus. One nurse interviewed said, "If we had the government behind us, to provide us the resources that we need, I think [the patient is named] would probably still be alive."

You are asked to be part of the review team who will follow up with Udell regarding the HIPAA violation. First, explain why this is a HIPAA violation. Second, what questions would you ask Udell? What action would you recommend taking, if any, against Udell? Focus on the issues of social media (the video posting), the information shared, and the ethical principles of justice, beneficence, nonmaleficence, and autonomy during the pandemic as you prepare your answer.

10.2 A nurse was caring for a toddler who required treatment and care in the intensive care unit at Texas Children's Hospital (Latner 2019). As the patient admitted was a toddler, he was too young to have received the measles vaccination. He had been taken to the hospital with a painful rash and high fever and was subsequently diagnosed with the measles. The nurse, a member of an anti-vaccine Facebook group, posted about the toddler to the group and noted that this instance may give those who oppose vaccination a reason to rethink their position. In her Facebook profile, the nurse noted that she worked at Texas Children's Hospital, but she did not post the patient's name.

The unvaccinated child of another member of the Facebook group was also a patient in the hospital when the toddler with measles was admitted. Concerned about contagion, she posted screenshots of the nurse's Facebook post on the Texas Children's Hospital's Facebook page.

As you think about this scenario, answer the following questions:
a. What makes this instance a HIPAA violation that warrants attention?
b. What action would you recommend the hospital take regarding the nurse who posted the information? What action would you recommend the hospital take to respond to the reposting of the information to the hospital's Facebook group?
c. What does this real-life event suggest to you about your work life and social media?

Check These Out

Want more information about the organizations and concepts discussed in the chapter? Check these websites out.

- American Medical Association Code of Ethics: Opinions on Physicians and the Health of the Community: www.ncmedsoc.org/physicians-health-program-offered-help-to-hundreds-last-year/
- American Nurses Association: www.nursingworld.org/default.aspx
  - Code of Ethics: www.nursingworld.org/Mobile/Code-of-Ethics
  - What Nurses Do: www.nursingworld.org/EspeciallyForYou/What-is-Nursing/Tools-You-Need/RNsAPNs.html
- North Carolina Medical Board Position Statement on Professional Obligations: www.ncmedboard.org/resources-information/professional-resources/laws-rules-position-statements/position-statements/professional_obligations_pertaining_to_incompetence_impairment_or_unethical
- Nursing Home Reform Modernization Act of 2020: www.congress.gov/116/bills/hr9021/BILLS-116hr9021ih.xml
- Society for Human Resource Management: www.shrm.org/pages/default.aspx
- Texas Nurses Association: www.texasnurses.org
- 1987 Nursing Home Reform Act: www.govinfo.gov/app/details/CHRG-110shrg37151/CHRG-110shrg37151/context

References

American College of Healthcare Executives (ACHE). 2017. "Code of Ethics." Amended November 13. www.ache.org/-/media/ache/ethics/code_of_ethics_web.pdf.

American Medical Association (AMA). 2021. "Physician Responsibilities to Impaired Colleagues." Accessed March 25. www.ama-assn.org/delivering-care/ethics/physician-responsibilities-impaired-colleagues.

Baldisseri, M. 2007. "Impaired Healthcare Professional." *Critical Care Medicine* 35 (2): S106–16.

Beauchamp, T., and J. Childress. 2019. *Principles of Biomedical Ethics*, 8th ed. New York: Oxford University Press.

Bright, R., and L. Krahn. 2010. "Impaired Physicians: How to Recognize, When to Report, and Where to Refer." *Current Psychiatry* 9 (6): 11–14, 20.

Candilis, P., D. Kim, and L. Sulmasy. 2019. "Physician Impairment and Rehabilitation: Reintegration into Medical Practice While Ensuring Patient Safety: A Position Paper from the American College of Physicians. *Annals of Internal Medicine* 170 (12): 871–79.

CNN. 2011. "Hospital Personnel Fired for Accessing Records of Tucson Victims." Published January 12. www.cnn.com/2011/US/01/12/arizona.hospital.records/.

Council on Mental Health. 1973. "The Sick Physician: Impairment by Psychiatric Disorders, Including Alcoholism and Drug Dependence." *Journal of the American Medical Association* 223 (6): 684–87.

De Mar, C. 2019. "Outrage After Video Shows Staffer Taunting, Terrorizing Woman, 91, at Glenview Nursing Home." CBS Chicago. Published August 8. https://chicago.cbslocal.com/2019/08/08/glenview-nursing-home-abuse/.

Elbein, S. 2011. "Intent to Harm." *Texas Observer*. Published March 17. www.texasobserver.org/intent-to-harm/.

Ellis, E. 2018. "Physicians Health Program Offered Help to Hundreds Last Year." North Carolina Medical Society. Published January 24. www.ncmedsoc.org/physicians-health-program-offered-help-to-hundreds-last-year/.

Federation of State Medical Boards (FSMB). 2019. "Policy on Physician Impairment: Towards a Model That Optimizes Patient Safety and Physician Health." Accessed August 22, 2021. www.fsmb.org/siteassets/advocacy/policies/policy-on-physician-impairment.pdf.

———. 2011. "Policy on Physician Impairment." Accessed March 25, 2021. www.fsmb.org/siteassets/advocacy/policies/physician-impairment.pdf.

Fitzgerald, R. 2021. "Caring for the Physician Affected by Substance Use Disorder." *American Family Physician* 103 (5): 302–4.

Gassen, S., and T. Williams. 2013. "Before Attack, Parents of Gunman Tried to Address Son's Strange Behavior." *New York Times*. Published March 27. www.nytimes.com/2013/03/28/us/documents-2011-tucson-shooting-case-gabrielle-giffords.html.

Goldstein, H., E. Pulakos, J. Passmore, and C. Semedo (eds.). 2017. *The Wiley Blackwell Handbook of the Psychology of Recruitment, Selection and Employee Retention*. Hoboken, NJ: John Wiley & Sons.

Greenberg, J., and J. Colquitt. 2005. *Handbook of Organizational Justice*. Mahwah, NJ: Lawrence Erlbaum.

Hensley, S. 2011. "Snooping Tucson Hospital Workers Fired in Records Breach." National Public Radio. Published January 14. www.npr.org/sections/health-shots/2011/01/14/132928883/snooping-tucson-hospital-workers-fired-in-records-breach.

Huff, J. 2011. "Caring for Each Other: Helping Health Care Professionals in Need." North Carolina Medical Board. Published April 26. www.ncmedboard.org/resources-information/professional-resources/publications/forum-newsletter/article/caring_for_each_other_helping_health_care_professionals_in_need.

Kane, C. 2019. "Updated Data on Physician Practice Arrangements: For the First Time, Fewer Physicians Are Owners Than Employees." American Medical Association. Accessed February 1, 2021. www.ama-assn.org/system/files/2019-07/prp-fewer-owners-benchmark-survey-2018.pdf.

Krakow, M. 2019. "Caregivers Taunted a 91-Year-Old with Dementia on Video, Lawsuit Says. They've Been Fired and Charged." *Washington Post*. Published August 11. www.washingtonpost.com/health/2019/08/11/caregivers-taunted-year-old-with-dementia-video-lawsuit-says-theyve-been-fired-charged/.

Krall, E., S. Niazi, and M. Miller. 2012. "The Status of Physician Health Programs in Wisconsin and North Central States: A Look at Statewide and Health Systems Programs." *Wisconsin Medical Journal* 111 (5): 220–27.

Kukulka, A. 2019. "Caregivers at Glenview Nursing Home Accused of Taunting 91-Year-Old Resident in Snapchat Video: Lawsuit." *Chicago Tribune*. Published August 12. www.chicagotribune.com/suburbs/glenview/ct-gla-collins-nursing-home-lawsuit-tl-0815-20190809-gilagfpsirex5nhkb4xivwhmjm-story.html.

Kurian, D. 2018. "Organizational Justice: Why Does It Matter for HRD." *Journal of Organizational Psychology* 18 (2): 11–22.

Lachman, V. 2009. "Practical Use of the Nursing Code of Ethics: Part I." *MEDSURG Nursing: The Journal of Adult Health* 18 (1): 55–57.

Latner, A. 2019. "Social Media Post Prompts Firing." *Clinical Advisor*. Published May 22. www.clinicaladvisor.com/home/my-practice/legal-advisor/social-media-post-prompts-firing/.

Lee, S., and C. Barnes. 2021. "An Attributional Process Model of Workplace Gossip." *Journal of Applied Psychology* 106 (2): 300–316.

Lowes, R. 2010. "Nurses in Texas Whistle-Blower Case Settle for $750,000." Medscape. Published August 12. www.medscape.com/viewarticle/726812.

Mannix, A. 2020. "In Wake of George Floyd's Death, Hennepin Healthcare Employees Fired for Accessing Confidential Medical Records." *Star Tribune* (Minneapolis, MN). Published September 24. www.startribune.com/after-floyd-s-death-5-hennepin-healthcare-employees-fired-for-accessing-medical-records/572505661/.

McLellan, A., G. Skipper, M. Campbell, and R. DuPont. 2008. "Five Year Outcomes in a Cohort Study of Physicians Treated for Substance Use Disorders in the United States." *British Medical Journal* 337: a2038.

Meadows, J. 2019. "Glenview Abington Ex-Staffers Plead Guilty to Teasing 91-Year-Old." *Patch* (Glenview, IL). Published August 28. https://patch.com/illinois/glenview/glenview-abington-ex-staffers-plead-guilty-teasing-91-year-old.

Mines, R., D. Kimlinger, Y. Moore, P. Hiester, M. Kent, and S. Hull. 2013. "The Organizational Impact of Impaired Health Care Executives or Physicians: A Review and Recommendations." *Journal of Workplace Behavioral Health* 28 (1): 1–12.

Murray, K. 2021. "Alcoholism and Medical Professionals." Alcohol Rehab Guide. Published February 19. www.alcoholrehabguide.org/resources/alcoholism-and-medical-professionals/.

Nelson, W. A. 2005. "An Organizational Ethics Decision-Making Process." *Healthcare Executive* 20 (4): 8–14.

Pendergast, W., and J. Scarborough. 2009. "Physician Health vs. Impairment: The North Carolina Physicians Health Program." *North Carolina Medical Journal* 70 (1): 59–61.

Rawls, J. 1971. *A Theory of Justice*. Cambridge, MA: Belknap Press of Harvard University Press.

Sack, K. 2010. "Whistle-Blowing Nurse Is Acquitted in Texas." *New York Times*. Published February 11. www.nytimes.com/2010/02/12/us/12nurses.html.

Society for Human Resource Management (SHRM). 2021. "Employee Records Confidentiality Policy." Accessed February 1. www.shrm.org/resourcesandtools/tools-and-samples/policies/pages/cms_009926.aspx.

Sweeney, E. 2017. "Former Florida Hospital Secretary Among 104 Charged with Identity Theft." *Fierce Healthcare*. Published February 2. www.fiercehealthcare.com/it/former-florida-hospital-secretary-among-104-charged-identity-theft.

Tian, Q., Y. Song, H. Kwan, and X. Li. 2019. "Workplace Gossip and Frontline Employees' Proactive Service Performance." *Service Industries Journal* 39 (1): 25–42.

US Department of Health and Human Services (HHS). 2021. "Health Information Privacy." Accessed March 25. www.hhs.gov/ocr/privacy.

———. 2019. "OCR Imposes a $2.15 Million Civil Money Penalty Against Jackson Health System for HIPAA Violations." Published October 23. www.hhs.gov/hipaa/for-professionals/compliance-enforcement/agreements/jackson/index.html.

Utah Code. 2011. "78B-3-425 Prohibition on Cause of Action for Negligent Credentialing." Accessed March 25, 2021. https://le.utah.gov/xcode/Title78B/Chapter3/C78B-3-S425_1800010118000101.pdf.

Utah State Legislature. 2011. "S.B. 150: Negligent Credentialing." Accessed March 25, 2021. http://le.utah.gov/~2011/bills/static/SB0150.html.

Wiet, M. 2005. "*Darling v. Charleston Community Memorial Hospital* and Its Legacy." *Annals of Health Law* 14 (2): 399–408.

Wilkie, D. 2014. "Workplace Gossip: What Crosses the Line?" *SHRM Blog*. Published February 26. https://blog.shrm.org/workforce/workplace-gossip-what-crosses-the-line.

CHAPTER 11
STRATEGIC PLANNING

Alice came to a fork in the road. "Which road do I take?" she asked. "Where do you want to go?" responded the Cheshire Cat. "I don't know," Alice answered. "Then," said the Cat, "it doesn't matter."

—Lewis Carroll, *Alice in Wonderland*

Important Terms

- Accountable care organization (ACO)
- Culturally competent and sensitive care
- Health policy
- Patient Protection and Affordable Care Act (ACA)
- Quadruple Aim
- Stigma
- Strategic planning
- Strategic planning cycle
- Triple Aim

Learning Objectives

Studying this chapter will help you to

➤ define health policy and understand its importance in healthcare strategic planning,

➤ define strategic planning and the strategic planning cycle,

➤ apply the ethical principles involved in strategic planning, and

➤ describe the lessons of the US military's humanitarian aid strategy and implementation for healthcare managers in nonmilitary organizations.

This chapter focuses on strategic planning, which addresses questions about the organization's mission (who it is) and vision (what it wants to be or do in the foreseeable future). The mission and vision, in turn, guide the creation of objectives, directions, assessment tools, and a formal implementation plan. Strategic planning involves collaboration among healthcare leaders who provide the overarching direction and employees participating on the front lines. The involvement of frontline employees matters because strategic planning is a dynamic process, and those providing direct care may be in a better position to recognize the challenges and conditions that the plan must accommodate and respond to (Harris 2017). In this chapter, we use several examples—featuring healthcare, corporate, and military organizations—to demonstrate how ethical organizations (through their leaders and managers) establish strategies and implement plans that are founded on ethical principles. In our discussions, you will see both intended and unintended consequences of these strategies when implemented.

CASE FROM THE FIELD
The Affordable Care Act

Health policy refers to strategies aimed at improving the health of the people and the communities in which they live. The United States advanced its health policy with the 2010 passage of the **Patient Protection and Affordable Care Act (ACA)**.

The ACA was designed to achieve three overarching goals:

1. Increase access to healthcare by making affordable health insurance available to more people
2. Expand Medicaid to cover all adults with incomes below 138 percent of the federal poverty level
3. Support innovative medical care delivery methods to lower healthcare costs

The provisions of the ACA provide rights and protections for healthcare consumers, including the following:

- People with preexisting conditions cannot be denied coverage.
- People are no longer subject to annual or lifetime healthcare spending limits.
- People who made an error on their insurance application can no longer lose their coverage.
- People's health insurance premiums must be spent on medical care. Insurance companies may spend no more than 20 percent of premiums on administration, overhead, and marketing. The remaining 80 percent must be spent on medical care.
- Insurance must cover preventive services.
- Adult children may stay on their parents' insurance plan up to age 26.

A key goal of the ACA was to expand access to healthcare by increasing the number of people with health insurance coverage. In 2010, 16 percent of the US population had no health

(continued)

---

health policy
The defining of health goals with a vision for improving the health of the people and the communities in which they live.

Patient Protection and Affordable Care Act (ACA)
A 2010 federal law that introduced extensive healthcare system reforms, including expanding access to private insurance and Medicaid coverage and strengthening consumers' rights and protections.

> **CASE FROM THE FIELD**
> The Affordable Care Act *(continued)*
>
> insurance; by 2020, that share had been reduced to 8.5 percent (Commonwealth Fund 2020). In this way, previously uninsured individuals and families were able to obtain insurance coverage without the barriers of high cost or denial because of a chronic illness. It is important to note, however, the effect of the COVID-19 pandemic on the distribution of health insurance coverage in the United States. By March 2021, the Congressional Budget Office predicted that about one million fewer people would have health insurance compared with March 2020, primarily because of the increase of unemployment (CBO 2020).
>
> In response to the pandemic, the US Congress passed the Families First Coronavirus Response Act (FFCRA), which increased financial federal support for Medicaid and the Children's Health Insurance Program (CHIP) to mitigate the anticipated loss of employment insurance coverage (CBO 2020). However, the reduction in coverage was less than expected. The overall number of insured increased from the passage of the ACA in 2010 to 2021, which created potential capacity issues for healthcare providers as many shifted their operations to accommodate more newly insured patients. This capacity issue is one consequence that healthcare delivery organizations may address in their strategic planning.
>
> Another goal of the ACA is to reduce healthcare costs. To achieve this end, many healthcare providers decided to form **accountable care organizations (ACOs)**. The Centers for Medicare & Medicaid Services (CMS) defines ACOs as "groups of doctors, hospitals, and other health care providers, who come together voluntarily to give coordinated high quality care to the Medicare patients they serve. Coordinated care helps ensure that patients, especially the chronically ill, get the right care at the right time, with the goal of avoiding unnecessary duplication of services and preventing medical errors" (CMS 2021). ACOs have existed since about 2005. Since then, this form has been adopted by commercial payers, state Medicaid programs, and Medicare. The exact makeup of individual ACOs differs but may include primary, specialist, hospital, emergency, outpatient, and home health care, as well as pharmacy and laboratory among its types of care, services, and settings. Providers of such care and services share data and information to monitor the patient's movement across the system, to find out the treatment ordered and the outcome achieved (intended to improve quality), and to prevent duplication of services (intended to reduce costs).
>
> In 2008, Donald Berwick, president and CEO of the Institute for Healthcare Improvement (IHI), and two IHI colleagues, Thomas Nolan and John Whittington, argued that barriers to integrate care may be politically based. To improve the US healthcare system, they held, efforts must focus on three aims (Berwick, Nolan, and Whittington 2008):
>
> 1. *Improving the patient experience of care;*
> 2. *Improving population health;* and
> 3. *Reducing the per capita costs of healthcare.*
>
> *(continued)*

accountable care organization (ACO)
A group of providers that collaborate to give coordinated and improved care and aim to reduce costs by being mindful of healthcare expenditures.

> **CASE FROM THE FIELD**
> **The Affordable Care Act** *(continued)*
>
> Practicing cost control, patient-centered care, integration and coordination of health services, and a focus on prevention would help accomplish this **"Triple Aim."** These practices are in alignment with the way ACOs operate, providing care at lower costs and increasing patient access to preventive measures such as vaccinations.
>
> Physicians Thomas Bodenheimer and Christine Sinsky (2014) subsequently added a fourth aim focusing on the provider. As a healthcare manager, it is your duty to create a work environment that discourages burnout and encourages job satisfaction. Thus, the term **"Quadruple Aim"** was coined to include another goal—ensuring a positive provider experience. ACOs share the goals of the Quadruple Aim (Wilson et al. 2020, 131):
>
> 1. *Improving the patient experience of care;*
> 2. *Improving population health;*
> 3. *Reducing the per capita costs of healthcare; and*
> 4. *Ensuring positive provider experiences.*
>
> Depending on the ACO's makeup, coordination is centered around the primary care physician, who is in charge of the patient's treatment. The primary care physician may participate in Medicare's Shared Savings Program, which requires providers to meet quality and cost metrics to benefit financially. Research has yielded mixed results regarding the impact of ACOs on financial gain, with only moderate to small savings reported (Colla et al. 2016; McWilliams et al. 2018; Ouayogode et al. 2021). However, research indicates positive outcomes of ACOs on the quality of care and patient experience (Harrison, Spaulding, and Harrison 2018; Kaufman et al. 2019; Shortell et al. 2017). Becoming or remaining involved in an ACO is yet another consideration for a healthcare organization's strategic plan.
>
> It is important to emphasize that health policy is political. Politics and the law have affected the provisions of the ACA, which in turn, influence healthcare strategic planning. Initially, the ACA intended that all 50 states would participate in Medicaid expansion. In 2012, however, the US Supreme Court determined that forcing states to expand Medicaid (or else the US Department of Health and Human Services could withhold all Medicaid funds) was unconstitutionally coercive (*National Federation of Independent Business et al. v. Sebelius, Secretary of Health and Human Services*, 567 US 519 [2012]). As a result, each state is now entitled to decide whether to expand Medicaid coverage for residents who earn up to 138 percent of the federal poverty level. If a state decides not to expand its Medicaid program, many of its residents—who otherwise would qualify for low-premium or free insurance coverage—lose the opportunity to take advantage of one of the ACA's main provisions. By 2021, 38 states and Washington, DC, had expanded their Medicaid programs (Kaiser Family Foundation 2021).
>
> *(continued)*

Triple Aim
The goals of improving the patient experience and the health of the population while reducing healthcare costs.

Quadruple Aim
The goals of improving the patient experience, the health of the population, and the provider's experience while reducing healthcare costs.

> **CASE FROM THE FIELD**
> **The Affordable Care Act** *(continued)*
>
> In 2017, President Donald Trump signed an executive order to "waive, defer, grant exemptions from, or delay" the implementation of some sections of the ACA, in preparation for repeal of the ACA. Ultimately, however, the ACA was not repealed. At the same time, public support for the ACA remained high, with 52 percent of Americans expressing a favorable opinion of the ACA compared with 39 percent unfavorable (Peterson 2020). That same year, the Tax Cuts and Jobs Act eliminated the individual mandate, which required all Americans to obtain health insurance for themselves and their dependents and imposed financial penalties for failing to do so (Jost 2017).
>
> Upon entering office in 2021, President Joe Biden signed an executive order revoking President Trump's executive orders pertaining to the ACA and strengthening Medicaid and the ACA by reopening the federal health insurance marketplace (HealthCare.gov) and extending the enrollment period for three months. During the extension, one million people enrolled in health insurance plans (Cirruzzo 2021).
>
> Healthcare organizations may face a variety of consequences of the ACA, both intended and unintended, and all of those consequences should be considered in strategic planning. These consequences include capacity issues (as more people have insurance), location (as states choose whether to expand Medicaid), and changes in the competitive market (as more providers join ACOs).

What Is Strategic Planning?

Strategic planning is the process of identifying a desired future state and then establishing goals and objectives to realize that state. It is a "process by which healthcare organizations determine their future direction" (Harrison 2021, 102). Additionally, strategic planning may serve as a response to either a legislative policy (such as the ACA) or a specific event (such as a preventable medical error that caused fatalities) that prompts the organization to reexamine its mission and realign its focus. In healthcare, leaders, managers, and other internal stakeholders typically engage in strategic planning every four or five years.

Think of strategic planning not as a linear process (with a clear start and an end) but as a cyclical one (with a continuous flow) called the **strategic planning cycle**. Organizational stakeholders involved in the strategic planning process work continually to create, implement, and assess plans; monitor, collect, and evaluate or compare data; watch, report on, and make predictions or projections about the threats and opportunities in the environment; develop and adjust strategies; and so on. In other words, the process does not end when a strategic plan is published and then distributed; so many other steps come before

strategic planning
The process of identifying a desired future state and then establishing goals and objectives to realize that state.

strategic planning cycle
The cyclical process of assessment, prioritization, and scheduling.

and after that point, and each step includes decisions and actions that are to be evaluated and corrected if needed.

The strategic planning cycle has three phases: assessment, prioritization, and scheduling (Johnson 2005). The assessment phase is when needs are identified. The prioritization phase is when resources are allocated for optimal effect. The scheduling phase is when the time frame of the implementation is laid out. These three phases are key to the strategic planning effort.

To illustrate these concepts, we present two cases: CVS's strategic initiative to expand its MinuteClinic and Vidant Health's initiative to acquire and later close a rural hospital. Additionally, we discuss how these strategies follow ethical principles. The ACA brought about changes in healthcare delivery that add to the many other considerations in an organization's strategic planning. In these cases, consider how this health policy affected the strategic initiatives of CVS and Vidant Health.

CVS's Strategy

CVS Health is a retail pharmacy chain where you may have had prescriptions filled, visited the MinuteClinic, or purchased over-the-counter medicine such as aspirin. CVS Health describes its strategy as follows (CVS Health 2021b): "Our mission at CVS Health is to take on many of the country's most prevalent and pressing health care needs by understanding and acting on what consumers want and need—personalized, people-centered care that treats them like a human being, not a number." CVS has locations in all 50 states, the District of Columbia, and Puerto Rico and operates about 1,100 MinuteClinics in 33 states and the District of Columbia (CVS Health 2021a; CVS Pharmacy 2021).

In 2000, a father who was frustrated that he had to wait three hours in a doctor's office for his son to be seen for strep throat launched the first MinuteClinic, then known by a different name, in Minnesota (Kaissi 2015). With his business partners, the father saw the need and opportunity for a walk-in clinic that could diagnose and treat common illnesses in a fast, convenient, and affordable manner. That assessment of the marketplace turned out to be true, and the clinic flourished.

In 2006, CVS acquired MinuteClinic, which now is located inside CVS stores and offers both acute and preventive care. The cost of this care is more reasonable than the cost of a visit to an emergency department or a doctor's office. Staffed by nurse practitioners and physician assistants, MinuteClinic accepts cash, credit card, and insurance payments. To avoid conflict of interest, the clinic does not require its patients to fill their prescription at the CVS pharmacy, although the clinic is located near the store's pharmacy.

MinuteClinic's continued success may be attributed to its convenience, availability (with evening and weekend hours), and affordability. According to a 2015 survey of healthcare consumers, 77 percent of respondents chose a retail clinic for convenience, 72 percent for speed of acquiring an appointment, 60 percent for after-hours care, and 58 percent for cost (Deloitte Center for Health Solutions 2015). Over time, MinuteClinic has established a positive reputation for ambulatory healthcare, receiving five consecutive accreditations from The Joint Commission (Levy 2018).

In response to the expected increase in the number of insured people attributable to the ACA (see this chapter's Case from the Field), CVS sought to provide greater access to ambulatory care. However, MinuteClinic has been met with resistance, particularly from physician lobbying groups. For example, CVS first attempted to gain entry into Rhode Island, where the company is headquartered, in 2005, but it ceased its efforts when physicians opposed the establishment of MinuteClinics on the grounds their presence might interfere with doctor–patient relationships (Freyer 2014). Up to that point, MinuteClinic's expansion strategy had followed the assessment, prioritization, and scheduling phases of the strategic planning cycle. During the assessment phrase, the clinic learned of the active resistance of physicians, and the cycle stopped there. As a result, CVS chose not to enter the market at that time. In 2014, CVS again requested entry into the Rhode Island market. The director of the Rhode Island Department of Health at the time, Dr. Michael Fine, approved the plan but with 22 conditions, including establishing measures to shore up primary care and providing charity care (Freyer 2014).

Even with some resistance, CVS continues to grow. Using the strategic planning cycle, CVS determined that it will help meet the nation's need for healthcare access with a lower total cost of care through the growth of its MinuteClinic. As Andrew Sussman and colleagues (2013) state,

> With the nationwide shortage of primary care providers, the addition of millions of newly insured patients through the Affordable Care Act and an aging Baby Boomer population, there is a significant and growing demand for care. MinuteClinic can help to meet that demand, collaborating with local provider groups, as part of a larger health care team.

Ethical Principles of This Initiative

By making convenience, lower cost, and increased access a priority, CVS is displaying the following ethical principles:

- ◆ Autonomy (respecting people's ability to decide when and where to see a healthcare practitioner)
- ◆ Beneficence (providing a service for minor healthcare needs that is an alternative to or could replace visits to the doctor's office, emergency department, or hospital)
- ◆ Justice (making good, affordable, and immediate care available to everybody, regardless of insurance status)

Moreover, CVS avoids potential conflicts of interest by informing MinuteClinic patients that any prescriptions they receive from nurse practitioners or physician assistants on the staff can be easily filled by another pharmacy; they do not have to patronize the CVS pharmacy in the store.

CVS's ethical principles are also reflected in its purpose and values. Its purpose is "helping people on their path to better health," and its values include innovation, collaboration, caring, integrity, and accountability (CVS Health 2021b). This purpose was evident in CVS's decision to stop selling cigarettes and other tobacco products in 2014, noting simply that it was "the right thing to do" (CVS Health 2014).

One of the 22 conditions of CVS's approval to enter the Rhode Island market was to provide charity care. Specifically, the condition states that MinuteClinic (Freyer 2014):

> include free care for all patients who can document that they qualify for charity care at a hospital, community health center, community mental health center or free clinic, limited to two visits per year for each patient and capped at 5 percent of total annual visits to MinuteClinics.

The ethical question here is, what ethical responsibility does an organization that prides itself on "helping people on their path to better health" have to patients who cannot pay? In response, CVS opened its first clinic in Rhode Island and has been "[c]ollaborating with the Rhode Island Free Clinic, providing care for free to its patients, as part of its overall commitment to increasing access to affordable health care" (MinuteClinic 2014).

By the beginning of the COVID-19 pandemic in 2020, CVS operated the largest network of walk-in clinics in the United States, receiving high customer satisfaction marks. The company responded to the pandemic by establishing new guidelines to assist its customers, including waiving delivery charges for prescriptions, providing vaccinations to those who qualify, as defined by the state in which they operate (e.g., by age, health condition), and conducting antibody testing for virus detection (CVS Pharmacy 2021). Its success has been noticed by other competitors, such as Walgreen's Healthcare Clinic, which has begun to offer full-service physicians offices co-located at its store (Walgreens 2020). This growth in services and competition illustrates that the classic strategic planning cycle really is a cycle. As competition increases, for example, CVS is already planning to increase its telehealth services (CVS Health 2020). Doing so will provide one more way to deliver its strategy to create "unmatched human connections to transform the health care experience" (CVS Pharmacy 2021).

VIDANT HEALTH'S STRATEGY

Vidant Health is a private, not-for-profit healthcare organization in eastern North Carolina. At the time it was considering what to do with Vidant Pungo Hospital, the organization consisted of "nine hospitals, home health, hospice, wellness centers, a freestanding surgery center and over 70 ambulatory care practices" (Jones and Dutton 2014, 48). One of its hospitals was Vidant Pungo, a 49-bed acute care hospital in rural Belhaven, North Carolina. It provided healthcare services to about 25,000 people. In 2013, Vidant Pungo's board of directors voted to close the hospital and replace it with a 24/7 multispecialty clinic.

Vidant Health's board mailed a letter to Pungo's community members to explain why the hospital had to close and what Vidant had already provided in uncompensated care—totaling $2.3 million (Beaufort County Board of Commissioners 2013). Vidant Health's president and CEO, David Herman, assured residents that Vidant Health would continue to provide care to the community (*Becker's Hospital Review* 2014). To provide sustainable care, its plan was to replace the old hospital with a new multispecialty clinic, indicating its commitment to provide care in rural North Carolina.

Herman noted that North Carolina's refusal to expand Medicaid was a factor in the decision to close Pungo Hospital (*Daily Reflector* 2014a). Alan Morgan, CEO of the National Rural Health Association, elaborated on the decision to close Pungo Hospital, referring to the financial challenges of keeping rural hospitals open if states chose not to expand Medicaid under the Affordable Care Act (*Daily Reflector* 2014b).

Vidant Pungo's closing would have resulted in 76 employees losing their jobs and in patients having to commute about 26 miles to reach the nearest hospital. Patients who required emergency care or other urgent high-level treatment would have to be transported by helicopter. Moreover, nine long-term care inpatients would have to be relocated to other facilities.

Response to the closing announcement was negative and swift. After lively and sometimes acrimonious discussions among the North Carolina NAACP, Vidant Health, and members of the Belhaven community, the decision was made to keep the hospital open but to transfer it to a new entity to own and manage (Voss 2014). Shoring up support, the Beaufort County Board of Commissioners voted to allocate $2 million to keep the hospital open. The town of Belhaven was required and the neighboring county was encouraged to raise another $3 million for the effort (Voss 2014). Even with this agreement, the funds were insufficient to maintain a hospital, and Vidant Health closed Vidant Pungo and opened a 24/7 clinic. However, it does not offer emergency care, and residents must travel 30 minutes to an hour to reach the nearest emergency care facility (Birch 2018).

When Vidant Health bought Pungo Hospital in 2011 (creating Vidant Pungo), the hospital was already in deep financial trouble, having declared bankruptcy ten years earlier. Vidant Health invested about $5 million to pay off Pungo's debts, to implement an electronic health record (EHR) system for the facility, and to repair the building and replace its equipment (Hoban 2015). In 2011, the ACA was already in effect, and the expectation was that all states would expand Medicaid. Thus, Vidant Health's assessment for its strategy to acquire Pungo factored in the need to expend funds, with the expectation that the state's Medicaid expansion would yield additional patient reimbursements. However, North Carolina opted not to participate in the Medicaid expansion, invalidating Vidant Health's strategic projections (an unintended consequence).

ETHICAL PRINCIPLES OF THIS INITIATIVE

Vidant Health's acquisition of the Pungo hospital illustrates that it was following these three ethical principles:

- Justice (serving Pungo's rural communities regardless of citizens' ability to pay)
- Beneficence (keeping Pungo open—at least for two more years—to ensure its patients could have access to healthcare close to home)
- Autonomy (enabling patients' choice of hospital site)

Moreover, Vidant Health has a history of corporate social responsibility. For example, at the time of acquisition, its 2011 community benefit report noted that the organization's unreimbursed Medicare and bad debt totaled $220 million (Vidant Health 2011). These ethical principles are also reflected in its mission to "enhance the quality of life for the people and communities we serve, touch and support."

The ethical questions here surround Vidant Health's decision to close the hospital. First, what ethical responsibility does an organization have to continue a service that is not economically sustainable? Being beneficent connotes that Vidant Health would have to provide charity care, and corporate social responsibility means that it should provide a social value. Second, what is the significance of fidelity—that is, being loyal to and acting in the best interest of the organization—in continuing to provide services to enhance its patients' quality of life? Vidant Health determined that it could not be all things to all people, and thus it planned to replace an unsustainable service with a more promising 24/7 multispecialty clinic.

LESSONS FROM THE US MILITARY'S HUMANITARIAN EFFORTS

This section details the implementation of a military strategic plan—the Cooperative Strategy for 21st Century Seapower—in response to the 2010 earthquake in Haiti. This US military effort offers applications for healthcare managers in both military and nonmilitary organizations.

QUICK AND ROBUST RESPONSE

In 2010, Haiti was struck by a major 7.0-magnitude earthquake. The earthquake severely damaged Haiti's infrastructure—including roads, buildings, and sanitation, power, and water systems—especially in the capital city of Port-au-Prince. The earthquake killed 230,000 people, injured 300,000 more, and left 2 million Haitians homeless (Walk et al. 2012, 370).

As photographer Tequila Minsky, who was in Haiti at the time, reported, "It was general mayhem" (Romero and Lacey 2010). With roads blocked by debris, hospitals leveled, and the water supply contaminated, government officials could not provide any disaster relief. Among the poorest countries in the Western Hemisphere (CIA 2018), Haiti already had scarce resources and thus was not equipped to handle the worst earthquake it had experienced in the past 200 years. Survivors urgently needed food, clean water, housing, and medical care. Help had to come from other countries.

Working under the principles of the Cooperative Strategy for 21st Century Seapower, a joint military and humanitarian strategy created in 2007 by the US Navy, Marine Corps, and Coast Guard, the US Navy deployed the USNS *Comfort* to Haiti the day after the earthquake hit. The *Comfort* is a hospital ship staffed and equipped to provide tertiary care. Primarily a medical service for US Marine, Air Force, and Army forces stationed overseas, the *Comfort* is also deployed for humanitarian relief missions. In Haiti, the ship's staff were joined by personnel from a variety of nongovernmental organizations (NGOs), numbering about 1,300 altogether. Their charge was to provide needed services to more than 1,000 Haitian people. Additionally, the US military deployed 20 Navy and Coast Guard ships to help in the effort.

In Haiti for 40 days, the *Comfort*'s medical team and NGO partners treated and cared for a steady flow of weakened, injured, or dying women, men, and children. The number of people who needed immediate attention rivaled the number seen by the USNS *Mercy* (the *Comfort*'s sister ship) in the aftermath of the 2004 tsunami in Indonesia. For comparison, the *Mercy*'s medical personnel admitted 176 patients and performed 193 surgical procedures, while the *Comfort*'s team admitted 817 people and performed 927 surgeries (Walk et al. 2012). (See exhibit 11.1 for more details.)

Exhibit 11.1 USNS *Comfort*'s Service During Haitian Disaster Relief Efforts, by the Numbers

Type and number of patients served	
Inpatient	817
Outpatient	55
Arrived as patient escort	185
Inpatient average length of stay	8 days
Average surgical procedures performed per day	21
Total surgical procedures performed	927
Total number of medical personnel (from US military and NGOs)	1,300

Sources: Information from Diálogo (2010) and Walk et al. (2012).

Culturally Respectful, Ethical Healthcare

To provide the most **culturally competent and sensitive care**, the medical team took this threefold approach (Etienne, Powell, and Amundson 2010, 141):

1. Use basic principles of healthcare ethics.
2. Respect communities, cultures, and traditions.
3. Respect the sovereignty of the host nation.

culturally competent and sensitive care
Healthcare that is aware, considerate, and respectful of patients' cultural and ethnic backgrounds and practices.

In addition, the team formed and consulted with a 12-member ethics committee. This committee comprised four physicians, four nurses, one healthcare administrator, one attorney, one chaplain, and one hospital corpsman (Etienne, Powell, and Amundson 2010). To ensure cultural diversity, two committee members were of Haitian heritage and thus knew the local language and culture.

Using the basic principles of healthcare ethics means adhering to the ethical principles of justice, beneficence, nonmaleficence, and autonomy. For example, 37 patients had to undergo amputations (Etienne, Powell, and Amundson 2010). In many Western cultures, such an intervention may be considered merely medically necessary. In Haiti, however, losing a limb has a **stigma** and has historically resulted in isolation (i.e., becoming a social outcast) for the afflicted person (Padgett 2010). Thus, when the team determined that a patient had to have an amputation, the team respected the patient's autonomy if he refused the procedure. The team instead administered antibiotics and wound care for the injury but performed no amputation (Etienne, Powell, and Amundson 2010). This decision was not made lightly. The patient and the healthcare providers thoughtfully weighed the issues of amputation as a short-term solution (life saving) and as a long-term handicap (causing unemployment, homelessness, and potential infection). In such situations, the ethics committee was called to provide both moral and practical guidance.

stigma
A mark that is defined negatively and, as a consequence, may cause an individual to be subjected to discrimination.

Respecting communities, cultures, and traditions was made easier because some of the members of the team and the ethics committee were Haitians themselves, and thus they understood the local language, customs, and culture. These members not only explained the Haitian cultural practices and mindset to the healthcare providers but also served as translators for patients. Diagnoses, options, and decisions were communicated to the patients, so the patients were well informed and thus more comfortable with their care and providers. Further, when deaths occurred, the "chaplain . . . provided culturally appropriate memorial services" for families who requested such a memorial (Etienne, Powell, and Amundson 2010, 143).

Respecting the sovereignty of the host nation refers to incorporating or deferring to the input and authority of Haiti's Ministry of Public Health and Population regarding the focus of care. Following the ministry's health policy at that time, the team provided no services or treatments that in the future (after the *Comfort*'s departure) would require a greater level of care than the local Haitian healthcare system could provide (Etienne, Powell, and Amundson 2010). However, the team did provide some necessary medical interventions. For example, patients who suffered severe traumatic brain injury were treated and then directed to a "well-regarded NGO" for continued care (Etienne, Powell, and Amundson 2010, 146). In this way, patients who required complex care were not abandoned, and the country's sovereignty was honored by not placing an undue hardship on its overburdened healthcare system.

Since the Haitian effort, the USNS *Comfort* has also provided medical care in Belize, Colombia, Costa Rica, the Dominican Republic, Ecuador, El Salvador, Guatemala, Honduras, Jamaica, Nicaragua, Panama, and Peru (Little 2015; Siens 2019). In 2020, the USNS *Comfort* treated US patients from New York and New Jersey for more than three weeks to support local hospitals overwhelmed by the COVID-19 pandemic (Bigley 2020; Fuentes 2020). Plans continue for the USNS *Comfort* to help fulfill the goals of the more recent 2015 Cooperative Strategy for 21st Century Seapower.

Mini-Case Study: Cooperative Strategy for 21st Century Seapower

Strategic planning is a process for looking seriously at who we are and what our environment is like and then thoughtfully considering where we want to go. The US Navy, Marines, and Coast Guard, like other nonmilitary organizations, follow that same principle. First, they base their strategies on their mission statements:

> US Navy (see www.navy.mil/About/Mission/): The United States is a maritime nation, and the US Navy protects America at sea. Alongside our allies and partners, we defend freedom, preserve economic prosperity, and keep the seas open and free. Our nation is engaged in long-term competition. To defend American interests around the globe, the US Navy must remain prepared to execute our timeless role, as directed by Congress and the President.
>
> US Marine Corps (see www.marines.mil): As America's expeditionary force in readiness since 1775, the Marines are forward deployed to win our nation's battles swiftly and aggressively in times of crisis. We fight on land, sea and air, as well as provide forces and detachments to naval ships and ground operations. Marines have a long history of developing expeditionary doctrine and innovations that set the example while leading other countries in multinational military operations. These unique capabilities and leadership qualities make the Marines our nation's first line of defense.
>
> US Coast Guard (see www.history.uscg.mil/home/Missions/): The mission of the United States Coast Guard is to ensure our Nation's maritime safety, security and stewardship.

Each of these military organizations is a sea service, with free use of the world's bodies of water to conduct their missions; employs experienced, committed personnel and equipment to fulfill their mission (both military and humanitarian); and has a history of supporting humanitarian aid efforts, as US hospital ships have served in the military since the 1860s (Hooper 1993). No other organization but the military can, on its own, provide such aid on a large scale. Even NGOs partner with the military to deliver aid to those who need it.

Although the US military does not develop health policy, it creates and implements military policy that responds to the current world environment. Sometimes, this environment encounters massive natural disasters (such as destructive earthquakes and tsunamis) that necessitate the military's deployment of medical interventions (such as hospital ships). The goal of military humanitarian efforts is to build trust, cooperation, and a mutual understanding with other countries. These efforts, in turn, promote peace and security. The Cooperative Strategy for 21st Century Seapower (US Navy, US Marine Corps, and US Coast Guard 2007) states,

> Although our forces can surge when necessary to respond to crises, *trust and cooperation cannot be surged*. They must be built over time so that the strategic interests of the participants are continuously considered while mutual understanding and respect are promoted.

The Cooperative Strategy for 21st Century Seapower is a joint strategy created by the US Navy, Marine Corps, and Coast Guard. This maritime strategy focuses on the aims of being forward, engaged, and ready, which are consistent with the aims of the three organizations: (1) to defend freedom and preserve economic prosperity with allies and partners; (2) to defend American interests around the globe; and (3) to ensure the United States' maritime safety, security, and stewardship. In 2015, the Cooperative Strategy was reassessed to focus on "all domain access," which includes engaging with identified partners in specific regions, such as the Indo-Pacific (US Navy, US Marine Corps, and US Coast Guard 2015). Nonetheless, the humanitarian aid delivered remained a strategic initiative as identified in the 2007 strategy. Implementation of this humanitarian aspect of the strategy entails deploying hospital ships (such as the *USNS Comfort* and *USNS Mercy*) on short notice and communicating with NGO partners that join the aid effort.

The success of humanitarian efforts is measured over time. The measurements include whether the area helped has achieved peace or maintained peace. Responses or public remarks from leaders of nations that have received humanitarian aid are also a good indicator of success. For example, the Haitian minister of health thanked the USNS *Comfort* crew for its "extraordinary efforts" (Kennedy 2010).

The Cooperative Strategy for 21st Century Seapower, like nonmilitary strategic plans, follows the strategic planning cycle of assessment, prioritization, and scheduling. Take, for example, the USNS *Comfort*'s mission in earthquake-ravaged Haiti. During the assessment phase, the needs identified included ship-operating and ship-medical personnel, NGO staff (primarily surgeons), and personnel familiar with Haiti's language and culture. During the prioritization phase, the top priority was determined to be the provision of appropriate, immediate treatment for the injured, being mindful of the country's constraints (lack of medical infrastructure, supplies, and personnel at present and near future) and opportunities in the environment (availability of healthcare providers and systems outside Haiti to which the worst cases could be transferred). During the scheduling phase, the time frame from deployment of the USNS *Comfort* to its return was mapped out. The *Comfort* stayed on Haiti's shores for 40 days, tending to as many wounded and injured as possible.

Mini-Case Study Questions

1. How does the USNS *Comfort* fit the US Navy's mission?
2. Explain how a medical relief or humanitarian aid effort fits with military strategy.
3. Explain how a medical relief effort is ethical, even though sometimes it does not or cannot perform complicated but urgent procedures (such as amputations).
4. The United States does not have universal healthcare. Explain the ethical issues that arise from the US military's healthcare ships offering free medical services to citizens of other countries when US residents do not get the same right. Consider in your answer that the USNS *Comfort* offered aid to patients from New York and New Jersey during the COVID-19 pandemic in 2020.

Points to Remember

- Health policy is defined by the World Health Organization (2021) as the decisions, plans, and actions that are undertaken to achieve specific healthcare goals within a society.
- Current health policy must be considered in an organization's strategic planning.
- Strategic planning is the process of identifying a desired future state and then establishing goals and objectives to realize that state.
- The strategic planning cycle is the cyclical process of assessment, prioritization, and scheduling.

Challenge Yourself

1. Consider the chapter-opening quote by Lewis Carroll. Think of an example in which this might be a forewarning as you prepare to become involved in strategic planning.
2. Explain how accountable care organizations may demonstrate autonomy, beneficence, and justice for patients.
3. Implementing a strategic plan may bring about unintended consequences and collateral damage. What does this mean?

4. Explain your opinion on Rhode Island's position on MinuteClinic's entry into the state's healthcare market. What would you have advised CVS to do regarding the conditions? Defend your recommendation by referring to the ethical issues involved.

For Your Consideration

11.1 Johns Hopkins Medicine elaborates six priorities in its 2019–23 strategic plan: make Johns Hopkins medicine easy, support the well-being of our people and our communities, push the boundaries of science and education, improve the quality and affordability of healthcare, work like one organization, and aim for precision in everything we do. Select one of these priorities and explain how the goals and strategies illustrate ethical principles. (The complete strategic plan can be found at www.hopkinsmedicine.org/strategic-plan/.)

11.2 A physician-owned practice comprising three clinics (pediatrics, women's health, and primary care) is considering strategies to respond to the entry of CVS MinuteClinics in the area. Given that MinuteClinic provides acute and preventive care, the practice is concerned that its current patients might start going to MinuteClinic, thus hurting the practice's business.

Should the practice offer evening and Saturday hours? Should it purchase the pharmacist-owned pharmacy next door to add to its offerings? Should it integrate its services with the local hospital and become part of an ACO?

Consider the following scenario, which illustrates how patients end up using MinuteClinic: A 12-year-old girl has allergies. Her pediatrician works at the practice and has treated her allergies since she was about four years old. The pediatrician knows the girl well and her family's medical history, and the two have established a trusting physician–patient relationship. On Friday night, the girl spends time with a friend who has a new kitten. By Saturday morning, the girl is wheezing, her eyes are watery, and her nose is running. When her mother hands the girl her inhaler, the girl discovers it is empty. Because the inhaler has no refills, her mother cannot just walk into her neighborhood pharmacy and get a new one. Because it is a Saturday, her mother cannot take the girl to the pediatrician's office. Meanwhile, the girl's symptoms are getting worse. Her mother decides to try the new MinuteClinic in her neighborhood. She takes the girl there to see a healthcare provider and perhaps to receive a prescription refill. Luckily, the nurse practitioner at the MinuteClinic is able to help and gives the girl a prescription for the inhaler.

Do you think this event might affect the relationship between the girl and her mother and the pediatrician? What should the practice do, if anything, to prevent a similar event from happening to its other patients? How may the practice strategically plan for MinuteClinic? Consider the practice's options but be mindful of the ethical principles involved in those options. What do you recommend, and why?

Check These Out

Want more information about the organizations and concepts discussed in the chapter? Check these websites out.

- Accountable care organizations (ACOs): General Information: https://innovation.cms.gov/innovation-models/aco
- Cooperative Strategy for 21st Century Seapower (2015): www.globalsecurity.org/military/library/policy/navy/21st-century-seapower_strategy_201503.pdf
- Cooperative Strategy for 21st Century Seapower (2007): www.hsdl.org/?view&did=479900
- Executive Order on "Minimizing the Economic Burden of the Patient Protection and Affordable Care Act Pending Repeal," January 20, 2017: www.federalregister.gov/documents/2017/01/24/2017-01799/minimizing-the-economic-burden-of-the-patient-protection-and-affordable-care-act-pending-repeal
- Executive Order on "Strengthening Medicaid and the Affordable Care Act," January 28, 2021: www.whitehouse.gov/briefing-room/presidential-actions/2021/01/28/executive-order-on-strengthening-medicaid-and-the-affordable-care-act/
- US Coast Guard: www.uscg.mil
- US Marine Corps: www.marines.com
- US Navy: www.navy.mil

References

Beaufort County Board of Commissioners. 2013. "Closing of Pungo District Hospital by Vidant." Published September 30. https://co.beaufort.nc.us/apps/downloads/downloads/board-minute-archives/2013-09-30-special-call-meeting.pdf.

Becker's Hospital Review. 2014. "North Carolina Mayor: Closing of Vidant Pungo Hospital is 'Immoral.'" Published January 21. www.beckershospitalreview.com/hospital-management-administration/north-carolina-mayor-closing-of-vidant-pungo-hospital-is-immoral.html.

Berwick, D., T. Nolan, and J. Whittington. 2008. "The Triple Aim: Care, Health and Cost." *Health Affairs* 27 (3): 759–69.

Bigley, S. 2020. "Comfort Admits New Jersey Patients." *Naval Air Station Patuxent River Tester*. Published April 19. www.dcmilitary.com/tester/news/local/comfort-admits-new-jersey-patients/article_aceb0ec3-2ca4-56f5-b535-8de8fdcc57b1.html.

Birch, J. 2018. "3 Years Later: Closure of Pungo Hospital Spurs Healthcare, Financial, Concerns in Belhaven." WNCT News. Published July 25. www.wnct.com/local-news/3-years-later-closure-of-pungo-hospital-spurs-healthcare-financial-concerns-in-belhaven/.

Bodenheimer, T., and C. Sinsky. 2014. "From Triple to Quadruple Aim: Care of the Patient Requires Care of the Provider." *Annals of Family Medicine* 12 (6): 573–76.

Centers for Medicare & Medicaid Services (CMS). 2021. "Accountable Care Organizations (ACOs): General Information." Accessed August 16. https://innovation.cms.gov/innovation-models/aco.

Central Intelligence Agency (CIA). 2018. "The World Factbook: Haiti." Accessed April 18, 2021. www.cia.gov/the-world-factbook/countries/haiti/.

Cirruzzo, C. 2021. "Biden: 1M Sign Up for Health Insurance During Obamacare Special Enrollment Period." *U.S. News & World Report.* Published May 11. www.usnews.com/news/health-news/articles/2021-05-11/biden-1m-sign-up-for-health-insurance-during-obamacare-special-enrollment-period.

Colla, C. H., V. A. Lewis, L.-S. Kao, A. J. O'Malley, C.-H. Change, and E. S. Fisher. 2016. "Association Between Medicare Accountable Care Organization Implementation and Spending Among Clinically Vulnerable Beneficiaries." *JAMA Internal Medicine* 176 (8): 1167–75.

Commonwealth Fund. 2020. "International Health Care System Profiles: United States." Published June 5. www.commonwealthfund.org/international-health-policy-center/countries/united-states.

Congressional Budget Office (CBO). 2020. "Federal Subsidies for Health Insurance Coverage for People Under 65: 2020 to 2030." Published September 29. www.cbo.gov/publication/56571.

CVS Health. 2021a. "Our Company at a Glance." Accessed August 27. https://cvshealth.com/about-cvs-health/our-company-at-a-glance.

———. 2021b. "Our Strategy." Accessed August 27. https://cvshealth.com/about-cvs-health/our-purpose.

———. 2020. *Corporate Social Responsibility Report.* Accessed April 18, 2021. https://cvshealth.com/sites/default/files/2020-csr-report.pdf.

———. 2014. "A Message from Larry Merlo, President and CEO." Published February 5. https://cvshealth.com/thought-leadership/message-from-larry-merlo-president-and-ceo.

CVS Pharmacy. 2021. "History." Accessed August 27. www.cvs.com/minuteclinic/visit/about-us/history.

Daily Reflector. 2014a. "County Candidates Discuss Medicaid." October 15.

———. 2014b. "Robertson: Vidant Remains Committed." September 28.

Deloitte Center for Health Solutions. 2015. *Retail Health and Wellness: Innovation, Convergence, and Healthier Customers*. Accessed April 18, 2021. www2.deloitte.com/content/dam/Deloitte/us/Documents/risk/us-risk-deloitte-retail-health-and-wellness.pdf.

Diálogo. 2010. "Hospital Ship USNS Comfort Completes Relief Mission in Haiti." Published March 15. https://dialogo-americas.com/articles/hospital-ship-usns-comfort-completes-relief-mission-in-haiti/.

Etienne, M., C. Powell, and D. Amundson. 2010. "Healthcare Ethics: The Experience After the Haitian Earthquake." *American Journal of Disaster Medicine* 5 (3): 141–47.

Freyer, F. 2014. "Health Chief Allows CVS to Open 7 MinuteClinics in R.I. Stores." *Providence Journal*. Published May 15. www.providencejournal.com/article/20140515/NEWS/305159874.

Fuentes, G. 2020. "Hospital Ship Comfort Ends NYC COVID-19 Mission After Treating 182 Patients." *USNI News*. Published April 27. https://news.usni.org/2020/04/27/hospital-ship-comfort-ends-nyc-covid-19-mission-after-treating-182-patients.

Harris, J. 2017. *Healthcare Strategic Planning*, 4th ed. Chicago: Health Administration Press.

Harrison, J., A. Spaulding, and D. Harrison. 2018. "Accountable Care Organizations: A Strategy for Future Success?" *International Journal of Organization Theory & Behavior* 21 (2): 113–21.

Harrison, J. P. 2021. *Essentials of Strategic Planning in Healthcare*, 3rd ed. Chicago: Health Administration Press.

Hoban, R. 2015. "Bill to Provide Relief to Rural Hospitals Complete." *North Carolina Health News*. Published September 29. www.northcarolinahealthnews.org/2015/09/29/bill-to-provide-relief-to-rural-hospitals-complete/.

Hooper, R. 1993. "United States Hospital Ships: A Proposal for Their Use in Humanitarian Mission." *Journal of the American Medical Association* 270 (5): 621–23.

Johnson, W. 2005. "The Planning Cycle." *Journal of Healthcare Information Management* 19 (3): 56–64.

Jones, A., and K. Dutton. 2014. "Patients and Families as Partners in Safety, Quality, and Experiences of Care." *Patient Experience Journal* 1 (1): 48–49.

Jost, T. 2017. "The Tax Bill and the Individual Mandate: What Happened, and What Does It Mean?" *Health Affairs Blog*. Published December 20. www.healthaffairs.org/do/10.1377/hblog20171220.323429/full/.

Kaiser Family Foundation. 2021. "Status of State Medicaid Expansion Decisions: Interactive Map." Accessed April 11. www.kff.org/medicaid/issue-brief/status-of-state-medicaid-expansion-decisions-interactive-map/.

Kaissi, A. 2015. *Flipping Health Care Through Retail Clinics and Convenient Care Models*. Hershey, PA: IGI Global.

Kaufman, B., B. Spivack, S. Stearns, P. Song, and E. O'Brien. 2019. "Impact of Accountable Care Organizations on Utilization, Care, and Outcomes: A Systematic Review." *Medical Care Research and Review* 76 (3): 255–90.

Kennedy, C. 2010. "Haitian Minister of Health Thanks Comfort's Crew." *Military News*. Published March 10. www.militarynews.com/norfolk-navy-flagship/news/front_center/haitian-minister-of-health-thanks-comfort-s-crew/article_dc36ba87-369d-5740-b42e-efa29c5a7699.html.

Levy, S. 2018. "MinuteClinic Gets Joint Commission's Gold Seal of Approval for Ambulatory Care." *Drug Store News*. Published November 20. https://drugstorenews.com/pharmacy/minuteclinic-gets-joint-commissions-gold-seal-of-approval-for-ambulatory-care.

Little, B. 2015. "WRNMMC Welcomes Home Sailors, Soldier From USNS Comfort." DCMilitary.com. Published October 8. www.dcmilitary.com/journal/features/wrnmmc-welcomes-home-sailors-soldier-from-usns-comfort/article_a7a0c6c3-d469-5437-b408-e218655efc4b.html.

McWilliams, J., L. Hatfield, B. Landon, P. Hamed, and M. Chernew. 2018. "Medicare Spending After 3 Years of the Medicare Shared Savings Program." *New England Journal of Medicine* 379 (12): 1139–49.

MinuteClinic. 2014. "MinuteClinic Expands in New England." Published October 29. www.multivu.com/players/English/7360151-cvs-minuteclinic-expands-in-new-england/.

Ouayogode, M., E. Meara, K. Ho, C. Snyder, and C. Colla. 2021. "Estimates of ACO Savings in the Presence of Provider and Beneficiary Selection." *Healthcare* 9 (1): 100460.

Padgett, T. 2010. "Haiti: What to Do with a Nation of Amputees." *Time*. Published February 17. http://content.time.com/time/world/article/0,8599,1964441,00.html.

Peterson, M. 2020. "The ACA a Decade In: Resilience, Impact, and Vulnerabilities." *Journal of Health Politics, Policy and Law* 45 (4): 595–608.

Romero, S., and M. Lacey. 2010. "Fierce Quake Devastates Haitian Capital." *New York Times*. Published January 12. www.nytimes.com/2010/01/13/world/americas/13haiti.html.

Shortell, S., B. Poon, P. Ramsay, H. Rodriguez, S. Ivey, T. Huber, J. Rich, and T. Summerfelt. 2017. "A Multilevel Analysis of Patient Engagement and Patient-Reported Outcomes in Primary Care Practices of Accountable Care Organizations." *Journal of General Internal Medicine* 32 (6): 640–47.

Siens, B. 2019. "Comfort Strengthens Partnership with Haiti Following Successful Medical Mission." US Southern Command. Published November 14. www.southcom.mil/MEDIA/NEWS-ARTICLES/Article/2016748/comfort-strengthens-partnership-with-haiti-following-successful-medical-mission/.

Sussman, A., L. Dunham, K. Snower, M. Hu, O. Matlin, W. Shrank, N. Choudhry, and T. Brennan. 2013. "Retail Clinic Utilization Associated with Lower Total Cost of Care." *American Journal of Managed Care* 19 (4): e148–57.

US Navy, US Marine Corps, and US Coast Guard. 2015. *A Cooperative Strategy for 21st Century Seapower*. Published March. www.globalsecurity.org/military/library/policy/navy/21st-century-seapower_strategy_201503.pdf.

———. 2007. *A Cooperative Strategy for 21st Century Seapower*. Published October. www.hsdl.org/?view&did=479900.

Vidant Health. 2011. *Community Benefit Report*. Accessed May 27, 2014. www.vidanthealth.com/vidant/dynamic-detail.aspx?id=17320.

Voss, M. 2014. "On the Table—$2 Million Offered to Aid Effort to Save Belhaven's Hospital." *Washington Daily News*. Published March 15. www.thewashingtondailynews.com/2014/03/15/on-the-table-2-million-offered-to-aid-effort-to-save-belhavens-hospital/.

Walgreens. 2020. "Walgreens and VillageMD to Open 500 to 700 Full-Service Doctor Offices Within Next Five Years in a Major Industry First." Published July 8. https://news.walgreens.com/press-center/news/walgreens-and-villagemd-to-open-500-to-700-full-service-doctor-offices-within-next-five-years-in-a-major-industry-first.htm.

Walk, R., T. Donahue, Z. Stockinger, M. Knudson, M. Cubano, R. Sharpe, and S. Safford. 2012. *Disaster Medicine and Public Health Preparedness* 6 (4): 370–77.

Wilson, M., A. Guta, K. Waddell, J. Lavis, R. Reid, and C. Evans. 2020. "The Impacts of Accountable Care Organizations on Patient Experience, Health Outcomes, and Costs: A Rapid Review." *Journal of Health Services Research & Policy* 25 (2): 130–38.

World Health Organization. 2021. "Health Policy." Accessed March 20. www.euro.who.int/en/health-topics/health-policy.

CHAPTER 12
OPERATIONS MANAGEMENT

You will not find it difficult to prove that battles, campaigns, and even wars have been won or lost primarily because of logistics.

—Dwight D. Eisenhower, 34th US president

Important Terms

- Compliance
- Internship
- Operations management
- Quality assurance
- Relators
- Supply chain management

Learning Objectives

Studying this chapter will help you to

➤ identify ethical issues in operations management,

➤ apply ethical principles to operations management, and

➤ evaluate the role of healthcare managers in ethical operations management.

This chapter discusses ethics in operations management. We define operations management, explain the connection between healthcare operations and ethics, and illustrate these points with cases. Healthcare operations management covers a wide range of activities. The healthcare personnel charged with managing, performing, monitoring, and evaluating these activities are expected to adhere to ethical principles and ensure that the activities fit with the organization's mission, vision, and values.

> **CASE FROM THE FIELD**
> Assessment, Training, and Ethics
>
> Fifteen years ago, Jean Zoeng established Full Motion Innovation Clinic Inc., a rehabilitation facility. Her vision, which her colleagues shared, was to create a workplace where all staff members were knowledgeable, friendly, and, above all, ethical. The clinic's mission was to provide the best quality that rehabilitative services had to offer and to help patients' bodies as well as recharge their minds and spirit. She worked with competent, honest healthcare professionals, including four physical therapists, three physical therapy assistants, five occupational therapists, two speech language pathologists, and three administrative staff assistants.
>
> At Full Motion Innovations, **quality assurance** (QA) was a part of routine operations. QA identified any unintentional mistakes in work processes, and it also reinforced the character and reputation of the clinic as a professional, ethical business that put the needs of its patients first. Patient records were reviewed every quarter, and training sessions for staff were held after that review, based on the QA results. Zoeng had been pleased with this process, especially considering reports by the US Department of Justice of questionable billing practices at some physical therapy practices.
>
> Carolina Physical Therapy (CPT) and Sports Medicine, Inc., a practice with nine locations in the state of South Carolina, resolved allegations that it had knowingly submitted fraudulent claims to Medicare billing as though patients had been treated individually, when they had not (DOJ 2019). The patients had not been receiving one-on-one care from a physical therapist or supervised physical therapy assistant.
>
> Acting as a **relator**, Hilary Moore, a former receptionist and patient appointment scheduler at the Sumter, South Carolina, branch of CPT, received $142,000 as a portion of the settlement (Constantine Cannon 2019). Moore brought the *qui tam* action under the False Claims Act, noting examples that demonstrated the fraudulent practice. Patients were stacked—that is, they would spend little or no time with a licensed therapist or therapist assistant, and then receive care from an unlicensed aide for the reminder or the entirety of the 60-minute appointment. Then, Medicare or TRICARE would be billed for the entire 60-minute therapy session as though it had been solely delivered by a physical therapist or supervised physical therapist assistant.
>
> *(continued)*

---

quality assurance
A program for monitoring and evaluating a product or service to ensure that quality standards are met and proper procedures are followed.

relator
A private citizen who sues on behalf of the government under the False Claims Act.

> **CASE FROM THE FIELD**
> Assessment, Training, and Ethics *(continued)*
>
> "It was not uncommon for a single therapist to bill for four 60-minute therapy sessions in a single hour" (*United States of America v. Carolina Physical Therapy* 2017, 7).
>
> The practice also had established productivity expectations by services provided (measured by income generated for the practice). If one physical therapist did not meet the expectations, no one at the office received a bonus. This push to meet expectations was overseen by an administrator for all the practice locations, suggesting that the firm was knowingly committing false billing.
>
> Another case that concerned Zoeng was that of a past owner of a home health agency who accepted federal COVID-19 funds to care for patients who did not exist. Amina Abbas was the former owner of a home health care agency called 1 on 1 Home Healthcare, located in Michigan. Although the business closed before the COVID-19 pandemic, Abbas applied for and received more than $37,000 to provide care for COVID-19 patients. Since she had no patients, she dispersed the federal funds to her family members instead. To be clear, the COVID-19 funds were designated for businesses that had patients, not for family members to spend as they wished (Snell 2021). Abbas was charged with embezzlement of government property (DOJ 2021).
>
> Zoeng hired a QA consultant, who was also the healthcare manager of another physical therapy practice. The consultant, aided by a team composed of an administrative assistant and a health informatics student intern, reviewed (or audited) the clinic's patient files from the past three months. For the previous quarter, the consultant discovered two errors in the records: a missing patient signature and an incorrect code used in a billing.
>
> At Full Motion Innovations, patients were asked to sign their name when they arrived for an office visit. This signature indicated that the patient had showed up for the appointment and received treatment on a particular day and time. The consultant found that Jim Yang, a patient receiving physical therapy following shoulder surgery, failed to sign in for his arrival and treatment two weeks ago, even though he was present. The plan of correction was to document the missing signature and to have Yang sign a note stating that he received treatment on that date. This documentation was placed in his medical record.
>
> The second error was a result of a physical therapist recording the wrong code for the services performed, which led to the submission of a reimbursement claim to Medicare (and subsequently receiving payment) that was lower than it should have been. The plan of correction was to document the error with a detailed explanation of how the discrepancy had occurred and then to complete a corrected claim and copy the remittance advice (Medicare documented payment) to Medicare with a cover letter stating the pertinent information (e.g., the incorrect charge, the correct charge, the difference between the two).
>
> Overall, the consultant noted a 3 percent error rate in the 60 randomly selected files that the team reviewed—a rate that is not unexpected or uncommon (even though Zoeng preferred
>
> *(continued)*

> **CASE FROM THE FIELD**
> Assessment, Training, and Ethics *(continued)*
>
> a zero error rate). To work toward the goal of "no errors next quarter" and avoid blaming her employees, Zoeng focused on course correction and did not disclose the names of the employees responsible for the errors. Additionally, she designed and led an all-staff training session on patient documentation and billing. The training session, which lasted 50 minutes, incorporated role-playing, which gave all employees a chance to practice coding, billing, and signing in patients while following necessary and specific steps. Both Zoeng and the staff were pleased with the training—not to mention the nonpunitive way she handled the matter.
>
> When the consultant and his team audited random patient files for the next quarter, they found no errors. To celebrate the success, Zoeng ordered a healthy lunch for the entire staff. This achievement proved that Full Motion Innovations was capable of truth in reporting, truth in billing, and truth in **compliance**.

compliance
An action that conforms to established rules.

WHAT IS OPERATIONS MANAGEMENT?

In the inaugural issue of the *Journal of Operations Management*, editor Lee Krajewski (1980, v) defined **operations management** as follows:

> Operations management refers to the management of any process [that] transforms some input into a useful output and covers a broad range of job titles and problem areas in manufacturing and service organizations.

operations management
The management of any product, service, process, resource, or activity that enables an organization to be productive and sustainable.

This broad definition points out that operations management is about *any* action to achieve that which is produced or served by the organization. In healthcare, products sold and services performed encompass a wide variety of actions. Title 45 (Public Welfare), section 164.501 of the Code of Federal Regulations (CFR) defines healthcare operations as encompassing six broad activities (*Federal Register* 2011, 862–63):

1. Conducting quality assessment and improvement activities, population-based activities, and related functions that do not include treatment
2. Reviewing the competence or qualifications of healthcare professionals, evaluating practitioner, provider, and health plan performance, conducting training programs where students learn to practice or improve their skills as health-care providers, training of non-healthcare professionals, accreditation, certification, licensing, or credentialing activities

3. Underwriting, premium rating, and other activities relating to the creation, renewal or replacement of a contract of health insurance or benefits
4. Conducting or arranging for medical review, legal services, and auditing functions, including fraud and abuse detection and compliance programs
5. Planning and development, such as conducting cost-management and planning-related analyses related to managing and operating the entity, including formulary development and administration, development or improvement of methods of payment or coverage policies
6. Managing and administrating activities of the entity, including customer service, resolution of internal grievances, sale, transfer, merger, or consolidation of the organization, creation of de-identified data set, and fundraising

While operations management covers a wide range of activities (as evidenced by this multilayered definition), healthcare managers are expected to move strategic plans into successful actions and respond appropriately to unforeseen events that occur in day-to-day operations. The connection between ethics and operations management is straightforward: Ethical operations management is compliant with laws and regulations, proactive in identifying and correcting problems and threats, focused on continuous improvement, and reliant on competent and ethical individuals.

Applying Ethical Principles to the Case from the Field

The ethical principles of justice, beneficence, nonmaleficence, and autonomy that we have been discussing throughout this book can be applied to operations management. Let's examine the Case from the Field to illustrate these principles in actual healthcare settings.

Zoeng worked with highly skilled, ethical people, and she herself managed the operations with integrity and honesty. Even with the best intentions, though, people made mistakes, as uncovered by the consultant. Nonetheless, the errors discovered at Full Motion Innovations are not comparable with the allegations made against CPT and 1 on 1 Home Health Care. One significant difference is that Zoeng's actions were deliberately ethical.

Justice

Zoeng handled all issues fairly and treated her staff members fairly as well. She hired an objective third-party consultant to assess the quality of the work performed and took the results of those assessments seriously. She provided interactive, enjoyable training based on the areas of improvement indicated by the errors found. Most important, she focused on fixing the mistakes and not blaming the people who made them. And, she celebrated the achievement of the goal. In a just workplace like Zoeng's, employees tend to be productive (a goal of operations management) and work hard to avoid repeating past errors.

In contrast, in the CPT case, personnel were charged with exploiting federally funded systems and violating their rules by billing for services they did not deliver. In the case of 1 on 1 Home Health Care, the charge was the acceptance of COVID-19 funds by a firm that was closed and thus did not require the relief. Despite their actions, the CPT personnel were treated fairly and given the option to resolve the claims; Abbas will be given her day in court (DOJ 2019, 2021).

Beneficence

Zoeng's adherence to beneficence is exemplified by three actions:

1. She staffed the clinic with knowledgeable, competent, and ethical professionals, all of whom contributed to patients' welfare.

2. She enforced the patient sign-in process, which supported the clinic's record keeping and thus its compliance with rules and regulations.

3. She ensured that QA was conducted every quarter, which shows her devotion to the clinic's patient-centered mission.

CPT, on the other hand, squandered its duty to do good. Instead of providing appropriate healthcare services to those who needed them, the firm allegedly gave limited care to patients by licensed, qualified personnel. These actions were the exact opposite of beneficence—that is, maleficence.

Nonmaleficence

While Zoeng did everything she could to not inflict evil or harm—the definition of nonmaleficence—Abbas is alleged to have accepted funds for a healthcare business that was no longer in operation; she was not following ethical operations management.

Autonomy

Zoeng exhibited respect for autonomy through two actions. First, she kept confidential the identity of the employees responsible for the missing patient signature and coding error. This act promoted trust and safety. Moreover, instead of finding fault, she recognized the need to train or retrain the entire staff. By doing so, she sent a message that everyone was responsible for appropriately performing the operational processes in place, not just a few people. Knowledge and a trusting environment, in turn, empower people to make the right, beneficent decisions.

Second, Zoeng followed an established quality process with the audit, and she followed up with training that reinforced respect for telling the truth. Conversely, CPT allegedly abused its patients' autonomy, as they were treated by unlicensed staff but billed for treatment provided by licensed staff. Abbas at 1 on 1 Home Health Care was not treating patients and accepted funds meant for patient access for care during a pandemic.

Connecting the CFR Definition to Operational Actions

As we stated earlier, definition of healthcare operations outlined in Title 45 of the CFR includes six activities. To illustrate the connection between this definition and operational actions, we examine activities 1, 2, and 5 in the CFR definition and give real-world examples of each.

Activity 1

Operations management involves "[c]onducting quality assessment and improvement activities, population-based activities, and related functions that do not include treatment" (*Federal Register* 2011, 862). An example of this activity is listening to and then acting on the feedback of those who receive and experience care to bring about quality improvement; this decision illustrates adherence to the ethical principles of beneficence and autonomy. Let's consider what occurs when this feedback is limited—as was the case when healthcare facilities were forced to restrict patient visitation during the COVID-19 pandemic.

The COVID-19 pandemic in the United States affected all aspects of healthcare delivery, including policies on who is allowed to accompany or visit patients in healthcare facilities. Along with other healthcare centers, Vidant Medical Center had to adapt its operations policies in response to the pandemic. Vidant Health is a private, not-for-profit health system in eastern North Carolina that comprises more than 1,700 beds in nine hospitals (eight of which are community hospitals), home health and hospice care, a freestanding surgery center, more than 100 ambulatory care practices, and four wellness centers (Vidant Health 2021a).

Vidant continued to update its restrictions on patient visitation throughout 2020 and 2021, in response to both the guidelines set by the Centers for Disease Control and Prevention (CDC) and the number of cases reported in eastern North Carolina. As shown in exhibit 12.1, Vidant updated its visitation policy again in March 2021, as COVID-19 cases began to decline and the number of people vaccinated increased.

Exhibit 12.1 Vidant Medical Center, Visitation Restrictions, March 2021

Thank you for trusting Vidant Health to care for you and your loved ones. The safety of our patients, visitors and team members is our top priority. As Vidant monitors and responds to the COVID-19 pandemic across North Carolina, we are taking steps to ensure the safety of all. Vidant remains vigilant with its screening process for all visitors, entry requirements and visitor restrictions by department. Vidant continues to closely track local data, including COVID-19 cases in our region and hospitals, and will adjust visitation restrictions accordingly.

In following the ADA (Americans with Disabilities Act) guidelines, visitors who need assistance due to a disability may have an additional individual with them when visiting a loved one in a Vidant Health facility to help navigate the current visitor guidelines.

All visitors will be screened and masked and asked to follow the entry requirements below.

Vidant strongly encourages visitors to consider virtual visitation options such as FaceTime and phone calls. Assistance with virtual visits, including iPads for patients without the necessary technology, is available on request. Virtual visitation is the safest way to stay connected with a loved one.

Visiting Hours and Restrictions by Department
All visitors must be screened and follow entry requirements:

Hospital inpatient departments, including surgical patients	Open hours	• One (1) healthy adult visitor screened and masked at all times. • Visitor must stay in patient's room unless visiting the café. • Visitor may switch out with one (1) other healthy adult visitor per day (12 a.m. to 11:59 p.m.).
Children's Hospital	Open hours	• Maynard Children's Hospital and pediatric patients at all inpatient Vidant facilities welcome two (2) guardians of the child at the bedside. Two (2) designated guardians are identified by the child's legal guardian on admission and are able to remain at the bedside throughout the duration of the child's stay. • Sibling visits are not permitted at this time; the health care team will work with families to facilitate virtual sibling visits as appropriate. • For pediatric palliative or end-of-life care, additional visitation will be considered with approval from leadership based on the needs of the child.

Women's Center, labor and delivery, maternity	Open hours	• One (1) healthy designated support partner screened and masked at all times. During the labor process, one additional labor support person over 18 years of age is also permitted at the bedside for the duration of labor up until two hours post-delivery.
Emergency Department	Open hours	• One (1) healthy adult visitor screened and masked at all times. • Visitor must stay in patient's room unless visiting the café.
Medical practices and outpatient clinics	During time of appointment	• One (1) healthy adult visitor screened and masked at all times.
Surgical outpatient procedures that require sedation or anesthesia	Open hours	• One (1) healthy adult visitor screened and masked at all times may wait with patient until that patient proceeds to their pre-surgical or pre-procedure area. Visitor may return at time of discharge.
Exceptions to Visitor Restrictions Include:		
End of life	Open hours	• Family members who are screened and masked may visit with guidance from care team and should call the unit for guidance.
Inpatient rehab facility at Vidant Medical Center	Open hours	• Visitors who are screened and masked may visit with guidance from care team and should call the unit for guidance.
Behavioral health	No visitors allowed	• No visitors allowed. Ask nurse for accommodations regarding virtual visits.
COVID-19-positive patients	No visitors allowed	• No visitors allowed. Ask nurse for accommodations regarding virtual visits.
		Thank you for helping us keep those we love safe.

Source: Vidant Health (2021b).

In July 2021, the CDC updated its recommendations in response to an increase in new COVID-19 cases caused by the delta variant—then the predominant variant of the virus—which is more infectious and more easily transmitted to both vaccinated and unvaccinated people. Vidant once again responded by adjusting its visitation policy in the Emergency Department (Vidant Health 2021c):

> To ensure the safety of patients, families, and team members, effective 7 a.m. Thursday, Aug. 12, visitors will not be allowed in the ED lobby or waiting areas. ED patients can have one healthy adult visitor screened and masked at all times once the patient has been placed into a room, as long as the patient is not COVID positive.

Vidant Health did not implement these changes without due diligence and careful thought. A few years earlier, the organization's leadership (senior management, board of directors, and physician leaders) had supported the systemwide implementation of a patient engagement initiative (Jones and Dutton 2014). This family-friendly, patient-centered policy of flexible visitation served as the guideline to promote active engagement by patients and families throughout the care experience. To that end, the Office of Patient and Family Experience was established to support patient engagement efforts, connect families to patient advisers, and provide other services. In 2013, when Vidant Health was awarded the John M. Eisenberg Patient Safety and Quality Award, more than 150 patient advisers were serving the organization's efforts (Atkins 2014).

Vidant's president and CEO, Brian Floyd, explained the system's COVID-19-related visitation restrictions (Ashley and Forsey 2020):

> One of the hardest things we have to do frankly is limit who can be with a loved one during a difficult time being sick in the hospital. . . . We don't take that lightly. I don't take that lightly. Our team doesn't take that lightly. We are only doing this because we feel it's in the best interest of safety.

Research has demonstrated that the presence of visitors is reassuring and soothing for patients and provides support during hospital stays. In a 2021 study, Geoffrey Silvera and colleagues examined the effect of visitation policy changes during the COVID-19 pandemic. Looking at the Hospital Consumer Assessment of Healthcare Providers and Systems (HCAHPS) survey, which covers 32 hospitals over a two-year period, the authors compared the scores of patients at healthcare organizations with open or limited visitation and those with fully closed visitation policies. HCAHPS measures include patient responses to their communication with physicians and nurses, their assessment of the responsiveness of hospital staff, their experiences with discharge planning, and their overall rating of the hospital (Silvera et al. 2021, 33).

This study found that patients' satisfaction scores were *slightly* lower at facilities with more restrictive visitation policies, particularly with respect to the responsiveness of hospital staff—that is, patients perceived that they waited longer for hospital staff to respond to their call. It is important to note, however, that these perceptions may have been influenced by two factors: First, patients were waiting alone for a response from hospital staff, and second, they may have needed to call for help more often because they did not have someone in the room to assist with activities of daily living (such as getting to the bathroom). Nonetheless, the slight reduction in patient experience reinforces the positive influence of visitor support.

Activity 2

Operations management involves "[r]eviewing the competence or qualifications of health care professionals, evaluating practitioner, provider, and health plan performance, conducting training programs where students learn to practice or improve their skills as health-care providers, training of non-healthcare professionals, accreditation, certification, licensing, or credentialing activities" (*Federal Register* 2011, 862). An example of this activity is partnering with an established student training or **internship** program of a local university, an action that illustrates adherence to the ethical principles of beneficence and autonomy. Let's consider the internship program of East Carolina University's Health Services and Information Management Department, Health Services Management program.

> **internship**
> Nonclassroom, practical training for students or new graduates in their field of study.

    Students in the Health Services Management program at East Carolina University—which is fully certified by the Association of University Programs in Health Administration (AUPHA)—complete a 160-hour internship, typically at a hospital, clinic, or physician practice (East Carolina University 2021). The university enters into a Health Services Management and Internship Site Affiliation Agreement with each site that accepts students for an educational experience. Students agree to work full-time (about 40 hours per workweek) under the direction of a preceptor (supervisor at the internship site) for course credit. The preceptor evaluates students on the basis of the competencies demonstrated—such as professionalism, communication skills, knowledge specific to the site, and performance of responsibilities assigned. Throughout their internships, students prepare portfolios detailing their experience; then, after the experience, they present their portfolios to peers, faculty, and visiting preceptors. During the 2020 and 2021 academic years, as healthcare and university sites responded to the COVID-19 pandemic by limiting in-person contact, students completed virtual internships, with the same responsibilities noted earlier, and presented their portfolios virtually to peers, faculty, and visiting preceptors.

    The internship site works with the university to ensure that students are ready and prepared for on-site experiences. Students undergo a background check, complete a health questionnaire, and sign site-specific confidentiality and security agreements. Some sites also ask students to complete an orientation, which includes information about the site (such as the mission, vision, values, and level of care provided). Moreover, some sites require students to take and pass a safety and compliance exam to ensure that they understand the

Health Insurance Portability and Accountability Act (HIPAA), privacy and confidentiality, infection control, and other fundamental concepts.

Internships are considered essential experiences for undergraduate students in AUPHA-certified programs. AUPHA (2021) publishes its certification guide and lists 28 criteria for undergraduate program certification. Certified programs must demonstrate that the internship provides at least 120 hours of experience and meets the stated goals and objectives of the program. Additionally, each program must have procedures for selection, orientation, and evaluation of the sites and preceptors.

ACTIVITY 5

Operations management involves "[p]lanning and development, such as conducting cost-management and planning-related analyses related to managing and operating the entity, including formulary development and administration, development or improvement of methods of payment or coverage policies" (*Federal Register* 2011, 863). An example of this activity is doing a cost-effectiveness analysis for a planned or current service and weighing that cost information against the benefits of the service. In other words, does the service meet the organization's mission, vision, and values? If not, what are the ethical costs of not meeting the mission, vision, and values? Let's consider how this concept applies to mobile mammography efforts.

The American Cancer Society (2019) estimated that in 2019 alone, 268,600 women were diagnosed with invasive breast cancer, 48,100 women were diagnosed with in situ breast cancer, and 41,760 died from breast cancer. Mammograms lead to earlier detection of breast cancer and better chances for survival. It is recommended that women have an annual mammogram beginning at age 45 and every two years thereafter for those 55 and older (American Cancer Society 2021). Women who live in rural areas are less likely to receive mammograms than women in nonrural areas, primarily because of cost (even though the Affordable Care Act mandates coverage) and distance (Hughes et al. 2020; Peppercorn et al. 2017).

A mobile mammography unit is one way to deliver this needed service to women who cite distance from a healthcare facility as a deterring factor. The mobile unit sets up temporarily in the community or neighborhood. Here are some examples of such a service:

- Portneuf Medical Center (2019), a regional hospital for southern and eastern Idaho and western Wyoming, has screened more than 100,000 women for breast cancer since 1994. In 2019, it replaced its 17-year-old mobile mammography unit with a coach equipped with 3D imaging.

- Hospital Sisters Health System (HSHS) Sacred Heart Hospital reported in 2019 that Charter Bank was helping fund a mobile mammography bus that was expected to serve about 25,000 women per year in rural areas. Fewer than 25 percent (30,750) of the 123,000 women in the outlying areas who are eligible for mammography are estimated to do so. The presence of the mobile unit allows greater access for these rural residents.

- ◆ Saint Alphonsus Mobile Health Screening Coach serves southwestern Idaho, a region where only about 30 percent of women over age 40 typically receive screening. Grants are available to those who cannot afford to pay for mammograms (Saint Alphonsus 2021b).

The evidence for the significance of mobile mammography is apparent. Many women in rural areas have greater access to and undergo breast cancer screening because these units exist.

An operations manager of a healthcare organization that operates or is considering mobile units must assess the cost-effectiveness of such a service. A 2009 study conducted in the United States indicated that mobile mammography is indeed more expensive than stationary (facility-based or in-hospital) mammography (Naeim et al. 2009, 286). Accounting for and comparing the costs—including mammography equipment, vehicle (for a mobile unit), real estate (for a stationary service), personnel salary, and operations—mobile mammography was found to be almost 2.5 times the cost of stationary mammography, at $102 per patient versus $41 per patient, respectively. However, the study also found that philanthropic support could reduce the mobile cost estimate by about $15 per patient (Naeim et al. 2009, 289). A more recent examination of the cost-effectiveness of mobile mammography conducted in France found that, as in the United States, mobile units were more likely to reach women in rural areas (De Mil et al. 2019). Likewise, this study found that the addition of a mobile unit increased costs while also providing women better access to breast cancer screenings.

Knowing that mobile mammography is more expensive to run than stationary mammography, you might wonder why healthcare organizations such as Portneuf Medical Center, HSHS, and Saint Alphonsus continue to provide mobile screenings. The answer lies in these organizations' mission, vision, and values statements. Part of the mission and values of Portneuf Medical Center (2021) is to provide world-class care to every patient, every time, and to give back to the community. Meanwhile, HSHS's (2021) vision is to be a "unique, high-quality health system providing exceptional care, centered on the whole person," with special attention to "our brothers and sisters who are poor, underserved and most vulnerable." Likewise, Saint Alphonsus (2021a) notes that reverence, justice, care of the poor, and integrity are among its core values.

For these organizations (and others like them) providing a necessary and possibly lifesaving service (which also fulfills the mission, vision, and values) outweighs the operating costs. This decision illustrates adherence to the ethical principles of justice and beneficence.

Healthcare Managers' Role in Ethical Operations Management

One of the roles of operations managers is to provide support and needed information to the decision-making team or authority, which, in turn, acts based on the information received. In this role, the manager should be vigilant of any organizational practices that could interfere with the fair distribution of limited resources and supplies when needed. Equally important, the manager should participate in the creation of solutions to help bring about continued fair distribution. The inadequate supply of personal protective equipment (PPE) for healthcare workers and patients illustrates the operational problems experienced during the COVID-19 pandemic (Patrinley et al. 2020).

Disruption of the Supply Chain

In healthcare, *supply chain* refers to the series of steps that take place from the sourcing of raw materials to the use or consumption of the final product. **Supply chain management** encompasses all the directed actions taken inside and outside the healthcare organization that enable this process, including identifying product needs, sourcing materials for production, making the product, transporting and delivering the product, and effectively using information systems needed for coordination (Handfield 2020).

Prior to the COVID-19 pandemic, healthcare managers followed standard business practices of obtaining quality products efficiently—both in supply and in cost. Outcomes included reduction of excess inventory (i.e., employing just-in-time inventory so as to have a supply of products for a designated time and reordering as that supply was used) as well as reduction of cost (e.g., buying products from overseas rather than from US suppliers). Before the pandemic, China was the leading exporter of respirators, surgical masks, medical goggles, and protective garments, producing more of these products than the rest of the world combined (Bradsher 2020). As the coronavirus spread in China, however, the Chinese needed these items at home, and travel was limited. Thus, the rest of the world experienced a decline in supply, leading to shortages that needed to be addressed (Evenett 2020).

By March 2020, the World Health Organization was calling for industry and governments to focus on increased production and distribution of PPE as healthcare workers and patients relied on these items to prevent COVID-19 infection (WHO 2020). The organization estimated a need for 89 million medical masks per month, while the prices for masks already had already increased six times their normal pre-pandemic price (WHO 2020).

Solutions to Address the Supply Chain Disruption

In July 2020, Mayo Clinic president and CEO Gianrico Farrugia criticized the healthcare industry's reliance on just-in-time inventory, arguing that this method of supply chain

---

supply chain management
Actions planned and taken to ensure that products needed for healthcare workers and patients are created, transported, and able to be used or consumed so that the process is efficient, timely, and cost-effective.

management "doesn't work for healthcare under a pandemic" (King 2020). The clinic responded by creating a larger network of suppliers to address gaps and work toward meeting demand in the future, developing point-of-care manufacturing to retrofit equipment for reuse and create a limited amount of PPE via 3D printing, and developing an internal network to better estimate supply demand for its use (O'Hara 2020). It also worked with group purchasing organizations and local manufacturers that redesigned their production processes to make needed PPE (Francis 2020). Further, the Mayo Clinic formed an aerosol-generating procedures group composed of healthcare employees representing infection control, anesthesia, pulmonary and critical care, respiratory therapy, and nursing to develop a three-tier system for appropriate PPE protocol (Sampathkumar et al. 2020).

The Mayo Clinic joined the COVID-19 HealthCare Coalition, an organization founded by private industries to coordinate effective responses to the coronavirus. The group's membership included universities, healthcare centers, healthcare services companies, information technology firms, and advocacy groups. The coalition's member organizations dedicated time and resources to form working groups, specific to their expertise, including a Supply Chain Working Group. In August 2020, this working group listed the following accomplishments (COVID-19 HealthCare Coalition 2020):

- Delivery of 675,000 masks to high-need locations
- Development of N95 mask-sanitizing procedures
- Creation of a PPE demand model to help balance supply and demand
- Establishment of networks for multiple PPE suppliers with buyers

James Francis, chair of supply chain management at the Mayo Clinic, summarized the lessons learned and the actions taken during the pandemic. The clinic worked to secure supply to meet the demands of healthcare workers and patients by encouraging creative thinking and applying expertise, illustrating adherence to the ethical principles of beneficence and nonmaleficence (see exhibit 12.2).

Exhibit 12.2
Ten Supply Chain Management Lessons Learned from the COVID-19 Pandemic

Lesson learned	Actions taken
Robust business continuity plans	Know potential issues that may impact production as healthcare is a participant in the global economy. Develop partnerships in-house, establish networks with other suppliers.
Agile and innovative culture	Encourage creative thinking to design and implement new methods to meet supply needs

(continued)

EXHIBIT 12.2
Ten Supply Chain Management Lessons Learned from the COVID-19 Pandemic (*continued*)

Lesson learned	Actions taken
Align communication	Communicate clearly and often and develop strong relationships with those who will be determining changes and those who will be communicating them.
Establish and adhere to PPE protocols	Collaborate with offices of safety, infection prevention and control, and nurses for protocol establishment.
Increase suppliers and capacity	Secure new manufacturers and increased production from existing suppliers. Develop creative partnerships; know who the contacts are with each up front.
Invest in information technology	Know days inventory on hand so to meet demand; run models to manage inventory.
Assess sourcing strategies	Determine needs for domestic and foreign suppliers with clinical input of products.
Determine inventory/distribution model	Assess and improve distribution models to distribute supplies where needed.
Achieve a balance between price and availability	Include the factors of availability and reliability as well as cost and quality.
Develop governmental/regulatory relationships	Identify contact person as recommended regarding suppliers and capacity.

Source: Information from Francis (2020).

MINI-CASE STUDY: CHANGE FOR THE BETTER

Vidant Health is a private, not-for-profit health system in eastern North Carolina consisting of more than 1,700 beds in nine hospitals, home health care, hospice care, a freestanding surgery center, more than 100 ambulatory care practices, and four wellness centers (Vidant Health 2021a). In 2006, as a result of a series of errors in one of the system's facilities, a patient received a transfusion with incompatible blood, causing the patient's death (Wynn et al. 2014). This event spurred the system to develop and implement major initiatives to change its operations for the better.

The improvements were so successful that Vidant Health received the John M. Eisenberg Patient Safety and Quality Award in 2013. Moreover, the system achieved an 83 percent reduction in serious safety events, a 62 percent reduction in hospital-acquired infections, a 98 percent optimal care score on the core measures of the Centers for Medicare & Medicaid Services and

The Joint Commission, and scored in the top 25 percent on the Hospital Consumer Assessment of Healthcare Providers and Systems (Atkins 2014; Wynn et al. 2014, 216).

These outcomes would not have been possible if Vidant Health had not rolled out systemwide changes in safety training, board leadership, transparency, patient–family partnerships, and leader and physician engagement. Safety training was implemented immediately after the patient's death, focused on improving the following areas:

- Safety habits for error prevention
- Situational awareness and sensitivity to operations
- Knowledge of daily on-site events and issues, which entails leaders and managers checking in with employees to discuss what happened in the past 24 hours, what is anticipated in the next 24 hours, and other points (such as safety priorities)

Board leadership included training for board members on quality care topics. Transparency became the organization's policy, entailing practices such as posting unexpected outcome and harmful event data on the system's website. (Patient–family partnerships are discussed earlier in this chapter.) Leader and physician engagement called for them to lead quality improvements "at the front line" (Wynn et al. 2014, 215).

Mini-Case Study Questions

1. Identify and explain how one action by Vidant Health illustrates what operations managers actually do.
2. Identify and explain how Vidant Health's actions illustrate the ethical principles of justice, beneficence, nonmaleficence, and autonomy in the workplace.
3. Go to Vidant Health's website (www.vidanthealth.com) and review its mission, vision, and values statement. How do Vidant Health's actions fit its mission, vision, and values?

Points to Remember

➤ Healthcare operations management covers a wide range of activities. The healthcare personnel charged with managing, performing, monitoring, and evaluating these activities are expected to adhere to ethical principles and ensure that the activities fit with the organization's mission, vision, and values.

➤ Operations management is the management of any product, service, process, resource, or activity that enables an organization to be productive and sustainable.

➤ Quality assurance is a program for monitoring and evaluating a product or service to ensure quality standards are met and proper procedures are followed.

➤ Ethical operations management is compliant with laws and regulations, proactive in identifying and correcting problems and threats, focused on continuous improvement, encouraging creative thinking in times of crises, and reliant on competent and ethical individuals.

Challenge Yourself

1. Consider the chapter-opening quote by former president Dwight D. Eisenhower: "You will not find it difficult to prove that battles, campaigns, and even wars have been won or lost primarily because of logistics." Think of an example in which this might be true for you as you prepare to become a healthcare manager.
2. Activity 4 of the CFR definition of healthcare operations is "conducting or arranging for medical review, legal services, and auditing functions, including fraud and abuse detection and compliance programs." Explain how the case of Full Motion Innovation Clinic illustrates activity 4.
3. Explain why weighing costs against organizational mission, vision, and values is important when determining action.

For Your Consideration

12.1 In 2020, the Office for Civil Rights (OCR) within the US Department of Health and Human Services reported that nearly 29.3 million healthcare records had been exposed or improperly disclosed and protected health information (PHI) compromised by privacy and security breaches. More than $13.5 million in fines have been levied against healthcare organizations found responsible for the breaches (Adler 2021). HIPAA was enacted in 1996 to protect patients' right to privacy in their dealings with the healthcare system and to access (and even have some control over) their own PHI. Moreover, healthcare providers are required to safeguard PHI and to identify and prevent "reasonably anticipated" disclosures of such data to unauthorized users. (See chapters 10 and 13 for more discussion of these topics.)

The following cases describe four organizations that violated HIPAA, each of which paid fines determined by the OCR (Adler 2021). Select one of these cases and explain the specific actions that violated ethical principles.

a. *Organization: Premera Blue Cross (PBC); settlement: $6.85 million; number of individuals affected: more than 10.4 million; year: 2015.* This settlement is the second-largest payment to the OCR related to a breach. PBC, the largest health plan in the Pacific Northwest, reported that cyber-attackers had accessed its information technology system and gained access to personal data, including Social Security numbers and bank account information, as well as patient data. The OCR found that PBC had not complied with HIPAA rules regarding risk analyses and auditing. Also, PBC settled a multistate action for $10 million and a class-action lawsuit on behalf of the breach victims for $74 million.

    b. *Lifespan Health System Affiliated Covered Entity; fine: $1.04 million; number of individuals affected: 20,431; year: 2017.* An unencrypted laptop computer was stolen from an employee's car. The OCR investigated and found that Lifespan had conducted a risk analysis and decided that encryption was required for mobile devices, but it failed to do so.

    c. *Organization: Aetna; fine: $1.0 million; number of individuals affected: 15,489; year: 2017.* Three data breaches were reported. The first concerned PHI exposure of plan members' information on the internet. The second was a mailing to 11,887 plan members in which PHI could be viewed through the window of the envelope—specifically, the words "HIV medication" were visible. The last was also a mailing, in which the name and logo of an atrial fibrillation study were visible. The OCR found a lack of administrative oversight and failure to have safeguards in place to ensure privacy. Additionally, Aetna negotiated a $1.15 million settlement with New York State, $935,000 with California, $99,959 with Connecticut, $175,000 with the District of Columbia, and $365,211 with New Jersey. Aetna paid $17.2 million to settle a class-action lawsuit filed on behalf of the plan member victims.

    d. *Organization: City of New Haven, Connecticut; fine: $202,400; number of individuals affected: 498; year: 2017.* In 2016, an employee was terminated from her employment with the New Haven Health Department during her probationary work period. The city neglected to terminate her access rights to the computer she used at work and access to information stored on the server. She returned to the department, used her work key to enter her office, and locked herself inside. She then used her log-in credentials to access the computer and copy data onto a USB drive.

12.2 Select one of the cases listed in 12.1 and discuss the recommendations that an operations manager might make to ensure that such actions do not occur again.

Check These Out

Want more information about the organizations and concepts discussed in the chapter? Check these websites out.

- Hospital Sisters Health System: www.hshs.org/
- Portneuf Medical Center: www.portneuf.org/
- Saint Alphonsus: www.saintalphonsus.org/
- Title 45—Public Welfare, section 164.501 of the *Code of Federal Regulations*: www.govinfo.gov/content/pkg/CFR-2011-title45-vol1/pdf/CFR-2011-title45-vol1-sec164-501.pdf

REFERENCES

Adler, S. 2021. "2020 HIPAA Violation Cases and Penalties." *HIPAA Journal*. Published January 13. www.hipaajournal.com/2020-hipaa-violation-cases-and-penalties/.

American Cancer Society. 2021. "Cancer Screening Guidelines by Age." Accessed May 3. www.cancer.org/healthy/find-cancer-early/screening-recommendations-by-age.html.

———. 2019. *Breast Cancer: Facts and Figures 2019–2020*. Accessed May 3, 2021. www.cancer.org/content/dam/cancer-org/research/cancer-facts-and-statistics/breast-cancer-facts-and-figures/breast-cancer-facts-and-figures-2019-2020.pdf.

Ashley, M., and M. Forsey. 2020. "Vidant Medical Center Is Enforcing New Visitor Restrictions Ahead of an Anticipated Jump in COVID-19 Cases." WNCT News. Published November 21. www.wnct.com/health/coronavirus/vidant-medical-center-restricts-visitation-during-covid-19-case-jump/.

Association of University Programs in Health Administration (AUPHA). 2021. "Certification Documents." Accessed May 3. www.aupha.org/certification/certification-docs.

Atkins, B. 2014. "Vidant Health Receives National Award for Quality and Patient Safety Initiatives." Published January 24. www.vidanthealth.com/vidant/newsroomdetail.aspx?id=17203.

Bradsher, K. 2020. "China Dominates Medical Supplies, in This Outbreak and the Next." *New York Times*. Published July 5. www.nytimes.com/2020/07/05/business/china-medical-supplies.html.

Constantine Cannon. 2019. "Carolina Physical Therapy and Sports Medicine, Inc." Published May 9. https://constantinecannon.com/2019/05/09/may-9-2019-2/.

COVID-19 Healthcare Coalition (C19HCC). 2020. "Delivering Impact and Value: COVID-19 Healthcare Coalition Members." Published July. https://c19hcc.org/static/catalog-resources/c19hcc_impact_report.pdf.

De Mil, R., E. Guillaume, L. Launay, L. Guittet, O. Dejardin, V. Bourvier, A. Notair, G. Launoy, and C. Berchi. 2019. "Cost-Effectiveness Analysis of a Mobile Mammography Unit for Breast Cancer Screening to Reduce Geographic and Social Health Inequalities." *Value in Health* 22 (10): 1111–18.

East Carolina University. 2021. "Bachelor of Science in Health Services Management." Accessed May 3. https://hsim.ecu.edu/undergraduate/health-services-management/.

Evenett, S. 2020. "Chinese Whispers: COVID-19, Global Supply Chains in Essential Goods, and Public Policy." *Journal of International Business Policy* 3: 408–29.

Federal Register. 2011. *Title 45—Public Welfare: Parts 1 to 199*. Revised October 1. www.govinfo.gov/content/pkg/CFR-2011-title45-vol1/pdf/CFR-2011-title45-vol1-sec164-501.pdf.

Francis, J. 2020. "COVID-19: Implications for Supply Chain Management." *Frontiers of Health Services Management* 37 (1): 33–38.

Handfield, R. 2020. "What Is Supply Chain Management (SCM)?" Supply Chain Resource Cooperative. Published February 19. https://scm.ncsu.edu/scm-articles/article/what-is-supply-chain-management-scm.

Hospital Sisters Health System (HSHS). 2021. "About Us." Accessed May 3, 2021. www.hshs.org/HSHS/About-Us/Mission-Values.

Hospital Sisters Health System (HSHS) Sacred Heart Hospital. 2019. "HSHS Foundations Receive $400,000 From Local Bank." Published June 4. www.hshs.org/SacredHeart/News/HSHS-Foundations-receive-$400,000-from-local-bank.

Hughes. A., S. Lee, J. Eberth, E. Berry, and S. Pruitt. 2020. "Do Mobile Units Contribute to Spatial Accessibility to Mammography for Uninsured Women?" *Preventive Medicine* 138: 106156.

Jones, A., and K. Dutton. 2014. "Patients and Families as Partners in Safety, Quality, and Experiences of Care." *Patient Experience Journal* 1 (1): 48–49.

King, R. 2020. "Mayo Clinic CEO Blasts 'Just-in-Time' Ordering as Pandemic Changes Supply Chain." Fierce Healthcare. Published July 7. www.fiercehealthcare.com/hospitals/mayo-clinic-ceo-blasts-just-time-ordering-as-pandemic-changes-supply-chain.

Krajewski, L. 1980. "The Inauguration of a Journal." *Journal of Operations Management* 1 (1): v–vi.

Naeim, A., E. Keeler, L. Bassett, J. Parikh, R. Bastani, and D. Reuben. 2009. "Cost-Effectiveness of Increasing Access to Mammography Through Mobile Mammography for Older Women." *Journal of the American Geriatric Society* 75 (2): 285–90.

O'Hara, J. 2020. "Mayo Clinic Q&A Podcast: Point-of-Care Manufacturing to Help Fight COVID-19." Mayo Clinic. Published March 30. https://newsnetwork.mayoclinic.org/discussion/mayo-clinic-qa-podcast-point-of-care-manufacturing-to-help-fight-covid-19/.

Patrinley, J. R., Jr., S. T. Berkowitz, D. Zakria, D. J. Totten, M. Kurtulus, and B. C. Drolet. 2020. "Lessons from Operations Management to Combat the COVID-19 Pandemic." *Journal of Medical Systems* 44 (7): 129.

Peppercorn, J., N. Horick, K. Houck, J. Rabin, V. Villagra, G. Lyman, and S. Wheeler. 2017. "Impact of the Elimination of Cost Sharing for Mammographic Breast Cancer Screening Among Rural US Women: A Natural Experiment." *Cancer* 123 (13): 2506–15.

Portneuf Medical Center. 2021. "Mission, Vision, Values." Accessed May 3. www.portneuf.org/about/mission-vision-values.

———. 2019. "Cutting the Ribbon to New 3D Mammography Coach." Accessed May 3, 2021. www.portneuf.org/cutting-the-ribbon-to-new-3d-mammography-coach.

Saint Alphonsus. 2021a. "About Us: Mission, Vision and Core Values." Accessed May 3. www.saintalphonsus.org/about-us/mission-vision-and-values.

———. 2021b. "Saint Alphonsus Mobile Mammography." Accessed May 3. www.freemammograms.org/details/saint-alphonsus-mobile-mammography.

Sampathkumar, P., E. Beam, L. Breeher, and J. O'Horo. 2020. "Precautions, Utilization of Personal Protective Equipment, and Conservation Strategies During the COVID-19 Pandemic." *Mayo Clinic Proceedings* 95 (9S): S11–13.

Silvera, F., J. Wolf, A. Stanowski, and Q. Studer. 2021. "The Influence of COVID-19 Visitation Restrictions on Patient Experience and Safety Outcomes: A Critical Role for Subjective Advocates." *Patient Experience Journal* 8 (1): 30–39.

Snell, R. 2021. "Michigan Woman First Charged with Stealing COVID-19 Medical Aid." *Detroit News*. Published February 11. www.detroitnews.com/story/news/local/michigan/2021/02/11/michigan-woman-first-charged-stealing-covid-19-medical-aid/6726933002/.

United States of America v. Carolina Physical Therapy and Sports Medicine, Limited Partnership. 2017. US District Court, District of South Carolina. Docket No. 3:17-cv-01952-CMC. Accessed August 18, 2021. www.courtlistener.com/docket/13474865/parties/united-states-of-america-v-carolina-physical-therapy-and-sports-medicine/.

US Department of Justice (DOJ). 2021. "Woman First in the Nation Charged with Misappropriating Monies Designed for COVID Medical Provider Relief." Published February 11. www.justice.gov/opa/pr/woman-first-nation-charged-misappropriating-monies-designed-covid-medical-provider-relief.

———. 2019. "Carolina Physical Therapy and Sports Medicine, Inc. to Pay $790,000 to Resolve False Billing Allegations." Published May 9. www.justice.gov/usao-sc/pr/carolina-physical-therapy-and-sports-medicine-inc-pay-790000-resolve-false-billing.

Vidant Health. 2021a. "System of Care." Accessed August 18. www.vidanthealth.com/about-us/system-of-care.

———. 2021b. "Vidant Medical Center Adjusts Visitation Restrictions in Emergency Department." Accessed August 28. www.vidanthealth.com/vidant-medical-center-adjusts-visitation-restrictions-in-emergency-department/.

———. 2021c. "Visitor Restrictions." Accessed August 18. www.vidanthealth.com/wp-content/uploads/2021/03/21-VH-851-VisitorRestrictionsMarch-Handout-PDF.pdf.

World Health Organization (WHO). 2020. "Shortage of Personal Protective Equipment Endangering Health Workers Worldwide." Published March 3. www.who.int/news/item/03-03-2020-shortage-of-personal-protective-equipment-endangering-health-workers-worldwide.

Wynn, J., E. Draffin, A. Jones, and L. Reida. 2014. "The Vidant Health Quality Transformation." *Joint Commission Journal on Quality and Patient Safety* 40 (5): 212–18.

CHAPTER 13
HEALTH INFORMATICS

All who work within healthcare and information systems must utilize and combine their technical, professional, and ethical expertise.
—Laurinda Beebe Harman and Frances H. Cornelius, *Ethical Health Informatics*

Important Terms

- Authorized users
- Business intelligence
- Confidentiality
- Data breach
- Digital health literacy
- Electronic health record (EHR)
- Health informatics
- Health information technology
- Health literacy
- Interoperability
- Meaningful use
- Privacy
- Security

Learning Objectives

Studying this chapter will help you to

➤ understand the field of health informatics and its function in the US healthcare system,

➤ explain the uses of and standards for electronic health records (EHRs),

➤ describe the current status of EHR use and health information exchange in the United States and future directions,

➤ examine how EHRs and related health information technologies create conflicts among the ethical principles of beneficence, autonomy, fidelity, and justice, and

➤ describe current health information security challenges for healthcare organizations.

This chapter focuses on health informatics and the ethical conflicts that arise in the use of health information.

HEALTH INFORMATICS

Health informatics can be defined as a "field that is concerned with the *optimal use of information, often aided by the use of technology, to improve individual health, health care, public health, and biomedical research*" (Hersh 2009, 2; italics in original). Healthcare managers are involved in health informatics because they create, use, and manage much of the health information that their healthcare organizations generate.

Health records have been kept for more than two centuries in the United States. Massachusetts General Hospital has bound patient records dating to the early 1800s. These early handwritten records are stored in large, leather-bound volumes more than two inches thick (Huffman 1963). The American College of Surgeons (2021) adopted the first "minimum standards" for hospital records in 1919 and, along with The Joint Commission, has continued to standardize the content of medical records.

A 1997 Institute of Medicine study discussed the limitations of paper records (e.g., legibility) and recommended that healthcare organizations begin converting to electronic health records (EHRs) (Atherton 2011; Dick, Steen, and Detmer 1997). Today, healthcare organizations—big and small—have developed and implemented their own EHR systems. This effort was aided by the passage of the Health Information Technology for Economic and Clinical Health (HITECH) Act in 2009, which provided incentives for adoption of EHRs and changed the reimbursement rates for Medicare to effectively penalize late adopters (Atasoy, Greenwood, and McCullough 2019).

To illustrate how healthcare organizations use EHRs, consider how a university's student health service might create a computerized health record for a patient, a college student.

Jordan has a sore throat, feels hot, and has difficulty swallowing. Feeling miserable, he calls his university's student health service to schedule an appointment. The receptionist asks him for basic information, including his name, date of birth, address, next of kin, and health insurance coverage. These patient demographic data are the first entries into Jordan's health record. The receptionist tells him to arrive 20 minutes early for his appointment.

health informatics
The study, invention, and implementation of structures and algorithms to advance communication, understanding, use, and management of health data and information.

> **CASE FROM THE FIELD**
> EHR: A Hero in the Storm
>
> Joseph P. Addabbo Family Health Center serves more than 38,000 patients at six sites across New York City. After Hurricane Sandy hit the city in October 2012, the center's doctors and staff, using laptop computers, searched its EHR system to see which diabetic patients urgently needed insulin. With contact information from the EHR, doctors and staff were able to identify patients in need and went door-to-door delivering the insulin. Dr. Jinpin Ying, the center's chief information officer, said that if it had still been using paper-based medical records, the patients would not have received their insulin. Dr. Ying considers the EHR "another hero in the storm" (NYC Health 2013, 3).

When he arrives, Jordan is given a paper form to complete. The form asks for the following information: medical history (e.g., previous surgeries and hospitalizations, past and current diseases or medical conditions, known family health history), current medications, and allergies. Completing a paper form is typical, but some patients are directed to enter their information at a computer kiosk or a laptop located in the office. When Jordan returns his filled-out form to the reception desk, a staff member adds the information from the form to his computerized record.

A nursing assistant calls out to Jordan to follow her into an examination room. There, or right outside of the room, the nursing assistant weighs him, measures his height, and takes his vital signs (temperature, pulse, blood pressure). A nurse comes into the exam room to confirm Jordan's medical history, current medications, and allergy information. All of this information is written down on paper and later transferred to his record.

When the physician comes into the room, she asks Jordan about his symptoms, when they started, whether he has experienced these symptoms before, and other detailed questions. The doctor then physically examines Jordan, taking note of his breathing and the sights and sounds he is displaying. Using a laptop, the doctor enters an order for a rapid strep test to help her diagnose or confirm the illness. For the test, the nurse comes back into the room to swab a sample of cells from Jordan's tonsils; the nurse then takes the sample to the lab while Jordan waits in the exam room.

In less than 30 minutes, the test result is ready and has been posted to his record. The physician confirms that Jordan has strep throat and orders a prescription for antibiotics. She asks him to come back for a follow-up. He is released, and the doctor quickly summarizes in a progress note the treatment he received.

Jordan's health record now contains every piece of information he provided in writing or verbally. It also includes the test administered, the lab result, the prescription ordered, and other physician notes. More information will be added to his record each time he visits this student health service. When he returns for a follow-up, more data and information will be added to his digital record.

WHAT IS AN ELECTRONIC HEALTH RECORD?

An **electronic health record (EHR)** is a computerized or digitized record containing a patient's health-related information. Based on the definition provided by an early organization, the National Alliance for Health Information Technology, a certified EHR must conform to nationally recognized **interoperability** standards so that health records can be created, managed, and consulted by **authorized users** across more than one healthcare organization (Hanken and Murphy 2017). Let's break down each component of this definition:

- *Computerized or digitized record of a patient's health information.* A health record—whether paper-based or electronic—contains medical and personal data and information accumulated by a healthcare provider from a patient's initial contact through subsequent visits to the provider or office. This might be referred to as the patient's *medical chart*. Many healthcare providers have shifted from paper to digital charts, thereby simplifying their processes for pulling files and looking up, reviewing, and updating the health-related information of each patient.

    As illustrated in Jordan's case, the chart includes the following information: patient demographics (name, address, birthdate, etc.), medical and family health history, progress notes (a physician's, nurse's, or assistant's brief description of the medical condition and treatment provided), list of health conditions (illnesses, injuries, symptoms, other complaints with dates and outcomes), list of medications, vital signs (temperature, pulse, blood pressure) at the time of visit, test results, diagnoses, procedures, and other relevant information.

- *Conforms to nationally recognized interoperability standards.* Interoperability is the capability of the EHR and related **health information technology (health IT)** products or applications to be shared and to be functional between at least two different organizations. Standards are detailed specifications that enable this exchange and that ensure the information's reliability, consistency, and accuracy. The Office of the National Coordinator for Health Information Technology (ONC) certifies technologies for meeting these standards (www.healthit.gov/topic/about-onc).

- *Created, managed, and consulted by authorized users.* Authorized users are those who need to access the patient's record to fulfill their official job-related

---

electronic health record (EHR)
A computerized or digitized record containing a patient's health-related information.

interoperability
The capability of electronic health records and related health information technology products or applications to be shared and to be functional across at least two different organizations.

authorized users
Individuals and groups that need to access a patient's record to fulfill their official job-related duties and responsibilities.

health information technology (health IT)
Electronic devices and systems used to store, share, manipulate, analyze, display, and generate patient- and provider-specific health data and information; also referred to as *health information* or *communications technology and systems*.

duties and responsibilities. For example, during Jordan's visit, the authorized users are the receptionist, the nursing assistant, the nurse, the physician, and the laboratory technician. Generally, types of authorized users includes the following:

- Healthcare organizations: health insurers, hospitals, physician offices, data warehouses, state and federal health agencies, pharmacies, durable medical equipment companies, vendors, and other health-related organizations on a need-to-know, work-related basis
- Individual healthcare personnel: healthcare managers, clinicians, payment specialists, consultants, pharmacists, clinical researchers, ward clerks, policymakers, medical social workers, psychologists, rehabilitation counselors, and other workers on a need-to-know, work-related basis
- Consumers: patients (or clients and residents), their families or caregivers, purchasers of health insurance (typically employers), members of/subscribers to the healthcare plan, and other personal users on a need-to-know basis

Typically, authorized users are assigned *credentials*—a user identifier and a password. With these credentials, they are permitted access to the EHR and to specific computer applications in the EHR. Unauthorized use occurs when the EHR is accessed by those who have credentials but no work-related purpose. Unauthorized use may be merely curious—for example, looking up the demographic data or medical condition of an acquaintance or a celebrity. As discussed in chapter 9, such breaches of patient confidentiality are considered unethical and can be traced back to the owners or holders of the credentials.

◆ *Across more than one healthcare organization.* This criterion relates to interoperability standards. Although small physician practices may have a basic EHR system used only in-house, most large healthcare organizations have EHRs that are government certified as meeting specific national standards. With this attribute, different types of organizations—such as large university hospitals, physician group practices, pharmacies, healthcare agencies, and health insurers—and individual personnel (such as counselors) can work together over a period to deliver services to the patient. Thus, having an interoperable EHR is necessary to fulfill the full vision of a national health information system.

For example, with an established EHR system, Jordan's doctor at the student health service would not need to ask about his previous bouts of strep throat because that information would already be in the system, entered by his hometown doctor. When Jordan goes home for a holiday break and sees his regular physician, that office would be able to pull up on the computer the record of his visit to the student health service.

EXHIBIT 13.1
Core Functionalities and Key Capabilities of Electronic Health Records

Core functionalities	Key capabilities
Health information and data	Longitudinal collection of electronic health information for and about individual persons
Results management	
Order entry and management	Interoperability that allows linkages among providers, such as individuals' personal health records
Decision support	
Electronic communication and connectivity	Security with access only to authorized users
Patient support	Immediate electronic access to individual and aggregate health information by authorized users
Administrative processes	
Reporting and population health management	Connections to external medical and health knowledge, decision support systems, and alerts
	Support of processes that enhance quality, safety, and efficiency

Source: Layman (2020). Reprinted with permission.

Elizabeth Layman (2020) describes eight core functionalities and six key capabilities of EHRs based on the Institute of Medicine's guidelines (see exhibit 13.1). The functionality needed will depend on the system's use—primary uses are related to delivering care and administration, whereas secondary uses involve education, research, and the promotion of public health.

GROWTH AND CURRENT STATUS OF EHR UTILIZATION

Healthcare has been slower than other industries (such as banking) to adopt information technologies. However, adoption and implementation of EHR systems has increased significantly since the first decade of the twenty-first century (Atasoy, Greenwood, and McCullough 2019). The HITECH Act likely helped spur hospitals to shift to electronic records (Adler-Milstein et al. 2014), and specifically to **meaningful use** of those records—for example, adding decision support capabilities to improve quality of care. As an illustration, the EHR system might identify all patients with diabetes and direct providers to assess A1C levels and counsel patients depending on their results.

The Centers for Medicare & Medicaid Services (CMS) offered financial incentives to healthcare organizations and individual providers that use EHRs in a meaningful way. To

meaningful use
The use of electronic health records and related technology within a healthcare organization to achieve specified objectives.

qualify for these incentives, hospitals and physicians had to show (separately) that they are meeting the requirements and objectives defined in three stages: (stage 1) data capture and sharing, (stage 2) advance clinical processes, and (stage 3) improved outcomes. Examples of meaningful use include electronically sending prescriptions to pharmacies (e-prescribing), routinely screening patients for high-prevalence risk factors or comorbidities, and embedding standardized protocols in the EHR and then submitting data on quality improvements in patient care. This program continues to be updated. CMS released a final rule establishing the criteria for reaching stage 3 in 2017 and beyond, focusing on the use of certified electronic health record technology (CEHRT) to improve health outcomes. In 2018, this initiative was renamed the Promoting Interoperability Program. This change reflected the shift to a new phase of EHR use with an increased focus on interoperability and improving patient access to health information (CMS 2021).

Researchers have studied the adoption and diffusion of health technology and EHRs as well as the extent of information sharing, meaningful use, and the promised impact of EHRs on safety and quality of care. By 2014, most hospitals had adopted EHRs and met basic criteria for meaningful use, such as recording demographics, vital signs, and tracking medications (Adler-Milstein et al. 2014). However, they were less likely to fulfill higher-stage criteria, such as sharing case summaries with outside providers or providing patients with online access to their health data. Three years later, hospitals continued to lag in the use of advanced EHR functions such as performance measurement and patient engagement. There was also evidence of a digital divide in advanced use, with critical-access hospitals (fewer than 25 beds in areas where access is limited) in particular lagging beyond other facilities (Adler-Milstein et al. 2017).

Advanced use of EHRs is seen as contributing to improved hospital performance. An early systematic review indicated that the majority of studies on the impact of EHRs on care reported positive consequences (Jones et al. 2014), although this finding may be tempered by selection bias, as these organizations were early adopters of and researched quality improvements. There is evidence that EHRs can improve preventive care for some conditions (e.g., cardiovascular disease) through electronic prompting (i.e., notification that the patient needs a test or treatment), increase provider access to information and communication with other providers, and improve patient safety for medication prescribing (Atasoy, Greenwood, and McCullough 2019). However, the literature on safety and quality improvements shows mixed findings; the effects of EHRs are likely modest, with positive outcomes on care depending on the extent of meaningful use (Baillieu et al. 2020; Lin, Lin, and Chen 2019). Similarly, providing patients with access to their health records and educational information through patient portals might increase their engagement, adherence to treatment and reduction of risk factors, or satisfaction with care—although the available evidence is still limited (Ammenwerth et al. 2021).

The interoperability of EHR systems and data sharing with other hospitals and clinics also remains a challenge. This difficulty is partly attributable to a lack of standardized protocols among EHR vendors. In addition, the movement toward electronic records has had some unintended consequences, such as the impact of failed expectations regarding the presumed benefits of health IT due to poorly designed or context-dependent studies, saturation of the EHR market and limited product innovation, provider burnout or resistance to increasing documentation requirements for nonclinical purposes, and possible obfuscation of relevant data (Colicchio, Cimino, and Del Fiol 2019).

THE FUTURE OF HEALTHCARE INFORMATION EXCHANGE

The eHealth Exchange, formerly the Nationwide Health Information Network, is an initiative intended to facilitate the exchange of healthcare information (Valle et al. 2016). Initially developed by the ONC in 2004, the eHealth Exchange is now managed by a nonprofit organization called the Sequoia Project. The initiative provides a set of standards, services, and policies that enable the secure exchange of health information. It is important to note that this initiative is not a physical computer network, but rather a future vision for the exchange of health information. Its main objective is to allow healthcare providers across the continuum of care to have access to the right data, at the right time, in the right place. When the healthcare industry achieves this vision, authorized users will be able to access comprehensive individual health records and population health information for multiple purposes:

- Clinicians, to provide patient care
- Patients and other healthcare consumers, to self-manage their care
- Public health workers, to conduct public health biosurveillance
- Healthcare organizations, to assess population-based health and community health initiatives
- Emergency responders, to provide care and services during natural disasters, threats to security, and other crises
- Leaders (e.g., government agency heads, industry experts who advise legislators), to develop healthcare policy, laws, regulations, and guidelines for the US healthcare system
- Organizational executives and administrators, to effectively manage their organization
- Healthcare researchers, to create or disseminate knowledge

This vision has not yet been realized, however, because of barriers to interoperability and delays in achieving meaningful use by healthcare organizations. Nevertheless, progress has been made in the development of open software that allows data sharing among government agencies (Project Connect), the development of regional health information exchanges, and increased access to health information for patients (Ahier 2012). Technological innovation continues. One proposed model for the growth of EHRs is the development of applications that connect with the major EHRs to augment their functionality, similar to smartphones (Colicchio, Cimino, and Del Fiol 2019). Although the initiative is still overseen by the ONC, the eHealth Exchange is now a public–private partnership comprising health information exchanges, healthcare providers with EHRs, secondary users of data (e.g., public health researchers), and healthcare consumers.

In 2020, the US Department of Health and Human Services published rules to address interoperability and patient access to their health information (HHS 2020). These rules affect healthcare providers, developers of certified health IT, and health information networks. The rules require greater information sharing, between systems, of data elements such as demographics, clinical notes, and medications, and prohibit unwarranted information-blocking practices (e.g., anticompetitive behaviors) so that users of certified IT can communicate more freely. They also give patients greater access to and control over their health records. Under the 21st Century Cures Act, signed into law in 2016, the HHS now requires organizations using certified EHRs to provide a secure, standards-based application programming interface (API) that allows patients to access their health records (open note provision), integrate their EHR with their health plan, and transport their information across providers. Hospitals participating in government health insurance programs (i.e., Medicare and Medicaid) must also send electronic notifications to other healthcare facilities or community providers to better coordinate care.

For the entire US healthcare system, the overall goals of EHRs, meaningful use, and the eHealth Exchange vision are (1) to improve quality and safety by increasing coordination and integration among providers and by fostering patients' engagement in their health, and (2) to lower costs by increasing efficiency and decreasing administrative costs. Future development of this vision will depend on the responses of healthcare organizations and their patients.

ETHICAL CONFLICTS IN HEALTH INFORMATICS

Health informatics is included in an ethics book for healthcare managers because the use of EHRs and related health information technologies involves ethical challenges. Specifically, the use of EHRs and health IT can create conflicts among the ethical principles of beneficence, autonomy, fidelity, and justice (Layman 2020; Rinehart-Thompson and Harman 2017).

The American Medical Association (AMA 2014, 2020) has periodically surveyed physician attitudes, motivations and perceived requirements for using EHR and digital clinical tools. Physicians generally approve of the use of EHR systems and appreciate the ability to access patient information remotely and the improvements in quality of care that EHRs make possible. However, physicians also report a number of perceived difficulties with EHRs. Common sources of dissatisfaction with EHRs include poor usability, time-consuming data entry, interference with face-to-face patient care, degradation of clinical documentation as a result of template-generated notes, and the inability to exchange health information. The AMA has developed a framework to improve EHR usability and works with the federal government and other stakeholders to improve interoperability and meaningful use. From 2016 to 2019, the number of physicians who perceived advantages to digital tools increased, particularly among primary care providers. This period also saw an increase in the adoption of digital tools (e.g., 37 percent of respondents reported using clinical decision support tools, up from 28 percent), with the largest increases in conducting virtual visits (28 percent) and remote patient monitoring to improve care (22 percent).

EHRs and related health information technologies are believed to be beneficent. However, poorly considered and imprudent use of the EHR and related health information technologies can come into conflict with the ethical principles of autonomy, fidelity, and justice.

Beneficence: Full Potential Unrealized

This chapter's Case from the Field is an example of the beneficence of EHRs—that is, digitization has a positive impact on access to health information. Layman (2020) discusses another situation that occurred after Hurricane Katrina hit the Gulf Coast. Fortunately, the Veterans Health Administration (VHA) had a functional EHR system at the time. As a result of this digitization, the VHA was able to transfer the records of 50,000 patients from flooded veterans' hospitals and clinics in New Orleans to facilities in Houston. At the same time, the ONC worked with pharmacies to create a medication database for 800,000 people in the region affected by the storm. The digitization of health records supported continuity of care and access to care.

However, these examples are probably exceptions. Many healthcare organizations are unable to fully use the mass of data they create. A typical small hospital creates 665 terabytes of data each year. To put this number in context, consider that the web archive of the US Library of Congress was estimated to contain less than 500 terabytes in total (Sejdic 2014). Despite this quantity of data, Grant C. Davies, a healthcare executive, described healthcare organizations as "information poor" (May 2014). **Business intelligence** and the use of **big data** are still in their infancy in the healthcare sector (Dash et al. 2019).

Corporations that generate enormous amounts of data, such as Amazon and Google, have long leveraged big data to create business intelligence. A simple form of business intelligence is the calculation of revenue and costs by service or by unit. More advanced forms of business intelligence include data mining and statistical analyses. Beyond enabling

business intelligence
Knowledge that organizations create by using computer-based techniques to identify, extract, and analyze their data for patterns.

big data
Extremely large data sets that are analyzed using specialized computational methods to reveal patterns and associations.

financial analyses and forecasts, business intelligence can help reduce medical errors, allow early detection of epidemics and health risks, and improve quality of care.

Experts in healthcare have been slow to use big data, however, and when they have tried to do so, they have found that the current state of EHRs does not allow data to be fully leveraged to create intelligence. The data in EHRs are sometimes inconsistent and can be incomplete or inaccurate. (Paper-based records were even more flawed.) For example, healthcare analysts and clinicians in North Carolina used big data to identify patients who may have been overexposed to ionizing radiation (Biola et al. 2014). Using Medicaid claims data, they identified 546 patients aged 18 to 64, without a diagnosis of cancer, who had received ten or more computerized tomography (CT) scans. Using these data was difficult because the coding of CT scans varied by the types of facilities and visits and because patients' Medicaid enrollment often was not continuous. We also know that EHR data are frequently inconsistent with patient reports (Echaiz et al. 2015; Valikodath et al. 2017). Such difficulties have led to a lack of trust in the integrity of EHR data and the reliability of research findings using such data. The use of EHR data is limited by the following (Savitz et al. 2020, 2):

- ◆ Missing data

- ◆ Errors or incorrect data entry

- ◆ Longitudinal inconsistencies due to changes in collection procedures or documentation practices

- ◆ Site and provider inconsistencies in how data are entered and organized

- ◆ Unstructured data in multiple areas, which challenges data standardization

- ◆ All relevant clinical data (e.g., radiologic images) may not be accessible

These limitations can be addressed by performance audits to improve entry and data checking (e.g., searching for implausible values), triangulation of measurement for the same condition, and standardization efforts across data research networks. EHR data can be valuable for healthcare research as they include rich clinical information but improving the quality of the available data remains a challenge.

Big data, by definition, refers to very large amounts of data that cannot be analyzed using traditional methods and require specialized strategies and tools for data management and analysis (Dash et al. 2019). The number of publications related to big data in healthcare has increased significantly in recent years. Clinical data from health records and from patients themselves can be integrated with biomedical data now being collected (e.g., genomics, images, mobile biosensors) to promote personalized medical decisions.

Describing the many sources of big data in healthcare and the data management and analytic tools currently in development are beyond the scope of this chapter. Despite

> **DID YOU KNOW?**
> Big Data
>
> Big data provide the tools, methods, and procedures to create, manipulate, and manage very large, complex, unstructured, and diverse data sets. Five dimensions—known as the "five Vs"—characterize big data: volume, velocity, variety, veracity, and value.

much progress, many barriers to meaningful use of EHRs persist, including data storage, integrity, unified format, image processing, visualization, sharing, and the need for metadata and querying. Students who are interested in health informatics might read further in this area to keep up with future developments (see, e.g., Anderson and Hardin 2017; Dash et al. 2019).

BENEFICENCE AND AUTONOMY IN CONFLICT

Autonomy, as explained in earlier chapters, is the right to self-determination. One proposed advantage of EHRs and related health information technologies is the increased engagement of patients (and family members) in their healthcare. The 21st Century Cures Act intended to put consumers in charge of their health information and, in doing so, enhance patients' autonomy and ability to make informed decisions. Patients' increased autonomy, however, may not be entirely achieved or distributed fairly.

Patients give healthcare providers personal data and information for specific purposes. Health information exchanges allow data and information to be combined in ways that patients did not imagine or authorize. Combining these data to create new information about patients without their knowledge or permission violates the principle of autonomy. More concerning is that this new information may be unknown to the patient. Thus, the extent to which patients' information is shared and new knowledge is created without their consent may reduce patients' autonomy. Subsequent use of EHR data raises ethical issues of **privacy** and consent as well as data validity, on which beneficence depends. Additionally, it is unclear whether patients perceive a benefit from or have an obligation to participate in learning health systems (Lee 2017).

Another threat to autonomy is patients' limited **health literacy**. In a seminal report on this topic, the Institute of Medicine estimated that "nearly half of all American adults . . . have difficulty understanding and acting upon health information" (Nielsen-Bohlman, Panzer, and Kindig 2004, 1). Low health literacy affects provider communication and

privacy
The right of individuals to limit others' access to their body, thoughts, and feelings.

health literacy
The ability to understand and act on health information.

collaborative care, necessitating efforts to improve patients' understanding of health information to facilitate disease management (Feinberg et al. 2018). Without health literacy, patients' autonomy is compromised because they are unable to understand the information needed to act in their own interest. Moreover, the concept of health literacy can be extended to the digital arena: **Digital health literacy** refers to patients' understanding not only of basic health information necessary to make decisions but also of online information and skills to use tools such as patient portals (Harris, Jacobs, and Reeder 2019).

digital health literacy
The knowledge and skills needed to use digital health information, including literacy skills, basic knowledge of computers, and understanding of online health information.

confidentiality
The expectation by individuals that the information they share is kept private or disclosed (to select, trusted parties) only when necessary and with their consent.

security
The use of managerial, personnel, operational, and technical controls to ensure that information systems and applications run effectively and support the confidentiality, integrity, and availability of data and information.

BENEFICENCE AND FIDELITY IN CONFLICT

Fidelity means keeping your promises. It encompasses privacy, **confidentiality**, and **security**, which healthcare managers—bound by their profession's ethical code—are mandated to protect. Specifically, managers "work to ensure the existence of procedures that will safeguard the confidentiality and privacy of patients or others served" (ACHE 2017). In addition, managers keep confidential their organization's proprietary data and their employees' information, such as performance evaluations.

Safeguarding patient confidentiality with EHR systems is paramount when records contain sensitive information, such as those relating to mental health treatment, substance use, or sexual health (Shenoy and Appel 2017). Most EHR systems include safeguards in addition to password identifiers, such as "soft stops," which remind physicians that they are requesting or "breaking the glass" to view sensitive information, or "hard stops," which restrict portions of a patient record to a small set of system users. Patients may be given some control over the sharing of their psychiatric records with other providers. As patients increasingly gain access to their own records, they will be able to add health monitoring information and correct any errors, but these advances require that patients trust the security of their records.

DID YOU KNOW?
Proprietary Data

Organizations safeguard their proprietary data to maintain a competitive edge. Proprietary data are considered property and may be protected by copyrights, patents, and trade secret laws. Examples are contracts, fee schedules and cost data, supplier lists, practice patterns, and strategic and long-term plans. Generally, these data are disseminated only to authorized organizational users. They are disseminated externally or publicly when mandated by local, state, and federal reporting requirements.

Ethical conflicts involving privacy, confidentiality, and security do not present simple, clear-cut solutions. These issues are complex because they lie at the intersection of the ethical principle of fidelity and multiple laws, regulations, and court decisions. The case of *Sorrell v. IMS Health* (564 US 552 [2011]) illustrates the conflict between prescribers' right to privacy and pharmaceutical companies' right to free speech through marketing (Petersen et al. 2013). Under the laws of almost every state as well as the federal Health Insurance Portability and Accountability Act (HIPAA) of 1996, pharmacies may sell prescription information to data-mining drug companies, but only after they have removed patient identifiers. However, the prescription information that is sold still contains data on prescribers (e.g., physicians, physician assistants, other eligible prescribers), as well as data on the drugs, dosages, and volumes. From these data, data miners create business intelligence that pharmaceutical companies use to market their drugs. In response, Vermont passed its own Prescription Confidentiality Law, which was at the center of the *Sorrell v. IMS Health* case, to prohibit the sale of prescription information without prescribers' consent. However, the US Supreme Court struck down the Vermont law, determining that it was too narrowly drawn because it restricted drug companies' right to free speech (Petersen et al. 2013). Although the case was decided based on commercial speech rather than privacy considerations, it has provoked ethical analysis of the use of big data, particularly considerations of individual versus public interests and research versus privacy (Kaplan 2016).

DID YOU KNOW?
What Do Privacy, Confidentiality, and Security Mean?

Privacy is the right of individuals to limit others' access to their body, thoughts, and feelings. It gives people the freedom to live without unwanted attention and public scrutiny. With respect to health records, privacy refers to the right of individuals to know about and have some (if not total) control over the collection, processing, storage, dissemination, and use of their personal health information.

Confidentiality is the expectation by individuals that the information they share will be kept private or disclosed (to select, trusted parties) only when necessary and with their consent. In terms of health records, confidentiality refers to the expectation that personal health information is stored in a secure, trusted system.

Security is the use of managerial, personnel, operational, and technical controls to ensure that information systems and applications run effectively and support the confidentiality, integrity, and availability of data and information. Security control measures protect facilities, systems, and data from interruption, loss, misuse, modification, theft, unauthorized access, damage, corruption, and other harms.

The case that opened part III, "Should a Good Risk Manager Worry About Cost and Price Transparency in Health Care?," addresses price transparency in health charges through the ethical lens of autonomy and justice. Both consumers and government have called for more transparency in healthcare charges, although hospitals have been reluctant to share their charges under different insurance plans. The US Department of Health and Human Services now requires hospitals to report their chargemaster prices, although these prices do not reflect what insurers or patients actually pay. What is needed is a system in which the true costs are clear and patients are provided information about their payments before obtaining services (Frakt and Mehrotra 2019).

BENEFICENCE AND THE SECURITY CHALLENGE

EHRs and other health information technologies are potentially beneficent because they ease access to health information. However, this beneficence comes with a price—increasing threats to security. Unfortunately, security breaches within the healthcare industry have been on the rise. By law, the US Department of Health and Human Services must publish a listing of **data breaches** involving protected health information if 500 or more individuals are affected. Large data breaches have involved major healthcare organizations, such as Trinity Health, Inova Health, Magellan, and Dental Alliance, each potentially affecting more than a million individuals (Jercich 2020). The data breach at Trinity Health involved Blackbaud, a widely used database vendor, and thus affected information at many individual hospitals across the country (Weston 2020).

Data breaches are generally classified as internal or external. Internal breaches may involve unauthorized access or internal disclosure, loss or theft (e.g., a laptop), or improper disposal of sensitive information. External data breaches are caused by an external agent and involve hacking, phishing schemes, and ransomware attacks. Such breaches are not only costly but also compromise the privacy of individuals and their trust in healthcare records and damage the reputation of the organization (Tully et al. 2020).

Research on data breaches has produced three important findings for the healthcare industry: (1) the healthcare sector is particularly vulnerable to attack; (2) the incidence of some internal breaches, such as theft or loss and improper disposal, has decreased; and (3) there has been a dramatic increase in hacking incidents, particularly aimed at email and network servers (Seh et al. 2020). In 2020, the Federal Bureau of Investigation, in concert with other agencies, issued a detailed cybersecurity advisory report describing this third threat (Joint Cybersecurity Advisory 2020).

Ransomware involves cybercriminals infecting a system with malicious software that blocks access to an organization's computer system and then threatening to publish the victim's data or block access unless a monetary ransom is paid. Healthcare organizations may be particularly vulnerable to ransomware attacks if they have outdated IT infrastructure. Some organizations may decide to pay the ransom because they cannot afford to lose access

---

data breach
The illegal use or disclosure of confidential health information that compromises the privacy or security of it and poses a risk of financial, reputational, or other types of harm to those affected.

to patient records. In 2020, ransomware attacks cost the healthcare industry an estimated $21 billion, mostly in downtime ($20.8 million), in addition to $2.1 billion in ransom payments (Horowitz 2021). To respond to this threat, healthcare organizations are investing in more sophisticated security measures and training staff to recognize security threats. Common security measures involve installing antivirus software, implementing firewalls, limiting VPN access to select computers (rather than the entire network), encrypting sensitive data, and using multifactor authentication (Dash et al. 2019).

Consider the difficulty of protecting against security violations in a health information network involving multiple healthcare organizations. Data security must protect real-time information that is shared across state boundaries and across hospitals, nursing homes, home health agencies, physician practices, pharmacies, health plans, and many other entities. Without adequate security, public concern for the privacy of patient information may limit the adoption of healthcare information exchanges, and patients may opt out of sharing their data with researchers to improve healthcare (Esmaeilzadeh 2019).

BENEFICENCE AND JUSTICE IN CONFLICT

Transparency and accountability, generally thought to be beneficent practices, are current trends in healthcare and government. In the spirit of beneficence, healthcare organizations and governments post online reports and data about their activities. However, these reports and data can be threats to justice, as well as to patients' privacy and confidentiality. For example, in the past, some states published data on Medicaid enrollees. These patients became individually identifiable because the data were organized by county or by services for small groups of people. When a cell on a report only contains one, two, or three people, a person's identity can be easily determined. In their efforts to be transparent and accountable, healthcare managers must take care not to present information in ways that unjustly expose individuals' or small groups' information.

Aggregate data in public databases can be broken down to identifiable information when databases are integrated and the data are cross-referenced. This is known as *re-identification risk*. For example, researchers have shown that hospital discharge records without individual identity information can be re-identified when they are cross-referenced with publicly available information such as voter registration lists using combinations of birthdate, gender, and residential zip code (Sweeney 2000; Walsh et al. 2018). As a result, under HIPAA, health data are only considered *de-identified* if 18 information features are removed, including names as well as "quasi-identifiers" such as zip codes in less populated areas and the exact ages of older individuals.

Of particular concern are genomic data (Aziz et al. 2019; Terry 2017)—an increasingly important area of health research. Patients with rare or uncommon diseases—such as cystic fibrosis, Huntington's disease, and phenylketonuria—receive care at only a few academic health centers. If the DNA of an individual is known, that patient can be identified as part of a membership class of people in a particular treatment study. These patients' right to privacy are then unjustly violated. Moreover, once identified as having a particular diagnosis, patients may be stigmatized or discriminated against by employers or insurance companies.

More and more, scientists and researchers are sharing data sets, both to verify their findings and to enhance scientific advances in areas such as psychiatry. However, the benefits of this open science initiative must be balanced with ongoing efforts to protect patient privacy (Walsh et al. 2018). These efforts typically involve contractual agreements in which the users of such health data promise not to try to re-identify data, as well as strategies to protect structured clinical data by suppressing or selectively replacing values (e.g., use of age ranges). De-identification algorithms also can be used with unstructured or qualitative text records to reduce (but not eliminate) the risk of re-identification. The development of such methods remains an active area of research.

BENEFICENCE: ENSURING THAT THE BENEFITS OF HEALTHCARE INFORMATION AND APPLICATIONS REACH ALL

As we have seen throughout this text, IT is ushering in new potential for patient education and engagement in their health, including informational webinars, telehealth programs, mobile applications, and access to patient portals. However, the potential beneficence of increased access to these services is not guaranteed. Healthcare managers can increase the likelihood of achieving beneficence by using *multiple* methods to publicize information about their organization and the services it offers. Many healthcare organizations use their website to post information that is important to patients and other healthcare consumers. Here are some examples:

- ◆ State health agencies and large pharmaceutical companies provide information about and applications for prescription assistance programs. Prescription assistance programs help patients who must take expensive medications, such as drugs for hepatitis C or transplanted organs, and patients who are poor and cannot afford their medications.

- ◆ Medical centers post their annual reports, medical encyclopedias, consumer guides, sets of disease- and procedure-specific discharge instructions, fact sheets on emergency care for injuries and poisonings, and other informational resources.

Healthcare managers can make a difference by ensuring that these informational resources are available in multiple languages and in multiple media, not solely on the internet. Using the internet as the only medium for disseminating has ethical implications. It minimizes the organization's capacity to do good, and it unjustly excludes many potential patients simply because they lack internet access. Therefore, the beneficence of increased access may not be fully realized.

Mini-Case Study: Ethical Principles of Physician Rating Websites

On the internet, consumers can review and grade professors; restaurants; car dealerships; movies; and many other services, products, and people. Patients who want to rate and share their experiences with their doctors may do so on sites such as HealthGrades.com, RateMDs.com, and Vitals.com. These sites present patients' feedback and the physicians' overall score on communication, access or availability, facilities, and staff. Most online ratings of physicians are positive (Kadry et al. 2011), although these systems have generated increasing physician distrust. Nevertheless, more individuals (particularly younger patients and patients with chronic diseases and high healthcare utilization) are now consulting these ratings (Murphy, Radadia, and Breyer 2019). Critics of these sites argue that anonymous ratings could be inaccurate because of their small numbers, or they could be maliciously manipulated. Both scenarios could damage a physician's reputation.

Physician rating sites present ethical conflicts involving the ethical principles of beneficence (for both the patient and the physician), patient autonomy, and justice (Samora, Lifchez, and Blazar 2016; Strech 2011).

Mini-Case Study Questions

1. Have you written a positive or negative online review of a service, product, or person? Were you scrupulously accurate in your assessment? What are the potential consequences of your rating?
2. Do you use the internet to find and rate physicians? Why or why not?
3. Despite initial findings suggesting a positive correlation between rating sites and patient care (Verhoef et al. 2014), it seems clear that such physician ratings are not proxies for clinical competence or patient outcomes (Murphy, Radadia, and Breyer 2019; Saifee et al. 2020). Rather, ratings are more likely to reflect factors related to the facility, such as wait times, availability of parking, and staff interactions. Despite these problems, online reviews can provide useful feedback to organizations (Murphy, Radadia, and Breyer 2019). As a healthcare manager, would you ask the organization's health IT department to set up an online rating tool to allow patients and other consumers to post anonymous reviews of the organization, its clinicians and other personnel, its billing and customer service office, and other departments? Why or why not?
4. A major concern with online reviews is that physicians are not able to respond to negative reviews without violating patient confidentiality. Responding to online reviews raises ethical challenges (Samora et al. 2016). What options or advice would you provide to a provider concerned about a very negative review?

Points to Remember

- Health informatics is the study, invention, and implementation of structures and algorithms to advance communication, understanding, use, and management of health data and information.

- Healthcare managers are involved in health informatics because they create, use, and manage much of the health information that their healthcare organizations generate.

- The overall goals of EHRs, meaningful use, and the eHealth Exchange vision are (1) to improve quality and safety by increasing coordination and integration among providers and by fostering patients' engagement in their health and (2) to lower costs by increasing efficiency and decreasing administrative costs.

- Government regulations and the development of a standard application programming interface will allow patients greater access and control over their health records.

- Health information and research exchanges continue to develop, based on the promise of using big data and sophisticated data analytics to personalize healthcare. However, the accuracy of data in EHRs can limit the promise of beneficence of digitized data and information.

- Poorly considered and imprudent use of EHRs and related health information technologies can come into conflict with the ethical principles of autonomy, fidelity, and justice.

- Cybersecurity and protecting healthcare data from external hackers and ransomware attacks is an ongoing and costly challenge for healthcare organizations.

Challenge Yourself

1. In a study of EHR adoption among psychology training clinics, the top-rated concerns among nonadopters were (1) financial costs, (2) lack of IT support, (3) difficulty getting the EHR to do what was wanted (flexibility), (4) implementation time, (5) computer system challenges, (6) increased security challenges, and (7) difficulty training staff (Cellucci et al. 2015). Only a minority of adopters had begun using EHRs beyond documentation to improve care.

    You are hired as the healthcare manager of a small obstetrics and gynecology practice that has an outdated EHR system that is used primarily for scheduling, documentation, and billing purposes, while still retaining some paper records. How would you go about working with the physicians and staff to assess upgrading their system? How might you address the concerns listed in the previous paragraph? How would you decide what EHR functionalities and capabilities the practice needs, both now and in the future?

2. Your mid-level managerial position was eliminated during a restructuring of the integrated healthcare delivery system where you worked. You were not offered a different position because one purpose of the restructuring was to reduce the system's personnel budget. You are now interviewing with other healthcare organizations. To make yourself more attractive as a job candidate, how much "insider knowledge" of your former system should you share with your interviewers?
3. You are a manager in a health plan's member services department. Your assistant, Taylor, wants to work from home over the Thanksgiving holiday. Taylor plans to download to a laptop several spreadsheets containing plan members' personal health information. How do you respond according to the ethical responsibilities of the health plan?
4. One of your staff members, MacKenzie, routinely claims "technophobia" and enlists coworkers' help with technology-related issues. For example, MacKenzie cannot assist patients who call the office with questions about the organization's patient portal. Instead, MacKenzie passes on to someone else even the most elementary questions, such as "How can I make an appointment on the website?" During their performance review in December of last year, you asked MacKenzie to attend at least three enterprise-wide technology training sessions, one of which had to be retraining on the patient portal. It is now November and MacKenzie has attended no training sessions. Ethically, what should you do?

For Your Consideration

13.1 Mahzarin Banaji, Max Bazerman, and Dolly Chugh (2003) are researchers and professors who specialize in ethics and organizational behavior. In a classic article, they suggest that managers ask themselves: "Answer true or false? 'I am an ethical manager.'"

They argue that most managers will say that they are ethical, but in fact, they are deceiving themselves. Although most managers will recognize bias and favoritism in other people's statements and actions, they are blind to their own prejudices and how those prejudices affect their beliefs and actions. The authors list four sources of bias that contribute to unintentionally unethical decisions:

- Implicit prejudice: Unconscious beliefs (e.g., elderly people are sickly or more likely to be infirm)
- In-group favoritism: Greater acceptance of people who are familiar than people who are different
- Conflict of interest: Favoring people who can do us a favor
- Overclaiming credit: Inflating the value of our own contributions

The combined effects of these prejudices lead managers to make decisions that are unfair and, more importantly, undermine their responsibilities.
   a. Describe how implicit prejudice and in-group favoritism undermine recruiting and retaining talented employees. What ethical and legal implications may result from these unintentional biases?
   b. Describe how conflicts of interest undermine the healthcare organization's relationships with purchasers and suppliers and with the community. What ethical and legal implications may result from this unintentional bias?
   c. Describe how overclaiming credit undermines individual, team, and organizational performance. What ethical implications may result from this unintentional bias?

13.2 You are a healthcare manager working for a state or federal healthcare agency. You may be called on to detect fraud in providers' activities through a covert operation. For example, investigators in the US Government Accountability Office (2008) conducted a covert operation in which they tested the billing enrollment procedures of the Centers for Medicare & Medicaid Services and its contractor:

Investigators easily set up two fictitious DMEPOS [durable medical equipment, prosthetics, orthotics, and supplies] companies using undercover names and bank accounts. GAO's fictitious companies were approved for Medicare billing privileges despite having no clients and no inventory. CMS initially denied GAO's applications in part because of this lack of inventory, but undercover GAO investigators fabricated contracts with nonexistent wholesale suppliers to convince CMS and its contractor, the National Supplier Clearinghouse (NSC), that the companies had access to DMEPOS items.

This operation revealed deficiencies in the billing enrollment procedures of CMS and its contractor. Criminals have used similar tactics to create fake companies with Medicare billing privileges. According to the report, once the fake companies are enrolled with CMS, they have access to Medicare beneficiary numbers and physician identification numbers. Subsequently, the criminals can use these numbers to defraud Medicare and Medicaid of millions of dollars.
   a. As a healthcare manager, do you believe it is ethical to deceive your peers at other government agencies? Why or why not?
   b. What ethical principles justify this particular covert operation? What ethical principles does this operation breach?
   c. Ethically, should healthcare managers conduct "sneak spot checks" of their employees' work products? Why or why not?
   d. Ethically, should healthcare managers covertly monitor their employees' email? Why or why not?

Check These Out

Want more information about the organizations and concepts discussed in the chapter? Check these websites out.

- eHealth Exchange: https://ehealthexchange.org/
- Office of the National Coordinator for Health Information Technology: www.healthit.gov/topic/about-onc
- Open Notes: www.opennotes.org/onc-federal-rule/
- Project Connect Health Systems Intervention: www.cdc.gov/std/projects/connect/default.htm
- 21st Century Cures Act: www.healthit.gov/curesrule/

References

Adler-Milstein, J., C. M. DesRoches, M. F. Furukawa, C. Worzala, D. Charles, P. Kralovec, S. Stalley, and A. K. Jha. 2014. "More Than Half of US Hospitals Have at Least a Basic EHR, but Stage 2 Criteria Remain Challenging for Most." *Health Affairs* 33 (9): 1664–71.

Adler-Milstein, J., A. J. Holmgren, P. Kralovec, C. Worzala, T. Searcy, and V. Patel. 2017. "Electronic Health Record Adoption in US Hospitals: The Emergence of a Digital 'Advanced Use' Divide." *Journal of the American Medical Informatics Association* 24 (6): 1142–48.

Ahier, B. 2012. "Reasons for Optimism About Health Information Exchange." Health IT Answers. Published November 27. www.healthitanswers.net/health-care-system-to-benefit-from-recent-hie-progress/.

American College of Healthcare Executives (ACHE). 2017. "Code of Ethics." Amended November 13. www.ache.org/-/media/ache/ethics/code_of_ethics_web.pdf.

American College of Surgeons. 2021. "The 'Minimum Standard' Document." Accessed September 1. www.facs.org/about-acs/archives/pasthighlights/minimumhighlight.

American Medical Association (AMA). 2020. *Digital Health Research: Physicians' Motivations and Requirements for Adopting Digital Health*. Published February. www.ama-assn.org/system/files/2020-02/ama-digital-health-study.pdf.

———. 2014. *Improving Care: Priorities to Improve Electronic Health Record Usability*. Accessed May 10, 2021. www.ama-assn.org/sites/ama-assn.org/files/corp/media-browser/member/about-ama/ehr-priorities.pdf.

Ammenwerth, E., S. Neyer, A. Hörbst, G. Mueller, U. Siebert, and P. Schnell-Inderst. 2021. "Adult Patient Access to Electronic Health Records." *Cochrane Database of Systematic Reviews* 2 (February): CD012707.

Anderson, B., and J. M. Hardin. 2017. "Data Analytics." In *Ethical Health Informatics: Challenges and Opportunities*, 3rd ed., edited by L. B. Harman and F. H. Cornelius, 95–118. Burlington, MA: Jones & Bartlett Learning.

Atasoy, H., B. N. Greenwood, and J. S. McCullough. 2019. "The Digitization of Patient Care: A Review of the Effects of Electronic Health Records on Health Care Quality and Utilization." *Annual Review of Public Health* 40: 487–500.

Atherton, J. 2011. "Development of the Electronic Health Record." *Virtual Mentor* 13 (3): 186–89.

Aziz, M. M. A., M. N. Sadat, D. Alhadidi, S. Wang, X. Jiang, C. L. Brown, and N. Mohammed. 2019. "Privacy-Preserving Techniques of Genomic Data: A Survey." *Briefings in Bioinformatics* 20 (3): 887–95.

Baillieu, R., H. Hoang, A. Sripipatana, S. Nair, and S. C. Lin. 2020. "Impact of Health Information Technology Optimization on Clinical Quality Performance in Health Centers: A National Cross-Sectional Study." *PLOS ONE* 15 (7): e0236019.

Banaji, M. R., M. H. Bazerman, and D. Chugh. 2003. "How (Un)Ethical Are You?" *Harvard Business Review* 81 (12): 56–64.

Biola, H., R. M. Best, L. M. Lahlou, C. Dewar, C. T. Jackson, J. Broder, L. Grey, R. C. Semelka, and A. Dobson. 2014. "With 'Big Data' Comes Big Responsibility: Outreach to North Carolina Medicaid Patients with 10 or More Computed Tomography Scans in 12 Months." *North Carolina Medical Journal* 75 (2): 102–9.

Cellucci, L. W., T. Cellucci, M. Stanton, D. Kerrigan, and M. Madrake. 2015. "Current Status and Future Directions of EMR Use in Psychology Training Clinics." *Health Policy and Technology* 4 (2): 91–99.

Centers for Medicare & Medicaid Services (CMS). 2021. "Promoting Interoperability Programs." Updated August 13. www.cms.gov/regulations-and-guidance/legislation/ehrincentiveprograms.

Colicchio, T. K., J. J. Cimino, and G. Del Fiol. 2019. "Unintended Consequences of Nationwide Electronic Health Record Adoption: Challenges and Opportunities in the Post-Meaningful Use Era." *Journal of Medical Internet Research* 21 (6): e13313.

Dash, S., S. K. Shakyawar, M. Sharma, and S. Kaushik. 2019. "Big Data in Healthcare: Management, Analysis and Future Prospects." *Journal of Big Data* 6: 54.

Dick, R. S., E. B. Steen, and D. E. Detmer (eds.). 1997. *The Computer-Based Patient Record: An Essential Technology for Health Care*, revised ed. Washington, DC: National Academies Press.

Echaiz, J. F., C. Cass, J. P. Henderson, H. M. Babcock, and J. Marschall. 2015. "Low Correlation Between Self-Report and Medical Record Documentation of Urinary Tract Infection Symptoms." *American Journal of Infectious Control* 43 (9): 983–86.

Esmaeilzadeh, P. 2019. "The Effects of Public Concern for Information Privacy on the Adoption of Health Information Exchanges (HIEs) by Healthcare Entities." *Health Communication* 34 (10): 1202–11.

Feinberg, I., E. L. Tighe, D. Greenberg, and M. Mavreles. 2018. "Health Literacy and Adults with Low Basic Skills." *Adult Education Quarterly* 68 (4): 297–315.

Frakt, A., and A. Mehrotra. 2019. "What Type of Price Transparency Do We Need in Health Care?" *Annals of Internal Medicine* 170 (8): 561–62.

Hanken, M. A., and G. Murphy. 2017. "Electronic Health Records." In *Ethical Health Informatics: Challenges and Opportunities*, 3rd ed., edited by L. B. Harman and F. H. Cornelius, 317–40. Burlington, MA: Jones & Bartlett Learning.

Harman, L. B., and F. H. Cornelius (eds.). 2017. *Ethical Health Informatics: Challenges and Opportunities*, 3rd ed. Burlington, MA: Jones & Bartlett Learning.

Harris, K., G. Jacobs, and J. Reeder. 2019. "Health Systems and Adult Basic Education: A Critical Partnership in Supporting Digital Health Literacy." *Health Literacy Research and Practice* 3 (Suppl.): S33–36.

Hersh, W. 2009. "A Stimulus to Define Informatics and Health Information Technology." *BMC Medical Informatics and Decision Making* 9 (1, Special Section): 1–6.

Horowitz, B. T. 2021. "2020 Offered a 'Perfect Storm' for Cybercriminals with Ransomware Attacks Costing the Industry $21B." Fierce Healthcare. Published March 26. www.fiercehealthcare.com/tech/ransomware-attacks-cost-healthcare-industry-21b-2020-here-s-how-many-attacks-hit-providers.

Huffman, E. K. 1963. *Manual for Medical Record Librarians*, revised 5th ed. Berwyn, IL: Physicians Record Company.

Jercich, K. 2020. "The Biggest Healthcare Data Breaches Reported in 2020." Healthcare IT News. Published December 30. www.healthcareitnews.com/news/biggest-healthcare-data-breaches-reported-2020.

Joint Cybersecurity Advisory. 2020. "Ransomware Activity Targeting the Healthcare and Public Health Sector." Report No. AA20-302A. Published October 29. https://us-cert.cisa.gov/sites/default/files/publications/AA20-302A_Ransomware%20_Activity_Targeting_the_Healthcare_and_Public_Health_Sector.pdf.

Jones, S. S., R. S. Rudin, T. Perry, and P. G. Shekelle. 2014. "Health Information Technology: An Updated Systematic Review with a Focus on Meaningful Use." *Annals of Internal Medicine*. Published January 7. www.acpjournals.org/doi/full/10.7326/M13-1531.

Kadry, B., L. F. Chu, B. Kadry, D. Gammas, and A. Macario. 2011. "Analysis of 4,999 Online Physician Ratings Indicates That Most Patients Give Physicians a Favorable Rating." *Journal of Medical Internet Research* 13 (4): e95.

Kaplan, B. 2016. "How Should Health Data Be Used?" *Cambridge Quarterly of Healthcare Ethics* 25 (2): 312–29.

Layman, E. J. 2020. "Ethical Issues and the Electronic Health Record." *Health Care Manager* 39 (4): 150–61.

Lee, L. M. 2017. "Ethics and Subsequent Use of Electronic Health Record Data." *Journal of Biomedical Informatics* 71: 143–46.

Lin, Y.-K., M. Lin, and H. Chen. 2019. "Do Electronic Health Records Affect Quality of Care? Evidence from the HITECH Act." *Information Systems Research* 30 (1): 306–18.

May, E. L. 2014. "The Power of Analytics: Harnessing Big Data to Improve the Quality of Care." *Healthcare Executive* 29 (2): 18–20, 22–24, 26.

Murphy, G. P., K. D. Radadia, and B. N. Breyer. 2019. "Online Physician Reviews: Is There a Place for Them?" *Risk Management and Healthcare Policy* 12: 85–89.

Nielsen-Bohlman, L., A. M. Panzer, and D. A. Kindig (eds.). 2004. *Health Literacy: A Prescription to End Confusion*. Washington, DC: National Academies Press.

NYC Health. 2013. "Using Technology to Weather the Storm." *Primary Care Information Project Bulletin* 7 (1): 1, 3.

Petersen, C., P. DeMuro, K. W. Goodman, and B. Kaplan. 2013. "*Sorrell v. IMS Health*: Issues and Opportunities for Informaticians." *Journal of the American Medical Informatics Association* 20 (1): 35–37.

Rinehart-Thompson, L. A., and L. B. Harman. 2017. "Privacy and Confidentiality." In *Ethical Health Informatics: Challenges and Opportunities*, 3rd ed., edited by L. B. Harman and F. H. Cornelius, 75–94. Burlington, MA: Jones & Bartlett Learning.

Saifee, D. H., Z. Zheng, I. R. Bardhan, and A. Lahiri. 2020. "Are Online Reviews of Physicians Reliable Indicators of Clinical Outcomes? A Focus on Chronic Disease Management." *Information Systems Research* 31 (4): 1282–1300.

Samora, J. B., S. D. Lifchez, and P. E. Blazar. 2016. "Physician-Rating Web Sites: Ethical Implications." *Journal of Hand Surgery* 41 (1): 104–110.

Savitz, S. T., L. A. Savitz, N. S. Fleming, N. D. Shah, and A. S. Go. 2020. "How Much Can We Trust Electronic Health Record Data?" *Healthcare* 8 (3): 1–4.

Seh, A. H., M. Zarour, M. Alenezi, A. K. Sarkar, A. Agrawal, R. Kumar, and R. A. Khan. 2020. "Healthcare Data Breaches: Insights and Implications." *Healthcare* 8 (2): 133.

Sejdic, E. 2014. "Adapt Current Tools for Handling Big Data." *Nature* 507 (7492): 306.

Shenoy, A., and J. M Appel. 2017. "Safeguarding Confidentiality in Electronic Health Records." *Cambridge Quarterly of Healthcare Ethics* 26 (2): 337–41.

Strech, D. 2011. "Ethical Principles for Physician Rating Sites." *Journal of Medical Internet Research* 13 (4): e113.

Sweeney, L. 2000. "Simple Demographics Often Identify People Uniquely." Data Privacy Lab. Accessed May 5, 2021. https://dataprivacylab.org/projects/identifiability/paper1.pdf.

Terry, S. F. 2017. "Genetic Information." In *Ethical Health Informatics: Challenges and Opportunities*, 3rd ed., edited by L. B. Harman and F. H. Cornelius, 469–86. Burlington, MA: Jones & Bartlett Learning.

Tully, J., J. Selzer, J. P. Phillips, P. O'Connor, and C. Dameff. 2020. "Healthcare Challenges in the Era of Cybersecurity." *Health Security* 18 (3): 228–31.

US Department of Health and Human Services (HHS). 2020. "HHS Finalizes Historic Rules to Provide Patients More Control of Their Health Data." Published March 9. www.hhs.gov/about/news/2020/03/09/hhs-finalizes-historic-rules-to-provide-patients-more-control-of-their-health-data.html.

US Government Accountability Office (GAO). 2008. "Medicare: Covert Testing Exposes Weaknesses in the Durable Medical Equipment Supplier Screening Process." Published July 3. www.gao.gov/products/GAO-08-955.

Valikodath, N. G., P. A. Newman-Casey, P. P. Lee, D. C. Musch, L. M. Niziol, and M. A. Woodward. 2017. "Agreement of Ocular Symptom Reporting Between Patient-Reported Outcomes and Medical Records." *JAMA Ophthalmology* 135 (3): 225–31.

Valle, J., C. Gomes, T. Godby, and A. Coustasse. 2016. "The Feasibility of the Nationwide Health Information Network." *Health Care Manager* 35 (2): 103–12.

Verhoef, L. M., T. H. Van de Belt, L. J. Engelen, L. Schoonhoven, and R. B. Kool. 2014. "Social Media and Rating Sites as Tools to Understanding Quality of Care: A Scoping Review." *Journal of Medical Internet Research* 16 (2): e56.

Walsh, C. G., W. Xia, M. Li, J. C. Denny, P. A. Harris, and B. A. Malin. 2018. "Enabling Open-Science Initiatives in Clinical Psychology and Psychiatry Without Sacrificing Patients' Privacy: Current Practices and Future Challenges." *Advances in Methods and Practices in Psychological Science* 1 (1): 104–14.

Weston, A. 2020. "Vidant Health Officials Say Some Patient Information Was Compromised in July Data Breach." WCTI News. Published September 14. https://wcti12.com/news/local/vidant-health-officials-say-some-patient-information-was-compromised-in-july-data-breach.

CHAPTER 14
HEALTH POLICY, HEALTH DISPARITIES, AND ETHICS

The idea that some lives matter less is the root of all that is wrong with the world.
—Paul Farmer, medical anthropologist and physician

Important Terms

- Downstream social marketing
- Enlightened self-interest
- Healthcare policy
- Health disparities
- Health equity
- Implicit bias
- Patient dumping
- Social determinants of health
- Social marketing
- Upstream social marketing

Learning Objectives

Studying this chapter will help you to

➤ explain the role of ethics in health policy and healthcare policy,

➤ understand the interrelationships of cost, quality, and access,

➤ assess how health policy may serve as an essential tool in times of crisis,

➤ explain social marketing and downstream and upstream approaches,

➤ assess the ethics of social marketing and public health initiatives through the lenses of ethical theories,

- explain the concept of health equity and discuss outcomes of health disparities, and
- understand structural racism and its effect on health.

healthcare policy
The implementation of health goals that affect costs, quality, and access to healthcare.

This chapter focuses on the role of ethics and professionalism in health policy and healthcare policy. Health policy refers to strategies aimed at improving the health of the people and the communities in which they live, while **healthcare policy** refers to policies that directly affect healthcare costs, the quality of care, and access to care for the people in those communities. The three variables of cost, quality, and access are referred to as the *iron triangle*—so called because it is challenging, if not impossible, to provide low-cost, high-quality care and offer wide access simultaneously (Kissick 1994).

As discussed in chapter 11, the Affordable Care Act is an example of health policy designed to improve the health of the American people by establishing the goals of increasing access to healthcare, expanding Medicaid eligibility, and supporting healthcare innovation to lower costs. The distinction between health policy and healthcare policy is sometimes blurry, as the actions of one may affect the actions of the other (Acuff 2014, 225). Health policy that affects one side of the iron triangle, such as access to care, will have an impact on at least one of the other two sides: cost and quality. The 1986 Emergency Medical Treatment and Active Labor Act (EMTALA) provides a classic example of this dilemma. Under this law, hospitals that offer emergency services are required to provide the following (CMS 2021):

- Medical screening examination when a request is made for an emergency medical condition (including active labor)
- Stabilization and further care as needed for all patients
- Transfer of patients to another healthcare facility as appropriate, regardless of the patient's ability to pay

However, the law allocates no funding to help hospitals provide these services. Thus, critical access hospitals and hospitals with emergency departments are left to figure out how to manage the costs incurred, which, in turn, may affect the quality of care and access to care.

Consider the iron triangle of cost, quality, and access with reference to this Case from the Field. The hospital administrators' focus on cost containment altered both the quality of care and access to care. Remember, though, that for emergency departments to provide quality care, they must remain open, and hospital administrators are acutely aware of the ethical dilemma they face—the need to provide care and the need to remain in business to do so. The practice of **patient dumping**—refusing care or transferring medically unstable patients because of their inability to pay—violates the principles of nonmaleficence, beneficence, and justice, as the refusal to provide care causes harm and creates no benefit to the patient.

patient dumping
To refuse care or transfer medically unstable patients because of their inability to pay.

> **CASE FROM THE FIELD**
> No Insurance, No Admission
>
> Documented real-life cases of patients being turned away from emergency departments or transferred from one emergency department to another helped spur the passage of EMTALA in 1986. For example, in 1980, a man in St. Louis, Missouri, arrived at a hospital with a steak knife in his back, but he was transferred from the emergency room because he did not have insurance. The hospital refused to provide aid to the patient because he could not pay $1,000 out of pocket prior to treatment (Annas 1986).
>
> A North Carolina general internist, Dr. Keith Wrenn, wrote to the *New England Journal of Medicine* to express his concerns about this "very disturbing trend" (Wrenn 1985, 373). In 1983, a car accident victim was brought to the emergency room at Wrenn's small rural hospital. The patient required neurosurgery, which the hospital was not equipped to provide. Dr. Wrenn recounted that during his attempt to transfer the patient to a private tertiary care center in a well-endowed university setting where the appropriate care could be provided, he was asked, "Does the patient have insurance?"
>
> A second experience occurred the following year and concerned another car accident victim who had experienced massive head trauma. The emergency room was able to stabilize her and attempted to relocate her for neurosurgery. However, the same tertiary care center refused to accept the patient on the grounds that she had no health insurance.
>
> In 1985, a patient named Mr. Lafon entered Parkland Memorial Hospital in Dallas, Texas. He had third-degree burns on his back and needed immediate care, which the hospital provided. However, prior to his arrival at Parkland Memorial, he had been turned away from three other hospitals because he could not pay the $500 to $1,500 deposit required to receive care. He was 56 years old, a laborer, and did not have health insurance. Lafon said of the experience, "Kind of makes you feel like a dog" (Taylor 1985).

Before the passage of EMTALA, some hospitals made admission decisions based on the patient's ability to pay, while other hospitals, such as Parkland Memorial, accepted patients because it was the right thing to do. However, the hospitals that accepted patients without insurance did so with increased cost responsibilities—to the tune of $1.05 billion each year (Ansell and Schiff 1987, 1500). Before EMTALA, emergency department transfers increased 600 percent in Washington, DC, from 1981 to 1984, and 520 percent in Cook County, Illinois (where Chicago is located), from 1980 to 1983 (Walker 2017). Consequently, concerns arose about patient dumping, access to care, and emergency department policy. The Joint Commission noted that people must be treated regardless of their ability to pay; the Hippocratic Oath requires that physicians must do no harm (Dossabhoy, Feng, and Desai 2018; Joint Commission 2010). Other public hospitals joined with Parkland Memorial and advocated for passage of the EMTALA (Parkland Hospital 2019). The US Congress passed the legislation, and President Ronald Reagan signed it into law in 1986.

However, EMTALA was passed without allocating funds to allow hospitals to cover the costs incurred to care for patients who cannot pay (this is referred to as an *unfunded mandate*). In this case, the elements of cost, quality, and access are motivated and driven by policy outcomes (Cellucci, Meacham, and Farnsworth 2019). By 2003, about 1,100 hospitals had determined that closing their emergency departments was the best strategic option (*Emergency Medicine News* 2003). The passage of EMTALA was not the only reason these hospitals decided to close; however, it is one factor that illustrates how health policy affects healthcare policy (see also the discussion of Pungo Hospital in chapter 11).

Other legislated policies have affected the healthcare industry's ability to plan and be prepared for unexpected events, such as terrorist attacks, natural disasters, and pandemics. The following section discusses the effects of the Pandemic and All-Hazards Preparedness Acts of 2006, 2013, and 2019 on healthcare organizations' ability to respond effectively and ethically. The key ethical principle in this case is beneficence—that is, being better prepared at the front end allows healthcare organizations to provide better patient care during a crisis, such as a pandemic.

PANDEMIC AND ALL-HAZARDS PREPAREDNESS ACTS OF 2006, 2013, AND 2019

The Pandemic and All-Hazards Preparedness Act (PAHPA; Public Law 109-417) was passed by Congress and signed by President George W. Bush in 2006. The law subsequently was reauthorized and updated by Congress and signed by President Barack Obama in 2013 (Public Law 113-5). The 2013 reauthorization included funding for public health medical preparedness programs to meet community needs during disasters and enhanced the authority of the US Food and Drug Administration. In 2019, President Donald Trump signed into law another updated version (Public Law 116-22), which added environmental health to the original components of public health and medical preparedness and response capabilities for emergencies.

Three events spurred the passage of the original 2006 law:

1. In September 2001, during President George W. Bush's first term in office, the United States experienced terrorist attacks on the World Trade Center in New York City and an attempted attack on the US Capitol.

2. In October and November 2001, anthrax attacks occurred in Washington, DC, New York City, and West Palm Beach, Florida.

3. In 2005, Hurricane Katrina devastated parts of Mississippi and Louisiana.

On September 11, 2001, four passenger planes were hijacked by terrorists. Two of the planes crashed into the World Trade Center, another crashed into the Pentagon, and a fourth crashed into a field in Pennsylvania. Both World Trade Center towers collapsed, the Pentagon was damaged, and all passengers aboard the four aircrafts died. In total, about 3,000 people died because of the attacks, 2,700 of them in New York City (Gold 2020). In the aftermath of 9/11, assessments praised community and healthcare organizations' response efforts while also identifying system-level weaknesses in the ability to prioritize, cooperate, and respond to emergencies and a lack of reporting structure to coordinate responses.

Exhibit 14.1 summarizes the actions of five responding organizations to meet the needs of the crisis (Comfort and Kapucu 2006; Klitzman and Freudenberg 2003). The National Commission on Terrorist Attacks (2004) concluded that the emergency response efforts were cumbersome at times, disorganized, and "hampered by problems in command and control and in internal communications." For example, even though air quality was known to be poor around the World Trade Center, personal protective equipment was not adequately supplied to those on-site. The events indicated a critical need to be better prepared.

Within a month of 9/11, the United States experienced a series of bioterrorist attacks, which also indicated a need for preparation. From October 4, 2001, to November 20, 2001, 22 people were exposed to deadly anthrax spores that had been prepared in a powder. People became exposed to the disease when they breathed or touched the spores. As the

EXHIBIT 14.1 Organizations and Actions Taken to Respond to 9/11

Organization	Example of actions taken
New York City Department of Health	Monitored food and drinking water to people at Ground Zero
American Red Cross	Set up emergency shelters
New York City Department of Health and Mental Hygiene	Provided crisis intervention via hotline to survivors, bereaved family members, and workers at Ground Zero. Followed up with the establishment of Family Assistance Centers to provide counseling and assist as appropriate (*e.g.*, file death certificates)
Agency for Toxic Substances and Disease Registry	Tested people around the Trade Center and residents in Lower Manhattan for asbestos and fiberglass fibers
Greater New York Hospital Association	Informed responders of medical transport bed availability at New York hospitals

Sources: Information from CDC (2014); Klitzman and Freudenberg (2003); National Commission on Terrorist Attacks Upon the United States (2004).

anthrax powder was enclosed in mailings sent to politicians and news media organizations (the three major networks—ABC, CBS, and NBC—as well as the *New York Post* and the Associated Press), it was more likely to infect mail workers and media company employees who had contact with the mail (Jernigan et al. 2002). This event indicated the need to be better prepared against a future bioterrorist attack.

In August 2005, Hurricane Katrina highlighted the need for more coordinated public health emergency preparedness and response to environmental disasters. Along the Gulf Coast, infrastructure was destroyed as schools, businesses, and neighborhoods were flooded and experienced severe wind damage. Houses that had stood for hundreds of years were destroyed (de Montluzin and de Montluzin 2011). Systemic organizational breakdowns occurred, and the Federal Emergency Management Agency was slow to respond, showing a lack "of visibility in the resource ordering process, difficulty deploying sufficient numbers of trained personnel, unreliable communication systems, and insufficient management controls for some assistance programs" (OIG 2006, 2). For instance, following the storm, Mississippi received less than 50 percent of the supplies needed, and in Louisiana, more than 22,000 people arrived at the Superdome for shelter but were met with woefully inadequate support—only two trucks of food and five trucks of water (OIG 2006). Stranded workers at Charity Hospital in New Orleans cared for patients there, rationing food and hydrating themselves intravenously while they waited for five days for help (Freemantle 2005). Hurricane Katrina indicated a need to be better prepared for natural disasters.

These three events underscored the need to develop a stronger infrastructure to address future terrorism, bioterrorism, and other crises that affect people's health. Senator Richard Burr of North Carolina introduced the PAHPA legislation, noting that "the federal [government] must ensure that all state and local public health departments and health care facilities are prepared and have the tools they need to confront the unpredictable challenges that [lie] ahead—whether it's a hurricane, a terrorist attack or a pandemic" (Morhard and Franco 2013, 146).

PAHPA provided important outcomes to help systems be better prepared. Most notably, it established a process to develop new vaccines quickly to respond to emergencies. This action had a significant impact during the COVID-19 pandemic. PAHPA also defined which organizations would serve as response leaders and established coordination protocols for organizations responding to disasters. Importantly, the legislation also included funding to strengthen biological laboratories so as to identify infectious diseases quickly and then distribute medicines appropriately. Another outcome was the identification and certification of medical volunteers to be ready for emergency response.

With legislation passed and updated to address health needs during times of crises, the next need concerned the importance of communicating to the public about public health crises and their responsibility to take action to protect their health and the health of others in their communities. This is illustrated in the concept of social marketing and efforts made to disseminate vaccines to address the COVID-19 pandemic.

SOCIAL MARKETING

Philip Kotler and Gerald Zaltman (1971, 5) are regarded as the founders of **social marketing**, which they defined as "the design, implementation, and control of programs calculated to influence the acceptability of social ideas and involving considerations of product planning, pricing, communication, distribution, and marketing research." Kotler and Zaltman proposed that marketing tools and techniques could be applied not only to selling products but also to influencing the behavior of individuals and the community to achieve a common good. For example, in 2021, social marketing was employed to persuade Americans to get the COVID-19 vaccine, both for their own good and for the good of those around them.

> *social marketing*
> Influencing the behavior of individuals and the community to achieve a common good.

Let's apply the concept of social marketing to the 2021 "We Can Do This" campaign of the Centers for Disease Control and Prevention (CDC), which aimed to increase vaccinations to prevent COVID-19 infections. This campaign communicated its message through a variety of channels, including television and social media platforms, and featured famous people such as actor Angela Bassett, singer John Legend, comedian and musician Steve Martin, and the Philadelphia Flyers hockey team receiving or talking about receiving their COVID-19 vaccinations (Adams 2021). Former presidents Jimmy Carter, Bill Clinton, George W. Bush, and Barack Obama and their spouses also participated in an "It's Up To You" public service announcement urging people to "protect those you love" and help "get rid of this pandemic" (VOA News 2021).

Corporations also joined the vaccination campaign. For example, Walgreens distributed ads featuring John Legend, who said, "COVID-19 has taken so much from so many, but this is our shot at returning to the faces and places we love and miss. . . . This is our shot at bringing our communities back together. . . . This is our shot" (Walgreens 2021). Walt Disney World and Universal Orlando supported Florida's campaign, "I Got My Shot," aimed at educating Floridians about the vaccine and encouraging vaccinations by providing a mobile vaccine unit to increase access (Adams 2021; WDW News Today 2021). McDonald's coffee cups displayed the message "We Can Do This" and featured stickers explaining where vaccines could be obtained (Kurtz 2021). Discussing the McDonald's campaign, Xavier Becerra, secretary of the US Department of Health and Human Resources, explained that "this effort will help more people make informed decisions about their health and learn about steps they can take to protect themselves and their communities" (Kurtz 2021).

The goals of the CDC's We Can Do This campaign were to educate people about the vaccines, to encourage them to get vaccinated, and to point them to available vaccination sites. Although the campaign primarily targeted those who had not yet obtained the vaccine, it also aimed to reach the vaccinated, in the hope that they would encourage others to do the same. The messages directed at this secondary group focused on affirming their action and the positive outcomes for family and community to build grassroots momentum for vaccinations.

Assessment Through an Ethical Lens

We can evaluate the ethics of social marketing efforts through the lenses of several ethical theories. In chapter 2, we discussed the ethical philosophies of deontology, consequentialism, Rawls's principles of justice, and the ethics of care. Here, we introduce another theory, called **enlightened self-interest**, which holds that individuals who act in the best interests of others ultimately serve their own self-interest. In other words, according to this philosophy, individuals maximize benefits to the self while minimizing harm to others. The concept of enlightened self-interest is rooted in corporate social responsibility policy. When it is applied to rationalize corporate social investment, for example, enlightened self-interest illustrates that companies invest in social and environmental causes that will "secure long-term economic performance by avoiding short-term behavior that is socially detrimental or environmentally wasteful" (Porter and Kramer 2006, 82). Simply put, a company may invest in the local environment; although this investment may not maximize shareholder value in the short term, it serves the company's best interests by creating goodwill, providing a service to its workers and families as well as the community at large, and encouraging prospective employees to work for the company.

A social marketing ethical assessment may aid in the process of evaluating social marketing efforts (Kirby and Andreasen 2001). This kind of analysis indicates how targeted groups will be identified and addressed through ethical philosophies (or lenses) that justify the campaign actions. For example, the targeted groups in the We Can Do This campaign were those who had received the vaccine as well as those who had not. The ethical theories that are relevant to this case include consequentialism, deontology, Rawls's principles of justice, ethics of care, and enlightened self-interest (review chapter 2 for the definitions of these theories).

Consequentialism focuses on the consequences of an action and holds that the result determines the moral rightness or wrongness of that action. In this case, the positive messaging was communicated to both targeted groups, acknowledging that those who had received the vaccine had done their part to promote health while encouraging those who had not received the vaccine do so for the benefit of themselves and their family, friends, and larger community.

Deontology centers on the action independent of the consequences. The focus is on the action done because it was the right thing to do the for the right reasons. The positive messaging communicated that the vaccinated had done the right thing and encouraged the unvaccinated to do so as well because it was simply the right thing to do.

Rawls's principle of justice emphasizes the importance of fairness. The positive messaging in this campaign educated all audiences, giving the same message to both the vaccinated and the unvaccinated. Moreover, the people communicating the message represented diverse backgrounds.

The ethics of care focuses on nurturing and relationships. Moreover, it highlights that care is an end in itself. The positive message in the We Can Do This campaign focused

---

enlightened self-interest
An ethical theory that holds that individuals maximize benefits to the self while minimizing harm to others.

on the benefit to self and others. The communications were inspirational, including video images accompanied by music that illustrated family and friends gathering in better times. This was possible, the videos communicated, because the vaccinated cared. The unvaccinated were encouraged to act with care as well and become vaccinated.

Enlightened self-interest is about maximizing benefit to yourself while minimizing harm to others. The positive messaging targeted the unvaccinated with the message that one person's choice to receive the vaccine could help stop the spread of COVID-19 while reinforcing the positive action already taken by the vaccinated to do their part.

The CDC's We Can Do This campaign focused on influencing and changing individual behavior; this is known as **downstream social marketing**. This approach allows social marketers to assess whether they are indeed creating and delivering a campaign that is ethical and, more importantly, to modify the campaign if ethical challenges are identified.

downstream social marketing
A social marketing campaign that focuses on influencing or changing individual behavior.

Upstream Social Marketing

Downstream social marketing efforts are usually more effective when they are coupled with **upstream social marketing** efforts—that is, efforts focused on influencing or changing systems, policies, or structural components. An example is a campaign aimed at changing laws to protect the health and well-being of a population. Essentially, upstream social marketing is about influencing policymakers and changing their behavior (Goldberg 1995). Upstream social marketing influenced legislation regarding COVID-19 vaccinations, but with mixed results. In July 2021, the US Department of Justice (DOJ 2021) concluded that "federal law does not prohibit public or private entities from imposing vaccination requirements for vaccines that are subject to emergency use authorizations from the US Food and Drug Administration."

upstream social marketing
A social marketing campaign that focuses on influencing or changing systems, policies, and other structural components.

Immediately following the DOJ's determination, the US Department of Veterans Affairs (VA 2021) mandated that all VA healthcare providers be vaccinated. That same month, California governor Gavin Newsom and New York State governor Andrew Cuomo issued vaccine mandates for state government employees. Cuomo remarked, "It's smart, it's fair, it's in everyone's interest" (Davis 2021). In August, Governor Ralph Northam in Virginia and Jay Inslee in Washington State mandated COVID-19 vaccinations for state employees, while in Hawaii, Governor David Ige mandated vaccinations for both state and county employees. Oregon governor Kate Brown mandated that all state healthcare workers must be vaccinated, and Maryland governor Larry Hogan issued a mandate for state employees in health, juvenile services, veterans affairs, and public safety and corrections (Davis 2021).

At the same time, however, governors in other states signed legislation limiting vaccine mandates, such as Arkansas governor Asa Hutchinson, who ordered that state agencies may not require vaccination as a condition of employment. Utah governor

Spencer Cox and Ohio governor Mike DeWine both signed orders stating that agencies (state agencies in Utah and state and private entities in Ohio) may not require vaccinations that have not been approved by the US Food and Drug Administration (Mitchell 2021).

Other public and private entities also established vaccination policies. For example, many public and private colleges and universities—838 as of August 2021—mandated that students, faculty, and staff be vaccinated to return to campus. Duke and Cornell Universities were the first to require students to be vaccinated (Best Colleges 2021). Harvard and Princeton mandated that all students, faculty, and staff be vaccinated, along with the university systems in California, Maryland, and Virginia (Thomason and O'Leary 2021). The University of Virginia disenrolled more than 200 students for the fall 2021 term for not reporting their vaccination status or filing for a medical or religious exemption (Best Colleges 2021).

Hospitals and assisted-living facilities also imposed vaccine mandates on their employees, including Vidant Medical Center in North Carolina, Benefits Health System in Montana, Houston Methodist Hospital in Texas, and Sunrise Senior Living, based in Virginia with facilities throughout the United States, Canada, and the United Kingdom (Basen 2021; Gooch 2021; Vidant Health 2021; Wu and Garcia 2021).

Examining both upstream and downstream campaigns using ethical perspectives is important because the outcomes of such efforts affect people. Healthcare professionals engaged in social marketing efforts should be mindful of behaving ethically and understand the value of applying an ethical lens to social marketing endeavors, especially with regard to public health initiatives, health disparities, and justice.

PUBLIC HEALTH INITIATIVES

In 1970, the Institute of Medicine was formed as part of the National Academy of Sciences. In 2015, the institute changed its name to the National Academy of Medicine (NAM), as it works with the National Academies of Sciences and Engineering to advise on matters of science, technology, and health (AJMC 2015). By 2021, NAM reported a membership of about 2,200 professionals in healthcare, sciences, law, administration, engineering, and the humanities whose primary goal is to provide information about health and healthcare in the United States. NAM's vision is to achieve a "healthier future for everyone" by "advancing science, accelerating health equity and providing independent, authoritative, and trusted advice nationally and globally" (NAM 2021).

In its now-classic report *The Future of Public Health* (1988)—written in response to concerns among the organization's broad membership that the United States had "lost sight of its public health goals"—the Institute of Medicine addressed the status of the public health system and defined public health, the public health mission, the substance of public health, and the organizational framework of public health. These four definitions serve as the foundation of today's public health initiatives in the United States (IOM 1988, 19, 40–42):

1. *Public health*. What we, as a society, do collectively to ensure the conditions for people to be healthy

2. *Public health mission*. To fulfill society's interest in ensuring the conditions in which people can be healthy

3. *Substance of public health*. Organized community efforts aimed at the prevention of disease and the promotion of health

4. *Organizational framework of public health*. Activities undertaken within the formal structure of government and the associated efforts of private and voluntary organizations and individuals

Fulfilling the mission of public health requires three actions:

1. Dissemination of information for the purpose of education

2. Allocation of resources to outreach programs through an organizational framework that includes participation by government agencies and private and voluntary organizations

3. Socially responsible behaviors by individuals and organizations

The success of public health initiatives depends on individuals and organizations acting ethically and responsibly. Again, let's apply these concepts to the COVID-19 vaccination campaign.

Sources of Information and Their Trustworthiness

The CDC and other government agencies produced and circulated information about COVID-19 and its harmful effects on individual and community health as well as resources to obtain the vaccine. The primary responsibility of the US surgeon general—the nation's doctor—is to provide the "best scientific information available on how to improve [people's] health and reduce the risk of illness and injury" (HHS 2021b). To that end, the Office of the Surgeon General generated and disseminated information about the vaccine and about public health threats such as COVID-19 (HHS 2021b; King 2021). Surgeon General Vivek Murthy spoke to the need to communicate with people, especially those in rural communities, about the need to get vaccinated against COVID-19.

For distributed information to yield the desired results and to serve as a guide, it has to be accurate, evidence based, and trustworthy. The majority of the public typically trusts the information generated by public health entities such as the CDC and the surgeon general. Simply put, we trust that certain people and groups are telling the truth because doing so is part of their job as stewards of public health. Additionally, they have nothing to gain—financial or otherwise—by giving false, outdated, or misleading information.

OUTCOMES

COVID-19 in the United States is a public health issue. The disease has cost many lives and poses a major threat to the country's economy. Direct economic losses attributable to the virus have been estimated at about $16 trillion (Cutler and Summers 2020). Thus, vaccination initiatives remain ongoing. However, the rollout of vaccinations beginning in January 2021 showed that Asians and white Americans were being vaccinated at higher rates relative to their shares of the population, whereas Hispanic and Black Americans were being vaccinated at slower rates compared with their shares of the population (see exhibit 14.2).

Responding to disparities in access to the vaccine, the CDC's We Can Do This campaign delivered messages in both English and Spanish, and the public health announcements

EXHIBIT 14.2
Vaccination Demographics as a Percentage of Total US Population, September 2021

Race/ethnicity	Received at least one dose (percentage among those with at least one dose)	Fully vaccinated (percentage among those fully vaccinated)	Percentage of US population in this demographic category
American Indian/Alaska Native, Non-Hispanic	1.1%	1%	0.8%
Asian, Non-Hispanic	6.2%	6.5%	5.8%
Black, Non-Hispanic	10.3%	9.8%	12.4%
Hispanic	17.2%	16.3%	17.2%
Native Hawaiian or Pacific Islander, Non-Hispanic	0.3%	0.4%	0.3%
White, Non-Hispanic	60.6%	62%	61.2%
Multiple/Other, Non-Hispanic	4.5%	4.1%	2.3%

Source: CDC (2021b).

featured people of diverse backgrounds. In addition, Secretary Becerra and Secretary of Housing and Urban Development Marica L. Fudge initiated a joint effort to increase equitable access to vaccinations by "meeting people where they are" (HHS 2021c). As Secretary Fudge elaborated (HHS 2021c),

> More than 100 million Americans are now fully vaccinated. Yet there are many others who still need help getting the vaccine. To raise our vaccination numbers even higher, we must continue to center our efforts around the guiding principle of equity.

Vaccination efforts to "meet people where they are" included setting up vaccination clinics in local community public health clinics, pharmacies, community centers, and churches, as well providing mobile vaccination units to reach those who lacked access to transportation (Adams 2021; CDC 2021c; Choi 2021). While the ethical principles of justice and beneficence justify such efforts, a key public health issue drove this effort. In May 2021, about 575,000 people had died from COVID-19: in 90 percent of these cases, COVID-19 was the underlying cause of death, while in less than 10 percent of cases, it was a contributing cause of death (CDC 2021e). While time will tell how effective the United States' social marketing campaign was in influencing behavior, to do nothing would have set the stage for unimaginable tragedy.

COVID-19 statistics show the disparate effect of the virus on the US population. We now turn our attention to the concepts of health disparities and the social determinants of health and discuss why they matter ethically.

HEALTH DISPARITIES

Research on **health disparities** began to appear in the 1990s (Milburn, Beatty, and Lopez 2019). In 2000, Congress passed the Minority Health and Health Disparities Research and Education Act to address health disparities, which, in turn, led to the creation of the National Institute on Minority Health and Health Disparities within the National Institutes of Health. In 2002, the Institute of Medicine published a landmark report titled *Unequal Treatment: Confronting Racial and Ethnic Disparities in Health Care* (Smedley, Stith, and Nelson 2003). Since then, addressing health disparities has been a focus of health researchers, government agencies, healthcare organizations, and professional groups.

Health disparities are measurable differences in health outcomes that are specifically linked to disadvantage. This emphasis on disadvantage is important, as all differences in health outcomes do not constitute health disparities. The concept of health disparities rests on a concern for fairness and social justice and the belief that all individuals have a right to health. Disparities are created when the benefits of health are unfairly constrained for certain groups (Braveman 2014; Braveman et al. 2011). This is captured

health disparities
A particular type of health difference linked to social, economic, or environmental disadvantage that is unjust and avoidable.

in the definition provided by the Healthy People 2020 initiative (Secretary's Advisory Committee 2008, 28):

> a particular type of health difference that is closely linked with economic, social or environmental disadvantage. Health disparities adversely affect groups of people who have systematically experienced greater social or economic obstacles to health based on their racial or ethnic group, religion, socioeconomic status, gender, age, or mental health; cognitive, sensory, or physical disability; sexual orientation or gender identity; geographic location; or other characteristics historically linked to discrimination or exclusion.

health equity
Pursuing the highest standards of health for all people, including the elimination of health disparities.

In contrast, **health equity** is a broader term that refers to striving for the best possible health for all people (Braveman 2014; Gómez et al. 2021). Health disparities are thus a moral or ethical concern for both the health professions and society. While Blacks and other racial and ethnic minorities have been the historical and continuing focus of health disparities research, those affected by health disparities encompass a wide range of populations that have experienced systematic discrimination and exclusion that has adversely affected their health (e.g., services for LGBTQ people; see Aleshire et al. 2019).

Health disparities exist across many areas of health, including infant mortality, asthma, cancer, cardiovascular disease, diabetes, HIV disease, obesity, mental health, and substance abuse. These disparities are associated with greater morbidity and mortality risk among low-income and minority groups, especially people of color. These disparities are attributable to differences in the quality of healthcare received and access to care, as well as social determinants of health, including the historical and current impact of racial discrimination in society (Joynt Maddox and James 2021).

SOCIAL DETERMINANTS OF HEALTH

social determinants of health
The environments and conditions in which people are born, grow, work, live, and age, including factors that affect their health, functioning, and quality of life.

Health and health outcomes are greatly influenced by "the environments in which people are born, live, learn, work, play, worship, and age" (Gómez et al. 2021, 1). The concept of **social determinants of health** was first embraced by the World Health Organization. In the United States, it has been articulated by a government-wide collaboration known as Healthy People (see https://health.gov/healthypeople). Now in its fifth decade, the Office of Disease Prevention and Health Promotion, an agency of the US Department of Health and Human Services, oversees this collaborative initiative, which establishes national health objectives, guidance, data, and tools every ten years for those working in public health, with the goal of achieving health equity for all.

The Healthy People 2020 initiative set trackable objectives in 42 topic areas, such as access to health services, environmental health, family planning, immunization and infectious diseases, and so on. The initiative's end-of-decade snapshot (Office of the Assistant

Secretary for Health 2020) showed that some leading health indicators (e.g., people with health insurance coverage, adults with controlled hypertension, adolescent smoking) significantly improved from 2010 to 2020, while others showed limited change (e.g., people diagnosed with diabetes, childhood obesity, dentist visits in the past year, reproductive health services). Overall, about one-third of the trackable objectives were met or exceeded goals, and about 20 percent showed improvement.

Within the Healthy People framework, the social determinants of health are organized into five place-based categories, as illustrated in exhibit 14.3. In addition to access to care and healthcare quality, people also need education, economic stability, safe neighborhoods, and communal support to lead healthy lives. Examples include preschool education, access to nutritious food, and health literacy.

Healthy People 2030, the initiative that began in 2021, focuses on these social determinants of health, with a goal to "create social, physical, and economic environments that

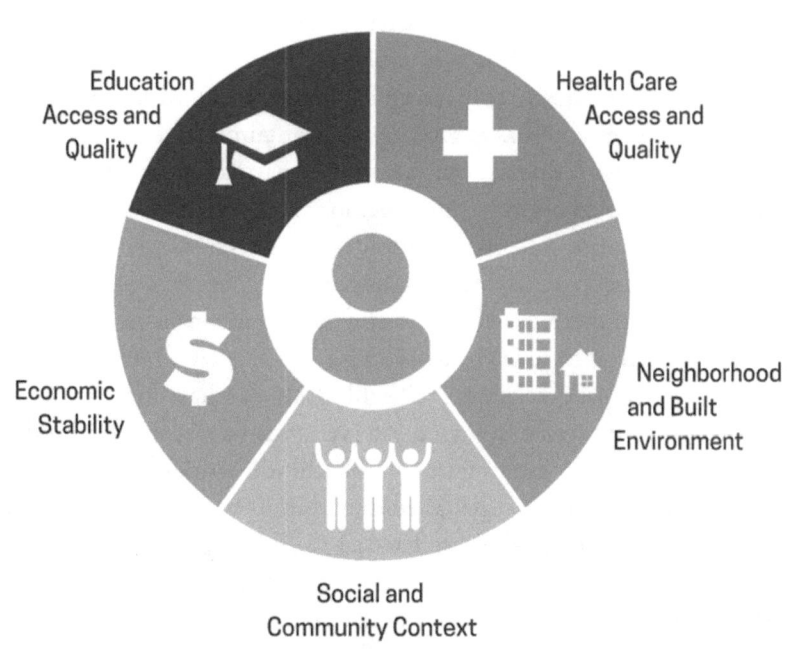

Exhibit 14.3
Social Determinants of Health

Source: Healthy People 2030 (2021).

promote attaining the full potential for health and well-being for all" (Healthy People 2030, 2021). These determinants are strongly related to the distribution of economic and other resources, and they are acknowledged to be the major contributors to health disparities (Gómez et al. 2021).

The COVID-19 epidemic highlighted the significance of health disparities. Minority groups, such as African Americans and Hispanics/Latinos, were affected disproportionately by the virus and had higher rates of hospitalization and death. Writing in the journal *Nursing*, Kathleen Pecoraro (2021) connects this increased risk directly to the social determinants of health and illustrates how these factors influence people's lived experience. For example, the coronavirus was passed through air droplets, yet social distancing was more difficult for individuals living in high-density areas or crowded apartments. Individuals with less education were also more likely to be working in essential service jobs and unable to work from home. Moreover, minorities in the United States have a greater burden of chronic disease (e.g., diabetes, hypertension) or comorbidities that put them at greater risk once infected. They are also more likely to be disenfranchised from healthcare in terms of historical mistrust and obstacles to seeking vaccination. During the COVID-19 pandemic, health inequalities translated into increased health risk for society generally.

Understanding the mechanisms by which social factors and life stressors shape health across the life span will require more research (Ehrlich 2020; Milburn, Beatty, and Lopez 2019). Retrospective research has demonstrated that cumulative adverse childhood experiences are associated with disease, but interdisciplinary longitudinal research, including research on biological markers (e.g., inflammation) and psychosocial conditions, is needed to understand the processes involved and to develop effective interventions. The Healthy People 2030 initiative recognizes this need. Its core objectives focus on high-priority public health issues for which there are reliable measurements and evidence-based interventions. Developmental objectives include health issues for which reliable public health baseline data are lacking. Research objectives pertain to health issues that have high burden or significant disparities but for which evidence-based interventions have not yet been developed (see Dankwa-Mullan et al. 2021 for a summary of health disparities research). Healthy People 2030 recognizes that no single organization, community, or sector of society alone can address the social determinants of health that cause health disparities or achieve health equity for the population. Greater social cohesion and collaboration will be needed to address the social determinants of health and the root causes of health inequalities (Gómez et al. 2021).

Disparities in Healthcare

It is critical for healthcare managers to understand the healthcare disparities that may arise from health polices, organizational practices, and provider interactions. Generally, the topic of health disparities within the healthcare sector starts with a discussion about access. Although the Affordable Care Act (introduced in chapter 11) helped increase the number of Americans

> ### ? Racism Affects Public Health
>
> Racism has long been recognized as a blight on American ideals. For too long, it has been a difficult conversation for Americans to acknowledge racism and discuss its legacy (Brown 2016). In 2021, CDC director Dr. Rochelle Walensky spoke about how racism threatens our nation's health and announced that the CDC would focus on developing interventions to address racism and its impact on social determinants of health (CDC 2021d; Wamsley 2021). Racism results in conditions that advantage some and disadvantage others throughout society. The impact of racism is deeply embedded in social conditions and determinants of health. As a result, racial and ethnic minority groups experience higher rates of illness and death across a range of health conditions.
>
> One example of the impact of racism on health is disparities in the incidence of cancer. African Americans experience disproportionate rates of cancer and have the highest death rates and the lowest survival rates for most cancers, including breast, lung, and prostate cancers. These disparities reflect a lack of insurance and access to care for early screening and detection, as well as chronic life stress exposure and depression. These factors lead to both more cancer-promoting behaviors, such as smoking, and biologic mechanisms, such as increased expression of pro-inflammatory genes and accelerated tumor growth.
>
> Another example is the known impact of structural racism on cardiovascular health. Black Americans experience 30 to 45 percent higher mortality from cardiovascular disease than other ethnic groups. State-level indicators of structural racism (e.g., voter registration, employment, judicial treatment) have been associated with higher myocardial infarction rates among Blacks. These higher rates also may reflect the effects of chronic stress and unhealthy coping methods (e.g., smoking) that affect health.
>
> The CDC has launched a web portal to serve as a hub for both scientific information and public discourse on the topic of racism and health.
>
> *Sources*: CDC (2021d); Coke and Hayman (2021); Minas et al. (2021).

with health insurance, in 2021, roughly 12 percent of people under age 65 still lacked insurance. Twelve states have not expanded access to Medicaid, leaving many working people without coverage. Minority groups are overrepresented among those (roughly 24 percent) without a regular healthcare provider (Office of the Assistant Secretary for Health 2020). Hospital closures in inner-city and particularly rural areas have had a negative impact on timely access to care; increased resources may be needed to support rural health clinics and Federally Qualified Health Centers that serve high proportions of individuals with limited means (Joynt Maddox and James 2021).

Examining the quality of care delivered by health organizations to disadvantaged groups and looking for quality improvements to address health disparities is another area requiring development (Wasserman et al. 2019). All too often, the care delivered to disadvantaged populations is suboptimal or does not meet the evidence-based recommendations for accepted practice standards. Understanding how care is delivered is critical to address health disparities; more quality improvement research (i.e., monitoring process and intervention outcomes over time) focused on known health disparities is urgently needed. We know that low-income patients with chronic and multiple health needs benefit from more case management. Similarly, we know the disadvantaged groups underutilize preventive health services, but we lack a full understanding of the reasons for this disparity (Wasserman et al. 2019).

The Agency for Healthcare Research and Quality (AHRQ) is the government organization that is charged with improving the safety and quality of America's healthcare system. The AHRQ develops knowledge through research and disseminates data and monitoring tools to healthcare organizations to assess and improve the quality of the services that patients receive. Here are a few examples of this work (AHRQ 2021):

> Project ECHO provides training and support for primary care clinicians in rural communities to provide specialty care for patients with conditions such as HIV and Hepatitis C and has been expanded to include behavioral health.
>
> EvidenceNOW is a grant program that provides practice support (i.e., knowledge, tools) to primary care physicians with the goal of increasing the capacity of practices to improve heart health.
>
> The Comprehensive Unit-based Safety Program (CUSP) promoted effective methods for reducing healthcare-associated infections (HAIs), and combines improvements in safety, teamwork, and communication together with a checklist of proven practices for preventing HAI in high-risk areas like intensive care units.

The AHRQ promotes the use of quality indicator surveys, such as the Consumer Assessment of Healthcare Providers and Systems, to provide valid assessments of patients' care experience in hospitals, nursing homes, and ambulatory care settings. The Centers for Medicare & Medicaid Services chose the hospital version of the AHRQ survey to be the measure used in its Hospital Quality Initiative.

Improving provider–patient interactions is also crucial for addressing disparate health practices. As American society has become increasingly diverse, it has become more important for healthcare providers and organizations to be recognize how patients' individual and cultural identities can affect the quality of care they receive and to provide culturally responsive care to all patients (Wasserman et al. 2019). Racial and ethnic minorities, individuals with limited English proficiency, and disadvantaged social groups may experience ineffective care if they are made to feel unwelcome or experience poor communication with their providers. Providers may appear more disengaged with disadvantaged minorities and therefore ask fewer questions, provide less health information, or offer fewer treatment options. This may be the result of less familiarity with a patient's culture, stereotypes, or implicit racial and ethnic biases that have been learned (Hall et al. 2015). Such biases can also affect clinical decision-making. An example of an **implicit bias** is associating drug use with people of color, and therefore writing fewer prescriptions for legitimate pain for minorities than other patients (Pecoraro 2021).

implicit bias
Unconsciously associating stereotypes with certain groups of people and behaving accordingly.

Training in cultural competence is meant to address such concerns in healthcare. Based on a review of studies, cultural competence training may improve the knowledge and attitudes of health professionals and promote greater satisfaction with care, but there is less evidence of improved outcomes and impacts on health disparities (Wasserman et al. 2019). Physicians may need a broader understanding of how social and environmental determinants of health affect a patient's ability to adhere to a care plan (Houlihan and Leffler 2019).

At the organizational level, healthcare facilities should evaluate whether they are meeting Culturally and Linguistically Appropriate Services (CLAS) standards of care. The National CLAS standards are meant to advance healthcare equity by ensuring that services are appropriately tailored to diverse patients (see https://thinkculturalhealth.hhs.gov/clas/standards). CLAS encompasses 15 standards that establish a blueprint for organizational action, including governance and leadership, patient communication and language assistance, community engagement, and continuous improvement. Healthcare organizations are asked to be respectful and responsive to patient health needs and preferences by considering each patient's culture and health beliefs, health literacy level, preferred language, and communication needs.

Finally, addressing disparities in the healthcare system will likely require the adoption of newer models of care (Houlihan and Leffler 2019; Wasserman et al. 2019). One such model is the *patient-centered medical home* (PCMH; see Jackson et al. 2013; Miller et al. 2017). According to the AHRQ, this framework promotes comprehensive care, patient-centered care, coordinated care, and accessible services and addresses quality and safety. Research suggests that the PCMH model has potential for improving patient and possibly staff satisfaction as well preventive services (Jackson et al. 2013). However, while PCMH enrollment has been associated with an increased likelihood of receiving recommended services (i.e., quality care), the data on racial disparities have been inconsistent to date (Swietek et al. 2020).

Most PCMH projects have been conducted in primary care settings serving populations with chronic illness and in consultation with payer organizations. The goal is not only to improve the quality of care provided to patients with complex needs but also to reduce the associated healthcare costs accrued in more fragmented health systems. Integral to this aim is the development of alternative payment systems (e.g., pay for performance, bundled payments, capitation) to incorporate behavioral health treatment (Miller et al. 2017).

The PCMH concept is closely related to the movement toward integrated healthcare. Healthcare leaders recognize that among the many health disparities, mental health equity is central to meeting the health needs of vulnerable populations and achieving health equity (Satcher and Rachel 2017). Mental health conditions such as depression greatly impact and interact with physical health conditions, such that screening for depression is now a recommended practice for all health settings. Given the many barriers to patients obtaining needed mental health services, integrated care—in which behavioral health services are integrated into primary care—has become the model for addressing these unmet needs of patients.

The shift to value-based care is a transformation in the way providers and payers address the social determinants of health (Houlihan and Leffler 2019). Many healthcare organizations now screen for social determinants such as food insecurity and other needs, linking patients to social services. Many states are now requiring managed care organizations serving the Medicaid population to incorporate such screening programs. For example, North Carolina requires participating managed care organizations to use a statewide screening tool covering housing, food, transportation, and interpersonal violence to better identify patients' unmet health-related needs. Researchers have found that healthcare spending is reduced when patients are connected to social services, demonstrating the business case for addressing social determinants of health as an overall population health strategy. It is expected that future payment arrangements for health services will not only incentivize quality improvements but directly measure and reward equity (Joynt Maddox and James 2021; Wasserman et al. 2019).

There is increased recognition that many of the root causes of disparate health outcomes are related to factors outside the clinic, although healthcare organizations have a definite role to play in promoting community policies and practices that improve opportunities for achieving health equity (Woolf 2017). Some health systems are staffing hospitals with social workers and case managers; they are also entering into community partnerships to meet patient needs.

One successful program, Racial and Ethnic Approaches to Community Health (REACH), involved the use of trained community health workers to meet the needs of different communities. By designing and implementing culturally tailored and community-led interventions, the program addressed existing gaps between healthcare services and ethnic community members, improved health knowledge and practices in designated areas, and built individual and community capacity to plan and implement future interventions (Cosgrove et al. 2014). Achieving health equity will depend on such programs and greater cross-sectoral collaborations between healthcare and education, business, and community leaders. It will also require further research on how sociocultural, behavioral, and health system factors converge and produce disparities in the quality of healthcare (Wasserman et al. 2019).

The US healthcare system compares unfavorably with developed European countries on standardized international measures of health, despite relatively higher expenditures; moreover, this gap appears to be widening (Schroeder 2016). This may be explained by the far greater portion of the US population that lacks health insurance and the greater income and wealth inequality in America. Steven Schroeder (2016) makes the case that the direct reason for the relatively poor health performance in the United States is the poor health status of Americans of lower socioeconomic class, predominantly living in the Southeast. He uses the example of cigarette smoking, which remains the most significant preventable health risk factor for associated deaths. While rates of smoking have declined significantly overall in the US population, smoking and other threats to health (e.g., obesity, diabetes, heart disease, HIV disease, violence, teenage pregnancies) are now concentrated among those living in poverty. Approximately 6 percent of the population (some 18.5 million people) are living in what is termed *deep poverty* (Abrams 2019), with incomes less than 50 percent of the federal poverty threshold. For a single person, that means living on $6,243 per year, and for a family of four, less than $12,170. People living in poverty experience higher rates of physical and mental health problems and face a stigma that results in cumulative disadvantage that persists over generations.

All of these factors underscore the inextricable relationships between cost, quality, and access when we view disparities through the ethical principles of social justice, beneficence, and nonmaleficence. We cannot improve the health of our nation without actions aimed at education and achieving greater income equality, with an explicit focus on the health of vulnerable populations. With the understanding that health disparities are complex, consider the following Mini-Case Study, which highlights the structural roots of racism and discrimination in lactation care.

MINI-CASE STUDY: THE STRUCTURAL ROOTS OF RACISM AND DISCRIMINATION IN LACTATION CARE

The practice of breastfeeding infants offers health benefits to both the infant (e.g., reduces the risk of developing asthma, type 1 diabetes, and gastrointestinal infections) and the mother (e.g., lowers the risk of high blood pressure and type 2 diabetes). Dr. Ruth Petersen (CDC 2021a), director of the CDC's Division of Nutrition, Physical Activity and Obesity, noted that "breastfeeding provides unmatched health benefits for babies and mothers. It is the clinical gold standard for infant feeding and nutrition, with breast milk uniquely tailored to meet the needs of a growing baby. We must do more to create supportive and safe environments for mothers who choose to breastfeed."

However, Black infants are 15 percent less likely to be breastfed than white infants in the United States (CDC 2021a). The Healthy People 2030 initiative set targets to increase the share of breastfed babies through six months of age from 24.9 percent in 2015 to 42.2 percent. Strategies to meet this goal include increasing education efforts and providing breastfeeding support to mothers in the hospital (HHS 2021a). Healthcare providers may seek certification to serve as an International Board-Certified Lactation Consultant (IBCLC). This credential requires a health sciences background, at least 95 hours of lactation education, clinical experience, and adherence to the International Board of Lactation Consultant Examiners' Code of Professional Conduct, which includes a personal integrity section (IBLCE 2015):

> 6.3. Treat all clients equitably without regard to ability/disability, gender identity, sexual orientation, sex, ethnicity, race, national origin, political persuasion, marital status, geographic location, religion, socioeconomic status, age, within the legal framework of the respective geo-political region or setting.

Thus, an IBCLC is a professional who provides lactation support for new mothers equitably and spends time to encourage, educate, and assist mothers with breastfeeding. Research fellow Erin V. Thomas (2018) interviewed 36 IBCLCs employed at hospitals. The interviews revealed differences in how mothers from different racial backgrounds were treated. Thomas categorized instances of overt racism, such as a caregiver making a stereotypical comment, as well as instances of implicit bias, such as providing less quantity or quality of care based on associated stereotypes. Examples of overt racism included statements such as, "We don't want these people having any more babies than they already do" (Thomas 2018, 1054). Implicit bias included actions such as designing educational literature and handouts that only showed white women breastfeeding, leaving women of color invisible in the educational literature. Tina, a 35-year-old Black IBCLC, explained her reaction when she saw the whites-only literature (Thomas 2018, 1056):

> In my opinion, for people to be successful at something, at anything, it is good for them to see images of people who look like them that are successful . . . I thought [choosing only white images for a pamphlet] was a great oversight.

When she pointed out the invisibility of Black women, her supervisor noted that it was too late to change the material, as it had already gone to print. The key point about implicit bias is that assumptions are made about patients of color, and subsequent actions—even if committed unconsciously—yield unequal treatment. Another example of implicit bias was reported by a 30-year-old Black IBCLC (Thomas 2018, 1054):

> I see Black moms come in there outside of means and no one really helps them with breastfeeding because the statistics say that they don't really breastfeed. So why waste the money if they are not going to do it?

Mini-Case Study Questions

1. Explain the concept of implicit bias as it is illustrated in Thomas's article.
2. Explain what ethical principles were violated by implicit bias.
3. Discuss the role of healthcare managers in addressing breastfeeding disparities.

Points to Remember

> - Health policy refers to strategies aimed at improving the health of the people and the communities in which they live, while healthcare policy refers to policies that directly affect healthcare costs, quality of care, and access to care for the people in those communities.
> - Social marketing is the practice of influencing the behavior of both individuals and the community for the common good.
> - Ethical theories serve as lenses through which to evaluate the ethics of social marketing efforts. One of them is enlightened self-interest, which maximizes benefits to self and minimizes harm to others.
> - Downstream social marketing focuses on influencing or changing individual behavior.
> - Upstream social marketing focuses on influencing or changing systems, policies, and other structural components.
> - Health status is greatly influenced by social determinants of health, which are related to the environments in which people are born, live, learn, work, play, worship, and age.
> - Health disparities are unjust differences in health attributable to disadvantage. Health disparities persist in many areas of health, with negative effects particularly on racial and ethnic minority populations and the poor.

Challenge Yourself

1. Consider the chapter-opening quote by Dr. Paul Farmer: "The idea that some lives matter less is the root of all that is wrong with the world." Think of an example in which you might witness or experience this in your work as a healthcare manager.
2. What factors influenced Congress to pass the 1986 Emergency Medical Treatment and Active Labor Act? Why do you think the legislation was not funded?
3. What factors influenced Congress to pass the Pandemic and All-Hazards Preparedness Acts of 2006, 2013 and 2019? Why do you think this legislation was funded?
4. How would you assess a healthcare organization's response to health disparities? Would the results of such an assessment influence your desire or decision to work for the organization? Why or why not?

For Your Consideration

14.1 Social determinants of health affect patients' physical and mental health outcomes. Consider one of the examples of social determinants of health examined in this chapter and assess how that determinant might be addressed in your community. For example, map out distances to locations that offer nutritious food. If transportation is an issue, the distance to a grocery store or farmers market may negatively affect a person's ability to eat well. Consequently, the lack of access to good nutrition may cause increased risk of heart disease, diabetes, and obesity. What could your community do to mitigate the negative effects of this social determinant of health so that people have better access to nutritious food? What ethical perspectives would influence your ideas?

14.2 The surgeon general leads the US Public Health Service Commissioned Corps, which is composed of public health professionals. Its mission is to "protect, promote and advance the health of our nation." Using the ethical lens presented, assess one of its priorities. This exercise requires you to become familiar with the Office of the Surgeon General's website (www.hhs.gov/surgeongeneral/index.html). For example, as of May 2021, the site included information on topics such as opioids and addiction, tobacco, and oral health. Gain an understanding of one of these priorities and the surgeon general's strategy to address it. Then conduct an ethical assessment, employing the method used to assess the CDC's COVID-19 vaccination strategy. Remember to identify the target markets as you work. Does the strategy fit the mission of the US Public Health Service? Explain.

CHECK THESE OUT

Want more information about the organizations discussed in the chapter? Check these websites out.

- Agency for Healthcare Research and Quality: www.ahrq.gov/cpi/about/profile/index.html
- CDC Racism and Health: www.cdc.gov/healthequity/racism-disparities/index.html
- COVID-19 Public Education Campaign: www.hhs.gov/coronavirus/education-campaign/index.html
- Emergency Medical Treatment and Labor Act: www.cms.gov/Regulations-and-Guidance/Legislation/EMTALA
- Healthy People 2030: https://health.gov/healthypeople
- National CLAS Standards: https://thinkculturalhealth.hhs.gov/clas/standards
- National Collaborative for Health Equity: www.nationalcollaborative.org/
- National Institute on Minority Health and Health Disparities: www.nimhd.nih.gov/about/overview/
- Pandemic and All-Hazards Preparedness Acts of 2006, 2013, and 2019: www.phe.gov/preparedness/legal/pahpa/pages/default.aspx
- US Department of Health and Human Services, Office of the Assistant Secretary for Preparedness and Response: www.phe.gov/about/aspr/Pages/default.aspx

References

Abrams, Z. 2019. "Pathways for Addressing Deep Poverty." *APA Monitor* 50 (7): 32.

Acuff, K. 2014. "Healthcare Ethics, Public Policy, and the Healthcare Organization." In *Managerial Ethics in Healthcare: A New Perspective*, edited by G. Filerman, A. Mills, and P. Schyve, 223–41. Chicago: Health Administration Press.

Adams, K. 2021. "10 Recently Launched COVID-19 Vaccine Ad Campaigns." *Becker's Health IT*. Published April 22. www.beckershospitalreview.com/digital-marketing/10-recently-launched-covid-19-ad-campaigns.html.

Agency for Healthcare Research and Quality (AHRQ). 2021. "Agency for Healthcare Research and Quality: A Profile." Accessed August 25. www.ahrq.gov/cpi/about/profile/index.html.

Aleshire, M. E., K. Ashford, A. Fallin-Bennett, and J. Hatcher. 2019. "Primary Care Providers' Attitudes Related to LGBTQ People: A Narrative Literature Review." *Health Promotion Practice* 20 (2): 173–87.

American Journal of Managed Care (AJMC). 2015. "Institute of Medicine to Be Renamed." Published May 4. www.ajmc.com/view/institute-of-medicine-to-be-renamed.

Annas, G. 1986. "Your Money or Your Life: 'Dumping' Uninsured Patients from Hospital Emergency Wards." *American Journal of Public Health* 76 (1): 74–77.

Ansell, D., and R. Schiff. 1987. "Patient Dumping: Status, Implications, and Policy Recommendations." *Journal of the American Medical Association* 257 (11): 1500–1502.

Basen, R. 2021. "Hospitals, Senior Care Systems Start to Require COVID Vax for Workers." Medpage Today. Published April 9. www.medpagetoday.com/special-reports/exclusives/92005.

Best Colleges. 2021. "What Colleges Require the COVID-19 Vaccine?" Published September 1. www.bestcolleges.com/blog/list-of-colleges-that-require-covid-19-vaccine/.

Braveman, P. 2014. "What Are Health Disparities and Health Equity? We Need to Be Clear." *Public Health Reports* 129 (Suppl. 2): 5–8.

Braveman, P. A., S. Kumanyika, J. Fielding, T. LaVeist, L. N. Borrell, R. Manderscheid, and A. Troutman. 2011. "Health Disparities and Health Equity: The Issue Is Justice." *American Journal of Public Health* 101 (Suppl. 1): S149–55.

Brown, L. C. 2016. "Dissecting Racism: Healing Minds, Cultivating Spirits." In *Living into God's Dream: Dismantling Racism in America*, edited by C. Meeks, 15–33. New York: Morehouse Press.

Cellucci, L., M. Meacham, and T. Farnsworth. 2019. *Essentials of Healthcare Management*, 2nd ed. Chicago: Health Administration Press.

Centers for Disease Control and Prevention (CDC). 2021a. "CDC's Work to Support & Promote Breastfeeding in Hospitals, Worksites, & Communities." Accessed May 27. www.cdc.gov/breastfeeding/pdf/breastfeeding-cdcs-work-508.pdf.

———. 2021b. "Demographic Characteristics of People Receiving COVID-19 Vaccinations in the United States." Accessed September 1. https://covid.cdc.gov/covid-data-tracker/#vaccination-demographic.

———. 2021c. "Mobile Vaccination Resources." Accessed May 19. www.cdc.gov/vaccines/covid-19/planning/mobile.html.

———. 2021d. "Racism and Health." Accessed May 19. www.cdc.gov/healthequity/racism-disparities/index.html.

———. 2021e. "Weekly Summary on COVID-19 Deaths." Accessed May 19. www.cdc.gov/nchs/covid19/mortality-overview.htm.

———. 2014. "Please Tell Me, Is It Safe to Go Home? After 9/11, Science Offers Comfort." Reviewed March 19. www.cdc.gov/about/24-7/protectingpeople/anthrax/safetogohome.html.

Centers for Medicare & Medicaid Services (CMS). 2021. "Emergency Medical Treatment & Labor Act (EMTALA)." Accessed May 15. www.cms.gov/Regulations-and-Guidance/Legislation/EMTALA.

Choi, C. 2021. "Faith-Based Organizations Help with COVID-19 Vaccine Outreach." WITN. Published February 17. www.witn.com/2021/02/18/faith-based-organizations-help-with-covid-19-vaccine-outreach/.

Coke, L. A., and L. L. Hayman. 2021. "The Impact of Structural Racism on Cardiovascular Health." *Journal of Cardiovascular Nursing* 36 (3): 196–97.

Comfort, L. K., and N. Kapucu. 2006. "Inter-organizational Coordination in Extreme Events: The World Trade Center Attacks, September 11, 2001." *Natural Hazards* 39: 309–27.

Cosgrove, S., M. Moore-Monroy, C. Jenkins, S. R. Castillo, C. Williams, E. Parris, J. H. Tran, M. D. Rivera, and J. N. Brownstein. 2014. "Community Health Workers as an Integral Strategy in the REACH U.S. Program to Eliminate Health Inequities." *Health Promotion Practice* 15 (6): 795–802.

Cutler, D., and L. Summers. 2020. "The COVID-19 Pandemic and the $16 Trillion Virus." *Journal of the American Medical Association* 324 (15): 1495–96.

Dankwa-Mullen, I., E. J. Perez-Stable, K. L. Gardner, X. Zhang, and A. M. Rosario (eds.). 2021. *The Science of Health Disparities Research*. Hoboken, NJ: Wiley-Blackwell.

Davis, E. 2021. "Governors Start Mandating the COVID-19 Vaccine for State Employees." *U.S. News & World Report.* Published July 29. www.usnews.com/news/best-states/articles/2021-07-29/these-governors-are-mandating-the-covid-19-vaccine-for-government-employees.

de Montluzin, E., and E. de Montluzin. 2011. *Dearest Arlette: Everyday Life in Postwar America and France, 1945–1955, as Recorded in the Letters of Two Reunited Families*. Columbia, SC: R.L. Bryan Company.

Dossabhoy, S., J. Feng, and M. Desai. 2018. "The Use and Relevance of the Hippocratic Oath in 2015—a Survey of US Medical Schools." *Journal of Anesthesia History* 4 (2): 139–46.

Ehrlich, K. B. 2020. "How Does the Social World Shape Health Across the Lifespan? Insights and New Directions." *American Psychologist* 75 (9): 1231–41.

Emergency Medicine News. 2003. "The EMTALA Paradox." *Emergency Medicine News* 25 (1): 46.

Freemantle, T. 2005. "Trapped Hospital Workers Kept Most Patients Alive." *Houston Chronicle.* Published September 18. www.chron.com/news/hurricanes/article/Trapped-hospital-workers-kept-most-patients-alive-1502571.php.

Gold, M. 2020. "New York City Marks 9/11 at a Time of Harrowing Loss." *New York Times.* Published September 11. www.nytimes.com/2020/09/11/nyregion/9-11-ceremony-September-11th.html.

Goldberg, M. 1995. "Social Marketing: Are We Fiddling While Rome Burns?" *Journal of Consumer Psychology* 4 (4): 347–70.

Gómez, C. A., D. V. Kleinman, N. Pronk, G. L. Wrenn Gordon, E. Ochiai, C. Blakey, A. Johnson, and K. H. Brewer. 2021. "Addressing Health Equity and Social Determinants of Health Through

Healthy People 2030." *Journal of Public Health Management and Practice*. Published March 8. https://doi.org/10.1097/PHH.0000000000001297.

Gooch, K. 2021. "Montana Health System Implements Mandatory COVID-19 Vaccinations." *Becker's Hospital Review*. Published April 16. www.beckershospitalreview.com/workforce/montana-health-system-implements-mandatory-covid-19-vaccinations.html.

Hall, W. J., M. V. Chapman, K. M. Lee, Y. M. Merino, T. W. Thomas, B. K. Payne, E. Eng, S. H. Day, and T. Coyne-Beasley. 2015. "Implicit Racial/Ethnic Bias Among Health Care Professionals and Its Influence on Health Care Outcomes: A Systematic Review." *American Journal of Public Health* 105 (12): e60–76.

Healthy People 2030. 2021. "Social Determinants of Health." Accessed August 25. https://health.gov/healthypeople/objectives-and-data/social-determinants-health.

Houlihan, J., and S. Leffler. 2019. "Assessing and Addressing Social Determinants of Health: A Key Competency for Succeeding in Value-Based Care." *Primary Care* 46 (4): 561–74.

Institute of Medicine (IOM). 1988. *The Future of Public Health*. Washington, DC: National Academies Press.

International Board of Lactation Consultant Examiners (IBLCE). 2015. "Code of Professional Conduct for IBCLCs." Updated September. https://iblce.org/wp-content/uploads/2020/07/Code-of-professional-conduct.pdf.

Jackson, G. L., B. J. Powers, R. Chatterjee, J. P. Bettger, A. R. Kemper, V. Hasselblad, R. J. Dolor, R. J. Irvine, B. L. Heidenfelder, A. S. Kendrick, R. Gray, and J. W. Williams. 2013. "The Patient Centered Medical Home: A Systematic Review." *Annals of Internal Medicine* 158 (3): 169–78.

Jernigan, D., P. L. Raghunathan, B. P. Bell, R. Brechner, E. A. Bresnitz, J. C. Butler, M. Cetron, M. Cohen, T. Doyle, M. Fischer, C. Greene, K. S. Griffith, J. Guarner, J. L. Hadler, J. A. Hayslett, R. Meyer, L. R. Petersen, M. Phillips, R. Pinner, T. Popovic, C. P. Quinn, J. Reefhuis, D. Reissman, N. Rosenstein, A. Schuchat, W.-J. Shieh, L. Siegal, D. L. Swerdlow, F. C. Tenover, M. Traeger, J. W. Ward, I. Weisfuse, S. Wiersma, K. Yeskey, S. Zaki, D. A. Ashford, B. A. Perkins, S. Ostroff, J. Hughes, D. Fleming, J. P. Koplan, J. L. Gerberding, and the National Anthrax Epidemiologic Investigation Team. 2002. "Investigation of Bioterrorism-Related Anthrax, United States, 2001: Epidemiologic Findings." *Emerging Infectious Diseases* 8 (10): 1019–28.

Joint Commission. 2010. *Advancing Effective Communication, Cultural Competence, and Patient- and Family-Centered Care: A Roadmap for Hospitals*. Oakbrook Terrace, IL: The Joint Commission.

Joynt Maddox, K. E., and C. V. James. 2021. "How the Biden Administration Can Improve Health Equity for Racial and Ethnic Minority Populations." *Journal of the American Medical Association* 325 (14): 1387–88.

King, N. 2021. "Local 'Trusted Messengers' Key to Boosting COVID Vaccinations, Surgeon General Says." National Public Radio. Published May 5. www.npr.org/sections/coronavirus-live-updates/2021/05/05/993754369/administration-plan-will-make-it-easier-to-get-access-to-vaccines.

Kirby, S., and A. Andreasen. 2001. "Marketing Ethics to Social Marketers: A Segmented Approach." In *Ethics in Social Marketing*, edited by A. Andreasen, 160–83. Washington, DC: Georgetown University Press.

Kissick, W. 1994. *Medicine's Dilemmas: Infinite Needs Versus Finite Resources*. New Haven, CT: Yale University Press.

Klitzman, S., and N. Freudenberg. 2003. "Implications of the World Trade Center Attack for the Public Health and Health Care Infrastructures." *American Journal of Public Health* 93 (3): 400–406.

Kotler, P., and G. Zaltman. 1971. "Social Marketing: An Approach to Planned Social Change." *Journal of Marketing* 35 (3): 3–12.

Kurtz, J. 2021. "McDonald's Teams Up with HHS on Pro-Vaccination Campaign." *The Hill*. Published May 11. https://thehill.com/blogs/in-the-know/in-the-know/552819-mcdonalds-teams-up-with-hhs-on-pro-vaccination-campaign.

Milburn, N. G., L. Beatty, and S. A. Lopez. 2019. "Understanding, Unpacking, and Eliminating Health Disparities: A Prescription for Health Equity Promotion Through Behavioral and Psychological Research—an Introduction." *Cultural Diversity and Ethnic Minority Psychology* 25 (1): 1–5.

Miller, B. F., K. M. Ross, M. M. Davis, S. P. Melek, R. Kathol, and P. Gordon. 2017. "Payment Reform in the Patient-Centered Medical Home: Enabling and Sustaining Integrated Behavioral Health Care." *American Psychologist* 72 (1): 55–68.

Minas, T. Z., M. Kiely, A. Ajao, and S. Ambs. 2021. "An Overview of Cancer Health Disparities: New Approaches and Insights and Why They Matter." *Carcinogenesis* 42 (1): 2–13.

Mitchell, H. 2021. "11 Bans on Vaccine Mandates—What States Have Them & Which Might Soon." *Becker's Hospital Review*. Published August 9. www.beckershospitalreview.com/workforce/11-bans-on-vaccine-mandates-what-states-have-them-which-might-soon.html.

Morhard, R., and C. Franco. 2013. "The Pandemic and All-Hazards Preparedness Act: Its Contributions and New Potential to Increase Public Health Preparedness." *Biosecurity and Bioterrorism: Biodefense Strategy, Practice, and Science* 11 (2): 145–52.

National Academy of Medicine (NAM). 2021. "About the National Academy of Medicine." Accessed May 19. https://nam.edu/about-the-nam/.

National Commission on Terrorist Attacks Upon the United States (9/11 Commission). 2004. "Executive Summary." Accessed May 23, 2021. https://govinfo.library.unt.edu/911/report/911Report_Exec.htm.

Office of Inspector General (OIG). 2006. "A Performance Review of FEMA's Disaster Management Activities in Response to Hurricane Katrina." Accessed May 21, 2021. www.oig.dhs.gov/assets/Mgmt/OIG_06-32_Mar06.pdf.

Office of the Assistant Secretary for Health. 2020. "Healthy People 2020: An End of Decade Snapshot." Accessed May 15, 2021. https://health.gov/sites/default/files/2021-03/21%20HP2020EndofDecadeSnapshot2.pdf.

Parkland Hospital. 2019. "Parkland Celebrates 125 Years of Service to Dallas Community." Published May 1. www.parklandhospital.com/news-and-updates/parkland-celebrates-125-years-of-service-to-dallas-1548.

Pecoraro, K. 2021. "How Social Determinants of Health Affect COVID-19-Related Morbidity and Mortality." *Nursing* 51 (5): 24–32.

Porter, M., and M. Kramer. 2006. "The Link Between Competitive Advantage and Corporate Social Responsibility." *Harvard Business Review* 85 (12): 78–92.

Satcher, D., and S. A. Rachel. 2017. "Promoting Mental Health Equity: The Role of Integrated Care." *Journal of Clinical Psychology in Medical Settings* 24 (3–4): 182–86.

Schroeder, S. A. 2016. "American Health Improvement Depends upon Addressing Class Disparities." *Preventive Medicine* 92: 6–15.

Secretary's Advisory Committee on National Health Promotion and Disease Prevention Objectives for 2020. 2008. "Phase 1 Report; Recommendations for the Framework and Format of Healthy People 2020." Published October 28. www.healthypeople.gov/sites/default/files/PhaseI_0.pdf.

Smedley, B. D., A. Y. Stith, and A. R. Nelson (eds.). 2003. *Unequal Treatment: Confronting Racial and Ethnic Disparities in Healthcare.* Washington, DC: National Academies Press.

Swietek, K. E., B. N. Gaynes, G. L. Jackson, M. Weinberger, and M. E. Domino. 2020. "Effect of the Patient-Centered Medical Home on Racial Disparities in Quality of Care." *Journal of General Internal Medicine* 35 (8): 2304–13.

Taylor, P. 1985. "Ailing, Uninsured and Turned Away." *Washington Post.* Published June 30. www.washingtonpost.com/archive/politics/1985/06/30/ailing-uninsured-and-turned-away/8d83c59d-15fa-4527-94a7-ef47b6779e50/.

Thomas, E. 2018. "'Why Even Bother; They Are Not Going to Do It?' The Structural Roots of Racism and Discrimination in Lactation Care." *Qualitative Health Research* 28 (7): 1050–64.

Thomason, A., and B. O'Leary. 2021. "Here's a List of Colleges That Will Require Students or Employees to Be Vaccinated Against Covid-19." *Chronicle of Higher Education.* Published September 1. www.chronicle.com/blogs/live-coronavirus-updates/heres-a-list-of-colleges-that-will-require-students-to-be-vaccinated-against-covid-19.

US Department of Health and Human Services (HHS). 2021a. "Increase the Proportion of Infants Who Are Breastfed Exclusively Through Age 6 Months." Accessed May 27. https://health.gov/healthypeople/objectives-and-data/browse-objectives/infants/increase-proportion-infants-who-are-breastfed-exclusively-through-age-6-months-mich-15.

———. 2021b. "The Surgeon General's Priorities." Updated January 26. www.hhs.gov/surgeongeneral/index.html.

———. 2021c. "HHS Secretary Becerra, HUD Secretary Fudge Announce Joint Effort to Increase Access to COVID-19 Vaccinations." Published May 5. www.hhs.gov/about/news/2021/05/05/hhs-secretary-becerra-hud-secretary-fudge-announce-joint-effort-increase-access-covid-19-vaccinations.html.

US Department of Justice (DOJ). 2021. "Whether Section 564 of the Food, Drug, and Cosmetic Act Prohibits Entities from Requiring the Use of a Vaccine Subject to an Emergency Use Authorization." Published July 6. www.justice.gov/olc/file/1415446/download.

US Department of Veterans Affairs. 2021. "VA Mandates COVID-19 Vaccines Among Its Medical Employees Including VHA Facilities Staff." Published July 26. www.va.gov/opa/pressrel/pressrelease.cfm?id=5696.

Vidant Health. 2021. "Vidant Health Announces COVID-19 Vaccine Requirement for Team Members to Protect Patients." Published July 30. www.vidanthealth.com/vidant-health-announces-covid-19-vaccine-requirement-for-team-members-to-protect-patients/.

VOA News. 2021. "Four Former US Presidents Promote COVID-19 Vaccination Campaign." Published March 11. www.voanews.com/usa/four-former-us-presidents-promote-covid-19-vaccination-campaign.

Walgreens. 2021. "Walgreens Teams Up with John Legend to Remind Americans This Is Our Shot to Get Back to What Matters." Published April 2. https://news.walgreens.com/press-center/news/walgreens-teams-up-with-john-legend-to-remind-americans-this-is-our-shot-to-get-back-to-what-matters.htm.

Walker, G. 2017. "Emergentology." *Emergency Medicine News* 39 (12): 10.

Walt Disney World (WDW) News Today. 2021. "I Got My Shot: Safer. Stronger. Together." Published May 19. https://wdwnt.com/2021/04/orange-county-florida-launches-i-got-my-shot-covid-19-vaccination-campaign-with-disney-world-and-universal-orlando-support/.

Wamsley, L. 2021. "CDC Director Declares Racism a 'Serious Public Health Threat.'" National Public Radio. Published April 8. www.npr.org/2021/04/08/985524494/cdc-director-declares-racism-a-serious-public-health-threat.

Wasserman, J., R. C. Palmer, M. M. Gómez, R. Berzon, S. A. Ibrahim, and J. Z. Ayanian. 2019. "Advancing Health Services Research to Eliminate Health Care Disparities." *American Journal of Public Health* 109 (Suppl. 1): S64–69.

Woolf, S. H. 2017. "Progress in Achieving Health Equity Requires Attention to Root Causes." *Health Affairs* 36 (6): 984–91.

Wrenn, K. 1985. "No Insurance, No Admission." *New England Journal of Medicine* 312 (6): 373–74.

Wu, G., and J. Garcia. 2021. "Houston Methodist Says It Will Fire Hospital Workers Who Refuse to Take COVID Vaccine." *Houston Chronicle*. Published April 22. www.houstonchronicle.com/news/houston-texas/health/article/Houston-Methodist-COVID-vaccine-refusal-fire-16121140.php.

CHAPTER 15
HEALTHCARE MANAGEMENT CONSULTING

Good counselors lack no clients.

—William Shakespeare, *Measure for Measure*

Important Terms

- Client
- Competence
- Good-faith duty
- Healthcare management consultant

Learning Objectives

Studying this chapter will help you to

➤ explain healthcare management consulting,

➤ describe the ideal characteristics of healthcare consultants endorsed by the codes of ethics of management and consulting associations, and

➤ discuss the ethical principles of autonomy, fidelity, honesty, and justice as they relate to healthcare management consulting.

Healthcare managers can offer consulting services as independent consultants, as members of consulting firms, or as internal consultants for a healthcare organization. Consulting roles are as replete with ethical issues as administration roles. In this chapter, we introduce you to those issues and the ideal responses of healthcare management consultants who learn and apply their profession's codes of ethics.

WHAT IS HEALTHCARE CONSULTING?

The profession of management consulting dates to 1911 and Frederick Winslow Taylor's publication of *The Principles of Scientific Management* (Redekop and Heath 2007). According to Elaine Biech (2019, 3), "Consulting is not a descriptor that identifies a profession in itself." Rather, people who consult are highly skilled professionals from a variety of backgrounds who apply their expertise to assess current business practices or spur innovative change. To illustrate, consider the following Case from the Field, in which Frank Gilbreth, an engineer, and Dr. Lillian Gilbreth, an industrial psychologist, worked as efficiency expert consultants in the early twentieth century. As you read about them, reflect on how consulting may help bring about improved patient care, a better work environment, and increased job satisfaction. An important note regarding management consultants is that they "provide services in the most ethical manner, to build relationships with the highest level of integrity, and to run a business with the highest principles" (Biech 2019, 256). Simply put, if consultants provide services to healthcare organizations ethically, they are more likely to provide recommendations that will improve care.

Organizations commonly become clients of management consultants when they need external, objective advice and counsel. In consulting, **client** is a generic term for an organization or person who hires an expert for their knowledge and advice on a defined issue.

client
In consulting, an organization or a person who uses the services of a management consultant.

CASE FROM THE FIELD
The Emerging Healthcare Consulting Industry: Frank Gilbreth (1868–1924) and Lillian Gilbreth (1878–1972)

As the United States underwent industrialization and reform in the late nineteenth and early twentieth centuries, the economy shifted from agrarian and handicraft to industrial and machine based. This change fundamentally altered the way Americans worked and lived, and it spurred the growth of management consulting. Early consultants were primarily engineers; they were quickly joined by psychologists, sociologists, and social workers who developed and applied management theory to real-life work environments.

(continued)

> **CASE FROM THE FIELD**
> The Emerging Healthcare Consulting Industry: Frank Gilbreth (1868–1924) and Lillian Gilbreth (1878–1972) *(continued)*
>
> The search for efficiencies in the workplace, spearheaded by Taylor, was expanded by consultants such as Frank and Lillian Gilbreth. They examined how healthcare providers performed their work, and then they offered recommendations to improve performance and worker satisfaction (Baumgart and Neuhauser 2009; Wiegmann and Sundt 2019). For example, they filmed surgeries and documented the time wasted as surgeons searched for the specific instrument needed. The Gilbreths identified inefficient actions, showed the time lost to surgeons, and recommended new methods to bring about more efficient and, as a result, better care. The outcome was what you see in an operating room today—an organized tray of surgical instruments, with nurses handing the specific tool requested to the surgeon (F. Gilbreth 1914, 1916). This change reduced the time required to perform surgery—a win for both healthcare providers and the patients in their care.
>
> While Frank Gilbreth worked as an engineer, he had no college degree; Lillian Gilbreth held a doctorate in industrial psychology. The combination of his experience and her education honed their focus on the worker as central to understanding work processes (L. Gilbreth 1914, 3):
>
>> The emphasis in successful management lies in the man, not the work; that efficiency is best secured by planning the emphasis on the man; and modifying the equipment, materials and methods to make the most of the man. It has, further, recognized that the man's mind is a controlling factor to his efficiency, and has, by teaching, enabled the man to make the most of his powers.
>
> The legacy of the Gilbreths' work spurred ergonomic research that described processes to improve patient care and reduced worker fatigue and injury (Jahn, Heiden, and Caldwell 2018; Rodman et al. 2020; Vaisbuc et al. 2018). Their human-focused approach brought about success for the organization and better outcomes for healthcare workers and patients. (For more detail on the Gilbreths' lives, see Yost 1949.)

Healthcare organizations engage **healthcare management consultants** for general and specific purposes, such as the following:

- Reviewing and auditing financial statements
- Providing temporary general management services, such as during the search for a new administrator

healthcare management consultant
A professional with skills, knowledge, and expertise in healthcare business operations and management who provides external, objective advice to clients.

- Assisting in the search for and recruitment of administrators, clinicians, and other professional staff

- Increasing profitability and productivity by addressing employee morale, enhancing reimbursements through improvements in coding and billing processes, and redesigning workflows and jobs

- Implementing changes, such as reengineering the organization's business and systems or restructuring the organization's compositional units and reporting lines

- Advising on special issues, such as strategic planning and forecasting, data analytics, marketing, public relations, external communications, conflict resolution, information technologies, negotiating provider contracts and fee schedules, and capital improvements

Some healthcare consulting services are temporary or short term, such as managing a business unit or department during the search for a new administrator. Other consulting services are long term, such as auditing financial statements.

IDEAL CHARACTERISTICS OF HEALTHCARE MANAGEMENT CONSULTANTS

Autonomy, integrity, competence, fidelity, honesty, justice, dignity, and a commitment to learning are the attributes that healthcare management consultants should display. Exhibit 15.1 illustrates the common characteristics endorsed by the codes of ethics of healthcare associations, such as the American College of Healthcare Executives (ACHE) and the Medical Group Management Association (MGMA), and management consulting associations, such as the Institute of Management Consultants and the Institute of Consulting. We discuss each characteristic in this section.

AUTONOMY

Autonomy is not listed in the codes of ethics, but it is nonetheless essential for consultants to possess because they must be able to make independent or unbiased assessments of their clients. The value of consultants' advice, recommendations, perspectives, reports, and overall service depends on their ability to be impartial.

An important foundation of autonomy is self-regulation. To self-regulate, consultants may turn to the codes of ethics of their respective professional association (such as ACHE or MGMA) and consulting society (see exhibit 15.1). The standards of conduct across all the codes are similar. Regularly checking your behaviors against these standards will help you not only correct or adjust your conduct but also develop and apply these standards.

EXHIBIT 15.1
Common Characteristics Represented in Healthcare and Consulting Codes of Ethics

Characteristic	American College of Healthcare Executives	Medical Group Management Association	Institute of Consulting	Institute of Management Consulting USA
Integrity	Having integrity		Having integrity	Having integrity
Competence	Maintaining competence		Showing competence	Showing competence
Fidelity	conducting professional activities with good faith; respecting professional confidences; disclosing financial and other conflicts of interest	Not abusing relationships in improper, economic, or other manner	Disclosing personal interests that may affect decisions; safeguarding confidential information	Appropriately treating all confidential client information; avoiding conflicts of interest
Honesty	Being honest		Being honest, open, and truthful	Not putting out deceptive advertising or misrepresentations
Justice	Being fair		Being reasonable and justifiable	Being objective and reasonable
Dignity	Enhancing dignity and image	Promoting the well-being of respective medical groups	Refraining from conduct that detracts from reputation	Not denigrating individual consultants, consulting firms, or the consulting profession
Commitment to learning	Continuing professional education		Continuing professional development	

INTEGRITY

In codes of ethics, integrity is a fundamental ethical principle and often one of the first desired attributes listed (see chapter 5). Healthcare management consultants who have integrity fulfill their commitments. For example, their *deliverables* (services or products delivered during or at the end of a project) meet the contract's specifications and schedules. Beyond keeping promises or agreements, managers with integrity are honest, fair, loyal, competent, and act with dignity. They know that their demonstrating integrity is "a factor of production as important as knowledge and technology" (Erhard, Jensen, and Zaffron 2016, 2). Integrity's placement at the top of the codes of ethics of consulting associations underscores its importance as the basis of successful client–consultant relationships.

Competence

competence
The ability to demonstrate and teach behaviors and skills associated with effective performance in a profession.

Effective and successful healthcare management consultants are exemplars of **competence**, defined as their being able to apply knowledge to carry out tasks, demonstrate high performance capabilities independently, and act with ethical awareness (Koskenvuori et al. 2019; Valizadeh et al. 2019; Vlasceanu et al. 2007). Competence is a common, expected attribute in the professional codes (appearing in three out of four columns in exhibit 15.1) because providing expert advice and sound recommendations not only benefits clients and their communities but also promotes the ethical principle of beneficence.

Moreover, as consultants show they are taking responsibility for their work and display their competence effectively, a trusting relationship builds between consultant and client as they enhance clients' abilities (Morin 2020). Thus, ethical competent consultants not only have the knowledge and skills but also the capability to teach what they know to clients, who may then spread or apply the information to their staff members, who may, in turn, develop their own competency.

Fidelity

Fidelity results when a promise or word is kept; like integrity, it is a foundational element of a successful client–consultant relationship. For healthcare management consultants, the ethical principle of fidelity is demonstrated through good stewardship. Good stewardship has two aspects: keeping confidences and avoiding conflicts of interest (see exhibit 15.2). Codes of ethics address both of these aspects multiple times and in multiple ways.

As good stewards, healthcare management consultants have a duty to maintain their clients' privacy and confidences. For example, they must not disclose to external parties the clients' proprietary data and information. In addition, healthcare management consultants have a **good-faith duty** to act solely on behalf of their clients' interests, not to practice self-dealing or act for personal gain. By being good stewards, consultants earn the respect of and build an ongoing relationship with their clients.

good-faith duty
The duty of healthcare management consultants to avoid conflicts of interests and self-dealing.

Honesty

The ACHE (2017) Code of Ethics states, "be truthful in all forms of professional and organizational communication, and avoid disseminating information that is false, misleading or

EXHIBIT 15.2
Two Aspects of Fidelity: Keeping Confidences and Avoiding Conflicts of Interest

Keeping Confidences

- Respecting professional confidence
- Keeping client information and records of client engagements confidential, and using proprietary client information only with the client's permission
- Respecting the intellectual property rights of clients, other consulting firms, and sole practitioners and not using proprietary information or methodologies without permission
- Not discussing with or disclosing to any person not authorized by the client or the client's delegated representative any information, data, results, report, or proposal arising from the assignment; not causing or allowing confidential information to be misused or to be published in any way without the permission of the client
- Safeguarding confidential information
- Safeguarding all confidential and proprietary information that comes into possession
- Treating appropriately all confidential client information that is not public knowledge by taking reasonable steps to prevent it from being accessed by unauthorized people
- Not using proprietary information or methodology without permission of its owner

Avoiding Conflicts of Interest

- Abiding by the good-faith duty
- Avoiding the improper exploitation of professional relationships for personal gain
- Disclosing financial and other conflicts of interest
- Not taking advantage of confidential client information for personal gain
- Disclosing to prospective or existing clients (before undertaking an engagement) any conflicts of interest (e.g., knowledge of specific client actions and information) that could compromise their success
- Not using information acquired during previous assignments that could in any way be detrimental to former clients
- Disclosing any personal interest that could affect managerial decisions
- Safeguarding confidential information and not seeking personal advantage from it
- Considering for each potential new engagement the possibility of it creating a conflict of interest or the perception of such a conflict, and, if such a conflict is identified, taking all reasonable steps to protect the interests and confidentiality of each client
- Neither offering nor accepting gifts, hospitality, or services that could create, or imply, an improper obligation
- Not taking advantage of proprietary or privileged information (either for personal use or the use of a client's firm or another client) without the client's permission
- Disclosing to the client any circumstances or interests that could influence personal judgment or objectivity

Sources: Information from ACHE (2017); Institute of Consulting (2018); Institute of Management Consultants USA (2018); MGMA (2015).

deceptive." The codes of ethics for consultants similarly address being honest and avoiding deceit and misrepresentations.

Honesty is more than just *not* lying. It is both a learned characteristic and a deliberate act of sincerity, frankness, candidness, and forthrightness. Honest consultants are scrupulously accurate, abiding by the many details of their deliverables. They are authentic and genuine when dealing with clients and others involved in their projects. By being honest, healthcare management consultants build trust and credibility among their clients.

Justice

Justice is represented in the codes of ethics by the terms *fair*, *objective*, *reasonable*, *legitimate*, and *justifiable*. Consulting fees and expenses, for example, should be reasonable, legitimate, and commensurate with the services delivered (Institute of Management Consultants USA 2018).

As mentioned earlier under the principle of autonomy, healthcare management consultants must avoid bias to maintain objectivity and impartiality. Avoiding bias requires attention and constant vigilance because consultants, like everybody else, have *unconscious* or *implicit bias*, which could cause consultants to unintentionally or incrementally commit unethical acts or big mistakes, such as fraud.

Unconscious bias refers to "associations or attitudes that reflexively alter our perceptions, thereby affecting behavior, interactions, and decision-making" (Marcelin et al. 2019, S62). As a result of unconscious bias, we may not spend the time or money or communicate sufficiently to provide benefit for someone who is of the "other" or not "like us." Research is replete with healthcare examples of racial disparities, including the ways in which patients are treated in healthcare and student selection to attend to healthcare professional graduate programs (FitzGerald and Hurst 2017; Maxfield et al. 2021; Narayan 2019). One step toward addressing potential unjust treatment of clients is to understand that unconscious bias exists, and then identifying your own biases. Self-awareness acts as a mitigating factor, and discriminatory behavior may be less likely to occur (Maxfield et al. 2021). Recognizing your own biases also may help you treat each client justly. However, recognition is only one step toward addressing the negative outcomes of unconscious bias. We discuss barriers to a just healthcare system and elaborate on the concepts of self-awareness, bias, and institutional and systemic discrimination in chapter 14. The main point here is that treating others justly—with honesty, fairness, and respect—is crucial to your successful performance as a consultant.

Dignity

Dignity and dignified behavior inspire clients' confidence in the competence and ability of the consultants particularly as well as in the healthcare sector generally. In the codes of ethics, dignity is reflected in the way consultants uphold the positive image and reputation of their profession by acting respectably and honorably. Consultants must not attack or disparage the work of other consultants and consulting firms (especially in the name of competition) because doing so is a disservice to not only the consultants' character but also the field. Simply put, if you sully the reputation of others and the career you represent, you sully your own character and honor.

Commitment to Learning

Healthcare management consultants must be able to perceive trends and detect changes in the healthcare environment, to identify problems and solutions common across the sector, and to apply current methods. Only by remaining up to date can consultants anticipate changes that will affect their clients. Thus, lifelong learning is an ethical imperative for consultants.

The Institute of Consulting's Code of Professional Conduct and Practice includes two standards for ongoing professional development. One standard addresses personal management and leadership practice, and the other standard is related to acting as a consultant and adviser. Consultants must stay informed on social and economic trends, upcoming laws and regulations, innovative analytic techniques, and projected or proposed changes. Taking continuing education courses, attending in-service training, and reading relevant publications are some of the ways consultants can acquire new knowledge or update their understanding.

Mini-Case Study: Consultants Settle, Pay $3.13 million

As a relator in a *qui tam* action, a former employee of V. J. Associates Inc. of New England blew the whistle regarding overbilling government contracts. Also known as *whistleblowers*, relators expose wrongdoing and can receive 15 to 30 percent of the recovered settlements from false claims actions. This whistleblower received 22.5 percent of the recovery.

More than half of the 50 states have their own False Claims Acts. In 2019, the defendants at the estimating consultant firm V. J. Associates settled allegations that it had overbilled, which is illegal under the False Claims Act. V. J. Associates had contracted with the states of Massachusetts, New Jersey, and New York on several building projects, one of which was the renovation of the Taunton State Hospital in Massachusetts (Briccetti 2020). From 2007 to 2018, the firm billed for hours not worked, and employees experienced pressure "from management . . . to not leave money on the table" (Fedderly 2020).

As an estimating consulting firm, V. J. Associates had been hired to forecast costs and resources for the project to be completed and estimate the time necessary to meet designated milestones in each project. Employees called this practice of overbilling "juicing"—they were billing for time spent working on other projects or tasks or even when they were not working (DOJ 2021). One former employee filed the lawsuit under the False Claims Act; the resulting investigation found that V. J. Associates had indeed overbilled by $1.2 million. V. J. Associates pleaded guilty to conspiracy to commit wire fraud; it was ordered to pay $3.13 million "in criminal and civil fines and restitution and be barred permanently from participating in contracts funded by the U.S. Department of Transportation" (DOJ 2021).

Mini-Case Study Questions

1. Which ethical principles and ethical standards were violated in this case? Refer to exhibit 15.1 and note which codes of conduct were not followed (e.g., the Institute of Management Consultants' position that consulting fees should be reasonable, legitimate, and commensurate with the services delivered).
2. If you were a consultant manager, how would you have avoided being in the position to "help manage" a fraudulent scheme? What would you do if you found yourself in this position?

Points to Remember

- The ideal characteristics of healthcare management consultants, as endorsed by codes of ethics, include autonomy, integrity, competence, fidelity, honesty, justice, dignity, and a commitment to learning.
- The value of consultants' advice, recommendations, perspectives, reports, and overall service depends on their ability to be autonomous and impartial.
- Integrity comprises many aspects of virtuous behavior, such as kindness, honesty, fairness, and uprightness.
- Competence is demonstrating a specific and measurable pattern of behaviors and knowledge that generates or predicts a high performance level in a given position or context of responsibilities.
- Fidelity is demonstrated through good stewardship in keeping confidences and avoiding conflicts of interest.
- By being honest, healthcare management consultants build trust and credibility among their clients.
- Justice is represented in the codes of ethics by the terms fair, objective, reasonable, legitimate, and justifiable. To maintain objectivity or impartiality, healthcare management consultants must avoid bias. In the codes of ethics, dignity is reflected in the way consultants uphold the positive image and reputation of their profession by acting respectably and honorably.
- Only by remaining up to date can consultants anticipate changes that will affect their clients. Thus, lifelong learning is an ethical imperative for consultants.

Challenge Yourself

1. The Shakespeare quote that opens the chapter is about lawyers. What characteristics and responsibilities do healthcare management consultants and lawyers share?
2. Your college friend works for a consulting firm that specializes in providing web services to large physician group practices and health plans. Your friend's boss has asked you to join the consulting firm, but you are concerned that you may not have the requisite competencies. You conduct a self-assessment using the Healthcare Leadership Alliance (HLA) Competency Directory at www.healthcareleadership alliance.org/directory.htm.

    You realize that three years of experience working as an associate administrator for finance at a medium-size community hospital has not prepared you for this consulting job. However, you decide that you want to pursue a consulting position two years in the future. Use the following worksheet as a guide (expand it as necessary) and list at least five competencies from the HLA Competency Directory that should be the focus of your continuing education. Remember, in chapter 3, we discussed the HLA's five competency domains: communication and relationship management, professionalism, leadership, knowledge of the healthcare system, and business skills and knowledge.

    Competency Worksheet

Domain	Competency
Domain 1: Communication and relationship management *Expand as necessary*	Demonstrate effective interpersonal skills

3. Your healthcare management consulting firm just received a request from the lead administrators of a small rural critical access hospital. The administrators are asking that your firm come on-site and then submit a report justifying a decision they have already made. Do you have an ethical problem with accepting this assignment? Why or why not? Relate your reasoning to the points made in exhibit 15.2.
4. You are a senior consultant in a large consulting firm. The director of the firm's human resources (HR) department is calling to inform you of a new client.

    One of the firm's partners and a senior consultant have already made a presentation, which the client liked so much that it engaged your firm. The scope of work, fees, and two-week schedule have been negotiated, and the contract has been signed. Just as the project is scheduled to start, however, the senior consultant who was involved in securing the account must step away from the project because of a family emergency. Per the firm's standard operating procedure, partners do not participate in project implementations but generate new clients and projects. Thus, you have been selected to take over with the other senior consultant's "junior" as a partner. You know this junior, but you have not worked with her.

The new client is a regional health center that is forming as a result of the merger of two community hospitals—one was run by an order of Catholic nuns, and the other was a for-profit associated with a national hospital corporation. The client wants your firm to assist with integrating and consolidating the two hospitals, including the following:

- Operating policies and procedures on employee evaluation, control, and compensation
- Hierarchy levels
- Reporting structures
- Executive titles

The HR director believes that you are the appropriate fill-in for this two-week project because you have been with the firm for six years and you have assisted with two healthcare organization–based projects. In one project, you guided a two-physician practice in setting up a scheduling system. In the other project, you helped a community hospital and a physician practice integrate their separate master patient indexes into an enterprise-wide patient index. As an incentive for you to accept the assignment, the HR director adds that the junior is an accounting whiz. However, you doubt your capability to help this time. It has been almost five years since you worked on healthcare operations–related assignments. Since then, your specialty has been strategic planning and product differentiation for competitive advantage. You wonder whether you should accept the assignment.

a. What should you say to the HR director?
b. How is your integrity involved?
c. What ethical principles are involved?

For Your Consideration

15.1 The ethical codes for healthcare managers and consultants emphasize the importance of integrity. Review the Case from the Field sections, the cases embedded in the chapter discussions, and the Mini-Case Study sections in this book (including this chapter), and select two examples of people acting with or without integrity. Then, using the following worksheet, identify the attributes of integrity depicted (+) or violated (–) in the selected cases. Include brief excerpts to illustrate or support your findings.

Check with your instructor to find out whether you

- have been assigned a Case from the Field, an example embedded in a chapter, or a Mini-Case Study, and
- will be reporting back to your peers to share your findings.

If you have not been assigned a specific case, make your selection based on what you find compelling. The worksheet example is Bob Allred's case in chapter 5, so you cannot select this case for this assignment.

Integrity Worksheet

Case Example: Crises Offer Us a Time to Reveal Our Character (Case from the Field, Chapter 5)

Attribute of integrity	Main person involved	Others involved (judge? other employees?)	Excerpt from case
	Bob Allred, administrator at Mountain State Hospital	Four psychiatrists who quit	
Truthful	(+) Did what he said he would	(+) Quit as they said they would	
Just	(+) Treated Bentley fairly	(−) Unfair, beneficence for patients but not for Bentley?	
Righteous	(+) Did the right thing		
Good	(+) Beneficence for all patients	(−) Beneficence for patients but not for Bentley?	
Coherent	(+) Behaviors matched beliefs	(−) Beneficence for patients but not for Bentley?	
Virtuous	(+) Acted with honesty, goodness, and fairness		
Compassionate	(+) Beneficence for all patients	(−) Beneficence for patients but not for Bentley?	
Willing to uphold values despite adversity	(+) Admitted Bentley despite staff members' opposition	(+) Quit despite having to find new positions	

15.2 Several ethical codes for healthcare managers and consultants mandate continuing professional development.
   a. Why do these codes mandate continuing education?
   b. What ethical principles does continuing education advance?
   c. Attending sessions at professional meetings to earn continuing education credits is one way to develop professionally. Describe at least three other ways that you could continue your professional development.

Check These Out

Want more information about the people, organizations, and concepts discussed in the chapter? Check these websites out.

- Healthcare Leadership Alliance Competency Directory: www.healthcareleadershipalliance.org/directory.htm
- Institute of Consulting: www.managers.org.uk/institute-of-consulting/
- Institute of Consulting Code of Professional Conduct and Practice: www.managers.org.uk/wp-content/uploads/2020/03/code-of-conduct.pdf
- Institute of Management Consultants: www.imcusa.org/page/ETHICS

References

American College of Healthcare Executives (ACHE). 2017. "Code of Ethics." Amended November 13. www.ache.org/-/media/ache/ethics/code_of_ethics_web.pdf.

Baumgart, A., and D. Neuhauser. 2009. "Frank and Lillian Gilbreth: Scientific Management in the Operating Room." *BMJ Quality & Safety* 18 (5): 413–15.

Biech, E. 2019. *The New Business of Consulting: The Basics and Beyond*. Hoboken, NJ: John Wiley & Sons.

Bricetti, P. 2020. "Estimating Consulting Firm to Pay $3.13 Million to Settle Overbilling Whistleblower Complaint." Whistleblower Network News. Published November 5. https://whistleblowersblog.org/2020/11/articles/false-claims-qui-tam-news/estimation-consulting-firm-to-pay-3-13-million-to-settle-overbilling-whistleblower-complaint/.

Erhard, W., M. C. Jensen, and S. Zaffron. 2016. "Integrity: A Positive Model That Incorporates the Normative Phenomena of Morality, Ethics, and Legality—Abridged." Working Paper No. 10-061, Harvard Business School Negotiation, Organizations & Markets Unit. Revised February 11. https://ssrn.com/abstract=1542759.

Fedderly, E. 2020. "NY Estimating Consultant Settles $3.1M Government Project Fraud Case." *Engineering News-Record.* Published November 3. www.enr.com/articles/50576-ny-based-estimating-consultant-settles-government-project-fraud-case-for-31m.

FitzGerald, C., and S. Hurst. 2017. "Implicit Bias in Healthcare Professionals: A Systematic Review." *BMC Medical Ethics* 18: Article 19.

Gilbreth, F. 1916. "Motion Study in Surgery." *Canadian Journal of Medicine and Surgery* 40: 22–31.

———. 1914. "Scientific Management in the Hospital." *Modern Hospital* 3: 321–24.

Gilbreth, L. 1914. *The Psychology of Management.* New York: Sturgis & Walton Company.

Institute of Consulting. 2018. "Code of Professional Conduct and Practice." Accessed April 9, 2021. www.iconsulting.org.uk/membership/professional_code_of_conduct.

Institute of Management Consultants USA. 2018. "IMC USA Code of Ethics." Accessed April 9, 2021. www.imcusa.org/?page=ETHICSCODE.

Jahn, M., S. Heiden, and B. Caldwell. 2018. "Identifying Improvements in Healthcare Systems Engineering Models for Chronic Care and Precision Medicine Applications." *Proceedings of the 2018 International Symposium on Human Factors and Ergonomics in Health Care* 7 (1): 218–23.

Koskenvuori, J., M. Stolt, R. Suhonen, and H. Leino-Kilpi. 2019. "Healthcare Professionals' Ethical Competence: A Scoping Review." *Nursing Open* 6 (1): 5–17.

Marcelin, J. R., D. S. Siraj, R. Victor, S. Kotadia, and Y. A. Maldoado. 2019. "The Impact of Unconscious Bias in Healthcare: How to Recognize and Mitigate It." *Journal of Infectious Diseases* 220 (Suppl. 2): S62–73.

Maxfield, C., M. Thorpe, N. Koontz, and L. Grimm. 2021. "You're Biased! Deal with It." *Journal of the American College of Radiology* 18 (1): 161–65.

Medical Group Management Association (MGMA). 2015. "Code of Ethics." Published September 29. www.mgma.com/MGMA/media/files/about/Code-of-Ethics-Approved.pdf.

Morin, K. 2020. "Is Consulting in Your Future?" *American Journal of Nursing* 120 (4): 51–57.

Narayan, M. 2019. "CE: Addressing Implicit Bias in Nursing: A Review." *American Journal of Nursing* 119 (7): 36–43.

Redekop, B. W., and B. L. Heath. 2007. "A Brief Examination of the Nature, Contexts, and Causes of Unethical Consultant Behaviors." *Journal of Practical Consulting* 1 (2): 40–50.

Rodman, C., N. Kelly, W. Niermeyer, L. Banks, A. Onwuka, E. Mason, and T. Chiang. 2020. "Quantitative Assessment of Surgical Ergonomics in Otolaryngology." *Otolaryngology—Head and Neck Surgery* 163 (6): 1186–93.

US Department of Justice (DOJ). 2021. "Government Contractor Sentenced for Fraudulently Billing Federal and State Construction Contracts." Published January 19. www.justice.gov/usao-ma/pr/government-contractor-sentenced-fraudulently-billing-federal-and-state-construction.

Vaisbuc, Y., J. Moore, R. Jackler, and J. Vaughan. 2018. "Operating Room Ergonomics: A Practical Approach for Reducing Operating Room Ergonomic Hazards." In *Advances in Human Factors and Ergonomics in Healthcare and Medical Devices*, edited by V. Duffy and N. Lightner, 462–68. Cham, Switzerland: Springer.

Valizadeh, L., V. Zamanzaeh, M. Deskandari, and S. Alizadeh. 2019. "Professional Competence in Nursing: A Hybrid Concept Analysis." *Medical-Surgical Nursing Journal* 8 (2): e90580.

Vlasceanu, L., L. Grunberg, and D. Parlea (compilers) and M. Seto and P. J. Wells (eds.). 2007. *Quality Assurance and Accreditation: A Glossary of Basic Terms and Definitions*, rev. ed. Bucharest, Romania: UNESCO. http://unesdoc.unesco.org/images/0013/001346/134621e.pdf.

Wiegmann, D. A., and T. M. Sundt. 2019. "Workflow Disruptions and Surgical Performance: Past, Present and Future." *BMJ Quality & Safety* 28 (4): 260–62.

Yost, E. 1949. *Frank and Lillian Gilbreth: Partners for Life*. New Brunswick, NJ: Rutgers University Press.

CHAPTER 16
BUILDING YOUR FUTURE AS A HEALTHCARE MANAGER

Knowing what's right doesn't mean much unless you do what's right.
—Theodore Roosevelt, 26th president of the United States

Important Terms

- Emotional intelligence
- Empathy
- Lifelong learning
- Motivation
- Self-awareness
- Self-development
- Social skill
- Toyota Production System
- Virginia Mason Production System

Learning Objectives

Studying this chapter will help you to

➤ answer why ethics matter in healthcare management,

➤ compare and contrast professional development and self-development,

➤ describe the five components of emotional intelligence,

➤ explain the role of ethics in emotional intelligence,

➤ develop a personal mission statement, and

➤ evaluate "walking the talk."

Based on our research for this book as well as our own experience, we propose that unethical behaviors by healthcare professionals often stem not so much from maleficence but from not understanding the ethical implications of one's actions. For example, contrast the acts to defraud Medicare and embezzle government property described in chapter 12 and the false claims schemes described in chapters 2 and 15 with the seemingly innocent day-in-the-life social media postings described in chapter 10. Often, healthcare professionals simply do not take the time to learn or consider thoughtfully the values and ethics of their professional responsibility. The work of healthcare professionals is important, and ethics matter.

In this chapter, we reiterate the importance of learning and applying ethical principles to healthcare situations. Our focus here, however, is professional and personal development—activities that will enable you to advance your career and encourage you to adhere to values and ethics. We draw on concepts and examples presented in earlier chapters to support this discussion. As you read the following Case from the Field, remember that this event spurred fundamental changes in the way Virginia Mason Medical Center operated. Virginia Mason still follows the guidelines and procedures implemented in this case, to the betterment of patient safety and care. Dr. Gary Kaplan (2018), Virginia Mason's chair and CEO, described how the organization built a culture of transparency:

> At Virginia Mason Medical Center in Seattle . . . every employee is considered a safety inspector regardless of job or title. All our team members are expected and encouraged to file a patient safety alert whenever he or she sees anything that poses an immediate or potential safety risk. This level of internal transparency is necessary because leaders and team members cannot correct problems unless they know they exist.

CASE FROM THE FIELD
Why Ethics Matter in Healthcare Management and Delivery

Mrs. McClinton

In 2004, a 69-year-old patient named Mrs. McClinton was undergoing treatment for a brain aneurysm at Virginia Mason Medical Center in Seattle, Washington. Instead of being injected with contrast dye or saline during the procedure, however, she was injected with a cleaning solution. She died 19 days after receiving the injection, during which time she had a stroke, two cardiac arrests, and her leg amputated below the knee in an attempt to save her life (Skolnik 2005).

What happened was a preventable medical error. No maleficence was intended. Three identical stainless steel bowls were placed next to each other in the procedure room. The first

> **CASE FROM THE FIELD**
> Why Ethics Matter in Healthcare Management and Delivery *(continued)*

bowl held saline, the second contrast dye, and the third a cleaning solution (chlorhexidine). The bowls were not labeled, and the liquids were all clear (Furman 2014). The solution to clean the skin used to be a brown povidone (iodine), but by the time of the procedure, it had been changed to the colorless chlorhexidine (Perry and Ostrom 2004).

Virginia Mason's chairman and CEO Gary Kaplan (2010) said this about the tragedy:

> *We failed her. She died of a preventable error. It was the deepest, darkest time in my career and in our organization's history. As soon as we found out what happened, we told our staff and then went public with the news.*

Kaplan's memo to the staff included this statement: "The essential truth of the matter was that no individual should be blamed—no individual would be blamed—because it was a system failure. Responsibility for the error rests with 'all of us'" (Kenney 2011, 59).

Virginia Mason

Virginia Mason was a tertiary care medical center that provided 336 beds and outpatient care and had regional clinics, a research center, and residency programs (Rakita et al. 2010, 882). When Kaplan became CEO in 2000, the healthcare industry reported a 3 percent error rate. To Kaplan, that rate was unacceptable, so he set out to direct Virginia Mason to perfect care as its goal. Moreover, when the board of directors asked, "Who's the customer?" he replied, "It's the patient" (Kaplan 2010, 146–47). The strategic team's examination of the work processes (*how* the work gets done), however, found that the patients were not the main customer—the providers were. That is, waiting rooms were designed for the convenience of the providers, not the patients; hours of operation reflected providers' work schedules, not patients' needs (Kaplan 2010, 147). From this assessment, the strategic planning team produced a strategic plan pyramid with the patient at the top. (To see this pyramid, visit www.virginiamason.org/workfiles/MIMP/VM_Strategic_Plan.pdf.)

Virginia Mason defined its vision, mission, and values by identifying what was important. The strategic plan detailed the organization's vision to be the quality leader; its mission to improve the health and well-being of its patients; and the values of teamwork, integrity, excellence, and service. Leadership had to communicate this plan to employees and gain their buy-in. Knowing the organizational values assisted leadership when a crisis occurred. As Kaplan (2010, 147) said about the placement of patients at the top of the strategic plan pyramid, "It is our true north and basic to everything we have done." At the bottom of the pyramid was the **Virginia Mason production system**, the foundation for achieving the vision.

(continued)

Virginia Mason production system
A policy that empowers employees to stop and report a process or practice that is unsafe or potentially harmful.

> **CASE FROM THE FIELD**
> Why Ethics Matter in Healthcare Management and Delivery *(continued)*
>
> ### VIRGINIA MASON PRODUCTION SYSTEM AND THE PSA PROGRAM
>
> Changing work processes was necessary to create and sustain a culture in which patients are first and to attain the overarching vision of being the quality leader. To help bring about these outcomes, Kaplan endorsed the Virginia Mason Production System, which was based on the **Toyota production system** (TPS). TPS was based on the assumption that humans make mistakes that are "reversible if they are caught soon enough" (Furman and Caplan 2007). On Toyota's production line, employees have the authority to stop production if they suspect something is awry.
>
> Introduced in 2002, the Virginia Mason production system promoted 100 percent patient safety by putting in place standardized, detailed descriptions of work processes as well as a culture that supported blame-free reporting. To this end, the Patient Safety Alert (PSA) program was instituted to give every employee the authority to "stop the line" (just as a Toyota worker would) when presented with "a situation that is likely to harm a patient to make an immediate report and to cease any activity that could cause further harm" (Furman and Caplan 2007). By 2006, managers, nurses, and nonclinical personnel were all making PSA reports.
>
> Typically, reports were made within 24 hours of the encounter with threats or incidents of error; the reports were then evaluated and resolved within two weeks. Personnel were not blamed for reporting but rather encouraged to do so, promoting a culture in which it was safe to speak up about mistakes (Furman and Caplan 2007). Moreover, Virginia Mason followed the practice of transparency, so unintended outcomes of errors had to be disclosed.
>
> An event that occurred at Virginia Mason between a nurse and a physician illustrates the organization's patient safety protocol. A nurse noticed that a patient had not received an echocardiogram or had a urine sample taken prior to receiving chemotherapy. It was protocol for a patient to have an echocardiogram to ensure a strong heart and a urine sample to test the patient's alkaline level (Kenney 2011, 53). The nurse informed the physician that the echocardiogram and the urine sample had not been done. In a patient-first culture, in which the patient is at the top of the pyramid, the physician's response should have been to order the tests. However, the physician did not do so and instead told the nurse to proceed with the chemotherapy treatment. The nurse refused and reminded the physician of the protocol; again, the physician ordered treatment to begin.
>
> Following PSA guidelines, the nurse stopped the line. She phoned the chief of Cancer Services to report the incident, and the chief contacted the physician and directed him to follow protocol (Kenney 2011). The physician then yelled at the nurse regarding her actions. The nurse again phoned the chief to report the physician's unprofessional behavior, and the chief backed the nurse. This event and the chief's support of the nurse following the PSA

Toyota production system
A policy of achieving zero defects, based on the assumption that mistakes are reversible if caught early enough.

> **CASE FROM THE FIELD**
> **Why Ethics Matter in Healthcare Management and Delivery** *(continued)*
>
> process gave credence to the program as a whole. Simply put, at Virginia Mason, once "You call in a PSA, we've got your back" (Kenney 2011, 53).
>
> ### THE ETHICAL RESPONSE
>
> Although the PSA program did not prevent Mrs. McClinton's death (which occurred two years into the program), it provided guidelines and created a culture that supported the organization's handling of the aftermath. First, Virginia Mason disclosed the incident and took full responsibility for it. Second, the chlorhexidine (the cleaning solution mistakenly injected into Mrs. McClinton) was placed on a swab to be applied on the skin, making the liquid impossible to put into a syringe. Third, the organization prioritized patient safety as its primary goal (Kenney 2011).
>
> In 2004, the Institute for Safe Medication Practices (ISMP), a nonprofit organization that educates people on safe medication practices, conducted the Medications Safety Self-Assessment Survey. Of the 1,600 hospitals that participated, 41 percent always labeled containers, 42 percent had inconsistent labeling practices, and 18 percent did not label at all (ISMP 2004). ISMP advocates the labeling of all solutions and medications. Healthcare professionals may confidentially report errors to ISMP; the primary purpose of such reporting is to educate and alert others about unsafe practices so that mistakes that happened in one place would not reoccur somewhere else.
>
> In the wake of Mrs. McClinton's death, Kaplan learned that two years earlier, the same medical error had been made "in another hospital in the Seattle community," but that hospital had not reported the event and had "kept quiet" (Kaplan 2010, 149). Cathie Furman (2014), senior vice president of quality and compliance at Virginia Mason, noted, "Just imagine if they had disclosed the error and we had been able to change our processes back then."
>
> At the time of this publication, the Virginia Mason production system remains in full force. The organization continues to train its employees on the system and annually sends more than 100 of its leaders to Japan to learn about TPS. Moreover, employees serve as certified leaders and conduct workshops. Furman (2014) described the impact of Mrs. McClinton's death this way: "Her death galvanized us. . . . On the one-year anniversary of her death, we came together as an organization to memorialize her. Her family joined us that day, and we committed then to setting aside a day every year to reflect on improvement of the past year in her memory and honor. It is the single most important day of the year at Virginia Mason." Mrs. McClinton's son said, "Mom fought to help and protect people all her life. It is only fitting that she helps people in death" (Lawrence Kahn Law Group 2020).
>
> *(continued)*

> **CASE FROM THE FIELD**
> Why Ethics Matter in Healthcare Management and Delivery *(continued)*
>
> ### Why Ethics Matter
>
> Mrs. McClinton's life—and the lives of many others who rely on healthcare professionals—is why ethics matter. Healthcare delivery organizations have a fiduciary duty to act in the best interest of others by disclosing their system failures in an effort to prevent further harm and, by extension, promote better practices. When Virginia Mason went public with the circumstances that led to Mrs. McClinton's death, it informed other hospitals so that they had information as they worked to improve their procedures and efforts on patient safety.
>
> Virginia Mason's transparency, production system, PSA program, patient-at-the-top organizational structure, and patient safety–focused culture adhere to the ethical principles of justice, beneficence, nonmaleficence, and autonomy. Such a conscious adherence to ethics enables the organization to foresee or prevent (as much as possible) an adverse event from occurring, but if it could not do so, to respond in the most appropriate manner.

Professional Development

lifelong learning
The practice of updating knowledge, learning new skills, and keeping up with trends and practices throughout a career to maintain professional competency.

Professional development requires a commitment to **lifelong learning**. The implicit message here is that we do not know everything and that healthcare is continually introducing changes that professionals have to know.

The responsibility for professional development is the professional's, although healthcare organizations do share in this responsibility. Virginia Mason, for example, provides its employees with professional development opportunities as part of its patients-first strategy and continuous improvement initiatives. Employees are trained on the PSA program and attend workshops focused on the Virginia Mason Production System.

Two components of professional development are membership in professional associations and self-development, which are discussed in the next sections.

Membership in Professional Associations

By simply becoming a member of a healthcare professional association, you are giving your career the opportunity to grow immensely. As a member, you may attend annual meetings, participate on committees, serve on the board, and sign up for seminars and webinars. Moreover, you could meet people with whom to network and to form a mentor–mentee relationship. You could learn much from these connections, many of whom will likely be experienced managers and leaders.

Consider, for example, the benefits of being a member of the American College of Health Care Administrators (ACHCA). Every year, ACHCA offers a Summer Leadership Conference, a weeklong themed educational program. (In 2021, the theme was "Lead with a Shared Vision," focusing on how managers can create a culture in which their employees are empowered to provide patients with better care and experience.) The conference is open to all members, who are encouraged to network with other professionals in long-term care settings. ACHCA also provides self-study courses that members can complete for continuing education credits. The content of these courses is reviewed by members of ACHCA's education committee to ensure that pertinent, current information is included.

No matter which professional association you join, you should keep this in mind: Learn the association's code of ethics, conform to that code, and practice the standards until you have internalized and made them part of your professional norms. The administrator of a state hospital in the Case from the Field in chapter 5 said that we should become familiar with the code of ethics for our profession because "if you haven't taken time in the front end to learn about values and ethics and views on important issues, you are likely to be weak when you are needed to be strong." Use this code as your ethical guide for as long as you work in healthcare management.

SELF-DEVELOPMENT

Self-development is the self-directed process of gradually improving character, knowledge, abilities, and other traits. While professional development is geared toward your career, self-development is aimed at your personal growth—although such growth contributes greatly to professional development.

Emotional intelligence, a written personal mission statement, and the inclination to walk the talk (earn trustworthiness) are three (of many) indicators that a person is engaged in self-development. Self-development is a process. Meeting your personal mission and improving your emotional intelligence skills help you to develop professionally. Moreover, serving as an ethical example once you have reached the mid- or senior level of your career encourages professional development in others.

Self-development is guided by personal values, professional codes of ethics, and general ethical principles (which are discussed throughout this book).

self-development
The self-directed process of gradually improving character, knowledge, abilities, and other traits.

EMOTIONAL INTELLIGENCE

Psychologist and journalist Daniel Goleman (1998) advanced the concept of **emotional intelligence**, which is the ability to manage oneself and one's relationships with others.

emotional intelligence
The ability to manage oneself and one's relationships with others.

Emotional intelligence comprises five components: self-awareness, self-regulation, motivation, empathy, and social skill. Each of these components is a skill that can be learned for the purpose of professional and personal development. In their article, health administration professors Brenda Freshman and Louis Rubino (2002) build the case for emotional intelligence as a core competency for healthcare leaders and managers (recall our discussion of competencies in chapter 3). Research has identified a number of positive outcomes of healthcare managers' ability to practice emotional intelligence; it may help with leadership development (Holt and Wood 2017), retention of nurses (Majeed and Jamshed 2021; Wang et al. 2018), bullying in the workplace (Meires 2018), and reducing stress (Cascio et al. 2017). We are not proposing that mastery is *the* key to all success, as research has found mixed support for positive outcomes (Lea et al. 2019), but we are suggesting that mastering emotional intelligence skills will benefit your professional development and your ability to serve the needs of others and your organization.

Mastery of a high emotional intelligence skill set helps people not only get along well with colleagues but also focus on delivering quality healthcare in a time of limited resources. Freshman and Rubino (2002, 2) note that as healthcare managers, we must contend with difficult questions, such as "How do we give access to our health care delivery system when there is a large percentage of the population with no ability to pay?" Moreover, we must address issues such as "How do we gain employee buy-in on measures designed to improve patient quality or ensure patient privacy?" Our ability to identify these issues and address them effectively may be enhanced by developing our emotional intelligence skill set.

Self-Awareness

self-awareness
In a professional context, one's understanding of her motivations, strengths, weaknesses, and effect on others.

Goleman (2013, 52) links **self-awareness** with the ability to hear an inner voice, a heartbeat. He writes, "How well people can sense their heartbeats has, in fact, become a standard way to measure their self-awareness." Can you sense your own heartbeat? Are you consciously aware if your heart is beating faster or slower and in what settings this occurs? If so, your self-awareness is higher than those who are not aware of their own beating heart.

Being self-aware is an asset both personally and professionally. That is, if you understand all the things that define you as a person—character, thoughts, attitudes, motivations, preferences, beliefs, desires, talents and skills, needs, weaknesses, strengths, and others' perception of you—then you tend to be better equipped (than those who are less self-aware) to identify areas for self-improvement and then create a change or development plan that suits you. For instance, as Goleman (1998, 96) suggests, if you know that deadlines "bring out the worst" in you, you can plan to complete work way ahead of the due date so as to prevent stress and unpleasant interactions with people. Moreover, self-awareness also helps improve the way you behave and the way you handle people and crises—in and out of the workplace.

Taking the time to reflect on who you are; doing self-assessments; listening to feedback from people (including peers, bosses, mentors, professors, and preceptors) who may give you their honest, objective opinions; and acting on the evaluations you received are just of the some steps to becoming self-aware. (See Dye 2017 for more strategies on becoming self-aware.) The last part of the previous sentence—acting—is especially important. It means doing something with the information, knowledge, or awareness (apply it; try it; teach it; use it as an example, evidence, or support material; build on it) so that something beneficial can emerge. Cultivating self-awareness allows you to "identify and overcome" your blind spots and help you achieve balance—what you do to serve others without forgetting to take care of yourself as well (Dye and Garman 2015, 17).

Although it is not related to self-awareness per se, consider the Case from the Field in chapter 9, in which we present the ideal example of doing something good with the information at hand. Dr. Frances Oldham Kelsey reviewed and approved drugs for the US Food and Drug Administration. Despite heavy pressure from a pharmaceutical company that wanted to sell thalidomide (an anti-nausea drug for pregnant women) in the United States, Dr. Kelsey delayed her approval until the company had conducted more tests to prove the drug's safety. During this delay, reports from other countries vindicated Dr. Kelsey's staunch refusal. The drug turned out to cause deformities in babies in utero. Her action prevented the drug's entry into the US market.

Self-Regulation

According to Goleman (1998), self-regulation is the ability to think before acting and to control disruptive impulses or moods. When you remain calm (especially during a crisis) and focused on the issues in front of you instead of allowing emotions to take charge (which could cloud your professional judgment), you are self-regulating.

Self-regulation is the mastery of remaining calm and focused on the issues, not on the mood. As an example, recall the Mini-Case Study in chapter 10 about the Texas nurses who served as patient advocates. The nurses questioned the physician's treatment of patients, including his sale of elixirs to patients. When the nurses tried to present their concerns to the hospital's board of directors, a board member interrupted them and effectively shut down their attempt to inform the board of improper physician conduct. The board member illustrated poor self-regulation (by interrupting and ending the discussion without listening to the nurses' concerns).

Additionally, in chapter 5's Case from the Field, some clinicians at a mental health facility displayed a lack of self-regulation. They delivered an emotional plea and threatened to (and some later did) resign from their positions if the administrator allowed a violent but mentally ill prisoner to be treated at the hospital.

Healthcare managers who cannot self-regulate may find themselves

- jumping to conclusions before seeking or learning all the facts;
- choosing sides in a conflict between two direct reports or between two patients, instead of being an unbiased mediator;
- acting in an abusive or a belligerent manner when they are upset or (worse) on a regular basis;
- being critical without offering corrective options or solutions; or
- holding a grudge, being too distant (which could read as cold or uncaring) or too friendly (which could read as unprofessional or needy) and having an inconsistent and unpredictable management style.

MOTIVATION

motivation
The reason for action.

Motivation is the passion to work and actively address challenges (Goleman 1998). Consider the motivation behind the US military's Cooperative Strategy for 21st Century Seapower (see the Mini-Case Study in chapter 11). This joint effort by the US Navy, Marine Corps, and Coast Guard was driven not only by the need to protect and defend American interests from threats but also by the desire to spread American goodwill to allied nations and people in need. The humanitarian part of this motivation is the reason hospital ships—like the USNS *Comfort*—are deployed to help with relief efforts. The *Comfort* itself has a set of motivations for each action it takes. During its mission in Haiti, for example, the clinicians and staff on the ship performed certain procedures but skipped others—because they were focused on providing culturally appropriate care, deferring to the local health policy at the time, and being mindful of the country's scarce resources and inability to supply further care.

As an aspiring healthcare manager, you should begin to identify your own professional motivations—your reasons for doing what you do. Why do you want to work in healthcare? Why do you think healthcare administration is the right field for you? Engaging in this exercise is good practice for the multitude of whys you will face and self-reflection you will need as a manager.

EMPATHY

empathy
The consideration of others' emotions and situations that allows one to feel the same way.

Empathy refers to the thoughtful consideration of others' emotions so that you may conduct yourself accordingly (Goleman 1998). The Tuskegee Study, discussed in chapter 8, lasted 40 years, during which the human subjects were exploited by the researchers, suffered painful conditions, witnessed their loved ones getting infected, and died without treatment. It was not until a whistleblower spoke to a reporter—who, in turn, passed the story to another reporter who wrote and published it in a small newspaper, which was then picked up by the *New York Times*—did the study finally come to end. The people involved in pointing out the immorality of the study, in reporting its existence, and in shutting down the program exhibited empathy.

By empathizing—or putting yourself in someone else's shoes, so to speak—you can better see the human implications of an action. Healthcare managers with empathy, for example, design and implement a work process while considering how such a change would affect the workers' daily functions, their satisfaction with their job, their ability to develop new skills, their relationship with each other and their superiors, and so on.

Social Skill

Social skill is the ability to "find common ground and build rapport" (Goleman 1998, 95). For healthcare managers, social skill can be defined as the ability to move "people in the direction you desire" (Freshman and Rubino 2002, 6). Moreover, this ability may aid you to inspire others and help them grow professionally, and they, in turn, may encourage still others to develop this skill (Drigas and Papoutsi 2018). Take, for example, Mahatma Gandhi (see the Case from the Field in chapter 6), who represents a servant leader who used his social skill to mobilize his community toward a better future. For Gandhi, that future was an independent India. Additionally, Gary Kaplan (see the Case from the Field in this chapter) introduced and worked to gain organization-wide support for the adoption of the Virginia Mason production system. For him, that future was a healthcare organization that promoted 100 percent patient safety.

social skill
The ability to form, manage, and sustain a connection or a relationship with others.

Personal Mission Statement

A personal mission statement is a written declaration of who you are, what you value or what is important to you, what goals you want to accomplish, and what you contribute (or aim to contribute) to society. This statement may be short (a few sentences) or long (a few paragraphs). Regardless of length, a personal mission statement speaks volumes about your convictions, your interests, your influences, and your aspirations. As such, it can be used as a guide for both professional and personal development.

Your mission statement should reflect an understanding of professional associations' codes of ethics and missions (see exhibits 5.1 and 5.2 in chapter 5 to review the vision, mission, and values statements of the American College of Healthcare Executives and ACHCA). It could also include your answers to the following questions (Dye 2017, 295):

◆ What is my purpose in life?

◆ What is my ultimate personal goal?

- What is my ultimate professional goal?
- What do I enjoy doing most?
- How and where do I make the most impact?
- How would I like my obituary to read?

Exhibit 16.1 offers two examples of a personal mission statement (written by students in an undergraduate health services management course).

A great illustration of a healthcare professional who follows her personal mission is detailed in the Case from the Field in chapter 12. In it, we discuss Jean Zoeng, the owner

Exhibit 16.1
Sample Personal Mission Statements

The following mission statements are used here (unedited) with permission from two students enrolled in a health services management program.

Mission Statement 1
I am at my best when I am working on things that encourage, enlighten and excite others.
I will try to prevent times when I feel restricted or in distress. I will enjoy my work by continuing to dream big, unite with others, and share my vision. I will find enjoyment in my personal life through making others laugh, meeting new people, being [adventurous] and traveling.
I will look for opportunities to use my natural talents & gifts such as acting, sense of humor, leadership skills and creativity. My journey in life is to enjoy every moment finding laughter, love, and happiness with each day that passes. I pursue to find success and significance in living. I will seek out and experience all of the pleasures and joys that life has to offer. I will be a person who has inspired limitless people to take control of their lives, love themselves for who they are, achieve anything they set their mind to, think big and live accordingly to their own guidelines. My most essential future contribution to others will be to show people that it is perfectly fine to be different, to think outside of the box and to have a creative mind. I will strive to incorporate characteristics such as confidence, honesty, and integrity into my life. I will continually replenish myself by focusing on the four dimensions of my life, which are God, family, friends, and fitness. I want to leave this world with no regrets.

Mission Statement 2
I am an honest, confident woman with a sense of humor who hopes to soon graduate college with honors and to find a job soon after that will lead to a career. I will do this by learning to set reachable goals for myself and I will strive for excellence while reaching these goals in both my academic and personal life. I hope to become a successful healthcare manager and do this by leading others by example while showing initiative, lifting others up, and being dependable. Above all else I will treasure the opportunities and challenges in my life and learn from all of them.

of a rehabilitation clinic who not only envisioned a facility in which the employees and the practices are ethical but also created such a facility and a culture to support it.

EARNING TRUST BY WALKING THE TALK

In Peter Drucker's (1988, 18) article "Leadership: More Doing Than Dash," he emphasized that "earning trust is a must." Trust is earned by acting consistently, exhibiting integrity, and meaning what you say. Simply put, trust is "walking the talk"—that is, keeping your promise, backing your words with action, and living by your values and personal mission.

Throughout this book, we have presented examples of healthcare leaders and managers who indeed walk the talk. The Case from the Field in chapter 4, for example, features executives at Virginia Mason Medical Center making the decision to implement a mandatory influenza vaccination policy for all employees. This policy is a walking-the-talk initiative in that it brings to life the organization's vocalized commitment to putting patients first.

Such an action earns trust. This trust may be between healthcare administration and employees and between the organization and the patients or public it serves. It shows that the organization is not just all talk but is also able and committed to do the walk. For healthcare managers, walking the talk is a foundation for their successful professional development.

MINI-CASE STUDY: PROBLEMS AT THE VA HEALTHCARE SYSTEM (2013–21)

In 2009, President Barack Obama appointed Eric Shinseki as secretary of the US Department of Veterans Affairs (VA), the federal department responsible for providing healthcare and federal benefits to American veterans and their dependents. Shinseki was assigned 16 initiatives to bring the VA into the twenty-first century. One of the 16 initiatives was to enhance veterans' experience with and access to healthcare (AMVETS 2011, 2).

In 2013, CNN was among the news outlets reporting that veterans were experiencing delayed care at the William Jennings Bryan Dorn Veterans Medical Center in Columbia, South Carolina (Bronstein, Black, and Griffin 2013). In fact, the delays were so serious that six veterans died while waiting for months to receive necessary diagnostic procedures. The waiting list for appointments had grown to 3,800 people in 2011. The VA launched an investigation into the GI Clinic at Dorn and found several issues, including low staff census (not enough clinical staff); leadership turnover that resulted in a lack of understanding of roles, responsibilities, and system processes; and program coordination (VA 2013).

Allegations of long wait times also emerged at VA facilities in Arizona and the VA Pittsburgh Healthcare System (Bronstein and Griffin 2014; Wereschagin 2014). However, such allegations were not new. Between 2005 and 2014, the VA Office of Inspector General (OIG) issued 18 reports about lengthy wait times (VA 2014). Moreover, the *New York Times* (2014) reported that VA patient wait times have been a problem since 1999. Delays, however, were not the only issues in these VA facilities. In the Phoenix VA Health Care System, for instance, there were claims of manipulated patient wait times, bad scheduling practices, and patient deaths.

In 2014, the IOG launched an investigation into these allegations. Two questions were addressed in this review (VA 2014, ii):

1. Did the facility's electronic wait list (EWL) purposely omit the names of veterans waiting for care and, if so, at whose direction?
2. Were the deaths of any of these veterans related to delays in care?

The investigators confirmed "inappropriate scheduling issues throughout the VA health care system" (VA 2014, iii).

At the Phoenix VA specifically, investigators found that 1,400 veterans did not have a primary care appointment but were listed on the EWL and that 1,700 veterans were waiting for a primary care appointment but were not listed on the EWL. (Until names are added on the EWL, the wait time does not officially begin.) Because veterans were not on EWLs, the Phoenix VA leadership "significantly understated the time new patients waited for the appointments" (VHA 2014, iii). Moreover, wait times varied by what was reported and by what actually occurred. Reviewing a sample of 226 appointments, the Phoenix VA reported an average wait time of 24 days for a first primary care appointment and less than half (43 percent) of these patients waited more than 14 days (VA 2014, iii). The investigators, however, found that the average wait time was 115 days for the first primary care appointment and about 84 percent of these patients waited more than 14 days.

The OIG report concluded as follows (VA 2014, iii):

> Our reviews have identified multiple types of scheduling practices that are not in compliance with VHA policy. Since the multiple lists we found were something other than the official EWL, these additional lists may be the basis for allegations of creating "secret" wait lists.

Secretary Shinseki called the finding "reprehensible" (Fahrenthold 2014) and resigned from his post on May 30, 2014 (Simon and Muskal 2014).

The outcomes of these "reprehensible" events included reduced trust in the VA system, loss of credibility in its system, and concerns about access to healthcare (Penn et al. 2019). The Veterans Choice Act of 2014 initiated the Veterans Choice Program and directed the expansion of access to care (with VA covering the costs) to the private sector, allowing veterans who have to wait longer than 30 days for an appointment or travel more than 40 miles to use a VA clinic to seek treatment at another facility (Gurewich et al. 2020). A review of wait times from 2015 to 2018 showed that the program did indeed reduce wait times for both Black and white veterans who lived in rural and urban communities (Gurewich et al. 2020). However, Black veterans had longer wait times for physical therapy (on average, three days longer), and 31 percent of Black veterans compared with 25 percent of white veterans experienced wait times of more than

45 days for dental or ophthalmology care. The concept of racial disparities was discussed in chapter 14 with regard to fairness and social justice for all. This disparity is also apparent in veterans' access to healthcare.

Comparing wait times in the private sector and VA medical centers from 2014 to 2017, researcher Madeline Penn and colleagues (2019) found improvement at the VA over time. In 2017, for example, wait times for new appointments were shorter than those in the private sector for primary care, dermatology, and cardiology, while orthopedic wait times remained longer for VA patients as opposed to the private sector (Penn et al. 2019).

In 2019, the Veterans Choice Act was replaced with the Maintaining Internal Systems and Strengthening Integrated Outside Networks (MISSION) Act, which allowed veterans to seek private sector healthcare (with the VA paying for the care) based on service availability, service quality, distance traveled to receive the service, and wait times of more than 20 days for primary and mental health care (28 days for specialty care) (Massarweh, Itani, and Morris 2020). However, given that wait times for veterans to receive services at the VA were shorter than those in the private sector, and given the extra costs associated to the VA, there are questions about the ability of the MISSION Act to address the underlying root issue—veterans' access to healthcare.

The COVID-19 pandemic also affected veterans' access to healthcare. VA facilities reduced operating hours and personnel, resulting in more veterans seeking care in the private sector. Between October 2019 and June 2020, veterans waited 41.9 days on average for an appointment in the private sector, still leaving veterans without timely access to healthcare (Selnick 2021).

Mini-Case Study Questions

1. Define the problems at the VA (in 2014 and 2021).
2. Evaluate the ethics of having 1,700 veterans who were not listed on the EWL wait for a primary care appointment at the Phoenix VA.
3. Explain why Secretary Eric Shinseki resigned his position.
4. Actions were taken to address the problems. With reference to the actions taken, what other issues have emerged that require attention? Evaluate the ethics regarding these "other" issues.

Points to Remember

➤ Professional development requires a commitment to lifelong learning.

➤ Two components of professional development are membership in professional associations and self-development.

➤ Self-development is the self-directed process of gradually improving character, knowledge, abilities, and other traits.

- ➤ Emotional intelligence, a written personal mission statement, and the inclination to walk the talk (or trustworthiness) are three (of many) indicators that a person is engaged in self-development.
- ➤ Emotional intelligence is the ability to manage oneself and one's relationships with others.
- ➤ The five components of emotional intelligence are self-awareness, self-regulation, motivation, empathy, and social skill.
- ➤ A personal mission statement is a written declaration of who you are, what you value or what is important to you, what goals you want to accomplish, and what you contribute (or aim to contribute) to society.
- ➤ Walking the talk means keeping your promises, backing your words with action, and living by your values and personal mission.

Challenge Yourself

1. Consider the chapter-opening quote by Theodore Roosevelt: "Knowing what's right doesn't mean much unless you do what's right." Think of an example in which this might be true for you as you prepare to become a healthcare manager.
2. When dealing with a crisis event, why do you think transparency in reporting is important?
3. How would you assess a healthcare organization's status regarding transparency? Would the results of such an assessment influence whether you would like to work there? Why or why not?
4. Identify professional activities that you plan to engage in to enhance your own professional development.

For Your Consideration

16.1 Executive search consultant Carson Dye (2017) created an Emotional Intelligence Evaluation Form (see the appendix at the end of this chapter). You can use this questionnaire as a tool for obtaining feedback from your peers, instructors, preceptors, and bosses. While the questionnaire was not originally developed as a subjective tool for evaluating yourself, it contains questions that help you reflect on certain aspects of yourself. Identify the questions about emotional intelligence, self-awareness, self-regulation, motivation, empathy, and social skill, and then assess yourself on those aspects. How did you rate your emotional intelligence? What strengths did you identify? What aspects would you like to improve?

16.2 Write your own personal mission statement. For reference, you may use the information provided in this and other chapters, and you may consider the questions presented in the emotional intelligence questionnaire. You may also review exhibit 16.1, which shows sample personal mission statements from two of our students, and you may Google the key term "personal mission statement" for more examples. Your search may take you to websites that offer tips and hints for not only writing a statement but also living that mission. Once you have completed writing, reflect on the ethics of your statement. What did you consider important? Why was it important to you?

References

AMVETS. 2011. "VA Performance and Accountability Report." Accessed June 18, 2015. www.amvets.org/pdfs/legislative_pdfs/2012/VA-Performance-and-Accountability- Report-11-15-11.pdf.

Bronstein, S., N. Black, and D. Griffin. 2013. "Hospital Delays Are Killing America's War Veterans." CNN. Published November 20. www.cnn.com/2013/11/19/health/veterans-dying-health-care-delays/.

Bronstein, S., and D. Griffin. 2014. "A Fatal Wait: Veterans Languish and Die on a VA Hospital's Secret List." CNN. Published April 23. www.cnn.com/2014/04/23/health/veterans-dying-health-care-delays/.

Cascio, M., P. Magnano, I. Parenti, and A. Plaia. 2017. "The Role of Emotional Intelligence in Health Care Professionals Burnout." *International Journal of Healthcare and Medical Sciences* 3 (2): 8–16.

Drigas, A., and C. Papoutsi. 2018. "A New Layered Model on Emotional Intelligence." *Behavioral Sciences* 8 (5): 45.

Drucker, P. 1988. "Leadership: More Doing Than Dash." *Wall Street Journal*, January 6, 18.

Dye, C. 2017. *Leadership in Healthcare: Essential Values and Skills*, 3rd ed. Chicago: Health Administration Press.

Dye, C., and A. Garman. 2015. *Exceptional Leadership: 16 Critical Competencies for Healthcare Executives*, 2nd ed. Chicago: Health Administration Press.

Fahrenthold, D. 2014. "How the VA Developed Its Culture of Coverups." *Washington Post*. Published May 30. www.washingtonpost.com/sf/national/2014/05/30/how-the-va- developed-its-culture-of-coverups/.

Freshman, B., and L. Rubino. 2002. "Emotional Intelligence: A Core Competency for Health Care Administrators." *Health Care Manager* 20 (4): 1–9.

Furman, C. 2014. "Terrible Tragedy—and Powerful Legacy—of Preventable Death." Posted March 26. www.virginiamasoninstitute.org/terrible-tragedy-and-powerful-legacy-of-preventable-death/.

Furman, C., and R. Caplan. 2007. "Applying the Toyota Production System: Using a Patient Safety Alert System to Reduce Error." *Joint Commission Journal on Quality and Patient Safety* 33 (7): 376–86.

Goleman, D. 2013. "The Focused Leader." *Harvard Business Review* 91 (12): 50–60.

———. 1998. "What Makes a Leader?" *Harvard Business Review* 76 (6): 93–102.

Gurewich, D., E. Beilstein-Wedel, M. Schwartz, H. Davila, and A. Rosen. 2020. "What Are the Predictors of Wait Times for Veterans Seeking Care in the VA and the Community Through VA-Purchased Care?" *Health Services Research* 55 (Suppl. 1): 57–58.

Holt, S., and A. Wood. 2017. "Leadership and Emotional Intelligence." In *Leadership Today*, edited by J. Marques and S. Dhiman, 111–38. New York: Springer Publishing.

Institute for Safe Medication Practices (ISMP). 2004. "Loud Wake-Up Call: Unlabeled Containers Lead to Patient's Death." Published December 2. www.ismp.org/Newsletters/acute care/articles/20041202.asp.

Kaplan, G. S. 2018. "Building a Culture of Transparency in Health Care." *Harvard Business Review*. Published November 9. https://hbr.org/2018/11/building-a-culture-of-transparency-in-health-care.

———. 2010. "Seeking Perfection in Healthcare." In *Lessons Learned in Changing Healthcare . . . and How We Learned Them*, edited by P. Batalden, 145–59. Toronto: Longwoods.

Kenney, C. 2011. *Transforming Health Care: Virginia Mason Medical Center's Pursuit of the Perfect Patient Experience*. Boca Raton, FL: CRC Press.

Lawrence Kahn Law Group. 2020. "McClinton vs. Virginia Mason Medical Center." Accessed May 31, 2021. www.lklegal.com/case-study-mcclinton-vs-virginia-mason-medical-center.

Lea, R., S. Davis, B. Mahoney, and P. Qualter. 2019. "Does Emotional Intelligence Buffer the Effects of Acute Stress? A Systematic Review." *Frontiers in Psychology*. Published April 17. https://doi.org/10.3389/fpsyg.2019.00810.

Majeed, N., and S. Jamshed. 2021. "Nursing Turnover Intentions: The Role of Leader Emotional Intelligence and Team Culture." *Journal of Nursing Management* 29 (2): 229–39.

Massarweh, N., K. Itani, and M. Morris. 2020. "The VA MISSION Act and the Future of Veterans' Access to Quality Health Care." *Journal of the American Medical Association* 324 (4): 343–44.

Meires, J. 2018. "The Essentials: Using Emotional Intelligence to Curtail Bullying in the Workplace." *Society of Urologic Nurses and Associates* 38 (3): 150–53.

New York Times. 2014. "Major Reports and Testimony on VA Patient Wait Times." Updated June 9. www.nytimes.com/interactive/2014/05/29/us/reports-on-va-patient-wait-periods.html.

Penn, M., S. Bhatnagar, S. Kuy, S. Lieberman, S. Elnahal, C. Clancy, and D. Shulkin. 2019. "Comparison of Wait Times for New Patients Between the Private Sector and United States Department of Veterans Affairs Medical Centers." *JAMA Network Open* 2 (1): e187096.

Perry, N., and C. Ostrom. 2004. "Hospital Details What Went Wrong: Woman Dies from Toxic Injection." *Seattle Times*. Published November 25. http://community.seattletimes.nwsource.com/archive/?date=20041125&slug=deathfolo25m.

Rakita, R., B. Hagar, P. Crome, and J. Lammert. 2010. "Mandatory Influenza Vaccination of Healthcare Workers: A 5-Year Study." *Infection Control and Hospital Epidemiology* 31 (9): 881–88.

Selnick, D. 2021. "A New VA Wait-Time Scandal Is Brewing." *Courier Times*. Posted March 8. www.buckscountycouriertimes.com/story/opinion/2021/03/08/op-ed-new-veterans-affairs-wait-time-scandal-brewing/4592183001/.

Simon, R., and M. Muskal. 2014. "Eric Shinseki Steps Down as VA Chief amid Wait List Scandal." *Los Angeles Times*. Published May 30. www.latimes.com/nation/nationnow/la-na-nn-shinseki-resigns-20140530-story.html.

Skolnik, S. 2005. "Woman's Family Sues Virginia Mason over Fatal Medical Mistake." Published March 23. www.seattlepi.com/local/article/Woman-s-family-sues-Virginia-Mason-over-fatal-1169307.php.

US Department of Veterans Affairs (VA). 2014. "Veterans Health Administration Interim Report: Review of Patient Wait Times, Scheduling Practices, and Alleged Patient Deaths at the Phoenix Health Care System." Published May 28. www.documentcloud.org/documents/1174886-vaoig-14-02603-178.html.

———. 2013. "Allegations of Mismanagement of the GI Clinic, Dorn VAMC Columbia, SC." Published March 25. http://i2.cdn.turner.com/cnn/2013/images/11/20/aibreport.pdf.

Wang, L., H. Tao, B. Bowers, R. Brown, and Y. Zhang. 2018. "When Nurse Emotional Intelligence Matters: How Transformational Leadership Influences Intent to Stay." *Journal of Nursing Management* 26 (4): 358–65.

Wereschagin, M. 2014. "Nearly 700 Pittsburgh Area Vets Stuck on VA Wait List." Published May 29. http://triblive.com/news/allegheny/6198875-74/veterans-care-list.

APPENDIX: CARSON DYE'S EMOTIONAL INTELLIGENCE VALUATION FORM

This form is reprinted with permission from Dye (2017, 375–83). Copyright Foundation of the American College of Healthcare Executives.

Emotional intelligence is a person's maturity quotient. Maturity is the ability to manage emotions, make sound decisions, positively influence others, and be self-aware. The questions in this instrument assess the emotional intelligence of a person in the workplace on the basis of the perception of those she/he works with directly or has worked with directly in the past.

Directions: Read each question carefully and circle the answer that most appropriately describes the person being evaluated. There are no right or wrong answers, but carefully reflect on each question and answer.

You have been asked to evaluate _____ along several interpersonal dimensions. Five or more individuals—peers and subordinates—are completing this questionnaire. When you are finished, please return your questionnaire to _____, who will compile the results and provide summary averages to the person named above. Because the questionnaire does not require your name, your participation is anonymous; please do not share your responses with anyone.

What is your relationship to the person being evaluated? Please check one.

_____ Peer (work at same organization)
_____ Peer (work elsewhere)
_____ Subordinate
_____ Superior (full-time paid boss)
_____ Superior (voluntary board member)
_____ Other

1. This leader creates the feeling that she/he looks forward to each day with positive anticipation.

Strongly Disagree	Disagree	Neither Disagree nor Agree	Agree	Strongly Agree
1	2	3	4	5

2. This leader truly believes that her/his work really makes a difference in her/his organization.

Strongly Disagree	Disagree	Neither Disagree nor Agree	Agree	Strongly Agree
1	2	3	4	5

3. This leader has an even temper.

Strongly Disagree	Disagree	Neither Disagree nor Agree	Agree	Strongly Agree
1	2	3	4	5

4. This leader rarely gets frustrated.

Strongly Disagree	Disagree	Neither Disagree nor Agree	Agree	Strongly Agree
1	2	3	4	5

5. This leader has the creative ability to solve problems among people.

Strongly Disagree	Disagree	Neither Disagree nor Agree	Agree	Strongly Agree
1	2	3	4	5

6. This leader truly enjoys being with other people.

Strongly Disagree	Disagree	Neither Disagree nor Agree	Agree	Strongly Agree
1	2	3	4	5

7. This leader has strong control over her/his emotions.

Strongly Disagree	Disagree	Neither Disagree nor Agree	Agree	Strongly Agree
1	2	3	4	5

8. When times get tough in the work setting, others can turn to this leader for guidance.

Strongly Disagree	Disagree	Neither Disagree nor Agree	Agree	Strongly Agree
1	2	3	4	5

9. When mistakes are made, this leader's first instinct is to take corrective action (rather than place blame).

Strongly Disagree	Disagree	Neither Disagree nor Agree	Agree	Strongly Agree
1	2	3	4	5

10. Other people would describe this leader as a person who does not "fall apart" under pressure.

Strongly Disagree	Disagree	Neither Disagree nor Agree	Agree	Strongly Agree
1	2	3	4	5

11. This leader is well suited for her/his career.

Strongly Disagree	Disagree	Neither Disagree nor Agree	Agree	Strongly Agree
1	2	3	4	5

12. If this leader had the chance to start her/his career all over again, she/he would still choose a leadership position.

Strongly Disagree	Disagree	Neither Disagree nor Agree	Agree	Strongly Agree
1	2	3	4	5

13. This leader respects other people.

Strongly Disagree	Disagree	Neither Disagree nor Agree	Agree	Strongly Agree
1	2	3	4	5

14. This leader is highly motivated.

Strongly Disagree	Disagree	Neither Disagree nor Agree	Agree	Strongly Agree
1	2	3	4	5

15. Others would say this leader has her/his ego under control.

Strongly Disagree	Disagree	Neither Disagree nor Agree	Agree	Strongly Agree
1	2	3	4	5

16. This leader has an appropriately high level of self-esteem.

Strongly Disagree	Disagree	Neither Disagree nor Agree	Agree	Strongly Agree
1	2	3	4	5

17. Although this leader may at times get upset or angry, she/he has the ability to control emotions.

Strongly Disagree	Disagree	Neither Disagree nor Agree	Agree	Strongly Agree
1	2	3	4	5

18. This leader has an appropriately high level of motivation.

Strongly Disagree	Disagree	Neither Disagree nor Agree	Agree	Strongly Agree
1	2	3	4	5

19. This leader always seeks win–win solutions in conflict situations.

Strongly Disagree	Disagree	Neither Disagree nor Agree	Agree	Strongly Agree
1	2	3	4	5

20. This leader would be the last person I would describe as a hopeless individual.

Strongly Disagree	Disagree	Neither Disagree nor Agree	Agree	Strongly Agree
1	2	3	4	5

21. Although impatient for positive results, this leader does not allow her/his impatience to create a negative working environment.

Strongly Disagree	Disagree	Neither Disagree nor Agree	Agree	Strongly Agree
1	2	3	4	5

22. This leader is a person whom others trust.

Strongly Disagree	Disagree	Neither Disagree nor Agree	Agree	Strongly Agree
1	2	3	4	5

23. This leader is appropriately self-confident without being overbearing.

Strongly Disagree	Disagree	Neither Disagree nor Agree	Agree	Strongly Agree
1	2	3	4	5

24. This leader is sensitive to others' feelings.

Strongly Disagree	Disagree	Neither Disagree nor Agree	Agree	Strongly Agree
1	2	3	4	5

25. This leader listens well.

Strongly Disagree	Disagree	Neither Disagree nor Agree	Agree	Strongly Agree
1	2	3	4	5

26. The last description you would expect to hear of this leader is "flies off the handle a lot."

Strongly Disagree	Disagree	Neither Disagree nor Agree	Agree	Strongly Agree
1	2	3	4	5

27. This leader maintains a good balance in life.

Strongly Disagree	Disagree	Neither Disagree nor Agree	Agree	Strongly Agree
1	2	3	4	5

28. This leader is emotionally stable and healthy.

Strongly Disagree	Disagree	Neither Disagree nor Agree	Agree	Strongly Agree
1	2	3	4	5

29. This leader faces setbacks and adversity well.

Strongly Disagree	Disagree	Neither Disagree nor Agree	Agree	Strongly Agree
1	2	3	4	5

30. This leader would not be described as hostile.

Strongly Disagree	Disagree	Neither Disagree nor Agree	Agree	Strongly Agree
1	2	3	4	5

31. This leader has developed good mechanisms to get feedback from others.

Strongly Disagree	Disagree	Neither Disagree nor Agree	Agree	Strongly Agree
1	2	3	4	5

GLOSSARY

accountability for reasonableness (A4R): A theory that uses due process to set priorities in healthcare decision-making.

accountable care organization (ACO): A group of providers that collaborate to give coordinated and improved care and aim to reduce costs by being mindful of healthcare expenditures.

advance healthcare directive: A legal document that specifies a person's preferences for treatments, life-sustaining technology, and other medical care; written before and used after the person becomes incapacitated or can no longer make decisions.

altruism: Sacrificing oneself for the public good.

American College of Health Care Administrators (ACHCA): The professional association for administrators of long-term care facilities.

American College of Healthcare Executives (ACHE): The professional association for those in the healthcare management profession.

authorized users: Individuals and groups that need to access a patient's record to fulfill their official job-related duties and responsibilities.

autonomy: The ethical principle of making decisions independently or for oneself.

Belmont Report: A report that provides the ethical foundation for biomedical and behavioral research in the United States; published in 1979 as *Ethical Principles and Guidelines for the Protection of Human Subjects of Research*.

beneficence: The ethical principle of acting to help or benefit others.

best interests standard: A standard whereby the patient's surrogate (or a court) makes healthcare decisions based on the best interests of the patient.

big data: Extremely large data sets that are analyzed using specialized computational methods to reveal patterns and associations.

boundary crossing: A deviation from an established professional role or boundary that may or may not be for a therapeutic purpose (e.g., provider self-disclosure, checking in on a former patient).

boundary violation: A boundary crossing that creates a reasonable risk of exploitation or harming the patient's care.

business intelligence: Knowledge that organizations create by using computer-based techniques to identify, extract, and analyze their data for patterns.

case consultation: The institutional ethics committee process of hearing and reviewing an ethical conflict and then advising all the parties involved on the next most appropriate steps to take.

casuistry: An ethical decision-making approach that relies on a case's facts, complexity, relevant laws, and unusual circumstances to determine a judgment.

categorical imperative: An unconditional, absolute (without exceptions or qualifiers) moral requirement.

certificate of need (CON): Required written approval issued by a state agency for proposed new services, buildings, and other plans.

charisma: The special personal appeal that disarms and draws in other people.

civil disobedience: The concept of resisting a law for the sake of standing up for what is morally right.

civil monetary penalties: Fines imposed by federal agencies for violating laws or regulations.

claim: An itemized request that a provider (organization or individual practitioner) submits to a payer (health insurance plan, Medicare, or another payer) for reimbursement of services rendered.

client: In consulting, an organization or a person who uses the services of a management consultant.

climate-smart healthcare: The implementation of resilient healthcare strategies for the more efficient use of materials and wise waste management to produce a healthier environment.

clinical ethics: A subset of bioethics in which the moral issues arise from the delivery of healthcare and services or from general clinical practice.

clinician: A professional—such as a physician, nurse, physician assistant, advanced practice nurse, physical therapist, counselor, clinical psychologist, or other clinical practitioner—who provides hands-on healthcare and services.

code of ethics: Standards of behavior and conduct for members of a profession.

Common Rule: Uniform set of regulations on the ethical conduct of research involving human subjects established by the federal agencies that fund such research; formally, the *Federal Policy for the Protection of Human Subjects.*

competence: The ability to demonstrate and teach behaviors and skills associated with effective performance in a profession.

competencies: The knowledge and skills needed to be considered proficient in a profession.

compliance: An action that conforms to established rules.

confidentiality: The expectation by individuals that the information they share is kept private or disclosed (to select, trusted parties) only when necessary and with their consent.

corporate social responsibility (CSR): A concept that refers to companies' commitment to working ethically, mindful of the social, economic, and environmental concerns of their stakeholders and the communities in which they work.

credentialing: The process of collecting, evaluating, and verifying the education and training, license, work history, references, and criminal background of physicians who apply for practice privileges.

cultural humility: Taking a humble and respectful interpersonal stance toward individuals from other cultures that involves challenging one's own cultural biases and approaching learning about other cultures as a lifelong process.

culturally competent and sensitive care: Healthcare that is aware, considerate, and respectful of patients' cultural and ethnic backgrounds and practices.

data breach: The illegal use or disclosure of confidential health information that compromises the privacy or security of it and poses a risk of financial, reputational, or other types of harm to those affected.

defense mechanism: A mental and emotional strategy to avoid feelings of anxiety or guilt over a wrongdoing.

digital health literacy: The knowledge and skills needed to use digital health information, including literacy skills, basic knowledge of computers, and understanding of online health information.

direct report: An employee who works under and is managed by an immediate superior or boss.

distributive justice: The unequal allocation of scarce resources according to morally relevant factors.

downstream social marketing: A social marketing campaign that focuses on influencing or changing individual behavior.

duty of care: A responsibility under fiduciary duty that requires an individual or a group to act with the care and prudence any reasonable entity would do.

electronic health record (EHR): A computerized or digitized record containing a patient's health-related information.

emotional intelligence: The ability to manage oneself and one's relationships with others.

empathy: The consideration of others' emotions and situations that allows one to feel the same way.

enlightened self-interest: An ethical theory that holds that individuals maximize benefits to the self while minimizing harm to others.

ethical branch: A major category of ethics composed of clusters and families of theories that share characteristics or functions.

ethical conflict: Any problem or situation that has an ethical component; a situation in which ethical principles seem to collide.

ethical decision-making process: The rational, step-by-step process of weighing facts, emotional and situational concerns, and ethical principles.

ethics: A system of beliefs and behaviors that people value and use to guide their conduct; the study of the moral life.

evidence-based management: A practice whereby the approaches that consistently yield desirable results are examined, tailored to fit a specific need, and strategically applied.

False Claims Act: A federal law passed in 1863 that prohibits businesses, groups, and individuals from defrauding the US government; healthcare organizations are subject to this law because Medicare and Medicaid are government programs involving claims and payments.

Federally Qualified Health Center: A clinic that receives government funds for providing affordable, good-quality, comprehensive healthcare services to an underserved community.

fee schedule: A list of medical services and procedures and their costs developed by healthcare providers for billing and claims purposes.

federal-wide assurance of compliance (FWA): A written, binding, formal commitment by an institution to comply with applicable regulations on research using human subjects.

fiduciary duty: The duty of an individual or a group to act in the best interest of another individual or group.

good-faith duty: The duty of healthcare management consultants to avoid conflicts of interests and self-dealing.

groupthink: A manner of thinking in which every member of the group supports the dominant perspective and thus fails to consider alternative or contradictory ideas.

healthcare management consultant: A professional with skills, knowledge, and expertise in healthcare business operations and management who provides external, objective advice to clients.

healthcare policy: The implementation of health goals that affect costs, quality, and access to healthcare.

health disparities: A particular type of health difference linked to social, economic, or environmental disadvantage that is unjust and avoidable.

health equity: Pursuing the highest standards of health for all people, including the elimination of health disparities.

health informatics: The study, invention, and implementation of structures and algorithms to advance communication, understanding, use, and management of health data and information.

health information technology (health IT): Electronic devices and systems used to store, share, manipulate, analyze, display, and generate patient- and provider-specific health data and information; also referred to as *health information* or *communications technology and systems*.

Health Insurance Portability and Accountability Act of 1996 (HIPAA): A federal law that set the standards for protecting the privacy of patients' health information.

health literacy: The ability to understand and act on health information.

health policy: The defining of health goals with a vision for improving the health of the people and the communities in which they live.

implicit bias: Unconsciously associating stereotypes with certain groups of people and behaving accordingly.

informational justice: The decision to give or share only pertinent information.

informed consent: A patient's written agreement to receive care, services, diagnostic or therapeutic procedures, and other medical interventions with full knowledge of the risks and benefits.

institutional ethics committee (IEC): A permanent organizational committee that provides advice and support on clinical ethics issues.

institutional review board (IRB): An administrative body established to protect the rights and welfare of human subjects recruited to participate in research activities.

integrity: A person's honest, virtuous, and thus trustworthy quality.

internship: Nonclassroom, practical training for students or new graduates in their field of study.

internship preceptor: An intern's practitioner supervisor.

interoperability: The capability of electronic health records and related health information technology products or applications to be shared and to be functional across at least two different organizations.

interprofessionalism: Healthcare professionals from different disciplines working together collaboratively for better patient care.

Joint Commission: An independent, not-for-profit organization that provides accreditation or certification to healthcare organizations and programs in the United States.

justice: The ethical principle of administering deserved rewards or penalties that are aligned with legal and moral standards.

law: A rule enacted by a legislative body, such as the US Congress or a state legislature; regulation is a rule established by an executive agency to carry out a law.

law fallacy: Invocation of the law when faced with an ethical conflict.

LEED-certified: Certification provided when a building is designed, constructed, operated, and maintained according to set environmental standards.

Lexington Model: A risk management program for disclosing errors that was instituted at Lexington Veterans Affairs Medical Center following a patient's death.

lifelong learning: The practice of updating knowledge, learning new skills, and keeping up with trends and practices throughout a career to maintain professional competency.

mandated reporter: An individual who holds a professional position (e.g., healthcare provider, counselor, teacher) and is required by state law to report specified information to an appropriate agency (e.g., child abuse to social services).

meaningful use: The use of electronic health records and related technology within a healthcare organization to achieve specified objectives.

medical futility: The professional opinion that continuing medical treatment is no longer a viable option for a patient.

Medical Group Management Association (MGMA): The professional association for medical practice administrators.

moral agent: A person who can rationally evaluate right and wrong; who has the power to take voluntary action; who has moral obligations, duties, and responsibilities to act; whose action can be evaluated; and who is accountable for his or her actions.

moral blindness: Insensitivity to or ignorance of the ethical implications of one's actions.

moral courage: The ability to stand up for what is ethically right with confidence and commitment

moral disengagement: The process of convincing the self that ethical standards do not apply to oneself in a particular context.

moral distress: Psychological distress that occurs when individuals perceive a moral obligation and feel constrained from acting ethically; consequently, they may experience symptoms and a compromised sense of agency.

moral injury: The end state of an egregious violation or repeated moral distresses that interfere with the ability to provide care in keeping with moral beliefs and expectations, leading to a state of burnout.

moral leadership: Leadership characterized by courage to do the right or ethical thing no matter what.

motivation: The reason for action.

National Alliance on Mental Illness (NAMI): A national mental health organization dedicated to building better lives for Americans affected by mental illness.

nonmaleficence: The ethical principle of refraining from actions that could harm others.

Nuremberg Code: A set of ten statements requiring that human participation in research must be voluntary and informed.

Office for Civil Rights (OCR): An office within the US Department of Health and Human Services that protects people's basic rights and investigates complaints of violations of the Privacy Rule of the Health Insurance Portability and Accountability Act of 1996.

Office for Human Research Protections (OHRP): The agency within the US Department of Health and Human Services (HHS) that protects the rights, welfare, and well-being of subjects involved in research conducted or supported by the HHS.

Office of Research Integrity (ORI): The agency within the US Department of Health and Human Services that oversees and directs activities for research integrity in the US Public Health Service.

operations management: The management of any product, service, process, resource, or activity that enables an organization to be productive and sustainable.

patient dumping: To refuse care or transfer medically unstable patients because of their inability to pay.

Patient Protection and Affordable Care Act (ACA): A 2010 federal law that introduced extensive healthcare system reforms, including expanding access to private insurance and Medicaid coverage and strengthening consumers' rights and protections.

persistent vegetative state (PVS): A clinical condition in which the patient is completely unaware of the environment or surroundings and is incapable of cognitive thinking or activity.

physician health program (PHP): A state-based program that helps impaired physicians get treatment and rehabilitation so that they can return to practice.

physician impairment: A physician's inability to provide safe, competent care to patients because of physical or mental illness or substance abuse or dependence.

precautionary principle: A decision-making rule developed in environmental law stating that in cases of serious or irreversible threats to the health of humans or ecosystems, acknowledged scientific uncertainty should not be used as a reason to postpone preventive measures (i.e., err on the side of prevention).

principle: A general prescriptive judgment.

principlism: An ethical decision-making approach that uses the four ethical principles—respect for autonomy (self-determination), nonmaleficence (do no harm), beneficence (do good), and justice (fairness)—as a standard for judgment or resolution.

privacy: The right of individuals to limit others' access to their body, thoughts, and feelings.

Privacy Rule: A regulation under the Health Insurance Portability and Accountability Act of 1996 that protects the privacy, use, and disclosure of people's own medical records and other health information.

privileging: The approval of a physician's privileges to perform designated procedures in a facility.

procedural justice: Fair procedures that ensure fair or equitable outcomes.

profession: A body of knowledge shared by a group of individuals with specialized education and training and common values.

professionalism: The knowledge, skills, abilities, and conduct expected of practitioners of a profession.

professional norms: Internalized standards of conduct to which professionals automatically and unconsciously conform.

professional role: The assigned and expected functions, responsibilities, and working relationships of a person in a professional position.

Quadruple Aim: The goals of improving the patient experience, the health of the population, and the provider's experience while reducing healthcare costs.

quality assurance: A program for monitoring and evaluating a product or service to ensure that quality standards are met and proper procedures are followed.

qui tam: A legal action, under the False Claims Act, filed by an individual (e.g., a whistleblower) on behalf of the government.

rationalization: Justification or plausible excuse for inappropriate actions or decisions.

referent: An entity, such as a professional association, to which its members look for guidance.

relator: A private citizen who sues on behalf of the government under the False Claims Act.

root-cause analysis: A comprehensive systems-based investigation of the factor(s) that caused an adverse event; the analysis not only addresses the event under investigation but also results in action plans to prevent future events.

security: The use of managerial, personnel, operational, and technical controls to ensure that information systems and applications run effectively and support the confidentiality, integrity, and availability of data and information.

self-awareness: In a professional context, one's understanding of her motivations, strengths, weaknesses, and effect on others.

self-development: The self-directed process of gradually improving character, knowledge, abilities, and other traits.

self-regulation: The ability to govern or monitor oneself.

situational context: The circumstances of a decision, such as aspects of the issue, organizational structure, ethical climate, leadership's expectations, and peers' influence, as well as the person's personal situation.

social determinants of health: The environments and conditions in which people are born, grow, work, live, and age, including factors that affect their health, functioning, and quality of life.

social marketing: Influencing the behavior of individuals and the community to achieve a common good.

social skill: The ability to form, manage, and sustain a connection or a relationship with others.

stakeholder: A person or group that has a stake in the organization and is affected by the organization's actions and decisions.

stakeholder theory: A theory that extends business ethics to address the rights and interests of people who interact with the business and are affected by its decisions.

stewardship: Acts that enhance the sense of the healthcare organization's commitment to the community and increase public trust in the healthcare organization.

stigma: A mark that is defined negatively and, as a consequence, may cause an individual to be subjected to discrimination.

strategic planning: The process of identifying a desired future state and then establishing goals and objectives to realize that state.

strategic planning cycle: The cyclical process of assessment, prioritization, and scheduling.

study protocols: A preestablished set of procedures for ethical research.

substituted judgment standard: A standard whereby a patient's surrogate makes healthcare decisions based on the patient's previously expressed preferences or known values and beliefs.

supply chain management: Actions planned and taken to ensure that products needed for healthcare workers and patients are created, transported, and able to be used or consumed so that the process is efficient, timely, and cost-effective.

surrogate: An individual appointed to make healthcare decisions for a person if that person becomes incapacitated or can no longer make decisions; also known as an *agent*, *proxy*, or *representative*.

systematic knowledge: Facts, tools, and theories of a field organized into a unique body of knowledge.

Tarasoff duty: The duty to warn a potential or intended victim about an imminent danger or threat recognized in many jurisdictions.

third-party payer: An entity that pays or reimburses a healthcare provider for the services rendered to a patient.

Toyota production system: A policy of achieving zero defects, based on the assumption that mistakes are reversible if caught early enough.

transparency: A policy of sharing information and communicating directly, honestly, and in a timely manner.

Triple Aim: The goals of improving the patient experience and the health of the population while reducing healthcare costs.

Tuskegee Study: A 40-year syphilis study on 600 African American men in Macon County, Alabama, that misinformed its subjects and prevented treatment for the syphilitic men in the group.

upstream social marketing: A social marketing campaign that focuses on influencing or changing systems, policies, and other structural components.

utility: The worth or value of an object to someone; in utilitarianism utility was proposed as a measure of goodness in promoting happiness.

value: A basic and fundamental belief of the members of a profession.

Virginia Mason production system: A policy that empowers employees to stop and report a process or practice that is unsafe or potentially harmful.

whistleblower: An individual who exposes and reports corporate wrongdoing.

INDEX

Note: Italicized page locators refer to exhibits.

Abandonment: informed consent and, 176
Abbas, Amina, 253, 256, 257
ABC: anthrax attack at, 306
Abington of Glenview Nursing Home (Illinois): social media and certified nursing assistant abusers at, 210–11
ACA. *See* Patient Protection and Affordable Care Act
Academic credentials: certification based on, 19; selected, *18*
Academic health centers: research conducted in, 148
Access: to care, in iron triangle, 302, 304; to healthcare information, beneficence and, 290; to healthcare services, distributive justice and, 180, 190; health disparities and, 316, 321; to nutritious food, 324
Accountability, 289. *See also* Transparency
Accountability for reasonableness (A4R): definition and key elements of, 180
Accountable care organizations, 7; definition of, 231; information about, website, 245; Quadruple Aim and, 232; Triple Aim and, 232
Accreditation: competencies and, 13; educational and training programs and, 19
Advanced practice nurses, 171
Advance healthcare directives, 96, 128, 184–85

Adverse childhood experiences: cumulative, disease and, 316
Adverse events: definition of, 188; root-cause analysis of, 189
Aetna: data breaches at and settlement related to, 269
Affective responses: judgments influenced by, 135
Affordable Care Act. *See* Patient Protection and Affordable Care Act
Agency for Healthcare Research and Quality: quality indicator surveys, 318; website of, 324
Agency for Toxic Substances and Disease Registry: actions taken to respond to 9/11, *305*
Agramonte, Aristides, 159–60
Alcohol abuse: physicians and, 215, 216
Allred, Bob, 86, 87, 88, 90, 92, 97, 345
Alt, Suzanne, 37
Altruism: definition of, 14
Amazon, 283
American Academy of Family Physicians: support for mandatory flu vaccination for healthcare workers, 65; website of, 78
American Academy of Medical Administrators, *18*
American Academy of Pediatrics: support for mandatory flu vaccination for healthcare workers, 65, 66–67; website of, 78
American Cancer Society: breast cancer statistics, 262

American College of Health Care Administrators, *18,* 134; Code of Ethics, 85, 90–91, 93, 95, 98; membership in, benefits of, 355; preamble and four expectations of members in Code of Ethics of, 91; vision, mission, and values of, 90, *91*; website of, 98

American College of Healthcare Executives, *18,* 47–48, 55, 134; Code of Ethics, 15, 21, 23, 56, 58, 59, 60, 85, 88–90, 93, 95, 98, 115, 135, 217, 338; common characteristics of healthcare management consultants in Code of Ethics, 336, *337;* Ethics Self-Assessment, 59, 60; Ethics Toolkit, 128; Gold Medal Award, 11; *Healthcare Executive Competencies Assessment Tool,* 51, 60; Health Information Confidentiality policy statement, 60; preamble and six parts of Code of Ethics, 88–90; vision, mission, and values, *89*; website of, 98

American College of Medical Practice Executives, 48

American College of Physicians: physician impairment position paper, 216; support for mandatory flu vaccination for healthcare workers, 65; website of, 78

American College of Surgeons: minimum standards for hospital records, 275

American Hospital Association, *18*; Patient Care Partnership, 173; support for mandatory flu vaccination for healthcare workers, 65; website of, 78

American Medical Association: electronic health record framework, 282–83; ethical guidelines of, 178–79; opinions on physicians and the health of the community, website, 224; physician impairment paper, 215

American Medical Directors Association: support for mandatory flu vaccination for healthcare workers, 65

American Nurses Association: Code of Ethics, 224; Code of Ethics, Provision 3 of, 220; support for mandatory flu vaccination for healthcare workers, 65; What Nurses Do, 224

American Organization of Nurse Executives, 48

American Public Health Association: support for mandatory flu vaccination for healthcare workers, 65; website of, 78

American Red Cross: actions taken to respond to 9/11, 305

American Society for Healthcare Risk Management: *Risk Management Pearls on Disclosure of Adverse Events,* 74; on risk managers' responsibilities, 206; website of, 78

Americans with Disabilities Act, 116, 179

Amputations: in Haiti, stigma attached to, 240

Anchoring trap, 137, *137*

Anthrax attacks, 304, 305–6

Antivirus software, 289

Application programming interface, 282

Applied ethics, 27, 29–30, 38; bioethics, 38; business ethics, 38; organizational ethics, 38; profession-specific ethics, 38

Aristotle, 33

Arizona Telemedicine Program, 181

Artificial intelligence: breast cancer care and, 115, 158; robotics and, 27

Artificial nutrition and hydration, 186

Asimov, Isaac, 45, 59

Assessment phase: in strategic planning cycle, 234, 242, 243

Assisted living administrators: licensure of, 19

Assisted-living facilities: vaccine mandates for employees in, 310

Associated Press, 306

Association for Professionals in Infection Control and Epidemiology: support for mandatory flu vaccination for healthcare workers, 65; website of, 78

Association of University Programs in Health Administration, 12, *18,* 19, 261

Atrial fibrillation, 158

Austin-Travis County Emergency Management Service, 71

Authorized users, 281; access to electronic health records and, 277–78; definition of, 277; types of, 278

Autonomy, 16, 23, 171, 204, 282, 285, 288, 340; American College of Healthcare Executives Code of Ethics based on, 90; clinical practice and, 171, 190; in context of post-shooting events at University Medical Center (Arizona), 219; CVS's Minute Clinic strategy and, 235; definition of, 213, 222; end-of-life decisions and, 184, 191; Full Motion Innovations Case from the Field and, 256–57; healthcare management consultants and, 336, 338, 342; human resources and, 213–14, 222; informed consent and, 173, 176; medical futility and, 128, 129, 142; organizational values and, 133; partnering with internship programs and, 261; physician impairment and violation of, 216; physician rating websites and, 291; price practices and, 199; professional *vs.* patient, 16; US military's humanitarian efforts in Haiti, 2010 earthquake and, 240; Vidant Health's acquisition of Pungo Hospital and, 238

Baby Boomers: MinuteClinic growth and, 235
"Balance after" bill, 205, 206
Banaji, Mahzarin, 293
Bassett, Angela, 307
Bazerman, Max, 293
Beauchamp, Tom, 212, 213
Becerra, Xavier, 313
Behaving ethically, 36–37, 39
Belmont Conference Center, 152
Belmont Report, 151, 152, 153, 158, 163; concept of autonomy and, 173; three ethical principles of, *152*; website of, 166
Beneficence, 20, 30, 113, 118, 159, 171, 282; American College of Healthcare Executives Code of Ethics based on, 89; *Belmont Report* and, *152*; clinical practice and, 171, 190; in context of post-shooting events at University Medical Center (Arizona), 219; COVID-19 vaccination campaign and, 313; crisis preparedness and, 304; CVS's Minute Clinic strategy and, 235; definition of, 111, 213, 222; duty to warn and, 177; end-of-life decisions and, 184, 191; Full Motion Innovations Case from the Field and, 256; health disparities viewed through lens of, 321; human resources managers and, 213, 222; informed consent and, 176; medical futility and, 128, 130, 142; mobile mammography efforts and, 263; organizational values and, 133; partnering with internship programs and, 261; patient dumping and violation of, 302; physician credentialing and, 218; physician impairment and violation of, 216; physician rating websites and, 291; promoting, ethical conflicts and, 180; supply chain management and, 265; US military's humanitarian efforts in Haiti, 2010 earthquake and, 240; Vidant Health's acquisition of Pungo Hospital and, 238; withdrawal of life support and, 185
Benefits Health System (Montana): vaccine mandates for employees at, 310
Bentham, Jeremy, 32, 33
Bentley, Harold, 86, 87, 88, 90, 92
Berkey v. Anderson, 174

Berwick, Donald, 231
Best interests standard, 129, 185
Bias: avoiding, consultants and justice and, 340, 342; in decision-making, 136, 142; four sources of, 293; implicit, 319, 322, 340; unconscious, 340
Biden, Joe, 233
Biech, Elaine, 334
Big data, 284, 285, 292; definition of, 283; "five Vs" of, 285
Billing, 211; false, 252, 253, 256, 257; overbilling, 341–42; surprise, 115, 200, 203, 205, 206; truth in, 254
Bioethics, 30, 38
Bioterrorist attacks, 305–6
Blackbaud: data breach at Trinity Health and, 288
Blue Cross, 22
Board of directors: disclosure of medical errors and, 74; fiduciary duty of a member of, 68
Bodenheimer, Thomas, 232
Body of learning: as core component of a profession, 10, 11
Boetto, Erik, 157
Boston University School of Medicine, 150
Boundaries: crossing/not crossing, clinical ethics and, 178–79, 190
Boundary crossing: definition of, 178
Boundary violation: definition of, 178
Bowen, Deborah J., 127, 132, 135
Brain death, 103, 107
Brain drain, 35
Brain injuries: end-of-life decisions and, 184
"Breaking the glass": in electronic health record systems, 286
Breast cancer: care for, artificial intelligence and, 115, 158; detection of, mobile mammography units and, 262–63; statistics on, 262
Breastfeeding: health benefits for infants and mothers, 321
Breuning, Stephen E., 155
Brown, Kate, 309
Bullying: workplace, emotional intelligence and, 356
Bundled payments, 205, 319
Burnout, 232; electronic health records and, 281; moral distress and, 139
Burr, Richard, 306
Bush, George W., 186, 304, 307
Business ethics, 30–31, 38
Business intelligence, 287; definition of, 283; reduction in medical errors and, 284

Business skills and knowledge domain: for healthcare management profession, 49, 343
Butler, Stuart, 6
Buxton, Peter, 161, 162

Calling, professional: answering, 15–16, 23
Cancer: racism and incidence of, 317
Candio, Christine M., 9, 11, 15
Canterbury v. Spence, 174
Capacity: definition of, 173
Capitation, 319
Capstone experience, 22
Cardinal virtues, 33
Cardiovascular health: structural racism and, 317
Career levels: different, professionalism and its development at, 50
Care ethicists: key concerns of, 35
Care ethics (or caring ethic), 35
Carolina Physical Therapy and Sports Medicine, Inc., 252, 256, 257
Carroll, James, 159, 160
Carroll, Lewis, 229, 243
Carter, Jimmy, 307
Case consultations: definition of, 186
Case from the Field: Affordable Care Act, 230–33; assessment, training, and ethics, 252–54; becoming professionals, 46–47; crises reveal our character, 86–88; electronic health record: a hero in the storm, 276, 283; emerging healthcare consulting industry: Frank Gilbreth and Lillian Gilbreth, 334–35; Man of the Year, 1930, 110–11; no insurance, no admission, 303; one lone voice, 171–72; social media and the certified nursing assistant abusers, 210–11; stewards of the community's health, 65–66; why ethics matter in healthcare management and delivery, 350–54. *See also* Case studies; Landmark Case from the Field; Mini-case studies
Case managers, 320
Case studies: distribution of complex communication responsibilities in surgical education settings, 102–8; emergency departments used as revenue streams despite needing to curb overutilization, question of, 2–7; role of risk manager in cost and price transparency in healthcare, 200–208. *See also* Case from the Field; Landmark Case from the Field; Mini-case studies
Cashi, Amanda, 28

Casuistry: definition of, 30
Categorical imperative: definition of, 32
CBS: anthrax attack at, 306
Celebrity patients: health record scandals and, 176
Censure, 14
Centers for Disease Control and Prevention, 204; COVID-19-related visitation policy changes, 257, 260; Diabetes Prevention Program, 57; Division of Nutrition, Physical Activity and Obesity, 321; flu vaccine recommendations, 65; history behind, 161; Racism and Health initiative, 317, 324; Tuskegee Syphilis Study Ad Hoc Advisory Panel, 162; vaping products report, 120; website of, 78; "We Can Do This" campaign, 307, 308, 309, 312–13
Centers for Medicare & Medicaid Services, 7, 267; accountable care organizations as defined by, 231; eligibility for telehealth services, 183; Government Accountability Office's billing enrollment procedures operation at, 294; Hospital Quality Initiative, 318; incentives for meaningful use of electronic health records, 279–80
Certificate of need, 113
Certification: educational and training programs and, 19; tests, 19
Certified Administrator in Physician Practice Management (CAPPM), *18*
Certified Assisted Living Administrator (CALA), *18*
Certified electronic health record technology (CEHRT), 280
Certified Healthcare Financial Professional (CHFP), *18*
Certified Medical Manager (CMM), *18*
Certified Medical Practice Executive (CMPE), *18*
Certified Nursing Home Administrator (CNHA), *18*
Certified Professional in Healthcare Risk Management (CPHRM), *18*
Chargemaster manipulation, 205–6
Chargemaster prices: hospitals and reporting of, 288
Charisma: definition of, 55
Charity care, 3, 4, 5, 55
Charity Hospital (New Orleans), 306
Charleston Community Memorial Hospital, 75, 76
Cheating: among college students, 36
Chemical restraints: informed consent and, 175, 176
Children: patients' right to self-determination for, 129, 130

Children's Health Insurance Program, 231
Childress, James, 212, 213
China: COVID-19 pandemic and supply chain disruption in, 264
Chugh, Dolly, 293
City of New Haven (Connecticut): HIPAA violation at New Haven Health Department, 269
Civil disobedience, 110–11; definition of, 114; examples of, 114; Gandhi and, 110–11
Civil monetary penalties, 156
Claims: definition of, 21, 113
Clark, Taliaferro, 160
Client: definition of, 334
Climate-smart healthcare: definition of, 71
Clinical ethics: definition of, 171
Clinical ethics, principles in, 172–80, 190; competence, 172–73, 190; confidentiality, 176–78, 190; crossing/not crossing boundaries, 178–79, 190; cultural competence, 179, 190; five Cs of, 172, 190; informed consent, 173, 175–76, 190
Clinical interactions, 170–92; access to healthcare and distributive justice, 180; end-of-life decisions, 184–86; important terms, 170; institutional ethics committee and ethics support, 186–87; learning objectives, 170–71; preventing medical errors, 187–89; principles in clinical ethics, 171, 172–80, 190; telemedicine and telehealth, 181–84
Clinical psychologists, 171
Clinician: definition of, 171
Clinton, Bill, 307
Cloning, 114
Cloud computing, 27
Cobbs v. Grant, 174
Code of Federal Regulations, 153, 154; multilayered operations management definition, based on six broad activities, 254–55; website, Title 45–Public Welfare, section 164.501 of, 269; website of, 166
Codes: Current Procedural Terminology, 21; International Classification of Diseases, 21
Codes of ethics, 51, 84–98; American College of Health Care Administrators, 85, 90–91, 93, 95, 98; American College of Healthcare Executives, 15, 21, 23, 56, 58, 59, 60, 85, 88–90, 93, 95, 98, 115, 135, 217, 338; American Nurses Association, 220, 224; application of, 93; becoming professional norms, once internalized, 91–92, 95; definition of, 20; development and enforcement of, 20, 23; fidelity, medical futility, and, 130; healthcare and consulting, attributes of healthcare management consultants endorsed by, 336, *337;* important terms, 84; learning objectives, 84; Medical Group Management Association, 21, 23, 85, 90, 95, 98; as moral compasses, 132; personal mission statement and, 359; primary purpose of, 20; of professional associations, learning, 355; values or ethical principles underlying, 20
Coding: definition of, 21
Coding errors: correcting, 253, 256; in orthopedics (mini-case study), 22
Cognitive heuristics, 137
Coles, Robert, 55
Collaboration: strategic planning and, 230
Collective moral choices: organizational goals and, 31
Commission on Accreditation of Healthcare Management Education, 19
Commitment to learning: healthcare management consultants and, 336, 341, 342; representation of, in healthcare and consulting codes of ethics, *337*
Common Rule, 152, 156, 158, 163
Communicable Disease Center, 161. *See also* Centers for Disease Control and Prevention
Communication and relationship management domain: for healthcare management profession, 49, 343
Communication and resolution programs, 189
Communication responsibilities in surgical education settings (case study), 102–8; abstract, 102; addressing futility, 107; case, 102–3; commentary, 103; communication education for trainees, 105–6; conclusion, 107; core competencies for leading difficult conversations, *106;* patient factors in poor communication, 103–4; physician factors in poor communication, 104; references, 108; surrogate factors in poor communication, 104–5; system factors in poor communication, 105
Community benefit, 55
Community benefit laws, 5
Community health centers: research conducted in, 148
Community health needs assessments, 3
Community hospitals: research conducted in, 148

Community stewards, 118
Comparative ethics, 28
Compartmentalization, 140
Competence: clinical ethics and, 172–73, 190; definition of, 173, 338; emotional, 173; healthcare management consultants and, 336, 338, 342; representation of, in healthcare and consulting codes of ethics, *337*; telehealth services and, 182
Competencies: assessing, 13; core, for leading difficult conversations, 106, *106*; definition of, 12; emergency services and, 204–5; emotional intelligence, 356; in evaluating professionalism of undergraduate interns, *53*; leadership, 54; mastering, healthcare managers and, 46; student internship programs, 261
Competency-based education: as norm in professional education, 12–13
Competent adult model: informed consent and, 173
Compliance: definition of, 254
Compliance Oversight: website, 166
Comprehensive Pain Specialists, 37
Comprehensive Unit-based Safety Program, 318
Confidences: keeping, fidelity and, 338, *339*, 342
Confidentiality: American Nurses Association Code of Ethics and, 220; autonomy and, 213; clinical ethics and, 176–78, 190, 278; definition of, 286; in employee–employer relations, 214; ethical conflicts involving, 286–87; internship programs and, 261, 262; meaning of, 287; nursing home residents and, 211; of performance reviews, 131; of proprietary data, 286; social media and, *212*; telehealth services and, 182–83
Confidentiality, human resources and, 214–17, 222; personnel, 214–15; physicians, 215–17
Confirming evidence trap, 137, *137*, 138
Conflicts of interest, 178, 221, 293, 294; avoiding, CVS's Minute Clinic strategy and, 234, 236; avoiding, fidelity and, 338, *339*, 342
Congressional Budget Office, 231
Consequentialism, 32, 308
Consequentialists: issues considered by, 32
Consultants settle, $3.13 million (mini-case study), 341–42
Consulting fees and expenses: justice and, 340
Consumer Assessment of Healthcare Providers and Systems, 318
Continuing education: consultants and, 341; training, maintaining competence and, 172

Contributing or giving back competency: professionalism and, *50,* 51
Controlling: Quadrant I: ethical and legal and, 113; Quadrant IV: unethical and illegal and, 116
Conventional morality, 29
Cooperative Strategy for 21st Century Seapower: culturally respectful, ethical healthcare, 240–41; implementation of, Haitian earthquake of 2010 and, 238–43; mini-case study, 241–43, 358; quick and robust response, 238–39; websites, 245
Copyrights, 286
Cornelius, Frances H., 274
Corporate ethics, 30
Corporate social responsibility: definition of, 55; enlightened self-interest and, 308; healthcare manager's role in, 56–57, 59; stewardship and, 70; Vidant Health and history of, 238
Cost: health disparities and, 321; in iron triangle, 302, 304
Cost-effectiveness analysis, 262
Cost transparency: healthcare inequities issues and, 201; limitations on, 204–5; as a moral imperative, 202–3; personal liberty and, 203. *See also* Price transparency
Counselors, 171
Courage, 33
COVID-19 HealthCare Coalition: Supply Chain Working Group, 265
COVID-19 pandemic, 223; CVS's network of walk-in clinics and response to, 236; deaths from, in United States, May 2021, 313; economic losses attributable to, 312; health disparities highlighted during, 316; hospital support provided by USNS *Comfort* during, 241; integrity of research submitted during, 157; new vaccine development process and, 306; precautionary measures implemented during, 65; supply chain disruptions during, 264; supply chain management lessons learned from, *265–66*; telehealth services during, 52, 183; uninsured population and impact of, 231; vaccination policies during, 309–10; veterans' access to healthcare and, 363; virtual internships during, 261; visitation policy changes during, 257, *258–59,* 260
COVID-19 Public Education Campaign: website of, 324
COVID-19 vaccination campaign: public health initiatives applied to, 311–12; social marketing and, 307, 308, 309

Cox, Spencer, 310
Coye, Molly Joel, 181
Credentialed by the American Academy of Medical Administrators (CAAMA), 18
Credentialing: definition of, 218; of physicians, human resources managers and role in, 217, 218
Credentials: for authorized users, 278; revocation of, 14
CRISPR, 27
Critical care situations: addressing moral distress in, 140
Critical thinking: ethics and, 110
Cruzan, Nancy, 186
Cultural competence: clinical ethics and, 179, 190; training in, 319
Cultural humility, 179
Culturally and Linguistically Appropriate Services (CLAS) standards of care, 319
Culturally competent and sensitive care: definition of, 240
Culture of safety, 189
Culture of transparency: at Virginia Mason Medical Center (Seattle), 350
Cumming, Hugh, 160
Cuomo, Andrew, 309
Current Procedural Terminology: codes, 21
CVS: strategic plan to expand MinuteClinic, 234–36
CVS Health, 234
Cybercriminals, 288
Cybersecurity, 288, 292
Cystic fibrosis, 289

Darling, Dorrence, II, 75
Darling v. Charleston Community Memorial Hospital, 75, 76, 218
Darsee, John, 155
Data: fabrication and falsification of, 157, 163; genomic, 289; proprietary, 286; sharing among government agencies, 282
Data breaches: definition of, 288
Data mining, 283, 287
Davies, Grant C., 283
Debriefing, 140
Decision-making: heuristics used in, 135–36
Decision traps, 142; avoiding, 138; major, descriptions of, 137, *137*
Declaration of Helsinki, *151*
Decompressive craniectomy, 102, 103, 107
Deductibles: uninsured and underinsured population and, 201

Deep poverty: health disparities and, 323
Defense mechanisms, 136; countering use of, 119; definition of, 118
Deficit Reduction Act of 2005, 115
De-identified health data, 289
Deliverables: healthcare consultants, integrity, and, 337
Denier, Yvonne L., 141, 144
Dental Alliance: data breach at, 288
Dentistry: price disclosure and, 203
Deontology, 32, 39, 308
Depression: screening for, 320
Descriptive ethics, 27, 28, 38
Descriptive models of ethical decision-making, 136
DeWine, Mike, 310
Dhaene, L., 144
Diacetyl exposure: e-cigarettes and, 120
Diagnosis Related Groups: chargemaster manipulation and, 205
Diagnostic errors, 188
Diaz, Carmen, 6
Difference principle, 34
Difficult conversations: leading, core competencies for, 106, *106*
Digital divide, 182, 280
Digital health literacy: definition of, 286
Dignity: healthcare management consultants and, 336, 340–41, 342; representation of, in healthcare and consulting codes of ethics, *337*
Dining rooms at the Legacy (mini-case study), 93–95, 96
Direct reports: definition of, 143
Disadvantage: health disparities linked to, 313
Disciplinary actions: codes of ethics as basis of, 21; professional associations and, 14
Discipline: as core component of a profession, 10
Discrimination: lactation care and (mini-case study), 321–22
Disparities in healthcare, 14, 316–21. *See also* Health disparities
Distributive justice: access to healthcare services and, 180, 190; definition of, 180; unmet need for, in US healthcare system, 202
Diversity: cultural competence and, 179
Doherty, Caroline, 57
Downsizing workforce: stakeholder theory and, 72–73
Downstream social marketing, 309, 323
Dreyfuss, Richard, 143
Drucker, Peter F., 54, 361

Drug abuse: physicians and, 215, 216
Duke University: student vaccination mandate, 310
Duke University Health System Inc.: settlement for False Claims Act suit, 117
Duty of care, 68, 70, 76, 77
Duty of loyalty, 68, 76, 77
Duty of obedience, 68, 76, 77
Duty to warn, 176, 177
DuVal, Merlin K., 162
Dye, Carson: Emotional Intelligence Evaluation Form, 364, 368–75

East Carolina University: Health Services Management internship program at, 261–62
E-cigarettes, 120, 121
Economic stability: social determinants of health and, 315, *315*
Education access and quality: social determinants of health and, 315, *315*
Education and training at a high level: as core component of a profession, 10, 13
E-health, 181, 184
eHealth Exchange, 281, 282; vision, overall goals of, for US healthcare system, 282, 292; website of, 295
Eisenhower, Dwight D., 251, 268
Electronic health records: advanced use of, 280; clinical notes in, 178; converting to, Institute of Medicine's recommendations for, 275; core functionalities and key capabilities of, *279*; definition of, 277; ethical challenges related to, 282; growth and current status in utilization of, 279–81; interoperability standards for, 277; limited use of data in, 284; meaningful use of, 279–80, 285; overall goals of, for US healthcare system, 282, 292; physicians and dissatisfaction with, 283; unauthorized use of, 278; university health service illustration, 275–77, 278
Emancipated minors, 175, 176
Embezzlement, 253, 256
Emergency departments: closing of, 304; patient dumping and, 302, 303
Emergency departments used as revenue streams despite needing to curb overutilization, question of (case study), 2–7, 52; abstract, 2; case, 2–3; commentary, 3; conclusion, 6–7; exploring solutions to General Hospital's dilemma, 5–6; General Hospital's deliberation about values, 4–5; hospitals'

legal obligations to communities, 3–4; references, 7
Emergency Medical Treatment and Labor Act, 3, 5, 6, 204, 302, 303, 304, 323, 324
Emergency services: competency and, 204–5
Emotional competence, 173
Emotional intelligence, 355–59, 364; definition of, 355; empathy, 356, 358–59, 364; five components of, 356, 364; motivation, 356, 358, 364; positive outcomes tied to, 356; self-awareness, 356–57, 364; self-regulation, 356, 357–58, 364; social skill, 356, 359, 364
Emotional Intelligence Evaluation Form (Dye), 364, 368–75
Emotions: judgments influenced by, 135
Empathy, 356, 364; definition of, 358; Tuskegee Study and, 358–59
Empirical ethics, 28
Encryption: of sensitive data, 289
End-of-life care, 97; ethical conflicts and, 184–86 191; multifaceted educational approach to communicating about, need for, 107; multifactorial reasons for poor communication in, 101, 103–5
End-of-life decisions: ethical issues involved in, 184–86
Enlightened self-interest, 308, 309, 323
Environmental sustainability: as a moral imperative, 70–72, 76
E-prescribing, 280
Epstein, Elizabeth, 138, 139, 140, 141
Equal access: telehealth services and, 183
Equality: justice and, 212
Equal opportunity principle, 34
Equipment failure, 188
Errors: in decision-making, 136, *137,* 137–38, 142; surgical, 189–90. *See also* Medical errors
Estimating and forecasting trap, 137, *137*
Ethical branches, 27–31; applied ethics, 27, 29–30, 38; definition of, 27; descriptive ethics, 27, 28, 38; moral psychology, 27, 29, 38; normative ethics, 27, 29, 38
Ethical conflicts, 111–12; defining, 111, 130–31; end-of-life care and, 184–86 191
Ethical conflicts in health informatics, 282–90; beneficence and autonomy in conflict, 285–86; beneficence and fidelity in conflict, 286–88; beneficence and justice in conflict, 289–90; beneficence and the security challenge, 288–89; beneficence: full

potential unrealized, 283–85; beneficence: increased access issues, 290
Ethical decision-making process, 127–44; choose or recommend from among the response options, *131,* 134; common errors in decision-making and strategies to avoid them, 137–38; consider the related ethical principles and organizational values, *131,* 133; definition of, 128, 142; determine the options for action, *131,* 133–34; identify the specific ethical question needing clarification, *131,* 133; important terms, 127; learning objectives, 127; poor communication and, 101, 103; recognizing and managing moral distress, 138–41; recognizing nonrational elements in ethical deliberations, 135–36; related resources and use of ethics consultation, 135; steps in, *131,* 132–34; understand the background and circumstances leading to the ethical conflict, *131,* 132–33; when medical futility and ethical principles collide, 128–32
Ethical deliberations: recognizing nonrational elements in, 135–36
Ethical dilemmas: poor communication and, 101, 103
Ethical framework, 109–24; ethical conflicts, 111–12; four-quadrant model, *112,* 112–16, 118; important terms, 109; learning objectives, 109
Ethical Health Informatics (Harman and Cornelius), 274
Ethical human resources: human resources managers' role in, 217–20
Ethical operations management, healthcare managers' role in, 264–65; addressing supply chain disruption, 264–65; disruption of the supply chain, 264
Ethical principles: of the *Belmont Report, 152*; colliding with medical futility, 128–31; CVS's Minute Clinic strategy and, 235–36; Full Motion Innovations Case from the Field and, 255–57; in human resources, 211–14, 222; learning and applying to healthcare situations, 350; organizational values and, *131,* 133; of physician rating websites (mini-case study), 291; US military's humanitarian efforts in Haiti, 2010, 240; Vidant Health's acquisition of Pungo Hospital and, 238
Ethical Principles and Guidelines for the Protection of Human Subjects of Research. See Belmont Report

Ethical research standards in healthcare: key documents for, 150, *151,* 152–53
Ethical theories, 32–35; deontology, 32, 39; ethics of care, 35, 39; Rawls's principles of justice, 34, 39; utilitarianism, 32–33, 39; virtue ethics, 33
Ethics: applied, 29–30, 38; basic concepts of, 26–40; bioethics, 30; business, 30–31, 38; of care, 35, 39, 308; as cornerstone of professionalism, 51; critical thinking and, 110; definition of, 27, 38; descriptive, 27, 28, 38; importance of, in work of healthcare professionals, 350; important terms, 26; law differentiated from, 112, 121; learning objectives, 26; legalistic approach to, 119, 122; normative, 27, 29, 38; operations management and, 255; organizational, 31, 38; patient safety and conscious adherence to, 354; profession-specific, 31; reasons for studying, 27. *See also* Clinical ethics, principles in; Codes of ethics; Four quadrant model of ethics and law
Ethics Code for Nurses, 178
Ethics consultation: use of, 135
Ethics heuristics, 164
Ethics of care, 35, 39, 308
Ethics of duty, 32
Ethics rounds, 187
Ethics Self-Assessment (American College of Healthcare Executives), 59
Ethics Toolkit (American College of Healthcare Executives), 128
Ethnic groups: cultural competence in serving patients from, 179
Evans, Alfie, 129
Everett, Wendy, 181
Evidence-based management: definition of, 47
EvidenceNOW program, 318
External data breaches, 288

Fabrication and falsification of data, 157, 163
Fairness, 14–15, 23, 30, 33, 34, 131, 206, 308; concept of health disparities and, 313; justice and, 212; organizational values and, 133; promoting society based on, 202
False billing, 252, 253, 256, 257
False Claims Act, 28, 116, 117, 122, 252, 341
Families First Coronavirus Response Act, 231
Family Smoking Prevention and Tobacco Control Act, 121
Farmer, Paul, 301, 323

Farrugia, Gianrico, 264
Favoritism, 293
Federal agencies: oversight of research in healthcare, 154–57, 163
Federal Bureau of Investigation: cybersecurity advisory report, 288
Federal Emergency Management Agency, 306
Federal Employee Health Benefits Program, 22
Federally Qualified Health Centers, 116, 317
Federal Policy for the Protection of Human Subjects, 153. *See also* Common Rule
Federal-wide assurance of compliance, 153, 154
Federation of State Medical Boards: physician impairment policy, 215–16
Feedback, 134, 357
Fee-for-service payment models, 6
Fee schedules: definition of, 116
Fellow in the American College of Medical Practice Executives (FACMPE), *18*
Fellow of the American College of Healthcare Executives (FACHE), *18*, 19
Fellow of the Healthcare Financial Management Association (FHFMA), *18*
Fernald School Study (Massachusetts), 149–50, 163
Fidelity, 20, 131, 171, 282; clinical practice and, 171, 190; definition of, 286; duty to warn and, 177; healthcare management consultants and, 336, 338, 342; medical futility and, 128, 130, 142; organizational values and, 133; representation of, in healthcare and consulting codes of ethics, *337*; research misconduct and violation of, 156; Vidant Health's acquisition of Pungo Hospital and, 238
Fiduciary duty, 68–70, 76; definition of, 68; three responsibilities of, 68, 76
Final wishes, 97
Financial realities: healthcare decision-making and, 4–5
Financial risk: distinguishing health risk from, 206–7
Financial stewards, 118
Fine, Michael, 235
Firewalls, 289
Florida Hospital Association, 15
Floyd, Brian, 260
Food and Drug Administration, 120, 121, 171, 304, 309, 310, 357
Food insecurity: screening for, 320
Ford, Eric W., 11
Formalism, 32

Formal training: professionalization and, 17
Four-quadrant model of ethics and law, *112*, 112–16, 118; Quadrant I: ethical and legal, 112, *112*, 113–14, 121; Quadrant II: ethical and illegal, 112, *112*, 114, 121; Quadrant III: unethical and legal, 112, *112*, 114–15, 121; Quadrant IV: unethical and illegal, 112, *112*, 116, 118, 121
Framing trap, 137, *137*
Francis, James, 265
Fraud, 117, 294, 340; Medicare, 37–38, 116, 294; rationales for committing, 122; research data–related, 155; scientific, 155, 156, 163; settlement in HCA probe of, 58
Fraud Enforcement and Recovery Act, 117
Freedom Riders, 114
Freshman, Brenda, 356
Fudge, Marica L., 313
Full Motion Innovation Clinic Inc., 252, 253, 254
Full-time occupation: professionalization and, 17
Furman, Cathie, 353
Futility: addressing, 107
Future career as a healthcare manager, building, 349–65; earning trust by "walking the talk," 361, 364; emotional intelligence and, 355–59, 364; important terms, 349; learning objectives, 349; personal mission statement, 359–61, 364; professional development, 354–55, 363
Future Healthcare Managers, 46, 54
Future of Public Health (Institute of Medicine), 310

Gandhi, Mahatma, 63, 77, 110–11, 359
Gardiner, Patti, 33
Gastmans, C., 144
Genetic engineering, 27
Genomic data, 289–90
Genomics, 284
Gerwig, Kathy, 71
Gey, George Otto, 157
Gibson, Count, 161
Giffords, Gabrielle, 218, 219
Gilbreth, Frank, 334, 335
Gilbreth, Lillian, 334, 335
Gilligan, Carol, 29, 35
Glasgow Coma Scale, 102
Glenkinsopp, John, 37
Glover-Thomas, Nicola, 129
Glucose monitoring devices, 158
Goals-of-care discussion, 103
Golden rule, 164

Gold Medal Award (American College of Healthcare Executives), 11
Goleman, Daniel, 355, 356, 3357
Good-faith duty, 338
Google, 283
Gossip, 131, 215
Graduate programs: accreditation of, 19
Gray v. Grunnagle, 174
Greater New York Hospital Association: actions taken to respond to 9/11, *305*
Green assignments: integrating into health administration curriculum, 78
Greene, A. Hugh, 14, 15
Green-powered electrical systems, 71
Groupthink: definition of, 159; Tuskegee Study and, 159–62
Guatemala: Sexually Transmitted Disease Inoculation Study in, 148

Hacking, 288
Haiti, earthquake of 2010: Cooperative Strategy for 21st Century Seapower responds to, 238–43, 358
Hajibabaee, F., 187
Hamric, Ann, 138, 139, 141
"Hard stops": in electronic health record systems, 286
Harman, Laurinda Beebe, 274
Harvard Medical School, 150
Harvard University, 310
HCA (or Columbia/HCA): fraud probe, settlement in, 58
Healthcare: unethical human experimentations in, 149–50
Healthcare access and quality: social determinants of health and, 315, *315*
Healthcare administration: virtuous traits and, 33
Healthcare-associated infections: reducing, 318
Healthcare consulting industry: emerging, 334–35
Healthcare decision making: financial realities and, 4–5
Healthcare Executive Competencies Assessment Tool (American College of Healthcare Executives), 51
Healthcare executives: six responsibilities of, to community and society at large, 85
Healthcare Financial Management Association, 18, *18*, 48
HealthCare.gov, 233
Healthcare Information and Management Systems Society, 48
Healthcare information exchange: future of, 281–82
Healthcare Leadership Alliance, 10, 47–49, 55; Competency Directory, 343, 346; on five competency domains for healthcare managers, 49, 343; leadership defined by, 54
Healthcare management as a profession, 9–23; characteristics of professions and professionals, 11–14; defining a profession, 10; important terms, 9; learning objectives, 9; stages of professionalization, 16–21; values and, 14–16
Healthcare management consultants: autonomy and, 336, 338, 342; commitment to learning and, 336, 341, 342; competence and, 336, 338, 342; definition of, 335; dignity and, 336, 340–41, 342; engaging, purposes for: 335-336; fidelity and, 336, 338, 342; honesty and, 336, 338, 340, 342; ideal characteristics of, 336–38, 340–41, 342; integrity and, 336, 337–38, 342; justice and, 336, 340, 342
Healthcare management consulting: defining, 334–36; important terms, 333; learning objectives, 333
Healthcare management profession: Healthcare Leadership Alliance on five competency domains for, 49
Healthcare managers: ethical conduct of research studies and, 148; mastering of several competencies by, 46; role in corporate social responsibility initiatives, 56–57, 59; role in ethical operations management, 264–65; role of stewardship in duties of, 64, 66–67, 76. *See also* Future career as a healthcare manager, building
Healthcare operations: defined in Title 45 of the *Code of Federal Regulations*, six activities tied to, 254–55, 257
Healthcare organizations: importance of human resources to, 210; professional development and, 354; risk managers' responsibilities to, 206
Healthcare policy: definition of, 302; distinction between health policy and, 302; ethics, technology use, and, 27; impact of health policy on, 304; important terms, 301; learning objectives, 301
Healthcare providers: claims submitted by, 21
Health disparities, 313–21, 323; in access to COVID-19 vaccine, *312,* 312–13; applying ethical lens to social marketing efforts and,

310; definition of, 313; important terms, 301; learning objectives, 302; social determinants of health and, 314–16, *315*. *See* Disparities in healthcare delivery

Health equity: achieving, 320; definition of, 314

HealthGrades.com, 291

Health informatics, 274–95; definition of, 275, 292; electronic health records, 277–82; ethical conflicts in, 282–90; important terms, 274; learning objectives, 274–75

Health information exchanges, 285

Health information technology: definition of, 277

Health Information Technology for Economic and Clinical Health (HITECH) Act, 275, 279

Health Insurance Portability and Accountability Act (HIPAA), 52, 59, 176, 211, 287, 289; compliance with research obligations under, 154, 163; duty to warn and, 177; firings following violations of, University Medical Center (Arizona), 219; internship programs and, 262; organizational violations of, 268–69; Privacy Rule under, 156, 166

Health literacy: definition of, 285; digital, 286; limited, impact of, 285–86

Health outcomes: determinants of, 314

Health policy: definition of, 230, 243, 323; distinction between healthcare policy and, 302; impact on healthcare policy, 304; politics and, 232

Health records: history behind, 275

Health Research Extension Act, 156

Health risk: distinguishing financial risk from, 206–7

Healthy People initiative: health disparities as defined by, 314

Healthy People 2020, 314

Healthy People 2030, 315, 316; breastfeeding goal, 321; website of, 324

Hedonic calculus, 33

HeLa cell line, 157, 158

Heller, Jean, 162

Hennepin Healthcare (Minneapolis): medical records violations at, 220

Herman, David, 237

Heuristics: avoiding over-reliance on, 164; used in decision-making, 135–36

High ethical standards: as core component of a profession, 10

HIPAA. *See* Health Insurance Portability and Accountability Act

Hippocrates, 142, 148

Hippocratic Oath, 4, 213, 303

Hiring process: confidentiality and, 215

HITECH Act. *See* Health Information Technology for Economic and Clinical Health Act

Hogan, Larry, 309

Honesty, 20, 131, 171, 206, 255; American College of Health Care Administrators Code of Ethics founded on, 91; American College of Healthcare Executives Code of Ethics based on, 89; clinical practice and, 171, 190; ethical human resources and, 217, 222; healthcare management consultants and, 336, 338, 340, 342; informed consent and, 176; organizational values and, 133; representation of, in healthcare and consulting codes of ethics, *337*; social media and, *212*

Honor: American College of Health Care Administrators Code of Ethics and, 91; American College of Healthcare Executives Code of Ethics and, 90; organizational values and, 133

Hospital-acquired infections, 188; elimination of Medicare payments for, 114–15

Hospital Consumer Assessment of Healthcare Providers and Systems (HCAHPS), 260, 267

Hospitals: closures of, 317; legal obligations to communities, 3–4; vaccine mandates for employees in, 310

Hospital Sisters Health System Sacred Heart Hospital: mobile mammography bus at, 262–63; website of, 269

Houston Methodist Hospital (Texas): vaccine mandates for employees at, 310

Human experimentation: primary purpose of, 149

Humanitarian relief efforts: Haiti, earthquake of 2010, 238–43

Human research subjects: evolution of protections for, 150

Human resources, 209–24; ethical, role of human resources managers in, 217–20, 222; honesty and, 217, 222; importance of, to healthcare organizations, 210; important terms, 209; learning objectives, 209

Human resources, confidentiality and, 214–17; personnel, 214–15; physicians, 215–17

Human resources, ethical principles in, 211–14; autonomy, 212, 213–14, 222; beneficence, 212, 213, 222; justice, 212–13, 222; nonmaleficence, 212, 213, 222

Human resources managers, role in ethical human resources, 217–20; employment termination, 217, 218–20; physician credentialing, 217, 218
Human resources stewards, 118
Human subjects committee, 153
Huntington's disease, 289
Hurricane Katrina, 283, 304, 306
Hurricane Sandy, 276
Hutchinson, Asa, 309
Hyatt, Josh Charles: cost transparency commentary by, 201–2
Hyman, David, 122
Hypertension, 111
Hyponatremia, 111

"Idaho Gives" day, 77
Identity theft, 220
Ige, David, 309
"I Got My Shot" campaign (Florida), 307
Illinois Department of Public Health, 211
Illinois Supreme Court, 75, 218
Immortal Life of Henrietta Lacks (Skloot), 158
Immunization Action Coalition: Influenza Vaccination Mandates Honor Roll, 66; website of, 78
Implicit bias: definition of, 319; healthcare management consultants and, 340; lactation support and examples of, 322
Implicit prejudice, 293, 294
Incentives: for adoption of electronic health records, 275; for meaningful use of electronic health records, 279–80
Income and wealth inequality: in United States, 320–21
Incompetent or incapacitated patients: informed consent and, 173, 175
Individual mandate: elimination of, 233
Indonesia: USNS *Mercy* deployed in aftermath of 2004 tsunami, 239
Influenza, 65
Influenza Vaccination Mandates Honor Roll, 66
Influenza vaccine: mandated for employees of Virginia Mason Medical Center, 64, 65–67, 77, 361
Informational justice, 213
Informational webinars, 290
Informed consent, 153, 157, 204; clinical ethics and, 173, 175–76, 190; definition of, 173; ethical conflicts under purviews of institutional ethics committees and, 187; legal framework for, 173, *174*; origins for, 150; pricing transparency and, 207; telehealth services and, 182, 183. *See also* Autonomy
In-group favoritism, 293, 294
Inova Health: data breach at, 288
Inslee, Jay, 309
Instagram, 211
Institute for Healthcare Improvement, 231
Institute for Safe Medication Practices, 353
Institute Management Consulting USA: common characteristics of healthcare management consultants in Code of Ethics for, 336, *337*
Institute of Consulting: Code of Professional Conduct and Practice, 341; Code of Professional Conduct and Practice, website, 346; common characteristics of healthcare management consultants in Code of Ethics for, 336, *337*; website of, 346
Institute of Management Consultants: website of, 346
Institute of Medicine, 279; electronic health records recommendation, 275; *To Err Is Human,* 187; formation of and name change, 310; interprofessionalism defined by, 51; on limited health literacy, 285; *Unequal Treatment,* 313
Institutional burdens: cost transparency and, 204
Institutional ethics committees, 175; definition of, 186, 191; ethics support and, 186–87; institutional review boards *vs.,* 186; three main goals or purposes of, 186–87
Institutional review boards, 153–54, 157, 163; composition of, 154; definition of, 153; institutional ethics committees *vs.,* 186
Integrated healthcare, 319
Integrity, 20, 171, 206, 255, 344; American College of Health Care Administrators Code of Ethics based on, 91; American College of Healthcare Executives Code of Ethics based on, 89; clinical practice and, 171, 190; definition of, 55; healthcare management consultants and, 336, 337–38, 342; organizational values and, 133; representation of, in healthcare and consulting codes of ethics, *337*; research misconduct and violation of, 156; trust and, 64, 361
Integrity Worksheet: crises offer us a time to reveal our character (Case from the Field), 345
Interdisciplinary teams, 51
Interest of others: as core component of a profession, 10

Internal data breaches, 288
Internal Revenue Code: Section 501(r)(3) of, 3
International Board-Certified Lactation Consultant (IBCLC), 321–22
International Board of Lactation Consultant Examiners' Code of Professional Conduct, 322
International Classification of Diseases: codes, 21
Internet, 290, 291
Internship preceptor: definition of, 53
Internship professionalism, 53–54
Internships: programs certified by the Association of University Programs in Health Administration, 262; definition of, 261
Interoperability: barriers to, 281; definition of, 277; of electronic health record systems and data sharing, challenges with, 280–81
Interprofessionalism, 64; benefits of, 52; definition of, 51, 58
Interviews: confidentiality and, 214
Iron triangle, 302
"It's Up To You" public service announcements, 307

Jackson Health System (Miami, Florida): medical records violations at, 220
Jameton, Andrew, 138
Janis, Irving, 159
Jewish Chronic Disease Hospital Study, 149, 163
Job satisfaction: poor, moral distress and, 139
John M. Eisenberg Patient Safety and Quality Award: Vidant Health receives, 260, 266
Johns Hopkins Medicine: six priorities in strategic plan of, 244
Johns Hopkins University Hospital, 157, 158
Joint Commission, 173, 267, 303; accreditation for MinuteClinic, 235; accreditation standards related to organizational ethics, 31; Code of Conduct, 69; on fiduciary duty, 69; mandates disclosure of medical errors, 73, 77; medical records standardization, 275; patient safety standards, 188; physician impairment requirement, 215; website of, 78
Jones, Albert, 55
Joseph P. Addabbo Family Health Center (New York City), 276
Journal of Business Ethics, 31
Journal of Healthcare Management, 11
Journal of Operations Management, 254
Journal of the American Medical Association, 160
"Juicing" (overbilling), 341–42
Julius Rosenwald Fund, 160
Justice, 20, 30, 33, 113, 159, 171, 282, 288; access to care and, 180; American College of Healthcare Executives Code of Ethics based on, 89; applying ethical lens to social marketing efforts and, 310; *Belmont Report* and, *152*; clinical practice and, 171, 190; in context of post-shooting events at University Medical Center (Arizona), 219; COVID-19 vaccination campaign and, 313; CVS's Minute Clinic strategy and, 235; definition of, 212, 222; distributive, 180; Full Motion Innovations Case from the Field and, 255–56; healthcare management consultants and, 336, 340, 342; human resources managers and, 212–13, 222; informational, 213; informed consent and, 176; John Rawls's principles of, 34, 39, 308; mobile mammography efforts and, 263; organizational values and, 133; patient dumping and violation of, 302; physician impairment and violation of, 216; physician rating websites and, 291; preserving, cost transparency issues and, 201–2; price practices and, 199; procedural, 40, 212, 213; representation of, in healthcare and consulting codes of ethics, *337*; telehealth services and, 182, 183; US military's humanitarian efforts in Haiti, 2010 earthquake and, 240; Vidant Health's acquisition of Pungo Hospital and, 238
Just-in-time inventory, 264
Juul, 120, 121
"Juuling," 120

Kachalia, Allen, 74, 75
Kahneman, Daniel, 135
Kaiser Permanente: environmental stewardship statement, 71
Kaiser Permanente Practice Greenhealth, 71–72
Kant, Immanuel, 32, 203
Kaplan, Gary, 350, 351, 359
Kelsey, Frances Oldham, 171, 172, 357
Kenseth, Deborah, 70
Kenseth v. Dean Health Plan, Inc., 70
Kickbacks, 178
Kidder, Rushworth M., 26, 37
Kirk, Shaylona, 140
Knowledge of the healthcare system domain: for healthcare management profession, 49, 343
Koek, Adriana, 189
Kohlberg, Lawrence, 29

Kotler, Philip, 307
Krajewski, Lee, 254
Kvedar, Joseph, 181

Lacks, Henrietta: legacy of, 157–58
Lactation care: structural roots of racism and discrimination in (mini-case study), 321–22
Lancet, 157
Landmark Case from the Field: unethical US Public Health Services studies, 148. *See also* Case from the Field; Case studies; Mini-case studies
Law: definition of, 110; ethics differentiated from, 112, 121. *See also* Four quadrant model of ethics and law
Law fallacy, 118, 119, 122, 137
Layman, Elizabeth, 279, 283
Lazear, Jesse, 159, 160
Leadership: competencies, 54; effective and moral, 54–55; values-based, 141, 144
Leadership domain: for healthcare management profession, 49, 343
"Leadership: More Doing than Dash" (Drucker), 54, 361
Leading and directing: Quadrant I: ethical and legal and, 113; Quadrant IV: unethical and illegal and, 116
Learning: lifelong, commitment to, 354, 363
Lederer, Edith, 162
LEED-certified: definition of, 72
Legend, John, 307
Lenox Hill Hospital, 69
Lewis, Tinslee, 129
Lexington Model: definition of, 74
LGBTQ population: health disparities and, 314
Liberty principle, 34
Library of Congress, 283
Licensure, 19, 20, 172
Life enhancement and extension technologies, 27
Lifelong learning: best practice guidelines and, 135; commitment to, 354, 363; consultants and, as ethical imperative for, 341, 342; definition of, 354
Lifespan Health System Affiliated Covered Entity: HIPAA violation and fine, 269
Life support: withdrawal of, 184, 185
Litigation risks: billing issues and, 204
Living wills, 96
Low-carbon healthcare, 71
Loyalty, 131; American College of Health Care Administrators Code of Ethics based on, 91; American College of Healthcare Executives Code of Ethics based on, 89; medical futility and, 128; organizational values and, 133
Lung disease: vaping-related, 120

Machiavellianism, 36
Magellan: data breach at, 288
Magill, Gerard, 64
Maintaining Internal Systems and Strengthening Integrated Outside Networks (MISSION) Act, 363
Maleficence, 256
Malicious software, 288
Mammograms: screening recommendations, 262
Managed care organizations: screening for social determinants and, 320
Management consultants, 334
Management consulting: history behind profession of, 334
Managerial ethics, 30
Mandated reporters: definition of, 177
Manhattan Eye, Ear and Throat Hospital, 68–69
Manhattan Eye, Ear & Throat Hosp. v. Spitzer, 68–69
Marine Hospital Service, 159. *See also* US Public Health Service
Martin, Steve, 307
Massachusetts General Hospital, 150, 275
Master of Business Administration (MBA), *18*
Master of Health Administration (MHA), *18, 19*
Master of Health Services Administration (MHSA), *18*
Master of Public Administration (MPA), *18*
Master of Public Health (MPH), *18*
Master of Science (MS), *18*
Mayo Clinic, 96, 265
McCullough, L. B., 103
McDonald's: "We Can Do This" campaign, 307
Meaningful use: definition of, 279; of electronic health records, 279–80, 285; overall goals of, for US healthcare system, 282, 292
Meaningful work: a sense of a calling and, 15–16, 23
Measure of Moral Distress for Healthcare Professionals, 139–40
Media attention, 164
Medicaid, 5, 6, 21, 115, 203, 231, 233, 282, 284, 317; Affordable Care Act and expansion of, 230, 232, 302; fraud, 294; Vidant Pungo's closing and North Carolina's refusal to expand, 237

Medical chart, 277
Medical errors: disclosing, stakeholders involved in, 73–75; number of deaths related to, 187–88; preventable, 187–89, 350, 351; reducing, business intelligence and, 284; total costs related to, 188, 191; types of, 188
Medical futility, 175; definition of, 128; medical necessity, rationing, and, 142; when ethical principles collide with, 128–31, 142
Medical Group Management Association, *18*, 48; Code of Ethics of, 21, 23, 85, 90, 95, 98; common characteristics of healthcare management consultants in Code of Ethics for, 336, *337*; mission of, 90; website of, 98
Medical homes, 7
Medical malpractice: and healthcare facility's responsibility (mini-case study), 75–76
Medical records: patient confidentiality and, 176. *See also* Electronic health records
Medical technologies: achieving benefits of associated research on, 158–59
Medicare, 3, 5, 21, 31, 142, 231, 252, 282; adoption of Diagnosis Related Groups, 205; fraud, 37–38, 116, 294; reimbursement for telehealth services, 183; Shared Savings Program, 232
Medicare for All, 6
Medicare Fraud Strike Force, 116
Medication-related errors, 188
Medications Safety Self-Assessment Survey, 353
Mental health equity, 319–20
Mentor–mentee relationships, 354–55
Mergers, 6
Meta, 211
Mexican-American War, 114
MHealth apps, 158
Mill, John Stuart, 32, 33
Mini-case studies: change for the better at Vidant Health, 266–67; coding error in orthopedics, 22; consultants settle, pay $3.13 million, 341–42; Cooperative Strategy for 21st Century Seapower, 241–43; dining rooms at the Legacy, 93–95, 96; ethical principles of physician rating websites, 291; groupthink and the Tuskegee Study, 159–62; medical malpractice and the healthcare facility's responsibility, 75–76; moral courage and fraud, 37–38; obligations to staff, 141–42; problems at the Veterans Affairs healthcare system (2013–2021), 361–63; serving as a patient advocate, 220–22; settlement in HCA fraud probe, 58; structural roots of racism and discrimination in lactation care, 321–22; surgical errors persist, 189–90; vaping becomes a health epidemic among youth, 120–21. *See also* Case from the Field; Case studies; Landmark Case from the Field
"Minimizing the Economic Burden of the Patient Protection and Affordable Care Act Pending Repeal," executive order on, website, 245
Minority Health and Health Disparities Research and Education Act, 313
Minors: informed consent and, 175
Minsky, Tequila, 239
MinuteClinic: expanding, CVS's strategic plan for, 234–36
Mission: American College of Health Care Administrators, 90, *91*; American College of Healthcare Executives, *89*; at CVS Health, 234; Medical Group Management Association, 90; mobile mammography efforts and, 262, 263; operations management and, 252, 267; stewardship and, 67; strategic planning and, 230; Vidant Health (North Carolina), 267; Virginia Mason, 351
Mitton, Craig, 141
Mobile biosensors, 284
Mobile mammography: cost-effectiveness analysis of, 263; evidence for significance of, 263; service examples, 262–63
Modern Healthcare: Community Leadership Award, 15
Mohr v. Williams, 174
Monitoring the Future Survey, 120
Moore, Hilary, 252
Moral agents: definition of, 33
Moral blindness, 118, 122, 137
Moral case deliberation process, 187
Moral character, 134, 136
Moral courage, 39; definition of, 37; fraud cases and, 37–38
Moral disengagement: definition of, 36
Moral distress, 142; addressing, strategies for, 140; definition of, 138; manifesting at multiple levels, 139; obligations to staff and, 141–42; recognizing and managing, 138–41; sources of, 141
Moral distress scale, 139
Moral engagement theory, 36
Moral injury: definition of, 139
Moral leadership, 38, 55

Moral psychology, 27, 29, 38
Moral reasoning, 29, 36, 39
Moral residue, 139
Moral stance: adopting, 130, 132, 137
Morgan, Alan, 237
Motivation, 356, 358, 364
Mountain State Hospital: American College of Healthcare Executives Code of Ethics applied to Bob Allred's experience at, 90; crisis at (case from the field), 86–88, 97, 345; professional norms applied to Allred's experience at, 92
Multifactor authentication, 289
Murray, Bill, 143
Murthy, Vivek, 311

Narcissism, 36
National Academies of Sciences and Engineering, 310
National Academy of Medicine: vision of, 310
National Academy of Sciences, 310
National Alliance for Health Information Technology, 277
National Alliance on Mental Illness, 86, 88; on treating people with mental illness in correctional settings, 86; website of, 98
National Center for Ethics in Health Care, 135
National CLAS (Culturally and Linguistically Appropriate Services) Standards: website for, 324
National Collaborative for Health Equity: website of, 324
National Commission for the Protection of Human Subjects of Biomedical and Behavioral Research, *151*, 152
National Federation of Independent Business et al. v. Sebelius, Secretary of Health and Human Services, 232
National Institute of Mental Health, 155
National Institute on Minority Health and Health Disparities, 313; website of, 324
National Institutes of Health, 313
National Patient Safety Goals (Joint Commission), 188
National Research Act of 1974, 150, *151*, 163
National Rural Health Association, 237
National Supplier Clearinghouse, 294
Nationwide Health Information Network. *See* eHealth Exchange
Natural disasters, 304, 306; benefits of electronic health records and, 276, 283

Nazi concentration camps, 161; Nuremberg Military Tribunals Doctors' Trial, *151*
NBC: anthrax attack at, 306
Neighborhood and built environment: social determinants of health and, 315, *315*
Nelson, William A., 40, 128, 134, 191, 212
Neo-Kantians, 32
Neuspiel, Daniel, 189
New England Journal of Medicine, 303
New Jersey Supreme Court, 186
Newman, Stephen L.: surprise billing commentary, 205
Newsom, Gavin, 309
New York City Department of Health and Mental Hygiene: actions taken to respond to 9/11, *305*
New York Post, 306
New York Times, 359, 361
Nicotine: vaping, 120
9/11 Commission Report, 305
9/11 terrorist attacks, 304; organizations and actions taken to respond to, 305, *305*
Nolan, Thomas, 231
Nonmaleficence, 20, 30, 171, 213; access to care and, 180; clinical practice and, 171, 190; in context of post-shooting events at University Medical Center (Arizona), 219; definition of, 213, 222; end-of-life decisions and, 184, 191; Full Motion Innovations Case from the Field and, 256; health disparities viewed through lens of, 321; human resources and, 213, 222; informed consent and, 176; organizational values and, 133; patient dumping and violation of, 302; physician credentialing and, 218; physician impairment and violation of, 216; supply chain management and, 265; US military's humanitarian efforts in Haiti, 2010 earthquake and, 240; withdrawal of life support and, 185
Nonprofit hospitals: Affordable Care Act and community benefit requirement for, 3
Nonverbal communication skills: leading difficult conversations and, 106, *106*
Nonviolent political action *(satyagraha)*, 110
Normative ethics, 27, 29, 38
Northam, Ralph, 309
North Carolina: declining Medicaid expansion under Affordable Care Act, protests against, 114
North Carolina Medical Board, 216; Position Statement on Professional Obligations, 224

North Carolina Physicians Health Program, 216
No Surprises Act, 115
Nuremberg Code, *151*; definition of, 159; website for, 166
Nuremberg Trials, 150
Nurses, 171, 204; moral distress and, 139, 140; as patient advocates (mini-case study), 220–22, 357
Nursing, 316
Nursing home: sample social media guidelines for, *212*
Nursing home administrators: licensure of, 19
Nursing Home Reform Act of 1987, 210, 224
Nursing Home Reform Modernization Act of 2020, 210, 224

Obama, Barack, 304, 307, 361
Office for Civil Rights, 156–57, 163, 166, 268
Office for Human Research Protections, 154–55, 163; Compliance and Reporting website, 156; enforcement powers of, 155; responsibilities of, strategies for, 154–55; website of, 166
Office of Inspector General, 31, 361, 362
Office of Research Integrity, 155–56, 157, 163; Misconduct Case Summaries, 166; website of, 166
Office of the National Coordinator for Health Information Technology, 277, 282, 283, 295; website of, 295
Office of the Surgeon General: COVID-19 information and, 311; website of, 324
Olansky, Sidney, 161
1 on 1 Home Healthcare (Michigan), 253, 256, 257
Open Notes: website of, 295
Open software development, 282
Operational actions, *Code of Federal Regulations* definition of healthcare operations connected to, 257–62; conducting quality assessment and improvement activities (activity 1), 257, *258–59,* 260–61; planning and development (activity 5), 262–63; reviewing competence or qualifications of healthcare professionals (activity 2), 261–62
Operations management, 251–69; definition of, 254; ethical, healthcare managers' role in, 264–65; ethics and, 255; important terms, 251; learning objectives, 251
Opioid use disorder: physicians and, 216
Organ donations, 97
Organizational ethics, 31, 38

Organizational framework of public health: definition of, 311
Organizational values: ethical principles and, *131,* 133
Organizing: Quadrant I: ethical and legal and, 113; Quadrant IV: unethical and illegal and, 116
Out-of-pocket expenses: dental, 203; uninsured and underinsured population and, 201
Overbilling, 341–42
Overclaiming credit, 293, 294
Oversight of research in healthcare: federal agencies responsible for, 154–57

Pandemic and All-Hazards Preparedness Acts of 2006, 2013, and 2019, 304–6, 323, 324
Pandemics: healthcare industry and preparing for, 304. *See also* COVID-19 pandemic
Parkland Memorial Hospital, 303, 304
Parsons, Talcott, 10
Patents, 286
Patient advocate, serving as (mini-case study), 220–22
Patient autonomy: professional autonomy *vs.,* 16
Patient-centered medical home, 319
Patient confidentiality. *See* Confidentiality
Patient dumping, 302, 303
Patient-family partnerships: at Vidant Health, 260, 267
Patient portals, 280, 290
Patient Protection and Affordable Care Act, 6, 115, 117, 235, 316; case from the field, 230–33; community benefit provision under, 3; definition of, 230; as example of health policy, 302; mammogram coverage mandated under, 262; overarching goals and provisions of, 230; passage of, 230
Patient rights: trustworthy information and, 103
Patients: disclosure of medical errors and, 73
Patient safety, 256; American Nurses Association Code of Ethics and, 220; electronic health record use and, 280; physician impairment and, 215; preventing medical errors, 187–89; primacy of, at Virginia Mason Medical Center, 351–54
Patient Safety Alert program: at Virginia Mason Medical Center, 352, 353, 354
Patient Safety and Quality Improvement Act of 2005, 188
Patient satisfaction: surprise billing and negative impact on, 203
Patient Self-Determination Act of 1990, 129, 186

Patient-specific factors: poor communication in end-of-life care and, 103–4, 107
Payers: claims submitted to, 21; coding and, 21
Pay for performance, 319
Payment reforms, 7
Pecoraro, Kathleen, 316
Penalties: civil monetary, 156
Penicillin: in treatment of syphilis, 148, 159, 161
Penn, Madeline, 363
Performance audits: of electronic health record data, 284
Performance reviews: confidentiality of, 131
Persistent vegetative state, 185; definition of, 184; right-to-die cases involving, 185–86
Personal coping, 140
Personal liberty: cost transparency and, 203
Personal mission statements, 355, 359–61, 364; answering questions in, 359–60; developing, 98; samples of, *360*; writing, 364–65
Personal protective equipment: COVID-19 pandemic and supply chain issues with, 264–65
Personnel: confidentiality and, 214–15
Perspective taking, 140
Petersen, Ruth, 321
Phenylketonuria, 289
Phishing schemes, 288
Phocomelia, 171
Phoenix Veterans Affairs Health Care System: wait times at, 362
Physical restraints: informed consent and, 175, 176
Physical therapists, 171
Physician assistants, 171
Physician credentialing: role of human resources managers in, 217, 218
Physician health program: referrals to, 215, 216
Physician impairment: confidentiality and, 215–17; definition of, 215
Physician offices: research conducted in, 148
Physician rating websites: ethical principles of (mini-case studies), 291
Physicians, 171; communication as professional duty of, 103; dissatisfaction with electronic health records, 283; moral distress and, 140; workplace violence and impact on, 204
Physician-specific factors: poor communication in end-of-life care and, 104, 107
Pierre-Paul, Jason, 59
Plagiarism, 163
Planning: Quadrant I: ethical and legal and, 113; Quadrant IV: unethical and illegal and, 116

Pneumonia, 65
Pocatello Free Clinic, 77
Poddar, Prosenjit, 177
Point-of-care manufacturing, 265
Policy and Procedure Order 129, US Surgeon General, *151*, 161
"Popcorn lung," 120
Portfolios: student internship programs, 261
Portneuf Medical Center: mobile mammography unit at, 262, 263; website of, 269
Postconventional morality, 29
Poverty: health disparities and, 323
Power of attorney, 96
Practical ethics, 29
Pratt v. Davis, 174
Precautionary principle: definition of, 129
Preceptors: internship programs and, 261
Preconventional morality, 29
Prejudice: avoiding, 14
Premera Blue Cross: HIPAA violation and settlement, 268–69
Prescription assistance programs, 290
Prescription Confidentiality Law (Vermont), 287
Prescription drug abuse: physicians and, 215
Prescriptive ethics, 29
Presidential Commission for the Study of Bioethical Issues, 147, 148; website of, 166
Preventive care: electronic health record use and, 280
Price discrimination, 203
Price fixing, 203
Price transparency, 199, 204, 207, 288. *See also* Cost transparency
Primary care physicians, 232
Princeton University, 310
Principles: definition of, 28
Principles of Scientific Management (Taylor), 334
Principlism: definition of, 30
Prioritization phase: in strategic planning cycle, 234, 242, 243
Privacy, 289; American Nurses Association Code of Ethics and, 220; autonomy and, 213; definition of, 285; ethical conflicts involving, 286–87; healthcare consultants as good stewards and, 338; of healthcare records, breaches of, 268; meaning of, 287; nursing home residents' right to, 211; social media and, *212*
Privacy Rule (HIPAA): definition of, 156; website for, 166
Privileging: definition of, 218

Procedural justice, 40, 212, 213
Profession, 11–14; adhering to professional norms and, 13–14; core components of, 10; definition of, 10, 22; possessing systematic knowledge and, 11–13
Professional Association of Healthcare Office Management, 18
Professional associations, 14, 17; benefits of, 18–19; codes of ethics and, 21; in healthcare management, selected, *18*; membership in, 354–55; primary purpose of, 18
Professional autonomy: patient autonomy *vs.*, 16
Professional competencies, 12–13
Professional credentials: certification based on, 19; selected, *18*
Professional development, 350, 354–55; lifelong learning and, 354, 363; membership in professional associations, 354–55, 363
Professional ethics, 29
Professionalism, 45–60; becoming professionals (case), 46–47; best practice guidelines and, 135; corporate social responsibility and, 55–57, 58; definition of, 10, 49; effective and moral leadership and, 54–55; ethics as cornerstone of, 51; important terms, 45; internship, 53–54; interprofessionalism, 51–52; and its development at different career levels, *50*; learning objectives, 45; of undergraduate interns, evaluating, 53
Professionalism domain: for healthcare management profession, 49, 343
Professionalization, stages of, 16–21, 23; code of ethics (stage 5), 20–21; formal training (stage 2), 17; full-time occupation (stage 1), 17; professional association (stage 3), 17–19; self-regulation (stage 4), 19–20
Professional norms: adhering to, 13–14, 22; definition of, 13, 49; examples of, *13*; internalized codes leading to, 91–92, 95
Professional role: definition of, 49
Professionals: adhering to professional norms, 13–14, 22; possessing systematic knowledge, 11–13, 22
Profession-specific ethics, 31, 38
Profitability: avoidable emergency department visits and, 6
Project Connect Health Systems Intervention: open software developments and, 282; website of, 295
Project ECHO, 318
Promoting Interoperability Program, 280

Proprietary data, 286
Protected health information: data breaches involving, 288; privacy and security breaches of, 268, 269
Provider-patient interactions: improving, disparate health practices and, 318–19
Providers: disclosure of medical errors and, 73. *See also* Nurses; Physicians
Prudence, 33
Prybil, Lawrence, 64
Psychotherapy: telehealth and, 182
Public: disclosure of medical errors and the, 73
Public health: definition of, 311; mission of, fulfilling, 311; racism and, 317
Public health initiatives, 310–13; applying ethical lens to social marketing efforts and, 310; outcomes, 312–13; sources of information and their trustworthiness, 311–12
Public health mission: definition of, 311
Public Health Reports, 160
Public service, 14, 23
Pungo Hospital: Vidant Health's acquisition of, 236–38

Quadruple Aim: definition of, 232
Qualitative futility: addressing, 107
Quality: health disparities and, 321; in iron triangle, 302, 304
Quality assurance, 252, 267
Quality improvement: electronic health record use and, 280
Quality of life, 184
Quantitative futility: addressing, 107
Quinlan, Karen, 185–86
Qui tam action, 252; consultants settle, $3.13 million (mini-case study), 341–42; definition of, 117

Race/ethnicity: COVID-19 vaccination demographics as a percentage of total US population, September 2021, *312*; health disparities and, 314; health disparities during COVID-19 pandemic and, 316
Racial and Ethnic Approaches to Community Health (REACH), 320
Racial disparities: unconscious bias and, 340; in wait times at Veterans Affairs Healthcare System facilities, 362–63
Racism, 179; lactation care and (mini-case study), 321–22; public health and, 317
Ransomware attacks, 288–89

RateMDs.com, 291
Rationalization, 136; definition of, 118; lessening, 119
Rawls, John, 202, 308; principles of justice, 34, 39, 308
Reagan, Ronald, 304
"Real Cost" tobacco prevention campaign, 121
Rectovaginal fistula, 165
Reed, Walter, 159
Reference-checking: confidentiality and, 214
Referent: definition of, 14
Reflection groups, 187
Reflection strategies: for addressing moral distress, 140
Re-identification risk, 289, 290
Reitz, Randall, 179
Relativism, 28
Relators, 117, 252, 341
Representativeness heuristic, 136
Reproductive rights: informed consent and, 175
Research ethics, 115
Research in healthcare organizations, 147–66; federal agencies responsible for oversight of, 154–57, 163; future ethical challenges, 158–59; important terms, 147; institutional review board, 153–54, 163; learning objectives, 147; major documents detailing ethical research standards in healthcare, 150, *151,* 152–53; unethical human experimentations in US healthcare, 149–50, 163
Respect, 206; American College of Healthcare Executives Code of Ethics and, 89; for autonomy (self-determination), in principlism, 30; autonomy and, 213; organizational values and, 133; for others, fairness and, 14–15, 23; for persons, *Belmont Report* and, *152,* 173
Respect for self and others: clinical practice and, 171, 190
Retention: emotional intelligence and, 356
Revocation of credentials, 14
Rhode Island Department of Health, 235
Rhode Island Free Clinic, 236
Right to die, 184, 191
Right-to-die cases, 185–86
Right to live, 184, 191
Risk management, 189; multifaceted nature of questions and concerns in, 202
Risk Management Pearls on Disclosure of Adverse Events (American Society for Healthcare Risk Management), 74

Risk managers: licensure of, 19
Risk manager's role in cost and price transparency in healthcare (case study), 200–208; abstract, 200; case, 200–201; chargemaster manipulation, 205–6; commentary 1, by Josh Charles Hyatt, 201–2; commentary 2, by Stephen L. Newman, 205; conclusion, 205; cost transparency as a moral imperative, 202–3; distinguishing financial risk from health risk, 206–7; limitations on cost transparency, 204–5; operational (normative) concerns, 203–4; personal liberty and cost transparency, 203; references, 207–8; risk manager's responsibilities, 206
Risk mitigation, 202
Roanoke Chowan Community Health Center: mission of, 57; website of, 60
Robotics, 27
Rolater v. Strain, 174
Role model, 164
Roosevelt, Theodore, 349, 364
Root-cause analysis: definition of, 189
Rubino, Louis, 356
Rural settings: mobile breast cancer screenings in, 262–63

Safe medication practices, 353
Safety risks: billing issues and, 204
Saint Alphonsus: website of, 269
Saint Alphonsus Mobile Health Screening Coach (Idaho): mobile mammography service, 263
Saint-Exupery, Antoine de, 209, 222
Salgo v. Leland Stanford Jr. University Board of Trustees, 174
Salt hunger, 111
Salt March, 110
Sanctions, 20
Sanctity of life, 20, 171; clinical practice and, 171, 190; end-of-life decisions and, 184, 191; opponents of withdrawal of life support and, 185
San Diego Medical Center: LEED-certified status of, 72
Schaffer, Adam, 74
Scheduling phase: in strategic planning cycle, 234, 242, 243
Schiavo, Terri, 185, 186
Schloendorff v. Society of New York Hospital, 174
Schneiderman, Lawrence, 128
Schroeder, Steven, 321
Schuman, Andrew, 189

Schwartz, Mark, 136
Scientific fraud, 155, 156, 163
Scientific misconduct: potential for great harm and, 157
Security: definition of, 286; electronic health records, beneficence, and challenge of, 288–89; ethical conflicts involving, 286–87; of healthcare records, breaches of, 268; meaning of, 287
Self-assessments, 357
Self-awareness, 356–57, 364; definition of, 356; emotional intelligence and, 356–57, 364
Self-care, 140
Self-determination, right to, 173, 285. *See also* Autonomy
Self-development, 355, 363
Self-diagnosis devices, 158
Self-management competency: professionalism and, *50,* 51
Self-regulation, 356, 357–58, 364; autonomy, healthcare consultants, and, 336; definition of, 15; as stage in professionalization, 19–20, 23
Sentinel events, 201–2; preventing, 188; root-cause analysis of, 189
Sequoia Project, 281
Sergeant, C. S., 129
Sexually Transmitted Disease Inoculation Study, 148, 163
Shakespeare, William, 333, 343
Shared Savings Program (Medicare), 232
Shashidhara, Shilpa, 140
Shinseki, Eric, 361, 362
"Sick Physician" (Council on Mental Health), 215
Silvera, Geoffrey, 260
Silverhawk peripheral plaque excision system, 28
Sims, J. Marion, 165
Sinsky, Christine, 232
Situational context: of ethical decision-making, 136
Skloot, Rebecca, 158
Snapchat, 210, 211, 213
Social and community context: social determinants of health and, 315, *315*
Social contract framework: Rawls's justice theory and, 34
Social determinants of health, 314–16, 323; definition of, 314; five place-based categories in, *315*
Social justice: concept of health disparities and, 313, 321; healthcare risk management profession and, 201

Social marketing, 307–10; assessment through an ethical lens and, 308–9; definition of, 307, 323; downstream, 309, 323; founders of, 307; upstream, 309–10, 323
Social media: certified nursing assistant abusers and, 210–11
Social media policy: creating, 211; sample, nursing home guidelines, *212*
Social skill, 356, 359, 364
Social workers, 171, 320
Society for Human Resource Management: sample policies offered by, 215; website of, 224
Socratic dialogue, 187
"Soft stops": in electronic health record systems, 286
Sorrell v. IMS Health, 287
Special knowledge and skills: as core component of a profession, 10, 11
Spitzer, Eliot, 69
Staff: obligations to (mini-case studies), 141–42; workplace violence and impact on, 204
Stakeholders: definition of, 64; fiduciary duty of a member of board of directors and, 68; identifying, ethical conflicts and, 132–33; moral context and, 72; price transparency and, 205; risk managers' responsibilities to, 206; strategic planning cycle and, 233
Stakeholders, organizational steward's responsibility to, 72–75; disclosing medical errors, 73–75; downsizing the workforce, 72–73
Stakeholder theory: definition of, 31; procedural justice and, 40
State licenses: applying for, 20
States: False Claims Acts of, 341
Statistical analyses, 283
Status quo trap, 137, *137*
Stefl, Mary, 47
Stewardship, 63–78, 118; of the community's health, 64, 65–66; definition of, 64; environmental sustainability and, 70–72, 76; fiduciary duty and, 68–70, 76; good, fidelity and, 338; important terms, 63; learning objectives, 63; responsibility of organizational stewards to stakeholders, 72–75, 76; role of, in healthcare manager's duties, 64, 66–67, 76
Stigma: definition of, 240; poverty-related, 321
St. Luke's Health Corporation (Missouri), 11
Strategic planning, 229–45; consequences related to Affordable Care Act and, 233, 237; at CVS, 234–36; definition of, 233, 243; important

terms, 229; learning objectives, 229; mission and vision and, 230; US military, in response to 2010 earthquake in Haiti, 238–43, *239*; at Vidant Health, 236–38
Strategic planning cycle, 236; Cooperative Strategy for 21st Century Seapower and, 242; definition of, 233; three phases in, 234, 242, 243
"Strengthening Medicaid and the Affordable Care Act," executive order on, website, 245
Students-in-training: codes of ethics and, 21
Study protocols: definition of, 153
Substance of public health: definition of, 311
Substituted judgment standard: definition of, 185
Sullivan, William, 13
Sunk-cost trap, 137, *137*
Sunrise Senior Living (Virginia): vaccine mandates for employees at, 310
Superintendents, 17
Supply chain: definition of, 264
Supply chain disruption: addressing, solutions to, 264–65; COVID-19 pandemic and, 264
Supply chain management: definition of, 264; lessons learned from COVID-19 pandemic, 265–66
Surgical checklists, 188
Surgical education settings: distribution of complex communication responsibilities in (case study), 102–8
Surgical errors: persistence of, 189–90
Surgical trainees: communication education for, 105–6
Surprise billing, 115, 200, 203, 205; mitigating litigation risk tied to, 206; risk managers' responsibilities in cases of, 206
Surrogate decision making: end-of-life conversations and, 104–5, 107
Surrogates: best interests standard and, 185; definition of, 128; informed consent and, 176; substituted judgment standard and, 185
Sussman, Andrew, 235
Sustainability, 55
Syphilis: Tuskegee Study, 148, 159, 160–61
Systematic knowledge: content areas and, 12; definition of, 11; possessing, 11–13, 22
System failures, 188
System-specific factors: poor communication in end-of-life care and, 105, 107

Tarasoff, Tatiana, 177
Tarasoff duty: definition of, 177
Tarasoff v. Regents of the University of California, 177

Taunton State Hospital, Massachusetts, 341
Tax benefits: nonprofit hospitals and, 3
Tax Cuts and Jobs Act, 233
Taylor, Frederick Winslow, 334, 335
Teams: interdisciplinary, 51
Technology: ethical issues and, 27
Telehealth, 181–84, 190; interprofessional teams and, 52; limitations with, 182; programs, beneficence and, 290; providing adequate safeguards for, 183; researching, websites for, 191; telemedicine *vs.*, 181
Telemedicine, 181–84, 190; historical context of, 181; limitations with, 182; telehealth *vs.*, 181
Telemonitoring: for congestive heart failure patients, 181; devices, 158
Telepsychology, 183
Temperance, 33
Termination: role of human resources managers in, 217, 218–20
Terrorist attacks, 304
Texas Children's Hospital, 223
Texas Medical Board, 221
Texas Nurses Association, 221; website of, 224
Thalidomide: banning of, 171–72, 357
Theory-based conversations, 187
Theosophical Society, 110
Therapy Dogs International: website of, 93, 98
Third-party payers: definition of, 64
Thomas, Erin V., 322
Thoreau, Henry David, 110, 114
3D printing, 27, 265
TikTok, 211
To Err Is Human (Institute of Medicine), 187
Toyota production system, 352, 353
Trade secret laws, 286
Training, 172; in cultural competence, 319; formal, professionalization and, 17
Transparency, 289; culture of, at Virginia Mason Medical Center, 350, 352, 354; definition of, 74; public concern about lack of, 200; social media and, 212. *See also* Accountability; Cost transparency; Price transparency
Transparency in Coverage Rule, 202
Treatment errors, 188. *See also* Medical errors
TRICARE, 252
Trinity Health: data breach at, 288
Triple Aim: definition of, 232
Truman v. Thomas, 174
Trump, Donald, 233
Trust, 256; broken, breach of fiduciary duty and, 68; earning, by "walking the talk," 355, 361,

364; gossip and violations of, 215; honesty of healthcare management consultants and, 340, 342; integrity and, 64; truthful communication and, 217
Truth: autonomy and, 213; in billing, 254
Truthful communication, 217
Turnover: moral distress and, 139, 140
Tuskegee Study, 148, 150, 163, 179; empathy and, 358–59; groupthink and, 159–62; medical officers and researchers involved in, 160; termination of, 162
Tversky, Amos, 135
Twain, Mark, 84, 95
21st Century Cures Act, 282, 285; website for, 295
Twitter, 211

Udell, Lillian, 223
Unconscious bias: healthcare management consultants and, 340
Undergraduate interns: evaluating professionalism of, *53*
Understanding professional roles and norms competency: professionalism and, 49, *50*
Unequal Treatment (Institute of Medicine), 313
Unethical human experimentations: in US healthcare, 148, 149–50
Unfunded mandate, 304
Uninsured and underinsured population, 320; Affordable Care Act and, 230–31; healthcare cost inequities and, 201; health disparities and, 317; price fixing and price discrimination and, 203
United States: ethical breaches in biomedical research in, 149–50
Universal Orlando: "I Got My Shot" campaign and, 307
Universities: vaccine mandates at, 310
University Medical Center (Tucson, Arizona), 218, 219; ethical principles in context of post-shooting events at, 219–20; zero-tolerance policy on privacy violations at, 219
University of California, Los Angeles, Health System: settlement for celebrity patients suffering medical record leaks, 176
University of Chicago, 17
University of Michigan: medical disclosure process, 74
University of Virginia, 310; telehealth interprofessional teams, 52
Upcoding, 22
Upstream social marketing, 309, 323

US Census Bureau, 201
US Coast Guard: Cooperative Strategy for 21st Century Seapower and maritime strategy of, 242; mission statement of, 241; website of, 245
US Department of Health and Human Services, 86, 87, 200; on benefits of telehealth, 52; chargemaster prices requirement for hospitals, 288; data breaches listing, 288; interoperability rules, 282; Office for Civil Rights, 156, 268; Office for Human Research Protections, 154–55; Office of Disease Prevention and Health Promotion, 314; Office of Research Integrity, 155; Office of the Assistant Secretary for Preparedness and Response, 324; protections for human subjects and, 153; Transparency in Coverage Rule, 202
US Department of Justice, 252, 309
US Department of Labor: Transparency in Coverage Rule, 202
US Department of the Treasury: Transparency in Coverage Rule, 202
US Department of Transportation, 342
US Department of Veterans Affairs: problems at healthcare system of (2013–2021), 361–63; vaccine mandate, 309
US Government Accountability Office: billing enrollment procedures of Centers for Medicare & Medicaid Services operation, 294
US Green Building Council, 72; website of, 78
US Marine Corps: Cooperative Strategy for 21st Century Seapower and maritime strategy of, 242; mission statement of, 241; website of, 245
US Navy: Cooperative Strategy for 21st Century Seapower and maritime strategy of, 242; deploys USNS *Comfort* during Haitian disaster relief efforts, 239, *239*; mission statement of, 241; website of, 245
USNS *Comfort*, 242, 358; medical care provided by, in Caribbean region, 241; service during Haitian disaster relief efforts, 239, *239*, 242–43
USNS *Mercy*, 242; service in aftermath of 2004 tsunami, Indonesia, 239
US Public Health Service: Commissioned Corps, 324; Division of Venereal Diseases, 160; historical context of, 159–60; unethical studies conducted by, 148
US Surgeon General: primary responsibility of, 311
Utah Code, 218

Utilitarianism, 32–33, 39
Utility, 118; definition of, 32–33; organizational values and, 133

Vaccinations: COVID-19, social marketing, and, 307–9
Value-based care: shift to, 320
Value-based leadership, 141, 144
Values, 14–16; American College of Health Care Administrators, 90, *91*; American College of Healthcare Executives, *89*; autonomy, 16, 23; a calling and meaningful work, 15–16, 23; mobile mammography efforts, 262, 263; operations management and, 252, 267; professional, definition of, 14; public service, 14, 23; respect for others and fairness, 14–15, 23; self-regulation, 15, 23; Vidant Health (North Carolina), 267; Virginia Mason, 351
Values-based payment, 6
Vaping: as health epidemic among youth, 120–21
Varkey, Basil, 170, 180, 189
Varsity Medical Ethics Debates, 158
Verbal communication skills: leading difficult conversations and, 106, *106*
Vermont: Prescription Confidentiality Law in, 287
Vertical gastric banding, 70
Vesicovaginal fistula surgical treatments, 165
Veterans Choice Act of 2014, 362, 363
Veterans Health Administration, 283; Lexington Model and, 74; support for mandatory flu vaccination for healthcare workers, 65
Vidant Health (North Carolina): acquisition of Pungo Hospital, 236–38; Advance Care Planning Expanded Toolkit, 96; change for the better at (mini-case study), 266–67; website of, 267
Vidant Medical Center (North Carolina): COVID-19 pandemic visitation policy, 257, *258–59*, 260; vaccine mandates for employees at, 310
Videoconferencing, 183
Violence in the workplace, 204
Virginia Mason Medical Center (Seattle): culture of transparency at, 350; identifying and prioritizing stakeholders at, 66–67; maintaining organizational integrity through reciprocity at, 67; mandatory flu vaccination program at, 64, 65–66, 77, 361; patient-at-the-top organizational structure at, 351–54; professional development opportunities at, 354; supporting and sustaining the organizational mission at, 67

Virginia Mason production system, 351, 353, 359
Virtual internships, 261
Virtue ethics, 33, 39
Vision: American College of Health Care Administrators, 90, *91*; American College of Healthcare Executives, *89*; mobile mammography efforts and, 262, 263; of National Academy of Medicine, 310; operations management and, 252, 267; strategic planning and, 230; Vidant Health (North Carolina), 267; Virginia Mason, 351
Visitation policy changes: during COVID-19 pandemic, 257, *258–59*, 260–61
Vitals.com, 291
V. J. Associates: consultants settle in overbilling case, pay $3.13 million, 341–42
Volunteering, 54
Vonderlehr, Raymond A., 160
Vulnerable populations: biomedical researchers and experiments conducted on, 148, 149–50, 163, 165; price fixing and, 203

Wakefield report on autism/vaccination link: allegations of fraud and, 157
Walensky, Rochelle, 317
Walgreens: "We Can Do This" campaign and, 307
Walgreen's Healthcare Clinic, 236
Walk-in clinics, 234–36
"Walking the talk": earning trust by, 355, 361, 364
Walt Disney World: "I Got My Shot" campaign and, 307
Washington Star, 162
"We Can Do This" campaign (Centers for Disease Control and Prevention): "meeting people where they are" and, 312–13; social marketing concept applied to, 307, 308, 309
Weinstein, Ronald, 181
Werhane, Patricia H., 31, 40
What About Bob (film), 143
Whistleblowers: definition of, 113; legal protection for, 114; Tuskegee Study and, 161–62; V. J. Associates overbilling case, 341
Whistleblowing: definition of, 38; in healthcare, research literature on, 37–38
White, Kenneth, 138, 139, 141
Whittington, John, 231
Wilkinson v. Vesey, 174
William Jennings Bryan Dorn Veterans Medical Center (South Carolina): delayed care for veterans at, 361
Willowbrook Hepatitis Studies, 149, 163

Wire fraud, 342
Workers' compensation programs, 21
Working with others competency: professionalism and, *50,* 51
Workplace violence, 204
World Bank, 71
World Health Organization, 314; call for increased personal protective equipment during COVID-19 pandemic, 264; health policy as defined by, 243; on influenza, 65; stewardship according to, 64; website of, 78
World Trade Center: 9/11 attack on, 304, 305
Worst-case scenario, 164

Wrenn, Keith, 303
Wrentham State School Study (Massachusetts), 150, 163
Wrong-site surgery errors, 188

Yale New Haven Hospital: Hand Hygiene Campaign, 76
Yang, Jim, 253
Yellow fever experimentation: US Public Health Service and, 160
Ying, Jinpin, 276

Zaltman, Gerald, 307
Zoeng, Jean, 252, 253, 254, 255, 256, 257, 360

ABOUT THE AUTHORS

Leigh W. Cellucci, PhD, MBA, is professor and associate dean for academic affairs in the College of Allied Health Sciences at East Carolina University. She received the University of North Carolina Board of Governors Distinguished Professor for Teaching Award and has coauthored four books and more than 45 articles on healthcare management. In previous positions, she served as program director and interim chair at East Carolina University and as program director and chair at Idaho State University. Most recently, she served on the board of directors and executive committee of the Association of University Programs in Health Administration.

Tony Cellucci, PhD, ABPP, is professor and clinic director of the Psychological Assessment and Specialty Services Clinic at East Carolina University. He is a board-certified clinical psychologist primarily involved in teaching and supervising health psychology graduate students. He is a past president of the Association of Psychology Training Clinics and serves on the editorial board of the journal *Training and Education in Professional Psychology*. Previously, he served as clinic director at Idaho State University, where he taught ethics for many years.

About the Authors

Tracy J. Farnsworth, EdD, MHSA, MBA, FACHE, is president of the Idaho College of Osteopathic Medicine at Idaho State University (ISU) and associate professor in healthcare management at ISU. He received the Kole-McGuffey Prize for excellence in education research and the Distinguished Author Award from the Association of Schools Advancing Health Professions. Previously, he served in executive-level positions with Intermountain Healthcare, Catholic Healthcare West, and the City of Hope National Medical Center. He serves on the board of trustees of Portneuf Medical Center and is the immediate past chair of the Association of University Programs in Health Administration.